Praise for *Elemental Philosophy*

"David Macauley's *Elemental Philosophy* is a wonderfully well-written tour de force. It combines close analysis of ancient philosophical sources with contemporary materials of astonishing intellectual breadth. This interdisciplinary work possesses theoretical rigor, cosmopolitan scope, and literary sophistication. It will appeal to general readers who may relish, as I have, this powerful invitation for philosophical regrounding and lyrical reflection about basic elemental principles that are critical to living wisely and well on planet earth today."

— Eric W. Orts, University of Pennsylvania

"One might suppose, in these days of quarks and black holes, that ancient Greek reflections on the elements of their landscape—fire, air, earth, and water—were too elementary to be worth recalling. Not so. David Macauley demonstrates their surprising relevance. Earth, air, water—even fire (energy, global warming)—are still central to the world agenda: sustaining life in a millennium of ecological crisis. From that day to this, wise philosophers keep their thoughts in touch with the sensuous, elemental Earth."

— Holmes Rolston III, author of *Environmental Ethics: Duties to and Values in the Natural World*

"The book is a multidisciplinary achievement which attests to the author's thorough acquaintance with, inter alia, ancient Greek cosmology, contemporary environmental philosophy, and literary and artistic traditions which have treated of the elements."

— David E. Cooper, *Environmental Values*

"After industrialization, knowledge became fragmented and people lost touch with the material realities of the places in which they lived. David Macauley blends ancient Greek precepts with twenty-first century circumstances: earth, air, fire, and water call upon us from across the millennia to reanimate humanity's connection to our home planet."

— David Spanagel, Worcester Polytechnic Institute

"In today's deforested, smog-choked, overheated world . . . earth, water, fire, and air are taking on renewed meaning as vital liminal sites in the ever-shifting human encounter with the more-than-human cosmos. Freighted with erudition yet buoyant with spirited wordplay, Macauley's intellectual history of the four elements is a delightful tour de force of environmental philosophy."

— *Seven Pillars House of Wisdom*

# Elemental Philosophy

SUNY series in Environmental Philosophy and Ethics
―――――――
J. Baird Callicott and John van Buren, editors

Elemental Philosophy

Earth, Air, Fire, and Water as Environmental Ideas

—— David Macauley ——

Front cover photo credit: Banyan tree, Goa Gajah (Elephant Cave Temple), Ubud, Bali, Indonesia. Photo by David Macauley, 2009.

Back cover art credit: "The Wheel of the Four Elements," by Shaila George, 2010. Reprinted by permission of the artist.

Published by State University of New York Press, Albany

© 2010 State University of New York

All rights reserved

Printed in the United States of America

No part of this book may be used or reproduced in any manner whatsoever without written permission. No part of this book may be stored in a retrieval system or transmitted in any form or by any means including electronic, electrostatic, magnetic tape, mechanical, photocopying, recording, or otherwise without the prior permission in writing of the publisher.

For information, contact State University of New York Press, Albany, NY
www.sunypress.edu

Production by Eileen Meehan
Marketing by Michael Campochiaro

Library of Congress Cataloging-in-Publication Data

Macauley, David.
Elemental philosophy : earth, air, fire, and water as elemental ideas / David Macauley.
    p. cm. — (Suny series in environmental philosophy and ethics)
Includes bibliographical references and index.
ISBN 978-1-4384-3245-8 (hardcover : alk. paper)
ISBN 978-1-4384-3244-1 (pbk. : alk. paper)
1. Four elements (Philosophy)   I. Title.

BD581.M25 2010
113—dc22
                                            2010004835

10 9 8 7 6 5 4 3 2 1

*Dedicated to my parents:
Howard Kane Macauley
and the late Marion Ernest Macauley*

Contents

Preface — xi

Acknowledgments — xv

Introduction — 1
    Four-Thought — 1
    Sheltering the Elements — 3
    Plan of the Work — 6

Part I: Elemental Encounters and Ideas — 11

Chapter 1. Philosophy's Forgotten Four — 13
    Earth — 14
    Air — 25
    Fire — 36
    Water — 43

Interstice: Stone — 51

Chapter 2. The Topology of the Elemental Environment — 59
    Elementary Letters — 60
    Elemental Places — 63
    Elements as Archetypes — 66
    Elemental Opposition — 67
    Elemental Substances — 69
    Chemical Elements — 72
    Cultural Comparisons — 74
    The Frame of the Four — 81
    Social Construction of the Elements — 84

Interstice: Wood — 93

Part II: Elemental Theories — 101

Chapter 3. The Flowering of Ecological Roots: Empedocles' Elemental Thought — 103
  Four-Play — 103
  The Problem of the Poems — 104
  Square Roots and Radical Rhizomes — 106
  Empedocles' Elemental Cosmology — 110
  Ecological and Political Equality — 113
  Organic Unity — 115
  Environmental Action — 117
  Anticipation of Evolution — 119
  Animal Empathy — 120
  Environmental Roots — 122
  Ecological Ethos — 122
  Crafting Nature — 124
  Purity and Pollution — 126
  The Rhizomes of Deleuze and Guattari — 131

Interstice: Ice and Snow — 137

Chapter 4. Plato's *Chora*-graphy of Earth, Air, Fire, and Water — 143
  The ABC of Everything — 143
  A Probable Physics — 144
  Derivation of Earth, Air, Fire, and Water — 145
  The Corpus of an Ecological Cosmos — 147
  Second Beginnings and Constrained Construction — 148
  Removing the Spell of the Elements — 150
  Elemental Recycling — 153
  Forms of the Four? — 155
  Elements Emplaced: *Chora*-graphy in the Matrix — 156
  Construction and Structure of the Primary Bodies — 160
  War and Play of the Elements — 163
  Dispatching the *Stoicheia*: Elemental S/endings — 165
  Husserl and the Mathematization of Nature — 168
  Postscript to Plato: Whitehead's Philosophical Footnotes — 170

Interstice: Cloud — 173

Chapter 5. The Place of the Elements and the Elements of Place: Aristotle's Natural Household — 179
  Four Accounts of Five Elements — 179
  A Dictionary of Elemental Definitions — 182

The Ancient Generation Gap	183
Pondering Weight	186
The Place of the Elements	188
The Elements of Place	192
Homecoming and Inhabitation	194

Interstice: Heat and Cold — 201

Chapter 6. The Economy and Ecology of the Aristotelian Elements — 209

Hot, Cold, Wet, and Dry	209
Converting the Contraries	213
Compounding the Quartet	216
Prime Matter as Persisting Problem	218
Extra Terrestrials: The Fifth Element	225
Elemental Contact: Beholding Tangible Bodies	228
In Touch with the Environment	233
The Soul and the External World	234
Aristotle and Ecology	238

Interstice: Light and Shadow — 243

Part III: Elemental Worlds — 253

Chapter 7. Domestication of the Elements — 255

Outside-In	255
Plumbing Philosophy	257
Watercraft and Landscape Aesthetics	260
From Waterways to Waterworks	264
Bottled Water	267
Fire and Water	270
Eclipse of the Atmosphere	271
Escape from Earth	273
End of the Elements?	275

Interstice: Night — 283

Chapter 8. In Touch With the Sensuous World: The Reclamation of the Elemental in Continental Philosophy — 293

Elemental Reveries: Bachelard's Poetics	295
Elemental Dwelling: Heidegger's Fourfold	300
Elemental Flesh: Merleau-Ponty's Re-membering	308
Elemental Sensibility: Levinas on Enjoyment	310

Elemental Imperatives: Lingis and Our Sensuous Surroundings ... 312
Elemental Passions: Irigaray on Breath and Body ... 316
Elemental Landscapes: Casey on Place ... 319
Elemental Nature: Sallis on Imagination ... 321
From Elements to the Elemental ... 324

Interstice: Space ... 327

Chapter 9. Revaluing Earth, Air, Fire, and Water: Elemental Beauty, Ecological Duty, and Environmental Policy ... 333
Elemental Ethics ... 334
Elemental Aesthetics ... 338
Environmental Action ... 345
Bewildering Order ... 352

Notes ... 357

Index ... 419

Preface

Many projects have a distant catalyst that sets them in motion, providing an origin, if not a guiding trajectory, for their unfolding. This one stretches back to my youth. In retrospect, the elemental world exerted a strong and abiding presence during the course of my development. I grew up along the Susquehanna—the longest river on the east coast of the United States—several miles outside of Bloomsburg, a sleepy college town in northeastern Pennsylvania. In our backyard, we put to use a well and maintained a large garden where my brother, sister, and I often were exiled to weed or harvest organic vegetables either to be enjoyed by the family or to be sold at a roadside stand the three of us operated in front of our property, an early venture perhaps in "natural capitalism." Cherry, apple, and pear trees punctuated the yard and supplied us intermittently with fruit when the bugs or birds didn't get to it first, while willow and maple trees offered us strategic perches on which to survey the neighborhood or erect arboreal forts, including a two-tiered structure with sliding board, "bat pole," and tent-top roof. The brick house contained a fireplace, a potbelly stove, and later on a wood-burning stove. We also maintained a fireplace in an outdoor pavilion and constructed a fire pit close to the river. Keeping the vestal flame alive necessitated cutting and splitting wood in the warmer months and then hauling and stacking it in the winter.

As a child, I witnessed firsthand the recurring force of seasonal ice floes and floods. Especially memorable was the fury of Hurricane Agnes, which subdued and swamped the northeastern quadrant of the Commonwealth and upstate New York, taking 129 lives and causing billions of dollars worth of damage in one of the worst storms in U.S. history. I watched the river deposit foreign objects from far-away upstream locales and sweep away belongings—picnic tables, garden posts, and firewood—from our backyard to unknown destinations as the water filled our basement and crested at three feet on the first floor. My father paddled over the mailbox in a rowboat to reach the island of our house, and when the floodwaters retreated, we spent the next several years slowly removing a pasty veneer of mud, dirt, and detritus from floors, furniture, and two garages.

This kind of event, however, represented one pole of a periodic personal oscillation between more common interactions with earth, water, night, sky, rock, snow, fire, and night and less ordinary and even sublime encounters with elemental phenomena. The former entailed regular camping, canoeing, hiking, rock climbing, distance running, and biking as well as years of scouting. As a ten-year-old, for example, I scavenged for and collected dozens of rocks and minerals, ranging from jasper and pyrite to calcite and talc and then proudly mounted and labeled my *objets d'art* on a shellacked wooden board that I still keep in my basement. The latter involved seeing the Aurora Borealis in Norway and, astonishingly, rural Ohio; exploring underground caverns and caves; visiting the Everglades, Petrified Forest, Grand Canyon, and Niagara Falls; journeying to glaciers in Europe and amazing limestone pillar hills in southeast China; or being caught without warning in an ocean undertow or violent lightning storm. These experiences, quite naturally, generated a lasting fascination with the physical world and an "accidental environmentalism."

The more proximate genesis for this book lies on the north shore of Long Island, where I set out late one night on a protracted run in the frozen silence of February. I had just moved into the carriage house of a cliff-top mansion that had been converted into a group home for graduate students. After loping along the beach at a brisk clip, I turned up into the woods and was shortly enveloped in what seemed like total blackness. A few minutes later, a severe thunderstorm began, and when the trail mysteriously stopped, I was lost wholly in unknown territory, barely able to discern the ground in front of me. Eventually, after tumbling blindly over low-lying wires that bloodied my shins, dead-ending in a bamboo grove, and then running on pure adrenalin in different directions for several miles, I found my way to a road that led me back to my new abode. Drying out by the calm of a fire, the opaqueness of the dark lifted and the bone-chilling cold was replaced by the warmth and incandescent light of a domesticated flame. This confluence of circumstances—the cloak of the night segueing into the palpable density of the woods, the revelation provided by intense fits of lightning giving way to a more steady pacifying fire, the serrated wind-driven waves of the Sound mingling with the beat of a driving rain—gave me pause to begin reflecting upon the sense and significance of the elemental into which I had been suddenly thrust and so deeply immersed. Given that I was then reading the Presocratic philosophers and their cryptic, if poetic, meditations on water, fire, air and earth, I drew inspiration tacitly from my youthful forays into wild, feral and semi-domesticated elemental regions, and a theoretical project was thus germinated and later given birth.

Despite initial appearances, this book, however, is not a wistful look back at or even simply a celebration of an ancient world lost to the inexorable march of time. The perennial elements, of course, continue to exercise profound influences upon our daily lives in new and challenging ways. Within the span of the past few years, Hurricane Katrina has ravished the Gulf Coast; a great tsunami has decimated parts of Indonesia; wildfires have been on the loose in San Diego, Los Angeles, and the Far West; and major earthquakes have rocked Haiti, Pakistan, and

Iran. "Extreme weather" outbreaks in the guise of tornados, sudden storms, flash floods, heat waves, cyclones, and El Niño are increasingly familiar and dangerous problems due in part to rising population densities, anthropogenic transformations of the environment, and poor social planning. We also have recently slowed and subsequently stopped in its invisible tracks the movement of light, a phenomenon so elemental as to appear and disappear outside our purview. At the very same time, we have created new chemical elements in the laboratory and proved with reasonable scientific certainty that a primal or elemental "dark matter" pervades the universe.

Environmental philosophers, however, have surprisingly neglected the perennial elements and elemental realms. We have tended, for example, to focus on the status of the snake molting on an outcropping of rock rather on than the underlying earth; we have embraced the bird in the sky or the fish in the sea but, until recently, ignored the air or water itself; and we have stressed the cultural objects forged by fire but not the flame per se. In a broader sense, this amounts to a philosophical disregard of meteorological entities and events as well. "There are seven or eight categories of phenomena in the world that are worth talking about, and one of them is the weather," notes Annie Dillard.[1] Although the present work engages multiple closely associated topics, a true discussion of the theoretical or empirical dimensions of weather would require another volume. This study likewise does not take up the elements in relation to esoteric subjects such as alchemy or astrology. Nevertheless, the project is multidisciplinary and interdisciplinary in orientation; while rooted firmly within philosophical traditions—and environmental philosophy in particular—I invoke the ideas and insights of other relevant fields, including literature, ecology, history, public policy, art, and natural science.

Two final notes are in order before commencing with the investigation: first, with respect to the use of Greek terms, I opt for the sake of accessibility to place them in transliterated form without the addition of diacritical or accent marks (e.g., *episteme*) rather than reproducing unaltered Greek letters (e.g., ἐπιστήμη). Second, should the reader not be interested in the nuances of fairly complex theoretical analysis or exegesis but instead be more prone to explore the ecological aspects or practical applications of the work, he or she may elect to skip selectively some of the material in Chapters three through six by using the section headers as a guide. Otherwise, the book develops through intersecting and interconnected philosophical, environmental, and historical lines, transitioning in due course from ancient thought to contemporary issues with interstitial respites devoted to reflections on other elemental phenomena: stone, wood, ice and snow, clouds, heat and cold, light and shadow, night, and space. To view some of my own photographs of these elemental entities, please see my Penn State University website: http://www.brandywine.psu.edu/Academics/faculty_dmm53.htm.

Acknowledgments

Martin Heidegger once remarked that "one's last thought should be a thank," playing on the related German verbs *denken* (to think) and *danken* (to thank). Although his intriguing idea suggests the possibility of appending an appreciative after-thought to the book, I follow the more customary approach of commencing rather than closing on a note of gratitude, if only for the concern that my acknowledgments might be lost in a forest of footnotes. Thanks and thoughts are owed to many individuals who helped to shepherd this work along both directly and indirectly. At Penn State University, I would like to thank George Franz, Sophia Wisniewska, Paul DeGategno, Sandy Gleason, Priscilla Clement, Molly Wertheimer, Phyllis Cole, Jeanette Reick, and Gail Wray as well as other academic colleagues—especially Arnold Markley, Pat Hillen, and Adam Sorkin—for their institutional and personal support. Research Development Grants from Penn State in 2004 and 2005 were very beneficial to me in completing the book. Thanks also go to the campus Writing Center and to librarian Sara Whilden and her reliable staff for cheerfully tracking down books and articles as I requested them.

At Oberlin College, David Orr provided a collegial, innovative, and good-humored setting in which to teach and write for two years, and an extended group of Environmental Studies faculty and staff there made my stay a pleasant one, including Harlan Wilson, Scott McMillan, John Petersen, Audra Abt, and Tom Newlin. While I served as a visiting scholar at Emerson College and subsequent to that time, David Spanagel offered a thoughtful and sympathetic sounding board for my ideas. Edward Casey and Peter Manchester, both at Stony Brook University, read much earlier drafts of the manuscript and gave me constructive comments and criticisms. Andreas Michel and Mike Kukral at Rose-Hulman Institute of Technology also contributed to my thinking through conversations.

At SUNY Press, special thanks goes to Jane Bunker for her patience and diligence in seeing through this work to its completion. I wish to acknowledge in particular the reviewers who shared helpful comments on the writing at a critical stage and to extend gratitude to the Series Editors, J. Baird Callicott and John van Buren, for embracing the project. In Germany, I thank Michael Dusche along with Klaus Held, who unknowingly facilitated the birth of this book in a graduate seminar on the Presocratics. Igor Jasinski, Christina Burris, Elena Figueroa, Natasha

Piletich, Deb Vetter, Barbara Zanelli, Liza Monroy, China Adams, Lauren Brown, Linda Weintraub, Doug Macauley, and Michele Dixon offered cheerful support and encouragement with the project, and discussions with Chris Hallman, Eliot Tretter, Gary Backhaus, Jhan Hochman, John Scott, Nicky Dyal, Eric Orts, Christy Schneider, Luke Fischer, and Mike Hill were all valuable to me. Emily Helms, who served as my undergraduate research assistant one semester, was also very helpful in locating texts and providing thoughtful feedback, while dialogues I had with Alex Lampros during an independent study I conducted on *Being and Time* forced me to clarify some of my views of Heidegger. Great thanks are due as well to my friend Shaila George for her artwork and design of the back cover illustration.

Place is a theme throughout this work, and a host of cafés in Oberlin, Philadelphia, New York City, Boston, and Bloomington, Indiana provided warm or, alternatively, cool, well-lit environments in which to tap away on my laptop. Thanks in particular goes to the Greenline Coffee House in West Philadelphia (where I ran a biweekly Philosophy Café) for its pleasant staff, fine coffee, and vegetarian fare. The good-spirited instructors at Wake Up Yoga and Studio 34 Yoga kept me attuned to the ever-important roles of breath and air as I labored through final revisions to the book. And I should not forget the contributions of several non-human companions, especially two Siamese cats (Yeti and Dante) and two black cats (Griffin and Nemo), who kept me company during the course of the writing.

Portions of this work were presented to the Society for Philosophy and Geography; the International Association for Environmental Philosophy; the International Association for the Study of Environment, Space and Place; and the Institute for Advanced Phenomenological Research. Parts of Chapters three, five, six, and seven have appeared, respectively, in an earlier or abbreviated form in scholarly journals: "The Flowering of Environmental Roots and the Four Elements: From Empedocles to Deleuze and Guattari," *Worldviews: Environment, Culture, Religion* 9, 3 (2005), pp. 281–314 (permission Koninklijke Brill N.V.); "The Place of the Elements and the Elements of Place: Aristotelian Contributions to Environmental Thought," *Ethics, Place and Environment* 9, 2 (2006), pp. 187–206 (permission Taylor and Francis Ltd.); "Night and Shadows: The Space and Place of Darkness," *Environment, Space, Place* 1 (Fall 2009), pp. 51–76 (permission Zeta Books); and "The Domestication of Water: Filtering Nature Through Technology," *Essays in Philosophy* 6, 1 (2005) (permission Michael Goodman, Editor). The right to use this material is gratefully acknowledged.

Finally, a very special appreciation is extended to my parents, Marion and Howard Macauley—to whom this book is dedicated—for their many forms of assistance, patience, and loving support during the entire course of my upbringing and education.

Introduction

> I am here . . . to confront, immediately and directly if it's possible, the bare bones of existence, the elemental and fundamental, the bedrock which sustains us.
>
> —Edward Abbey, *Desert Solitaire*

> I suspect that even today when the most erudite ask what is the nature of anything, they are haunted by the answer, "of earth," "of water,," "of air," or "of fire"—the solid, the flowing, the gaseous, the caloric.
>
> —Frederick Woodbridge, *Essay on Nature*

Four-Thought

"The world today," proclaimed writer Henry Beston in the 1920s, "is sick to its thin blood for lack of elemental things, for fire before the hands, for water welling from the earth, for air, for the dear earth itself underfoot."[1] Beston's diagnostic remark about our relation with the environment points to the potential significance of taking into consideration—philosophically, geographically, and psychologically—not just individual organisms, distinct species, or identifiable ecosystems but the elemental places, forces, and phenomena of the surrounding and sensuous world as well. Such a perspective suggests that environmental dilemmas are, in part, a result of our historical, cultural, and experiential relationships with earth, fire, air, and water. The ever-threatening pollution of the skies and atmosphere (air); risks to oceans, lakes, rivers, and aquifers (water); conversion of fertile soil and forested land (earth) into fallow deserts and toxic dumps; and overreliance on fossil fuels and high technology (fire) provide compelling reasons for exploring this idea. As inhabitants of an increasingly human-made world—where we live literally inside of artifacts and they reside routinely within our bodies—most of us have forgotten or even foresworn the primacy and place of elemental "four-thought."

    We are, in effect, increasingly sheltered from rather than brought into closer contact with the elements, which, in turn, have retreated from the forefront of daily thought and experience. If the current ecological crisis is partly a predicament involving our changing relations to earth, air, fire, and water, it more specifically concerns what we may term the domestication of the elements and environment, a transformation and social taming of other-than-human entities, animals, and locations. This domestication has fostered forms of forgetting, kinds of cultural and philosophical amnesia. The elements often appear dimmed down or diminished as they enter the human *domus*. Although physically near, they nevertheless remain existentially remote, covered over, or concealed. One task, then, of ecological philosophy is to encourage a renewed understanding of and critical encounter with air, fire, earth, and water and to make us aware of the complex—and sometimes very necessary—mediations that exist between us and the environment, between humans and the more capacious world. It implies the need for elemental *anamnesis*—recollection or, literally, "loss of forgetfulness." Put differently, addressing environmental problems necessitates *finding our own element* and place within an encompassing and abiding manifold.

Ecology—the household of nature—and correspondingly an ecological human community provide a fitting theoretical abode for understanding the elements, which in Aristotle's ancient view are themselves seeking to return to their respective places—endeavoring to find their way home. The tetrad of water, earth, fire, and air, however, need not be construed solely as objective things-in-themselves, unmediated presences or first principles—in short, as simple, indivisible constituents of the material world by way of analogy with the chemist's periodic table. Rather, through putting ourselves in sustained touch with the perennial elements, we might begin to discover ways in which traditional notions of nature can be amended and perceived cleavages between the natural and cultural realms can be mended, even eclipsed. This goal is facilitated by tracing the terrain of the changing and often submerged idea of the elements historically within the compass of a philosophy of the physical world so as to reveal the ways in which they are culturally "constructed" by human faculties, philosophies and practices while this process is still "constrained" by what lies beyond, beneath, between, and before us.

The ultimate purpose, however, of an inquiry into conceptions of earth, air, fire, and water is not simply to see the manner in which the four elements have been elevated into philosophical ideas—indeed one of the hundred "great ideas" of Western thought according to Mortimer Adler—but to help lead this thinking back to engaged experience and practical environmental action.[2] In puzzling perpetually over the origin and meaning of life as well as our place within the world, we ruminate invariably on the elemental composition of these realms, attempting to find or create an order out of the bewildered and be-wildering—both confusing and becoming wild—abundance of sensual perceptions that we encounter. And whether we identify the elements as atomic or eternal, theoretical principles or physical places, generated or pregiven, or we number them as 4, 5 or 117, they will no doubt hold an enduring philosophical fascination. As Alfred North Whitehead observed, the ancient theories of earth, air, fire, and water continue to testify "to the undying vitality of Greek philosophy in its search for the ultimate."[3] An examination of the classical elements serves this ongoing task of bearing witness, but it also opens up the promising possibility of putting to use such knowledge in the service of ecological sustainability.

Sheltering the Elements

In the forthcoming chapters, we pursue the idea of the elements from their origins in early Western thought to their more recent expressions in contemporary fields, such as phenomenology and post-structuralist thought, situating the investigation within the broader context of environmental philosophy. Through a "stoicheology"—from the Greek *stoicheia* (elements), thus literally a study of the elements—we articulate, examine, and attempt to reanimate the notion and experience of the elemental, to unearth and exfoliate, as it were, some of the sedimented layers of philosophical and cultural history that have overlain and masked this idea. It is necessary first to provide a brief overview of the trajectory and broad plan of the present work and to make a few introductory points in anticipation of several preemptive challenges that might arise with respect to an attempt to recover critically and extend creatively the canonical elements.

In this latter regard, one may inquire reasonably why the four elements, rather than the more familiar concept of nature, are being invoked. Additionally, one could object plausibly that fire, earth, water, and air are no longer considered "elements" but rather chemical compounds (in the case of air or water) or admixtures (with forms of earth) or rapid oxidation processes (in the instance of fire) and that one is in danger of courting anachronisms by resuscitating them. As Hegel puts it in *The Philosophy of Nature*, "The concept of the four elements, which has been commonplace since the time of Empedocles, has been rejected as puerile phantasy." "No educated person," he adds, "is now permitted, under any circumstances, to mention [it]."[4] Why then, we might ask, after acknowledging the intellectual stigma attached to interest in the elements—Hegel's words nearly suggest a taboo—would one proceed to consider their meaning, to take seriously and even to take up this ancient idea? Furthermore, why would Hegel deign to undertake such an inquiry himself in the same work and write in his *Lectures on the History of Philosophy*: "In the idea of the four elements we have the elevation of sensuous ideas into thought"?[5]

Hegel's observations are significant because they gesture toward recognizing in some small measure that the collective notion of the elements as earth, fire, air, and water is both quite ordinary—perennial, pervasive, and commonplace to most cultures—and at the same time very extraordinary—belonging to the realm of dream, mythology, and imagination or, indeed as he notes, to fantasy. In light of this characterization, we may well be inclined to relegate these once-fundamental "building blocks" of nature to the status of philosophical fossils, or to picture them as being a bit like the large wooden toy alphabet cubes that are arranged and rearranged by many children seeking to construct—or spell out—a secret corner in the cosmos. That is, the four elements strike many philosophers and natural scientists as something palpable and primitive but also as something to be outgrown or overcome in time. Indeed, as something that has in fact been superseded with time. Such an attitude, we shall see, is mistaken.

One rationale for taking up earth, fire, air, and water is that they are more concrete and less abstract than an often elusive and elastic notion of nature. It is easier, in brief, to engage these entities with the senses and to experience them physically or viscerally and then, in turn, to know them intellectually. We can draw a lighted flame before our eyes, inspect dry earth in our hands, relish cool air in our noses and lungs, and appreciate the distinct textures or tastes of water with our tongues. Nature, by contrast, is a more amorphous and contested notion lying in a terrain that often leads across philosophical precipices, through conceptual quicksand and into a theoretical *cul de sac* that poses a thicket of epistemological, ontological, or metaphysical problems. This point is evidenced by the spate of recent books with such titles as *The Death of Nature, The End of Nature, Against Nature, Reinventing Nature?* and *The Social Creation of Nature*. Because of this anxiety over its uses, limits and value, nature is increasingly deployed or intoned with clothespin quotes that guard the word and idea like semantic sentries ("Nature") as if it were being written cautiously under a form of protest or erasure.[6]

In undertaking this study, then, we will not be referring *back* to "Nature" itself as an entirely stable sphere of meaning—a repository of the ontologically pregiven—so much as gesturing *forward* (sideward and wayward) to the possibility of discovering a more fluid, open and unfolding philosophical framework and ecological field. That is, we will be seeking less a *re-rooting* of the elements in a supposedly firm and intractable soil or ground of being (and, correspondingly, a notion of nature counter-posed sharply to culture) but instead their *re-routing* through the shifting sands of becoming and, we could say, a nascent *culture of nature* that embraces not only the forces of air, water, earth, and fire but the formative human presence in the environment as well. Here an analysis of the *domestication of the elements* rather than the *domination of nature*—an expression used widely by environmentalists—provides an alternative and ultimately more coherent theoretical model for understanding many of our interactions with the physical world.[7] Fire, for example, is domesticated most traditionally in the hearth—the heart of the home—but also as technology in the form of lighting, electricity and weaponry (i.e., "firepower"). Similarly, water is domesticated in fountains, bottles, pipes, tubs, and engineering projects as it is routed into the social sphere where its cultural meanings are defined, magnified, or multiplied.[8]

A second and related reason for investigating earth, air, fire, and water is that they are part of our everyday lifeworld in ways that the widely respected elements of the periodic table are not. One can even say that in some sense the scientific elements and those of philosophy, cosmology, or mythology are antipodal. "H_2O and water are opposites," the noted writer Ivan Illich has remarked.[9] That is, the elements of modern chemistry are not the elements of our more immediate, somatic, cultural, or imaginative experience even if they are now recognized as the *Urstoff* of the universe. Most recently discovered—and more accurately, *invented*—elements of the periodic table, in fact, survived only a few seconds before vanishing into atomic debris through radioactive decay. There are, in short, very practical and determinate empirical dimensions related to earth, air, fire, and water arising from our bodily needs to locate drinkable fluids, adjust air temperature and quality, secure fire for cooking and heating, or find cultivable earth to grow food, and our daily language and goals concerning the environment are usually couched in these specific elemental terms.

Third, we need to historicize our ideas of nature and our relations with our surroundings: tell a story and so, in the process, view ecological restoration as a narrative and form of *re-story-ation*.[10] In this sense, we must keep in mind the origins of Western science and philosophy in the accounts of the four elements and thereby better understand their initial appearance, later disappearance and surprising reappearance. As the philosophers Frederick Woodbridge and Gaston Bachelard have both declaimed, even the most learned scholars and natural scientists today may still be intrigued or troubled by earth, air, fire, and water when investigating the physical universe. In the late eighteenth century, scientist Joseph Priestley—who himself helped to undermine the primacy of two of the classical elements—announced in ambivalent words: "There are, I believe, very few maxims in philosophy that have laid firmer hold upon the mind, than that . . . atmospheric air . . . is a simple elemental substance, indestructible, and unalterable, at least so as water is supposed to be."[11] We should remember that the idea, theory and influence of the so-called fifth element *aether* (ether) persisted into the twentieth century and recall that scientists thought Aristotle's ethereal quintessence filled the space between stars and inside atoms. Renowned physicist James Clerk Maxwell once waxed that the universe is "full of this wonderful medium; so full that no human power can remove it from the smallest portion of space, or produce the slightest flaw in its infinite continuity."[12] In the case of Plato—who advanced a complex theory of the four elements as geometric shapes—it is clear that modern physics seems in many respects to be "returning" to this early thinking or at least reaching conclusions that are often compatible with it. Even the language of the Presocratics is being invoked, as contemporary scientists speak of hot and cold dark matter or speculate on the existence of a uniform primordial and material "soup" that resembles Anaxagoras' "all things were together."[13]

This book does not concern itself in the main with the basic constituents of modern chemistry, such as Promethium, Nitrogen, or Germanium, but rather focuses on the elements as they appear in early cosmology, Presocratic thought, classical Greek philosophy, nature writing, phenomenology, Continental theory, and, to a lesser extent, literature and art. These latter understandings of the elements are at once both quotidian and richer in social and philosophical meaning than are their chemical counterparts.[14] Humans are surely symbol-creating animals, even if we are also rational ones, as Aristotle knew, and so one must attend to this cultural dimension in an investigation of the environment and elemental regions.[15] The classic—as opposed to modern scientific—conception of the elements connects us, as is seen throughout this work, to issues related to place and pollution, cosmological order and geographical orientation, human dwelling and animal domestication, ecological perception and environmental poetics, and the bodily senses and body politic, among other topics.

Fourth and finally, one must acknowledge that in returning to bygone eras, we encounter numerous potential difficulties in applying retrospectively such concepts as ecology, anthropocentrism or evolution, to mention but a few terms. It will not be argued, however, that Empedocles, Plato, Aristotle, or other early philosophers were "environmentalists" in the current sense of the word. Rather, we need to explore their orientations, sensibilities, and attitudes toward the physical world and especially the elements—not merely the literal truth of their often outdated philosophical and scientific claims—and to consider the relevance, influence, insights, and shortfalls of this thinking for contemporary predicaments. John Rist puts the issue well—although perhaps a bit too strongly—when he observes:

> We may identify a paradoxical situation: Ancient thinkers evince little overt concern for the environment, while normally possessing a mental universe in which they have the resources for justifying such concern, while we moderns often exhibit concern for the environment but have few theoretical resources on which such concern can be grounded.[16]

In this light, the matter is not simply whether these philosophers were in fact interested in natural processes (they clearly were) or environmental subjects as we now say (they obviously were not) but whether their thought is still germane to or productive for our own. And, more importantly, the question now arises whether given the benefit of hindsight we are wise enough to learn from the experiences and ideas, the errors and insights, of our forebears.

Plan of the Work

In the following work, we reflect initially, in turn, on earth, air, fire, and water individually as they appear in the physical and cultural realms, exploring some of their manifestations in the lifeworld so as to encourage an active recollection and ongoing encounter with the elemental. Although introduced separately at this preliminary stage, we will later see how they relate to one another conceptually and materially. The ensuing chapter recalls and considers the elements in Presocratic and classical Greek thought and looks at some of their philosophical and social meanings, characterizations and characteristics, relations with one another, and ties to the broader environment. This enterprise includes brief comparisons with the cosmologies and myths of non-Greek and non-European cultures, where the elements arise with frequency. Additionally, we will discover that the elements not only help to provide the frame and axis of our perceptual order but also that they are "constructed" themselves in part through existing social, political, and linguistic practices. As throughout this work, these arguments and observations are cast within a wider context so as to underscore the enduring pertinence of the ancient Greeks to contemporary problems.

We then take up the philosophical, poetic, and religious works—*Peri Phuseos* (*On Nature*) and *Katharmoi* (*Purifications*)—of the Presocratic thinker Empedocles in terms of their perspectives on the natural environment. Through an ethical, political, and material framing of the four *rhizomata* (roots or elements) of earth, fire, air, and water into a coherent cosmology, Empedocles provides an early but important understanding of ideas and issues that remain relevant today, including conceptions of pollution and social equality, the treatment of nonhuman animals, descriptions of organic processes, the status of nature, and the speculative underpinnings of evolutionary theory. We can reasonably view Empedocles as a kind of shaman-naturalist who is keenly aware of and empathetic with the workings of the physical world even if he is not strictly an "ancient environmentalist." We also explore the poststructuralist (net)work of Gilles Deleuze and Félix Guattari, where we find a critique of the kind of "roots" Empedocles identifies and a defense of a notion of "rhizomes" that enables us both to observe continuities with the Presocratic philosopher and to make creative or constructive links with our modern environment.

We subsequently investigate the place and displacement of the elements in the alembic of Plato and Aristotle's respective writings. In the case of Plato, we look at the construction of the elements in his physical treatise, the *Timaeus*, examining their state and status within the Platonic *chora*-graphy and cosmology, including their manner of derivation, transformation, and geometrization. There are ecologically significant dimensions to his physics—especially his view of place and conception of the cosmos—but Plato's treatment of the natural world ultimately reduces the elements to a secondary, tertiary, or lesser status. We see that in quantifying and qualifying earth, water, air, and fire, Plato dispatches the "letters" of nature to posterity in several different ways: necessitating elements of the erstwhile "elements," offering a method for the mathematization of nature, and providing a model now amenable in certain respects to modern chemistry and physics. In the process, we forge philosophical and environmental connections to contemporary Continental thought through the works of Alfred North Whitehead and Edmund Husserl.

With Aristotle, there is a return to a qualitative framework in which, despite initial appearances, the elements can once again be interpreted as primary and ultimate. Aristotle, in fact, advances multiple accounts of the elements in works ranging from *On the Heavens* and *On Generation and Corruption* to the *Physics*, *Meteorology*, and *On the Soul*. We reconstruct and relate these various accounts, showing the unrecognized or unacknowledged logical threads through these texts, discussing his differences with and divergence from Plato and the Presocratics, and exploring problems tied to the generation, transformation and compounding of earth, water, air, and fire as well as the status of a fifth element. We identify four major components of Aristotle's theory of the elements related to weight, place, motion, and contrariety. We find, too, that an implicit ecology of the elements can be discerned and developed from their cyclical economy, one that concerns natural place, physical and bodily contact, geocentricity, organic unity, and philosophical naturalism.

The next chapter examines the domestication of the elements as a way of understanding their mediation, transformation, or ostensible disappearance in both everyday life and critical or creative thought. The notion and practice of domestication is articulated in relation to attempts to escape the earth, alter the air and atmosphere, or transfigure and tame fire as a form of technology. Special focus is placed on inveterate efforts to control, channel, and corral water in its many modalities as an illustration of these processes, including river redirection, fountains, and bottled water.

In the penultimate chapter, we explore the return, recovery, and reclamation of the elements and elemental realms in twentieth- and twenty-first-century Continental thought and attempt to fashion an avenue out of some of our environmental dilemmas through an encounter with the contributions of selected phenomenologists, postmodernists, and philosophical naturalists. We identify and elucidate the respective roles of dwelling through Martin Heidegger's elemental fourfold, reverie by way of Gaston Bachelard's elemental poetics, and the body using Maurice Merleau-Ponty's notion of elemental "flesh" as integral to re-animating, re-membering, and re-cycling the four elements. We also look at ideas of recent philosophers, such as Luce Irigaray (elemental passions), Alphonso Lingis (elemental imperatives), Edward Casey (elemental landscapes), John Sallis (elemental nature), and Emmanuel Levinas (elemental sensibility), for environmental connections with place, gender, corporeality, and perception. Each of these figures helps to put us potentially into closer contact with the sensuous world by offering a fresh vocabulary or voice for ecological discourse and a competing, if often compatible, vision of our elemental surroundings. We conclude the investigation by suggesting some ways of relating earth, air, fire, and water to aesthetics, ethics, and public policy so as to encourage a turn toward environmental values and action.

One final note: eight "interstices" are positioned as segues between the individual chapters and represent short meditations on other elemental phenomena that constitute our world. Two reflections are devoted very loosely to each of the four perennial elements. Thus, stone and wood bond us with the subtending earth; ice and cloud tie us to the shifting realm of water; heat and light join us with the force of fire; and night and space link us to the canopy of air. These interstices serve as concrete counterpoises to the theoretical dimensions of the work but, hopefully, provide in addition small openings for a closer and more robust consideration of these entities or subjects in their own right.

— Part I —

Elemental Encounters and Ideas

— 1 —

Philosophy's Forgotten Four

The four elements [are] the hormones of the imagination.
—Gaston Bachelard, *Air and Dreams*

Now I a fourfold vision see, / And a fourfold vision is given to me.
—William Blake, Letter to Thomas Butts

Western philosophy commences as a profound, if protracted, contemplation of the natural environment in an attempt to discern the workings of the world and to reflect on its origin, constitution, and meaning. The first *physiologoi*, or natural philosophers, speculated not just on the human *psyche* (soul or mind) but also focused foremost on the vaulting sky, the flickering turns and reversals of fire, the eddies and rhythmic flows of water, and the hidden depth or silent beauty of rock and earth—in short, the four elements. By way of an engagement with the elements as well as living plants and animals, they searched for a hidden *arche* (ruling principle), an underlying *logos* (order) and a guiding *telos* (purpose or goal). Interrogating and building on ideas advanced by the Presocratics in the sixth and fifth centuries B.C.E., subsequent philosophers and incipient scientists like Aristotle and Theophrastus were able to provide the underpinnings of later ecological thought by integrating close observation of the natural world with rational explanation and justification.[1]

In these early historical periods, theories of nature were not yet separated sharply from or supplanted by more human-centered theories of mind, nor was philosophy itself distinguishable clearly from nascent science. This ancient thought remains relevant today not because it is empirically accurate but because it is embedded in a vision of the world much vaster than humanity alone. It also is marked frequently by a generosity of spirit, sensitivity to the subtleties of environmental change, openness to nonhuman otherness, and an ontologically egalitarian orientation. As environmental thinkers seek to "green" philosophy and to "deepen," "widen" or even "democratize" ecology, it is vital to recall these initial and bold theoretical strides. It is equally imperative to grasp the slow departures from a philosophical perspective rooted in a vision of an intelligible, rational, and beautiful cosmos, the transitions out of myth and stories about animal figures, the increasing breaks with the organic and biological realms, and eventually the attempts to escape or transcend this world altogether. In so doing, we can benefit from an inquiry into how the elements—including matter, motion, and causality—were construed or constructed and ask how social and ecological changes involving deforestation or domestication, for example, altered these notions and allowed transformations of land, sea, sky, and fire power to proceed with little encumbered speed.[2]

The four elements—water, air, earth, and fire—have exercised an enormous, if often unnoticed, impact on the Occidental imagination. It may be reasonably said that they have helped to organize an influential view of the lifeworld and to frame a compelling picture of the universe. But they also served as the *materia prima* with which philosophy erected its founding edifices. This four unfolds—sets itself forth—into philosophical and literary history, too, where we can trace its unexpected resonances through the four ancient humors, the Pythagorean *tetraktus*, alchemical speculation, or the opuses of modern poets such as William Blake, T. S. Eliot, and Ezra Pound, to name but a few.

Nonetheless, it is an apparent, if at times unfortunate, truth of the human condition that we often only become aware of circumstances, conditions, and objects when they change suddenly, when they fail to function in predictable manners, or when they disappear inexplicably from our circadian rhythms. This is especially the case with things elemental. When a flame leaps out unexpectedly from a campfire and licks the surrounding brush or when lightning fissures a halcyon night sky, we become cognizant of the awesome and transfiguring force of fire. When a pipe bursts in the bathroom or when a river breaks its banks and floods communities, we no longer take the calm course of water for granted. When the atmosphere thins as we ascend a mountain or when the pressure in our ears pops on a plane, we sense quickly the presence of what formerly seemed to be missing entirely in the invisible air. When the ground is cleaved and wrenched open or when an avalanche of rock and snow is launched like a toboggan down a precipitous slope, we stand up and take immediate notice of the stirrings of the seemingly solid, stolid, and stable earth. In order, then, to foreground the four classical elements and place them before us from the outset—and prior to examining the theories of their emergence, transformation, and endurance—let us first meditate upon earth, air, fire, and water individually and consider some of the ways they enter into our everyday worlds so as to make their presence felt both as an ecological necessity and a robust cultural resource.

Earth

O sweet spontaneous / earth how often have / the /doting / fingers of / prurient philosophers pinched / and / poked / thee /, has the naughty thumb / of science prodded / thy / beauty . . . / (but . . . / thou answerest / them only with / spring).

—e. e. cummings, "O sweet spontaneous"

> The earth is not a mere fragment of dead history, stratum upon stratum like the leaves of a book, to be studied by geologists and antiquaries chiefly, but living poetry like the leaves of a tree, which precede flowers and fruit.
>
> —Henry David Thoreau, *Walden*

Earth is confoundingly complex—"wild bewildering" to borrow a pregnant phrase from Edgar Allan Poe—because it is encountered and conceived in a vast variety of ways: as dirt, humus, soil, compost, stone, land, silt, mud, clay, loam, dust, sand, mineral, and excrement, among others. At the same time, we subsume these distinctions when we speak not only of earth as ground but as planetary whole—the Earth—our life-supporting home. In many of its manifestations, earth is posited as a creative matrix, material base, or generative mother for both human civilization and philosophical speculation. These associations are evident in, for example, the religious belief that we are but a handful of shaped dirt (Adam is Hebrew for red clay) that will return to the dust; in the profound cultural attachments to land and landscape; and in attempts to recycle or reuse earthy wastes.

Just as the atmospheric air is multilayered, so is earth more than monolithic. It is extremely differentiated across an ever-proliferating surface in the form of continents, bioregions, valley basins, alpine ranges, deserts, dells, fields, and forests. It is distinguished vertically as sedimented tiers ranging from the bountiful and cultivable epidermal "skin" of the topsoil to the darker subsoil to the deep and deader realms of the interior and ultimately molten center. We live on and interact not only with *terra cognita* but also *terra incognita*, both a revealed and revealing surface and a concealed and self-secluding core, or underground. It is through the earth's "held-back silence," its "taciturn" and sequestered features, to use Rainer Rilke's words, that the fertile face of the land is held up and made manifest. As the poet asks, "Earth, isn't this what you want: to arise within us, *invisible?*"[3] Reciprocally, then, the telluric sphere sinks back into the unseen insides where in withdrawal it is kept in reserve before it is ready to emerge again.[4]

However, when the "doting fingers of prurient philosophers" explore the earthiness and underworld of dream, myth, and imagination, they frequently find—in accordance with classicists—three distinguishing psychological levels of earth: first and uppermost, Demeter's green plain of growth and fertility (the topsoil); second and below, *Ge*, the subsoil, dark earth or underground as well as physical and psychic ground (or place) of persons and communities; and third, *Chthon*, the realm of depth, coldness, and the dead beneath earth as we normally speak of it. In essence, this Demeter–Ge–Chton stratification conceives a less physical or more "pure" earth beyond the ground we normally walk on.[5] As Jung observes, when we begin to plumb the place of the unconscious, we discover invariably a vital relationship of body and earth via chthonic powers, the force of the dark and elemental, the maternal and material ground. It is this bodily belonging to earth that over time expresses our many affinities and binds our emerging identities to specific or peculiar places.

The etymologies of "earth" bespeak its multicultural manifestations and, by extension, its multinatural dimensions because the land is shaped and subsequently experienced in a variety of manners. But underlying these differences are some common connections. Our English word has cognates in many languages, including *Erde* in German and *aarde* in Dutch. It is related to *ert* ("ground") in Middle Irish and *ertha* in Old Saxon. Semitic languages possess words for "earth" that are close to those in Indo-European tongues. One finds in Arabic, *ard*; in Aramaic, *araa*; in Akkadian, *irtsitu*; in Phoenician, *erets*; and in Hebrew *arets* or *erets*. Latin roots *terr-* (as in "terrestrial") or *tellur-* (as in "tellurian") also refer to the earth. The Earth has been personified widely as a deity, too, especially a goddess, as in the Greek, *Gaia*, or the figure of "Mother Earth" (*Terra Mater* or *Tellus Mater*). The Chinese earth goddess and embodiment of fertility is Hou-Tu, who serves in a capacity similar to Gaia. In Norse myths, Jord is the divine earth mother and the parent of Thor. An exception to these gender roles can be found in ancient Egypt, where sky in the figure of Nut is a female goddess while earth appears in the form of Geb, who is male.

The nomenclature of earth underscores its vast differentiation and heterogeneity: there are ten soil orders, more than twenty designations for soil characteristics, and more than fourteen thousand individually named soils. The storied layers of earth are known appropriately as horizons, implying both an accumulated horizontality and a demarcating liminality, a line measuring the passing sands (and soils) of time. An assembly of horizons is referred to as a profile, which bears the mark of a particular soil and is fashioned through the dynamism of earth, fire, air, and water. The relatively passive earth provides a substrate in the form of igneous, metamorphic or sedimentary rock on which water works its terra-forming and soil-building powers, sending silica, clays, aluminums, and irons into lower tellurian depths. Through chemical changes and wind transferences, air also exercises an assertive role. Carbon dioxide, for example, is pivotal in the production of calcium horizons in the soil profile. Finally, soil grows hotter as one moves deeper into the earth, and chemical reactions, in turn, increase dramatically with temperature rises, thereby providing a place for elemental fire in the process. Minerals are transformed; iron is oxidized; and acids and salts are freed to actively engage the earthen medium. Ultimately, the soiled surface—what geologists call regolith—is subject to a grand form of circulation akin to air and water cycles as it erodes, blows away, flows, and eventually sinks at a pace of more than ten tons per acre each year in the United States into the suture that recycles it toward a subterranean fire.[6]

Look closely at a handful of rich soil, and you can frequently unearth a cornucopia of delights resting in the palm of your hand: shards of marble, slivers of leaf fiber, specks of sand, fragments of roots, splinters of wood, the remains of tiny organisms. Soil derives from the Latin *solium*, meaning, "seat," and it is likely related to *sedere*, "to sit." In this capacity, it is the outermost earthen "stuff" and "skin" on which we position our bodies and place our cultures. In order to maintain itself, soil employs a labor force of specialists in demolition, disassembly, and regeneration, including a million and a half species of fungi and between two and three billion species of bacteria, most of them part of a silent army of the unknown.[7] When it is fertile, soil provides the materiality of and matrix for life itself. A shortage of this substance, however, can contribute to the decline and demise of whole cultures. The Mayan, Greek, and Roman empires, for example, all eroded and fell apart from within, in part due to poor soil management, a fact to which our own society should remain alert as we consume and vanquish this invaluable resource.[8]

In his natural history of dirt—what he calls earth's "ecstatic skin"—William Bryant Logan recounts that the sea was once a kind of liquid proto-soil, a place "where Earth, air, water and the solar fire met for the first time" before life oozed onto land.[9] Although we routinely acknowledge that larger terrestrial organisms are located mainly where the earth meets the air—where the tip of the topsoil greets the base of the sky—we may forget that the soil, too, is percolating with biological activity. Environmentalists, in fact, invoke the image of a soil pyramid and often describe the land itself as living. A rich forest soil contains as many as 5,500 individual organisms and as many as seventy different species in a single square foot, including a bevy of mites, millipedes, pill bugs, termites, earthworms, and nematodes.[10] Worms are, in many respects, the embodiment of this earthy materiality—biotic citizens in the best sense—as they feast on and excrete dirt, and deposit castings that enrich the soil they inhabit. Although technically blind, they sense and "see" by way of the polarities of wet/dry and hot/cold, qualities Aristotle identified as being the essence of the four elements. As Darwin himself recognized, "It may be doubted whether there are many other animals which have played so important a part in the history of the world."[11]

In one sense at least, we can "make" earth in a way that we cannot create water or air. The "brown gold" of compost is the result of a process whereby we speed up the decomposition of organic matter. Lawn clippings, coffee grounds, leaves, rotting wood, kitchen scraps, and animal manure can all be assembled into a warm distillate that will decay over several months through the work of bacteria. There are many ecological merits of compost that are produced largely through the contributions of its main ingredient, humus. The benefits of this "buried treasure" to the ground or garden include improving soil integrity and structure; increasing the ability of the earth to hold water for growing food; absorbing solar energy to warm the soil; breaking down organic matter through a host of microorganisms to provide plants with needed elements; and restoring to the earth chemicals removed through agriculture. For the American gardener, generating compost has been elevated to the level of a moral virtue not merely because it reinvigorates the land but because it is viewed as rekindling our humanity by reasserting our interdependence with the earth and our independence from the petrochemical industry.[12]

Earth is more resistant to the force of light and thus more opposed to displaying protean qualities than the remaining triumvirate of canonical elements. Virginia Woolf caught sight of this point when she waxed: "earth absorbs colour like a sponge slowly drinking water. It puts on weight; rounds itself; hangs pendent; settles and swings beneath our feet."[13] In the fifteenth century, Basil Valentine likewise noticed that earth is both porous and gross so that it latently "receives all that the other three project onto it."[14] Geographically, earth offers girding support for the primary dimensions of place. It is an encompassing "matrix of matrices" relative to its tendency toward downward motion, providing a region of orientation for human and nonhuman bodies.[15] In landscape art, like the physical world it strives to represent, earth is routinely underlying—below water and sky—so that it both defines and delimits topographical features. As a subtending placeholder, it solicits and draws forth our beholding faculties of aesthetic appreciation.

Earth is marked more demonstrably and visibly than other elemental realms by human activity, though we can also see the signature effects of moving air, flowing water, and catalytic fire upon its surface and subsurface. "Wind and water and ice and life / have powdered our planet's obdurate skin," John Updike rightly notices."[16] More specifically, earth is inscribed with a concatenation of anthropogenic lines: a complex skein of roads and highways, urban grids, wending fences, and twisting borders. When viewed from above, these markings assume a variety of shapes and meanings in relation to geographic and cultural place. I am often entranced, even hypnotized, when staring out the window of a plane onto the geometric patterns and shifting colors of the landscape far below, especially when the view suggests a deeper sense of geologic time or a foreign cultural frame of reference. The outlines of farms appear as if a patchwork of embroidered quilts; odd shapes seem to coalesce magically into interlocking jigsaw puzzle pieces; great shadows borne of hovering clouds or distant mountains spill over vast spans of ground and generate the illusion of dimensionality, even texture, where topographical relief barely exists; and the albedo of the planet morphs from snowy alpine whites to desert browns and tans to the blues and greens of more liquid-saddled terrain.

Upon learning of the equator in grade school, a geographer friend of mine who grew up in Kenya biked a great distance to the region where the line, which lies equidistant from the planet's poles, was supposed to be. He was crestfallen, however, to discover after a fruitless search that this most famous terrestrial marking was not literally tattooed upon the earth but exists only in our collective imagination and upon cartographic creations. The Nazca lines of Peru are, by contrast, one very material kind of geoglyph or "earth carving." Etched into the desert pampa two thousand years ago through the removal of rock so as to reveal pale pink sand beneath, these lines depict several hundred figures, including pictures of a humming bird, monkey, lizard, whale, and pelican among many animals, along with concentric circles, spirals, and other geometric patterns. The fact that they are only visible from high in the air has led to speculation that they represent effigies of animal gods, ancient roads or "walking temples," star pointers, images of constellations, primitive landing strips, or astronomical observatories. Here we gain a glimpse of earth as a kind of archival palimpsest, a tableau written or imaged upon over and over through time before being erased inexorably by elemental processes.

Throughout much of history and lasting into the Renaissance, however, normative prohibitions existed against digging too deeply into the bowels of the life-giving earth and wantonly removing minerals from it, actions believed to encourage human greed. The Roman Pliny thus wrote:

> We trace out all the veins of the earth, and yet . . . are astonished that it should occasionally cleave asunder or tremble: as though, forsooth, these signs could be any other than expressions of the indignation felt by our sacred parent! We penetrate into her entrails, and seek for treasures . . . as though each spot we tread upon were not sufficiently bounteous and fertile for us.

The earth was, in short, perceived as animate, sacred or capable of responding to such "violations" with earthquakes or other disasters, and such constraints on mining tended to protect the landscape, water, and human inhabitants from poisons and pollution.[17]

The stolidity and reliability of the often rock-solid earth lies in contrast with the overarching and ever-fluctuating sky. One is mostly stationary and stable; the other is transitory and largely transparent. Together, they form an elemental partnership and pairing around which our optical and corporeal worlds are organized. For the Greeks, the dynamism of earth and sky was expressed in terms of a division between gods and humans—between the "heavenly ones" (*epouranioi*) and "earthly ones" (*epichthonioi*)—as well as a distinction between Olympian and chthonian divinities.[18] But Thomas Moore registers a gentle protest: "A piece of the sky and a chunk of the earth lie lodged in the heart of every human being," he proclaims.[19] When the earth quakes or cleaves, as it does roughly 150,000 times each year, we are dislocated and disoriented, unsettled from our ingrained habits and forced to come to terms with the epiphanic insight of Heraclitus that everything does in fact flow and change. Of such events, Seneca once inquired, "What can one believe quite safe if the world itself is shaken, and its most solid parts totter to their fall . . . and the earth loses its chief characteristic, stability?"[20] As a seeming comment on this rhetorical query, Maurice Merleau-Ponty declared, "One earthquake does more to demonstrate our vulnerability and mortality than the whole of the history of philosophy."[21] During those instances in which we do lose contact with earth, however, we discover ourselves not in a formless void or vacuum of empty space but rather in the air and wind or in the open water, in the throes of another primal element.

On rare occasions, we sense our bodies in earth's embrace, deported into the hold of an encompassing hole, a below buried beneath the topsoil base but above a bottomless abyss. Earthen holes tend to signify an admixture of archetypal danger, delight, and discovery. What child has not clawed joyfully into shoreline sand, overturned shovelfuls of clay dirt, or imagined tunneling through the rocky earth to China (or alternatively America) as part of an early environmental expedition? John Ruskin recalled that in his youth he was enthralled with digging holes but that to great chagrin his parents did not countenance this kind of avante-gardening.[22] "Who needs to travel thousands of miles to find the new?" Logan aptly wonders. "The most mysterious place on Earth is right beneath our feet."[23] When we are surveying the strata of rock formations and outcroppings in such locations, we may become acutely aware of deep geologic time—an other-than-human scale of temporal processes fed by inexorable erosion, death, decay, and petrifaction. The rates of this transformation, of course, differ from place to place but the end result of turning stone into soil remains eternally the same. Meanwhile, resistant granites don the mountaintops; marbles shore up the high lands; and soft sandstones are recumbent in the valley bottoms. In this way, the landscape itself testifies like an expansive canvas to the ongoing influence of elemental processes and the forces of weather on earthen minerals.

The place of earth within philosophy is largely concealed—or folded into the wider concept of nature—befitting its own tendency toward darkness and self-seclusion. Earth is the one classical element not identified specifically by a major Presocratic thinker as an *arche* (origin or governing principle), with the proviso that Xenophanes of Colophon reputedly held that "For all things come from the earth, and all things end by becoming earth."[24] But philosophers, like poets, have intermittently discovered its archaic beauty and illuminated its enduring primacy and potency. The Benedictine monk Venerable Bede thus gave voice to the idea of earth as an egg—a cosmological motif also found among ancient Egyptians, Orphics and Gnostics—and in the process incorporated the three other classical elements in his vision. "The Earth is an element placed in the middle of the world as the yolk in the middle of an egg: around it is the water, like the white surrounding the yolk; outside that is the air, like the membrane of the egg; and around all is the fire, which closes it in as the shell does."[25] Indeed, earth assumes a distinct shape and status in Plato's cosmology, a unique position in Aristotle's geocentric physics, and a vital role in recent phenomenological and ecological investigations. Earth must be recognized for its centrality to notions of human perception, territory, motility, and materiality as well as its indispensable connections with other elemental zones. Earth is in many respects the keystone of the four perennial elements, providing a physical base and philosophical basis for an understanding of geographical and cultural place, one concept integral to sustainable environmental practices.

Hesiod imagines "broad-bosomed Earth" as a "sure standing-place" that comes into being aboriginally and only subsequent to "Chaos." As an illustration of Earth's fecundity and autonomy, she then gives birth through a kind of parthenogenesis to the starry heaven (Ouranos), who as a spouse covers her from above and conceives with her the hills and sea and "deep-whirling" Okeanos, the mythical river that encircles the Earth. Homer, too, acknowledges earth as the "well-formed . . . mother of all" whose "beauty nourishes all creatures that walk upon the land."[26] Plato, who uses similar language at times as Homer, posits the existence of what we might call a "second earth" in the *Phaedo*, a "true earth," given that we live in a "hollow" of Gaia, about a central sea "like ants or frogs round a pond." He hypothesizes that we dwell unknowingly of the real nature and decidedly large size of our spherical homeland, which he portrays vividly in his role of an early geographer as being like a ball "made of twelve pieces of skin, variegated and marked out in different colors."[27] In the *Laws*, Plato characterizes the land as an "ancestral home," counseling "we must cherish it even more than children cherish their mother." The earth is a "goddess" and "divine mistress" who deserves the same respect accorded other "spirits of the locality." [28] As is discovered here, Plato also privileges the position of earth within his *chora*-graphy of the elements, making it the *terra firma* of a transformational schema in the *Timaeus*.

Earth subtends and supports; it carries and bears the weight of the world, even if its ecological carrying capacity is finite and being stretched to the limit. Despite "her strong thighs," earth is still vulnerable and can "grow exhausted with bearing / too much, too soon too often," speculates poet Marge Piercy in one of her "Elemental Odes."[29] It is to this supportive dimension that Edmund Husserl refers when he describes the earth as *Ur-ark*, "the original ark," the "basis body" or "ground-body" (*Bodenkörper*) for all other bodies.[30] In doing so, he highlights its fundamental function as a permanent "here" for us as well as underscores the way that in its proto-primordiality—and contrary to Copernicus' claim—it does not actually move. In commenting on Husserl, Jacques Derrida observes of the earth that it is "the most universal, the most objectively exhibited element given to us" because it provides us with "the first matter of every sensible object." The earth is the "*exemplary* element" because it is "more naturally objective, more permanent, more solid, more rigid . . . than all other *elements*."[31] Merleau-Ponty also warns of the "forgetfulness of the earth"—as Martin Heidegger had explored a more abstract "forgetting of being"—and indicates that it serves as the "ground [*sol*] of experience" and "the root of our spatiality, our common homeland."[32]

In an effort to reveal its complex and multihued features, Gilles Deleuze and Félix Guattari speak of the Earth as a "body without organs," an entity "permeated by unformed, unstable matters, by flows in all directions, by free intensities or nomadic singularities."[33] The earth is not simply a singular force or phenomenon among many, nor is it a substance possessing form; nor again is it the same as territory. It is instead a "close embrace of all forces" and "an intense point in depth or in projection" that might be explored through what they style as "geo-philosophy."[34] In a broadly compatible vein, Stephen David Ross calls attention to the fecundity and seeming inexhaustibility of earth. In contrast to the hallmark ecological traits of stability and order, he finds a dizzying and disorienting superabundance on display.[35] The profundity and generative production of the earth—creatures beyond counting, depths past fathoming, surfaces always proliferating—expresses an unpredictable diversity and a bewildering disorderliness that exceeds expectations, upending our neat taxonomic or perceptual assumptions. And, finally, it is worth registering that John Sallis specifically identifies a uniquely *elemental* index for earth, comparing it with a conception of the individual earth and the universal earth. From this view, what we need is to think the earth "not as the *from which* of material composition but as a *from which* of manifestation."[36] This enterprise, in turn, entails perceiving things of the earth in terms of their self-showing, their revelation. In many of these philosophical characterizations, earth is cast as exceptional, singled out as special in an elemental or ontological sense.

Images of earth in poetry, literature and art allow us to further pinch, poke, and prod (to use e. e. cummings' language) the elemental world. In this work, we can distinguish introverted and invisible aspects of terrestrial repose—in the recesses of caves for example—from more extroverted dimensions accessible through human action upon stone, metal, and mineral. As is seen later, Gaston Bachelard reveals how the creative forces and dynamic features of earth are opposed by a potential for telluric destruction and ultimately renewal. He shows the ways that writers imaginatively find or fashion a view of the materiality of earth that is a complex combination of resistance and acceptance so that in its precarious equipoise in the laboring hands of the body, we are able to locate our notions of relative hardness and softness.

Originating as out-of-doors descendents of Minimalism and Conceptual Art, Earth Art and Land Art leave human marks and creative traces upon the landscape in an other-than-human setting rather than in a museum or gallery. Robert Smithson's 1970 "Spiral Jetty"—a coiling fifteen-hundred-foot pedestrian-scale earthwork built up out of stone, earth, and algae into the Great Salt Lake of Utah—is the most well-known instance of this genre, but other artists labor with or upon the earth as well, employing it as a medium, an extension of other media, or literally as a swath of canvas. Hamish Fulton and Richard Long, for example, both rely on the action of the walking body to reveal the nuances of the earth in particular locales, either through the documentation of photographs accompanied by haiku-like words or by unconventional site-specific sculptures. On a grander scale, Michael Heizer has undertaken a massive and controversial work on the Mormon Mesa of Nevada entitled "Double Negative" in which 240,000 tons of earth was displaced to create two giant trenches fifty-feet deep and fifteen-hundred-feet long. These excavations refer creatively to the empty or "negative" space generated by human and natural processes, commenting on the blurred distinction between sculpture and elemental rock.

Mapping is, of course, a primary way to discern and define the vast physical stretches of earth. Most basically, a map takes measure of the earth. Edward Casey distinguishes four broad kinds of mapping in an effort to identify the ways in which earth is marked: cartography (representation of geographic areas in the greatest possible exactitude), chorography (maps of particular regions), topography (maps of distinct places like cities) and, finally, a less traditional body-mapping (where the body charts or marks the earth through artistic action). Casey also astutely differentiates earth—what underlies our bodies and personal experiences as a stable place—from land, a mediatrix and middle term between earth and world. "Land turns earth inside out, as it were, putting its material contents on display, setting them out in particular places, so as to become subject to articulation in language and to play a role in the history of those who live on it."[37] Landscape, then, is where and how the earth appears; the place in which it is shaped by the cultural world. However it is evoked, the map is, of course, not identical with the represented earth, except perhaps in the fantastical tale told by Borges in which cartographers continually enlarge a map until it is coincident with the entire kingdom.

Although yielding to our efforts, earth is characterized above all by its tendency to regularly oppose our endeavors. Aviator and author Saint-Exupéry, who sets his famous story *The Little Prince* upon our own planet but speaks of tiny extra-terrestrial orbs in an unknown elsewhere, declares that "Earth teaches us a lot more about ourselves than all the books in the world, *because it resists us*." "Man," he surmises, "only finds himself when he measures himself against an obstacle."[38] To listen to, to celebrate and even to love this material resistance, this weighty opposition and unseen force we name gravity—even as we seek to surmount it—enables us to better apprehend this element. I am reminded here of one of my former students who stood in a marshy bog, a field of moist sediment and muck, during an entire spring afternoon on Earth Day in order to experience this magnified terrestrial pull and visceral earthen presence. Such a feeling is also conveyed by playing with or relaxing in viscous mud, burying oneself in sand, crawling up a slippery pyramid of gravel, climbing out of a deep hole, or even lying prone in an open grave (yes, try it!). This double moment of elemental embrace and elemental resistance is captured eloquently by Robert Frost in his lyric poem, "To Earthward": "When stiff and sore and scarred / I take away my hand / From leaning on it hard / In grass and sand. / The hurt is not enough; / I long for weight and strength / To feel the earth as rough / to all my length."[39]

It is expressed, too, in the "Burial Hymn" of the ancient *Rig Veda* when the subtending ground is addressed in prayer, along with Death and the community of mourners: "Creep away to this broad, vast earth, the mother that is kind and gentle. . . . Open up, earth; do not crush him, wrap him up as a mother wraps a son in the edge of her skirt."[40] Similarly, during yoga, in *Shavasana* or "corpse pose," one lies supine at the end of a day's practice and passively sinks into the earth, which bears one's weight generously, offering us a glimpse of that final resting state we will experience. Appropriately, perhaps, as a friend of mine was lying in *Shavasana* on a beach in Costa Rica, the spaces in the sandy earth beneath her began to slowly wiggle, shift, and open, and a whole army of ants—emissaries of the earth—emerged to crawl gently over and claim her outstretched body.

"Earth" and "world" often seem to be in a perpetual but productive strife with one another—an ongoing and ultimately unassimilated *agon* (contest) that in certain ways mirrors a widely perceived tension and antagonism between the spheres of nature and culture. Earth is a "serving bearer" that is capable of emerging, rising forth, and issuing upward. It is a self-dependent, effortless and inexhaustible entity that provides an elemental shelter and anchor for humans and other animals. The earth withholds from our attempts to fathom it. It is self-concealing in contrast to the world, which is more self-revealing. As Heidegger argues, it is only *on-the-earth* that we can understand ourselves *in-the-world* we create. It is here that we can find a harmony with the environment because "all things of earth, and the earth itself as a whole, flow together into a reciprocal accord."[41]

The elemental imagination points not just to the importance of more definite earthen entities such as stone, mountain, and mineral but to less determinate terrestrial matter such as mud, which can function as a primitive and plastic substance. The earthy material and paste of excrement, in particular, inhabits our theories, bodies, and psychological lives as well as fertilizes agricultural soil. Excrement can, in fact, serve as an ecological and cultural aliment because waste is but food in a different context, sustenance for other organisms. Shakespeare gestures directly toward this connection when he professes in *Timon of Athens*, "earth's a thief / that feeds and breathes by composture / stolen / from general excrement."[42] One of the lasting contributions that contemporary ecological criticism might make is to demystify, or at least to openly discuss, this seemingly sacred taboo but very profane subject. One would not be going too far, in fact, to regard the political and social cause of environmentalism itself as a kind of *bowel movement* that asks us to reconsider the relationship between body and earth, excrement and aliment, anality and animality, consumption and waste, and even death and dung. As Peter Sloterdijk speculates, "The grand act of ecology in the history of ideas that will have an impact as far as philosophy, ethics, and politics are concerned will be to transform the phenomenon of refuse into a 'high' theme."[43]

"Division into sky and earth— / it's not the proper way / to contemplate this wholeness," Wislawa Szymborska reminds us, perhaps with the idea in mind that the earth extends its broad embrace to include the largely invisible atmosphere with which it is contiguous and continuous.[44] When we are sequestered inside the ground itself—*in*-habiting it—like the spelunker in a cave, this "wholeness" transforms earth into both a subterranean base and a soiled sky, both a firm footing and canopied ceiling. At such times, we are quite literally encompassed and *surrounded* by earth, as the English word "environment" (from the French *en*, in, and *viron*, circuit, turn, or circle; hence, "to encircle") implies or the comparable German *Umwelt* (linguistically, the "around world") suggests. This sense of being enclosed by the terrestrial is magnified in limestone caverns, where at a languid pace the earth simultaneously accrues from beneath as conical pillars in stalagmites and drips down from overhead to form stalactites. Reflecting on my own experiences exploring caves in Pennsylvania, Kentucky, and Virginia, I can recall clearly the damp, cool, underground air; the moist earthen walls replying with soft echoes to human voices; the slow trickling water; and the dance of fire from flickering torches or flashlights. For me, these caves were not Platonic pits from which to escape but rather elemental worlds to behold.

In a very significant way, then, we are *autochthones* (autochthonous), creatures born of the earth as the Greek term *gegenes* suggests—combining notions of genesis and earth—and as implied by the English *human*, a word that is cognate with *humus*, the dark organic material in soils. It is probably more true to say that we emerge *out of* the earth rather than being born or thrown *into* it, as Existentialists assert. In fact, there is a persisting belief in many cultures that children "come from" the recesses of the earth, from local ravines and caverns or, alternatively, from rivers, springs, and ponds. Despite these superstitions and stories, it is earth-boundedness and earth-bondedness that give us our corporeal shape, our peculiar human posture and comportment, our legs that carry us as swinging pendulums across the unfolding landscape. Thus, as Nietzsche counsels, it behooves us "to remain faithful to the earth"[45] and to guard against what might be termed *earth alienation*, the attempt to surmount or escape the earth entirely.[46] Like the phenomena of fire, water and air, earth is less abstract and more primordial, particularized and localized than the notion of nature, and so it is worthy of focus not only as "our planet" but also as a canonical element. In a letter, poet Wallace Stevens appropriately reflects on "how utterly we have forsaken the Earth, in the sense of excluding it from our thoughts. There are but few who consider its physical hugeness, its rough enormity. It is still a disparate monstrosity, full of solitudes, barrens, wilds. It still dwarfs, terrifies, crushes."[47] Indeed, even as the world seems to shrink in magnitude at the same time. Actively remembering earth—and the Earth—therefore is surely one key to better appreciating, honoring and respecting its singularity and uniqueness. "O earth!" the Greek playwright Aristophanes opines, "what a sound, how august and profound! It fills me with wonder and awe."[48]

Air

This blue wilderness of interminable air.

—Lord Byron, *Cain*

Air is our second skin. / It enters us like a lover, or we die. / . . . the intimate element, in / and out of our bodies all day, feeding / us quietly, stoking our little fires.

—Marge Piercy, "What goes up"

Over the course of our lives, we will take in on average 650 million breaths.[49] Each day, that amounts to roughly thirty-five pounds of air entering and exiting our bodies by way of the cavity of our mouths and the cadenced bellows of our lungs which, if flattened like a sheet of paper, would be large enough to cover a tennis court. As with our passing awareness of the surrounding atmosphere, we rarely pause to consider this involuntary but essential activity sustaining our world and accompanying us like a trusty metronome, except perhaps when we are gasping for elusive oxygen. In his most well-known romantic tragedy, Shakespeare comments cleverly on this point when Juliet inquires of a nurse, "How art thou out of breath when thou hast breath to say to me that thou art out of breath?"[50]

Through a protracted story whereby our animal ancestors shuttled back and forth between surf and turf—water and earth—as fish, then amphibians, then reptiles and finally mammals before settling on solid soil, we evolved the ability to breathe in the open air. Later, when we stood upright, our bipedal posture altered our biological comportment and decoupled respiration from locomotion, which were allied closely in our quadrupedal forebears.[51] This change may have contributed fortuitously to the development of distinctly human speech—which relies on the subtle adjustment of the flow of air in the larynx, pharynx, and nasal hollow—and hence indirectly to our self-understanding as the animal possessing the glorious gift of language. "A living being capable of speech" (*zoon logon ekhon*), as Aristotle puts it. Sylvia Plath even seems to intuitively associate commonplace respiration and the regularity of the pulse with existential identity. "I took a deep breath and listened to the old bray of my heart: I am, I am, I am," she exclaims.[52] Taking inspiration from this epiphany, we may find the kind of certainty and conviction Descartes sought in his intellectual meditations on the *cogito* but arrive instead on a more fundamental and temporally prior, corporeal truth: *I breathe therefore I am*. Like the cry of a newborn infant gulping her first breath as she is eased into an unfamiliar world, this insight might well be worth celebrating.

The physiology of individuated and deeply personal breathing, however, passes quickly into more communal territory when we reflect on the notion that our breath is routinely circulated and shared with others, especially in the closed quarters of an office, airplane, classroom, or hospital, but also on a walk through the woods. Some of the very air you are now imbibing and shunting through your body may recently have been eddying around the majestic peak of the Matterhorn, passing out of the swollen corpse of an opossum by the side of a gravel road, trailing gently off the tail feathers of a migrating Canadian goose or whistling through the snow-ballasted branches of a Douglas fir tree. This can all be rather breathtaking. We are *conspiring*—literally, breathing together—and to contemplate this fact can dramatically change our lives to reveal new ways that human others and nonhuman otherness are woven into the very elemental conditions of our existence.

In the surviving fragments of his thought, the Presocratic Anaximenes identifies air as the source of all things. Indeed, air is linked intimately with life and life-processes in the physical, psychological and philosophical connections it shares with the wind and breathing, conceptions of the soul or spirit, and ideas or reputed experiences of the divine. Like earth, the atmosphere is neither homogeneous nor self-same. It is instead layered and multileveled. It has, in short, its own kind of "geography" or more exactly aeolian zones such that we can even speak of *airsheds*—regional "basins" without determinate physical boundaries where pollutants move or collect—by way of analogy with the more familiar concept of watersheds and the emerging notion of foodsheds.[53] We dwell in the lowest and densest layer, the troposphere, which extends from the surface of the earth upwards to a height of about seven miles. It is here that clouds, storms, and the weather occur. Breathing is made possible in this sphere, and air moves vertically with ease because of constant changes in temperature. Above the troposphere lies the stratosphere, which reaches up roughly seven to ten miles from the earth's surface. The troposphere contains ozone, the poisonous and explosive blue gas that protects life on the planet from ultraviolet rays. The air continues to thin here and becomes even more dissipated in the third layer, the ionosphere, where we find the fierce, unfiltered rays of the sun. The outermost layer is the exosphere, which merges in its furthest depths with the very thin atmosphere of the sun and which holds only a few hundred atoms of air per cubic centimeter.

Like water, air has distinct flows and movements. In fact, water and windy air share in the ability to move as waves, circulating and swirling in similar patterns so as to carry soil or transport sediment and other debris. It is not simply aesthetic exaggeration to say that in some sense animal life evolved from one sea to another insofar as it moved from the early oceans to the emerging oceanic air, a point suggested by the ancient Greek belief in Okeanos, the river coursing around the earth.[54] The air also conducts and makes possible communication and the modulation of animal voices. Language may be less a written carving or semi-permanent engraving than it is a "curl of breath" or a piping "breeze in the pines."[55] In this view, words are "clipped breath" or tiny parcels of spirit that permit us to listen to the weather. "Our 'tongues' taste the world we eat."[56] As Malcolm de Chazal holds in an aphorism with lyrical flourish, "Water talks with its mouth full; the air with its mouth open." This, presumably, is a reason we strive harder to comprehend the "messages" of the wind than those of the burbling brooks.[57] Giambattista Vico has argued, too, that celestial signs, markings or soundings in the sky, such as lightning or the formations and flights of birds, were the first languages, occurring before phonetic forms and representing a kind of *theo-logi* (language of god) that could be grasped via divination.[58] It is clear as well that from the earliest of times, many civilizations have been sky-worshippers, stargazers, contemplators[59] of the constellations, and surveyors of the geometry of the heavens, seeking signals from above so as to better understand or communicate with animals, humans, and the cosmos itself.

The sky is air's primordial home and spacious playground. This is where air reveals itself as wind; clots or clusters into clouds; articulates itself through the idiolects of light and color; and conjures up storms and precipitation. Szymborska artfully dissolves the common distinction we rely on between the interior and exterior in remarking that sky is "A window minus sill, frame, and panes. / An aperture, nothing more, / but wide open." She observes expansively, "I've got the sky behind my back, at hand, and on my eyelids. / The sky binds me tight / and sweeps me off my feet."[60] Metaphorically, the sky can be relocated indoors. Within buildings, high ceilings seem to facilitate speculation, wonder and elevated thoughts; lower architectural horizons are conducive to exacting and detail-oriented tasks. Rilke takes this idea a step further when he invites the firmament into the hidden recesses of our porous bodies. "The inner—what is it? If not intensified sky," he avows.[61] And Bachelard grants us license to interact imaginatively with what others have defined as off-limits materially in quoting approvingly of a poet who surmises, "The sky is waiting to be touched by a hand / of fabulous childhood."[62]

Due to its many mysteries, the sky has been subject of abiding speculation and the residence or real estate of the divinities in myriad cultures. In India, it was thought to pour forth from the navel of a man with a thousand eyes and heads. In Egypt, it was conceived and cast as a great iron lid. In Greece, a whole pantheon of gods populated this sphere. John Ruskin identifies eloquently some of the sky's ineffable attraction: "Sometimes gentle, sometimes capricious, sometimes awful, never the same for two moments together; almost human in its passions, almost spiritual in its tenderness, almost divine in its infinity its appeal to what is immortal in us."[63] The color of the sky, in particular, has engendered widespread wonder, especially among philosophers, poets, and scientists who have feuded over whether the hallmark blue is the result primarily of suspended particles of earth, properties of the air itself, aspects of water vapor, or features of fiery light—to invoke loosely the four elements as causal agents—among other explanations that include the perceptual work of the mind and the physical activities of molecules. For the Greeks and Chinese, azure suggested something profoundly nonhuman, in part because death transforms the healthy shades of red in the body to hues of blue through cyanosis.[64] Plato seemed to believe that sky blue resulted from an amalgam of darkness and brightness. And in his influential color theory, which is part of a broader *Naturphilosophie*, Goethe characterizes this blue in affective terms as cold, recessive, and remote, while nevertheless tending to draw us to chase after and contemplate its anomalies. "As the upper sky and distant mountains appear blue, so a blue surface seems to retire from us," he says.[65] Enigmas and controversies surrounding this phenomenon still remain, and Peter Pesic argues thoughtfully in *Sky in a Bottle* that the quest to comprehend the nature of sky and its color directs us equally inward and outward—toward both atomic theory and distant galaxies.

"Sky" is a word that is akin to the old English term *sceo*, meaning cloud, and one that harks back in Indo-European roots to *skeu*, a kind of covering or canopy of shifting colors. The sky should not best be thought of—although it often is—as an absence, emptiness, or stillness on the one hand or a reflective mirror on the other hand. "Light as air" may be a poignant turn of phrase, but it is strictly inaccurate. The atmosphere is more of a visceral, thickened. and ponderous presence, weighing more than five thousand trillion tons and rife with life, activity, and movement. We often forget that it is full of moving gases (especially hydrogen, oxygen, and nitrogen), dust, fungi, spores, and viruses, along with animal life, including the larger species of birds, butterflies, bees, and bats.[66] Aerial ecosystems contain dense soups of floating plankton as well. There are as many as twenty five million flying insects over a single square mile of the earth's surface, and microbes thrive at heights of up to fifty miles. Naturalists have even observed "organic rain" in the atmosphere when invertebrate "fallout" occurs due to temperature changes after small organisms have first been carried aloft by wind, which they experience presumably as a vertical rather than horizontal force. Such beings, in fact, may be transported so high in an hour that it can take three weeks for their return to the ground. And if that odyssey is not thrilling enough for them, hungry predators often are lying in wait, such as a species of spider that has been found at altitudes higher than four miles.[67]

Bound, then, to the planet by the sucking pull of gravity, the airy sky begins quite literally at your feet, merging with and emerging in geological time from the rocks of the earth and, with the development of oxygen, destroying, and displacing most forms of anaerobic life. Atmosphere derives from the Greek *atmos*, meaning "vapor," and *sphaira*, meaning "ball" (or the Latin *sphaera* meaning "sphere"), and it shares a linguistic connection with the Greek *aenai*, "to blow." The ancient Greeks—who constructed a Tower of Winds in Athens in the second century B.C.E—used *anemos* (wind) as a synonym for direction, placing geographic markers on their maps with puffy and pointed cheeks so as to indicate North, South, East, and West, the cardinal directions that many cultures associate with the four elements. The Roman thinker Seneca defined the wind as "air flowing one way," and Christian mystics such as Hildegard von Bingen regarded the winds as moving the firmament and maintaining planetary order. As the so-called "wings of God," the four winds were thought to keep the four elements apart and in harmony. Thus, the air has helped to provide for physical and metaphysical orientation within geographic space and place. The atmosphere, we might suggestively say, is a kind of "*Atman*-sphere"—*Atman* being the Sanskrit conception of the unchanging self and a word related to the German word for breathing (*atmen*)—in the sense that it is like the innermost breath or essence of an individual. And if we continue this analogy, the atmosphere may also be viewed by extension as akin to the universal All (*Brahman*), the ultimate ground of being in Hindu philosophy.[68]

Air, too, exercises a strong aesthetic and emotional influence on us through the ever-changing weather, affecting our daily feelings and dispositions. The fact that there are so many different kinds of and names for wind—by one count, more than four hundred around the world—indicates the manifold "moods" and formless forms that air assumes from breezes, gusts, gales, and zephyrs to tornadoes, siroccos, cyclones, and hurricanes. Add to that long list the vast variety of local and regional winds such as the Santa Ana (southern California), foehn (Alpine region), chinook (northern U.S. plains), bora (Dalmatian coast), *Trauben-kocher* ("grape cooker" of Switzerland), or harmattan (Sahara), and the moving currents around and above us take on increasing complexity. Air encompasses and encloses us in a sensible, if nonvisible, thickness. As poet Robert Browning puts it, equating *atmos* and *anima*: "that puff of vapour . . . man's soul."[69] Except perhaps as wind or smoke, however, air often does not occur as a mode of presence for many individuals, who believe habitually that there is nothing but absence in the air because we do not clearly butt up against a thing or a being. Such a view is misguided if, as Luce Irigaray argues, the ambient air, rather than the house of language, is our first home and what unites and embraces all physical bodies as well as conducts our speech.[70]

From runners, swimmers, and cyclists to more stationary weightlifters, archers, and gymnasts, most athletes realize the commanding importance of disciplined breathing for excelling at their sports. Through vigorous exercise, we can nearly double our aerobic capacity, adding to the volume of air that reaches our lungs and the amount of oxygen that nourishes our muscles. The cultivation and governance of breath is especially integral to yoga, where it is as vital to this ancient and enduring practice as the bodily postures (*asanas*) themselves. *Pranayama*—the art of breath control—assists the digestive, nervous, respiratory, and circulatory systems, and it helps to yoke both the errant senses and mind. Hatha yoga traditions consider *prana* not only to involve rhythmic inhalation and exhalation but also frequently to be equatable with life itself, as in one's "life breath." One of the most significant of the many forms of *pranayama* is *ujjayi* (victorious) breath, which entails partially closing the glottis, thereby producing an audible sound, akin to the ebb and flow of the sea or to wind moving through a stand of pines. Another is *kapalabhati* (cleansing breath), which is forceful exhalation followed by passive inhalation in rounds of breath to clear the nasal passages.

In the Brihadaranyaka Upanishad, the paramount role of breath is underscored by way of a thought experiment in which the bodily senses and faculties (*indriyas*), who are quarreling over which is best, take their disagreement to Brahman, who replies that the honor belongs to the one whose departure makes the body worst off. After each, in turn, takes leave of the body, which in its absence still manages to survive, the breath is about to exit "like a great stallion pulling up the stakes by which he was tethered," until the others beg it to stay because they realize suddenly how they all depend on *prana* for their own existence.[71] The *Bhagavad Gita*, too, speaks of the "pure calm of infinity" that may be attained by one who "shuns external objects, / fixes his gaze between his brows, / and regulates his vital breaths / as they pass between his nostrils."[72] Judging by the serene countenances and prolonged lives of those who adopt meditative breathing, there is little doubt about the merit of this claim.

The historical Buddha may be credited with the surprisingly simple but extremely significant discovery and promotion of the power of human breath. His *Anapanasati Sutra* is devoted to the subject and counsels awareness in this most quotidian of processes. Referring to the monk and his daily practices, the sutra commences with the words, "Always mindful, he breathes in; mindful he breathes out."[73] It proceeds to recommend sixteen basic exercises involving air so as to bring great benefits to the attentive mind and receptive body. These activities range from a focus on the length and constancy of the breath to the related tasks of calming mental chatter and nurturing a dispassionate disposition. For those just embarking on meditative breathing, two ways to facilitate this process and to rein in a wandering psyche involve counting during alternating in-breaths and out-breaths and consciously following the movement of the breath as it progresses from the nose (beginning) to the chest (middle) and navel (end).

The father of Western medicine, Hippocrates, remarked, "there is one common flow, one common breathing," adding that in this way "all things are in sympathy" (*sympatheia ton holon*).[74] This claim points to the unity of all beings through the medium of air and its articulation in breath. Chanting, in fact, has been described as a protracted communal exhalation that extends expiration so as to generate higher pressure in the abdomen and lungs.[75] More generally, those who meditate usually alter their breathing so as to reduce the amount of air they take in and to lengthen exhalations, which calm and quiet the brain. In seated meditation, some monks can even reduce their average number of breaths to as few as four to six per minute, two to four times fewer than most humans by comparison. In doing so, they also spend a much greater percentage of the breathing cycle in the expiratory phase.

Of breath and the "breath breathing human being," the thirteenth-century poet and mystic Rumi wisely denies it custody by any religion or philosophical perspective. It is "Not Christian or Jew or Muslim, not Hindu / Buddhist, sufi, or zen." Its ontological status is, in fact, redolent with paradox: an oxymoronic nothing strutting along the razor edge separating it from an incipient something; a supremely fulfilling, if ordinary, activity recoiling back gymnastically upon its own emptiness and extraordinariness. "I am not . . . / composed of elements at all. I do not exist. / My place is placeless, a trace of the traceless. Neither body or soul. / I belong to the beloved, have seen the two / worlds as one."[76]

Today, we know that the content of the air is critical to the maintenance of life, and that the bulk of it is produced not by photolysis of water (chemical decomposition through radiant energy) but by the burial of carbon, which is fixed in the organic matter of algae and green plants, in sedimentary rocks. The percentage of oxygen in the air (now about twenty-one percent) cannot increase more than a percentage or two from its current state (to an upper limit of about twenty-four percent) or vegetation throughout the world would burst into a tremendous conflagration that would consume tropical rain forests and even Arctic tundra.[77] Nor can it move to a much lower range or many living species, including humans, would not be able to respire and survive. This surprisingly constant and stable level of oxygen in the air—which is in chemical disequilibrium at the same time—has been proposed as evidence for the claim that the planet functions like a living organism that actively alters its environment so as to sustain life processes.[78] The air is composed as well of other gases that serve important roles in preserving life and planetary conditions: nitrogen (about seventy-eight percent), which builds pressure in the atmosphere and helps to extinguish fires; traces of carbon dioxide, which allows for photosynthesis and climate control; and relatively minute but extremely important amounts of methane (which regulates oxygen and ventilates the anaerobic zone), nitrous oxide (which governs both oxygen and ozone), and ammonia (which controls the acidity of the environment), along with sulfur, methyl chloride, and methyl iodide.

Philosophers have on occasion peered into the invisible air to discover the vital role of respiration. Aristotle's *On Breath*—although some scholars contest its authenticity—examines the physiological and metaphysical aspects of breath, which he links with the emotions and a conception of the soul. Aristotle, in fact, envisions breath as "the purest substance of the body," giving it a flickering and evanescent materiality.[79] Heidegger implies that breath is a "temporal extension" of our lives, providing voice in a terse phrase to the idea that along with our heart, breathing keeps time and tempo for us. It functions, we might say, as kind of biological clock, even to the point that it may be more revealing for us to imaginatively count the number of breaths, rather than the remaining years, we have left in our lives. And Derrida speaks of air—and by extension breath, which partakes as a portion of it—as the "*apeiron* of Presocratic physiology, the *tehiru* of the Kabbalah, the possibility of presence, of visibility, of appearance, of voice," a phenomenon that comes to mean at heart "*this-is-trying-to-say-that*" so that we are ever in the "present infinitive."[80]

As noted, Anaximenes boldly proposes air (*aer*) as the element that can explain all that exists. He advances an early form of hylozoism—the belief that matter is living—and offers a different determinate entity in the stead of Thales' water, abandoning as well Anaximander's *apeiron* (boundless) for an infinite but definite element.[81] In his proto-scientific and philosophical theory, the invisible is rendered visible through the processes of condensation and rarefaction. Warm air changes to fire through dilation; cold air is transformed to wind through condensation, then cloud via further compression, then water by additional thickening, and finally earth and stone—hence a progressive solidification. At the same time, Anaximenes is able to account for changes in temperature because relative hotness arises through rarefaction and relative coldness through condensation. Expressed in more modern language, he finds that the appearance of air is altered by density and direction of motion such that changes in quantity are translated into changes of quality.

As to why air is advanced as the most basic and originative element, we can reach conjectural conclusions based on extant philosophical fragments, everyday human experiences, and the early Greek tradition. The central role of breathing in the maintenance of animal life is undoubtedly a primary reason for this choice and a factor contributing to a defense of hylozoism.[82] Furthermore, air occupies a vast, if frequently overlooked, portion of the perceivable world. It is the medium in which we dwell, through which we smell, and by which we support ourselves physically in daily rhythms. Finally, for Anaximenes at least, air is divine, and in this sense it participates in that which is immortal and eternal, thus providing an additional source for his hylozoism.

In fact, the atmospheric air and beyond is thought to be an abode of the gods by many of the ancient Greeks. As Theophrastus preserves Anaximenes' claim, "The air within us is a small portion of God."[83] The Milesian asserts as well: "As our soul, being air [*aer*] holds us together and controls us, so does wind [*pneuma*] and air [*aer*] enclose the whole world."[84] This remark suggests that air acts as a kind of thin "material" and metaphysical glue and that the life-soul (or breath-soul) is comparable to cosmic air, which is likewise alive and animate. Although it remains speculative, Anaximenes might be suggesting that air serves not only as an originative and binding force from both the outside and inside but that the cosmos resembles an organism of some kind that manifests life because it is like the human body, which is similarly bound or controlled by air.[85] A clear parallel is established in any case between macrocosm and microcosm, and the significance of air, wind, and breath in life processes is underscored very early in Western thought.[86]

But if the world is born in many religious and philosophical traditions with an animating breath, its demise or end is also anticipated commonly with the cessation of cosmic respiration, as when four angels stand at four corners of the earth, holding off the four winds in the Biblical "Book of Revelation." Mircea Eliade suggests that the sky encourages religious experiences because it is perceived and represented as "wholly other." In its very being, the sky "reveals transcendence, force, eternity. It *exists absolutely* because it is *high, infinite, eternal, powerful.*"[87] Thus, many of the most important deities for primitive people possess names that signal height or meteorological activity: the supreme god of the Maori is Iho, meaning "elevated"; the Selk'nam of Teirra del Fuego call their divine being "Dweller in the Sky"; and the Sky God of the West African Yoruba is known as Olorun, literally "Owner of the Sky."

Rather than being entombed in the earth, some Buddhists opt for "sky burial," a funerary practice in Tibet involving the ritual dissection of a corpse that is placed in pieces on a mountaintop. Exposed to the force of the elements (*mahabhuta*), the eviscerated body becomes food for vultures and other birds of prey, and the custom is even referred to as "giving alms to the birds" (*jhator*). This gifting of the body to the natural world—the funeral as feast—is more environmentally friendly than interment and cremation because it does not entail the use of fuel or land. And although the ritual may have emerged because of the extreme elemental conditions in the local environment—especially the rocky earth and scarcity of trees for timber—there is something ecologically poetic in the act of bequeathing or rejoining one's body and last breath with the dancing winds and becoming carrion for taloned creatures in the airy canopy. Perhaps with this kind of notion in mind, Ralph Waldo Emerson once spoke of "the blue sky in which the private earth is buried, the sky with its eternal calm, and full of everlasting orbs."[88]

As referred to previously, the Gaia hypothesis has recently revived interest in the idea that our planet functions like an animate organism by emphasizing the elemental role of the air and the atmosphere in supporting the development and protection of life.[89] Put simply, Lovelock proposes that through cybernetic processes—homeostasis and negative feedback loops—that actively adjust and regulate the composition of the atmosphere (air) and oceans (water), modify the albedo or surface coloration of the land (earth), and alter the changing rates of temperature, ozone accretion and depletion, oxidation, and terrestrial burning (broadly, the transformative power of fire), the planet is able to support itself in a manner similar to a complex living system.[90] This view not only recalls a similar Greek notion and a perennial belief held by many Native American cultures, but it stands in an uneasy relation with the increasing concern raised about anthropogenic changes to the content and chemistry of the air.[91] When writer Gregory Nagy asks metaphorically "what is blowing in the wind," he is compelled by empirical evidence and literary panache to conclude: "The answer, my friend, is that the world may be running out of breath."[92] Even if this view overstates the nonfigurative case, we would be best admonished to care for "world-mothering air, air wild"—to borrow the words of poet Gerald Manley Hopkins—and the atmospheric commons given its vital role for the health of most living organisms and the well-being of the planet itself.

Quite clearly, then, we need to be concerned about the changes we are making to this elemental realm. Inhaling the air of Mexico City, for example, on a daily basis is roughly like smoking two packs of cigarettes a day. Our senses often signal to us that something is indeed afoul. The air may smell noxious or toxic, like it is saturated with oil, laced with asphalt, or laden with smoke. Visually, its color may blur to the browns and oranges of smog, or it may darken as particulate matter, exhaust, and ash smother the intensity and clarifying power of sunlight. Our bodies also offer us feedback about air quality through the symptoms of coughs, respiratory stress, burning eyes, and headaches. When the wind shifts, our mood may either lighten and lift or become more sober and sullen. In his essay, "The Psychedelics of Pollution," Harold Fromm proposes that a new twist can be given to an old commentary on the question of free will. In addition to the influence of our genes, parents, psychological history, and class or ethnic background on our perspectives of the world, Fromm worries about the role of the chemical composition of the air. "How 'free,' " he asks, "is a creature whose worldview at a given moment has literally been concocted miles away in the vat of a steel mill? If one can be drugged without pills, soused without Scotch, depressed without precipitating psychological events, irritable without irritants, and pessimistic without philosophy... then what does it mean to have a mind or a will of one's own?"[93] Curiously, despite the paramount importance of clean air to our health and happiness, weather reports rarely mention pollution levels and related dangers in their reports.

Over time and by degrees, we have, it seems, slowly amended an imaginative vision of the heavens into an optical experience of the sky and then turned that into a meteorological conception of the atmosphere and ambient air. Whereas the firmament was once thought to be teeming with deities like Jupiter, Odin, and Thor or, according to Paracelsus, crowded with sylphs, it is fair to say that it is now largely the province of impersonal gases and inert human objects. With soot, smoke, and smog hovering increasingly above our heads concurrently with the emergence of an ever-pronounced yearning to journey into outer space, the sky is likely to become more and more a contested arena. If, as a result, it is further "disenchanted," we might hope that the growing recognition of its fragility—or alterability—may encourage future generations, in turn, to "re-enchant" or, at least, better protect it. Given that the sky of Mars, our closet planetary neighbor, is dull ochre rather than deep blue in color, perhaps, as Pesic notes, this, too, will give us pause to consider what we are doing or undoing and what kind of airy dome we are willing to bequeath to our children or our children's children.

At the level of "existential ecology," a turn toward yoga, regular walking, or running, and practiced meditative breathing techniques might enable us to appreciate more fully the encompassing medium in which we live and on which we depend. Biologist Joan Maloof has observed that many Americans tend to discount the allure of air, especially what she terms "old-growth air," in their treks to and through the forest. By contrast, the Japanese acknowledge and even name this presence, which they call *shinrin-yoku* or "wood-air breathing."[94] In this regard, Rilke summons us toward an inspiring gesture of corporeal expression: "Don't you know yet?" he asks. "Fling the emptiness out of your arms / into the spaces we breathe; perhaps the birds / will feel the expanded air with more passionate flying."[95] If indeed poetry helps us not just to dream and to experience awakened reverie but to open up the occluded world and even to inhale and exhale with greater ease and grace, such advice may be more valuable than we initially think. Breathe... and drink deeply and freely with Byron and the rest of us of "this blue wilderness of interminable air"!

Fire

> To preserve and use fire is the oldest of humanity's ecological duties, its most distinct trait as a biological organism, the first of its quests for power and knowledge, the genesis of its environmental ethics.
>
> —Stephen Pyne, "Consumed by Either Fire or Fire"

> The reverie by the fireside has axes that are more philosophical. Fire is for the man who contemplates it an example of sudden change or development. ... [F]ire suggests the desire to change, to speed up the passage of time, to bring all of life to its conclusion, its hereafter.
>
> —Gaston Bachelard, *The Psychoanalysis of Fire*

With the domestication of fire and the wedding of *techne* (art, craft, or skill) with *logos* (reason, order) to form the concept and practice of technology, we discover a decisive turning point in the transformational capacities of humanity, one not far in importance from the development of bipedalism or the acquisition of language. It is literally firepower—which soon after takes the form of soldiering, forging, melting, and burning—that inaugurates a new era in the chapter of human history relative to the natural world.[96] In the *Protagoras*, Plato relates the story of Prometheus, who steals this element from the gods once they fashion creatures from a mixture of earth and fire. The mythic acquisition of fire is what defines humans because Epimetheus (whose name means after-thought) had already distributed the qualities of speed, strength, and flight to other beings. Recognizing that we need to be protected, Prometheus (whose name means fore-thought) thieves fire and with it the capacity for the mechanical arts (*techne*) from Zeus, bestowing it upon us. As Plato remarks: "In this way man acquired sufficient resources to keep himself alive," adding, however, that he "had not political wisdom."[97] In playing too loosely with fire, humans are often "out of their element," we might say, although we are the single species to possess and use it. Fire opens up not only previously unthinkable possibilities but also a Pandora's box of problems, including questions of how it is to be controlled in the form of technology.

Heraclitus was among the first to identify fire (*pyr*) as an extraordinary element. It is fire that is "everliving, kindled in measures and in measures going out."[98] Fire is the universal *logos* (order) and that which neither a god nor human has made. Although quenched in degrees, he maintains that it endures in its transformations or turnings (*tropai*) into water and then earth. Such change, Heraclitus claims, can occur via the medium of *prester* (literally "burner"), the "thunderbolt [that] pilots all things" (fr. 119). "All things are requital for fire, and fire for all things" (fr. 40). The soul (*psyche*) as fire is extinguished when it becomes water and earth, and Heraclitus suggests that through this physical association—and coordination of the individual with the cosmos—a time will arrive when reason is subordinated to excessive desire. But, he believes, fire eventually discerns and catches up with all existing things, and so the soul can be rebirthed should it choose the path of wisdom. In pointing to the powers of primal *pyr* (fire), the ungrounded "ground" of his metaphysics, Heraclitus invokes a form of plurisignation or polysemy, deliberately marshalling multiple meanings of the term together for the first time to create a magisterial and hydra-headed concept.[99] Here, we should take note that "fire" derives from the Middle English, "fir," and the Old English "fr," and that it has roots in Latin and Germanic tongues. Our English word has antecedents and descendents with both an active (animate, personified) and passive (impersonal and neuter) linguistic lineage, indicating in a sense the dual and paradoxical nature of the flame. "Ignite," for example, comes from *ignis* (Latin) and *egnis* (Indo-European), and it conveys the decidedly dynamic dimensions of fire, as does the kindred Sanskrit, *agni*, embodied in the eponymous Hindu deity of fire.

There are a number of perennial and still potent myths connected with fire, including the Prometheus complex (fire and respect), the Hoffman complex (spontaneous combustion), and the Empedocles complex (destruction of the world).[100] Culturally, fire has played an enormous role in religious rituals, social rites, and primitive taboos.[101] One common myth involves the theft of fire by trickster animals or birds that pass it off in an animal relay but in the process are burned, providing them with their many-hued colors. Elemental fire fascinates and entrances, even functioning as a hypnotic medium for persons who sit before it. Whether its origins lie ultimately in rational explanations stressing the value of harnessing and controlling the element for practical use, more psychological associations such as sexualized rubbings, or religious, and mythological frameworks invoking connections with gods, sacrifice, and worship (as in Zoroastrianism), fire is as much a social phenomenon as a natural one, fostering both respect and fear and often becoming a first object of prohibition. Fire, as Bachelard recognized, may no longer be a force for scientific study—although it surely exists in the scientific unconscious—but it is nevertheless a phenomenon with important philosophical and cultural dimensions.

Fire provides heat for cooking and comfort, light for the capacity to turn night into day, and immense power to alter and shape our surroundings and the elemental world.[102] Although it is the one element in which nothing can live and thrive (even if some organisms breed in charcoal), Thoreau rightly associated animal life with the internal fire of animal heat.[103] The hearth, where fire is traditionally domesticated, too, has been the social center of the home-sphere since humans took to the confines of the cave, then the cottage, and now the condominium, although the television currently supplies the electronic flickering images around which many families gather.[104]

Low-intensity fires are necessary to the ecology of wooded areas, restoring soil composition by recycling biomass and thinning out older growth.[105] As a major ecological player—an amoral protagonist—fire has helped to govern evolution and fuse the physical landscape to the biological world. Its contributions range from specific actions such as encouraging geotrophic orchids to blossom following a local burn to more general inputs into the ecosystem through carbon cycles and the release of greenhouse gases via forest fires. Plants and animals adapt to fire patterns by developing protective traits such as thick barks and leaves, underground biomass, and subterranean burrows. Jack pines use the heat of fire to crack open their tough cones and release their seeds in propagation, and fire promotes the growth of many grasses, fruits, and tubers. Most mammals and birds, too, will repopulate regions that have been burned within a breeding season or two.

Contrary to a widespread impression, Native Americans employed fire actively and routinely in their interactions with the landscape. They used it to drive, enclose, and kill mule deer, buffalo, and white-tailed deer. They ignited fires to trigger the growth of new plants, to clear brush and undergrowth, and to augment the proliferation of nuts, seeds, and berries. They burned to communicate with each other about the prospects of war, sightings of prey, and the threat of white settlers. They deployed the flame to drive off enemies and strangers. Intentionally or not, these activities exerted considerable impact on grassland ecosystems, chaparral, and forests. And although Native Americans exhibited nuanced and deeply empathetic understandings of the land, they did not control fires in a systematic way, and they sometimes failed to responsibly tend or extinguish their campfires.[106] As an ancient, albeit meta-organic, technology, fire thus requires cultivation, control, and care rather than domination or elimination. It necessitates, so to speak, an enlightened cultural "atmosphere" or "air" in which to breathe, move, and consume in regulated manners as opposed to ideological "water" that would attempt to smother or squelch it.

Concerning the centrality of fire to human civilization, pyro-historian Stephen Pyne goes as far to speak of a synergistic pact that eventuated in an environmental ethic through which we obtained the power of the flame while the biota of the world acquired regimes of fire and the capacity to propagate through us. Fire both segregated us from and bonded us to the natural world. Our relationship with fire thereby has been deeply reciprocal. "If humans used flame to promote their food stocks, wildlife often depended on anthropogenic burning to fertilize and ready the landscape and stimulate the fodder which they, the indigenous fauna, also required in order to thrive."[107] In this way, the land expressed a symbiosis and was sculpted by fire into territory for hunting.

Pyne identifies three historical periods and corresponding kinds of fire. "First Fire" is nature's flame beginning roughly 450 million years ago—if we leave out volcanoes and lightning—and ignited regularly for millennia through a triumvirate of fuel, oxygen, and heat (or more accurately a tetrahedron if we include a necessary chemical chain reaction) before being captured and kindled by enterprising early hominids, who co-evolved with fire. "Second Fire" is broadly an agricultural regime, an era of anthropogenic origin, where fire use through the control of combustible fuel sources has profoundly shaped and reshaped the planet's landscape by changing the configuration and character of fields, forests, and vegetation. "Third Fire," our present period, is the industrial process set off and conducted through combustion, whereby fire burns in confined spaces and draws its strength from energy sources born of fossil fuels long buried in the earth (stored solar fire in effect) rather than through the more immediate effects of sunlight on the planet's surface.

As Pyne surmises accurately, fire is more like a domesticated animal than it is a traditional technology such as a tool with handles. It is, in short, less like a hammer, axe or saw—which can be picked up and put down at will—and more akin to a work horse, ox, or farm dog. Like animals brought under the yoke and the shelter of the human *domus*, fire must be "conceived, fed, protected, put to bed, awakened, trained, controlled, exercised, bred."[108] In fact, it can be selectively reproduced into different "breeds," including fire for hunting, cooking, heating, farming, and the like.[109] Feral fire, once tamed and tended, in turn domesticated us, encouraging people to settle down, till the soil, and gather around a ballasting central hearth in the house. Fire dramatically altered our diets (from hunting on fire drives to exorcising parasites in our food and cultivating new culinary arts); it enabled us to read, write, and work in places or times otherwise cold, wet, and dark; and it provided us—via the Faustian bargain we brokered for it—with the capacity to find and use new technological prowess in our interactions with the natural world. Unlike water, air or earth, fire can be summoned up with a kind of magical legerdemain from next-to-nothing in widely varying climates and geographical locales, making possible further Diasporas of the human species and spawning more complex and awe-inspiring technologies. The ripple effects of fire as *techne* are truly prolific. "Fire distilled seawater into salt, wood into tar, resin into pitch and turpentine, grain and grape into alcohol; it transformed wood into ash and then into soap, and cooked calcitic rock into lime. Plaster and cement, in turn, encouraged new construction," to cite one example provided by Pyne.[110] If, as Arthur C. Clarke claims, all advanced technologies are not in the end distinguishable from magic, then surely fire seems to have deep and original connections with both arts. Indeed, fire qua technology has shared with magic a seeming ability to influence or manipulate the natural world, to work in mysterious or ineffable ways, and to mesmerize and entrance the human mind.

At the same time that fire has expanded—and in a simultaneous sense contracted—into the industrial realm where it tends to be rendered into a largely invisible form of combustion, there has been a loss of regular contact with the elemental flame that humans have tended, worshiped, celebrated, and shepherded for centuries. The force of fire is everywhere felt—even in the manufacture of materials designed to resist it—while the flame increasingly remains unseen, especially in urban environments. The closest many of us come to a relatively unmediated fire on a daily basis is at the end of a three-inch cigarette. More than any of the other three primal elements, fire has been reduced widely to a mere symbol. Speaking of the calendar of fire rites in Europe, Pyne recounts that as the flame vanished from everyday life, fire ceremonials also disappeared until very few within the educated classes were able to discern a role for them. Fire rituals were perceived in terms of superstition rather than as evolving from "fire's practical biology, its capacity to purge and promote," and eventually they were diminished to "votive candles and eternal flames over memorials."[111]

As fire has been transmuted into pyrotechnics and high technology, the flickering flame has been channeled into a bestiary of machines, or been coaxed into and tamed by electrical wires. And although public health has benefited noticeably, the air is still marked with the signature effects of sequestered fire in dirty smoke, exhaust, and emissions. A process of substitution in service of efficiency or profit has been in operation: the light bulb for the candle; the gas heater for the fireplace; the electric range for the flame-bearing stove; and so on. Pyne puts the story of fire's ontological and cultural demise from "universal cause to chemical consequence" in succinct but elegant terms as anthropogenic fire supplanted aboriginal fire, as hidden combustion replaced open burning, and as the near omnipresent regime of Third Fire smothers the flames of First and Second Fire:

> Industry invented new pyrotechnologies, then suggested that heat engines were an analogue for animal heat. Natural philosophy found other ways than fire to explain the world, and then used that revealed world to explain fire. Chemistry downgraded flame to an atomic reaction. Thermodynamics split fire from Heraclitean universality to a laboratory demonstration. Once the manifestation of the deity and the source of life, fire had become alien, a destroyer of cities, a savager of soil, a befouler of air, and emblem (in science as in agriculture) of the hopelessly primitive.[112]

What, we might ask, then, is the place or geography of fire? Like water, fire flourishes unevenly in hotspots around the earth's surface and appears in a variety of forms, but unlike water—its ostensible antagonist and opposite—life cannot thrive directly within its clutches, even if fauna and flora are powerfully sustained by it. Although dependent on the underlying earth for fuel sources and the encompassing air to nourish and stoke its flame as well as provide a sink for smoke and carbon, fire is unlike both earth and air in that it does not seem to possess distinct individuated layers and zones in quite the same way as those two elements. Fire, however, does proceed through three identifiable stages: the incipient (preheating, distillation, and slow pyrolysis); the smoldering (full pyrolysis, ignition, and initial combustion); and the flame (rapid reaction, heat transfer, and full fire). As Aristotle argued, fire is characterized by the physical qualities or differentiae of hot and dry in contrast to earth (cold and dry), air (hot and wet), and water (cold and wet). As such, it tends to rise, its proclivity and "natural place" being upward and toward the circumference and limit—in contrast to the downward-tending earth—as it reaches for oxygen, and even as it moves laterally with rapidity, searching like a famished lion for food.

Although fire has been domesticated indoors and serves itself as a prime agent of human domestication, it travels and sojourns widely in various guises outside the human house to all continents and corners of the planet, even touching the frozen water of Antarctica, which collects the ashen effects of industrial burnings in its ice. In other words, fire in effect now crosses water, cuts easily through air, and finds a comfortable home within the depths of earth itself.

Fire burns magnificently and often freely in the forests of North America, Southeast Asia, and Australia, even if it is often out of human sight. And nomadic people have regularly carried the burning flame with them on sticks for long spans of time as they moved from place to place—a practical feat that finds a parallel today in the ceremonial passing of the Olympic torch from one city, state, or country to the next.

Europe's colonization of other lands—aptly via fire power itself in the weapons of war—provided the predominant means for transmitting industrial fire throughout the world. As Pyne reveals, countries that have largely eliminated open fires are encouraging or coercing nations with practices and policies permitting outdoor burnings to curtail them. "The open flame—fluttering in the wind—remains, for modern economics and environmentalism, a symbol of defiant primitivism," and so goes the argument advanced by developed nations, "only by quenching it can a people cross the threshold to modernity."[113] In the United States, suburbia is typically less rich in fuel sources than dense city interiors, where fires can take root through arson, for example, in vacated lots and buildings. Since the origins of domestic life took root, fire has been located, of course, within the protected interior of homes in stoves, furnaces, candle-holders, and lamps as well as its primary locus, the hearth or fireplace, which radiates warmth and light to the setting. However, Pyne shrewdly observes that "no Paleolithic hunter would recognize the fire in a pump-action shotgun; no Neolithic swiddener, the flames buried in a tractor or the nitrogenous fertilizer sprayed by a portable power pump; no priest the theophanous fire behind a fluorescent lamp; no natural philosopher, the fiery prime mover fed on fossil fuel, turning the geared wheels of industry; no poet, the quintessential combustion that makes software possible."[114]

Philosophy is born out of the chrysalis of poetry and myth as well as the archaic and enduring experience of the elemental world. It is not surprising, then, that fire continues to beguile the contemplative mind. Heidegger, for example, reflects on the figure and hallmark fire (*pyr*) of Heraclitus, whom he believes should be honored as "the Lucid," rather than with the more familiar appellation, "the Obscure." Heraclitus reveals "the lighting whose shining he attempts to call forth into the language of thinking."[115] Fire is the "ever-enduring rising," what "always already rests in itself" as *physis* (nature). Heraclitus' conception of *pyr* is expansive and names sundry nouns such as "sacrificial fire, the oven's fire, the campfire, but also the glow of a torch, the scintillation of the stars."[116] Fire can be understood, too, in terms of active verbs like blazing, glowing, and shining, though equally welding, cauterizing, consuming, and extinguishing. In short, Heidegger claims it is "lighting governance" that marks Heraclitus' fire, a directing force that provides measure and yet it is capable of taking it away. Meditative fire gathers and sets things into presence before us. Fire is a lighting that not only illuminates but sets all into the open, and the event it lights up is designated by nothing less than the world itself. Or, as Heidegger expresses it, the cosmos is fire that endures.

Derrida focuses on the flame and its relation to spirit, ghosts, ashes, and technology in an encounter with Heidegger's own thought and "un-thoughts," although he does not consider the latter's engagement with Heraclitus. *Geist* (spirit) is in-flamed—transformed to fire—in the German's dangerous embrace of Nazism and his associated interpretations of the poets, Trakl and Hölderlin. "Jetzt komme, Feuer!" (Now come, Oh fire!), says Hölderlin in language that invariably causes us to hear the benighted world of cremation, incineration, crematoria, and the Holocaust, even if these words are not uttered directly. Rather, in Derrida's reading, this "cleansing" fire is stoked by Heidegger's own inflammatory political speeches and the invocation or inspiration of the German "spirit," drawing by small degrees perhaps on the Greek *pneuma* (breath) and Christian *spiritus* (spirit), but bypassing the Hebrew *ruah* (breath, spirit). As Derrida shows, *Geist* in the end becomes a wild "fire, flame, burning, conflagration."[117]

Fire and with it the age of pyrotechnology present us, then, with philosophical, environmental, and political questions as well as Promethean powers. Is fire in danger of becoming a cultural ember as we continue to ignore our awesome capacities to transfigure the planet, wantonly burn up fossil fuels and transit toward an era of "algeny" and biotechnology?[118] Perhaps as the visionary Blake suggests: "Unless the mind catch fire / The God will not be known."[119] Bachelard himself confessed that he would rather fail to provide a good lecture in philosophy than neglect to light his fire in the morning,[120] while filmmaker Jean Cocteau responded to the common question, "If your house should catch fire, what objects would you carry off?," with the appropriately uncommon poetic riposte: "the fire."[121] It is a long way from Heraclitus to the hydrogen bomb, but a reflection on the central role of fire in human thought and experience can help us to better understand our history and precarious place in the broader environment. Having seized it from the natural world or, as the myths suggest, stolen it from a supernatural order, we are now wedded like domestic partners—for better and for worse—to fire's seductive charms and incendiary threats. Like our relationship with other elements, we would be well advised to act with measured responsibility toward it. Failing to heed such a message, the only alternative may be to accept Robert Frost's apocalyptic prediction: "Some say the world will end in fire; / Some say in ice. / From what I've tasted of desire / I hold with those who favor fire."[122]

Water

Water is H$_2$O, hydrogen two parts, oxygen one, but there is also a third thing, that makes it water and nobody knows what it is.

—D. H. Lawrence, *Pansies*

The H$_2$O which gurgles through . . . plumbing is not water, but a stuff which industrial society creates. . . . The twentieth century has transmogrified water into a fluid with which archetypal waters cannot be mixed.

—Ivan Illich, *H$_2$O and the Waters of Forgetfulness*

Water is pervasively and powerfully present within both Western and Eastern philosophical, literary, and geographical thought. The Presocratic physiocrat Thales—widely regarded as the first Greek philosopher—claimed that water is, in some sense, the source of all things. In other words, he judged it to be an abiding, albeit often hidden, constituent of the plethora of sensible phenomena. In arriving at this conclusion, he may have reasoned from the fact that moisture appears to nurture and inhabit all living things—thus providing them with a source of warmth—and that such wetness is contained in seeds and sperm, progenitor-agents of much life.[123] We can speculate, too, that supplementing this physiological analysis was the centrality of meteorological conditions, especially the cycling of water in the Mediterranean regions.[124] By suggesting that the world arises in some fashion from water or primeval waters, Thales anticipated indirectly the modern biological view that life on earth originated in the oceans.[125] And in moving from a manifest multiplicity of observable phenomena to a singular basis *within* the world for explaining all of nature, he made a lasting contribution to science while assisting in the early animation of elemental philosophy.[126] As Nietzsche puts it, Thales' proclamation rose to the level of philosophical insight for three reasons: "First, because it tells something about the primal origin of all things; second, because it does so in a language devoid of image or fable, and finally, because contained in it, if only embryonically, is the thought, 'all things are one.' "[127]

Around the same historical time of 600 B.C.E., water predominates as an image and metaphor in the Eastern philosophical thought of Taoism and especially its key text, the *Tao Te Ching*. The central idea there of the Tao 道 is presented both as an abstract principle and in concrete physical terms such as vases and pots, which can hold water. Like water, the Tao is best understood in terms of fluidity, movement, process, and *rhythm*—a word related to "flow." The "supreme good" is compared with water because it "nourishes all things without trying to / It is content with the low places that people disdain." The Tao is depicted repeatedly in terms that are appropriate to this fluid: "muddy and yet . . . limpid," "at rest and yet . . . slowly comes to life," or a "shape that has no shape." "Nothing in the world," we read, "is as soft and yielding as water / Yet for dissolving the hard and inflexible, / nothing can surpass it."[128]

The properties of water, too, are like characteristics of the Tao, which is identified through a form of *via negativa*—that is, by way of what it is not. Water is typically colorless, tasteless, and odorless. It lacks form but becomes a matrix of form for other things, providing shape, contour, and texture to the landscape as well as more discrete objects. Morphologically, hearts, ears, eyes, intestines, bones, and antlers bear strong resemblance to or the influential mark of the spiral and spherical shapes of water and water drops, as do snails and shells.[129] As the poet Novalis announces boldly, "There is not doubt that our body is a moulded river."[130] And Gary Snyder advances an even more synoptic thesis about this type of ecological influence on our bodies, avowing "the 'place' . . . gave us far-seeing eyes, the streams and breezes gave us versatile tongues and whorly ears. The land gave us a stride, and the lake a dive. The amazement gave us our kind of mind."[131]

Water may lack an innate rhythm, but it serves as a source of rhythm in the meteorological and physiological spheres, regulating body temperature, mediating, and reflecting gravitational pulls in the tides, and playing an integral role in changes of the weather and seasons. Like the Tao, water is a link between life and death (especially in deserts) and darkness and light (e.g., rainbows). Water also lies between the acid and alkaline, as well as between conduction and radiation within the realm of heat exchange (facilitating the transference of warmth), functioning in this regard like the Tao, which lies between and dismantles opposites such as male and female, black and white, or passive and active. As with the Tao, water possesses putative powers of purification, the ability to mend, cleanse, and heal the cleavages between the natural world and society.

"Water is the *koan* of water," Zen Buddhists have observed.[132] We can construe this *koan*—a meditative conundrum used to attain *satori*, sudden enlightenment—to mean that the way of things, the process of elemental nature, is paradoxical and that it also contains the solution to its own riddling contradiction. Such sentiments recall Heraclitus' notion of *panta rhei* ("all flows" or "everything changes") and his celebrated remark using water imagery that "one cannot step twice into the same river" (fr. 51). The Tao is understandable, however, by analogy not identity with water. We are thereby better able to grasp a difficult idea through a material image, an element, rather than apprehending it only qua abstract idea.[133] Who, for example, has not been caught in the excitement of an unanticipated torrential downpour and been submitted to an unforeseen shower that pelts one's limbs, saturates one's clothing and soaks one's belongings? Staring hypnotically into—or walking through—an uncurtailed curtain of water, expressions like "the rain beats upon the rain" or "the sound of rain needs no translation" might leap to mind and seem entirely apt. We are receiving an education about water through water in the midst of its very improvisational music.

"How inappropriate to call this planet Earth, when it clearly is Ocean," comments Arthur C. Clarke, no doubt emboldened by the fact that about seventy-one percent of the earth's surface is water.[134] Ninety percent of a baby's body is fluid, mostly water, and it can even be said that humans are a kind of "muscular water," especially given that before birth we lie protected in an envelope of the liquid.[135] In composition, seawater is, in fact, close to that of blood with a main difference being that blood contains iron (and less salt) while seawater possesses magnesium. Our connection with the oceans is still evident in the fact that our eyes must be bathed frequently in salt water, and our body—like the sea—requires a prescribed range of saline in order to sustain life.[136] These corporeal ties to elemental waters, then, are more than mythic or metaphorical. In *Your Inner Fish*, paleontologist Neil Shubin details the astonishing ways that our hands resemble the fins of fish; shows how our head is organized like an extinct creature of the sea; reveals the manner in which our jaw evolved from gill arches; and points to the similarities existing at the cellular level between humans and aquatic sponges. We can apparently thank our tadpole past, too, for hiccups and hernia, among other "gifts," as we ruminate on "What a piece of work is a man," to invoke Hamlet's observation.[137]

Water may not be alive (although even this has been challenged),[138] but it is in many ways the primordial stuff of life, as Thales knew, accounting for or playing a part in nearly all chemical and other physical changes within living organisms. Being without material determinateness, it is nevertheless the source of material change. Thus, in order to understand concepts like change, form, flow, and even life itself, it is instructive to meditate upon the qualities and powers of this most universal of substances. Indeed, as Herman Melville remarks in *Moby Dick*, "meditation and water are wedded for ever."[139] Or as a recent "biographer" of water puts it, "William Blake's grain of sand, in which he saw the world reflected, is more properly a raindrop."[140]

Many religious texts and traditions are anchored deeply in such speculation about watery origins. A common figure in creation stories like those of the Maidu Indians and the Yauelmani Yokuts of California is an Earth Diver, an aquatic bird, amphibious creature or deity who plummets to the bottom of the seas to transport up a generative seed from which the world springs.[141] In the "Creation Hymn" of the *Rig Veda*—a key early work of Hinduism—we find: "There was neither non-existence nor existence.... What stirred? Where? In whose protection? Darkness was hidden by darkness in the beginning . . . all this was water. The life force that was covered with emptiness."[142] "Genesis" also advances the claim, in effect, that in the beginning the world emerges from the matrix of a primordial sea—even if creation is ultimately *ex nihilo*—since God separates the water below from the water above to fashion the vaulting heavens and the dry earth, while *The Koran* asserts: "we made every living thing from water."[143]

Real or imagined bodies of water from the Ganges and Nile to the river Styx, too, are associated with divinities or the journeys of the dead. Both mythically and meteorologically, water serves as a destructive force in addition to a creative catalyst, as illustrated by the flood motif in the *Gilgamesh Epic* and the Bible or recent natural disasters like Hurricane Katrina and the South Asian tsunami. In symbolic terms, primordial waters can be both *fons et origo* (spring and origin). They precede life in an evolutionary and ontological sense, but also continue to nourish it. Water easily and equally suggests disintegration, hence death, as well as its counterpart, regeneration, and rebirth. Eliade develops this idea through a distinction between *emersion* from water and *immersion* in it, where the former "repeats the cosmogonic act of formal manifestation" and the latter "is equivalent to a dissolution of forms."[144] Because of their profound depth and mystery, oceanic waters even come to represent the entire unconscious, and it is plausible to maintain that all experiential leaps into the unknown amount psychologically to leaps into water, as dangerous initiations or passages.[145]

Just as there are multifarious forms of earth and air, so there are differentiations within water with respect to color, strength, course, purity, and location. These phenomenal or ontological distinctions play themselves out culturally and environmentally in terms of how we relate to deep or surface liquids, stagnant or running waters, meandering or linear flows, fresh or salt water, and clear or muddy fluids. Water emerges in the process of this translation as maternal, violent, baptismal, therapeutic, feminine, and the like. In this regard, as it grows denser, darker, and deeper, it becomes increasingly material.[146] Water, of course, exists in combination with other elements, assimilating, diluting, and permeating substances to create mud or paste (earth and water), alcohol or thermal springs (fire and water), and cloud or fog (air and water). Indeed, it may be the case that serious thinkers confronted by the exotic marriage of fire and water must abandon the security of rationality in order to accept this amalgam or its offspring.[147]

Like fire, water facilitates introspection and reflection, mirroring what it "sees" and so doubling the surrounding world and providing a sister body to the blue sky. In offering a round-the-clock reflecting pool for the stars and constellations—the traditional markers of both temporality and eternity—water holds itself forth as a reliable image of passing time and a metaphor for life, especially in the flows of rivers and streams. In pointing to the inherent flux of all of physical reality, Heraclitus offers us a generative and generous source for a philosophy of water, whereby all materiality is liquefied into flows of various rates and viscosities, and where even static nouns and seemingly inert things can be dissolved potentially or set into motion—"verb-ed" we might say—so as to indicate their aboriginal fluidity and ongoing change. A building qua fixed or permanent structure (and noun), for example, thereby passes theoretically into an ever-evolving action or unfolding event—that is, building qua process (and gerund as in the verb, "to build"). With the presumption that all truly does flow, even the singular or solitary self eventually disintegrates into a pool of associations, concatenations, and assemblages. Stated differently, if all that exists involves the doing or un-doing of something else, then trees are tree-ing, things are thing-ing, and you are you-ing. Thus, in the realm of the imagination at least, "everything that *flows* is water; everything that flows participates in water's nature."[148] And Bachelard takes this idea a step further to proclaim that psychoanalytically water is a form of joyful nourishment, an insight expressed in ancient India by a Vedic hymn that reads: "The waters, which are our mothers and which desire to take part in the sacrifices, come to us following their paths and distribute their milk to us."[149]

So important is this "milk" to sustaining civilization that the quest for fresh water helped to draw the map of the world and to guide human settlement, urban development, and public health concerns. Geographically, however, water is not evenly or equitably distributed, despite the fact that that there might possibly be enough water contained in minerals within the earth to refill the oceans of the world numerous times over, and water molecules have been found in interstellar gas and, astonishingly, within the sun itself. Throughout many parts of the world, people still walk very long distances to fetch and carry home their daily supply of water. Residents of the United States and Canada are fortunate to be supplied by the largest fresh water system on the planet in the Great Lakes. At the same time, approximately 1.2 billion people worldwide (roughly one in five), including great swaths of Africa and the Middle East, do not have access to clean drinking water—a child dies every eight seconds from contamination—and nearly three billion are without access to regular sanitation services.[150]

While collecting and coalescing in basins, the very hallmark of water, however, is restless movement, which takes on archetypal patterns, especially the spiral, sphere, vortex, and wave. Water tends to seek organic wholes and to enter into large and small networks of circulation. For example, in the ebb and flow of rhythmic waves—that express the polarities between water and windy air, which tends to behave as a fluid—the surface of a lake or sea registers minute impacts and vibrations and becomes as if a sense organ for the body. Water, in turn, is literally moved in interpenetrating and intersecting circles as a wave passes until it reaches shallow territory and is flattened into an ellipse.[151] More broadly, there exists a great global conveyance system for water, which is constantly in transit from place to place, its flow retarded, restrained or redirected by the earthen landscape, conditions in the air and gravity. Water experiences both deep "thermohaline" circulation—which is affected by changes in temperature—and movement on or close to the surface, as it is driven primarily by winds. Residence time, which varies greatly for rivers, lakes, and seas, is the duration that water stays in a given region, and up to three thousand years may be required for an amount equivalent to all that dwells in the oceans to pass through the atmosphere.

As in the forest, life in the sea is distributed in a rich array of loosely defined tiers and levels. In both spheres, it is most prolific near the glistening top, where sunlight is abundant and organisms bask in solar radiance. As one descends, darkness takes taut hold and temperatures drop. Creatures, in turn, compete for energy in the form of food or light that filters down from above. In the sea, one enters into a zone of blackness within several hundred feet of the surface. Yellows and reds are the first to be expunged from the color spectrum given that longer waves of light are absorbed most quickly; purples and blues stretch further into the abyss. Averaging more than two miles in depth, the oceans become for we earth dwellers the embodiment of foreign and unfamiliar worlds. Dry land juts out as a kind of accident on a water-ballasted globe, a consequence of ancient geological upheaval. Plankton—deriving from the Greek for "wandering," like the word "planet"—rule this realm numerically, but strange and exotic figures drift along at great depths, forced to adapt and evolve in a highly pressurized and light-deprived environment. Below one thousand feet, they tend to possess large eyes, to be completely blind or to develop bioluminescence both to attract prey and repel predators. Here, we find ferocious and bizarre-looking creatures whose names alone seem to induce an amalgam of fear, wonder, and awe: the Atlantic Hagfish or "Slime Eel" (which eats its victims from the inside-out), the Giant Squid, the Dragonfish, the Giant Tube Worm, the Hatchetfish, the monstrous Fangtooth and the Viperfish, among many others.

The oceans, then, contain a vast variety of qualitatively different regions and depths, a sea of shifting colors and a kaleidoscopic display of flickering and competing surface characteristics. This complex world is extremely difficult to fathom, especially because visual perception is drawn largely to the façade and roiling play of the waterline. Ruskin, however, felt that for artists it is relatively easy to provide a "degree of depth and transparency to water; but that it is next to impossible, to give a full impression of the surface."[152] An exception to this observation is provided by the work of Vija Celmins, who skillfully explores in realistic detail the flickering and evanescent skin of water in her seascapes through graphite-field drawings to impart texture to the peaks and troughs of waves. Among other artists who have played with the tendencies and power of water, Olafur Eliasson created in 2008 four giant waterfalls ranging in height from 90 to 120 feet in the very heart of Manhattan. The water, which is pumped through pipes from the East River, cascades down great towers of scaffolding, offering itself visually to the residents of the city in a public display that bends and blends aspects of the natural and cultural worlds.

Despite what we know of water's properties and proclivities, much remains in a cloud of obscurity. Water still exhibits random and unpredictable movements as it flows; it requires inexplicably a great amount of energy to be heated; and unlike other substances, it contracts rather than expands when it changes from solid to liquid form upon being warmed.[153] Writer Tom Robbins captures some of its elusive nature in this playful description:

> Water—ace of elements. Water dives from the clouds without parachute, wings or safety net. Water runs over the steepest precipice and blinks not a lash. Water is buried and rises again; water walks on fire and fire gets blisters. Stylishly composed in any situation—solid, gas or liquid—speaking in penetrating dialects understood by all things—

animal, vegetable or mineral—water travels intrepidly through four dimensions . . . a mathematics turned wrong side out, a philosophy in reverse, the ongoing odyssey of water is virtually irresistible."[154]

On a celebratory note, Szymborska observes, "There are not enough mouths to utter / all your fleeting names, O water." "Whenever wherever whatever has happened / is written on waters."[155] And toward the goal of offering expression to some of water's manifold voices, artist and critic Linda Weintraub has constructed an immense instrument out of a stream that courses through the land in upstate New York. As it progresses on its way, the water whistles, hisses, and gurgles in amplified musical manner, hitting high and low notes, modifying its pitch, and sending its song into the countryside.

Like air, fire, and earth, water is susceptible to overuse and abuse. The litany of global problems is long and far-reaching in its magnification of other baleful ecological, economic, and health effects. It includes lake eutrophication (algae proliferation); agricultural, industrial, and chemical runoff; illegal dumping; unsustainable dams (causing silt accumulation, seismic faults, altered river temperature and flow, and changed saline mix in deltas); water over-drafting; shrinking aquifers and irrigation land; over-fishing; wetland disappearance; groundwater contamination; water-borne and water-vector diseases like cholera, malaria, and bilharzias; terrorist threats to water supplies; and the poisoning or death of large aqueous bodies such as the Aral Sea (perhaps the worst anthropogenic ecological disaster in history). Because water travels quickly like air across geographical and political boundaries, it is undoubtedly wise to adopt the environmental axiom that in a very real sense "we all live downstream." Despite its seeming abundance, fresh water is not an easily or a cheaply renewable resource in arid climates and regions suffering severe pollution.

There is a reasonable chance we will witness the emergence of geographical water wars in the not-too-distant future, given that the fluid is at once vital, scarce, and unevenly distributed.[156] In fact, Mark Twain's dictum that "Whiskey is for drinkin'; water is for fightin' " has been made manifest not just in films like *Chinatown* or *Waterworld* but in real-life situations that include threatened wars in the Middle East and a military standoff in 1944 when the heavily armed Arizona National Guard intervened to stop California's reputed theft of water during dam construction on the Colorado River. As one authority on the subject points out, "The trouble with water—and there is trouble with water—is that they're not making any more of it."[157] At the same time, we are making more people who are each dependent on the regular availability of fresh drinking water. We have substituted, it seems, a luxurious addiction to dirty oil for a more sustainable recognition of our utter dependence on and necessary interdependence with clean, clear water.[158]

As noted earlier, Heraclitus observed that, "One cannot step twice into the same river" (fr. 51) because "other and still other waters flow upon them" (fr. 50).

Less famously and more recently, Norman Weinstein counters with the metaphysical quip: "No river steps into the same person twice."[159] We might raise the stakes on this Presocratic philosophical game with the further riddle: if all is water (as the popular interpretation of Thales suggests), how is it that water is held by itself? What, in other words, is the difference between the container and the contained? Such is the nature of this fluid to promote paradox, engender literary and philosophical reflection, and multiply mystery.

Having meditated on earth, air, fire, and water individually, we now transition to consider the more general ways that the elements appear together in the physical and cultural perspectives of the West and the East. Emerson aptly inquires about what might have given birth to "these splendid ornaments, these rich conveniences, this ocean of air above, this ocean of water beneath, this firmament of earth between? This zodiac of lights, this tent of dropping clouds, this striped coat of climates, this fourfold year?" He points out that older generations beheld this intricate and dazzling world "face to face," whereas more recent ones have tended to encounter it indirectly and though earlier eyes. But he proceeds to ask quite simply and legitimately, "Why should not we also enjoy an original relation to the universe. Why should not we have a poetry of insight" as well as one of tradition.[160] Keeping the spirit of this question in mind, we look at both the occluded tradition and the emerging ideas and insights about the elements. It is hoped that in the process we will gain a greater understanding of the lay of the elemental environment and perhaps even begin to develop a more original relation to the world around us.

Interstice: Stone

> Picture the scenes that might be staged by a very skillful stonemason practicing a kind of lithography with his chisel or by the philosopher writing at the limit of philosophy, . . . writing a text doubly on stone, making stone speak of itself.
>
> —John Sallis, *Stone*

> To contemplate rocks . . . is to entertain the possibility of being crushed by them.
>
> —Gaston Bachelard, *Earth and Reveries of Will*

Stone, of course, does not speak, let alone refer to itself. Or does it? To speak of it speaking or remaining mute, one must imagine an account of its cryptic language, a dialogue with its inner essence or, alternatively, a story of its elemental silence. The Polish poet Wislawa Szymborska provides one such confabulation in "Conversation with a Stone" when the unnamed speaker in her poem—who wants to "have a look round"—knocks repeatedly at the door of a stone, who refuses entry to its interior but in doing so nevertheless displays a voice. The stone is more, or at least other, than what it is normally perceived to be. "You may get to know me, but you'll never know me through / My whole surface is turned toward you, / all my insides turned away." Despite the many entreaties and varied assurances that the speaker will not seek refuge and will leave "empty-handed," all the requests are summarily denied. "You lack the sense of taking part," says the stone. And, it turns out, no other sense is an adequate substitute for this absence, not "even sight heightened to become all-seeing." "You shall not enter, you have only a sense of what that sense / should be, / only its seed, imagination." Appropriately and humorously, the stone's last response is "I don't have a door," as the speaker and reader are thrown back to their separate realities.[1]

We easily forget that Western philosophy commences, quite astonishingly, with contemplation of a rock rather than a thought or a human action or a deity.

As tradition touts it, Thales ponders a magnesium stone that reveals to him a world in which soul (*psyche*) is kinetic and the world is alive and "full of gods." He holds forth boldly that the loadstone possesses soul—which, whether associated with spinal fluid, breath, or blood, was considered widely to be the source of life or consciousness—because it, the stone, literally moves iron. In other words, what manifests the capacity to stir and change of its own accord is animated. Thales' words were not written in stone; in fact, they survive only through the deteriorated parchment of doxographers and later commentators, who enable him to speak from beneath a gravestone, but his extant fragments of speculation possess the potential to move a new material discourse into existence.

Thus, the Philosopher's Stone (*lapis philosophorum*)—the mythic material of alchemy—was thought to allow us to turn lead to gold. Hegel still falls under its metaphoric sway when he writes, "In regard to Nature, it is agreed that philosophy ought to know her as she is, that if the philosopher's stone is hidden anywhere, it must at any rate be within Nature herself."[2] In a strange way, it continues to fascinate through stories, film, and institutions such as Freemasonry, offering up the enticing idea of transmuting elemental substance into a more magical metal, or even providing an elixir of immortality. Likely bewitched by this kind of lure, Aristotle's student, Theophrastus, devoted an entire volume to the investigation of stone, classifying rock based on its response to heat, organizing minerals according to their revealed properties, describing precious stones, and remarking on the relative hardness of earthen entities.[3]

At times, the names of rocks seem capable of conjuring up secret realms themselves, like foreign words hinting at unfamiliar worlds. Perhaps, they should be intoned slowly, like incantations: malachite, schist, mica, onyx, agate, flint, garnet, quartzite, turquoise, feldspar, and gneiss. Whole human eras have been claimed for rocks and minerals, including the Stone Age, Iron Age, and Bronze Age. Indeed, the history of civilizations and the natural history of the land eventually become fixed in layers of stone stacked above one another like cuneiform tablets waiting for archeologists, anthropologists, climatologists, and paleontologists to unearth and patiently decipher them. As "recordings" or "texts," stone is far from silent, incommunicative or cold to the well-trained ear, eye, and touch. "To a geologist," writes Marcia Bjornerud, it tells "gothic tales of scorching heat, violent tempests, endurance, cataclysm, and reincarnation." Through a four-billion-year story registered "in beach sand, volcanic ash, granites, and garnet schists, the planet has unintentionally kept a rich and idiosyncratic journal of its past."[4]

Culture permits us to posit a distinction between ordinary or profane stone, on the one hand, and extraordinary or sacred stone, on the other hand, and to explore the "soft side" of rock, including the values, meanings, and imaginative associations it evokes for us.[5] The Kaaba, for example, is a revered stone building in Mecca toward which Muslims pray and around which pilgrims promenade during the Hajj. Resting near the eastern cornerstone of the Kaaba is a massive black monolith with great religious significance for the devout, who often kiss or touch the venerated object—which may actually be an ancient meteorite—in an act of homage to their prophet, Mohammad. In a very loose sense, Christianity is also founded upon the certainty of stone in the proclamation that "The Lord is my rock" and the famous utterance to the apostle Peter (whose name derives from the Greek, *Petros*, meaning rock) in the Gospel of Matthew: "And I say unto you, you are Peter; and on this rock [*petra*] I will build my church."[6]

Stone figures prominently, too, in Zen gardens, where it serves to organize space and generate the "yang" element of a yin–yang polarity. In these visual koans—or picture-poems and contemplative puzzles—sand may appear to eddy around the perimeter of rocks like water channeling through a stream as artfully positioned stone registers itself in thoroughly artless ways on the meditative mind, providing a focal point for cathexis, catharsis, or creative flights of fancy. And lunar rocks, transported like purloined treasure back to the Earth by astronauts, carry the status of stone from the realm of the commonplace to the culturally significant. Like the terrestrial-bound Rosetta Stone, space rocks collected from meteorites or the surface of Mars and the Moon may provide a key to better interpreting the hieroglyphic clues of the solar system, silently informing us whether or where we can expect to find signs of water or life. As outcroppings of the sacred, stones exhibit adamantine qualities; they betoken power and permanence. "The hierophany of a stone is pre-eminently an ontophany; above all, the stone *is*, it always remains itself, . . . it *strikes* man by what it possesses of irreducibility and absoluteness," notes Eliade.[7]

Despite a reputation for quiet strength and solidity, stone, like everything else, weakens, deteriorates, shifts shape, and perhaps even flows. Strictly speaking, Hawthorne was wrong when he posited, "Mountains are Earth's undecaying monuments."[8] They, too, fall apart from gravitational pulls and erosion at about the same rate at which they rise. "Something there is that doesn't love a wall," Robert Frost astutely observes, "That sends the frozen-ground-swell under it, / And spills the upper boulders in the sun; / And makes gaps even two can pass abreast."[9] Walk along a wall of rock, and it seems to adopt a kind of movement and a rhythmic life of its own. For three exceedingly slow hours en route to and from the cloud forests of Monte Verde in Costa Rica, I drove on a river of very rough rock that was once an ox-cart trail traversed by self-exiled Quakers seeking an avenue out of a more violent world. The stones appeared to conduct and carry, if also resist, my vehicle as I bounced in and out of worn hollows and deep ruts for miles, while being transported like a wooden top buoyed along by a meandering stream. Artist Andy Goldsworthy has explored some of this malleability and liquidity of stone in fashioning elegant arches, cairns, and serpentine walls. In one surprising earthwork, he even extracts red pigment from rock he extricates from a streambed, dissolving it to transform the water into a crimson conduit, a tributary of fleeting blood. Ansel Adams likewise photographed mountains and cliffs not so much as monuments of enduring stone but more as evanescent expressions of weather, wherein one might be able to discern through black and white images ranging the gamut of subtle shades like the eighty-eight keys on a piano, the particular time and temperature or the humidity and wind direction of a geographic place.[10]

Some stone is granted a second existence as sculpture once it has been quarried, shaped, and chiseled into diverse forms. Artists like Arp, Rodin, Brancusi, and Moore have enlarged our experiences and conceptions of marble, granite, alabaster, sandstone, jade, and soapstone. Michelangelo, who believed that a statue lay waiting to be discovered inside every slab of stone, once proclaimed, "With chiseled touch / The stone unhewn and cold / Becomes a living mould / The more the marble wastes / The more the statue grows."[11] Aesthetically, stone cries out for appreciation not just through sight but also via the senses of touch, sound, and even smell. Some rocks possess the property of resonating like a bell when hit with a sharp object, a phenomenon that can be witnessed in Ringing Rocks Park in Bucks County, Pennsylvania. When struck individually in a lab outside of their native environment, these rocks generate tones with frequencies that the human ear cannot discern. It is only when the tones interact with and echo one another outdoors that a sound with a high enough pitch to be heard by humans is produced.

The three main languages or "literary genres" of stone offer clues to how we might read rocks and hence interpret the broader environment they ballast, adorn, and help to define. In a nutshell, sedimentary rocks like limestone, shale, and sandstone are produced through the recycling action of elemental water and air on existing rocks and tell us much about surface conditions and the epidermal forces of the Earth. Igneous rocks ranging from pumice and obsidian to basalt and quartz are of volcanic (extrusive) or plutonic (intrusive) provenance and apprise us of deeper tellurian stories. Rocks of metamorphic (literally "shaped after") origin such as marble, slate, and schist start in igneous or sedimentary territory and change form as they engage new surroundings. They are the petrological "polyglots" and "travel writers of the rock world, chronicling their astounding journeys through the crust."[12] Together, they provide a hermeneutical key of sorts to the stratigraphy on which we live, and an opportunity for ecological cartography.

Stone can also be produced through petrifaction, a process that occurs gradually through the substitution or infiltration of each cell in a buried log or other organic matter by very hot, silica-laden water, which preserves intact and exact detail the original structure of the wood as a kind of jewelry teeming with "agitized rainbows." "Coming unexpectedly upon such a trove," Edward Abbey remarks, "a man is sometimes overcome by greed; by the mad desire to possess it all, to load his pockets, his knapsack, his truck with these hard lustrous treasures and somehow transport them all from the wilderness to the ship, garage, and backyard."[13] This sentiment, incidentally, was something like what I experienced as a young teen wandering around the Petrified Forest of the American southwest and tempted to pilfer souvenirs wrought by the earth's exorbitant workings. Abbey, in fact, describes one of his books—which we might imagine as the fallen fruit of a former tree—itself as a type of tombstone, a petroglyphic monument to the disappearing beauty of the austere desert.

Stone, then, is also a final signpost, a place to inscribe a terse epitaph or the sparest of words about the bare biological facts of the mortal coil that lies beneath it. A geologist whom I know desires to be buried below a large unmarked boulder in the middle of nowhere, finding it the most fitting way to return to earth-driven cycles that grind rock and bone without the slightest suggestion of judgment into dirt and dust. In the Woodlands Cemetery of West Philadelphia, an urban necropolis where I often run, deer graze on clover amidst the stony graves that are anchored by craggy trees that grow from the corpses, shooting their outstretched limbs into the sky like *Vṛkṣasana*, a dynamic yoga pose. Wandering through this undulating graveyard or another local potter's field, I am reminded frequently how elemental all this is and ever will be: an elaborate tapestry of earth, rock, sky, shadow, night, and death.

Imputing intentionality to the stone but making a point in the process, E. W. Eschmann speculates: "Rocks, too, long for existence. If we but knew their instincts and the means to stimulate and fecundate them, perhaps we might raise different species of marble just as we do dahlias and Siamese cats."[14] Stone, in any event, can both fascinate and be-calm us; it offers a passing promise of security but seems to resist our best efforts at understanding it because of an apparent impassivity or blankness of expression. We lug small rocks home from beaches, hikes, and foreign lands as mementos, tokens, and traces of the places we visit, but also as tiny attempts to comprehend them. The Grand Canyon confounds and stupefies us through its sheer depth and immensity; fossils entrance us for the bewildering sense of a cavernous time to which they allude but that we fail to fully fathom. The Great Wall of China; the Pyramids of Egypt; the Mesopotamian ziggurats; Mount Rushmore; the Taj Mahal; the catacombs of Rome, Paris, and Ukraine; the Crazy Horse memorial currently being cut from the Black Hills of South Dakota; the statues of Easter Island; the Wailing Wall of Jerusalem; Stonehenge; and the Parthenon all stand out as grand emblems of the muscular power of stone. But so do thousands of more common temples, cathedrals, synagogues, and mosques; castle ruins, ordinary basement walls, commercial banks, and even the vast network of concrete highways that runs like a series of dendritic rivers throughout the United States.

Like the ancient Egyptians, the Incans put stone to use in remarkable ways, hauling it long distances—from up to forty miles away—through great ingenuity, cobbling together enormous slabs to form impenetrable walls or sophisticated irrigation systems, and integrating military, religious, astronomical, and economic functions into aesthetically-pleasing structures. Perched amidst the clouds at nine thousand feet, the well-preserved ruins of Machu Picchu represent an apotheosis of such engineering skills. Here, one finds an abandoned city and citadel of sculpted rock glistening in the sun, a place of mystery that remained sequestered from the marauding Spaniards. The visitor is struck by how this entire world seems organized around one elemental substance. Stone tools were used to break and polish quarried rock. Stone troughs channel water down steep hills. Stone frames and houses temples; it forms cascading sets of steps; it delineates boundaries; and it integrates the city with the surrounding canyons, misty firmament and precipitous cliffs. Most of the blocks, which were cut and fitted without the benefit of mortar through a technique called "ashlar," are so tightly assembled that one cannot even insert a razor blade between them. Through respect, even reverence, rock is raised from the bonds of the earth to the showcasing sky and elevated as well from the realm of the prosaic to that of the poetic. In the process, one can imagine the way human character and personality itself have also been shaped and sculpted by this materiality. The Imperial system of weights and measures in Great Britain even uses "stone" to refer to a unit of mass—one is equal to fourteen pounds—such that we can express the heaviness of our bodies as, for example, twelve stone. Of the Incan stonecutters, Alphonso Lingis writes, "the whole life, the identity of the artisans was absorbed without leaving signs. We know them only, as they knew themselves as, laborious bodies, bodies devoted to effacing the rough traces of the quarrying, the signs of human intervention from the surfaces of the stones, bodies becoming patient, impenetrable, indecipherable as the stones."[15]

On the other side of the earth, in China, I made a trek to see Dafu, the great seated Buddha in the southwestern part of the country. Located at the confluence of the Dadu and Min Rivers, the 230-foot statue with eyes and ears spanning more than twenty feet each in diameter, was chiseled by several monks (including the original artist who gouged out his eyes to obtain funding) from the side of a hill over a ninety-year period beginning in 713 C.E. What struck me as I ate a picnic meal on one of his giant toenails was the voluminous nature of the stone and the contrast of his serene countenance—which watches over passing ships at night—with the pre-existing but still enduring face of the cliff that frames the setting and dwarfs human figures scuttling up or down the steep staircase with nine turns. The Chinese adage that "the mountain is a Buddha and the Buddha is a mountain," applies literally and figuratively in the case of Dafu, whose presence reveals magisterially the stuff of elemental substance.

Although now viewed widely in terms of their grandeur, mountains were once considered to be ugly disfigurations of and protuberances on terrestrial symmetry—carbuncles on the earth's face or alleged evidence of God's wrath.[16] It was not until Romantic poets praised them for their beauty and glory that a shift in perception began to occur. Mountains, however, are not just objects to be mined for aesthetic, theological, or scientific significance but earthen outcroppings of the most elemental kind to be bodily engaged and viscerally experienced. Rock and mountain climbing, along with spelunking, foster a primal contact with stone, and these activities are fraught with psychological connotations ranging from antagonism, fear, and resistance to communion, love, and sublime acceptance. "Great things are done when men and mountains meet; this is not done by jostling in the street," writes William Blake.[17] Climbers undoubtedly take something from the rocks they scale, but they also leave a bit of themselves upon the stone escarpments, cliffs, and peaks, which outlast and often continue to overshadow their lives, placing human events in a broader perspective. "Whoever climbs the highest mountains laughs at all tragedies, real or imaginary," observes Nietzsche.[18]

The myth of Sisyphus tells the tale of an "existential" Greek hero condemned endlessly to push a rock up a mountain before it invariably rolls back down to the bottom, and the labor begins again. Camus imagines the scene of this elemental encounter:

> One sees merely the whole effort of a body straining to raise the huge stone, to roll it, and push it up a slope a hundred times over; one sees the face screwed up, the cheek tight against the stone, the shoulder bracing the clay-covered mass, the foot wedging it, the fresh start with arms outstretched, the wholly human security of two earth-clotted hands.

Camus surmises that "a face that toils so close to stones is already stone itself!"[19] But in the descent, when Sisyphus is all-too-aware of his tragic plight, he becomes greater than his allotted fate and hence stronger than the stone. Bachelard, however, offers another interpretation, pointing out that we should remember that there is a vibrant struggle with an actual rock going on, something that we may discount because we have foregone daily familiarity with stone or intellectualized it too much. And whereas Camus finds a human face become stone, Bachelard discovers precisely the opposite possibility: "a rock which is the object of so prodigious a human effort becomes itself human!" It is, in other words, capable of explaining manual labor and of serving as an "objective correlative" for biceps that become aware of their own strength.[20]

If philosophy begins in part with the *terra firma* of rock or rock-solid foundations, including Empedocles' reputed embracing leap of fate into a volcano, it is on more slippery ground with elemental earth and stone from that time forward. Plato presents the cave as a dark and unenlightening place to be escaped. Aristotle contrasts voluntary activity negatively with that of a rock, which has no capacity for deliberation. Heidegger denies stone a world because it has no access to experience or other entities as such; it is indifferent to itself and, in effect, erased from the deeper realm of Being. Sartre agrees, insisting that we are not humans in "the way a rock is a rock."[21] But a slow resuscitation begins, as if rock presses itself forth and obtrudes into the philosopher's hard-headed consciousness. Deleuze and Guattari, for example, speak of the intriguing possibility of a "geology of morals." Derrida interrogates critically Heidegger's "crossing-out" of stone, commenting, "You cannot say that a stone is indifferent to its Being without being anthropomorphic. It is neither indifferent nor not indifferent."[22] And John Sallis reveals Heidegger's complex relationship with ancient Greek temples, ruins, and deformed elemental rock. To hold that stones are worldless, Sallis rightly notes, is not to say that they are unable to become part of a world that may open above or around them, as happens with tombstones, sculptures, and architecture.[23] Bachelard, in turn, celebrates mineral, metal, and molten material as elemental entities through an active literary and psychological encounter with rocks as sign of defiance and a rendezvous with "monstrous powers." Finally, when poetry becomes phenomenological, writers like Rilke show how stone can shine forth to illuminate a world, as when he meditates on the torso of Apollo, which is "suffused with brilliance from inside, / like a lamp, in which his gaze, now turned to low / gleams in all its power." Indeed, the poet suggests that when one truly observes the way sculpted stone can radiate light and "glisten like a wild beast's fur . . . from all borders of itself" so that "there is no place that does not see you," only one option exists to embrace: "You must change your life."[24]

Stone nonetheless rests at the very outer limit of our understanding of both life and language, of what is possibly animate and what can conceivably communicate. Literary critic Walter Benn Michaels has written skeptically of landscapes "speaking" and more specifically of investing rock with a voice. In this view, claiming that the angles of stone are like expressive gestures involves an illicit anthropomorphism. Teaching a stone to talk, as Annie Dillard phrases it, however, need not be taken so literally. Another option is teaching a human to "listen," meaning broadly to perceive in a way that permits entities to be revealed in their "given-ness"—their "thus-ness" or "such-ness"—and for us to become receptive to the other-than-human dimensions of the environment.

Admittedly, works of art as well as buildings are increasingly made of steel, glass, and plastic rather than marble, granite, and slate. While stone has always been used to signal territory, memorialize, and delimit or establish boundaries through fences, walls or obelisks, its status took a strange twist when it was theriomorphized and sold across the United States in the 1970s as "pet rocks" in little boxes containing sprigs of straw and a set of instructions on how to care for them. Still, stone and rock, whether assuming the shape of wedding rings and jewelry, construction material or metaphoric music as in "rock and roll," will continue to impact our cultural lives in unexpected ways as long as the third immense and exceptional "rock" (planet) from the sun stays secure in its orbit. Along the way, we might begin to hear or perhaps even converse with a kind of muffled voice in this very primitive material. Charles Simic writes: "From the inside the stone is a riddle: / No one knows how to answer it. / Yet within, it must be cool and quiet." But because we can see sparks generated when stones are rubbed together, Simic speculates, "Perhaps there is a moon shining / From somewhere, as though behind a hill— / Just enough light to make out / The strange writings, the star-charts / On the inner walls."[25] "Let the stones speak," Dylan Thomas avers, "with tongues that talk all tongues."[26]

— 2 —

The Topology of the Elemental Environment

He sang how in the mighty Void, the seeds of Earth and Air and of Ocean, and of Fire—that pure thing—range themselves together; and how from these principles all the Elements arose, systematically cohering in the tender globe of the World.

—Vergil, *Sixth Eclogue*

One dreams in front of his fire, and the imagination discovers that the fire is the motive force for a world. One dreams in front of a spring and the imagination discovers that water is the blood of the earth, that the earth has living depths.

—Gaston Bachelard, *The Poetics of Reverie*

The doxographic tradition of the Greeks records the views of early philosophers on a variety of subjects in an order that was followed regularly: principle, God, universe, earth, sea, rivers, Nile, stars, sun, moon, milky way, meteors, wind, rain, hail, snow, thunder, rainbow, earthquakes, and animals.[1] If we survey this curious list, we see the four elements are present repeatedly in both direct and indirect ways: water as sea, rivers, Nile, and rain; earth as earth itself and earthquakes; air as wind and possibly as rainbow or thunder; and, finally, fire as stars and sun. In a subtle manner, these ancient references point to the formative and enduring influence of the elemental world on philosophical thought.

Speaking broadly, we can identify a number of related and often overlapping frameworks of meaning for the concept of "element," including, but not limited to, substances, places, archetypes, letters, opposites, and chemicals. Most of these senses of the term convey the idea of something fundamental, ultimate, or basic—that is, elemental. As we sketch out a typology or topology of types—an "archetopology" so to speak—it is important to recognize that "elements" are not necessarily singular or univocal entities.[2] Like the notion of "nature," elements have been understood through a host of very different approaches. Indeed, there is a polysemous, promiscuous, and even polymorphous quality to their appearances or representations, especially when we consider them historically and take into account their re-emergence in recent Continental philosophy, where we discover notions of elemental flesh, elemental landscape, elemental imperatives, elemental reveries, elemental passions, and elemental sensibility. Many of the particular meanings of element, too, possess an implicit or explicit tie to the ambient environment with which they are associated deeply, one that is explored more fully as we proceed.

After locating some of the fundamental forms in which the elements express themselves, we look, in turn, at several non-Greek or non-Western perspectives so as to gain a sense of the way in which other cultures have incorporated elemental experiences and thought into their philosophies, religions, and stories, focusing on ancient and perennial views within China, India, and Japan, among other locales. We then inquire into some of the reasons why the elements typically appear as four in number, connecting such explanations with the physical environment and body. Finally, it is argued that the elements are socially mediated and constructed through institutional, linguistic, and political practices or beliefs, including those related to marriage, the emotions, war, sex, community structures, and morality.

Elementary Letters

If part of the grand task of philosophy is "to preserve the force of the most elemental words" as Heidegger boldly claims, then surely some of the most fundamental terms, ideas, and concepts concern the elements themselves, the constituents of the physical realm and the regions basic to the lifeworld.[3] Human linguistic patterns, vocabulary, and thought processes are related intimately to the manifestations of water, air, earth, and fire. In Greek, the word *stoicheion*—translated into Latin as *elementum*—is based on a comparison of physical principles with letters of the alphabet and may have referred originally to what is placed in a row or line.[4] Aristotle thus comments on the numerous ways in which letters can be rearranged to form words and texts so as to show the seemingly infinite power of these units. These *stoicheia* or letters are the elements that compose the great "Book of Nature," as it was called regularly, or literally *spell the cosmos* from qualitatively distinct components. In Plato's dialogues, the *stoicheia* retain some of the multivalent senses of both letters and elements, implying an attenuated connection between written discourse and theories of world-construction evident especially in the *Timaeus*.

The early Greeks, however, were not the only people to fall under the mesmerizing spell of the elements. English vocabulary, too, is fraught with links between the elements and the more cultural sphere of language. Water, for example, is continually present in our language and mental deliberation when we speak of *streams* of consciousness; *currents* of thought; *floods* of insight; *flowing* words, ideas, and time; *watershed* events; *well-springs* and *pools* of information; *waves* of success; *turning* tides; and so on. In the case of water, such tropes and metaphors tend to underscore wholeness, cyclicality, and rhythm.[5] Interestingly, Emerson developed a view of language that calls attention to such ties between the natural world and language, arguing first that words are signs of what he terms "natural facts"; second, that such particular natural facts are symbols of what he calls "spiritual facts"; and finally that nature itself is the symbol of spirit. With respect to the first claim, he holds that every word that expresses an intellectual or moral fact (truth) when followed to its root is derived from a material appearance. In support of this perspective, he offers examples such as right (meaning straight), wrong (meaning twisted), spirit (meaning wind), transgression (as the crossing of a line), and supercilious (from the raising of an eyebrow). He also points to the picturesque and poetic qualities inherent in early language, holding that the same natural symbols compose "the original *elements* of all languages."[6]

Keeping this Emersonian notion in mind, we may observe that in Mandarin, the present ideograms (Chinese characters) for earth, air, fire, and water are descendants of pictograms (picture-letters) that embody the primordial elements as they were visually and sensuously present themselves to ancient Chinese hands, eyes, ears, and minds. Fire 火 (*huo*) initially appears as a simple enclosed flame at a campsite and later looks more like the flickering form of fire itself, with two sparks on either side of a central flame. Earth 土 (*tu*) evolves from a plant blossoming perpendicularly out of the ground, and it retains this basic appearance to the present day. In its current state, it is composed of three strokes: an upper horizontal line (the cultivable crust), a lower horizontal line (the fertile but stony subsoil), and a vertical line joining the other two and extending beyond it into the air (all living things that emerge to the surface from the subsoil). In its ancient form, air 氣 (*qi*) first represented sun and fire, which together produce steam, whose appearance as air was portrayed as squiggly lines of vapor. When air is combined with the character for fire, it gives us "wrath" or "anger" (*huo qi*), as in the dangerous and unpredictable admixture of wind and flame. Finally, water 水 (*shui*) originally resembles either a winding stream or river when etched on bone and bronze or it depicts the eddies, currents, and drops of this fluid, and in contrast to fire—whose lines leap upward—the movement is predominately downward. Written adjacent to the character for "flower," it creates the word "spray," just as "fire" placed next to flower produces "spark."

In each case, as "radicals"—essentially roots of a linguistic character—these elemental and "alphabetical" building blocks are used to form terms with referents in the natural world. Other examples from China convey this connection as well.[7] *Feng shui* 风水 (literally a combination of the characters for wind and water) is an important concept that denotes an appropriate location in which to build a house, bury the dead, or locate furniture, and the idea can be understood in terms of ecological relationships that exist between objects, emphasizing as it does the primacy of place. Home dwellers and interior decorators who subscribe to the geo-spatial philosophy of *feng shui* position furniture or utilities based on their perceived connection with an element and that element's relation to other elements within a larger placial context. Rather than simply coordinating colors, textures, or dimensions within a given environment, the art of *feng shui* involves creating a gestalt of earth, air, fire, water, and sometimes metal or wood so as to complement and complete one another.[8] Through a long history of associations, each element is connected with characteristics ranging from direction and materiality to shape,[9] color, and emotion.[10] One should not, for example, situate a fireplace (fire element) next to a sink, toilet, or fountain (water element). *Feng shui* recommends adding water where there is too much noise or when one seeks to improve transmission of ideas and thoughts; when sluggishness occurs, it is advisable to bring in a fire element; and where relaxation is necessary, earth and water should be added. As in some of the early Greek theories, there exists something akin to positive, negative, and neutral relations between the various elements. Thus, the positive remains of fire produce earth, whereas earth itself relates negatively to fire in its capacity to squelch out a flame.

Shan shui 山水 is a linguistic and literal unity of *shan* or mountain (i.e., rocky earth) and *shui* or water that means "landscape," and it provides another illustration of an elemental combination that forms an environmental concept, in this instance the action of moving water on stone, hill, and soil to create the topography and geography.[11] A well-known calligraphist expresses this relation between the natural realm and written Chinese language when he observes of his art: "Every horizontal stroke is like a mass of clouds in battle, every hook like a bent bow of the greatest strength, every dot like a falling rock from a high peak, every drawn-out line like a dry vine of great old age and every swift and free stroke like a runner from his start."[12] Because of this link between the concrete things of the physical environment and their pictorial representations in script, it is plausible to surmise that in certain respects Chinese culture is (or has been) connected more closely with the ambient elements and the surrounding environment than it might otherwise be (or have been) if the language was tied solely to a system of abstract signs. Over time, however, the language has shifted increasingly from the use of pictograms (picture-words) to phonograms (sound-words) and then to ideograms (idea-words) and thus distanced itself—and perhaps Chinese society too—from the elemental world.

On this more general point concerning the attenuation or domestication of an elemental connection within language to the broader environment, Richard Nirenberg speculates that there once existed a time, perhaps "a dim mythological past," when what he calls Spirit "sounded in the K's of the crackling fire, in the furious F's of raging storms, the R's of thunder, and in the serpent's sibilant S's or Z's." In his view, with the growing control over natural phenomena, "our tongue became slacker, the sound gradually tamer: we evolved an aspiration, a breathing, something inner, almost intangible."[13] In a similar vein, Max Horkheimer observes: "Today nature's tongue is taken away. Once it was thought that each utterance, word, cry, or gesture had an intrinsic meaning; today it is merely an occurrence."[14] And Jung echoes this point when he writes, "Thunder is no longer the voice of an angry god, nor is lightning his avenging missile. No river contains a spirit, no tree is the life principle of a man, no snake the embodiment of wisdom, no mountain cave the home of a great demon. No voices now speak to men from stones, plants, and animals, nor does he speak to them believing they can hear."[15] Although there is clearly no possibility of "going back" to another era, a working knowledge of the elements and the elemental aspects of language might assist us potentially in better understanding not only our words but also the manner in which they still bind us to the more capacious world.

Elemental Places

Greek geography undoubtedly contributed to the inspiration and source for the theories of the four elements.[16] The colorful commingling and optical interplay of the fire in the bright golden sun with the warm air in the luminous blue sky, the dry brown earth of the rugged mountainous landscape, and the azure water in the Aegean and Mediterranean seas—the latter name conjoins two elements, earth and water, to mean the "sea of the middle earth"—surely impressed themselves indelibly on the first Western minds contemplating the origin and constitution of physical things. In fact, it was commonly believed by the Greeks that in the best climate no one meteorological force prevails but rather there exists proportionality and harmony among them, a view that accords with the seeming parity of the four elements and four humors. Earth, air, fire, and water have been correlated widely to the massive elemental places of land, sky, stars (or heavens), and sea, and this is true even of the early Greek mythological and religious writings in which the universe is partitioned into provinces in which the gods dwell and rule. In the poetic work of Hesiod in eighth century B.C.E, for example, the world is divided into the realms of Earth (*Gaia*), Sea (*Pontos*), and Sky (*Ouranos*), which are assigned to Hades, Poseidon, and Zeus.[17] In Plato's *Timaeus*, by contrast, the elements come into being in a Receptacle (*hypodoche*), which functions as a primordial place of places, and they occupy distinct regions based on the movements therein. Aristotle, too, stresses the importance of place proper (*topos*), and natural place (*topos oikeios*) in his accounts of the elements. In brief, each of his four simple bodies eventually finds its rest in an appropriate locale when it is no longer under the force of some constraint. Each strives, in other words, to find its native place and domestic home.

As part of an investigation of the theories of the elements, it is valuable, then, to keep in mind their geography, the order and orientation that they help to sustain and in which they are ever implicated. Thought appears to plot its own coordinates and to demand reference points, resting places, positions, and even dispositions. Given that humans are goal-oriented beings, we seek directions and directionality (e.g., progress, ends, plateaus, and benchmarks), and so it is reasonable to believe that philosophy, too, requires a kind of compass, map, or chart so as to move, navigate, and stake out territory and claims. Gilles Deleuze puts it this way: "thought itself presupposes axes and orientations according to which it develops." Thus, "it has a geography before having a history" that "traces dimensions before constructing systems."[18] Indeed, the Presocratic philosopher Anaximander helped to found geography as a science in the sixth century B.C.E by devising the first map of earth as a physical whole, even if his map was more of a theoretical than a practical contribution.[19]

As place-based and place-defining entities or forces, the elements provide us with physical location on the planet and even metaphysical orientation in space, being bound in many philosophical frameworks with human corporeality, aesthetics, and psychology. The intersection of air (sky) and earth in the landscape, or water and air (sky) in the seascape, constitute the horizon—what Blake, a poet of the fourfold, called *Urizen*, which we can read as "your reason." As the Greek term *horos* suggests, the horizon establishes the bounds and limits of our perceptual experiences.[20] The horizon grants depth to vision and serves as a "zonal place" where colors and shapes fade or become indeterminate.[21] When we move toward it, the horizon seems mysteriously to recede and withdrawal from us. "The horizon of the far sphere includes the enormous concave dome of the sky as well as the land or sea that spreads out before us as it draws into remoteness," notes Edward Casey. It is "the ultimate *perimeter of places*" that simultaneously "holds and distributes the places within its embrace" through the continual animation of the human body.[22] Progressing in the direction of the horizon, we discover it disgorging new and sometimes unexpected features of a place, offering across its threshold billowing cauliflower clouds or serene panoramic vistas, verdant woods or monochromatic fields, the blues of the sea or the browns of desert earth, and enticing us all the while to endless worlds beyond our discerning gaze.

We can differentiate multiple forms of this phenomenon, including an apparent horizon—such as the meeting point of sky and earth—and a sensible horizon, which is the tangent plane relative to the earth's surface where an individual is positioned. The encircling horizon is another perceptual form that offers a vanishing point or edge-line in observation and functions as a reference for sight. It often serves, in effect, as an occluding edge for objects. In moving about, we frequently find the earth-sky horizon consuming or revealing overhead objects like the stars, moon, and sun, which shrink or wax in magnitude depending on the time of day or the earth's motions. When the flat ground opens up before us, the horizon becomes part of an ambient perceptual array. There may even exist an "implicit horizon" available to us when distant objects are not obscured by fog, trees, or rocks. By focusing on the stationary horizon, we can orient our bodies in both place and time during a hike, walk, or journey through bearings gleaned from minor changes in our perceptions of elemental surroundings. The earth-sky line establishes an external frame of reference and allows us to govern our upright bodies, which move perpendicularly to the horizon though the physical world. The horizon, as eco-psychologist James J. Gibson argues, is not strictly an objective or subjective phenomenon. Instead, it reveals the reciprocity of an observer with his or her environment so as to become a stable feature of perception.[23] Or, as Merleau-Ponty says, it guarantees the persistence of entities as we investigate them, serving as "the correlative of the impending power which my gaze retains over the objects which it has just surveyed, and which it already has over the fresh details which it is about to discover."[24] In this regard, the natural world itself is "the horizon of all horizons" in that it secures the unity of all our experiences as a given lying beneath the upheavals and disruptions of our lives.[25]

Still, there exists an aura of the ineffable around the horizon. Heidegger suggests boldly "what lets the horizon be what it is has not yet been encountered at all." The horizon is "the side facing us of an openness which surrounds us." It appears akin to a region, perhaps even "an enchanted region where everything belonging there returns to that in which it rests."[26] Derrida likewise claims of the horizon that it is a virtual presence in all experiences, being both a unity and an incompletion of those experiences, an "always-already-there" of an open future.[27] And Merleau-Ponty describes the horizon as "a new type of being, a being of porosity, pregnancy, or generality, and the one before whom the horizon opens is caught up, included with it."[28] Nevertheless, the horizon is integral to showing and bestowing beauty on the places we inhabit or cherish, a point that did not escape Emerson's notice. "There is a property in the horizon which no man has but he whose eye can integrate all the parts, that is, the poet," he remarks. For Emerson, although the eye forms nature's "first circle," the horizon that it constitutes becomes the second instance of this engaging and repeated geometric figure, which when we behold as beautiful allows us to take pleasure in our own nature as well.[29]

In contrast with a horizontal axis and point of reference, we find in perspectives such as Aristotle's philosophy that up and down (i.e., verticality)—as well as circumference and center—are defined by the distinct movements of elemental bodies, providing us with a further possible basis for environmental orientation. Aristotle, in fact, considers the enigmatic question whether there might be a top and bottom as well as left and rights sides to the heavens.[30] In many Chinese and Native American cosmologies, the cardinal directions of north, south, east, and west also are allied closely with the elements, offering another possible way of thinking about travel through the landscape. Finally, as massive and voluminous places—if at times amorphous and indeterminate—the elements often generate a profound sense of primordial depth or a numinous feeling when we witness or encounter their dramatic interactions, especially if we are enveloped by, carried along with, or immersed in moving water, wind, or earth. As playwright Henrik Ibsen once observed in this regard, "The sea possesses a power over one's moods that has the effect of a will. The sea can hypnotize."[31] Place, then, exhibits both a palpable density and innate intensity that can be expressed through elemental forces, one that is explored more fully as this study progresses.

Elements as Archetypes

Carl Jung characterizes the four elements as archetypes, which are ideas or forms of thought emanating from the experiences of a people in such a way that they are powerfully present in the collective unconscious of individual lives.[32] Archetypes—literally, original models—are the hidden underpinnings of the conscious mind, "the roots which the psyche has sunk . . . in the earth."[33] Using an analysis of dreams, symbols, icons, and myths throughout the world, Jung argues that fourfold schemes, designs, and objects such as crosses, limbs, and squares represent an attempt to find a reconciliatory center in the world as a whole or within a particular person. He speculates that the four elements were likewise born as an expression of unity and wholeness. "The idea of those old philosophers was that God manifested himself in the creation of the four elements," and that the four represents dimensions or qualities of a One.[34] Jung attaches special significance to the phenomenon of squaring the circle in mandalas which, by bringing together a celestial circle with the squareness of the earth, symbolize the four elements as a union, and he proposes, too, that the mind is composed concomitantly of four fundamental functions or faculties: sensation, thinking, feeling, and intuition.[35] In this view, "the quaternity is an organizing schema par excellence, something like the crossed threads in a telescope. It is a system of coordinates that is used almost instinctively for dividing up and arranging a chaotic multiplicity."[36] As Jung observes, it likely derives in part from marriage quaternio, a primitive form of cross-cousin marriage that differs from early kinds of sister exchange.

Arising as they do within early forms of religion, myth, and poetry before acquiring a more secure, if still tenuous, philosophical, and scientific status, it is not surprising that the elements are portrayed commonly in aesthetic, nondiscursive manners and modes. They conjure up mythic and material images and are often cordoned closely with the faculty of imagination. Bachelard, in fact, refers to them as "hormones of the imagination." Multiple times in the course of his dialogues, Plato invokes the elements in the context of a dream, implying not just that they are less than metaphysically ultimate or real but also suggesting connective tissues and ties between, on the one hand, the oneiric life of the mind and, on the other hand, fire, water, air, and earth.[37] Bachelard, too, notices of himself: "Sometimes even when I touch things I still dream of an element."[38] In this regard, he shows how conceptions of the elements are internalized and re-lived in aquatic or aerial daydreams of dwelling within seemingly uninhabitable places such as nests, shells, or drawers. For Bachelard, all significant and enduring images reveal a psychological state, and in a passage especially pertinent to the Presocratics, he maintains:

> In order for a reverie to continue . . . it must find its *matter*; a material element must give the reverie its own substance, its own law, its specific poetics. And it was not without cause that the primitive philosophies often made a decisive choice in this direction. They associated their formal principle with one of the four elements, which thus became marks of *philosophical temperaments*. In these philosophical systems, learned thought is linked to a primitive material reverie; calm, durable wisdom is rooted in a substantive permanence.[39]

According to Bachelard, these early perspectives remain fonts of inspiration and conviction because we discover in them image-generating powers. Philosophy is thereby only able to persuade through powerful reveries, by providing an avenue, in effect, through dreams for thought, or for what Bachelard calls "awakened oneirism." This ability to stimulate the imagination, to suggest reveries, and to elevate sensuous ideas into serious thought is central to understanding the elements, particularly as they assume cultural forms and social modes. The canonical four elements thus figure prominently not only in philosophy but also in the paintings of artists such as Archimboldo in the sixteenth century, in the works of Shakespeare, in the texts of alchemy, astrology, and chiromancy, and in the ontological aspects of numerous poets.[40]

Elemental Opposition

The notion of opposites such as hot–cold, dark–bright, dry–wet, and male–female was widespread among Hippocratic writers and is brought to bear repeatedly in the earliest Greek philosophy, as in Heraclitus' remark, "Cold warms up, warm cools off, moist parches, dry dampens" (fr. 49). In such fragments, we see the presence of four primary opposites—cold, warm, wet, and dry—which are correlated subsequently with four elements. Opposition, in fact, appears to be "elemental" to experience, arising as the antonym of "to be" or "to exist" as a negation or *not* and then appearing in the form of the disjunctive either/or. Something is, for example, perceived to be either cold or hot. One cannot have both, especially if we follow Aristotle's law of noncontradiction. Opposites are not simply different and distinct; they also are ostensibly exclusive. In nearly all cultures, we find a functioning role for common oppositions such as life and death, good and evil, truth and falsity, love and hate, fate and chance, and freedom and slavery, even if these familiar pairs break down on closer inspection. From this early "faith in opposite values," as Nietzsche styled it later, the notion of elements may have arisen, in part, or at least been given widespread credence.

Opposition can be construed as well in terms of strife, as in one's opponent or enemy in an athletic contest or war. In the early elemental philosophies, opposition qua strife often characterizes the interactions of earth, air, fire, and water, which are competing for power or place. For example, the cosmology of the Roman poet and philosopher Lucretius makes the oppositional conflict into a source of growth and decay: "There is always this great elemental deadlock, / This warfare through all time."[41] Our language reflects this potent experiential phenomenon and fact as well. On rainy and windy days or when we are in the throes of a natural disaster such as an earthquake, mudslide, or avalanche (earth); hurricane or tornado (air); flood, tsunami, or drought (water); and forest fire or electrical storm (fire), we speak frequently of "battling the elements." The perceived discord between the elements themselves is thus transferred to a tension between humans and environmental forces.

Contributing to the interpretation of the elements as antithetical pairs is the clash of opposing forces that we find in Heraclitus' riddling thought. For example: "War is the father of all and king of all; and some he has shown as gods, others men; some he has made slaves, others free" (fr. 83). In such startling statements, we find a reevaluation of all experience in terms of oppositions that are not only interpretations of the world of flux but affirmations of struggle as necessary to existence. War is an ongoing strife and interchange of oppositions, and it is proposed as the divine basis for human community and law, including the transformations between life and death, young and old, and slavery and freedom. While presenting us perpetually with images of opposition, Heraclitus nevertheless resolves these tensions in images and artifacts such as a bow or lyre that reveal either a dynamic "fitting-together" (*harmonia*) or a more mechanical unity wrought through nexus and contiguity (*sunapsis*). Accordingly, "a thing agrees at variance with itself" (fr. 83) when two opposing forces eventually work in unison via a third term to create a "hidden attunement" (fr. 80) or invisible harmony.

"Nature loves to hide"—*Physis kryptesthai philei* (fr. 10)—Heraclitus tells us, a cryptic remark that captures the tautness between the ostensible opposites of appearance and hiddenness, revelation and concealedness, light and darkness, life and death. From the notion of the opposites, it is but a short step to the four elements, which Heraclitus identifies in the statement: "The reversals of fire: first sea; but of sea half is earth, half lightning storm" [or whirlwind] (fr. 38). Here, the ongoing cycle of water (the sea), earth, and air (storm or whirlwind) is maintained by the exchange of all things for fire, Heraclitus' *logos*. Generation and corruption are brought about by way of inter-transformations of the opposites. In developing this perspective, Heraclitus is less concerned than the older Milesians in the purely physical aspects of the elemental changes, avoiding such terms as rarefaction and condensation, and focusing instead on the way that unity is derived from opposition.

As some of the Presocratics had proposed in a less-developed fashion, Aristotle argues that the elements are contraries, which he considers among the most basic principles of nature. Aristotle not only agrees with Empedocles and Plato that the elements of nature are four in number and articulates a fourfold scheme of causation, but he formulates as well a fourfold classification of opposition, distinguishing *contrary* opposites (e.g., odd–even, just–unjust), *correlative* opposites (e.g., double and half), opposites of *affirmation and negation* (e.g., man and not-man), and opposites of *possession and privation* (e.g., sight and blindness).[42] In the field of logic, he advances too, a formal fourfold linguistic scheme of opposition—commonly referred to as the "square of opposites"—that exhausts all possible forms of propositional statements used in arguments by dividing them into the universal affirmative, the universal negative, the particular affirmative, and the particular negative.[43] This quadrangular schema allows us to determine kinds of logical compatibility or contradiction. Thus, for example, "All water is blue" (a universal affirmative statement) and "Some water is not blue" (a particular negative statement) cannot both be true because the former is contradictory (complete opposite) of the latter.

Opposition occupies a central place throughout other Presocratic philosophy. We discover it in Pythagorean thought and in particular their table of contraries (*sustoichia*), which recognizes two columns of opposites that are grouped in pairs such as even and uneven or female and male. We see it in Parmenides' poetic "Way to Opinion" in the opposition of light and night and the juxtaposition of fire and earth. We discern it in Anaxagoras' remarks on the opposition of cold and hot, and locate it in Anaximander's references to the qualities of hot, dry, cold, and moist. In all these instances, there are explicit or implicit connections to and influences on later notions of the elements. These positions also provide the basis for Aristotle's criticisms of earlier theories, whether they are forms of what we might call "elemental monism" (e.g., Anaximander's *apeiron*, Thales' water, or Parmenides' One), "elemental dualism" (e.g., the Pythagoreans), "elemental triadism" (e.g., Ion of Chios), or "elemental tetradism" (e.g., Empedocles).

Elemental Substances

Matter

The early Greeks were not materialists in the modern sense of the term because their notion of "matter" (*hyle*) was not separated sharply from or divested of "mind" as it is in the post-Cartesian period. However, another influential interpretation of the elements has been in terms of their distinct materiality or, less directly, their characterization as material principles. Aristotle, in particular, anachronistically attributes the Presocratics with having discovered the "material cause" in their identification of one or more of the elements as the source or first principle (*arche*) of all things.[44] Thus, Thales' water, Anaximenes' air, and Heraclitus' fire could be considered the immanent parts out of which "substance" is formed. In this regard, Aristotle proceeds to develop his own conception of "prime matter" (*prote hyle*)—however coherent or controversial it may be—which, although differing from the four elements, still bears a definite relation to them.

The Atomists are probably the most thoroughgoing materialists of ancient Greece. Their "element" is the nonqualitative atom, which is an outgrowth of the thought of Empedocles and which has a lineage that lasts into contemporary physics.[45] Because of the recurrent attempts to find something basic and fundamental, atoms bear strong similarities with the elements, and indeed can be regarded as being a kind of element of elements. *Atomon* means not-divisible, and it is noteworthy that the ancient Atomists removed all qualitative properties of the basic units—including Empedocles' metaphorical forces of love and hate, which unite and divide earth, air, fire, and water—leaving only the quantitative properties of weight, shape, and size and thus preparing the way for the emergence of a more mechanical philosophy. Atoms, unlike elements per se, are an infinite number of indivisible units. They are imperceptible and possess no qualities except solidity. Characterized as moving in a void, it was believed that those alike in size and shape are brought together to form such entities as the elements. According to Aristotle, in fact, the only distinctions in the "elements" of the Atomists are contour (*rhysmos*), contact (*diathige*), and inclination (*trope*).

Bodies

A related characterization of air, water, fire, and earth is in terms of physical bodies. Plato's elements, for example, are corpuscles, sensible bodies with a determinate shape and constructed by a Demiurge (divine craftsman) but derived through reasoning and argumentation. Aristotle also speaks of the elements as "simple bodies" with distinct kinds of natural movements in the celestial and sublunary spheres. The ancient Greeks commonly thought of the body, too, as being composed of the four elements, which correspond to four humors (*chymoi*), thus providing a theory of ecological and physical health that carries possible significance for us today given that there is increasing evidence of environmental diseases caused by the rapid breakdown, simplification, and pollution of natural systems. Ancient medical writers warned regularly not only about excesses in consumption of drink and food but about sudden changes in the winds and weather, believing that illness can arise through the surrounding environment.

Elemental philosophers like Empedocles implicitly or explicitly refer to the theory of the four bodily humors, which flourished until the eighteenth century when it was challenged by Johann Gottfried von Herder and others. It was believed widely that the human body resembles in many ways the universe as a whole, thereby indicating a complex connection between microcosm and macrocosm. The four elements and their relation to the humors were respectively: (a) air—hot and moist—as blood, (b) fire—hot and dry—as yellow bile, (c) water—cold and moist—as phlegm, (d) earth—cold and dry—as black bile or melancholy. The origin of the doctrine, evident in Hippocratic texts around 400 B.C.E., is not known for certain, although it may derive from theories of the elements or from Egyptian medicine. Health in the body as in the environing world results from a balance of the four, a harmony of antagonistic forces. Disease, on the contrary, comes about when one element transgresses or oversteps its bounds.[46] Plato writes: "The origin of diseases is no doubt evident to all. Since there are four kinds which compose the body, earth, fire, water, and air, disorder and diseases arise from the unnatural prevalence or deficiency of these, or from their migration from their own proper place to an alien one; or . . . from any bodily part's taking in an unsuitable variety."[47] Excess of fire produces continuous heats and fevers; excess of air, quotidian fevers; excess of water, tertian fevers; excess of earth, long-lasting quartan fevers.

Construed as corporeal entities, the various theories of the elements underscore tacitly the importance of touch, contiguity, and interconnection between the natural environment, animal beings, and humans, offering what amounts to as an epistemology or ontology of contact. For example, in a passage that is arguably one of the most important in the history of environmental theory because of the suggestion that a people may be affected greatly by their physical surroundings, we find the Renaissance thinker Jean Bodin asserting a link between contemporary life and the geographic environment in the distribution of the elements and humors:

> This savagery [of the Southerners, probably meaning the Egyptians and Carthaginians] comes partly from that despotism which a vicious system of training and undisciplined appetites have created in a man, but much more from a lack of proportion in the mixing of humors. This, in its turn, comes from elements affected unequally by external forces. The elements are disturbed by the power of the celestial bodies, while the human body is encompassed in the elements. . . . So it happens that those who are in the furthest regions are more inclined to vices.[48]

Despite the prejudicial and stereotypical aspects of this view, we can observe here the perceived relationships between the elements, the body, and the environment that have exercised an enormous influence on historical beliefs and practices from the time of the ancient Greeks onward.

Roots

Empedocles refers to earth, air, fire, and water as *rhizomata*, a term commonly translated as "roots." In so doing, he regards the elements as something originary and primary, the cause and source of all that exists. The term *roots* derives from the biological and genealogical realms and despite the fact that Empedocles' *rhizomata* are not generated, this notion nevertheless suggests natural growth, change, and movement, perhaps even a fluidity that is capable of reversibility. Speaking of air, fire, water, and earth as *rhizomata* indicates the vitality of the substructure of the physical world, and Empedocles' attribution of divine names to them implies their great power and sempiternity. Empedocles is the first philosopher to thematize the four elements as necessary and sufficient agents to explain the entire world order, and by ostensibly using the terminology of roots, he sets the tenor and trajectory for later thinking about them.[49] The language of roots is significant because it continues to function in philosophy in the sense of something elemental, grounded or foundational, including even etymological "roots." It becomes associated with metaphysical frameworks and schemata in particular, and it is allied closely with notions of systems and arboreal structures, as in the invocation of "branches" of knowledge, evolutionary "bushes," and grammatical "trees."[50]

Chemical Elements

A final illustrative contrast for the classical elements is provided by modern chemistry, which assigns elements with atomic numbers and plots a periodic system.[51] At present, there are one hundred seventeen known and confirmed elements, of which ninety-four have been found throughout the universe (ninety-three on earth); the remaining ones are produced synthetically.[52] Contemporary scientists defend the radical stability of these elements, in line with the view of Empedocles. The elements of chemistry can be combined into approximately four million compounds, ninety-five percent of which include carbon (so-called organic compounds). As is generally known, they are composed of atoms with a dense center or nucleus (containing positively charged protons and electrically neutral neutrons) that is surrounded by distant electrons with negative charges. When chemistry correlates the formula of H_2O, for example, with the make-up and properties of water, we find an extension and application of ancient Pythagorean ideas. In the early nineteenth century, John Dalton wedded the theory of the element with the theory of the atom—as Plato had done two thousand years prior in a different way—and concluded that only as many atomic forms exist as elements. Shortly before Dalton's work, the French chemist Antoine Lavoisier established the conception of chemical elements or "simple radicals" in the modern sense, which he defined following Robert Boyle and the ancient Greek tradition as substances that cannot be further decomposed.[53] This idea was supported by experiments that showed conclusively that compound bodies are the combined weight of the simple bodies of which they are composed. The modern elements were then divided into four groups, including gases and the "imponderables" (e.g., light and heat); those yielding acid on oxidation; metals; and the "earths" such as lime, alumina, and silica.

As late as 1780, some chemists held that there exists a strong rationale for referring to water, air, fire, and earth as elements if they are conceived in great purity. However, Lavoisier argued that "the fondness for reducing all the bodies in nature to three or four elements . . . proceeds from a prejudice which has descended to us from the Greek philosophers."[54] In his view, the conception of the four elements is but a hypothesis that was relied on prior to the discovery of the first principles in chemistry or experimental philosophy. We must remember chemistry supplants alchemy, which had provided the elements with a significant place in its framework.[55] Here, however, we see one of the most telling challenges presented to the canonical elements because ancient thinkers were generally unable to distinguish clearly and adequately an "element's" chemistry from its physics or, put differently, its essential internal structure from its changing outward manifestations. Thus, when Thales' water becomes ice it is seen as more like earth—in that it is solid and hard—and when it evaporates it appears more like air because it is no longer visible.

The shortcomings of the ancients can be attributed in part to their relative lack of technical sophistication and equipment and an associated tendency to rely heavily on observation and the senses. When we judge solely by appearances, a host of transformations occur within the realm of the "elemental" as when salt seems to change into water after it is added to the liquid. Ever since the work of Boyle, Priestley (who discovered pure oxygen), and Lavoisier came to a critical head in the 1770s, we have realized that water, to choose one of the primal four, is not an indivisible element in the chemical sense but a compound of hydrogen (etymologically, a "water-former") and oxygen (literally, an "acid-former").[56] As we have suggested, however, water, air, earth, and fire may prove to be elemental in other senses—phenomenological, experiential, somatic, aesthetic, or environmental.

Again, the foregoing typology and elemental topology identifies some of the more significant understandings of "element" that have been given currency by early Greek philosophers and later thinkers and that remain extant and active in Western cultures. This overview, however, is not exhaustive of possible perspectives and, furthermore, the senses and meanings of element are not necessarily exclusive. We return to a more complete consideration of some of these subjects—particularly the notions of place, roots, bodies, letters, and material images—in the course of the forthcoming discussion as well as elucidate in the process key environmental issues at stake. We also examine new or emerging views of the "elemental" within

Continental philosophy, including conceptions of elemental poetics, elemental passions, elemental imperatives, elemental sensibility, elemental flesh, elemental landscape, and elemental nature, among others.

Cultural Comparisons

In coming to understand the Greek and Western views of the elements, we need to grasp some of the general differences from and similarities to other worldviews, many of which once conceived or still consider earth, air, fire, and water to be primary components of their philosophical, religious, or cosmological perspectives. In this way, we can observe at once both the near universality and cultural particularity of conceptions of the elements. In those philosophies and societies retaining strong relations with the ambient elements, one often finds either an active or latent environmental sensitivity or sensibility—an ecological *mentalité*—present or preserved in them, especially insofar as they continue to behold and internalize the places, bodies, matter, language, and images associated with air, fire, earth, and water. Like the ancient Greeks, these cosmologies, religions, myths, and writings often are deeply intertwined but, as Paul Radin has argued in the case of primal cultures, "primitive man" is still an incipient philosopher (or, alternatively, philosopher-shaman, philosopher-poet, or philosopher-healer), and we should extend this judgment potentially to non-Western people as well.[57]

China and Japan

As in other Eastern classics, the Chinese work, *The Three Characters*, refers to water, fire, wood, metal, and earth as the five elements, that from which all things derive their origin. These elements correspond to inner organs—kidneys, heart, liver, lungs, and spleen—which are related, in turn, to one another in a manner analogous to the exterior elements. That is, they adhere to a cyclical movement, as do the seasons or compass directions. A second century Confucian comments:

> The five elements move in a circle in proper order, each of them performing its specific functions. Therefore, wood is located in the East and characterizes the *chi* [breath] or ether of Spring. Fire is located in the South and characterizes the *chi* of Summer. Metal is located in the West and characterizes the *chi* of Autumn. Water is located in the North and characterizes the *chi* of Winter . . . Earth dwells in the center and is called Heavenly Nourisher (a natural source of nourishment for the four elements).[58]

These "five movers," as they were sometimes called, are identified further with five numbers (in a first and second cycle, respectively: water = 1 and 6, fire = 2 and 7, wood = 3 and 8, metal = 4 and 9, earth = 5 and 10). Thus, each of the correlative organs contains odd and even numbers and the qualities of both *yin* (feminine) and *yang* (masculine) that reputedly operate through the elements.

Not only are the elements associated with seasons, directions, organs, senses, atmospheric conditions, virtues, and numbers, but they are connected to and embodied by particular colors and animals: wood with the Blue Dragon, fire with the Red Bird, metal with the White Tiger, and water with the Black Turtle. They assume as well a definite relation to human affairs—and justice in particular—as each of the elements is linked to a political minister (wood, metal, fire, water, and earth with the Ministers of Agriculture, Interior, War, Justice, and Works, respectively) who is kept in check by another office and element. For example, when the Minister of War "turns to evil and slander, deceiving the ruler, then he who administers the law shall carry out punishment."[59] In this case, it is water that exercises punitive authority so that one may claim that water overcomes fire. As seen here, a surprisingly similar notion of cosmic rule and justice is found in the ancient Greek elemental theories of Anaximander and Empedocles.

The elements in Chinese philosophy often both generate and overtake each other by a definite cyclic procedure of "five goings" (*wu xing*). Thus, in one account metal supplants wood, which conquers earth, which in turn displaces water, which overcomes fire, which finally occupies the place of metal.[60] In contrast to the tradition that posits five primal elements, Taoist thought within China recognizes a fourfold, even if it cannot be assimilated completely to the Western understanding: "Man follows the ways of the Earth / The Earth follows the ways of Heaven / Heaven follows the ways of Tao / Tao follows its own ways."[61] As noted earlier, water assumes pride of place within Taoism, where it is given feminine associations of receptivity and passivity. In part because of the attentiveness shown to the vital roles of air, earth, water, and fire, Eastern thought generally and Taoism in particular have been well received within some schools of environmental thought, especially among deep ecologists.[62]

Traditions within Japan likewise refer to "five great" (*go dai*) elements, although occasionally a sixth immaterial element of consciousness is added. Deriving largely from Chinese and Buddhist cultures, the elements are in increasing order of power: earth 地 (*tsuchi* or *chi*), water 水 (*sui* or *mizu*), fire 火 (*ho ka* or *hi*), wind 風 (*fu* or *kaze*), and the void 空 (*ku*). In the East, their scope and meaning differ from both ancient and Western understandings, so that in Japan earth includes most hard and solid objects; water represents flowing, fluid, and formless things; fire is associated with energetic entities (including animals); wind signifies free movement, growth, and expansion; and the void suggests that which lies outside ordinary experience (from atomic forces to nuclear reactions and higher forms of consciousness). Some of the most common representations of the elements in Japan can be seen within Buddhist architecture. For example, pagodas are often constructed so as to display five tiers starting from earth at the base and continuing to the sky or void at the apex, whereas Japanese lanterns in Buddhist temples and

Zen gardens frequently symbolize the five elements in respective parts ascending from the bottom (earth) to a lotus flower (water) to a flame or light (fire) to the top sections gesturing upward (wind and void/sky).

India and Persia

The Indian and specifically Hindu view of the elements is complex, but it regularly embraces a fivefold framework, as in Chinese thought, although sometimes a more triangular pattern is emphasized. In this latter schema, a primal triad or trinity exists in the group of the most significant gods: Brahma (the Creator), Vishnu (the Preserver), and Shiva (the Destroyer). They are referred to as the *Trimurti* (three forms) and represent manifestations of the impersonal Brahman. Frequently, they are correlated respectively with earth (which brings life), water (which sustains life), and fire (which destroys life). Traditional cosmologies tend to depict the elements as arriving through creative action:

> In the beginning ... there was that only which is, one only, without a second. ... It thought, may I be many, may I grow forth. It sent forth fire. That fire thought, may I be many, may I grow forth. It sent forth water. ... Water thought, may I be many, may I grow forth. It sent forth earth. ... That being (that which had produced fire, water,, and earth) thought, let me enter those three beings (fire, water, earth) with this living Self, and let me then develop names and forms.[63]

In one ancient work, we find the following sequence of elemental birth: "From that *Brahman*, which is the Self, was produced space [*akasa*]. From space emerged air [*vayu*]. From air was born fire [*tejas*]. From fire was created water [*ap*]. From water sprang earth [*prthvi*]."[64] Here, the ordering that emerges is premised upon diminishing material subtlety, but the five great elements (*pancamahabhuta*) are interdependent articulations of primal energy with unique aspects and locations that are connected with the ultimate reality of a unifying *Brahman*. *Akasa* (space) is added to the classic tetrad, but it is to be conceived of as an expansive openness that fills a void rather than thought of as emptiness. In their subtle forms, the elements are linked with the five bodily senses: water to taste, wind or air to touch, earth to smell, fire to sight, and space to sound. Upon death, many Hindus believe that our gross (as opposed to subtle or causal) body, which consists of the five elements, dissolves and returns to the natural world. Within some Hindu traditions, worship services are commonly preceded by a purification of the elements through offerings made to a deity so as to bring about a harmony of microcosm and macrocosm: Incense represents the wind, flowers stand for the sky, water itself is used for water, light symbolizes fire, and fragrances evoke the earth.[65]

In the early Vedic age, the divinities are bound closely with elemental forces. Agni is the personification of fire; Indra is associated with thunderstorms and weather; Varuna is tied with the sky and rain; and Surya is linked with the sun. In a subsequent period marked by the more philosophical texts known as the Upanishads, ancient sages believed that one must possess intimate knowledge of a deep Self (*Atman*), which is considered to be immortal, in order to break the inveterate bonds of *samsara*—the cycle of birth and death. "What is the rule for this elemental self," asks the Maitri Upanishad, "whereby, on quitting this body, it may come to complete union with the Self?"[66] In short, they understood it variously as being like—or even made of—water, breath, or fire, phenomena that seemingly endure, assume multiple forms, possess subtle qualities, and are integral to human existence. Water was a prime candidate because, in addition to being necessary for life and incessantly altering its forms and states, there existed an ancient belief that upon death, the life fluid of the deceased migrates from the body on a funeral pyre and ascends as smoke to the moon, where it is gathered before returning to earth to form new life. If liberated from the cycle, however, a door in the moon—viewed as a drinking bowl brimming with life-sustaining liquid—would open and one could pass through it. The Self was also conceived as breath. "Wind is that which gathers everything together," declares the Chandogya Upanishad, just as breath brings together all for the self or even the gods.[67] When the life breath at last exits individuals, it was thought we become part of encompassing winds. Finally, the notion of the Self was tied to ritualistic fire that presumably transports offerings to the gods. As support for this view, people likely reasoned from observation: When the body dies it quickly turns cold; heat is needed to digest food, hatch eggs, and trigger growth of living things; and fire is tied ceremonially with the deity, Agni.[68]

Given the appeals to the five elements underlying physical reality and to the central Hindu tenant that the individual Self (*Atman*) is ultimately united with the universe (*Brahman*)—as the air inside a jar is substantially the same air outside it, although obscured by the veils of *maya* (illusion)—there is a sense in which this philosophy tends to encourage a decentered "cosmo-centric" environmental perspective. Theoretically, one's *dharma* (duty) might thereby be enlarged to include a recognition and respect for all that exists, including not just humans (anthropocentrism), living beings (biocentrism), ecosystems (ecocentrism), or the Earth itself (planet-centrism) but the elemental forces in the universe, too, if this view proves coherent.[69]

The Hindu system of Samkhya—one of six orthodox schools of thought—also offers an account of the elements, one that appears to correspond in some respects with the Western hermetic view. According to this framework, the *bhutas* (corporeal elements) belong to the material world, and they are correlated with the same number of *tanmatras* (essential measures) that reside in the thinking individual. Ultimately, both the *bhutas* and *tanmatras* originate from *prakriti* (nature), which is akin to prime or cosmic matter. As primordial determinations, they pass through *ahankara* (ego-consciousness) and are split into the subjective and objective dimensions of the revealed world. In some ancient Indian texts, there is an acknowledgment of the four classical elements along with ether. Thus, Bhargava—a devotee of the ultimate *Brahman*—questions a sage as to the means by which the body is held together and as to which power is greatest and most manifest. The sage replies that in addition to the sense organs, the elements of air, fire, water, earth, and ether compose our physical beings but that *prana*, the primal energy of the world, actually divides itself fivefold so as to keep together and support the body.[70]

Fire, water, earth, and air likewise occupy a special place within early Buddhism—which develops out of but breaks with Hinduism on key beliefs—where the elements are thought to provide potential assistance in the emancipation from suffering (*dukkha*). They are considered fundamental components of form, which is the first category of the "five aggregates" (*skandhas*) that in turn function as the basis for the Four Noble Truths of the philosophy. The four elements serve as focal points for meditation, given their constitutive roles in the human body. In the Buddhist sutra, "One Truth, Countless Teachings," earth, air, fire, and water are singularly and collectively invoked to illustrate the complex dynamic of multiplicity and unity with respect to wisdom and the world.[71] Nirvana—the exalted goal of enlightenment and the end of the finite self and desire—is even described on occasion as a condition wherein there is not earth, water, fire or air, and it means more literally to "blow out," "extinguish," or "quench," terms that refer implicitly to fire, air or water. In fact, in "The Parable of Fire," Tathagata—the honorific name given to Siddhartha Guatama and the historical Buddha—is compared to a burned-out fire in that nothing substantial remains of his being subsequent to enlightenment except the ashes (earthy remains) of his worldly deeds.[72]

Persian sources, too, acknowledge the elements, as in Omar Khayyám's famous eleventh-century philosophical and poetic *Rubáiyát*, which derives from the Arabic word *rubá* meaning foursome, and which is written in quatrains. Bearing interesting and occasionally uncanny resemblances to Empedocles' elemental work, the text declares: "You who are product of the four elements and seven planets / And because of that Four and this Seven in perpetual agitation / Drink wine; I have told you more than a thousand times / There is no coming back for you, when you're gone, you're gone."[73] The first word alphabetically in Farsi is, in fact, a classical element, *ab*, which means water. *Ab*, in turn, forms the root of *abad* (abode) and *abadan* (civilization), underscoring the importance of water to their understandings of home, place, and civilization.

Native Views

The elements appear regularly in many indigenous cultures, especially in expressions related to an animate world suffused immanently with "spirit" or "soul." A common Native American prayer begins: "Earth, water, air, and fire combined to make this food. Numberless beings have died and labored that we may eat. May we be nourished that we may be nourishable."⁷⁴ The Thompson Indians of the North Pacific Coast offer a story of the origination and transformation of earth, fire, water, and woman by a primal "Old One" or chief who descends from an airy cloud and upper world to pull hairs from his head and hence "throw down" or create the elemental world.⁷⁵ The Apache of North America also present a cosmogonic tale involving the founding and establishment of the earth, which is at first a soft, weak, unsteady, and composite entity. Four friends, who speak among themselves about the difficulties they face, decide to work together and find a solution to this problem. As if holding the edges of an outstretched cloth tent, each pulls at the earth from a different side—marked by the directions of north, south, east, and west—and each secures his or her piece via a colored cane covered with metal thorns in the alternating colors of white, blue, black, and yellow. In turn, however, three figures personified in the form of wizened men and representing the other elements (Black Wind Old Man, Black Water Old Man, and Black Thunder Old Man) batter the earth with their tempests, making it cold, weak, and wet. But the four friends respond to the challenge by providing the earth with hair (grasses, bushes, and trees) for warmth, bone (mountains and rocks) for strength, and veins (flowing streams) for breath.⁷⁶ In this way, the elements participate actively in the world-creating process.

The Maori—the first people to settle in New Zealand and close cultural relatives of the Polynesians—espouse what amounts to a theory of elemental matter in some of their works, most of which still survive through oral traditions. Matter is made of four basic ingredients—earth, air, fire, and water—although none of these elements as such are alive or given form. Air is understood to be a complement of every existing entity, "that which continues or holds the life of all things,"⁷⁷ a description that bears resemblance to Anaximenes' characterization of the same element as a binding force. The elements only exist in states of combination, but individually they are still *sui generis*. In fact, uniqueness adheres to everything in the universe, which consists of unrelated monads given unity through the existence of Io, the cosmic deity. "It is through the earth, water, fire, and air combined that all things have form and life."⁷⁸ Within the Maori tradition, the environment is viewed not merely as a resource to be appropriated but as a community of kinship in which other members are considered *tapu* (sacred or forbidden) even if the natural world can still be made available for use when justified. Such a relationship between humans and the other-than-human world finds parallels within modern science, and Maori traditions can be interpreted reasonably as symbolic expressions of ecological notions.⁷⁹

Creation Myths

Creation accounts of many cultures often begin with one or more of the elements out of which the world, humans or gods are fashioned. Cosmogony, we should remember, precedes theogony, with which it is frequently continuous. In the Babylonian epic, *Enuma Elish*, the gods Apsu and Tiamat are born of primeval waters.[80] In the mythology of Japan, air in the form of wind is responsible for creation by ushering out the mists that surround the islands. Ancient Sumerian priests and priestesses, too, identify four primary powers with which the main gods and goddesses are linked: Ki (Goddess of the Earth), Nammu (Goddess of Water), An (God of the Sky), and Enlil (God of Storms). These deities rule the four elemental regions of earth, water, heavens, and lower atmosphere.

Monotheistic traditions retain veiled or explicit references to the elements, which usually are perceived as being more endemic to pagan cultures. In the Biblical story of Genesis, for example, the first human is created out of the dust of the earth, which is separated from the heavens above, and both emerge from a watery chaos.[81] Within Christianity, Francis of Assisi—considered by some Catholics as the patron saint of the environment—offers "The Song of Brother Sun and All Creatures," which celebrates the powerful place of air, fire, water, and earth:

> Praise to Thee, my Lord, for Brother Wind, / For air and cloud, for calm and all weather, / By which Thou supportest life in all Thy creatures. / Praise to Thee, my Lord, for Sister Water, / Who is so useful and humble / Precious and pure / Praise to Thee, my Lord, for Brother Fire, / By whom Thou lightest the night; / He is lovely and pleasant, mighty and strong. / Praise to Thee, my Lord, for our sister Mother Earth / Who sustains and directs us, / And brings forth varied fruits, and coloured flowers, and plants.[82]

According to the apocryphal book of Enoch, the elements even take the oath of the covenant.[83] At the same time, we often find a theological counterbalance to these largely marginal or residual aspects of the tradition, as in Thomas Browne's remark, "There is surely a piece of divinity in us, something that was before the Elements, and owes no homage unto the Sun."[84]

Such admittedly very brief comparisons help to show that the elements have occupied a cross-cultural and trans-historical place in philosophy, religion, myth, and literature. There are decided differences, of course, between pre-philosophical and early philosophical perspectives of earth, air, fire, and water, but these are usually matters of degree. In both cases, the elements frequently make their initial appearance in the guise of gods who govern the universe, but then they are transformed into more rational principles. Speaking of the early contemplators of the cosmos, Vico observes: "The world of the theological poets was composed of four sacred elements: the air whence Jove's bolts come, the water of the perennial springs whose divinity is Diana, the fire with which Vulcan cleared the forests, and the tilled earth of Cybele or Berecynthia." Each of the four participated in divine ceremonies involving, for example, auspices, water, spelt, and fire until physicists eventually characterized and studied them as elements. In Vico's view, these theological poets provided sensible and often humans forms to the elements and in the process created diverse divinities, offering philosophers like Plato with the later "opportunity to intrude [a] doctrine of minds or intelligences: that Jove was the mind of ether, Vulcan of fire, and the like."[85]

The Frame of the Four

Thales, Anaximenes, and Heraclitus are clearly the direct precursors to Empedocles' notion of the elemental fourfold. Each, in turn, emphasized the primacy of a different element—respectively water, air, and fire—claiming that everything can be explained by it or derived from it. To these three, Empedocles supplies a fourth in the element of earth, and the classic quartet reaches closure and completion, with the possible exception of Aristotle's introduction of *aether* (ether), a fifth extraterrestrial phenomenon. Still, one may reasonably ask, "Why four?" In addition to the psychological and cultural role of the archetypes that Jung explores, there are multiple relevant variations on the number four, each of which possesses a firm ground in the natural environment or lived body.

There are four seasons of winter, spring, summer, and fall; four cardinal directions of north, south, east, and west; and four corporeal modes of being in the positions of standing, sitting, lying, and walking. There are four parts of a day as morning, afternoon, evening, and night, and four primary taste buds—sour, sweet, salt, and bitter—that enable us to enjoy a vast variety of foods and flavors.[86] Although early thinkers would not have been aware of this fact, the DNA of all living creatures consists of four bases—adenine, cytosine, guanine, and thymine—which serve as the alphabet of existence, the genetic spelling for organisms. Modern physics now identifies four basic forces—electromagnetism, gravity, a weak nuclear force, and a strong nuclear force—as enterprising scientists attempt to find a single theory that will unify them. And even though modern chemistry has expanded the number of elements to more than a hundred, the main "ingredients" of the universe and our atmosphere in particular are far fewer in number, consisting mainly of four: carbon, hydrogen, oxygen, and nitrogen. In fact, the valence of carbon, which serves as the basis of planetary life, is four.

We readily discover additional biological, chemical, or physical aspects of the world governed by a fourfold that point beyond coincidence or randomness to the significance of structural features and functions related to this number. For example, many chordates possess four stabilizing legs or feet; the hearts of mammals have four chambers; there are four human blood groups; and the fabric of the universe may be four-dimensional when we add time to the three dimensions (height, depth, width) of space. Four is considered an old limit in counting, and with one, two, and three, it belongs among the very few numbers used as an inflected adjective. The break-off juncture and point of change may occur here because there are four fingers (not including the thumb, which functions like an exceptional number one, the antithesis of plurality[87]) and because quantities greater than four cannot be grasped frequently or directly with perceptual ease.[88] In the mathematical realm, there are four fundamental operations involving addition, subtraction, division, and multiplication, and four is both the smallest composite number and first positive non-Fibonacci number.

Four provides us with the interlocking sides of a square, suggesting solidity, order, and stability, the "frame" of a world-picture or cosmos, language used specifically by Plato, who also espouses four key moral virtues.[89] As he puts it in the *Timaeus*, "the frame of the world took up the whole of each of these four; he who put it together made it consist of all the fire and water and air and earth, leaving no part or power of any one of them outside."[90] Four gives us the walls of a typical dwelling unit, which orients us daily and deeply in a given place.[91] It provides us with the supporting posts of the temple—that is, the columns that hold the dome of the heavens—and, as the ancient Greeks believed, both the quartet of bodily humors and set of primary colors out of which all others are derived.[92] Later, too, in the Bible, we find references in "Revelation" to the four angels of the apocalypse who hold the four corners of the earth as well as mention of the four winds of heaven in the Book of Daniel.

The Pythagorean four, which transfers mathematics onto the material world and frames it within a *tetraktus*—the combination of the first four natural numbers into a new number such as ten—may represent in veiled respects the collective elements of fire, water, air, and earth. Here, the fourth term (solidity) results from three constituent "elements": points (one), lines (two), and surfaces (three). Considered as sacred, it is described in terms that are expressed subsequently in Empedocles' poetic philosophy. The *tetraktus*, for example, contains "the springs and root of everlasting nature" (*pagan aenaou phuseos rizoma*).[93] The unity to which the Pythagoreans traced the physical elements was not itself material—as it was for the Ionians—but rather the more immaterial principle of number, even if they regarded number as extended in space. Aristotle advances this interpretation as well, maintaining that they viewed the elements of numbers as the elements of all things.[94] The Pythagoreans, who were among the first to call the universal whole by the term *kosmos*, celebrated the fourfold with ecstatic prayer: "O holy, holy *tetraktus*, thou that contains the root and the source of the eternally flowing creation! For the divine number begins with the profound, pure unity until it comes to the holy four; then it begets the mother of all, the all-comprising, the all-bounding, the first born, the never-swerving, the never-tiring holy ten, the keyholder of all."[95]

Four is enormously important, too, in many Eastern philosophical and religious traditions. Within India, and Hindu thought in particular, the life of an individual is divided into four stages or *asrama* (student, householder, retired person and *sannyasin*—i.e., renouncer of the social order) with four respective aims or goals (*purusarthas*): pleasure (*kama*); worldly success (*artha*); social duty (*dharma*), and liberation (*moksha*). Society is similarly partitioned into four broad stations or castes (*varnas*) that are said to have emerged in mythological fashion when a primal human was severed in four parts: *brahmins* (priests and intellectuals); *kshatriyas* (warriors and administrators); *vaishyas* (merchants and farmers); and *shudras* (unskilled workers). There are four main paths or practices (yogas) designed to foster discipline and insight: *Bhakti* (love), *Jnana* (knowledge), *Karma* (action or work), and *Raja* (experimental or psychological approaches). Within Buddhism, we find the Four Noble Truths of suffering (*dukkha*), desire (*trishna*), releasement (*nirvana*), and the eightfold path to enlightenment. The Om, a Buddhist and Hindu mantra, considered to be the soundless sound of the universe, is likewise composed of four elemental parts that correspond to four primary states of consciousness represented by letters: A (waking); U (dreaming); M (deep sleep); and the integration of these dimensions into a unifying silent whole or ultimate reality. As the Mandukya Upanishad claims, "The elements are the fourths; the fourths, the elements."[96] Finally, the symbol of the swastika—often depicted as an equilateral or crooked cross containing right angle arms—expresses a primal fourfold in the East. Originating in Neolithic India, it represents both the sun and the wheel and serves widely as an auspicious sign in art, architecture, and religious ceremonies.

Although there is a close association between the elements and "framing" or "fouring" so as to find, found or fashion a stable ontological, perceptual or aesthetic order in the environment, it must be borne in mind that there is nevertheless a danger in committing too simply or rigidly to a conception of a fourfold that encourages a calcification of categories or a reification of ideas. In this regard, it is helpful to heed the constructive—and deconstructive—aspects of contemporary philosophical critiques of the frame, "enframing" (*Gestell*) and the "world-picture" (*Weltbild*) articulated by Heidegger and Derrida.[97] Derrida, in particular, has sought to dismantle, displace or scatter fourfolds and the frame of the four (e.g., the "square roots" of Empedocles, Pythagorean themes, the square earth, the picture frame, and the four-cornered book with a closed meaning, including the so-called "Book of Nature"), even as he endeavors to break open the tight closure of dialectics (the movement of three) with a fourth or fifth philosophical moment. Toward this end, his writing revels in the play of "the prior" and "the preface" (which becomes a fourth text) along with the open or splayed square, in contrast to unities, dyads, dualisms, trinities, and triangles.[98] In his view, the "opening of presence is surface number four." Although "claiming to be originary, wild, and irreducible like the incessant, ever-virginal arising of the world, it has its own 'history' or rather it is plunged by that 'history' into a limitless time that is neither a 'present' nor a 'history.'"[99]

Stated differently and more simply, cosmological, political, or environmental order must possess certain structures of reliability and intelligibility, but we must also recognize that the natural world is too complex, too wild, and bewildering, to be reduced to a numerical formula, despite historical attempts to do so. As seen in due course, a recent and intriguing development within Continental philosophy has been to speak not so much about singular elements per se as a notion of or encounter with the "elemental," thus building on a long tradition but breaking productively with it as well.

Social Construction of the Elements

One of the most contested topics within philosophy and cultural theory today concerns the question of social construction, including its meaning, truth, and limits.[100] This issue also is being raised within environmental philosophy as a discussion over whether nature is an independent or, alternatively, socially constituted entity. On the one hand, there are positions holding to the objectivity of natural processes, anchoring their claims in a natural order and ontology that is presented as relatively separate from us.[101] On the other hand, there are perspectives that defend the view that there is no nature in-itself, given that it always constructed by and through human actions and institutions.[102] The practical and political implications of this question are far-reaching because they bear on whether the natural world should best be left alone, managed ("tended," "stewarded," or "shepherded"), reconstructed, restored, or even "reinvented" as some writers argue.[103] More specifically, the debate has the potential to impact issues related to genetic engineering, cloning, terraforming other planets, restoration ecology, permaculture, national parks, zoos, and the preservation of endangered species. In brief, if we want to "control" nature, help it to "realize" a goal, be "at one" with it, or simply "let it be," then we may need to come to terms with what *it* is or is not, as well as how it may evolve, change, or even disappear through anthropogenic actions.

That the early characterizations of the elements are culturally mediated is evident in the distinct kinds of social relations through which they are regularly viewed or portrayed. The elements are almost always socialized to one degree or another, presented through the language of familial relationships, kinship structures, social bonds, or individual and community antagonisms. For the first-known Western philosophers and poets, the natural world was generally considered to be moral, just, and even sacred because it was seen as an extension of—and hence continuous with—the human community. In ancient and primitive thought, *physis* (nature) in fact becomes a kind of *nomos* (law) in that the perceived essence of something is harmonious with and even identical to its significance for the social group. The essence of an entity—and by implication the natural world—is understood in terms of its social functioning.[104]

In this regard, ancient understandings of the elements are based frequently on a departmental division of the cosmos, one determined by and through social custom. Early people often thought that gods governed natural phenomena and that the deities emerge from the natural world rather than vice-versa. For example, the Greeks associated thunder and lightning with Zeus, while storms and earthquakes are connected to Poseidon. Such a perspective suggests a recurring socialization of nature—an inveterate attempt to render it understandable and meaningful to the community in human terms—even if it initially takes the form of a personification or anthropomorphism.[105] As the physicist James Clerk Maxwell has remarked provocatively, "The only laws of matter are those which our minds must fabricate, and the only laws of mind are fabricated for it by matter."[106] Thus, the Platonic Demiurge is depicted as a divine craftsman of the cosmos but a builder and artificer nonetheless, one modeled on human capacities for invention, artisanship, geometrization, and construction. Or, as Cicero puts it in commenting on an ancient understanding of *physis*, "nature is a craftsmanlike fire, proceeding methodically to the work of generation."[107] Here, Bachelard both reminds and cautions us: "Interpretations of ancient texts are often *overly clever readings*. The modern reader too often pays homage to the ancients for their 'knowledge of natural phenomena.' He forgets that knowledge thought to be 'direct' is a part of a system that can be very artificial; he also forgets that the 'knowledge of natural phenomena' is closely connected with 'natural' reveries."[108] In what follows, we identify several kinds of common elemental mediation so as to observe the role of "social construction" in the earliest Western philosophy.

Sex and Marriage

Marriage and sex are paradigmatic forms for expressing an important kind of elemental relation, one that quite literally socializes the elements and the natural world in the symbolic act of communal union. The bond formed when the female-gendered earth is fertilized by the male-gendered sky was a primary dimension of the mythological life of the Greeks. Aeschylus thus writes: "The pure Sky longs passionately to pierce the Earth, and passion seizes the Earth to win her marriage. Rain falling from the bridegroom sky makes pregnant the Earth. Then brings she forth for mortals pasture of flocks and corn, Demeter's gift, and the fruitfulness of trees is brought to completion by the dew of their marriage."[109] The four elements also were viewed widely as a pair of divine couples in which, for example, Zeus is paired with Hera, and Hades is linked with Persephone. Jung, in fact, found a correspondence between the four-element theory and "marriage quaternio."[110] Empedocles, too, was likely familiar with the incest motif in marriage quaternio—as in Zeus' coupling with his daughter Persephone—and so the idea of a double marriage appears to reside deeply in the origins of the theory of the four elements.[111] In both Hesiod's work and the Chinese *Tao Te Ching*, we find as well the sundering by chaos of the elemental regions of sky and earth, which were originally one, and so capable of reunion. And the force of this association can be discovered many centuries later in Blake's poetry, where he conjures the notion of joining elemental opposites in "Marriage of Heaven and Hell."[112]

One significant effect of this portrayal of elemental interactions is that it indicates an early way of "domesticating" earth, air, fire, and water, an avenue for acculturating, emplacing or even pacifying parts of the natural world. In the *Sophist*, for example, Plato's Eleatic stranger remarks critically on the ideas of previous thinkers and their treatment of the opposites of hot and cold or dry and wet, including one unnamed philosopher who "marries [them] off, and makes them set up house together."[113] The genesis of the elements themselves is, in fact, a kind of "birth" as the term suggests, and so it is reasonable to see such birthing as resulting from a "marriage"—usually the male sky with the female earth—and the prior or subsequent establishment of a household and elemental economy. This point is evident in Plato's *Timaeus*, where the Receptacle is compared with a mother; the model is likened to a father; and the natural world (the four elements) that arrives via these "parents" resembles an offspring. We may add to this consideration of marriage, sex, and the elements that the form (*eidos*) and matter (*hyle*) combination that composes the elements generally entails a gender distinction so that earth, air, fire, and water can be "wedded" either by mutual union or an arranged matrimony, so to speak.[114] In primitive myth, too, the world is often presented as originating from an egg that is hatched by a bird who governs the gap (*chaos*) and whose role is to bring together the two elemental domains of earth and sky. In such instances, we find a kind of "taming" of formless disorder derived through the facilitation of an animal, one who could conceivably be domesticated herself.

Love and Hate

As in most relationships with which we are familiar, the ancient elemental couples and couplings are regularly imputed human emotions. Two of the most common ascriptions concern affinity and division, likeness and difference, particularly the binding ties of friendship or love and the dividing drives of wrath or hate. In Empedocles' cosmology, the four *rhizomata* of earth, fire, air, and water are united and separated by the forces of *philia* and *neikos*, love and hate. Originating in the sphere of nature, *philia* and *neikos* operate in both the organic and inorganic realms, functioning as agents of unity and multiplicity. They are human metaphors or emotions transferred to or discovered within the natural world and not simply mechanical causes of attraction and repulsion. Love is in many ways comparable to Hesiod's use of *Eros*, which assumes a cosmogonic role in his work, and it is the source of unity between male and female—as in the case of elemental marriage—as well as a bond in the universe as a whole. When a state of "oneness" has been achieved, however, it is eventually and inevitably sundered by the powers of hate, which possesses a status as vital as love.

War and Strife

A related mode for expressing elemental interactions in language that may be characterized as socially constituted is in terms of struggle and conflict. Such representations of earth, fire, air, and water are often expressions of antagonism writ large, difference, and division rendered social and political. This opposition is not immediately or easily sublated into a higher unity through, for example, the senses or trust (*pistis*), as it is in the work of Empedocles, who allows for resolution to occur potentially by way of the mind. Heraclitus' fragments are especially emblematic of this elemental dynamic. For Heraclitus, war or strife is the "father of all and king of all" (fr. 83) in that it describes the relation of opposites and typifies most forms of change and growth. In his account, the absence of elemental conflict would signal the end of the universe, which depends on a productive ontological tension. To be sure, Heraclitus provides for temporary respites from the ongoing cosmic battleground, but his predominating images and metaphors are borrowed from the realm of warfare. One important issue raised by such elemental philosophy is the extent to which the natural world functions competitively or cooperatively, a subject broached more fully in Empedocles' thought and within evolutionary theory.[115]

Justice and Morality

The manner in which the elements are portrayed is frequently suffused with moral and political language: requital, injustice, making reparation, the paying of penalties, and the like. Anaximander's Presocratic cosmology exemplifies a fourth characterization of elemental relations, relying as it does on legalistic language drawn from the human community. For Anaximander, *tisis* (payment, penalty, punishment) and *dike* (justice) govern the processes of elemental change and interchange. When one elemental opposite oversteps its domain at the expense of its contrary, "injustice" results. The moral order is disturbed due to a transgression of borders. To grasp the perspective that gave rise to this notion, we can invoke an analogy drawn from biology. In the case of human or animal bodies, which might be said to be composed of elemental earth, it is necessary for such corpora to appropriate (i.e., rob) from other elements so as to survive and flourish: to take from air so as to acquire breath, to take from water so as to obtain blood and bodily fluids, and to take from fire so as to secure animal heat. Over time, however, "payment" comes due, and this demand results in the death and dissolution of the body. Each of the elements returns to its kind: water to water, fire to fire, air to air, and earth and to earth. The hydrological cycle works on a similar basis when airy clouds "thieve" water from other provinces—lakes, rivers, and seas—but are forced eventually to pay requital and to release their "captive" back to its proper realm.

Heraclitus likewise declares the existence of a law (*nomos*) for the natural world that is analogous to human law but supersedes it in strength, breadth, and significance, though strife turns out ultimately to be related to justice in his philosophy, whereas for Anaximander, it represents a kind of injustice.

In recent times, many artists, intellectuals, and environmentalists regularly depict their societies not only as unsustainable but also as patently unjust, out-of-balance, overly competitive, and even corrupt. That the natural world is commonly presented in like-sounding phrases that emphasize its supposed stinginess, cruelty, amorality or indifference is significant. Among other possibilities, it suggests the value of a critical social ecology that extends its analysis to an understanding of the organic environment and the ambient elements as well as the built world and human communities. In other words, issues of environmental justice and ecological ethics are bound closely with questions of human equity, fairness, liberty, and happiness so that social and political theory must account necessarily, and even dialectically, for our normative interactions with, projections onto and transformations of the natural world.[116]

Tribal Structure

Following the anthropological and sociological theories of Émile Durkheim and Lucien Lévy-Bruhl, classicist F. M. Cornford has argued convincingly that the early classification and division of the world into distinct regions is likely premised on tribal groupings, which were often split into fours.[117] Many ancient communities, it seems, cut themselves into four parts or two phratries (a subdivision of a tribe) due to population increases and other cultural pressures. Pursuant to these divisions, the structure of the universe was seen, in turn, as a reflection or representation of the customary social groupings. For example, the Ponkas, a tribe of the Sioux Indians, separated the camp into two phratries and four quarters, which are possessed by a pair of clans of earth, wind (i.e., air), thunder (i.e., fire), and water. Similarly, the aboriginal people of Mexico acknowledged four dimensions of the pueblo—the Indian village or the communal dwelling of this collective unit—and correspondingly four parts of the heavens and four primary gods. Viewed in this manner, the elements may be grasped once again in terms of their mediated relations with the human order. The microcosm (smaller social grouping) is reflected outward or projected onto the macrocosm (larger natural order). Nature—more specifically the elements—is seen through a filtering *nomos* (custom).

In the case of Anaximander, we find the separation of the elements through the whirling movement (*diné*) of the universe into distinct regions as a temporary order and then their protracted return to what he calls the *apeiron* (boundless)—literally, that without limit. As Cornford points out, this cosmology is "a transcript in representation of an organic structure such as we find in a totemic tribe, in which the primitive unitary tribal group and the organic nexus of clans reappear as two separate stages—the primary *physis* and the four elements separated out of it."[118] If we follow out this line of thought, we are able to speak in terms of a "politics of cosmology" in that the universe is represented as a kind of *polis* (political community), one that is coextensive with the dictates, demands, and divisions within the human order.[119]

Physical and Metaphysical Construction

Finally, the role humans have played in the social construction or, more pointedly, co-construction of the elements is evident from the very outset of Western philosophy, and so it is appropriate to explore briefly Thales' contribution in this regard. The traditional portrait of Thales is that he was the first of the Ionian *physiologoi* (natural philosophers) who speculated disinterestedly on the world's origin, finding water to be the source of all things, the *point de repère* for the differentiation of matter. Overcoming *mythos* (myth) through the use of *logos* (reason), and scientific observation—so the story goes—he was able to discern an underlying unity to all reality in the "substance" of water, the only "stuff" able to take on or transform itself into all three states—what we now identify as the liquid, gaseous, and solid—the gamut of material possibility. An anecdote about Thales' redirection of a river for King Croesus' army is not widely believed[120]—it was rejected by the historian Herodotus who tended to support and recount most stories he heard[121]—although it is commonly repeated that Thales fell into a well while stargazing, thereby becoming a prototype for the absent-minded professor. Thus, we find an image of Thales, and concomitantly of the philosopher more generally, as an individual given to withdrawal into the self due to either the necessity of or preference for disengagement from practical affairs and worldly matters.[122]

There are strong reasons, however, to believe to the contrary that Thales was engaged directly and deeply with water in many of its modalities as a geometer (earth-measurer), a hydraulic engineer (water-worker), and a traveler (sea-farer) as well as a philosopher. As a result of his interactions with and investigations of this element, he may have been permitted and privileged to discover some of its seemingly universal qualities, properties, and powers.[123] It is likely that Thales actually was able to divert the Halys River in Anatolia[124] so as to make it fordable for Croesus to pass into Cappadocia on an expedition and campaign.[125] In short, there may literally have been a *physical* (and social) "construction" project with elemental waters that helped to provide insights into the more *metaphysical* workings and ways of this liquid, which was in turn characterized through and marked by such practical and technical experiences. As the historian Mott Greene observes of Thales and water:

> He navigated across it, he moved it, he measured distances across it. He speculated on the causes of the Nile flood. He experienced water

as a means of transportation, as a source of wealth (he knew to corner all the olive presses because it had *rained* a lot), and as an elemental substance, capable of a variety of forms.... As a resident of a hydraulic civilization, nothing could be less strange than that he developed his skills and his ideas on the basis of water.[126]

Moreover, Miletus lay only four hundred miles from the western delta of the Nile (a three- to four-day trip by boat); it was both a port and river city through which the Meander River flowed; and like Egyptian society—with which Thales was familiar—it was oriented and informed culturally by the dangers and possibilities of powerful bodies of water.[127]

Ancient engineer-philosophers such as Archimedes, Ptolemy, and Hero also put water to practical work, helping to found in the process what is now called hydrostatics, the study of fluids at rest. After Aristotle's death, the center of Greek thought moved from Athens to Alexandria, which lay at the mouth of the Nile. Around this same time, philosophy acquires increasingly a more practical orientation. Hero, for example, developed a kind of slot machine for delivering "holy water" in temples and realized that the evaporation of water can be employed to perform work as vapor expands. In other words, he was able to foresee and use the power of steam. The philosopher-poet Empedocles, too, provided the rudiments of an early water clock, the *klepsydra*, which is a cone-shaped vessel with holes in the base and apex that sinks slowly as it fills with water—the time taken to sink remains the same and provides a unit of measurement.[128]

The first three millennia of recorded history, in fact, were marked by an extremely active involvement with water, especially the building of dikes, dams, and bridges, the prediction of seasonal climate changes such as floods, the creation of irrigation systems and leveling of fields to receive water, and the construction of vessels to sail the seas, lakes, and rivers. Nearly all ancient civilizations established themselves in river valleys and undertook water projects and forms of river management: the Akadian, Sumerian, and Babylonian along the Tigris, and Euphrates; the Egyptians along the Nile; the Shang along the Yellow River; and the Harappan along the banks of the Indus, to name several of the most important.

On this point, Frankfurt school theorist, Karl Wittfogel, has argued provocatively but persuasively that civilization itself arose through massive feats of hydraulic engineering and the need to coordinate both large pools of labor and resulting bureaucracies in such waterworks. In these huge projects, water flows were interrupted, altered, or rechanneled for irrigation in areas as far apart as ancient Egypt, Mesopotamia, China, and India.[129] When this theory and these facts are taken into account along with the centrality of water to all life—Thales dies ironically of heat and thirst—we can begin to fathom how the world may be seen through the very transparent element of water and how this greatly malleable matrix and medium in turn might be viewed and shaped through the lens (and partially constituted through the associated language) of laboring practices, physical construction, social projects, and psychological projections of the developing human world. In short, with the incipient domestication of water, like the earlier domestication of fire, we can locate a bellwether historical process—a watershed event so to speak—that permits us to observe our changing relationship with the natural world, our technical devices and each other.

It is no coincidence that the elements have reappeared in recent Continental thought with the breakdown of ecological stability and the increasing domestication of organic and inorganic diversity. Before considering their philosophical re-emergence and elaborating on their contemporary relevance, we must first reconstruct and examine the major elemental theories in the works of Empedocles, Plato, and Aristotle. As is evident later, there is a distinct transitional sequence in the movement from one thinker and philosophical framework to the next in terms of whether the elements are conceived qualitatively or quantitatively on the one hand and unchanging (eternal) or changing (capable of transformation) on the other hand. In the perspectives advanced by these early Greek philosophers, we witness the first, boldest, most original and influential views of air, earth, water, and fire. We begin with Empedocles.

Interstice: Wood

> What sense can it make to suggest that everything is made from air, fire, earth, and water? All the sense in the world is the answer—at least when we are talking of trees... so the old Greeks were absolutely right. Trees, at least, are compounded from earth, water, and air, and the sun that powers the whole enterprise is the greatest fire of all.
>
> —Colin Tudge, *The Tree*

> If ever you have come upon a grove that is full of ancient trees which have grown to an unusual height, shutting out a view of the sky by a veil of bleached and intertwining branches, then the loftiness of the forest, the seclusion of the spot, and your marvel at the thick unbroken shade in the midst of the open spaces, will prove to you the presence of deity.
>
> —Lucius Annaeus Seneca, *Moral Epistles*

Wood enters the fiber of our lives in little noticed but significant ways. My grandfather worked regularly with this material. On birthdays and Christmas, he would gift my siblings and me wooden mallets, coasters, and paperweights that he had lathed or carved from rich brown oak, bird's eye maple, and light-hued poplar. I grew up splitting logs and dried stumps for the fireplace and enjoyed applying the repetitive rhythmic strokes of a sharp, wood-handled axe and sledgehammer to timber or to a metal wedge lodged within it, as I learned to read and follow the lead of the grain. A smattering of carpentry skills I acquired from my father through helping to remodel a house, build a deck, and frame a dormer—as well as by making an occasional towel or gun rack in shop class or a small vehicle for a pinewood derby—also taught me about the peculiar textures and nuances of the substance.

Trees and wood possess the unique capacity to at once record passing time through growth rings and, like wise elders, to "witness" quietly and affect a deeper current of ecological events, usually being among the oldest organisms in a biotic community and living thousands of years in some cases. The *truth* of a *tree* is revealed through language given that the two words share a similar etymological root, and both suggest rectitude and aspiring heights. Ezra Pound must have sensed this link when he wrote, "I stood still and was a tree amid the wood, / Knowing the truth of things unseen before, / Of Daphne and the laurel bough / And the god-feasting couple old / That grew elm-oak amid the wold."[1] The potential bond between wisdom and wood is evidenced too in experiential encounters with the vast scope of arboreal flora from the birch and beech to the banyan and bamboo. As anyone who has spent a span of time in the forest knows, the effects can be both calming and contemplative, like the consolation in coming home. "The wonder is that we can see these trees and not wonder more," Emerson appropriately opined upon visiting the sequoias of Yosemite.[2]

Eastern stories are especially telling. When a monk asks the Zen Buddhist Joshu, "What is the meaning of Bodhiharma's coming to China?," Joshu replies, "The oak tree in the garden." When another monk likewise inquires of Zhaozhou, "What is the living meaning of Zen?," Zhaozhou says, "The cypress tree in the yard."[3] Wood, in fact, is one of five elements in Chinese traditions, typically being associated with qualities like new growth, the direction of east, and attributes such as flexibility and strength. In Taoism, an uncarved block *(Po)* of wood is a key material image connoting our supposed original nature, which can be shaped, cut or sculpted into different expressions or simply be left alone in its pristine condition. Indeed, this particular philosophy emerged in the wooded south of China, where iconoclasts and rebels often flourished and took refuge from the law in the interiors of the forest. And in India, the Buddha attains *nirvana* beneath a tree—likely a Bodhi or Peepul.

Trees, which hold a special status in most cultures, were once considered to be the wooden spines and sacred spires of the earliest forest shrines, especially in places like ancient Greece. Speaking more recently from an outpost in the Sierra Mountains, John Muir waxes in a religious vernacular:

> A few minutes ago every tree was excited, bowing to the roaring storm, waving, swirling, tossing their branches in glorious enthusiasm like worship . . . Every hidden cell is throbbing with music and life, every fiber thrilling like harp strings, while incense is ever flowing from the balsam bells and leaves. No wonder the hills and groves were God's first temples, and the more they are cut down and hewn into cathedrals and churches, the farther off and dimmer seems the Lord himself.[4]

While traveling through Scandinavia, I visited the largest wooden church in the world in Kerimäki, Finland, which was built in the 1840s and seats more than three thousand people. Positioned near a beautiful lake, which is so clear and pure that one can drink directly from its waters, the church is a masterwork of carpentry and a celebration of the uses and beauty of wood with its many arches, pews, galleries, columns, beams, and domes that have been hewn from the material, as the forest has been repositioned and reshaped into hallowed architecture.

The sylvan sphere has always occupied our thoughts and dreams as an elemental realm upon which we project our secret anxieties, desires, and fears. Forests, argues Robert Pogue Harrison, are "shadows of civilization," enigmatically offering sites of danger, darkness, and asylum for lawbreakers as well as generating places of reverence, enlightenment, and revelation. "In the forest the animate may suddenly become inanimate, the god turns into a beast, the outlaw stands for justice, Rosalind appears as a boy, the virtuous knight degenerates into a wild man, the straight line forms a circle, the ordinary gives way to the fabulous."[5] As Harrison makes clear, institutions in the west from the church and family to the government and city founded themselves in opposition to the perceived wildness of woods, and this antagonism has greatly guided our conceptions of and actions toward these areas ever since. In fact, the word "forest," has a juridical origin deriving from the Latin *foresta* and likely *foris*, meaning "outside," and it is related to the verb *forestare*—to exclude or place off limits. The forest, then, was first conceived in the Middle Ages as land beyond the public domain belonging to the king for hunting or recreation and not to be cultivated or trespassed upon by commoners. Nevertheless, while defined over and against the public sphere, one unintended result of this delimitation was that forests came to be protected in Europe by "accidental environmentalist" kings and the sets of forest laws they promulgated.

Appreciating wood and the trees from which it derives demands an active, open, and embodied engagement with forests and a perspective not based solely in art—since the arboreal is not birthed from artists—but also in the sciences of botany, biology, and ecology. Holmes Rolston, who characterizes forests as among the most archetypal and elemental forces on earth, argues that we may first need to disenchant the woods so they can be enjoyed as living museums while permitting them to re-enchant themselves spontaneously on their own, too. One needs to understand photosynthesis, oxidation, nitrogen cycles, carbon bonding, glucose, and more. "Science takes away the colors, if you insist; apart from beholders, there is no autumn splendor or spring green. But science gives us the trees solidly there, photosynthesizing without us, energetically vital to the system of life."[6] An ancient forest, Gary Snyder concludes, is "a place of organisms, a heaven for many beings, a temple where life deeply investigates the puzzle of itself."[7] The association between trees and a sense of the sacred is a perennial one, and in his classic work, *The Golden Bough*, James Frazier identifies the many people—from the Celts, Germans, and Greeks to the Ojibwa, Koreans, and Chinese—who have considered trees to be divine or populated their woods with fairies, sprites, elves, and gods. This belief in animate wood frequently led to prohibitions on the use or abuse of many groves, helping to preserve them for posterity.

Analogous to the "life span" of mountains, a tree requires roughly the same length of time for it to return to the soil through decay once it has fallen as it did for it to rise to its final height. Until that happens, great trees may stick around for a while to relish "dead verticality," as Snyder phrases it. "How curious it would be to die and then remain standing for another century or two," he ruminates. "If humans could do it we would hear news like, 'Henry David Thoreau finally toppled over.'"[8] When a tree does fall in the forest without a human around, it likely makes a sound for the simple reason that there are many other organisms around to experience the event, linking percept with perceiver in the way that mountains and valleys are logically tethered together. Once we humans disappear entirely, move on to inhabit other worlds or merge and evolve with technology, forests will spread to cover again great portions of the planet, and such philosophical questions may become moot. In his provocative thought experiment, *The World Without Us*, Alan Weisman envisions precisely this kind of scenario if humans should suddenly vanish, and he describes in detail how the indefatigable elements would systematically corrode and collapse our infrastructures and reclaim buildings, farms, and cities, leaving little more than bronze artifacts, plastic, anthropogenic molecules, and radio waves while rural areas would revert to original forest. In the damp climate of Europe, for example, aspen and birch would hastily take over potato fields, and within twenty years farming pastures would give way to woodland. Under the protection of this new canopy, spruce, elm, oak, and maple would proliferate as birds and other former denizens return and multiply.[9]

We evolved with trees, and without them "our species would not have come into being at all," posits science writer Colin Tudge.[10] In fact, the reason we possess "dexterous hands and whirling arms" stems from the fact that our ancestors spent eighty million years in their midst.[11] Trees—and the wood they bear—can serve as connections and quite possibly compacts between human generations. Planting a tree binds one to biota and the living landscape but also ties one through time to future persons or, genealogically, to one's own family tree, especially when a young elm or maple, for instance, is established as a "green headstone" above the grave of a departed relative. Jeremy Bentham once proposed that we embalm our ancestors and line them up along country roads in alternation with trees after protecting our relative's faces from the elements with a special coating of resin. In the United States, the local carpenter traditionally was the one who "undertook" care of the dead (hence the designation, undertaker) and constructed pine boxes for their remains. Although coffins are now often made of steel or fiberglass, many are still assembled with pine boards or hardwood like mahogany or cherry.

Wood like wine, of course, is not all the same by any measure, and several key distinctions are worth noting. One is between heartwood and sapwood. Heartwood is the fibrous substance that has died but because of its genetic structure is resistant to decay. Usually older, harder and darker, it forms the discolored circles at the center of a tree's trunk, branches, or cross-section. Sapwood, by contrast, is the living wood between the bark and heartwood that carries water from roots to branches and then to leaves as well as stores the tree's sustenance. A second distinction is between hardwood, which comes from trees with broad leaves like the oak or birch, even though the wood is not in every instance actually hard, and softwood such as cedar or balsa, which derives from conifers and can sometimes be harder than certain hardwood trees, as is often the case with yew.

Many individual species of trees have rooted themselves justifiably in our collective minds. We gather around the evergreen during winter holidays; the oak provides us with shade and inspiring images of endurance or strength; the willow evokes wistful emotions; and the redwood and sequoia suggest majesty and grandeur. Writer Michael Pollan has identified a number of additional species that inhabit the Western worldview, including the Political Tree, the Romantic Tree, the Colonial Tree, and the Puritan Tree, among others. Puritans, for example, will clear trees in order to redeem nature while romantics worship them in order to restore culture:

> Puritan Trees tend to get chopped down sanctimoniously. Colonial Trees get chopped down unceremoniously. In stable times Political Trees get planted, but in revolutionary times, they get chopped down—albeit ceremoniously. And the Romantic Tree? Its proper fate is to find itself in a park or wilderness you preserve, rather than plant, since much of its spiritual authority derives from its independence from man.[12]

My neighbors and I planted a weeping snow cherry that bursts into snow-white petals each spring, marking the exact divide between our properties but also giving us a common entity for which to care. Like stone, trees are used widely to mark human territory and political lines, but they can also indicate the more pregiven boundaries of bioregions, signaling changes in microclimates, influencing watersheds, and affecting feeding grounds and predation.

From trees, we obtain dyes and drugs, ointments and incense, resins and varnishes, gums and glues, fibers, fruit and fuel, paper and paints, nuts, and much more. Wood is valued above all for utilitarian reasons, and it has been whittled, molded, and cut into weapons, writing instruments, utensils, homes, ships, and furniture, among many other objects. I have a particular fondness for hardwood floors and once spent a week tearing up the glue-laden tiles in my New York apartment in order to reach the original flooring, which I then sanded down and stained. I work on an old roll-top desk, and when I write I am usually surrounded by a "grove" of books. Each of these things—the grainy floor of the "forest" beneath me, the "canopy" of my desk, and the towering "trunks" of bookcases—tends to mitigate a severed connection with trees and even to delight me at times with a very latent scent of wood or the deep woods. On top of this, I live in a residential section of Philadelphia that bespeaks, like many towns across the country, the past and present ties with trees in its street names: Larchwood, Hazel, Cedar, Spruce, Chestnut, Locust, and Pine.

Plastic is a poor substitute for the biological affinities we share with wood, ones that take us back to our evolutionary beginnings when we bounded from tree to tree. We grow to appreciate the supporting curves of cedar chairs, the solid sounds of a sharp kitchen knife clicking against a stiff chopping block—my own consists of ten different kinds of wood from Costa Rica—and the reassuring grip and balance of a well-honed wooden tool, straight-grained hard rock maple pool cue stick or persimmon-headed golf club in our hands. Baseball players sometimes develop such a rapport with their bats that they can be discovered talking to them or meticulously counting the grains in the barrels. The white ash, used to make a flexible but dense bat of choice, however, is currently under assault both from rising temperatures that soften the wood and from non-native emerald ash borer beetles that have decimated twenty-five million trees of this species, making professional hitters legitimately concerned.

If, as Aldo Leopold suggests, it is possible to "think like a mountain," it might be even more plausible to "run a business like a Redwood forest," as one major advocate of biomimicry suggests. Such forests are instances of mature ecosystems that tend to be energy efficient, reuse their own waste, rely on diversity, avoid fouling their territory, and optimize resources in ways that other less developed systems and, by extension, human businesses fail to do.[13] For comprehensible reasons, trees tend to inspire such creative thinking and worldly applications. Several years ago, a friend of mine spent ten days in Vermont designing and building a sustainable tree house after first identifying a suitable growing support to use as the structure and frame. Like a bird's nest, constructing a wooden residence in an arboreal hold is a perfect organic and aesthetic fit, as if the one blossomed from the other.

In the last act of Shakespeare's "Macbeth," the trees of the forest seem to march and advance upon Macbeth in the guise of an opposing army, which is camouflaged in boughs and twigs, so as to exact poetic vengeance. Today, trees are more literally on the move and increasingly in the news because of climate change, industrialization and pollution. The world now loses twenty million acres of woodland each year to deforestation. The causes are legion but often related to over-consumption and slash-and-burn activities driven by cattle ranching, petroleum extraction, agribusiness and urban development, though wildfires, acid rain, and logging do contribute heavily to this process. In China alone, forty-five billion pairs of chopsticks are discarded annually, a figure that amounts to roughly twenty-five million mature trees.

It took 350 million years for evolutionary forces to assemble the world's great forests through a complex concatenation of trial and error, of research and development, as it were. It has taken far less time for us to disassemble most of these magnificent realms where the great wealth of the planet's species make their respective homes. "Forests precede civilizations and deserts follow them," Chateaubriand astutely noticed.[14] And if there is insight contained in this claim, we should take heed ourselves as the former disappear with alacrity and the latter emerge in their stead. Trees, of course, provide a host of ecological functions and environmental services, including sequestering carbon (about 330 pounds annually for a typical tree), creating shade, reducing noise, generating oxygen (two trees give off enough for one person), providing food, shelter, and habitat for many organisms, and holding soil in place. The economic value of trees is enormous given that they also remove pollutants from the atmosphere—about ten pounds per tree each year on average—mitigate storm water damage, increase the value of homes, and cool buildings up to twenty degrees in the summer. In effect, trees collectively act as a vital organ of the planet, like lungs on the animal body.

On my university campus, we are establishing a fifty-acre arboretum with walking trails, benches, binoculars for bird watching and activities designed to better connect place with pedagogy. Toward this end, I regularly take students on walks in the woods and am always surprised to learn how unusual this kind of outing is for them. Some of the students, who are largely of an urban or suburban upbringing, admit to never having been to a forest, just as many of them have not ever visited a farm, gone camping or swum in a body of water larger than a chlorinated pool. They may be experiencing something like what Richard Louv calls "nature deficit disorder" in his book, *Last Child in the Woods*. This is unfortunate because the woods offer a place of learning and mystery; they provide an outdoor course in botany, ecology, and natural history; and they encourage encounters with philosophical wonder, the depths of time and the intoxicating puzzle of beauty. "The human community, when healthy, is like an ancient forest," Snyder remarks. "The little ones are in the shade and shelter of the big ones, even rooted in their lost old bodies." [15] One suspects Dr. Seuss' Lorax, the "mossy, bossy" creature who famously speaks for the trees, might agree.

Part II

Elemental Theories

— 3 —

The Flowering of Ecological Roots

Empedocles' Elemental Thought

To the elements it came from / Everything will return / Our bodies to earth, / Our blood to water / Heat to fire, / Breath to air. / They were well-born, they will be well-entomb'd!

—Mathew Arnold, *Empedocles on Etna*

Primary images have a philosophical advantage: by studying them, we may examine in connection with each of them practically all the problems of a metaphysics of imagination. The image of the root is particularly suitable in this respect.

—Gaston Bachelard, *Earth and the Reveries of Repose*

What is at question in the rhizome is a relation to sexuality—but also the animal, the vegetal, the world, politics, the book, things natural and artificial—that is totally different from the arborescent relation: all manner of "becomings."

—Gilles Deleuze and Félix Guattari, *A Thousand Plateaus*

Four-Play

As environmental philosophers, geographers, and historians explore the thought and practices of ancient civilizations,[1] one period that has been largely neglected is occupied by the Presocratics, the first *physiologoi*—natural scientists and philosophers—to inquire with penetrating insight into the physical universe. Within this early Greek era, a distinctly important figure who has been widely ignored is Empedocles. Such oversight is especially surprising given how present-day environmental problems are related in a deep manner to our experiential, cultural, and historical understandings of the four elements, which Empedocles, a native of Acragras (Agrigento) in Sicily, first thematized in the fifth century B.C.E. In order to help encourage a more widespread ecological sensibility[2] and to forge a more environmentally sustainable society—one that is attuned to the significance of the underlying earth, encompassing air, circulating waters, and transfiguring force of fire in the landscape and human technology—it is valuable to return in a creative and critical manner to the elemental "roots" themselves.[3]

This chapter examines the origins and initial representations of the perennial notion of the four elements or "roots" by Empedocles, drawing out their implications and suggesting the relevance of this ancient philosophy for environmental concerns. In the process, we see how "radical"—in the political, biological, and philosophical senses—such roots are by way of their theoretical formation and potential flowering in contemporary contexts. More specifically, it is argued here that Empedocles' ideas may be reasonably interpreted so as to show an anticipation or foreshadowing of the theory of evolution, an attentiveness to and deep sympathy with sentient organisms and nonhuman entities, and a discourse germane to comprehending environmental contamination. As part of this exploration, we discuss the meanings of pollution, the social construction of nature, the treatment of animals, and other issues raised by his two extant contributions: *Peri Phuseos* (*On Nature*) and the *Kartharmoi* (*Purifications*). Finally, we take up a recent critique of the notion of roots and a reanimation of the notion of rhizomes in the post-structuralist work of Gilles Deleuze and Félix Guattari for new possible ways of thinking about the elements and our own environmental dilemmas.

Although he should not be identified anachronistically as an "ancient environmentalist," we can think of Empedocles as engaged in the multiple—but at that time undistinguished—roles of naturalist, poet, religious prophet, philosopher, and perhaps even shaman-healer. In these and other capacities, he seeks a coherent explanation of the cosmos by focusing on the force of the four now classical elements and through his meditations and speculations displays an acute sensitivity and knowledge of the surrounding natural world. Understanding roots also connotes finding our own "element" and place of belonging on the earth. "To be rooted," Simone Weil has remarked, "is perhaps the most important and least recognized need of the soul," and, she rightly adds, it is one of the hardest to define and secure.[4] It is here that Empedocles can be of assistance to cultures such as our own that are uprooted increasingly and no longer as actively aware of the fourfold of fire, water, air, and earth as it might befit us.

The Problem of the Poems

The Empedocles whom we most frequently encounter is through the eyes of Aristotle—and this is true more generally for all of the Presocratics—but this portrayal is commonly encumbered by Aristotle's preoccupation with finding in advance anticipations, misinterpretations or contradictions of his own outlook and our overreliance, in turn, on Aristotle for reconstructing earlier accounts.[5] It is more illuminating to read Empedocles within his own historical and philosophical context even as we carefully adapt or adopt his insights and ideas within a present-day setting. In this regard, one must eventually come to terms with the extra-philosophical dimensions of his work and life that concern natural magic, political reform, shamanism, and poetry as well as the "materialistic" sides of his writing that can be construed more narrowly as philosophical, physiological, or cosmological. In many respects, Empedocles' texts defy traditional classifications and distinctions in thought.

Much controversy exists, too, over the relation of Empedocles' two ostensibly very different works, *On Nature* and *The Purifications*. Many commentators find it a difficult task to reconcile the foci and fragments of these poems. The former work is devoted in the main to natural philosophy, the claims of reason and the goals of nascent science, describing a cosmological process in which the universe is cyclically generated and destroyed through the primordial actions of two forces—a unifying "love" and separating "strife"—that act on the elements. The latter text attends more to religious matters, specifically the trek of an "impure" spirit (*daimon*) who has been banished from the realm of contentment and peace to experience a series of incarnations in various earthly forms (vegetable, animal, human) until reaching a final state of "purity."

Among the perspectives held on the relation of these works, two predominate. One position finds a scientific view contradicted clearly by the religious mysticism, magic, and metempsychosis (transmigration of the soul) of the other such that a rational or even imaginative synthesis is not possible.[6] This view, however, generally depends on a sharp and, in the end, untenable, dichotomy between religion and science, belief and reason, that does not hold up as well for Empedocles time period in question as it might in later historical epochs. The categories of thought and experience were not so starkly crystallized and separated in an era that located a place for both Apollonian rationalism and Dionysian excess.[7] A second perspective tries to assign Empedocles' works to different periods of his life, claiming that his ideas changed dramatically over time as evidenced by an analysis of his writing style, temperament, and explicit or implicit concerns. Some interpreters argue that *On Nature* is his early work and that this kind of investigation was abandoned for the religious comfort he sought in older years, whereas other scholars hold to the reverse, seeing the *Purifications* as a fiery product of youth that was eventually set aside for calmer and more sober reflections.[8]

Both views, however, are ultimately dependent on controversial, subjective, and still-disputed biographical information and interpretations, tending to downplay or ignore the points of intersection of the actual texts and focusing instead on questions of character, personality, and authorship. That Empedocles addresses to a close personal friend named Pausanias the work, *On Nature*—his so-called scientific treatise that would presumably be for a learned and larger audience—while exuberantly and openly shouting to all friends who dwell in the city in the opening lines of the *Purifications*—his supposed religious writings that might normally be restricted to a smaller, more familiar, and less secular crowd—is the reverse of what we might expect of "public" and "private" matters. It also provides us with another clue that Empedocles is upsetting traditional expectations and divisions.

In contrast to these perspectives, it is plausible and more reasonable to see the two works as compatible, even complementary. In many ways, *On Nature* presupposes or further articulates ideas advanced in the *Purifications*, holding as well to the doctrine of the immortality of the soul, declaring the cosmic sphere to be divine, and the *rhizomata* to be immortal deities (*daimones*), and appealing likewise to notions of purity and piety. Empedocles also proclaims the grand powers of a divine love that serves to unify the cosmos as an organizing principle both within and outside of us and which can be correlated to the migrating spirit (*daimon*) in the *Purifications*. In this way, we can read Empedocles as seeking a location for this spirit or soul in the struggle and harmony of the elemental roots within the sensuous, physical world. The realm of nature (*On Nature*) and the realm of spirit (*Purifications*) are thereby best seen as two parts of one integrated whole bound through an underlying or overarching panpsychism—the notion that all is endowed with intelligence, mind or a mind-like property. In short, the "other-worldly" and Orphic strains in his "religious" writings often find points of agreement or analogy within his naturalistic work.[9]

Square Roots and Radical Rhizomes

To the water of Thales, the air of Anaximenes, and the fire of Heraclitus, Empedocles adds the earth, completing the canonical tetrad as we have inherited it.[10] In a style that might be called either poetic philosophy or philosophical poetry,[11] he writes: "And first the fourfold root of all things hear! / White gleaming Zeus, life-bringing Hera, Aidoneus / And Nestis whose tears bedew mortality" (fr. 6). No small amount of ink has been spilled in the last two thousand years in attempts and accompanying disputes concerning how these names should be correlated with the elements.[12] It is clear and incontestable that Nestis, the Sicilian deity of rivers, represents water. This interpretation is suggested directly when Nestis is spoken of as moistening mortals with her tears, an outpouring in essence of water. Ancient interpreters tended to agree that Zeus should be assigned to fire, although confusion and controversy have been created because recent commentators are more prone to equate *aither* with air instead of fire (correctly it seems) and so place Zeus with air after bestowing Aidoneus to fire. This correlation of Zeus with *aither* makes a certain sense because one of the most lasting Greek traditions has been to regard the heavens as the home of this great god.

Aidoneus, however, means "invisible" and so also implies air, which is the element that makes vision possible but is not itself seen. At the same time, Aidoneus is another poetic name for Hades—god of the underworld—and could represent earth as some modern writers argue or even fire because of the connection to the underworld and the association with the volcanoes of Sicily to which Empedocles alludes. To Hera is applied the phrase, "life-bringing" (*pheresbios*), suggesting the bountiful and fecund earth as in Hesiod's *Theogony* but possibly air on which life depends as well. If a choice were forced on the basis of this information, it would most likely seem that Zeus, who is associated with the upper reaches of the sky, represents air; Hera, who supports life, stands for earth; Aidoneus, who governs the netherworld, symbolizes fire; and Nestis, who as deity of rivers, signifies water. In any event, *aither* should be treated (and translated) as air rather than fire or a combination of fire and air. In the fifth century, B.C.E. *aer* was only considered an isolated instance of what we call air, especially the conditions of cloud or mist. As the scope of the word *aer* increased and expanded, the scope of the term *aither* was accordingly diminished, so that by early in the fourth century B.C.E. it comes to mean only the highest or most divine realm of air.[13]

Despite the scholarly controversy, the crucial point remains that in granting them divine names, Empedocles implies that the tetrad of earth, air, fire, and water are the new governing powers (*archai*) of the world, posited and so positioned to supplant traditional mythology or at least imbue it with a *logos* (reason or order).[14] The attribution of divine monikers is not simply poetic flourish. The *rhizomata* are god-like because they are regarded as eternal and immortal, even if we now no longer characterize them as elements in the chemical sense. As Aristotle recognizes, "The elements too are gods."[15] In referring to the roots as Hera, Zeus, Nestis, and Aidoneus, Empedocles also socializes—even personalizes—the physical world, providing a basis for kinship and familiarity with the elements that we experience or "battle" on an everyday basis. The incessant controversy over the correlation of the divine names (and more secular terms)—which themselves change over the course of the poems[16]—with the individual "elements" suggests, first, that Empedocles' did not have as hard and fast a terminological classification as we might imagine given the eternality of earth, air, fire, and water but more of a loose and "growing" net-work or "system of roots." Second, it implies that the *rhizomata*, as understood through the mediations of human senses, language, and convention (along with the compounds composed of them) are capable of a form of nominal change, even if the *rhizomata* themselves are not (a point reinforced later).

In *On Nature*, we find the elemental forms are represented as the sun, stars, rain, and earth and then as the sun, earth, heaven (*ouranos*), and sea. Empedocles also offers an analogical understanding of the roots, implying although not explicitly mentioning the four basic colors—black, white, red, and yellow—with which the Greek artists supposedly worked.[17] The Atomists and later Plato and Aristotle will replace this analogy from painting with one from writing, as the *stoicheia*—a word translatable as both elements and the letters—assume greater philosophical importance, but at this historical juncture Empedocles frames a very colorful, visual, and vivid cosmological picture. Just as the four colors in the hand of a skilled painter can produce the panoply of all visible objects, so the four elements are able to constitute all that exists in the world: plants, animals, and humans in particular. "For from them hath budded all / that was or is or evermore shall be" (fr. 21). Even the "long-lived gods" belong by necessity to this process of eternal change.

Empedocles calls them *rhizomata* (or "roots" as they are generally translated or mistranslated) and refers to them variously as the "roots of all" or "the fourfold root of all things" or the "primeval four" and not strictly "elements" (*stoicheia*), which is a philosophical appellation of later usage, originating most likely with Plato.[18] This distinction is important. Strictly speaking, *rhizomes* are subterranean plant stems akin to bulbs and tubers that are frequently thickened by the accumulation of deposits of food material. They send off shoots above and roots below but, unlike roots, they possess nodes, buds, and scaled leaves. In this sense, they have no true beginning or end; instead, they are an overflowing middle that grows in all directions. This point bodes significant for the recent philosophical (net)work of Deleuze and Guattari—to be considered later—because as pragmatic naturalists they oppose images and metaphors of the root, radical, or tree in preference for that which moves nomadically and through multiplicity as a rhizome.[19]

The notion of "roots"—a biological and genealogical image—nevertheless suggests something both primary and originary but also a living source of growth, like the etymological "root" of *physis* (nature) itself—from the Greek for plant—whose first meaning implies biological development. It can be (and was) attributed to one's ancestry—persons prior in time—and also applied to one's offspring[20]—persons later in time—indicating a reversibility, fluidity, and mobility to the concept, much like the roots of trees, which move in many directions, including downward into the earth, laterally into water, and even upward into the air. Water (*hudor*), fire (*pyr*), earth (*ge*), and air (*aer* or *aither*) also are the great visible masses of the world respectively thought of as the oceans, heavens, land, and sky. In this regard, Empedocles suggests that the senses provide a good basis for understanding these "elements," even if our sight, hearing, taste, touch, and smell are not infallible.[21] The sense of tactility has a particularly important role to play given that it is distributed over the entire body, and so with his epistemological trust in the senses, Empedocles begins to puts us quite literally *in touch with the elements*.[22]

Empedocles, of course, did not discover the four elements because they were already current in common Greek belief. Rather, like other Presocratics, he created a *frame-work*—a picture-poem in effect—for understanding and interpreting physical change. He *squares the roots* into a coherent cosmic picture. Contrary to the claims of some commentators, we do not find this same emphasis in the earlier Greek thought of the Milesians, even if a vague poetic or mythic tetrad can be found in Hesiod's *Theogony* and in Homer as earth, sea, underworld, and heaven (*ouranos*), perhaps contributing to the gradual emergence but rapid acceptance of the later doctrine.[23] In Homer's *Iliad*, the partitioning of the cosmos is such that Poseidon rules the sea; Hades governs the misty darkness; Zeus holds the heavens; and earth belongs to all in common.[24] The early cosmologies, however, do seem to make frequent recourse to a fourfold division—either as qualities, material entities, or "substances"—and frequently in the form of wet/dry and hot/cold characterizations.

Although Presocratics such as Melissus and Diogenes, too, mention earth, air, fire, and water as basic units of the universe, their elements are not exhaustive or sufficient explanations because other entities like iron, wind, and stone play roles, and they are, moreover, but phases in a transformational process. Empedocles' insight is to stress the primacy, necessity and seeming sufficiency of the four roots, something that had not been done previously by either poets or philosophers. He then proceeds to offer us a "larger vision of the whole and all" (fr. 2). Empedocles thus makes an advance not only over Thales, Anaximenes, and Heraclitus but also over Anaximander, who rejected single element theories and posited an *apeiron* (boundless) in which order comes about through the clash of opposites but is governed by a definite law.

Rhizomata serve, first, as the name for earth, air, fire, and water; refer, secondly, to the visible masses in the world corresponding to these names, and indicate, thirdly, what we might now call a mythic or symbolic dimension, as when Empedocles associates fire with the sun, or the sea (water) with "Earth's sweat" (fr. 55). In terms of this characterization, *rhizomata* are (a) eternal, (b) uncreated (*ageneta*), and (c) constitutive of what the world is made—"for these are all" (fr. 26). The first two properties imply "elemental" in the sense of original "substances" (although not in the later Aristotelian sense). The third trait suggests "elemental" in the manner of basic, primary, even simple. Thus, a distinction emerges between compounds and that of which they are composed. Each root, however, possesses its own individual prerogative or character (*ethos*) so that individual qualitative differences of kind are recognized. Empedocles attests to the universality and eternity of the *rhizomata*: "And how, besides, might they to ruin come / since nothing lives that empty is of them?" (fr. 17).

One is able to grasp the *rhizomata* and correspondingly the cosmic process of mixture (*mixis*) and separation (*diakrisis*) because they reside and abide in us as well. This fact is evident from the fragments: "Behold her now with mind, and sit not there / With eyes astonished, for 'tis she inborn / Abides established in the limbs of men" (fr. 17) and "For 'tis through Earth that Earth we do behold / Through Ether, divine Ether luminous / Through Water, Water, through Fire, devouring Fire, / And Love through Love, and Hate through doleful Hate" (fr. 109). The four roots are able to take one another's place without the introduction by Empedocles of empty space (*kenon*). They possess the capacity for movement and division, even if the change is through rearrangement, and in this sense it is thus more apparent than real. Earth, air, fire, and water are at one with their parts that have been separated off, and so there is not truly birth or death. Division occurs because the roots "run through" each other and so alter their appearance. Despite such divisibility, Empedocles does not need "roots of roots" or, as Plato requires in the *Timaeus*, "elements of elements" as it were. Earth, for example, can consist of smaller parts, but these parts are of the same type as the root itself. Empedocles' solution to the problems of mixture and separation is, in brief, to develop a theory of microscopic pores, through which the roots pass, thereby explaining how and why some entities combine more freely than others. The roots, in short, require the existence of particular sizes of pores in order that they can mix.

Empedocles' Elemental Cosmology

Before exploring the connections between Empedocles' philosophy and environmental thought, we need to convey briefly a sense of his elemental cosmology. *On Nature*, in short, attempts to unite the Eleatic doctrine of "being" with the Ionian notion of "becoming." This work occupies a place between the monism of Parmenides and the extreme pan-metabolism of Heraclitus. Empedocles follows Parmenides (who also wrote in verse) in the thesis that being neither comes into existence nor passes away. It cannot arise from nonbeing or become nonbeing. Becoming—understood as qualitative change in an original "substance"—is impossible. "From what-is-not what-is can ne'er become; / So that what-is should e'er be all destroyed" (fr. 12). But Empedocles also attempts to reconcile this position with the evidence of change, the apparent fact that particular things seem to arise, change, and decay. This reconciliation is effected by presenting generation as "commingling" and decay as "separation" from a primal elemental stuff, which itself does not change.

Empedocles posits two primordial, everlasting forces: namely love (*philia*), which is variously identified as Aphrodite, Harmony, and Kypris, and strife, which is spoken of as Hate, Wrath, and Neikos. Thus, like the elemental roots themselves, they are given mythical names. As an agent of organic unity, love brings together the roots (and cosmos) while strife, in turn, disperses them, causing differentiation (and chaos). Love and likeness are clearly associated—"each through Love draws near and yearns for each" (fr. 21)—while strife is assimilated to difference: "hostile chiefly are those things which most from one another differ" (fr. 22).[25] These active and opposed forces, which have antecedents in Heraclitus' tension between "war" and "harmonia" and perhaps vague latter-day analogues in Freud's instincts of *eros* (love) and *thanatos* (death), alternate in predominating. "The world-wide warfare of the eternal Two . . . whiles into one," Empedocles claims (fr. 20). The roots are not always in a state of separation or mixture, and because they are neither generated nor perishable, Empedocles has implicitly critiqued and ingeniously developed the Parmenidian position that something either *is* or it *is not*.

In the end, the four roots are actually not sufficient agents for change in the visible world; they require the efforts of love and strife, which serve as forces analogous to positive and negative electrical charges—catalysts in effect for change, or in Aristotelian vernacular "efficient causes." Yet they cannot be understood as comparable in status to the four roots, constituting as it were two additional "elements," although some interpreters have suggested this view.[26] Love and strife are not perceptible to the senses but understood only via mind (*nous*). They are not "things" like the roots. It is more likely that love and strife are coextensive with the roots in that the world requires their presence in order to change. They are motivating principles that work on the *rhizomata*. But if moving agent and movable element are distinguishable, they are not separated in a Cartesian or Newtonian sense. Love and strife are both physical and psychological principles, and Empedocles' language is clearly here, as elsewhere, situated at the intersections of poetry and philosophy, myth, and science.

Empedocles' cosmic process is circular and each cycle continues for an extremely long, if unspecified, time. The roots, too, move "around the circle of the world" (fr. 17). They appear out of the vortex, whose origin is not explained fully but which is perhaps due to a disturbance of the equilibrium or from strife. Four main stages of the process can *apparently* be distinguished even if Empedocles is not explicit in these divisions:[27]

1. The solitude of the sphere, where an apogee is attained;
2. The dispersion or unrest, which is marked by what is called the quaking "limbs of God";
3. The triumph and rule of strife; and,
4. The re-conquest of chaos by the force of *philia* and the attainment of a perigee.

Stated in other terms, there is both a unifying, absorbing movement "into the One and All" and a Plotinian-like process of emanation where "the Many, and the Many, again / Spring from primeval scattering of the One" (fr. 26).

Both strife and amity separate and unite, but the result is different for each. Strife gives birth to chaos, the separation of the elements, and monstrous forms while amity yields living beings, the "multitudinous tribes of mortal things" (fr. 35). Neither hate nor love is completely destroyed during the rule of the other. Love is not able to fully conquer and rule because hate waits "out yonder on the circle's utmost bounds" (fr. 35). Empedocles implies that during his (and our) lifetime strife is reigning and that the period of love is an historical memory, perhaps of Aegean or Minoan pre-Greek civilization.

The first apparent phase of the cosmic cycling is marked by the complete predominance of love (*philia*) such that strife is driven outward, exiled in effect spatially to the most extreme limits of the sphere like a heinous criminal. In this stage, the four roots are most perfectly intermixed and blended in their equality. They are so endeared to one another that any competing characteristics they might possess are mitigated and vanquished. The Sphere (*Sphairos*) is the acme of perfection where no distinctions of quality exist. There is neither becoming nor decay. It is sometimes expressed in negative terms, like the later medieval notion of *via negativa*. For example, it has no reproductive organs, no feet, and no knees,[28] as Empedocles refuses to give it the characteristics of animal or human. It is rounded, "like unto itself" and "exultant in surrounding solitude" (fr. 29, 27). It is implied that the Sphere is unlimited because it is without end or beginning, but it is nevertheless still given a definitive shape. On this point, the ancient Greeks typically displayed unease at the boundless and limitless, and this fear finds expression as well in Empedocles.[29]

But the Sphere is only one phase in the endless cosmic cycle that will be continually dissolved and reconstituted. While it persists, there are no animals, plants, humans, or gods of which to be spoken. Humans and the world of mortal things appear only when the Sphere is altered through strife, and the universe as we know it comes about through this dynamic tension. During the rule of the Sphere (and love), however, the four roots still retain their respective qualities. As to how strictly complete and perfectly united is this state, there exists room for question since if *philia* joins the foursome into one, it would theoretically eliminate their individuality and distinctness. There is nonetheless a marked peace, tranquility, and rest to this initial phase.

In contrast to the unity and stasis of the first stage, the second stage introduces both plurality and movement. The parts or "limbs" of god[30] begin to quake, a description not unlike that given by proponents of the Big Bang theory, in which the cosmos is produced by a great explosion of compact matter. Again, Empedocles does not offer an explanation in physical terms for this transition from an unmoving sphere to a moving world (a point for which Aristotle criticizes him), although the broad cosmic oath to which he refers suggests a metaphysical cause of change in that it operates like Anaximander's universal justice, which allows no power to gain complete control. The waning and waxing of love (*philia*) and strife (*neikos*) must follow the eternal way of things and the time allotted to them. Each elemental root starts to seek its own kind (or likeness) with which it is still "friendly," and through this process, separation, and differentiation come about. Love slowly loosens its grip on things. The world, our world, begins to be formed as great masses of the elements are separated off: earth, sea, sky, and fire. At this point, each mass still possesses some of the other roots. Thus, waters spring from the earth; air sinks down to the ground; fires burn in the deep beneath and so on. As with Anaximander, cosmogony begins with the encroachment on the borders of the given elemental provinces, and the *rhizomata* appear themselves to evolve and change. Following the ongoing ordering and arrangement of earth, air, fire, and water on the cosmic scale, living beings begin to emerge from the primal mixture, with trees—the visible, living, and growing embodiment of "roots"—appropriately arriving first and containing the four "elements" in a very thoroughly mixed manner.

A third phase—essentially an extension of the second—as the complete triumph of strife in the cosmic process whereby all the roots have been thoroughly separated. This stage is the most completely removed from the unity and peace of the Sphere. It also is short and transitional. A fourth and following phase is the reassertion of *philia* after strife reaches the bottom-most depth of the vortex. Love assumes increasing power and place over the roots, and strife is driven to the outer bounds. Just as *philia* was banished, so will strife again be removed. The roots come together to form another world of living creatures. However, rather than animate "whole-natured" clumps blooming into individuated organs and limbs under the influence of strife, isolated limbs combine to form odd creatures at first before they develop into more familiar species. In this way, the universe oscillates between unity and diversity.

Throughout the extant fragments, one finds a repeated stress on the twofold nature of the cosmic process and a "twofold truth" that is concomitantly expressed. "Twofold the birth, twofold the death of things," writes the poet-philosopher (fr. 17). Creation thereby is depicted simultaneously as (like) a birth but also (like) a death (of the Sphere). Strife scatters and disperses but also begins anew the process of constituting the material world. Empedocles remarks in an aphoristic style, "What must be said, may well be said twice o'er" (fr. 25), and indeed there is a repetition of key pronouncements in his fragments.[31] Empedocles develops this two-fold nature of cosmic proceedings at length with metaphors and analogies drawn from the physical and perceptual world. "One vision of two eyes is born" (fr. 88) and "The joint binds two" (fr. 32) are typical pronouncements. The cyclical, repetitive nature of the Empedoclean universe recalls as well the teachings of Heraclitus, who proclaimed, "For beginning and end are shared on the circumference of a circle" (DK 103) and Parmenides who remarked, "It is all the same to me where I should begin for that point I shall again at some time reach" (fr. 5). It also points us forward to Nietzsche's more recent notion of the "eternal recurrence of the same" (*die ewige Wiederkehr des Gleichens*)—the idea that all events return in time—and his attempt to bring together being and becoming, albeit in a different manner than Empedocles.[32] Finally, at a very fundamental level, it underscores what religious scholar Mircea Eliade identifies as the indissoluble bond between archaic humans and deep cosmic rhythms, especially those involving ritualistic repetition that generates "sacred history" as it is transmitted through myth and archetype.[33]

Ecological and Political Equality

In terms of the contemporary relevance of Empedocles' teachings, we can discern or develop a number of philosophical links between his work and broadly construed environmental subjects so as to critically reclaim the ecological sensibility of his orientation. The thrust of key aspects of Empedocles' thought is toward an understanding of our respectful place in the natural environment as the four "elements" (*rhizomata*) of earth, air, fire, and water are accorded a central role within a perspective that makes fertile connections to the capacious world. A first potentially significant aspect of Empedocles' philosophy for environmental thought lies in the ontological equality of the elements.[34] They rest in equipoise (*atalanton*) and are equal with respect to, first, origin and age (*elika gennan*); second, strength (and its related concept of honor, *time*); and, third, rule, which is carried out in turn. As Empedocles writes: "Behold those roots own equal strength / And equal origin; each rules its task; And unto each its primal mode; and each prevailing conquers with revolving time" (fr. 17).[35] In this sense, they function like the role of the *demos* (people) of the Greek *polis* (civic community), whereby rule (political governance) follows a democratic notion of rotation or "successive supremacy,"[36] an idea that is eventually undermined by the hierarchical divisions of later Greek thought and cultural life. "In turn they [the roots] conquer as the cycles roll / And wane the one to other still, and wax / The one to other in turn by olden Fate" (fr. 26). It is worth bearing in mind that Empedocles himself was an egalitarian and a defender of democratic principles. He also helped to bring about the dissolution of an oligarchic organization known as the Thousand and was even said to have refused the kingship of his own city.[37]

The realm of nature and politics for Empedocles—and to a lesser extent Presocratic thought more generally—is thus marked by a radical *isonomia* (equality) that is not static but rather informed by a sense of proportion and blending equilibrium (*krasis*) and infused by a broader concept of cosmic justice (*dikaiosyne*).[38] The influence of the Pythagoreans on Empedocles is apparent on these points. For them, justice is a number. As a square number (*isakis isos*)—one multiplied into itself—it is thus a perfect harmony because it consists of equal parts, like the four (square) roots of Empedocles. Furthermore, justice is premised on the arrangement of a *polis* composed of equal parts, and as long as those parts remain equal, so theoretically does the *polis*. By divesting aggressors of the profits they have acquired from victims and restoring it to these latter individuals, equality is actively maintained. Justice therefore requires requital as well. The *polis* is considered the sum total of equal participating members, and its goal is the adjustment and harmony known as justice.

As another Presocratic thinker, the medical writer Alcmaeon, puts it with respect to the physical environment: "What preserves health is equality (*isonomia*) between the powers—wet and dry, cold and hot, bitter and sweet and the rest, and monarchy (*monarchia*) among them is the cause of sickness."[39] In this sense, an autocratic ontological or social rule is viewed as detrimental to individual persons, the political sphere (*polis*), and the entire natural realm. Well-being relies on a relative equality, diversity of forms, and dynamic equilibrium, principles that generally operate in mature ecosystems or stable ecological communities in the case of human societies.[40] The multiple elemental *archai* can be viewed as challenges to the possibility of a single person or power presiding (a *mon-archia*). The cosmo-*polis* is quite literally a "radical" democracy of all that (or who) exists. Empedocles expresses a perspective that bears out and articulates Alcmaeon's criteria of health, thus leveling older inequalities that had been established by religious teachings and traditions. Zeus, who was formerly considered "king of kings," most blessed among the blessed, and the mightiest sovereign of all is now placed on the same level as the nearly unknown divinity named Nestis.[41] Social ecologist Murray Bookchin places this particular Presocratic contribution in an historical and ecological context, arguing persuasively that: "it simply becomes silly to emphasize that Presocratic thought was riddled by demonstrably false 'archaisms' when . . . exploring its *orientation*, not its 'scientific' merits." "Nature philosophy," he adds, "lost not only its grounding in *isonomia* [equality] but its sense of ecological meaning."[42] It is this ecological significance and its associated reparative egalitarianism that arguably needs to be recovered when we inquire into the early cosmologies and elemental philosophy. There are, in fact, emerging parallels and analogues within modern environmental thought in the perspectives of biocentrism, deep ecology, and some forms of religious pantheism that often exhibit disparate forms of ontological or ecological egalitarianism, perceiving living creatures, physical entities, and processes, or even all dimensions of the cosmos as meriting equal consideration or as endowed with relatively equivalent moral worth. By contrast, social ecology focuses on achieving a radical democratic vision of polity and in reaching a greater equality in human communities, in particular.[43]

Organic Unity

Empedocles' generous panpsychism accentuates the fundamental unity of all material elements, entities, and organisms. Intelligence courses through the entire cosmos: "One holy mind, ineffable, alone, / And with swift thoughts darts through the universe" (fr. 134). The *rhizomata*, too, are accorded a kind of animate awareness. We find Empedocles claiming, for example, "all things have fixed intent [*phronesis*] and a share of thought" [*noma*] (fr. 110). In "minding" nature, Empedocles presents knowledge in physical terms as his physiology passes into psychology. He establishes a direct correspondence between the corporeal elements and our awareness of them. The natural world and our perception of it are bound together in a close communing relationship because our feelings and thought bear a direct relation to the elemental combinations within us. Like is known by like, and Empedocles is perhaps the first Western thinker to highlight this "elective affinity"—as Goethe terms it—of all things. Earth is perceived via earth, water with water and so with the rest of the roots. We can interpret this position as connecting each elemental root with a corresponding sense within us, such that touch involves solidity (earth), taste is linked to that which is moist (water), sight implies light (fire), and smell entails some form of vapor (via air).[44]

We are, in other words, intimately entangled with the forms and fortunes of the four elements. For the first time, emotions such as love (*philia*) and hate (*neikos*) are discovered in the bonds, separations and motions of earth, air, fire, and water. An intensive, volitional dimension is invested in the physical world and designated as an objective motivating factor. There is, in brief, the development of what we could call *e-motional matter*. Value is construed as an integral and immanent part of the study and knowledge of the natural world. Strife continually disturbs and destroys the cosmological process, but it is finally *philia* (love) that wins out, even if we interpret this dimension as a powerful utopian wish, as Ernst Bloch conjectures.[45]

In portraying this organic unity, Empedocles often relies upon metaphoric language that bends, blends, and blurs the human and transhuman. Arms become branches; the sea is the sweat of the earth; olives give birth to eggs; the ear is a fleshy twig; and so on. Empedocles, too, shows a keen insight into the homology of biological entities by observing the relationship of leaves, hair, feathers, and scales (fr. 82), but in further characterizing these organismic epidermal surfaces and extensions as the "same things," he immediately creates a kind of *be-wildered order* that undermines familiar and expected understandings.[46] The multiplicity and variety of things is not so much "reduced" to an undifferentiated oneness as it is repositioned so as to reveal its similitude.[47] Feathers, scales, hair, and leaves implicitly correspond to four forms of life—bird, fish, mammals, and plants—and represent as well air, water, and earth. (Fire seems to be excluded because organisms cannot literally survive in it.) The cumulative effect of this portrayal is to build up a picture of an animate cosmos in which distinctions between things are graded, labile, mobile, and fluid. Since the physical barriers between all kinds of organisms are theoretically broken down or dissolved, one can more readily comprehend how and why a *daimon* (spirit) in the *Purifications* could conceivably change from the form and corresponding place of a boy or girl to a bush (both earth-dwelling) or to a bird (air-dwelling) or to a fish (water-dwelling) (fr. 117). Empedocles suggests that the parts that compose us—indeed all things—will eventually be broken up, recycled, and reunited as something else. In fact, the first humans are said to spring from the earth, and so we are considered autochthonous beings.

Admittedly, there are a range of related terms and theories that fall into the philosophical orbit or under the conceptual umbrella of panpsychism and the view that all things have a share in mind, including animism (everything possesses soul), hylozoism (all matter is alive), pansensism (everything senses), pantheism (all is God), panentheism (all is *in* God) and panexperientialism (everything experiences). Empedocles' own form of panpsychism appears, as David Skrbina notes, to rely on three overlapping "arguments" for collapsing the sharp distinction between the animate and inanimate and, more pointedly, advocating the position that everything partakes of a modicum of awareness or thought. First, Empedocles appeals to an "indwelling powers" argument whereby everything is claimed to possess noetic qualities or the capacity of thought; second, we find a "continuity" argument involving the notion that if the elements possess soul (*psyche*), so by inference and extension does all they constitute because it is not reasonable or possible to draw a clear line between entities with *psyche* and those without it; and finally, there is a "first principles" argument that views mind as essential—we might say "elemental"—rather than incidental to the universe.[48]

The history of panpsychism is long and involved, but the intuition, argument, or worldview that matter and mind are intimately intertwined—or at least not polar opposites—continues to surface within environmental discourse and to affect debates related to intrinsic and instrumental value in the natural world, the scope and depth of our ethical obligations, and critiques of mechanistic theories of nature, as well as the ontological status of elemental forces and phenomena. There are strands, resonances, or outcroppings of panpsychist views in the outlooks of many indigenous peoples; the works of H. D. Thoreau, Aldo Leopold, and John Muir; and the thought of Charles Hartshorne, Alfred North Whitehead, and Gregory Bateson, among others. Within environmental ethics more properly, J. Baird Callicott's contrasting interpretation of European and North American Indian philosophical perspectives point to the suggestive possibility of a more inclusive ethos toward the land that characterizes elemental entities and forces like wind, water, rock, and earth as participating in the same consciousness that humans experience.[49] In the end, it is likely that panpsychism is not entirely provable or disprovable and that at heart it expresses a kind of ontological sensibility, aesthetic or ethic toward the surrounding world. Skrbina may be right that there is something like a "greater virtue" argument and value to the philosophical framework as well because it encourages a "more integrated, compassionate, and sympathetic cosmos" to the extent it is "life-affirming and life-enhancing" and critical of narrowly mechanistic, manipulative materialistic values, and views of the world.[50] In this regard, Empedocles deserves credit for helping to initiate a robust tradition that endures to the present-day.[51]

Environmental Action

There is reason to believe that Empedocles himself—whom Lucretius extols as "scarce seems of human stock"[52]—actively and physically worked with the four elements so as to effect change and benefits for the human and broader ecological communities. With regard to water, for example, it has been recorded by a number of doxographers that Empedocles was instrumental in slowing a plague by alleviating pollution problems in a local river through the diversion of two streams into its flowing waters. In terms of air, it has been reported that he was able to redirect winds that were damaging crops, possibly by developing an early form of a windbreak. And it has been claimed that he kept alive for nearly a month a woman whose animating breath and vital pulse had failed or were failing.[53] We might also speculate that the reason he climbed Mount Etna, the legendary place of his perishing,[54] was to admire the landscape and to investigate the four elements and their simultaneous interactions: "the great upheaval of earth; air in the winds that constantly sweep the summit; water in the melting ice and snow; and fire in the glowing seething caldera."[55] His actual or mythical death—his "descent" following Orpheus to the underworld—is, in fact, curiously prefigured in one of his own texts when the *daimon* (spirit) is cast from earth into "beams of radiant Sun" (i.e., fire [fr. 115]). Like Plato's "mixing bowl" for the four elements in his dialogue, the *Timeaus*, the volcano (fr. 52) can be seen as a kind of primordial kettle out of which the four ingredients of the world ebb, cycle, and flow, the site of intersection of enveloping and erupting earth, swirling air, molten fire, and cooling or condensing water in the ice caps.[56] Commenting on the anecdote of Empedocles and his death in Etna, Deleuze observes:

> The Presocratics placed thought inside the caverns and life in the deep. They sought the secrets of water and fire. . . . In a deluge of water and fire, the volcano spits up only a single reminder of Empedocles—his lead sandal. To the wings of the Platonic soul the sandal of Empedocles is opposed, proving that he was of the earth, under the earth, and autochthonous.[57]

In certain respects, Empedocles represents a figure as old as—and probably even older than—the philosopher, prophet or priest: namely, the shaman-magician. In this capacity, he combines the as-yet distinguished roles of naturalist, public advisor, magician, reflective thinker, healer, poet, and preacher. Or, to use the words of Empedocles himself, he is among those persons who are "seers at last, and singers of high hymns / Physicians sage, and chiefs o'er earth-born men / Shall they become, whence germinate the gods" (fr. 146). Put briefly, a shaman is an individual who through rigorous mental and physical training (e.g., fasting, solitude, and abstinence) develops a character—often psychologically flexible or deliberately destablized through dissociation—so that he or she acquires new powers (either assumed or real) and is thereby able to pass into other states of consciousness.[58] Through their *askesis* (self-discipline) and resulting experiences, shamans are thought to acquire the art of divination, medicinal magic, extra-normal wisdom, poetic, and religious insight, and the ability to bi-locate so that they can reside simultaneously in different places. Thus, the many anecdotes surrounding Empedocles—including his own claims which in many respects are the source of his legend—of bringing on or forestalling rain, staying the driving winds, and resuscitating the dead, as well as his disappearance from this world into a fiery crater so as to supposedly become a god, prove more comprehensible.

This line of interpretation also helps to explain how he could have written two so seemingly disparate works and, moreover, written philosophy in a poetic style (or vice-versa). Viewed as a shaman or natural magician as well as a natural philosopher, Empedocles' goal is not necessarily to "dominate," "master," or "control" the elements as the classical scholar Hermann Diels has claimed[59] but to understand and facilitate their natural actions and tendencies so as to benefit humans and other creatures, as he may have done in his interactive work with the winds, weather, and waters.[60] Through a kind of "sympathetic magic" that originates in the idea of like seeking like, Empedocles (and the practices he propounds) might be seen as influencing events in the natural world. As a mediating presence between "civilized" humans and "wild" nature, the shaman is theoretically able to commune more freely and clearly than others with animals, trees, rocks, or clouds. Empedocles' remarks regarding a separation of body and soul can be reasonably interpreted, too, as the desire to engage in a form of "travel" to other locations so as to attain wisdom (rather than simply as a form of philosophical dualism as some scholars assert), and his claims of being a bush or a tree can be contextualized in terms of the shaman's attempts at shape-shifting and "becoming other."[61] As Theodore Roszack speculates: "From the shamanic vision-flight we inherit the religious and mythic connotations that cling so stubbornly to all thinking about rising and falling, up and down, light and heavy." Indeed, from the vantage of vision-flight, levity is the basic trajectory of the human soul.[62]

Anticipation of Evolution

In Empedocles' texts, one can discern a faint foreshadowing of the much later theory of evolution and natural selection and, more generally, an acute observation of changes in natural phenomena. In his cosmological "ecology," animal genesis occurs when the force of *philia* (love) increases, and the various parts of creatures are the first to be formed. These are scattered about and "there budded many a head without a neck / And arms were roaming, shoulderless and bare / And eyes that wanted foreheads drifted by / In isolation wandered every limb / Hither and thither seeing union meet / . . . These members fell together where they met / And many a birth besides was then begot / In a long line of ever varied life" (fr. 57–59). The evolutionary process, in short, advances not by divine purpose or intelligent design, as many of his forebears had thought, but through the interplay of the forces of attraction and repulsion exercised on material elements.

In Empedocles' view, the world evolves and the singular elements are transformed into organisms who, or species which, require a fitness in order to reproduce and survive, a point reinforced by Aristotle's interpretation in the *Physics*: "Whenever then all the parts came about just what they would have been if they had come to be for an end, such things survived, being organized spontaneously in a fitting way; whereas those which grew otherwise perished and continue to perish, as Empedocles says his 'many-faced ox-progeny' did."[63] Aristotle takes Empedocles to task for an anti-teleological view of nature that divests it of purpose and direction and presents animal development as fortuitous, although Empedocles' perspective is closer in this regard to most current views of evolutionary theory.[64] Simplicius remarks on this issue as well:

> Empedocles says that during the rule of Love there came into being at random first of all parts of animals such as heads and hands and feet, and then there came together those "ox-kinds with the foreparts of men," while on the other hand "there sprang up," naturally, "men with the heads of oxen," that is, compounded of ox and man. As many of these parts as were fitted together in such a way as to ensure their preservation, became animals and survived, because they fulfilled mutual needs—the teeth tearing and softening food, the stomach digesting it, and the liver converting it into blood. The human head, when it meets a human body, ensures the preservation of the whole, but being inappropriate to the ox-body it leads to its disappearance. All that did not come together according to the right formula perished.[65]

Through a kind of "accidental compounding"—as it has been called—which bears some resemblance to the modern idea of mutation, life evolves.[66] This ancient theory, however much it contains the first rudimentary aspects of the idea of the evolution of life, shows no signs of recognizing the notion that *individuals* within a species must be fit in order to survive. It "evolves" from an entirely different cosmological framework and does not speak in terms of the present (existing) era as did Darwin. Nevertheless, there are significant affinities with and similarities to latter-day ideas, as with other areas of Empedocles' work. One fragment, for example, that begins, "But separate is the birth of human limbs / For 'tis in part in man's" (fr. 63) offers a vague anticipation of modern embryology in that it seems to acknowledge that both sexes supply parts for the possibility of offspring.[67]

Animal Empathy

For Empedocles, humans exist on a par with other creatures, and we are only everlasting insofar as the elements are eternal. We do not own a distinctive soul since entities other than humans, including plants and animals, can possess it as well. "And when as mortals we be loosed apart / we are as nothing" (fr. 15), he writes. The elemental gods, too, are of this world. Nothing stands outside, above, or behind the phenomenal realm. Animals and plants are presented not in terms of a hierarchy—as they are later in Aristotle's thought—but are understood as members of a broad community.[68] Empedocles, however, perceived a great imbalance existing in the world that, in his view, was signaled, first, by perjury and, second, by animal slaughter. Like his Pythagorean brethren, he holds to a strict vegetarianism that precludes the consumption or sacrifice of living things whenever possible. In the *Katharmoi* (*Purifications*), he counsels, in particular, the avoidance of animal flesh and beans, the latter taboo probably based on the similarity in shape to an egg, the source of life. In this regard, there is continuity and no doubt an indirect influence on the contemporary animal rights philosophy and movements.[69] Like Heraclitus, Empedocles also makes a strong plea from empathy against animal sacrifice, calling it a "monstrous crime" (fr. 139) as do many anti-vivisectionists today: "Will ye not cease from this great din of slaughter? / Will ye not see, unthinking as we are, / How ye rend one another unbeknown?" (fr. 136).[70]

Although there are strong similarities in the use of language, the implicit critique of what we now call anthropocentrism, and the desire to extend care and concern to other creatures, it must be acknowledged that the above analogy does break down. Contemporary critics of factory farming and animal experimentation direct their arguments and opposition in the main against repetitive, unnecessary and commercial research rather than less common religious sacrifice. And, in general, they challenge the crowded, cruel, unhealthy, and inhumane conditions in agribusiness rather than individual, small-scale, and subsistence agriculture, and animal husbandry. Even if the critiques are continuous and in many ways compatible, neither of these former practices and institutions existed 2,500 years ago. There are, of course, interesting philosophical and historical ties—as well as tensions—between animal rights views and positions within environmental ethics, although these subjects are not discussed here.[71] On these topics, Empedocles should be seen neither simply as an early animal rights advocate nor as an ancient environmental ethicist. Instead, he is a complex thinker, whose works and orientation cut across a variety of present scientific and philosophical subfields, opening up areas of debate rather than foreclosing them with easy answers.[72]

Empedocles does clearly recommend that we owe other creatures justice because of our kinship with them and a common breath that pervades our beings. But we should inquire critically about Empedocles' image of a golden time when "All things were tame, and gentle toward men / All beasts and birds, and friendship's flame blew fair" (fr. 130). If read literally, this characterization tends to romanticize the natural world, though it also could be seen as providing a needed counterweight to an image of struggle, survival, and ruthless competition, which is surely only a one-dimensional representation of ecological interactions and biological evolution.[73] In this sense, Empedocles sensibility shares some affinities with the much later arguments and ideas of figures such as Ernst Haeckel and Peter Kropotkin. Kropotkin, a nineteenth-century scientist and anarchist, stressed the cooperative, mutualistic, and altruistic aspects of animal and human societies and argued that mutual aid is as important to evolution as competition, thereby providing the basis for a radical theory of human or social ecology.[74] Haeckel, also a nineteenth-century scientist, coined the term *ecology* and investigated—as the word now suggests—the science of relations between organisms and their environment. Like Empedocles, he tended to portray the cosmos as unified, placing humans and nonhuman animals on the same biological and moral levels and depicting the natural world as a relatively benevolent source of wisdom. From Haeckel's perspective, the energy in the universe is constant and matter is immortal, and as a result of the law of the conservation of energy there is no place for an after-life.[75] One may even say, then, that via the direct or indirect influence on the work of such individuals that Empedocles helped to inaugurate an eco-philosophical tradition that continues to inform present day thought.

Environmental Roots

We might locate a more metaphoric ecological tie between an Empedoclean conception of "roots," which cooperatively sustain and regenerate the natural world, and the actual roots of growing plants, which support and nourish life above ground. Presently, ecologists are discovering that plants and their root systems are not as passive, individualistic, or competitive as they had once thought. Through a process known as hydraulic lift, plants ranging from the sugar maple to the sagebrush draw water up during the night with deep earth roots and, rather than storing it for the next day, flush it out through shallow roots into the surrounding ground, watering neighboring plants and helping to maintain a community ecology or local ecosystem.[76] Among other things, this finding—which helps to upset entrenched notions of plant competition—may provide impetus for exploring the role of roots in global water cycling and the shaping of the environment and lead toward ecological models that account more fully for mutualism, cooperation, interaction, and co-participation in nature, as does the "counter-culture" tradition of Empedocles and his literary, philosophical, and scientific heirs.[77] Neil Evernden, for example, following the phenomenological insights of Merleau-Ponty and Heidegger, proposes that we think of organisms in terms of sets of relationships and processes with extended fields of being:

> A tree, we might say, is not so much a thing as rhythm of exchange, or perhaps a centre of organizational forces. Transpiration induces the upward movement of water and dissolved materials, facilitating an inflow from the soil. If we were aware of this rather than of the appearance of a tree-form, we might regard a tree as a centre of a force-field towards which water is drawn. . . . We do not mistake the bark for the dog, but we habitually mistake the shape for the tree.[78]

Ecological Ethos

With respect to the rudiments of an ecological ethos or environmental ethics suggested in Presocratic thought (and Empedocles' works in particular), it may only be present implicitly and as part of totality of general value-terms like *dike* (justice), *time* (honor), *arete* (virtue), and *agathos* (the good). Within Empedocles' worldview, one cannot escape the continuous cosmic cycle of birth and death, although one's soul can conceivably improve its lot by refusing to bring additional suffering and harm into the world. In the surviving fragments, we find a constant cosmic cycling or *recycling* at work, analogous to a fundamental dimension of ecosystem theory that views biological and organic processes in terms of energy flows and material cycles, including the circuits of carbon, nitrogen, oxygen, phosphorous, water, and plant succession.[79] As Empedocles remarks, "this long interchange shall never end" (fr. 17). In fact, his characterization of the condition of the pre-cosmic Sphere is similar to what is now termed *thermodynamic equilibrium*. This state is secured in part through a reliance on a Parmenidean "rule of conservation" of real (i.e., actual) things that guarantees the continuity of life and the indestructibility of the elements. No clear scale of values is posited, although an embedded ethics may lie in his cosmic conception of things, where nature is just and justice is natural. Speaking of Presocratic thought, Gregory Vlastos points out: "Cosmic justice is a conception of nature at large as a harmonious association, whose members observe, or are compelled to observe, the law of the measure. There may be death, destruction, strife, and even encroachment (as in Anaximander). There is justice none the less, if encroachment is invariably repaired and things are reinstated within their proper limit."[80]

Historian Donald Hughes, who has explored the thought of the Pythagoreans and early Greek and Roman philosophy generally for its ecological dimensions, in fact, argues that of all the philosophical viewpoints that began in ancient Greece, Pythagoreanism contains an ethics that on the whole appears to be the most environmental in orientation, in that it is based on a respect for living beings and an organic worldview.[81] And, as we have seen, it is a body of thought that influences Empedocles. Hughes finds in the works of those associated with the Pythagorean School a sensitivity to the natural world that is lacking in earlier and later Greek thought, but he rightly cautions against the doctrine of the separation of body and soul.

Empedocles' Orphic influences are also potentially compatible with—and perhaps contribute to—some nascent schools of environmental ethics. Orpheus, a legendary Greek figure, was often represented pictorially with trees and animals that were attracted to his song. Through music, he was able to impart rhythmic dance to the natural world, to heal others, and even to alter the course of rivers, all abilities that have been associated with great shamans. In this regard, one can find in the musical aspects of the Orphic legacy a relationship to ecological currents in their attention to wholeness, roundness, harmony, and mood.[82] Ranier Maria Rilke has dedicated a series of sonnets to Orpheus' name, offering a kind of phenomenological poetry that celebrates the earth and its inhabitants, beginning with the lines: "A tree ascended there / Oh pure transcendence! / Oh Orpheus sings! Oh tall tree in the ear! / And all things hushed . . . Creatures of stillness crowded from the bright / unbound forest, out of their lairs and nests."[83] Like the Orphics and Pythagoreans, Empedocles advocates a form of metempsychosis (transmigration of the soul)—whereby selves are enwrapped "in unfamiliar tunics of the flesh" (fr. 126)—and claims to have been incarnated as a boy, girl, thicket, bird, and fish. Whether one chooses to believe him or not, the doctrine underscores his universal empathy for all beings, including plants, animals, and humans (both male and female).

Crafting Nature

Finally, Empedocles' writings suggest indirectly and latently an early understanding of how the notion of nature—more exactly, the elements—is represented as crafting (constructing) and maybe even in some sense "fashioned" or "fabricated" itself, although *prima facie* the four *rhizomata* must be regarded as eternal and ungenerated in his work.[84] Here, we are provided with a small bridge between ancient and contemporary controversies concerning the status of "nature." Throughout the surviving fragments, Empedocles repeatedly relies on images and metaphors drawn from the sphere of arts and crafts to describe the four roots, the perishable combinations of things formed of them, and the natural world more generally. Earth, air, fire, and water are compared with paints and dyes in linen. The elements are kneaded together in dough, and those "ingredients" that do not mesh or coagulate well reject one another as would water and oil. Analogies from the realm of *techne* (art, craft, or technology) are repeatedly asserted, including those involving cooking, the making of cheese. and metalwork as well as images connected with wheels, lanterns, and the clepsydra.[85]

In this sense, Empedocles' *philia* (love) anticipates Plato's Demiurge (*Demiourgos*), who is literally a "worker of the people" and one who constructs the natural world in the manner of a manual worker and often more particularly as a metallurgist. To make vision possible, Empedocles' *philia* similarly "rivets" roots together for use as eyes. *Philia*, too, adds water to earth like a potter and sets the resulting product in an oven. "As Kypris [love], after watering Earth with Rain / Zealous to heat her . . . To speed of Fire that then she might grow firm" (fr. 73). The elements, then, are not generated but they are still "fashioned"—at least in the manner of cosmetic decoration—when they are given color, qualities of moisture or heat, and the like. Recall as well that the *rhizomata* are personified as individual gods. For Empedocles, they are real, eternal entities but nonetheless still seen through fallible, fabricated, and perhaps even "fabricating" human lenses, although they are clearly not fashioned by human hands because Empedocles appears to reject what environmentalists now call "strong anthropocentrism." The elements are accordingly socialized, as they are in many early cosmological and mythical views where they are presented in terms of human relations involving sex, warfare, and domestic marriage. Because they are considered divine and eternal, they are not fully (meta)physically "constructed" as they will be in Plato's *Timaeus*.

In this regard, one particularly important fragment can be read in two ways: "Nothing that is has a birth (*physis*) / But only mixing and parting of the mixed / And birth (*physis*) is but a name given them by men" (fr. 8).[86] *Physis* here could mean *genesis* as opposed to death (*thanatos*), and this is the sense that most translators have followed. But it is also possible to see *physis* in terms of *ousia* (substance) as Aristotle recognizes in quoting this fragment,[87] and so to read the remark as calling into question the essential constitution or nature of all things.[88] One way to construe this fragment is that temporary compounds such as flesh and bone do not have a *physis* (nature) themselves; only the four *rhizomata* possess an immortal *physis*. We must rely—at least in part—on convention and human nomenclature to provide us with an account of the stuff (or *Urstoff*) of things, and minimally the perishable mixing compounds (*thneta*). The very next fragment, in fact, begins, "When they [the roots] have mixed in the form of a man . . . then people say that this is to be born," with Empedocles adding that "I follow the custom" so as to use such language himself, even if it is not wholly accurate (fr. 13).

Thus, although Empedocles seeks to speak of and articulate the unchanging way of things—eternal elements and an abiding nature (*physis*)—he must pass through an inexact and often erring *nomos* (human convention) to arrive there. And the equivocal meaning of the fragment in question seems to convey some of the "undecidability" of this enterprise—to use a phrase of Jacques Derrida—working against the seemingly overt intention of the author so as to undermine a stable textual claim.[89] Indeed, in one sense, the roots do come into being insofar as they grow from one into many and vice versa. The broader matter at issue here, however, concerns the complex *physis/nomos* debate that emerged in Greek thought and the question of the invention, discovery, or convention of nature. Historians, philosophers, playwrights, and poets all contributed to this controversy, with figures like Antiphon, Callicles in Plato's *Gorgias*, Thrasymachus in the *Republic*, and Thucydides lining up in defense of *physis* (nature) as an evaluative standard for individuals or the community, and those like Critias, Protagoras, and Iamblichus coming to the aid of *nomos* (custom, law, convention).[90] In discussing the notion of nature and its tension with *nomos*, G.E.R. Lloyd sums up the matter well and argues persuasively that early writers or theorists like Hesiod, Homer, Plato, and Aristotle "did not (so much) discover nature—like Columbus hitting America." Instead, "they created, they invented, their own distinct and divergent ideas, often in direct and explicit confrontation with their rivals."[91] The paradox arose—and still remains—that *physis* is supposed to represent what is simply and objectively there in the world and can thereby be taken for granted, but what exactly that comprises is contested in every possible manner: scientifically, morally, and politically. As seen in Chapter two, these concepts and concomitant disagreements persist to the present day, where we find staunch advocates on both sides of the spectrum, especially regarding the question of the social construction of nature.

Over time, the elements are transferred, as Sidney Feshbach has observed, from an explanatory notion within natural science to an organizing idea within human culture. For Empedocles, the four *rhizomata* "appear together as a unit, with each element presenting a polarity in which *destruction* is countermanded with *construction*: e.g., the unwearying winds which lay waste the cultivated fields are checked and, implicitly farming and harvesting are renewed."[92] But Feshbach may overstate the case that Empedocles is not really engaged in direct ways with the forces of the natural world because his focus is on comprehending them solely through "organizing ideas and principles," specifically the framework of the four elements.[93] As we have seen, the poet and philosopher was also very likely a man of practical action and not only just a speculative thinker. We might even say that through his work, nature and *nomos* are delicately interfused and balanced. In multiple ways then—from his claims about and undertakings with the physical world to his ethical and religious orientation—Empedocles' seminal ideas, suggestive metaphors and empathetic sensibility open up potential bridges to contemporary environmental issues even if he lives in a very different era from our own and works under another set of circumstances. Let us turn to look lastly at his value for understanding one widespread ecological problem.

Purity and Pollution

One of the most visible contemporary concerns in Western society and recent environmental philosophy and politics in particular is pollution. Indeed, since the 1960s with the public policy stances and written work of Rachel Carson, Barry Commoner, and many local and grass-roots groups that have called attention to this issue, pollution is one of the most serious problems that confronts modern culture and the natural environment.[94] We are regularly warned—and usually with good reason—of the dangers that transform and threaten water (e.g., wells, aquifers, rivers, oceans, and human reservoirs), air (e.g., the atmosphere and ozone layer), and earth (e.g., topsoil, forests, and beaches). In other words, three of the vital four elements are under sustained assault. And, if we include the ecological and political problems associated with the domestication of fire as technology, we can add the fourth of the classical elements to this list.

Landfill leakage, acid rain, littering, excessive noise levels, oil spills, toxic chemical waste, auto exhaust, and factory smoke are problems of the first order of social and political importance.[95] We cannot review the facts and figures here, although it is necessary to point out that the dangers are pronounced and worldwide in prevalence, necessitating "glocal" (global and local) and "intermestic" (international and domestic) responses.[96] For example, leading hydrologists estimate that as much as one fifth of the world's population does not have regular access to unpolluted drinking water.[97] Throughout the United States, aquifers that support human and animal life are under threat because of the destruction of wooded regions. Each year, too, ships and pipelines *legally* dump hundreds of millions of tons of waste in the seas and coastal waters. Where earlier historical cultures had on the whole a more direct daily contact with water in its transition from source to use (e.g., the bucket and well or washing in the stream)—and so better understood the necessity of respecting it and recognizing the dangers of disrupting its flows and content—we have largely lost this connection with the elemental processes, which have become more and more concealed.

Concurrent with the increasingly visible spread and pervasive existence of *physical* pollution itself (e.g., landfills, smog, petrochemicals, noise, and runoff waste), we find that the examination of pollution as a *theoretical* (i.e., moral, religious, and political) discourse remains quite hidden and nearly invisible. As it turns out, however, pollution is both a conceptual and a physical problem, having its historical origins in ancient philosophy, religion, and myth. Pollution, in fact, seems to be an idea that is endemic to all societies such that our own notions of contamination are not so distant from those of so-called primitive cultures.[98] All communities appear to identify what is threatening and hostile to the surrounding environment and their own way of life through the development of a framework of connected physical and symbolic locations where what is not considered to be in its proper place is a danger to the network, system or order of things. "Pollution" and "purity" must be viewed as inextricably intertwined. What constitutes pollution needs to be seen in contrast to what counts as unadulterated, clean, pristine, unblemished, virgin, or pure.

In this sense, the etymology of pollution (from the Latin, *pollutionem* and *polluere*, to soil), meaning corruption, profanation, and desecration—and suggesting that which is dirty, stained, tainted, or befouled—is instructive.[99] In the Greek, *miasma* (noun), *miaino* (verb), and *miaros* (adjective) all connote something that stains the blood, implying as well ritual impurity. For the ancient Greeks, pollution tended to be less a quantifiable phenomenon—as it is today with the use of pollution ratios (e.g., parts per billion), indices, allowances, taxes, and credits—and more a qualitative human experience. Due to the gravity associated with such acts of violation—which were thought to bring on divine retribution in many cases—quite a number of ancient texts recorded taboos against various types of pollution.[100]

Many forest groves, for example, were considered sacred such that one was not permitted to chop down trees, despoil the ground, or remove brush from these areas. Prohibitions were established so as to protect such diverse "eco-steries" (in contrast with singular sites of the sacred such as churches and "mona-steries"). Hesiod warned against relieving oneself of bodily fluids and other discharge into flowing waters, conveying not only a prohibition backed by religious injunction but also imparting a measure of insight regarding health practices and environmental awareness in the process.[101] Because the natural world was viewed as alive and full of "elemental gods"—as characterized by Thales or Empedocles—it was a direct affront to or an attack on these deities and their notions of order to selfishly, unthoughtfully, or wantonly disturb the environment. Such actions of social and cosmic injustice could lead, in turn, to natural disasters because of the perceived close linkages between humans, the natural world, and the gods, who meted out justice and retribution. The importance attached to natural place was such that a reorganization of the elemental masses—especially the transformation of water (sea) into earth (land)—was considered an arrogant threat to Zeus, who had originally overseen and ordained their division and arrangement. Thus, Herodotus reports that when the inhabitants of Cnidus, who had attempted to run a canal from their city to Asia Minor, met with repeated injuries, they eventually discontinued their work on learning that the oracle at Delphi had responded to their inquiry with the admonitory counsel: "Do not fence off the isthmus; do not dig. / Zeus would have made an island had he willed it."[102]

The actual ecological problems of Greek civilization were manifold, even if they were a far cry from what modern societies now experience. Then, as now, pollution took the form of an assault on the elements as places and environmental conditions. Mining technologies and the timber industry in particular adversely affected air, earth, and water. The quest for mercury, lead, and arsenic—which contributed to bone, brain, and blood diseases—often caused streams to be redirected, dried up, or contaminated. The increasing removal of forests visibly scarred the landscape. Herodotus, for example, took note of the fact that an entire mountain was upended in search of gold. Emerging metallurgy emitted smoke and poisonous gases into the air in addition to the wood and charcoal burned as fuel. And high noise levels were often reached in urban centers.[103]

In Empedocles' writings especially and early Greek thought more broadly, one can locate a valuable place of inquiry and point of departure for shedding some light on our own dilemmas about this subject. As observed earlier, the ancient Greeks themselves had problems with both physical pollution and bodily or psychic impurity, and they tended to convey their concerns in moral and religious language. In the *Timaeus,* for example, Plato remarks on the pollution of the part of the soul that is divine and recognizes the separation from others that must occur as a result of *miasma,* an action resembling the isolation of Empedocles' *daimon.* In the *Euthyphro,* the priest who is prosecuting his own father, and whom Socrates is interrogating, insists that justice is so important and, correspondingly actions of pollution so heinous, that it does not matter whether the perpetrator is one's relative: "The pollution is the same if you knowingly keep company with such a man and do not cleanse yourself and him by bringing him to justice" (4c). And in the *Critias,* Plato comments on the physical degradation that had been wrecked on the forests, soil, springs, and streams of his Attic homeland to provide wood for furniture, fuel, temple roofs, and weapons and, especially, to fill the increasing demand for ships. He observes that "by comparison with the original territory, what is left is . . . the skeleton of a body wasted by disease; the rich, soft soil has been carried off and only the bare framework of the district left."[104]

Empedocles repeatedly counsels against pollution, and his own actions such as the clearing of a plague-ridden stream attest to his commitment in this regard. The title, too, of the *Katharmoi* refers to the process of purifying (or purging) oneself via *katharsis*, a term with both medical and religious dimensions that we find among the Pythagoreans,[105] in Socratic discourse and Platonic dialogues,[106] and in Aristotle's work.[107] Because of impure actions, bodily defilement, and a reliance on strife, Empedocles suggests that a culpable individual (*daimon*) will be hounded by the four elements: "Air hunts them onward to the Sea" which "disgorges them on Land" and then "Earth will spue toward beams of radiant Sun" which "will toss them back to whirling Air" (fr. 115). Like their cosmic rule, the four *rhizomata* take turns in exacting justice for the polluting deeds against the cosmos and, in essence, against the four divine and personified elements themselves. Empedocles implies that the guilty individual will be punished through rebirth into the ongoing cycle and will not be at home in his or her element as a result. Punishment assumes a personal tone in the *Purifications*. But the same process is in operation in both works, as evidenced by the fact that Empedocles refers at crucial moments to a broad "oath" that governs cosmic things. In each instance, this invocation occurs after the reign of *philia*. It is bloodshed of humans or animals especially that brings on the wrath of the elements, a point that assumes additional importance because of the special significance attributed to blood in *On Nature*, where it is presented as the seat of the soul and the site of thought and perception.[108]

The banishment of the *daimon* (spirit) for his polluting crimes follows the tradition in Athens and Sparta of exiling from the city those convicted of murder.[109] In Greek tragedy, there are numerous instances of the four elements collectively, singularly or in tandem rejecting a person who is responsible for a heinous, polluting act and hence unworthy of their presence. For example, in Sophocles' most well-known play, Oedipus, having killed his father (parricide) and slept with his mother (incest), is sent inside by Creon away from the sun, "the holy rain," earth, and the light.[110] In Euripides' *Medea*, a visceral disgust is shown toward Medea because she is still able to see the earth and sun after she kills her own children.[111] This idea, as expressed in Greek legal theory and poetry, not only reveals the necessity of responsibility to other humans, but it suggests our accountability to the elements and the environment. Just as the epic heroes must accept the consequences of their actions, so must Empedocles, other ancient Greeks and, by extension, we (post)moderns as well.

We can further read Empedocles as suggesting that our own era is one of excess pollution due to our continual reliance on strife, bloodshed, and disrespect for other life forms, including not simply plants and animals but the elements as well. This view is in accordance with Empedocles' claim that the present age is one in which strife has the upper hand. As purifying rituals, Empedocles recommends forms of abstinence, asceticism, and self-discipline, especially the avoidance of bloodshed and the embrace of vegetarianism. If we are to heed any of his wisdom, we need to be aware, however, that *purification* can eventuate—at least potentially—in a fanatical *Puritanism*, or even worse in attempts to "clean up" and expunge "impure elements" when treating so-called pollution. On this point, individuals in environmental movements themselves should take mindful note. Within these movements, there are both weak (basically innocuous) currents and strong (potentially noxious) strains of asceticism, moral hypochondria, and self-proclaimed purity.[112] These tendencies have sometimes displayed themselves in forms of monasticism, quietism, neo-stoicism, uncritical primitivism, and romanticism at one end of the spectrum to a willingness to embrace forms of coercion or a facile and reactionary rejection of everything "modern" at the other end of the continuum due to the perceived urgency of the situation (a "Leviathan or oblivion" perspective).[113] In large part because of the waste and excess (read: pollution) generated by industrial cultures, overdeveloped countries, and consumption-oriented economies, environmental movements have fostered countervailing and understandable tendencies to emphasize simplicity of living, avoidance of nonrenewable materials, and a reliance on small-scale, local, and decentralist technologies in which one can trace the flows of energy and facilitate the re-use of material resources.

What is also at issue with pollution, then, is the idea of order itself in its ontological, environmental, social, and political dimensions. And when environmentalists and industrialists argue, it concerns as much contamination or preservation of ideas and ideals of order, including "nature" and the "natural" and "proper or "improper," as it does disagreements over levels of material contamination. As anthropologist Mary Douglas has shown through a consideration of primitive and modern societies, dirt, defilement, and pollution are connected with the perception of disorder, and attempts to eliminate them should be viewed more as ways of organizing the environment than as actions originating in fear. She argues that reflection on dirt entails meditation on "the relation of order to disorder, being to nonbeing, form to formlessness, life to death."[114] Thus, rituals associated with purity or impurities are attempts to forge personal or social unity in experience. Dirt is essentially matter that has lost its place, and it should not be considered a unique, isolated phenomenon. "Where there is dirt, there is system. Dirt is the by-product of a systematic ordering and classification of matter, in so far as ordering involves rejecting *inappropriate elements*."[115]

In this sense, we might say that whereas industry has tended to set itself up as representatives and interpreters of human law so as to admit new kinds and combinations of "dirt" and to reject the "elements" that they no longer find appropriate, environmentalists have tried to establish themselves as arbiters of an existing or older order—sometimes appealing to "nature's laws"—so as to question or exclude such forms of "pollution" and to protect the place of the "elements."[116] Beneath the relatively clean surface, this debate often seems to center around ethical and political issues concerning the quality of life in a given community, standards of living and competing ideas of the good life and not simply scientific discussion about acceptable amounts of pollution.[117] Increasingly, we must also be aware of the ethnic and racial dimensions to the problem of pollution (and purity) both in terms of ideas and sites of dumping—which inordinately affect the poor, minorities, and the people of developing or "underdeveloped" countries—and attempts at "cleansing" or cleaning up social pollution.[118] This issue is especially important because the racial, gendered, or animalized "other" often has been segregated, violated, or dominated through conceptual and practical social pollution taboos and an association with a "threatening" wildness or "brute" nature.[119] As one green literary critic puts it, "Ecology has introduced a sense of radical contingency into political thought. It is not the *polis*, but pollution, which now acts ironically as the materialized 'universal' through which power and freedom may be mediated. Questions of race, gender and class are never very far away from questions of who is dumping what onto whom."[120]

In the course of examining the discourse of pollution, we should be careful not to view the elements or nature as "polluted" by the mere presence of human activity and thought because humans often play a "co-constructive" epistemological and physical role in this process.[121] We also need to engage continually in a critical discussion about what actually constitutes pollution; what is being made less pure; who defines these terms; and who (or what) is responsible for creating pollution or eliminating it. There are clearly different implications for homogeneous cultures than for more heterogeneous societies, in which perceptions often differ sharply as to what makes up dirt, waste, and refuse. Empedocles highlights for us the problem in a more closely knit culture than our own, but in the process he helps us to come to terms with our own perceived relations to matter "out of place" by pointing to the larger elemental dimensions of this issue that involve order and disorder.

Finally, with regard to the ancient Greeks, we would do well to keep in mind the image of Hygeia, a personification of Athena and the inspiration for our word for "hygiene." In this figure of wisdom, we can discern a source that suggests that people can remain healthy in body and mind when they use their reason, respect their physical surroundings, and extend concern to others as they would to themselves. These ideas, too, are advanced in a less abstract way by the Hippocratic writers who reveal how our well-being is dependent deeply on the environment, climate, and terrestrial elements.[122]

The Rhizomes of Deleuze and Guattari

Before turning to Plato's theory of the elements, we need to raise the issue in a preliminary manner whether there is another more contemporary way to make a critical recovery of—or return to—the elemental "roots" as envisioned by Empedocles.

Recently, root images and attendant metaphors have fallen into disfavor as they have been critiqued in some philosophical circles, especially those associated with post-structuralism. Jacques Derrida, for example, argues: "if a text always gives itself a certain representation of its own roots, those roots live only by that representation, by never touching the soil, so to speak. Which undoubtedly destroys their *radical essence*, but not the necessity of their *racinating function*." He elaborates:

> To say that one always interweaves roots endlessly, bending them to send down roots among the roots, to pass through the same points again, to redouble old adherences, to circulate among their differences, to coil around themselves or to be enveloped one in the other, to say that text is never anything about a *system of roots*, is undoubtedly to contradict at once the concept of system and the pattern of the root.[123]

This kind of challenge, in turn, has begun to influence positions within environmental philosophy as such claims are taken up and debated.[124] Even if fire, air, water, and earth are no longer accepted reasonably as completely unchanging entities in an ontological sense or as indivisible chemical elements, we cannot afford to reject them altogether as conditions, places, and forces that are fundamental to our life-world, perception, and language, as well as the surroundings of other beings. How might we reinterpret and reconceive them so as to question their philosophical status while maintaining their environmental and political relevance? One possibility—among others to be explored later—is suggested by the post-structuralist work of Deleuze and Guattari.

Like Empedocles, Deleuze, and Guattari develop the concept of the rhizome in *A Thousand Plateaus*, a rhizomatic text itself that continues a line of flight initiated in their earlier work, *Anti-Oedipus*. For them, however, rhizomes are clearly distinct from roots and trees and their accompanying epistemology of hierarchical systems above or basic foundations below (e.g., Plato, Descartes, and Kant), which they criticize as oppressive. "We're tired of trees. We should stop believing in trees, roots, and radicles," they write. "They've made us suffer too much." In their view, we live an arborescent culture—from biology to linguistics, from anatomy to theology and all of philosophy[125]—which is founded on tree and root metaphors.[126] "Nothing is beautiful or loving or political aside from underground stems and aerial roots, adventitious growths and rhizomes."[127] Because rhizomes are subterranean stems such as bulbs or tubers that can be connected to anything else, they differ from trees and roots that plot points or establish an order or a structure (e.g., Chomsky's grammatical trees). The two models of thought, language, and writing however, are not completely opposed even if they are considered to be different given that one can find "knots of arborescence" in some rhizomes and "rhizomatic offshoots" in some roots.[128]

In contrast to roots and trees, rhizomes are anti-genealogical, nonhierarchical, a-centered, nonsignifying multiplicities that are made of "plateaus" that are connected to other multiplicities. They are maps, not tracings; associated flows rather than points or linear movements; becomings not imitations. Unlike Empedocles' *rhizomata*, they are not eternal or divine. Rhizomes are animated by desire not obedience or command (as in the "command trees" of information science). They are nomadic conjunctions (and + and + and) with no beginning or end. Like an underground bulb, they are a middle overflowing in all directions. But by—and through—extension, rhizomes can be (or, rather, *become*) animals that move in packs or deterritorialized "colonies" (such as rats and ants); plants that spread wildly and freely (like weeds, potatoes, couchgrass, and crabgrass); heterogeneous entities that deterritorialize and reterritorialize one another (e.g., the orchid and the wasp); viruses that link with other animals;; music that sends out lines of flight in all directions;cities (e.g., Amsterdam, with its stem-canals), and so on.[129]

Mindful of the significance of tree, root, and rhizome metaphors, Deleuze and Guattari identify several kinds of books. First, there is the classic root-book that develops by binary logic and imitates or mirrors the world, being derived from the tree as the image of the cosmos or the root as the image of a world-tree (e.g., the Bible as Book of books). A second kind of book is based on a radicle-system or fascicular root in which the main root has been aborted or its end been destroyed so that a multiplicity of new roots can graft onto it while a shattered unity nevertheless remains (e.g., William Burroughs' cut-up texts, Nietzsche's aphorisms, or works by Joyce). A third and alternative image is provided implicitly by the writers of the text they collectively produce—"since each of us was several, there was already quite a crowd"—which makes use of nearly everything that comes into their sights and whose plateaus (chapters) can be played (read) like a record or CD in any order. Like a rhizome, the text makes connections to geologic, literary, philosophical, biological, technological, psychoanalytical, and other resources. Rhizomatics, too, distinguishes itself by its relation to desire, rather than power, which occurs where rhizomes harden and crystallize into roots. The nomad, like the rhizome, breaks with Oedipal forces—for example, God, father, and country. She, he, and it are opposed to State thought, which channels and controls desire and flows of all kinds (money, people, capital, etc.). Their lines of flight can be shattered or ruptured but such lines remain affirmative and creative, not only resistant as in Foucault's micro-analysis of power.[130]

It might therefore be possible to re-read and *re-route*—rather than *re-root*—Empedocles' *rhizomata* away from a form of philosophical essentialism and toward a pragmatic environmentalism and maybe even to reconsider an entire philosophical, literary, and ecological tradition of the elements.[131] What Deleuze and Guattari appear to argue is that the so-called "Book of Nature" is a work of human fiction, without real author and authority, lacking foundations, and absent true origins and originary elements or "roots." Despite Empedocles' claims, rhizomes—which Deleuze and Guattari construe much more broadly than the Presocratic thinker—are always already in the process of change, transition, and becoming, and in this regard at least they are more like the elements of Plato (chapter four) and Aristotle (chapters five and six) which undergo transformation. We can even raise the bold possibility that various entities "rhizomatically" become-other—evolve, change, or morph into creatures and forms that dwell in or embody earth, air, and water. They might do so by, for example, acknowledging their existing places within elemental flows, viscosities, frequencies, intersections, and exchanges of which they partake and belong or by actively situating themselves in these elemental regions.

With our feet hurrying across the porous ground, our bodies planted in a hole, or our torsos planted prone on a shifting beach, we already are part of the territorial tracings and movements of earth. With our heads immersed in the thickness of the atmosphere or our lungs and limbs engaged with the swirling winds, we repeatedly breathe, think, and dream in the regions of the air. With our bodies thirsting and consuming, pumping and perspiring, absorbing and ejaculating, floating and swimming in various fluids and their flows, we are constantly mixing with water. And with our backs basking in the sun or our fingers and hands extended with a burning cigarette, candle, or blowtorch, we are involved increasingly with the play and power of fire. In this sense, we are rhyzomatic (rhyz-somatic) organisms—"rhyz-orgs" one might say—entities making elemental linkages, affinities, and connecting lines of flight through symbiosis, seduction, alliance, and contagion. When we consider the degree to which we have become cybernetic organisms (cyborgs), this tendency to interact with other elemental realms is altered and magnified significantly through prosthetic attachments, even if it is mediated frequently and less than direct.[132] The use of scuba gear or jet skis, for example, can be seen as way of becoming-fish or becoming-waterbug, respectively, as the lungs and feet are extended to make aquatic breathing and movement possible. When traveling in planes, rockets, and submarines or through underground caverns, mines, and tunnels, we literally leave the soiled surface of the planet and are coursing through the air, water, and earth itself like birds, eels, or worms. In these senses, we are bulbous, many-directional rhizomes, branching upward, downward, sideward, and wayward into elemental zones.

Deleuze/Guattari, like Empedocles, then, provide for new ways of seeing the interrelations between humans and nonhumans and their surrounding environments in terms of a multiplicity of modes and moments in which living forms alter their characteristics and appearance. Whereas Empedocles suggests the things inherent in placial change or shamanic flight and holds to the eternality and immutability of the four elements, Deleuze and Guattari bespeak the potentialities existing in "rhizomorphing," shape-shifting, and becoming-other of both the elements themselves (or nature) and human beings. Like *A Thousand Plateaus*, Empedocles' two works move in multiple, overlapping, and seemingly contradictory ways, making connections in disparate spaces and places: to poetry, embryology, cosmology, physics, zoogony, politics, and environmental pragmatics. In many respects, they are rhizomatic texts themselves, not attempts to create or reflect an existing "Book of Nature." The power of Empedocles' four *rhizomata* is not monarchical but poly-archical, even if still inured to elemental gods who, however, are not Oedipalizing entities. As a biological image and metaphor, rhizomes—like roots—already suggest the ability to grow and change, to reverse directions and branch out to new regions, even as Empedocles' specific language seeks to contain this apparently inevitable "contamination" (leakage, seepage, and creepage) in an animate world with polysemous or indeterminate meaning. At many points in Empedocles' cosmology, there is in fact, a mixing, intermixing, and commingling of earth, air, fire, and water so as to form heterogeneous places and hermaphroditic creatures. As elemental entities ourselves, Empedocles thus provides one basis for believing in our ability to become-other in a manner similar to that suggested by more recent, post-structuralist thinkers. And if we reread the *rhizomata* with Deleuze and Guattari in mind, we can potentially "weed out" and extirpate the unwanted aspects of root metaphors and admit the possibility of elemental change.

Deleuze and Guattari are both more *and* less "radical" than Empedocles. On the one hand, they develop a new view of philosophy as practice, which conceives its task as the creation of new concepts, one that nullifies beginnings and endings, undermines and overthrows ontology. On the other hand, they perform an up-rooting, deracinating operation—removing both root and reason, or *ratio*—on those philosophies that rely on false foundations, fictitious origins, or fabricated roots. In the process, they offer an alternative notion of evolution, which Empedocles helped to introduce into intellectual history. They argue that evolutionary thought rids itself of a linear ordering in favor of an evolutionary tree but that it now needs to abandon the model of the tree with its idea of descent.

> Under certain conditions, a virus can connect to germ cells and transmit itself as the cellular gene of a complex species; moreover it can take flight, move into the cells of an entirely different species, but not without bringing with it "genetic information" from the first host. . . . Evolutionary schemas would no longer follow models of arborescent descent going from the least to the most differentiated, but instead of a rhizome operating immediately in the heterogeneous and jumping from one already differentiated line to another.[133]

Like Empedocles, their view of evolution is nonteleological, although they place additional emphasis on the claim that it is nondeterministic as well.[134] Deleuze and Guattari stress the significance of symbioses in this process, greatly extending Empedocles' notion of attraction (like to like) and the forces of *philia* (love) to include beings of different kingdoms with no conceivable filiation.[135] Their notions of "becoming-animal"—through, among other ways, sorcery—and even *becomings-elementary*, -molecular or -cellular are especially relevant to an understanding of the elements, the environment and Empedocles.[136]

Deleuze, in particular, espouses a kind of "naturalism" but not one that opposes nature to human culture or custom. Instead, it is influenced by the thought of empiricism, pragmatism, and immanent causality. It challenges philosophical orientations governed by the supernatural, transcendental, and dualistic, finding in the natural world (which might also work against itself) a basis for a rhizomatic view of evolution that underscores the importance of diversity, the insights of ethology, and the significance of a milieu, which is defined in surprisingly ecological terms. Rhizomes are clearly greater than four in number, but they are still earth-bound becomings. In fact, Deleuze and Guattari develop what they term *geo-philosophy*, pointing out how thinking always occurs in a relationship with earth and territory. "Thinking consists in stretching out a plane of immanence that absorbs the earth (or rather, 'adsorbs' it)."[137] Earth is not simply one element among the existing others but instead that which "brings together all the elements within a single embrace while using one or another of them to deterritorialize territory."[138] Finally, like Empedocles, their "ecology," too, is bound closely with a radically democratic view of politics,[139] one that emphasizes the interrelated areas of what Guattari calls environmental ecology, social ecology, and mental ecology.[140]

In this way, we can observe a long, if discontinuous and serpentine, thread from ancient Greek philosophy and religion to Continental theory that rekindles, animates and transforms the elements as rhizomes and makes suggestive connections to the encompassing earth. We have attempted to interpret and extend Empedocles' thought in ways that are compatible with and true to the spirit, if not the elemental letters, of his poetic works and to make creative and constructive links to the present. Empedocles' works offer us more a philosophical and poetic sensibility than an exact science of ecological relations; more an ethical disposition and example that we might debate or cautiously emulate—as well as improvise with and improve on—than a moral map we should faithfully follow. By returning critically to ecological origins in Presocratic thought, we may observe some of the historical "roots" of Western perceptions of the natural world and, given time and patience, perhaps eventually witness the flowering of this ancient wisdom in contemporary environmental actions.

Interstice: Ice and Snow

> Winter is refuge and deathbed, monastery and ivory tower, cave and ghost.
>
> —Gretel Ehrlich, *The Future of Ice*

> Whoever will be an inquirer into Nature let him resort to a conservatory of Snow or Ice.
>
> —Francis Bacon, *Sylva Sylvarum*

"Ice," Thoreau once announced, "is a fit subject for contemplation."[1] Perhaps this is so because it seems to refract back not just our physical images but to encourage mental ruminations—our very own reflections—radiating them in return in slightly altered form to their points of origination, enchanting us like a mirror but denying us entrance like an inscrutable stone. As with fire and water, ice possesses a curious coterie of paradoxical qualities. Covering a tenth of the Earth's land and slightly less of the planet's oceans, it is both fragile and extremely strong; rock solid but slipping easily into liquidity. Ice is also in its own way quite "hot," always lurking relatively near its melting point and floating as well in its own melt, the juice of its disintegration. As Mariana Gosnell tersely puts it:

> It is more brittle than glass. It can flow like molasses. It can support the weight of a C-5A transport plane. A child hopping on one leg can break through it. It can last 20,000 years. It can vanish in seconds. It can carve granite. It can trace the line of a windowpane scratch. It can kill peach buds. It can preserve mammoths for centuries, peas for months, human hearts for hours.[2]

Ice, of course, assumes many garbs and guises, existing as the most common of more than a dozen possible solid phases of water and transmuting itself as well into an earthen mineral or the celestial rings of Saturn. From ice cubes and icicles to rime and glaciers, ice is a shape-shifting and protean substance. As frozen rain, it tethers itself to the gables of a house or dangles delicately from tree branches so as to trigger a kaleidoscopic display of silver light. As a continuous sheet, it blankets over like translucent cement an entire aquatic world for months at a time. Some scientists even believe that the first life on earth may have been birthed slowly by way of water molecules that hitched a ride through the cosmos with ice-encrusted comets before crashing to our planet. If stone, iron, and bronze are each honored with an era in human history, ice belongs to the ages, likely to return again and again to encase and preserve the geologic and cultural jewels of our planet like fossils buried in amber. Such is its elemental importance.

If we stretch language to its embodied limits, ice almost seems to possess a melodic, moody, or melancholic voice. For anyone who has resided along a river that freezes in winter and breaks up in spring, the sound of it murmuring is quite memorable. The first tide of vibrations to register upon your senses is the heaving groans: the friction and frisson, the clanking and creaking moans. Birth pangs. Smooth serene silence crackles; something seems to be hatching. In "The Rime of the Ancient Mariner," Coleridge speaks of ice itself conversing: "It cracked and growled, and roared and / howled / Like noises in a swound!"[3] Indeed, the expressive grunts, sighs and pings of ice have inspired songs and whole concerts. For example, the British Antarctic Survey commissioned Peter Maxwell Davies' "Antarctic Symphony" on the fiftieth anniversary of Ralph Vaughan Williams' "Symphonia Antarctica" (1953), which conveys the raw wonder, deep mystery and frigid chill of this ghostly realm, including the thunderous movements of icebergs. Of the polar world, Admiral Richard Byrd proclaimed:

> There is no other music like the toneless music of millions of years of accumulated silence, through which come bars of unearthly colours. There is no need for ears to hear the fugues played on this ice organ. Here nature has set aside for man a domain of beauty and inspiration such as he cannot know elsewhere on this planet.[4]

Indeed, given that less than three percent of its landscape is defined by outcroppings of rock, Antarctica is without much exaggeration a continent constructed almost entirely of one substance fused to itself and to the elemental world assembled about it. It is as if water were seeking to build an intricate cathedral—part architecture, part sculpture, part glorious throne—of, by, around, and to itself. Here, ice links "land to land, land to sea, sea to air, air to land, ice to ice," notes Stephen Pyne.[5] The atmosphere in Antarctica is made of ice vapor and clouds; the hydrosphere consists of seas and streams of ice; and the lithosphere is formed of ice plateaus and hills. As Pyne proceeds to detail, there exists a vast hierarchy and tapestry in this southernmost sphere from icebergs, sea ices, and coastal ices to mountain ices, ground ices, polar plateau ices,, and finally atmospheric ices. A brief sampling of one kind of sea ice includes "pack ice, ice floes, ice rinds, ice hummocks, ice ridges, ice flowers, ice stalactites, pancake ice, frazil ice, grease ice, congelation ice, infiltration ice, undersea ice, vuggy ice, new ice, old ice, brown ice, rotten ice."[6]

At the other end of the globe lies the great ice of the north, a region that resembles a desert in its apparent austerity, calmness, and barrenness but that suddenly becomes more vibrant with unexpected shifts in weather, changes in the tundra, or the appearance of harp seals, caribou, and flocks of seabirds. In *Arctic Dreams,* Barry Lopez describes his experiences at this pole. Of the land, he observes that it grows immense and seems to be alive like an animal. In this world, light and darkness are tied together in such a way one could judge this to be the ground floor of creation. Ice, of course, figures prominently, and most of the bergs are chiseled from the Greenland ice cap. Reaching far below the waterline—the rule of thumb is that seventh-eighths of its mass and four-fifths of its height is hidden away—these monoliths glide along like prehistoric vessels, calling life to the base of their towering walls, where fish feast in nutrient-bearing waters and Arctic denizens in turn prey on them. Lopez characterizes his first encounter with these stately entities in revealing prose: "It was as if they had been borne down from a world of myth, some Götterdämmerung of noise and catastrophe. Fallen pieces of the moon."[7]

One of the more interesting encounters I've had with ice was basking in the sun atop a glacier to which I had hiked near Interlaken, Switzerland. Lying out on this colossal monument, an offspring of ancient geological processes that was inching along at an imperceptible pace, I thought about how the earthen ice reached back deeply in time and how it spilled its moraine and leaking fluids forward into the surrounding landscape, feeding the fields and forests with water for miles. Despite their majestic stature, glaciers are everywhere on retreat. Huge sheets of ice are daily calving and collapsing into the sea. With rising planetary temperatures, the rapid disappearance of ice is a harbinger of baleful environmental change. Whereas arctic sea ice floats like a cube on the waters of the north, Antarctic ice sits atop land. When the former melts, it does not contribute to rising sea levels; as the latter vanishes, it adds to the surrounding water. But as a result, under even moderate projected rates of ice shrinkage, two-thirds of the estimated 22,000 polar bears will be extinct in the Arctic by the year 2050.[8] And many other disruptive, even catastrophic, events are likely on the way fueled by worrisome ecological feedback mechanisms and loops.

As a form of crystalline ice itself, snow often begins in a slow trickle, as an apparent leak in the pregnant plenum above us. Large lazy flakes wend their way capriciously to the ground, suiciding themselves like kamikaze pilots against stone, sidewalk, or tundra. White petals crash quietly and hush the landscape, as air meets earth en route to water and eventually again the sky, perhaps again through the detour of ice. We amble along in the midst of this spectacle, not so much enveloped as curtained and silhouetted. Falling snow reminds us—or so it should—that we live *inside* this blue-green terrarium of a planet rather than sit passively on it.

The childlike wonder we experience with the first snow of winter became fully evident to me during my freshman year of college in Williamsburg, Virginia when dozens of students who had grown up in Southern states rushed outside to witness and celebrate the event, some touching and tasting snowflakes for the first time in their lives. The geometry of snow likely contributes to its beauty and our fascination with it. Flakes, which can appear as needles, plates, and columns and that measure in size up to fifteen inches wide, possess six radiating arms, the hexagonal symmetry emerging as a mirror of the crystalline structure of ice from which it grows. As to the specific shape that a flake assumes, that depends on the humidity and temperature conditions when these flowers of ice form. What accounts for the symmetry may in fact be a sort of "information sharing" between the connected arms. Another possible explanation is that the flake is responding identically on all sides to the same atmospheric factors it encounters. Gretel Ehrlich portrays this kind of precipitation with more poetic élan: "Snow starts far up in the sky with one dust mote cartwheeling through cloud. As it free-falls, moisture encarnalizes dust: faceted crystals are born. The one becomes many and they go where wind blows: everywhere and down and touching."[9]

Similar things are not the same; and it is important to recognize that there are numerous types of ice and snowfall, including squalls, flurries, blizzards, graupel (frozen fog that condenses on flakes of snow), thundersnow, and lake effect snow, among sundry others. On the ground, snow takes a variety of forms ranging from crust, corn (wet granular snow), firn (long-lying snow) and slush to drifts, powder, penitents (tall blades), and watermelon snow (pink snow caused by algae). Being predominately white, a landscape of snow is especially susceptible to our projections. In the mesmerizing light, it can seem akin to a desert of sand that plays tricks with our eyes and gives birth to hallucinogenic images like multiple suns and moons. A popular view asserts that the Inuit possess many different words for snow—far more than other cultures—thus reflecting their own intimate experiences with and linguistic dexterity regarding this elemental stuff. Likely originating with anthropologist Franz Boas, who identified just four Eskimo terms for snow, the legend grew as the number of words expanded and stories were embellished. The controversy turns in part on the complexities of what qualifies as a word and what counts in particular as a separate word for "snow." Still, the Inupiat people of Alaska's northwest Arctic, among others, do distinguish numerous kinds of ice, including land-locked ice (*tuvaq*), young ice (*sikuliaq*), and pack ice (*sarri*), indicating a nuanced vocabulary for understanding and interacting with their terrestrial and watery worlds.[10] And writer Jay Griffiths offers a voice of dissent in the cross-cultural debate, challenging the notion that there is a single root word or category encompassing "snow." As she senses more generally, the terms for elemental substances in the wild north are fast disappearing like the ice itself. "As the words for ice and snow are melting away with each elder's death, so the knowledge they contain is melting."[11]

In an unaltered or relatively unadulterated state, ice poses a slippery challenge to traditional aesthetic evaluation because of the amalgam of disparate qualities it is capable of displaying, ranging from plasticity to solidity and from evanescence to long-spanned endurance. Commenting on Antarctica, Pyne suggests it is "a minimalist landscape that requires a high order of esthetics to be appreciated. Where the ice is ensconced within ice within more ice, art finds itself without information; the senses are stripped; perception vanishes into white nirvana."[12] As he has accomplished with other elemental phenomena, Andy Goldsworthy helps us, however, to appreciate snow and ice in a novel light by moving them into a hybridic sphere, where the wild physical order grounds us but the artistic imagination is permitted to take flight. During cold winter months in Scotland, Goldsworthy created thirteen large, one-ton snowballs, which he then kept in refrigerated storage. Months later, on a warm summer night, he transported them quietly into London's financial district, where he deposited them on the sidewalks. In the morning, Londoners gazed and gawked at these "sculptures" with a mixture of fascination and amusement as pedestrians were provided with a temporary tie to a different place and seasonal time: the outlying countryside and the vanished winter. As the snowballs melted and evaporated, their interiors revealed a smattering of pinecones, seeds, feathers, branches, barbed wire, stones, or wool. For five more days, the artist and public observed the action of wind, heat, and human hands on the changing size, texture, color, and shape of the snow. Experimenting with pond ice, icicles and large blocks of frozen water as well, Goldsworthy fashions sculptures and cairns out of elemental substance, offering his fabrications over to the energies of the natural world, which will gently annihilate them in due course.

In addition to hypnotizing us with the beauty of glistening surfaces, ice and snow serve critical environmental functions and provide untold benefits to humans in the process, even if they also spark thousands of accidents each year or threaten vital services like the delivery of electricity. Melting snow is a significant source of water in many parts of the world, where the mountains catch and retain snowfall in the winter and then release it as runoff in the spring. Snow also provides a layer of insulation that conserves the internal heat of the earth, thereby protecting plant life in extremely cold weather. At the same time, it reflects the sun's rays away from the planet, helping to cool the land in the summer and contributing to ongoing hydrological cycles. Because ice, like freshwater, is distributed unevenly, a quixotic attempt to address existing and anticipated water shortages once involved hauling icebergs by boat to parched areas in the Middle East. Icebergs and glacial ice, however, do contain some of the purest water on the planet, and perceiving this fact as an opportunity, vodka voluptuaries and cognoscenti have taken to blasting off chunks of ice from glaciers with shotguns and rifles in order to create perfect cubes for their drinks. And, lest we forget, the strange slipperiness of ice—which defies the way two solids usually slide against one another with friction and resistance—challenges the ability of our bodies to negotiate and navigate through the precarious world as we amble down the sidewalk or test ourselves in athletic endeavors from skating and skiing to bobsledding and hockey.

In these and other ways, ice and snow summon peculiar effects upon the human psyche. They provide a serene but sometimes uneasy counterpoise to the containing lid of the sky, particularly when the heavens are benighted or troubled, certifying that a cold season has arrived or is en route. Perhaps as much as any other major visual engagement with ice, Frederic Edwin Church's painting, "The Icebergs," evokes such enigmatic power and eerie beauty in a seascape image that also points toward an elemental encounter with the sublime. After completing the fifty square foot canvas, Church added a shattered mast of a ship in the foreground in order to make it more accessible to the public when it debuted in 1861 because, to the chagrin of many art patrons, there was no evidence of humanity in the original version. But the net outcome is that we are still strangely seduced and then abandoned in this alien and frozen realm, drawn in alluringly though left alone at a cold distance from the icebergs in the end. "Beware," the picture seems to say; "you are out of your element."

Snow and ice are able to still the land and silence a busy street, temporarily calming the noisy machinery of our technological society. In a society rife with mechanical reproduction and the rule of artificial objects, they remind us of the sheer force of elemental processes. One also wonders if they "remind" themselves along the way that they were—and will be again—primordial water. "I slip on these 'elements,'" Merleau-Ponty remarks, "and here I am in the world."[13] To be sure. Such is the ever-present potential of ice and snow to yank the rug out from under our ingrained habits and expectations and to confirm the exteriority and striking impermanence of the world around us. As Wallace Stevens says, "For the listener, who listens in the snow, / And, nothing himself, beholds / Nothing that is not there and the nothing that is."[14]

— 4 —

Plato's *Chora*-graphy of Earth, Air, Fire, and Water

We must . . . consider in itself the nature of fire and water, air and earth. . . . For to this day no one has explained their generation, but we speak as if men knew what fire and each of the others is.

—Plato, *Timaeus*

Life must be lived as play, playing certain games, making sacrifices, singing and dancing. . . . [Thus] men will live according to Nature since in most respects they are puppets, yet having a small part in Truth.

—Plato, *Laws*

But how can one state the elements of an element?

—Plato, *Theaetetus*

The ABC of Everything

In Plato's cosmological dialogue, the *Timaeus*, we encounter a powerful new account of earth, air, fire, and water, one that continues to partake of the complexities of both myth (*mythos*) and reason (*logos*) but in a decidedly different way than had Presocratic philosophy.[1] The elements, in short, become geometrical and proportional. "Matter" is mathematized within a feminine matrix, the place of its becoming. Plato cordons and connects the elements in a definite relationship with one another and gives them a novel transformational capacity. He transplants Empedocles' four roots (*rhizomata*) into his own philosophical framework but endows them with a change in status—above the disorder that exists at the lowest level yet beneath the realm of a benevolent Demiurge and the Forms that provide this master-craftsman with true models. And it is likely Plato who first confers on us the term, *stoicheia* (elements). As he remarks, the elements can be construed as "the ABC of everything" (*stoicheia tou pontos*) (48b).[2]

Plato's work has been drawn of late into environmental debate about the status of nature (*physis*) and, to a lesser degree, the subjects of natural science, ecological history, vegetarianism, and technology (*techne*).[3] Absent from this discussion, however, has been a critical consideration of the role of the elements (*stoicheia*) and their relation to the more encompassing outlook afforded by the influential theory in the *Timaeus*. In this chapter and the two that follow, we examine the accounts of the elements that Plato and Aristotle advance, showing their original responses to the difficulties they perceive in their predecessors and the depth of the debt still due to these forebears. Along the way, we demonstrate that in their willful adoptions of a Presocratic perspective that gave primacy to the elements, they also skillfully adapt earth, air, fire, and water to the demands of their own philosophical systems. They seek and secure a definite place for the elements, a stay against the confusion in the fray of cosmological creation. In finding locations for the elements of the tetrad singularly and collectively and treating the universe itself in rational terms, Plato and Aristotle ensure that the natural world is still "minded." Although there is a marked departure from the views of the Presocratics, their thought retains broad ecological dimensions and strands, connections with the capacious environment beyond the human *polis* (civic community) as well as insights that prove valuable to twentieth-century physics. In the process, we develop ties to more recent philosophy, including that of Edmund Husserl, Alfred North Whitehead, and Jacques Derrida, each of whom provides tools to interrogate, critique, or extend ideas within elemental thought.

At the same time, Plato's "stoicheology" (study of the elements)—especially the emplacement of the four to the extent that it is a procrustean—helps to fit the elements for their eventual philosophical displacement and later disappearance. In the end, the elements qua earth, air, fire, and water do not prove to be entirely elemental, first, or fundamental. Something else precedes and is more primary. In the instances of both Aristotle and Plato, new philosophies of nature also come into being, views that gain a great measure of sophistication in their explanatory force but lose something vital as conceptions of the natural household with the accompanying abandonment of forms of animism—the notion that matter is alive. In order to more fully comprehend the state and status in which we presently find earth, air, fire, and water in our own changing natural environment and emerging postnatural lifeworld, it is necessary to reconstruct and reconsider the accounts advanced by Plato and Aristotle and to examine some of the related dimensions of their work that concern nature, place, physical contact, domestication, and geocentricity, along with more traditional philosophical matters such as genesis and motion.

A Probable Physics

Turning to the *Timaeus*, we see that it is presented in the form of a myth, but that it is spoken of as a "probable" story or explanation. The proposed cosmology is a verisimilar account (*eikos logos*) because a true account (*alethes logos*) cannot be offered and probably not even a self-consistent one. Philosophy of nature (or physics), Plato suggests, is an inexact science. The narrative concerns the creation of a "secondary" world and so it offers a metaphysics of change and becoming rather than one of permanence and being. It relates how a Demiurge, a craftsman or fabricator, brings order out of disorder, imposes reason on necessity (*ananke*), so as to produce the best possible cosmos, one that is a "likeness" (*eikon*) of a most perfect model. We can divide the dialogue into three sections. The first part bespeaks the making of the world's body and soul, and then the human body and soul. The second part presents a cosmogonic view of the order imposed on a chaotic Receptacle, along with the resultant compounds and varieties of bodies. The final section outlines the structure and workings of the human body in relation to the human soul, the differentiation of the sexes, and the generation of animals. Plato's theory of the elements emerges primarily within the account of the world—which consists of four primary bodies or elements—and the description of the physical disorder that precedes the eventual emergence of cosmological order.

According to the *Timaeus*, the universe is engendered by the Demiurge as a visible, corporeal entity. That is, it must come into being as a body (*soma*). Although the world's body and the four primary bodies are introduced first in the dialogue, soul (*psyche*) is given ontological and temporal priority over them as in Plato's outlook more generally. There is—to use the later Scholastic distinctions—a difference between the order of discovery (*ordo cognoscendi*) or, we could say, order of invention (*ordo inveniendi*), where the body appears first—and the order of being (*ordo essendi*), where soul is privileged. More exactly, the soul exists between mind (*nous*) and body (*soma*), between that which has no genesis and is being always (*to on aei*), and that which comes to be and has a beginning (*arche*). Structurally, these distinctions reflect a broader order divided between the intelligible and eternal realm of being and mind on the one hand, and the sensible and temporal realm of becoming and the bodily on the other hand. As intermediaries and mediators between the extremes, we find soul set at the center of the world's body and enveloping it from the outside and the Demiurge, who must turn to the eternal before fabricating.

Derivation of Earth, Air, Fire, and Water

Plato derives the existence of the elements early in the dialogue. In order for the world to be seen, there must be light (fire), and so that it can be touched, there must be solidity, thus implying the necessity of earth. In this way, Plato introduces the requirement of two elements, fire and earth, which are also the most extreme elements. These primary bodies are "put together" (*sunistanai*) by the Demiurge. Furthermore, a bond (*desmos*) is needed between these elements in order to keep them united. Two elements with one mean proportion would suffice for a two-dimensional world if the body of the universe had been without depth as a plane surface. However, two proportions are necessary for a three-dimensional world because the body of the universe is solid. Thus, we have the addition of water and air—which are placed between fire and earth—and the subsequent relations of earth to water, as air is to fire. From these constituents, the corpus of the cosmos is composed as a unity of proportions (*analogia*), bound through concord (*philia*) and not dissoluble, except through the unmaking of the master builder. At this early stage in the dialogue, the quantities have simply been determined and set in a fixed proportion, one that is geometrical rather than mechanical. The elements will later be formed through the imposition of determinate and fixed geometrical shapes upon their powers (*dunameis*) and motions, which are still unordered.

It is important to note that in this cosmological account Plato employs the notion of *philia* (friendship, concord, love) introduced earlier by Empedocles. Conspicuously absent from the *Timaeus*, however, is a corresponding contrary akin to Empedocles' strife (discord or hate). Amity of the elemental bodies is thereby achieved through their proportionality, but there is not an eventual periodic destruction of the world as Empedocles had foretold. Whereas the *rhizomata* appear, too, as given for Empedocles, Plato deduces the necessity of the elements through argumentation and at the same time ascertains that they must be four in number.[4]

Plato does not specify the exact numbers in his geometrical proportion, and there has been no small amount of controversy as to what he meant and whether such claims are plausible.[5] Although one can debate the merit and success of his procedure, it is significant first of all, that Plato offers a rational account for the existence of the elements rather than simply positing them, even if he does merely assert the names of air and water after deriving the need for two additional bodies. The elements come about through reason, the work of intelligent and intelligible design, and necessity plays a role as well. The Demiurge, as we is seen here, fixes and fashions them with a rational geometrical form. Thus, we can come to know them because of their structure, which is comprehensible.

Second, Plato agrees with Empedocles about the number of elements but diverges as to their exact constitution and nature. They are four in total, but they are not eternal.[6] In the *Philebus*, Plato speaks of the elements as constituting the body (*soma*) of the universe and our individual bodies, as he does in the *Timaeus*. In the *Gorgias*, he characterizes the world as a togetherness (through *philia* and *kosmiotes*) of heavens, earth, gods, and humans, a depiction that shares affinities with Heidegger's later notion of *Geviert* or fourfold (see Chapter eight). Understood as primary bodies, the elements are limited in quantity but nevertheless linked mathematically. The world's body is thus bound inherently through the glue of geometric proportion. It will not dissolve because of a cyclical strife or through a lack of internal harmony of the elemental parts. The four primary bodies form the "frame" of a visible, tangible cosmos, which requires no more or no less of these entities, and the Demiurge leaves nothing of earth, air, fire, and water outside this picture.[7]

The Corpus of an Ecological Cosmos

Plato represents the world's body as a living being that is whole and complete, with parts that are themselves whole and complete. It is singular and unique such that another cannot come from its being, and free from sickness and age—thus everlasting. It is spherical in shape because the sphere is the most homogeneous shape, possessing too the traits of being uniform, smooth, and without organs or limbs (hands and feet).[8] Fitting to its corporeal form, its motion is such that it turns around in the same place, rotating on its own axis. In brief, the body of the universe is self-sufficient in all respects, even to the point that it is "designed to feed itself on its own waste" (33c)—an *ecologically sustainable entity* to be sure.

In this characterization, Plato challenges the older Ionian view that an indefinite mass surrounds the universe, providing it with a supply of "raw materials" with which to construct worlds, and he rejects as well the Atomists' notion of an infinite void containing an unlimited amount of matter. But he does make it clear that the cosmos is still a living being (*zoon*). This position carries forward the claims of many of the Presocratics who had characterized the cosmos as a living animal. Democritus first spoke of the individual as a microcosm (*mikros kosmos*) and thereby forged an analogy between an animal as a miniature cosmos and the universe itself as a large animal. Anaximenes developed the notion, portraying the cosmos as alive and breathing, held together and maintained by air (*aer*) and breath (*pneuma*), as it is with humans. Plato's view also exhibits resonances with the recently rejuvenated theory that the earth functions like a self-regulating living organism. His cosmos is, in short, rational and self-maintaining rather than lifeless, inert matter, although his conception concerns the universe as a whole, whereas the Gaia hypothesis focuses on the earth as a planetary system.[9]

In connection with this description of the world's body, Plato, too, refers to the primary bodies as "hot and cold things" (33a) with powers of acting on composite entities. Hotness is a quality of fire, evinced when fire causes the sensation of heat or turns something else hot. Coldness, by contrast, is a corresponding quality of that which suffers the affection. In this sense at least, the *powers* (*dunameis*) of the four primary bodies are *qualitative* properties even if the *form* these bodies take is distinctly *quantitative* (regular and geometric). In his description of the chaos Plato suggests that the elements are qualified by these "other affections" and possess "vestiges of their own nature" (52d–53b). If the elements could exist outside the cosmos, they would only survive as powers that have not yet been formed. They might thus act violently upon the world body, a possibility that Plato precludes with the singularity and uniqueness of the universe, which is all-containing and pan-encompassing. Nothing *without* can wreck havoc on it for no thing exists outside the world; nothing *within* can cause dissolution because the parts are whole and harmonious in their proportion. As constituents of this cosmos, the elements are so positioned and composed as to help support like spokes the turning sphere of world, which is "equidistant every way from center to extremity" (33b).

Following an elegant if elliptical description of the birth of time as "a moving likeness of eternity" (37d) that imparts a measure of constancy to the inconstant flux and makes the cosmos in the process more like its model,[10] a quartet of living creatures is placed within the Living Creature itself so as to complete the likeness of the world's pattern. The cosmos as entity is itself copied at the microcosmic level. And the four elements are represented as stars, birds, fish, and animals. Each kind of being inhabits a given location qua element. Each finds an *appropriate environmental place*. Stars are allotted with souls and set in the outer fire, which is bright and visible. They are embroidered across the heavens as an adornment and given a double motion, at once rotating and forward moving. Winged beings (birds) find their place in the air. Fish dwell in their element, water. Finally, animals move by foot across dry land, or earth. The elements are thus particularized and then these embodiments are emplaced. Each form of life is *in its own element*, even if it is constituted of all four.[11]

Human souls are wrought from the same "mixing bowl" as the soul of the universe and then sown into the earth and the planets. As newly incarnated beings, we are formed of portions of earth, air, fire, and water that are borrowed from the universe on the condition that they will be returned to it, through a sustained and *sustainable recycling of the elements* one might say. We are bound to and subjects of natural and cosmological processes rather than agents standing outside of them. An indissoluble bond does not hold together the human body, although there is a unity of the portions of the four elements. In terms of the elemental structure of the human body itself, the eyes in particular are fabricated of a fire that yields light and that is kindred to the fire of daylight. The resultant sight is considered as the cause of what benefits us in the highest degree, including the invention of number, the notion of time, and investigation of the world—hence philosophy itself. In suggesting the eye in terms of a pure fire within us, Plato follows Empedocles who had compared the eye to a lantern, explaining that fire within the eyeball is fine enough to pass through tissues that water cannot penetrate. Via the susceptible and sensing body, the motions of the qualities of objects also assail the human soul—driving winds, flowing waters, solidifying earth, or encroaching fire. In other words, we must do occasional "battle" with the elements.

Second Beginnings and Constrained Construction

In contrast to the first section of the dialogue—which describes the operations of reason from above—the second section begins from below in an explanation and analysis of the "tumultuous welter" of earth, air, fire, and water along with the chaotic regions of the body and space. The elements are products of reason *and* necessity (also called an errant cause), just as the realm of becoming is a combination of both factors. "Necessity" (*ananke*), however, should not be construed in the modern sense of the rule of fixed and unchanging natural law but rather as something not formed by intelligence (i.e., that which is without purpose or mindful design).[12] As Plato puts it the *Laws*: "Fire and water, earth and air—so they say—all owe their being to nature and chance, none of them to art; they, in turn, are the agents, and the absolutely soulless agents, in the production of the bodies of the next rank, the earth, sun, moon, and stars" (889b). In this view, the four elements come together in "inevitable casual combinations" not through the agency of mind or art, or a god, but rather by nature and chance (*phusei kai tuche*) or by necessity (*ex anankes*) (889c).[13] If left alone, the elements would proceed randomly and blindly in such a manner. Therefore, as the *Timaeus* holds, reason is required in order to "persuade" necessity. The elements will be harnessed, in effect, to subserve a conscious design. With respect to a broader ecological framework, the role of necessity thus provides a vital internal sense of limit and a horizon of constraint, one that must be acknowledged and respected in human interactions with the material world.

The four bodies, then, are constructed by a Demiurge mind (*nous demiourgos*), but this construction is also constrained by what is visibly and physically there in a "discordant and unordered motion" (30a). The recalcitrance of the elements (or primary bodies) limits the activities of the divine intelligence, who can only craft a universe "as good as possible." Earth, air, fire, and water are partially intractable. They cannot be completely subordinated to the work of the Demiurge. A *constrained constructivism* is the method set forth by Plato.[14] This philosophical position lies between an extreme "idealism" (in the Berkelean sense) or creation from nothing (along Biblical lines) on the one hand and a recourse to "materialism"—which Plato could by no means fathom—on the other hand. Plato's leaning toward idealism—specifically a form of objective idealism—is doubly evident: first in the imposition of mind upon the existing "stuff" of the Receptacle (more loosely "matter" to use Aristotelian terms) so as thereby to "construct" the elements, and second in the resultant bodies that take the "form" of ideal geometric figures.

In this regard, the second section of the *Timaeus* is a second beginning. In order to fully explain the cosmos, Plato must start once more with the nonrational factors, the so-named elements, which had been understood by the Presocratics as first principles (*archai*). This second start considers what the earlier physiocrats had taken to be primary but what Plato will argue are, in fact, secondary qualities. This second look—which takes "second place" (46d)—is fitting for bodies of a lesser, subordinate status. Plato seeks to show that original, first causes of motion and world-construction do not belong to the elements themselves, as many of the Presocratics had claimed. Most previous philosophers, he suggests, considered them as capable of producing effects through heating and cooling or compacting and rarefying, but this is not possible for entities without the abilities of planning or intelligence. He declaims: "the only existing thing which properly possesses intelligence is soul, and this is an invisible thing, whereas fire, water and earth, and air are all visible bodies" (46d). Plato strives to explain the generation of the elements from simpler, prior, and more fundamental beginnings, even though his analysis will not necessarily have arrived at a first principle or principles. His account, again, is a probable one but, he adds, "more so" than others. In this second discourse on necessity, we can discover more clearly the exact nature of Plato's elements and become more cognizant along the way as to what they are not. We need to keep in mind that the elements are, first of all, primary bodies, visible and tangible entities.

Removing the Spell of the Elements

The realm of the oneiric greatly abetted Dmitri Mendeleyev in 1869 with his discovery of the Periodic Table of the Elements. "I saw in a dream," he wrote, "a table where all the elements fell into place as required. Awakening, I immediately wrote it down on a piece of paper."[15] In the dream, the Russian chemist noticed that when the elements were ordered in terms of atomic weight, their properties could be seen to repeat in a series of periodic intervals—hence, the name of the table. Dreams enter the elemental theatre as well in the *Timaeus* at a critical juncture, when the concept of the *chora* is introduced as the place in which all that exists comes into being. But because we perceive this point in a dream state and through a kind of "bastard reasoning," the distinction between appearance and truth or, more pointedly, between the image of *chora* and *chora* itself, is shaken and complicated, indeed effaced.[16] As with Mendeleyev and Descartes—who was seated within his philosophical "cave" before a meditative fire and uncertain if he was truly awake—dreaming (whether as an active oneirism or a more passive sleep) thus powerfully facilitates the finding and founding of a new universal order, if still a bewildering one, where the elements are constructed, classified, and framed.

The first known philosophical reference to the word, element, occurs in the *Theaetetus*, where, interestingly again, Socrates recounts a dream. In this case, it is one in which unspecified persons (possibly Pythagoreans) claim that the elements—the ABC of things, as syllables (*syllabai*) and words—are composed of letters (*logon ouk echei*). Following a rejection of the argument that true belief is equivalent to knowledge (a position recapitulated in the *Timaeus*), Socrates examines the view that one can give an account of a syllable through spelling (e.g., the first syllable, S-O, in the name *Socrates*) but not of the individual letters (elements) themselves. As Socrates relates the dream, the world (including "ourselves and everything else," 201e) consists of complexes and their more simple elements. Complexes possess a *logos* (account of their elements), whereas elements themselves do not. The elements can only be named. One cannot attribute anything further to them (even existence or nonexistence) for that would be a type of predication. One may not even add terms such as "just," "each," or "this" to them. According to the position (and dream) under investigation, the elements are perceivable by the senses (*aistheta*) and namable, but nevertheless unknowable and inexplicable, unlike the syllables (complexes), which are knowable and explicable. The Greek letter "Σ" (Sigma), for example, of "Socrates" is only an audible noise, "like the hissing of the tongue" (203b). In Plato's *Cratylus*, Socrates also suggests that the letter "P" (Rho) expresses "rapidity, motion and hardness" while "Λ" (Lambda) connotes "smoothness, and softness" (434c). In these remarks, we espy the identification of an implicit connection between language and natural phenomena (considered in Chapter two) since the sound of a tongue, for example, could just as easily be associated with the warning noise of a snake or the crackling of a fire on which wet wood has been tossed.

The broader position under scrutiny here concerns whether the addition of an explanation or account (*logos*) can convert true belief into knowledge. There is, too, a logical problem of how to acquire knowledge of individual members within a species and a related epistemological problem of the relationship between individual things and the elements of which they are composed. In the language of Wittgenstein, it is the difficulty of determining a singular use of the terms, *simple* and *composite*. But it also concerns the status of the rudimentary *stoicheia*, which can be understood as the fundamental sounds of which letters are symbols.[17] Here the elements are not directly named as earth, air, fire, and water (the four primary bodies of the *Timaeus*) or as simple qualities (e.g., fiery, yellow, hot, etc.) but are more generally construed as elementary, unanalyzable parts. Socrates challenges this view by showing that if one has knowledge of the first syllable in his name (S-O), then one must know the "S" and the "O" because to claim the contrary would be tantamount to being led into an absurd and untenable position.

If the syllable is equivalent to the aggregate of its two letters and one perceives each of the letters, the addition of an account that was held to produce knowledge would only lead to two distinct perceptions of two unknowable objects. If, however, the syllable is something different from an aggregate of two letters such as a unity or single entity beyond its letters or elements, it is not a whole and cannot have the letters as its parts. Because one cannot discover anything other than letters to be the parts of the syllables, it would follow that both syllable and letter are equally incapable of explanation, hence unknowable. The illustration, in other words, proves itself to be an objection to the theory that it purportedly served. Knowledge of the elements (letters) must be clearer than the knowledge of syllables, but the theory (dream) holds that perception of the elements (letters) is inferior to an account provided of the syllables (complex). So as to bolster this position, Socrates appeals to the experience of actually learning the letters (*stoicheia*) of the alphabet. One tries to learn through sight and hearing each letter and not to confuse it with written or spoken words. Similarly, in music school, the goal is to follow each note and correlate it to its given string since the notes are commonly thought to be "elements of music" (206b). For Plato, then, scientific knowledge (*episteme*) requires knowing not only the complexes but also the simple constituents or elements of which they are made.[18]

As noted already, the term *stoicheia* means both elements and letters of the alphabet. When the elements are understood as primary, first, and fundamental (e.g., as *archai*), they are the most basic constituents of "Nature's book," to invoke a common metaphor that was familiar to Plato and a term of regular use in the Academy. They be-spell the K-O-Σ-M-O-Σ.[19] Plato's position in the *Timaeus*, however, is that the four elements are not even syllables, let alone individual letters. Syllables are derived directly from letters, but what passes for earth, air, fire, and water is not pure. The elements are compounds, hence reducible to something simpler. Even the corpuscles of the "pure" elements are not configured directly from Plato's "letters," which turn out in the end to be two in number, considerably fewer than the twenty-four contained in the Greek alphabet. Rather, they are formed indirectly because their "faces" are first cast from two primary triangles (somewhat like the example in the *Theaetetus* that discusses only two letters of "Socrates"). The (sur)faces, then, of the solid corpuscles are most like "syllables," whereas the corpuscles are analogous to "words" and the bodies formed by a number of such corpuscles are akin to "sentences" in the so-called "book" of nature—if we extend the metaphor.

Thus, we may say, that Plato adheres more to the "spirit" than the "letter" of the elements qua earth, air, fire, and water. He continues to put to use the *stoicheia*—the word and idea—but in the process he appears to remove much of their earlier "animating" force. In taking away the letter-carrying capacity of the elements, Plato posts another message to posterity. *No longer under the spell of the four elements*, as had been the Presocratics—Thales, Anaximenes, Heraclitus, and Empedocles—Plato directs us, at least tacitly, away from the primacy of earth, air, fire, and water, delivering us from elemental words and elementary worlds and, at length, from the letter-bound writing itself of those realms.[20] The elements, as seen here, seem to have pure "spiritual" Forms, but they are no longer nature's alphabet, the true or full embodiments of physical things, places, or regions.

Plato's elements are not material *substances* or *things* because such terms retain the notion of an enduring identity. In other words, earth, air, fire, and water do not appear continuously as the same "thing." That is, they are transient appearances. The elements constantly "slip away," (49e) eluding an opportunity to be described as entities in particular. Because of their evanescent character, they are not a "this" or a "that." Plato makes it clear that they are not to be described in any way that would impute permanence to their existence. Nothing that changes its character (*allote alle gignomenon*) should be called "this" (*touto*). *Gignomena* (that which becomes), he suggests, can be ascribed adjectives and adjectival pronouns—words that represent phases of an elemental process for example but not substantives or their equivalent pronouns. The elements are more "this-like" (*toiouton*) or, as Francis

Cornford renders it, "what is of such and such a quality" (49d). The elements, in short, have a *qualified* rather than a perduring status. They are, at best, dependent, quasi-entities whose nominal and ontological status is insecure, fuzzy, fleeting. "It is hard to say," Plato admits, "with respect to any one of these [elements], which we ought to call by any given name rather than by all the names together or by each severally, so as to use language in a sound and trustworthy way" (49b).

Prior to their construction, the elements are the *discontent contents* of the Receptacle—what is contained precariously in the *hypodoche*—but they are held as a quality (*poiotes*) understood as a "such-ness." As qualities—qualified qualities—they are distinct from material objects and substances. Some kinds of qualities, however, Plato seems to concede, are similar enough in resemblance to one another as to permit the use of a name to group them, thus allowing us to say "fire" or "earth" and the like. Whereas Empedocles sought to eliminate changes of quality by seeing genesis and perishing in terms of interchange and mixture, Plato pursues a distinctly different approach, granting the possibility of change in quality but without positing unalterable elements or an underlying substrate. The elements at this stage—"before the generation of the Heaven" (48b)—are known primarily through their nomenclature. They are names for a set of shifting qualities, which are not yet characterized as existing in figures of any particular, determinate shape. As *names* of qualities, the elements are not exactly emblems (or incarnations) of a qualitative cosmos in the way they were for many of the Presocratics. Moreover, with the later geometrization of the primary bodies—and the accompanying "mathematization of nature," to use Husserl's phrase—we find quality itself yielding to quantity. In contrast to the four elements, the Receptacle is permanent. It is only through their location or that "in which" they appear that it makes sense to speak of the elements as "this" or "that." The "matrix" is where the qualities appear and where events occur, even though it does not strictly possess qualities or occur. To call the elements something properly, we must recall their *whereabouts*, put them in their proper place.

Elemental Recycling

Plato's elements, then, must be understood in terms of their becoming-ness rather than their being-ness. They are not Empedocles' *rhizomata*, which are eternal and unchanging. Instead, they are *seemingly* and continuously transformed from one into another, for Plato adds the proviso to his first characterization of the phenomenal transformations, "as we imagine" (49b).[21] When compacted, water becomes earth (and stones); when dissolved and dispersed, it becomes air (and wind). Air, in turn, is transformed into fire through being enflamed. Reversing this cycle, fire condenses and is extinguished, returning to the form of air. Air becomes water through condensation into cloud and mist, growing gradually more compacted as it changes into liquid form. Water is transmitted once again into earth by the same process.

This kind of cyclical permutation of bodies was common to some of the Presocratics. Anaximenes, in particular, advanced a first theory of the process, selecting air as his chosen element. Through packing (*pilesis*), air becomes water and then earth; whereas through rarefaction, it is transformed into fire. Plato's use of terms such as "condensation" and "rarefaction" signal a degree of debt to Anaximenes. However, in invoking the notion of the cycle—a concept now central to ecological theory—he also borrows, in part, from Heraclitus, who had spoken of the constant exchange of all things for fire and fire for all things (DK 90). The *semblance* of permanence to this elemental process is attributable to the sheer ongoing-ness, repeatability and stability in the elemental exchanges.

In terms of a further comparison with Empedocles, Plato's theory is slightly more economical in that Empedocles requires four distinct types of "matter." Plato's stoicheology also avoids empirical criticisms to which Empedocles appears to succumb because it acknowledges that changes take place between earth, air, fire,, and water. Empedocles did not permit change of one root into another, but as Plato (and later Aristotle) argues perceptual experience teaches otherwise as, for example, when water is transformed into vapor (air) and vice-versa.

Fire (*pyr*), air (*aer*), water (*hydor*), and earth (*ge*) are transformed into one another, but the "cycle" is truncated. It appears more like the top arc of a circle set on an earthen base. We are able to move upward from air to fire and downward from water to earth, for example, but with earth we reach a *cul de sac*, a temporary repose, since it cannot be changed into fire. The "square dance" of the elements whose *dunamis* (power) means as well "square roots" or numerical "squares"—a characterization we attributed to Empedocles' four *rhizomata* or roots—is momentarily halted. The *chora*-graphy of the elements demands a respite.[22] Earth is exceptional—truly *terra firma*—the wallflower of the four that refuses to carry on. It is incommutable and to this degree privileged, as in the later philosophical accounts by Aristotle, Hegel, Heidegger, and Deleuze.[23] This intransigence is due to its shape, a cube whose surfaces are squares. Earth is the least mobile and most stable of the elemental bodies. Squares, as we would expect, provide for greater stability than triangles. Of the recalcitrant earth, we might even ask with Socrates, who queries at the outset of the dialogue: "One, two, three—but where, my dear Timaeus, is the fourth?" (17a). In this sense, the transformational schema can most accurately be described as a kind of "tri-cycling."

The exclusion of earth indeed appears to be contrary to observational evidence, as Aristotle points out.[24] However, we can defend Plato here in part because he does not ignore earth entirely when considering the *observable* changes of elements. Earth is only singled out in the *geometric* description of the mixtures. This omission is explicable because the figure given to earth cannot mix with the others and so resists basic transformations. The difference between the observable or phenomenal changes and the geometric transformations also indicates a difference in the *Timaeus* between the various and related verisimilar accounts, which dialectically correct one another throughout the course of the dialogue. What initially seems to be the case is later revised to give a better, more likely version, so as to come closer to a true account.

Forms of the Four?

Although the elements are transient and transformed entities in the world of becoming, we need to inquire whether there might not be elements with enduring and unchanging status in the realm of being. Might not Empedocles' *rhizomata* lie there in timeless rest? As Plato puts the question, "Is there such a thing as 'Fire just in itself' or any of the other things which we are always describing in such terms, as things that 'are just in themselves'?" (51b). Alternatively, is the earth, air, fire, and water we perceive through our bodily senses all that has reality qua element? The issue, in short, is one concerning whether there are Forms independent of the sensible elemental four.

Plato speaks of "copies" (*mimemata*) of earth, air, fire, and water as being received by the Receptacle. And so it is implied that there could be original models for such copies just as there supposedly is a genuine and perfect model for the universe. The copies, however, are not shapes of the primary bodies but rather the qualities that we perceive when we feel water or fire or one of the other elements. Plato proceeds to affirm the reality of the Forms of Fire, Air, Water, and Earth even though he does not want to enter into a protracted discourse on the subject, having dealt with the Forms in other dialogues. His implied view is nevertheless continuous and consistent with the arguments in the *Phaedo* and the *Republic* as to the independent reality of the Forms. There is no prima facie reason, in other words, to think that he has altered his position on the stark division between the sensible and the intelligible realms.[25] Intelligence and true belief are considered separate and distinct, and this split parallels the division between instruction and persuasion in the *Timaeus*. Knowledge comes about through instruction and is accompanied by a true account of its grounds (*alethes logos*), which cannot be shaken through persuasion. The Forms follow from the distinction between rational understanding (*nous*) and true belief.

There is, then, "fire just in itself," which is an object of intellection, known through reason. And the true meaning of the name "fire" accords to this ideal object, although Plato is reticent about anything more belonging to its essential nature. By contrast, the sensible fire of the phenomenal world involves the changing qualities and combinations of qualities that we perceive at any given time such as "hotness," "yellowness," or "dryness." We do not physically sense the corpuscles of the elements or their shapes such as the pyramid in the case of fire.

In two other dialogues, Plato expresses mixed positions about whether the elements actually have corresponding Forms. In the *Parmenides*, Socrates admits to being puzzled as to whether there is a Form for fire or water, although he is certain that it would be absurd to think that mud, dirt, hair, and other "trivial" or "undignified" entities have independent unchanging realities—denigrating earthy things in the process. In the *Sophist*, however, it is suggested that the four elements are originals as the "offspring" of divine craftsmanship and that each of these products is accompanied by images, which are more specifically dream images as well as shadows or reflections. Thus, when Plato speaks of the elements he once again invokes the notion of the dream, as he had in the *Theaetetus*. In holding to the independent reality of Forms of the elements, Plato seems to demote further the status of the earth, air, fire, and water in terms of how we sensuously feel, breath, see, and taste them in our environmental surroundings. He locates their true being in a realm that we can know but not bodily perceive, even as he finds the site of their genesis in an enveloping matrix. The elements are copies, dependent qualities, not that which is ultimately real.

Elements Emplaced: *Chora*-graphy in the Matrix

The subject of place is wedded deeply and inextricably with ecological concerns ranging from an understanding of animal niches in ecosystems to the building of human homes, and from the growing phenomena of cultural placelessness and philosophical place-alienation to theoretical or political attempts to cultivate "topophilia" (love of place) and bioregionalism in response to such problems. In this regard, the elements of the *Timaeus* are not without a circumambient abode and environmental place. Plato refers to this location variously as a "Receptacle" (*hypodoche*) of becoming, a "matrix" (*ekmageion*) and "recipient" (*dechomenon*) as well as a "mother" (*meter*) and a "nurse" (*tithene*). This third type of thing (*eidos*)—more accurately, a fourth entity—is postulated as necessary to the account along with the intelligible model and the visible copy, to which we can add the Demiurge. As "actors" in this emerging dialogue, we meet the Maker (the mindful master-craftsman), the Models (the formal father and elemental errant offspring), and now the Matrix (the massive, moving mother). This cast of characters and characterless participants conspire in the dramatist's text to create the cosmos. Plato frequently uses the term *God* (*theos*) to describe the Demiurge and so to distinguish him from lesser gods in the dialogue. The Demiurge, however, is not a religious figure to be worshipped; that is, he is not like the later conceptions of

God in Judaism, Christianity, and Islam. In fact, he is probably more mythical and symbolic in nature, an entity that not only brings about the emergence of order from disorder but also helps to facilitate the movement of the narrative. In many respects, he comes to represent the reason that Plato perceives as permeating the universe.

Although the term is not introduced until later in the dialogue, *chora* with its multivalent and graded senses of space, region, place land, locale, room, and even country—along with its associated place names or personal identities—serves in this capacity as a kind of super-locator, functioning as a Platonic placer for the elements, a "matrix for everything" (50c).[26] It becomes a "stage"—setting, place, and seat—to view the relations of our "characters" and subsequently a locale for the four elements to work out their intricate and ordered steps, their *chora*-graphy—*choreia* means dance, from *choros*, dance or place for dancing—which we might also define in the footsteps of Paul Virilio as "the systematic description of regions or districts."[27]

Through its violent rocking motion—constant yet irregular—it brings about order from primordial disorder. It is first swayed and shaken by the powers and qualities of the elemental bodies that pervade it and then it, in turn, separates, winnows, and carries the bodies of earth, air, fire, and water into different regions according to likeness and unlikeness. Heavy and dense things move one way while lighter and more rare things settle in another place. This regionalization thus amounts to a form of placing in which perceptible qualities or things are configured and shaped, as the Demiurge (Plato's "efficient cause," to use Aristotelian vernacular) enters almost *deus ex machina* to give form to a soupy chaos, the void from which Plato retreats.

The creation is not *ex nihilo*—as in Genesis—but *chora* is, however, simply posited as "our new starting point in describing the universe" (49a)—it appears *ex hypothesi*. It possesses a kind of negative but superabundant essence; it has a precarious nature, "clinging in some sort to existence on pain of being nothing at all" (52c). Plato thereby endeavors to define what it *is* by what it *is not*, a method that emerges more fully in Neoplatonism and Medieval thought as *via negativa*. The imperceptible, indestructible, amorphous Receptacle is "free from all characters" (50e) and is *not* to be called earth, air, fire or water, nor components or compounds of these bodies (i.e., qualities into which elements could be further analyzed). We would *not* be mistaken, he tell us, if we refer to it as an invisible, all-receiving and characterless entity that participates puzzlingly in the intelligible realm and remains difficult to apprehend, although the question remains of course as to how we will informed.

This impressive, impressionable medium is described through a series of similes that slowly build up a dim picture of its elusive garb. It is like the scentless base oils used in perfumes, like a plastic block of wax (for molds or dyes) that receives impressions, like a mirror in which fleeting images appear, and like soft gold that can be fashioned into many different shapes such as jewelry.[28] Presented in this way—and passively present in its evasive absence—it takes on traditional maternal and feminine associations, especially because it is given to "receive" (*dechesthai*) sensible copies of immutable realities and to be worked on by an active Demiurge, who predominates over the matrix as a kind of fictive and illicit male "dominatrix" we could playfully say. So described, it is understandable that Plato does not attribute to it a form (*eidos* or *morphe*) of its own. Its appearance (and disappearance) is bound with its description as a sort of shimmering adornment or accessory, wrought from images of precious metal, glass, and pleasant smells, recalling for us, too, the cosmetic "fashioning" process of the Empedoclean "elements" or *rhizomata*.

With its indeterminate nature, *chora* bears some resemblance to Anaximander's *apeiron* (boundless), but this indeterminateness is brought into tension with the precisely established nature of the elements, for which we need a reliable account in order to know the Receptacle. The Receptacle is thus indeterminate but determining; neutral (like Democritus' atoms) but not permitting of blind necessity. It is shapeless yet receptive, providing a seat (*edra*) for sensible becoming. This plastic, permanently pregnant plenum—to extend Plato's metaphors—is the embodiment in many respects of a *be-wildered order*—and so described as partaking in a "bewildering way" (51a–51b) of the intelligible—because the pre-elemental birthing place of earth, air, fire, and water is disordered, chaotic, or pre-cosmic. It is, in brief, not fully domesticated by the Demiurge or the bodies that are born within it. Before the genesis of the world, this cosmic container does not "house" the elements proper—to use the language of domestication—only an ignited part or a wet part that appears as fire or water rather than the copies of the elements as we have come to know them. Its occupants possess but traces of themselves even if the Receptacle is being "fired" and "wetted" for the craftsman who works by "splicing," "measuring," "molding," "cutting," and "pouring," appearing more like a manual laborer than a god.[29]

Plato thus notes the instability of perceived objects and distinguishes between (a) what comes to be; that is, through genesis, and (b) that *in which* (*en ho*) it comes to be—as opposed to *out of which* (*ex hou*) it derives.[30] The former realm relates to the four elemental bodies and the latter to the Receptacle of becoming. Plato proceeds to offer us not just an elemental cosmological principle but also an insightful *ecological maxim*—namely, that "anything that is must be in some place [*topos*] and occupy some room [*chora*], and that what is not somewhere in earth or heaven is nothing" (52b). In other words, the "what-ness" of something is bound with its "where-abouts," its location, so that a body is literally not a body—it is no-body or no-thing—if it is nowhere, if it does not have a worldly or environmental place. In this sense, place can be said to precede space because space takes its definition and bearings from the organisms and things that *occupy* (or co-constitute) the world.[31] *Chora* provides a "situation" (52b) for things to come into existence and to take shape.

On first blush, *chora* seems to be equated with "matter" (a word not used in the text). Neither the matrix nor the elements, however, is entirely substantive even if the *hypodoche* (Receptacle) is subtending or underlying, as the term in Greek implies. *Chora* is not empty. And it is not strictly accurate that Plato gives us a cosmology of pure form without matter.[32] What "matters" for Plato is not the prime material (*prote hyle*) of Aristotle nor the extended bodies (*res extensa*) of Descartes; rather, as suggested earlier, *chora* is instead closer to occupied place than undifferentiated space, although ultimately it resists adequate translation. And the "stuff" that is generated is prone to move, to wander, and to "slip away," eluding not only *predictability* but also *predicability*—that is, resisting clear classification or predication, except anachronistically. The ancient Greeks may not even have possessed an operative word for "space" in our sense because they arguably experienced the spatial not in modern terms as extension but more like *topos* (place). They experienced it as *chora*, which, as Heidegger holds, means more exactly neither space nor place "but that which is occupied by what stands there." As he speculates, "Might *chora* not mean: that which abstracts itself from every particular, that which withdraws, and in such a way precisely admits and 'makes place' for something else."[33]

Although it is not identified by name with the *stoicheia*, Plato speaks of the earth as planet (rather than element) in terms comparable with the Receptacle as "our nurse" and "guardian." This association is understandable because the earth literally provides us with a dwelling place and home. It nourishes and "nurses" us as beings who emerge like offspring from it, as opposed to creatures merely "thrown into it." Similarly, in the more narrowly human realm, it is the *polis* (civic community) that provides a locus of orientation.[34] In a sense, it functions as the analogous sphere of political placing, ordered, and legitimized in one Platonic account by an autochthonous myth of the metals.[35] For Plato, the realms of "the political" and "the natural" are never too far apart. For example, in the utopian *Republic* (both good place and no place), Plato claims that the guardians must consider the land in which they dwell as a "mother and nurse" (414a–414e), language that recalls for us the *Timaeus*. This connection between the "laws" of the natural and social worlds, the *kosmos* and the *polis*, is made earlier by Heraclitus when he suggests that just as the Furies could hunt down the sun should it leave its course, so the people must fight for their law as they protect the city's wall, although he does not progress much further than paralleling the two realms. In Plato, these relations are much more deeply embedded, as evidenced by the fact that the *Timaeus* begins with a discussion that summarizes, in part, the *Republic* and addresses the question of "the best form of society and the sort of men who would compose it" (17c). Whereas an analogy is drawn between soul and city-state in the *Republic*—each is divided into the rational (*logistikon*), spirited (*thymoeides*), and appetitive (*epithymetikon*)—the *Timaeus* forges a link between human life and universal order, completing the connection between citizen, soul, and cosmos or, alternatively, politics, morality, and cosmology.

Nevertheless, there are potential concerns that arise in gendering the earth or cosmos in female terms—as a nurse or "mother of becoming"—because such characterizations can provide impetus—when extended beyond the sphere of cosmology—for domesticating "otherness." In the *Timaeus*, the *chora* cloaked in the imagery and metaphors associated with woman is presented as formless order, mystery, and invisibility upon which order must be imposed—frequently in violent fashion—by the male Demiurge. Strictly speaking, the Receptacle is not even a parent (*tocheus*) but only a host (*xene*) or nurse who supplies the elemental offspring with room (*chora*) and "board." And it can only be apprehended though a kind of "bastard reasoning" (52b). The last section of the *Timaeus* (90e–92c) also speaks of the generation of women and animals, conceiving them as fallen, dissolute, and foolish men. Both women and animals are depicted as "disobedient and self-willed," creatures "that will not listen to reason" (91b). Such cosmic characterizations may not in themselves always be objectionable, but they can provide a ready pretext for the subordination of both the natural world and women, which are often casually but deeply linked in the philosophical mind, as modern-day ecological feminists have pointed out.[36] This is a problem that arises in other Platonic dialogues—and in Greek thought more generally—as, for example, in the *Menexenus* where Plato surmises that "The woman in her conception and generation is but the imitation of the earth and not the earth of the woman" (238a).[37]

Construction and Structure of the Primary Bodies

In their pre-cosmic condition, the elements are but "traces" (*ichne*, meaning footsteps or imprints) of themselves, tossed about "without proportion or measure." The containing Receptacle is in a state of continual flux, and so nothing is sufficiently stable to be termed a particular "this." Because of their perpetual transformations, the elements are not elemental enough. Elements of these "elements" are required, and for Plato this necessitates their geometrization. Earth, air, fire, and water thus need to be "framed" by the Demiurge with the "greatest possible perfection" (53b), a dimension that is absent earlier in the account. The bodily is broken down—deconstructed so to speak—to its most basic beginnings in the *chora* but it must be built up again—constructed or reconstructed—through the imposition of regular geometric shape. This requirement involves a two-step process. First, we find the construction of four types of primary bodies out of two "elemental" triangles. Second, the resulting figures are each assigned to fire, earth, water, and air. Following on this process is a *redescription* of the transformational capacity of the primary bodies and a qualified correlation of the geometric shapes with the qualities that affect our sense organs in the activities of perception or sensation.

Plato did not have recourse to algebra, which had not yet been developed, or other higher forms of number theory, and so he turns to geometry to provide a basis for the mathematization of "matter." He reasons that since earth, air, fire, and water are all bodies (*somata*), they must possess depth (*bathos*) and be bounded by surface (*epipedon*). All rectilinear surfaces can be analyzed into right-angled triangles, of which there are two: the isosceles (two equal sides) and the scalene (unequal sides with the hypotenuse double the length of one side). As Plato says, this is "the first beginning" of what we term the elements and his way of "saving the appearances" (as we might now say) of what passed for the account given earlier. There is the additional suggestion, however, that something might be more ultimate than the triangles themselves, "principles [*archai*] yet more remote than these are known to Heaven and to such men as Heaven favors" (53d). Here one can only conjecture that Plato has Pythagorean principles in mind with this cryptic reference. The suggestion seems to be that geometric properties of figures such as the triangle are the visible appearances of the properties and relationships of numbers themselves and perhaps even ultimately of the first number, one. Right-angled triangles, for example, have sides in the ratios of 3:4:5, and so one can "reduce" the triangle itself to numerical relations. Put briefly, this kind of thinking lies at the heart of the Pythagorean position that all things are numbers.[38]

Proceeding according to the dictates of likelihood and necessity, Plato is interested in finding a manner in which the four bodies deduced earlier—most perfect and dissimilar ones—might be constructed in such a way that they can be generated from one another through the process of resolution. He then demonstrates how the triangles can be used to build these four solid, regular bodies, selecting the equilateral triangle as the best triangular face for such a method, one that is common to the shapes of three of his bodies. The first, simplest, and smallest body formed is the pyramid, which has four surfaces, four angles, three surfaces per solid angle, and twenty-four elementary triangles. The second body composed is the octahedron, which is made of eight surfaces, six angles, four surfaces per solid angle, and forty-eight elementary triangles. The third constructed body is the icosahedron, consisting of twenty surfaces, twelve angles, five surfaces per solid angle, and one hundred and twenty elementary angles. Unlike the other three, the fourth body is made from isosceles triangles, four of which form a square, with six squares making a cube. It has six surfaces, eight angles, three solid surfaces per angle, and twenty-four elementary triangles. Finally, a fifth figure, the dodecahedron, is constructed of twelve pentagons. In terms of their assignment, the first body is fire, the second is air, and the third is water. The fourth body is earth, which is generated in sets of four. The fifth figure is used by the Demiurge for the sphere that is the whole—the heavens—on which are patterned animal shapes in the zodiac and the many constellations. This representation and placing of nonhumans in the heavens is significant because the domestication of the elements—a subject explored throughout this work—often occurs historically through control exercised over animals or their symbolic manifestations.[39]

Because fire, air, and water can be broken into the same kind of equilateral triangles made from scalene triangles, each is able to dissolve into its component figure and then be reformed as one of the other two. Furthermore, because all are composed of an exact number of elementary scalene triangles (in their respective instances, fire has twenty-four; air possesses forty-eight; and water has one hundred twenty), they exist in a quantitative relation to one another such that one water is equivalent to one fire plus two air; one air is equivalent to two fire; and five air are equivalent to two water. Plato's geometrical account also enables him to provide for the relative lightness and heaviness of these bodies. Of the three, water—being composed of one hundred twenty elementary triangles—is the heaviest, followed by air and then fire. As a cube, earth moves least of all due to the fact that its structure is different from the other bodies, and so it cannot be transmuted into water, air, or fire.

Thus, the bodies of the elements are stereometrically formed; that is, they possess or represent a simple measurable solid form. Their geometrization permits them to nest together temporarily but prevents them from bulking. The *shapes* of earth, air, fire, and water comprise their materiality—they are what matters. The elements are configured; they possess a patterned structure and surface. Furthermore, earth, air, fire, and water may not be numbers per se (as a strict Pythagorean perspective implies), although they are connected closely with the proportions and relations of numbers. As to their size, all the bodies are too small to be visible individually, but they can be seen as aggregate masses. Because of the fact that Plato's two true "elements" (triangles) are produced in a variety of sizes and then mixed with others, there exists a vast diversity in the grades of size. Finally, so as to bring all of this into an exact perfection, the motions, numbers, and powers of the bodies are adjusted in proper proportions.

Once their pattern emerges from the disorder of the Receptacle and the entirety is held within the sphere of the dodecahedron, the cosmos emerges. We transit, in effect, from a *bewildered* (as confusing) *disorder* to a *be-wildering* (as beautiful and beyond human) *order*. The elements continue to be formed, transformed, and reformed within a plenum because there is no vacant space, "no room to be left empty" (58b). This ongoing movement is attributable to the revolution of the whole, and within the whole, first, to the differences in size of the components of the bodies and, second, to the compounds going to their distinct individual places: earth in the center, followed by a surrounding water, then air, and last fire. The smaller units enter into the larger ones (e.g., a fire pyramid penetrates air) and the larger units quench or shatter smaller ones (e.g., water destroys air).

Put differently, Plato brings together Empedocles with the insights of the Atomists, who earlier likened atoms to letters: each element has a corpuscular structure. But he also transforms Atomism. There are only four types of corpuscles, each with a distinct structure: (a) tetrahedra with four sides or pyramids (fire); (b) cubes with six sides (earth); (c) octahedra with eight sides (air); and icosahedra with twenty sides (water). The mathematics of Plato's system is relatively complex, but it is more significant to stress that the arrangement at the lowest level of nature accounts for the arrangement at subsequent levels. Reason and mathematics rather than mere chance shape the universe.

War and Play of the Elements

A final task is to correlate loosely the shapes, sizes, and movements of the four elemental bodies with the sensible qualities that act upon our sense organs, which are supposed to be composed of the same elements. Thus, we turn to the topics of sensation and perception and the contact between the soul that acquires knowledge and the surrounding sensible environment. For example, in the case of fire as flame and light, we have the corresponding sensible qualities of hot and vision, respectively. Alternatively, in the case of air as *aether*, mist, or darkness, we find bright, odors, and black, respectively.

Plato undertakes this enterprise "for the sake of recreation" and as "an innocent pleasure" for sport or amusement (*paidia*) (59c). He sets aside for a moment thought of eternal subjects to consider the *interplay* of the elements with the sensing body and sensuous world and, in effect, to engage in a constructive play with the elements himself—in contrast no doubt with the difficult work of pure mathematics (the Pythagorean dimensions of his work) or pure theory (the science of knowing as an understanding of Being). Instead of exactitude, he is concerned with plausibility and probability and to this extent his use of mathematics is not so much discontinued as diminished.[40] There is room to maneuver more freely and time to play.

Heraclitus had emphasized the combat and opposition involved with the elements. Each is at war, seeking to annihilate the other, even if they still eventually compose a cosmos that is harmonious and just.[41] "We should know that war is common, and strife is justice and that all things happen according to strife and just necessity" (DK 80). Anaximander also underscored the necessary encroachment and combat that occurs in elemental interactions. Plato, too, speaks of the elements in conflict and as one being "overpowered" by another or as "cutting" with sharp edges, "enveloping" another or "suffering" changes in the transformational process. Like soldiers on a battlefield, the elements are engaged in "thrusting," "quenching," and "shattering." "Weaker" and "stronger" bodies "contend" with one another before a "resolution" is reached. At this point, one can declare a figure that "prevails" or a "victorious" body (56e–57b).

Although strife might characterize one dimension of the elemental interactions, the dance of the elements in the Receptacle—their tightly tuned *chora*-graphy—is more ludic in the *Timaeus* than in many earlier cosmologies. We have entered the fleeting sphere of nature and the realm of "recreation," which should be read playfully as well in terms of cosmic *re-creation*, since Plato reconstructs the universe from the elemental shards and philosophical fragments that he inherits like puzzle pieces from Heraclitus, Empedocles, Parmenides, and other Presocratics. Plato hereby plays the order of nature and thereby helps to create or to re-create the cosmos through a kind of *poiesis*. In fact, an analogue to this process exists in the Hindu notion of *lila* (play or divine play) that suggests that the universe is at play with itself in a grand but light-hearted game.[42] Plato's play thus takes us into the realm of the mythic or sacred. As the noted historian of play John Huizinga has argued, "The human mind can only disengage itself from the magic circle of play by turning towards the ultimate," for logical or rational thought does not proceed far enough.[43] In this sense, Plato's vacillation between *mythos* (myth) and *logos* (reason) is more understandable because mythic consciousness apprehends and interjects itself into the physical world, participating in it as a lived reality, while at the same time gesturing beyond it to something more enduring.[44]

> Archaic man plays the order of nature as imprinted on his consciousness . . . the change of seasons, the rising and the setting of the constellations . . . the course of the sun and moon. And now he plays this great order of existence as sacred play, in and through which he actualizes anew, or "recreates" the events . . . and thus helps maintain the cosmic order.[45]

Like the Demiurge himself who turns upward to the eternal model before turning downward to the sensible copies, Plato repeatedly turns between the physical and eternal realms, between the true and verisimilar accounts, between the geometric description of the elements and their phenomenal appearance.

Plato's late work is, then, still quite serious but it no longer denigrates play as the philosopher tended to do in his earlier dialogues. In *The Laws*, for example, Plato asserts that "though human affairs are not worthy of great seriousness . . . I say that a man must be serious with the serious" and postulates further that "God alone is worthy of supreme seriousness, but man is made God's plaything, and that is the best part of him." "Therefore," he continues, "every man and woman should live accordingly and play the noblest games and be of another mind from what they are at present" (803b–803d). Presumably, it is philosophy that Plato has in mind as being among the noblest games, but—as the *Timaeus* implies—one can also contemplate the natural world and particularly the elements so as to live the life of play he recommends in the *Laws*.[46] As Huizinga puts it in a comment that could be applied in part to the *Timaeus*:

> [I]n acknowledging play you acknowledge mind, for whatever else play is, it is not matter. Even in the animal world, it bursts the bounds of the physically existent. From the point of view of a world wholly determined by the operation of blind forces, play would be altogether

superfluous. Play only becomes possible, thinkable and understandable when an influx of mind breaks down the absolute determinism of the cosmos.⁴⁷

In this observation, we can see the vital thread between the physical world, intelligence, and play—even serious and competitive play that produces strife and a victor. There is something more than matter that emerges, permitting the bewildering and wild world to be ordered and understood. Mindfully having witnessed this process, Plato is now ready to take in the delightful tonic of play itself in the permutations of the elements.

This is one theme that Plato bequeaths to the Neoplatonist Plotinus, who commences his meditations upon the natural world with a playful note, suspending seriousness for a spell. "Suppose we said, playing at first before we set out to be serious, that all things aspire to contemplation, and direct their gaze to this end—not only rational but irrational living things, and the power of growth in plants, and the earth which brings them forth."⁴⁸ Like Plato, Plotinus is quite serious about his play, even though "there will be no risk in playing with our own ideas," for play takes us into contemplation (*theoria*) and leads as well into the natural sphere (*physis*). The eternal realm is approached not only through interior reflection or mysticism but also via the external world of nature, which serves as a conduit for comprehending an ultimate One.

Dispatching the *Stoicheia*: Elemental S/endings

On the one hand, the elements are corporeal and positioned entities. They are, in fact, at least *thrice embodied*: as corpuscular entities themselves; as present in human and animal bodies; and as part of the body of the universe. They are concentrically enclosed in the viscera of physical existence. In so belonging to the human body, Plato is able to invoke the elements in order to account for somatic disease, and even environmental health and illness. An excess, deficiency or misplacement—migration from their proper place to a foreign location—of one of the four primary bodies was thought to create problems for the human body. From an ancient perspective, for example, a surfeit of fire causes continuous heats or fevers; an overabundance of air produces quotidian fevers; a surplus of water leads to tertian; and an excess of earth (the most sluggish of the elements) provokes quartan fevers. Through elemental emplacement, Plato finds a definite locale for their genesis in the containing *chora* and accounts for their structure in part through the activity in this super-locator.

On the other hand, it turns out that the "elements" are *not true elements*. We encounter steps in a slippery reduction of earth, air, fire, and water from first principles (*archai* among the Milesians) to secondary qualities and more strictly *names* of qualities—rather than the powers themselves—in a secondary world of becoming (rather than the primary realm of being, where doubt is even expressed as to their existence); from bodies to their component shapes; from their particular shapes (triangles) possibly even to number; and finally—if we follow out the trajectory of Pythagorean ideas—even from number to the unity (oneness) on which number itself is predicated. Plato does not carry through this "de-grading" process—at least not systematically—to its very end because there is no physical science of becoming, only a probable account, but the point should be clear that the elements are, in many ways, a vestige of what they were in earlier thought. In some ways, they are like the "traces" that we encountered earlier in Receptacle—*trace elements*, we might say—since they are like "footprints" and remainders of their more robust status in the Presocratic cosmologies. In the end, Plato insists that elements of the four elements are needed. Fire, air, water, and earth are not elementary enough.

Furthermore, the four elements are no longer accorded the status of letters in "Nature's book." Instead of letters, they are more like syllables and most like polysyllables. Plato's disposition toward displacing the elements to a lesser role—beneath *nous* (mind) and *psyche* (soul) in cosmogenesis within the *Timaeus* is also in curious accord with the veiled fourfold and its foreshadowing role in a central epistemological Platonic myth, the Allegory of Cave, in the *Republic*. In that myth, earth is represented as the seat of solidity and shadows, of denseness and darkness most removed from knowledge in the innermost interior of this "choric" cavern, or philosophical womb. Fire, the element most opposed to earth, is the source and medium of light and sight but clearly not enlightenment, except symbolically and secondly as the Sun. Water—first encountered outside the cave—is merely a medium of reflection for images. And insofar as it is implicitly present, air provides visibility, conducts the sound of the echo transmitted in the cave, and serves as a medium for fire, but it no longer binds the world as it had in Anaximenes' philosophy. None of the elements individually or collectively, then, is a direct conduit to the eternal and immutable, except perhaps playfully and indirectly.

In certain respects, Plato nevertheless still appears as a strong precursor to modern physics and chemistry. In combining the earlier views of the elements and atoms in a preliminary manner, he anticipates much later scientific theories and developments in the study of nature. Even though the modern atom can be split and significant differences exist with Plato's polyhedra, which lack energy and are bound through proportion rather than a dynamic force, the atomic models as characterized in the early twentieth century by Neils Bohr and Ernest Rutherford possess a geometric structure. Plato's universe as a whole is teeming with activity (*energeia*), which is bound intimately with his "matter" as modern theories would suggest rather than being added as motion like in many ancient views. The chemical elements of the periodic table with their atomic numbers and weights are not Plato's four elements, but they are reducible to something else more basic (atoms of one kind), just as Plato speculates (triangles in his case). Heisenberg, too, has argued that the two most fundamental and influential contributions of early Greek natural philosophy for later science were the claims, first, by the Atomists that very small particles make up matter and, second, by the Pythagoreans that the universe is structured by mathematics.[49] In Plato, we find these beliefs elegantly combined.[50]

In many ways, Plato is closer to the current view of atomic substructure than the Atomists. Elementary particles are presently given mathematical form (although now generally as equations), and stereochemistry (which studies the spatial positions of atoms relative to chemical and optical properties) can be compared favorably with Plato's corpuscular theory. Some molecules and atoms, too, can be represented as pyramids, tetrahera, and octahedra. For example, methane is now characterized spatially as a regular pyramid with four hydrogen atoms surrounding a carbon atom.[51] Finally, there are interesting parallels that can be drawn between the cosmological view advanced in the *Timaeus* and the Big Bang model of the universe in terms of the role played by sensible perception of the realm of change, the formalizations of scientific explanation, and the inventiveness of the human mind.[52]

With regard to an inquiry into and critique of the idea of the "domination of nature"—or what we have been terming the domestication of the elements—there are competing and countervailing tendencies in Plato's dialogue. The *Timaeus* seeks to give intelligence, order, and beauty an expansive place in the universe. Mind operates in nature even if it can exist outside or beyond it—"intelligence cannot be present in anything apart from soul" (30b)—and nature can be understood because of its inner rational order. Plato, like Aristotle, maintains a teleological framework, although in many respects it gestures toward a divine teleology rather than an immanent, naturalistic one. Expanding on the view of Anaxagoras that *nous* (mind) is the initial cause of the universe, Plato arrives at the idea of a single craftsman-deity, a Demiurge who facilitates the birth of the cosmos. Like Anaxagoras, Plato begins with the principle that mind sets the primordial confusion—the bewildering chaos—in order but unlike him, he continues to hold to it as the basis for which conclusions about the cosmos depend.

In positing a Demiurge and locating the true world in the realm of the Forms, however, Plato takes a step away from the earlier philosophical strains of hylozoism—in which all pronounced units of "matter" are endowed with life—that were inherent in many Presocratic theories. The elements themselves as primary bodies are not alive as they literally or figuratively were for some of the Presocratics—recall Heraclitus' "ever-living" fire or Empedocles' animate *rhizomata*—nor are they self-moving. Rather, they attain to movement initially through the shaking of the *chora*, prior to the presence of the world soul, which is also not responsible for their animation because it has a higher order existence.

In the *Laws*, the question is raised, "When we see that this [power of] motion has shown itself in a thing composed of earth, water, or fire... how should we describe the character resident in such a thing" (895c). The immediate, unreflective response is that one can suppose such things to be endowed with life. But upon further investigation, it is revealed that soul and the primal power of movement are one and the same. As "the first-born of all things" soul is the supreme ruler in the realm of nature (*physis*) so that the status of the natural world insofar as it is identified with the four elements and the body is demoted to "second in the scale, or as low down as you please put" (896b).[53] Through its motions, soul "stirs all things in sky, earth, or sea" (896e). The works of nature and nature itself, Plato argues, are "secondary and derivative" (892b) from mind and art, and the elements, too, need something external to animate and motivate them.[54]

Husserl and the Mathematization of Nature

In the *Timaeus*, the four elements are mathematized, specifically geometrized, even if it is acknowledged that one cannot speak of the *exact* application of the principles and constructs of these fields within the realm of becoming. For Plato more broadly, the study of mathematical sciences is a requisite propaedeutic of philosophy, and its centrality to his work is evidenced by his educational plan in the *Republic* (ten years of such training), his use of geometry as a model upon which to ground knowledge (*episteme*), and his frequent recourse to Pythagoreanism. The related subjects (*mathemata*) of arithmetic, geometry, astronomy (then considered a branch of pure mathematics), and music (harmonics) have the capacity of turning the soul from the material world to objects of pure intellection. These true sciences yield *a priori*, exact and certain understanding of immutable truths as, for example, when an uneducated boy "learns" what his soul (mind) already "knows" through prodded recollection in the dialogue, the *Meno*. What we presently call natural science—the study of the physical world—is not true science at all for Plato.

In many respects, then, we might view Plato as a largely unrecognized precursor or even progenitor of what Edmund Husserl calls in the 1930s the "mathematization of nature," a phenomenon that has been linked to increasing historical attempts to control the natural world.[55] In *The Crisis of the European Sciences*, Husserl undertakes an investigation of the meaning of nature within the context of the knowledge gained through scientific advances, finding that as we have attained to greater cognitive control over the cosmos, we have also acquired greater mastery of the surrounding environment and greater dominion over other humans. The crisis of the sciences is characterized as a manifestation of a "radical life crisis" of humanity, and it is presented in terms of a loss of their significance for human life. The purpose of the inquiry is to explore how this loss arose, and what is at issue is the concept of science itself. The origin of modern philosophy and the distinct achievement of modern science, Husserl argues, are mathematical in character: the ideal of a universal science premised on the model of mathematics and geometry. And the "mathematization of nature" of which he speaks can actually be analyzed itself into two substeps: the *geometrization* of nature attempted by Galileo and the *arithmetization* of geometry achieved by Descartes and Leibniz.

Corresponding to the division within the spheres of human activity—the pre-scientific lifeworld (*Lebenswelt*) and the scientific world—is a division within nature itself. On the one hand, there is an intuited nature (*lebensweltliche Natur*)—the experienced nature of everyday life—and, on the other hand, there is a scientific nature (*wissenschaftliche Natur*)—the abstract-universal, mathematized nature of the physical sciences. The methods of science become in turn significant for the tasks of philosophy. According to Husserl, the first step in this transition is an abstraction, focusing on the shape dimensions of the world to the exclusion of secondary qualities. The second step involves interpretation and, more particularly, the consideration of spatial relationships as ideal so as to treat them with geometric exactness. In the process of abstraction and interpretation, as Husserl points out, science "forgets" the lifeworld—as we have largely forgotten the four elements on which our lives depend—and the nature that is "mastered" is that of everyday life. The true meaning of the world is thus expressed *more geometrico* by divesting it of the "merely subjective." Ontologically, *to be* comes to mean *to be measurable* in ideal, geometric terms for philosophy.

Although Husserl traces this transformation most specifically to Galileo, thereby attributing it more to the modern age than to the Greeks,[56] it must be acknowledged that Galileo himself inherits "pure geometry" from the Greeks as a science that seeks exact knowledge over its objects, and that Plato shares some of the ostensible procedures and goals of this enterprise, even if he does not complete this process into the "infinitization" that Galileo and modern science sought.[57] As Husserl recognizes, ancient thinkers following Plato's notion of the Forms had "idealized empirical numbers, units of measurement, empirical figures in space, points, lines, surfaces, bodies; and they transformed the propositions and proofs of geometry into ideal-geometrical propositions and proofs."[58] Plato does not go so far as to treat *everything* about the world as an example of a geometric object or relationship even if its importance in the *Timaeus* is evident in the analysis of the elements as resulting from number and shape. But he does create an influential view of the world in which a realm of eternal, unchanging objects exists beyond the deceptive flux of sensory experience, and this position corresponds in many manners to Husserl's characterization of the division between the scientific world and the lifeworld, which is devalued as the sphere of subjective experience.

Moreover, within this framework, Plato's Demiurge functions, too, a bit like the actor (i.e., scientist) in Husserl's analysis of modern science in that he remains behind the investigation, never quite *appearing* on the scene. Plato's configuring craftsman is hard to find, "and having found him it would be impossible to declare him to all mankind" (28c). So as to be all-encompassing, Galileo also treats "secondary qualities," which are not measurable directly in geometric ways (e.g., warmth, smell, color, weight), in terms of their geometric correlates. Plato likewise considers "secondary" sensible qualities that act on sense organs as correlatable to geometric shapes. Finally, there is some evidence in the so-called "unwritten doctrines"—coming via Aristotle—to suggest that Plato thought of the Forms themselves as generated by numbers—the "one" and the "indefinite dyad"—and that "the mathematicals" are intermediate between forms and particulars, signifying the many ideal objects that are required by mathematical statements.[59] Even if controversial, one of the larger goals Plato seems to have in mind, is to unify the various branches of knowledge, and mathematics clearly serves a key role in this process. When this undertaking is seen in relation with the secondary status of nature in Plato's writings, we can more easily ascertain a link between the two projects, a connection embodied especially in the *Timaeus* and carried forward today.[60]

Postscript to Plato: Whitehead's Philosophical Footnotes

In the twentieth-century work of Alfred North Whitehead—who famously saw all Western philosophy as but a series of footnotes to Plato—and especially his *Process and Reality*, we can discover a modern analogue and more contemporary response to the *Timaeus*—which Whitehead felt should be read at dawn, "as of a world just created and still becoming." We also can find a *postscript* to Plato's elemental "letters" and their ending or sending to posterity. Whitehead remarked that the ancient treatments of elements "bear witness to the undying vitality of Greek philosophy in its search for the ultimate" and are "factors of the fact disclosed in sense-awareness."[61] Plato's perspective in the *Timaeus*, he argues, is comparable to the matter and ether of modern science in terms of having a molecular view of the four elements and, although sounding at times fantastic, it embodies ideas that any reasonable philosophy of nature needs to identify and explain.

Although he does not develop the idea of the elements directly, Whitehead's whole cosmology, like Plato's, revolves around the bewildering issue of order—its emergence, endurance or absence. Such order ranges in kind from personal order in which an individual is considered to be the same person from birth to death (i.e., where there is identity over time) to social order that exists in his notion of societies, and finally to cosmological order that comes into being in a fashion bearing a striking resemblance to Plato's mythic framework in the *Timaeus*, where an aboriginal disorder is present. In Whitehead's "order of nature" there is continuity as opposed to hierarchy as we progress from molecules to single cells (organized republics of molecules) to plants (democratic societies) to animals and eventually to humans. In the *Timaeus*, the forms of structure that come about in the *chora* through extension are geometrical in nature, and this view finds a parallel in *Process and Reality*, where mathematical relations are part of the order of extensiveness that characterizes the "cosmic epoch" in which we live.[62]

It is also perhaps not until the arrival of Whitehead and his philosophy of process, his cosmology of becoming and his metaphysics of flux that we can return critically to a Platonic view of nature because mind or what Whitehead terms *subjective aim,* exists throughout all forms of life.[63] In fact, one might go as far to assert that mind in Whitehead's cosmology is not only *in* nature, as per the *Timaeus,* but that it *is* nature. That is, nature as process is mind at work. Evolution is therefore not perceived as a mindless, random movement because subjective aim is present, or omnipresent, in matter. It is a creative, conscious advance into novelty, and each entity in the universe is presented as a microcosmic reflection of this grand procession. The purposive goal of this advance, too, is the enlargement of mind, or what Whitehead terms "evolutionary expansiveness." It is important to note, however, that for Whitehead subjective aim is not simply intellectual in nature—rather it is the "lure for feeling" that is "the germ of mind"—and that "mental operations do not necessarily involve consciousness" so that inorganic matter (or nonliving "societies") can be included within what has been termed his "process ecology."[64]

In addition to change, motion, and becoming, a philosophy of nature must also account for relative permanence, a theme that also returns us to Plato. For Whitehead, eternal objects, in contrast to enduring ones, provide for the "very being of the process."[65] Thus, his metaphysics, although primarily one of fluidity, entails an element of durability. Against the flowing rivers of change, we find the stability of the "solid earth, the mountains, the stones, the Egyptian Pyramids, the spirit of man, God."[66] This aspect of his thought, like others, is derived from Plato and, in particular, his universals. Unlike Plato, however, Whitehead does not lead us into a hierarchy that ends with a transcendent God. Eternal objects are not Forms that are copied on the shadowy earth. The metaphysical status of eternal objects, on the contrary, is pure potentiality, the possibility for an actuality.

In this way, objectivity influences Whitehead's system and, if the sketch of the position being advanced here were fleshed out, it also clearly informs his "process ecology." For Whitehead, an objectivist position means that "the things experienced and the cognizant subject enter into the common world on *equal terms.*"[67] As with his reworking of the mind–body problem, he gives new meaning to the subject–object distinction. He defines object in terms of its potentiality for being a component of feeling and subject as being constituted by feeling. He also introduces the notion of "objective immortality" by which he means the "stubborn facts" that persist after actualities of the past have perished while retaining their foregone "decisions." This notion allows Whitehead to escape falling into the Platonic trap of unduly denigrating the physical world and preserves his potential for environmental philosophy. His emphasis on objectivity raises interesting issues regarding the possibility of an ecological ethic—questions that can be asked likewise about Platonic thought because both thinkers find ethical and aesthetic order in the cosmos. In such a view, reason, freedom, and value can be seen as part of and emergent from nature rather than imposed on it from a narrowly human perspective.

There are, of course, dis-analogous dimensions between the cosmologies of Whitehead and Plato. Most notably, the Platonic Demiurge is decidedly different from Whitehead's God, the "great Companion—the fellow sufferer who understands" in that it is not so strictly defined or so easily locatable in Plato's metaphysics, nor is his cosmology as overtly complex as Whitehead's thought. In the last analysis, Whitehead's "essay in cosmology"—as he subtitles *Process and Reality*—extends and points toward the possibility a new productive engagement with the Platonic philosophy of nature and cosmological myth, but it can also be said that by repeating it and giving us a "new form of Platonism," albeit in a different language, it renews and resacrilizes not only the *Timaeus*, but the cosmos that has been brought into being.[68] As Mircea Eliade points out, the repetition of a cosmogony leads to the consecration of place, and it is to this notion, among others, that we now turn in a consideration of Aristotle's philosophy and the potential it demonstrates for rescuing the elements for further environmental work.

Interstice: Cloud

I am the daughter of earth and water, / And the nursling of the sky; / I pass through the pores of the ocean and shores; / I change, but I cannot die.

—Shelley, "The Cloud"

They are the celestial Clouds, the patron goddesses of the layabout. From them come our intelligence, our dialectic and our reason.

—Aristophanes, *The Clouds*

Oscar Wilde once remarked that until poets and painters first revealed the beauty of fog no one could really see or appreciate it fully.[1] The same might be said of clouds, fog's higher-flying cousins. Clouds were, in effect, "invented" by an amateur meteorologist who was instrumental in creating a new nomenclature for the sky.[2] By identifying and cataloging them based on Linnaean notions of classification, Luke Howard was able to momentarily freeze ephemeral entities and bring into existence a new way of perceiving elemental reality. Of the English Quaker and chemist, Goethe wrote, "Howard gives us with his clear mind / The gain of lessons new to all mankind; / That which no hand can reach, no hand can clasp / He first has gained, first held with mental grasp."[3]

As phenomena situated broadly between air and water on the elemental scale, clouds mark a transitional zone between the overarching heavens above and the ballasting earth below. They also become instant Rorschach tests formed of moving, if inchoate, pictures whereby we see what we seek. This point is underscored in Shakespeare's most famous play when Hamlet cries out to Polonius, "Do you see yonder cloud that's almost in shape of a camel?" but then decides it looks more like a weasel and changes his mind again to claim it is assuming the outline of a whale.[4] Amidst the wide horizons and shifting canvases of prairies or plains, where the activity on the ground is often slow to unfold and evolve, the eye is forever drawn to the drama of the sky. Of a typical day in the desert, Edward Abbey observes: "The clouds multiply and merge, cumuli-nimbi piling up like whipped cream, like mashed potatoes, like sea foam, building upon one another into a second mountain range far greater in magnitude than the terrestrial range below."[5] He details their development when they arrive as "unfurling and smoking billows in malignant violet, dense as wool." Eventually, the clouds "thicken, then crack and split with a roar like that of cannonballs tumbling down a marble staircase; their bellies open—too late to run now—and the rain comes down."[6]

Clouds are most basically condensed water vapor that forms very small ice crystals held in the atmosphere as a visible mass. They are generally created in one of several ways: when air reaches a temperature below its saturation point, when air masses intermingle, or when air absorbs additional water vapor until it reaches its line of saturation. Color is one key to comprehending the cloud's contents—or grumbling discontent—and it ranges the gamut from white to blue-gray to black. Clouds are usually milky white at the top because they are highly reflective of light, though they become gray or darker farther into their depths as solar radiation diminishes due to density or water absorption. Very thin clouds tend to take on the hues of their surroundings, and they are illuminated and hence colored by non-white light, as happens at sunrise or sunset. Clouds with hints of green come about when the light of the sun is dispersed by ice, whereas rare yellow clouds are generated by smoke from forest fires.

Because they are equally so elemental and extraordinary, artists have a hard time resisting the beckoning charms of clouds as subjects. Magritte used them iconically in paintings to create dream-like images, to evoke mystery and surrealist possibility or impossibility, and to investigate the grammar of the sky through false walls or window frames. The English artist John Constable—"the man of the clouds" as he once described himself—devoted much of his work to an exploration of the aerial world, believing clouds in particular to be "the key note, the standard of scale, and the chief organ of sentiment" in the landscape.[7] In "Seascape Study with Rain Cloud" of 1824, for example, he shows beautifully the *force majeure* of a rain shower by exploiting dark slashing brushstrokes to link blackened clouds with the surface of the ocean. In offering advice to other artists of this time period, John Ruskin commented on a "great peculiarity" about the sky: namely, that "clouds, not being much liable to man's interference, are always beautifully arranged," unlike other aspects of the landscape.[8]

One could even chart a cultural history of clouds to reveal the ways they have been understood as emblems of freedom, harbingers of doom, and symbols of the divine. Powerful elemental phenomena—and representations of them—are almost always multivalent because they are cut from and hence reflect the rich and arguably paradoxical or contradictory fabric of reality. Clouds are no different in this regard. Societies throughout the world have used them to suggest the presence of supernatural forces, frequently employing clouds as a throne or a means of revelation. The Egyptians linked clouds with creation, fertility, and divine protection. The Dogon of western Africa, who live a very difficult life in a rocky landscape and are utterly dependent on rainfall, understandably connect clouds with all symbolic dimensions of their view of the universe. The insubstantiality of the cloud permitted Hebrews to invoke it as a visible stand-in for the invisible Yahweh because they could not use physical icons as a mode of divine representation. Thus, through the cloak of a pillar of cloud, God guides the Jews out of Egypt into Canaan, appears in the tent of the Ark of the Covenant, and communicates to Moses on the mountain. In the Bible, Enoch also experiences an intense vision of a cloud: "There I saw the locked reservoirs from which the winds are distributed: a reservoir for the hail . . . for the fog and the mist, and the cloud coming from them has been floating over the Earth since the beginning of the world."[9] Within Christianity, clouds can connote mystery or mysticism, and they are often associated with the figure of Jesus, who ascends to heaven in a cloud.

Writers like Shelley, Goethe, and Coleridge celebrate clouds with paeans to these floating, drifting sky ponds. The Romantics are drawn especially to their transient, indefinite, and distant aspects, delighting in the attempt to render fleeting forms into transcendent objects. For them, clouds are not merely another feature of the landscape and atmosphere or a way to soften or sharpen lighting but entrancing entities in their own right. Clouds, however, can signal not just a sense of the sublime but also destruction and death, as in plumes of smoke and dust suspended above the fallen World Trade Center towers in New York, ominous hurricane storm clouds threatening to assault a populated area, or mushroom clouds triggered by nuclear explosions.[10]

In Switzerland, architects have fashioned the startling Blur Building as an artificial cloud that bends and "blurs" notions of space, stability and structure, creating an ever-changing field of air subject to the whims of wind and water. Its lightweight "tensegrity" frame measures sixty-five feet in height, two hundred feet in depth and three hundred feet in width, and its pavilion area is created from water sent from the surrounding Lake Neuchâtel into the sky to become mist and fog through thousands of nozzles. Individuals approach this anthropogenic atmosphere on a four-hundred-foot ramp that takes them into the heart of a billowing mass. Although all buildings contain and circulate air, Blur is in a very real sense constructed of it, disorienting visitors who may become lost without normal perceptual clues in the ragged and changing edges of an ill-defined shroud. The relative amorphousness of this embryonic and evolving "air work" resembles well the indeterminate nature of clouds, whose ethereal "bodies" seem suddenly to appear and evaporate—manifest then dematerialize—as they are embroidered with a strange but hypnotic texture that emerges through a dialectical dance of surface and depth.

The fascination with clouds has a long intellectual history. Within philosophy, this first theorized that clouds are formed through the thickening of air, which he conceived as the primary stuff of the universe. In Anaximenes' view, when air is further condensed, rain is pressed out; when falling water coalesces, hail occurs;

and when moisture combines with wind, snow descends. Not long thereafter, Socrates is portrayed in parody by Aristophanes as a comic figure hanging in a basket and hence having his head lost in the clouds. The playwright makes the gadfly of Athens deliver speeches like the following:

> I'd never come up with a single thing / about celestial phenomena, / if I did not suspend my mind up high, / to mix my subtle thoughts with what's like them— / the air. If I turned my mind to lofty things, / but stayed there on the ground, I'd never make / the least discovery. For the earth, you see, / draws moist thoughts down by force into itself— / the same process takes place with water cress.[11]

Here we find the suggestion that those who study meteorological phenomena, or more specifically nephrology, are not to be taken seriously—that they are but "airheads." This view, naturally, is far from the truth. Aristotle commences his *Meteorology* with the question, "why do not clouds form in the upper air as one might on the face of it expect?" and proposes a mechanistic theory based on interactions of the elements of air, earth and water with the sun.[12] Seneca subsequently portrays clouds as driving agents of change in the atmosphere. And Descartes seeks to disenchant clouds of their mystery in order to usher in a new philosophy of nature since painters and poets regularly portray them as "the throne of God and pretend that He uses his own hands to open and close the doors to the winds, to sprinkle dew on the flowers, and to hurl lightning against the rocks."[13] More recently, Bachelard speaks of clouds as a kind of "imaginary matter" with which one can work or play as in a hypnotic daydream. From this perspective, reverie "controls a changing phenomenon by giving it a command that has already been carried out or is being carried out. 'Great elephant! Stretch out your trunk,' says the child to the cloud that is growing longer. And the cloud obeys."[14] Would that the rest of reality respond so well to our wishes.

Owing its orientation to the genius of Howard, the operative scientific taxonomy starts with a visual distinction between *stratus* (think: to stratify) or "layered" clouds that resemble flat blankets and *cumulous* (think: to accumulate) clouds, which are more piled up and convective in nature and appear in the sky as great cotton balls or bunches of cauliflower. These two types are then subdivided into four families based on the general altitude of the cloud: high, middle, low, and vertical. Cirrus clouds form above five thousand meters—about three miles—in the cold troposphere and tend to be wispy and transparent, like curls of white hair. Among other kinds, we find both cirrocumulus and cirrostratus clouds in this region. Between two thousand and five thousand meters lie "alto" clouds, including those that compose the memorable mackerel sky. Below two thousand meters are low-lying clouds and fog, which is generated when stratus clouds touch the earth. A final family is vertical clouds that form at multiple altitudes and that rise high from their bases, often containing up-currents of air.

What is sequestered within the seemingly empty pockets of clouds—which cover sixty percent of the surface of the earth—must impress the most dexterous of magicians. Out of these "rabbit hats" comes a litany of precipitation, including a dazzling array of rain, snow, hail and sleet. A large rain cloud can contain as many as 150,000 tons of water, enough to fill a pond that is one mile long, three hundred feet wide and five feet deep. Falling hail is sometimes large enough to kill antelope, and it has reached the size of a grapefruit. The wonder generated by these objects crashing to the earth must have inspired Basho's haiku encouraging us to experience the elemental world as immediately as possible: "Look, children, / Hail stones! / Let's rush out!"[15]

Thunder and lightning serve as the admonitory voices of more commonly muted and pacific clouds. Lightning is, in essence, electricity produced in cumulonimbus clouds when ice crystals and water drops collide, which generates positive and negative charges that move down on the ground, leap from cloud to cloud, or transit within clouds. When lighting strikes, the light actually moves upward from the earth toward the cloud despite appearances of the opposite, and the superheated air expands so quickly that it sends out a shock wave that we ear-witness as an explosion. Perhaps the sheer force and revelation afforded by these events help to account for Heraclitus' identification of the thunderbolt as that which steers all things in the cosmos. Sculptor Walter de Maria has explored some of this elemental clout in New Mexico by arranging four hundred gleaming stainless steel poles into a large geometric grid in a desert field that responds not only to the occurrence of lightning but also to atmospheric conditions, especially storms and the play of light, which produces mesmerizing optical effects. The work—designed for viewing over a twenty-four-hour period—provokes a reception that ranges from the cerebral to the emotional, and it spawns a productive tension between ground (earth) and sky (air). When a tempest arrives on the scene, lighting (fire) and rain (water) are added potentially to the aesthetic mix of the four elements.

The ability to accurately read the sky and especially the portents of clouds has been vital to farmers, military leaders and ship captains in many ages. The watchwords, "Red sky in morning, sailor take warning; red sky at night, sailor's delight," redound through the centuries. Very lightweight or scattered clouds in a clear sky commonly point toward strong winds. Bad weather may be in the offing when clouds move quickly and multiply in number or thicken and descend suddenly. The rapid departure of such clouds indicates that atmospheric frenzy is immanent, and sailors learn to avoid deadly cyclones in warm climates by watching for cirrus clouds carrying heavy rain ahead of a storm.

As residents of the tropics and subtropics know, clouds are not just confined to the upper reaches of the sky. "Cloud forests" can be formed in evergreen areas where there is a frequency of low-level water vapor, usually found at the level of the canopy. In these regions, misty air reduces the amount of direct sunlight arriving on the ground, and precipitation routinely takes the form of fog drippings. The high moisture content in the environment, in turn, encourages the growth of many kinds of moss, ferns, orchids and exotic epiphytes (or aerophytes)—plants that live on top of other plants. When cloud forests emerge on mountains, as they do in Costa Rica and Peru, one may further observe the beautiful confluence of shimmering light against rock, wood, sky and water—truly an elemental encounter.

As screens of fleece for our mind's eye, clouds offer therapeutic and aesthetic opportunities as well as chances to participate in elemental play. Bachelard observes:

> In its dynamic intoxication, the imagination uses the cloud like an ectoplasm that sensitizes our mobility. In the long run nothing can resist the invitation of the clouds to travel as they patiently float by, again and again, far up in the blue sky. It seems to the dreamer as if the cloud could carry everything away with it: sorrow, steel, screams.[16]

I gaze through the window of my plane and see fields of poppies, stalks of broccoli, wraithlike glaciers cleaving. I am suddenly within a blizzard of white, lost in a Sahara of shifting sand. It seems as if I am inside a vast aerial brain, the sky's cerebral cortex. The steward hands me a coffee. Appropriately, milky cream wells up and swirls upon the surface. More clouds. Given their widespread and free availability, we should all feel indulgent enough at times to engage in this entertainment and cognitive escape, for it appears that clouds, too, are almost relishing in the creation of short-lived sculptures of ice, air and water. It is as if they are saying with Shelley, "I silently laugh at my own cenotaph, / And out of the caverns of rain, / Like a child from the womb, like a ghost from the tomb, / I rise and unbuild it again."[17]

— 5 —

The Place of the Elements and the Elements of Place

Aristotle's Natural Household

Give me a place to stand and I will move the world.

—Archimedes

The potency of place [is] marvelous . . . and takes[s] precedence of all other things.

—Aristotle, *Physics*

I find the elemental to be deeply binding. Each phenomenal element, whether it be air or water or rock, is intimately linked to every other and in this capacity helps to tie together the landscape I witness.

—Edward Casey, *Representing Place*

Four Accounts of Five Elements

The secret to understanding Aristotle, Santayana once observed, is to see him as a thoroughgoing naturalist given that "everything ideal has a natural basis, and everything natural an ideal development."[1] Indeed, for Aristotle, elemental entities possess natural places and movements; objects of knowledge are apprehended through bodily and earth-bound senses; there is frequent reference to biological models or analogies; and even the concept of the soul *(psyche)* is naturalized. Such approaches tend to make his work amenable to ecological thought and deliberation—even if it might sometimes be problematic in its application—and as a whole more germane in its orientation to emerging issues than many other philosophical frameworks. Aristotle's vision of the natural world and human community, in fact, continues to affect environmental discourse in constructive ways as evidenced by social ecology, a contemporary school of thought that has embraced some of his main ideas.[2]

Aristotle introduces his own original understanding of earth, air, fire, and water after launching a sustained critique of the elemental philosophy of the Presocratics and Plato. In the process, we encounter a strikingly new account of nature (*physis*) and its relation to place, motion, change, contrariety, and causality, one that transforms thinking about the environment and exercises an influence even past the objections of Descartes, Spinoza, and Newton. Aristotle attends to the *whereabouts* of the elements (*stoicheia*). He provides in effect a *household* for earth, air, fire, and water—a place for their homecoming and an abode for their return and "domestication"—just as Plato provided a locale for their genesis, their arrival into the world through a Receptacle (*hypodoche*). In brief, Aristotle takes up Plato's offer to "put the matter to the test" and find a better method for the construction of the elemental bodies such that "his will be the victory, not of an enemy, but of a friend."[3] The challenge for him is to defend the primacy of the elements understood by Empedocles as unchanging building blocks while showing that they are nevertheless generated, although not as Plato envisioned.[4]

Given that Aristotle's writings on the elements appear in a variety of texts, the question can be raised whether he proffers distinct and differing accounts of earth, air, fire, and water. There is, it seems, a psychological theory (*On the Soul*), a cosmological view (*On the Heavens*), a more restricted physical outlook (*On Generation and Corruption*), and a meteorological version (*Meteorology*) of the elements.[5] In many key respects, these four frameworks dovetail just like the four elements themselves to form a relatively coherent picture of the Aristotelian universe and the physical world of the ancient Greeks. Ultimately, however, Aristotle provides a kind of jigsaw puzzle theory of the elements, one with a few stray or missing pieces, a couple of questionable fits, and several leftover items but also one that can be cobbled together creatively to present a powerful perspective of the environment.

Whereas Aristotle's *Physics* examines place and change in general, *On the Heavens* (hereafter *De Caelo*) takes as its topic the more narrow range of local movement and treats earth, air, fire, and water in terms of their lightness or heaviness. It also introduces *aether* (ether) as a fifth element that splays open the frame of the four, exposing it to the sidereal realm beyond "the above," and ostensibly, but not actually, altering the economy and ecology of earth, air, fire, and water. *On Generation and Corruption* considers the elements as contraries and simple bodies, exploring the types of transformation between them. Aristotle thereby analyzes change of substance (generation), change of quality (alteration), and change of magnitude (growth). *On the Soul* (hereafter *De Anima*), in turn, tackles the subject of the *psyche* (soul) and whether it is composed of elements as some earlier philosophers had presumed. Finally, the *Meteorology* studies combinations and mutual influences of earth, fire, air, and water in the environment.[6]

Aristotle's stoicheology (study of the elements) takes its primary point of departure from two main sources: Empedocles and Plato. Aristotle finds affinities with each thinker, but only partial ones. He agrees with Empedocles that the elements are four in number, but he does not maintain that they are immutable and eternal. Likewise, he accepts with Plato the notion of "forms" but is unwilling to remove them from the fleeting physical and phenomenal world. And whereas Plato treats earth, air, fire, and water in terms of a more basic mathematics, Aristotle's theory functions completely without recourse to numbers and must be considered instead in terms of his notions of nature and place as well as the controversial status of prime matter (*prote hyle*). There is, too, an important return to qualitative aspects of explanation and interpretation, as in the Empedoclean framework, features that had been rejected by the Atomists and as for the most part by Plato.

In some ways, it appears as if Aristotle, like Plato, also abets in the marginalization and eventual displacement of the classic elemental tetrad, helping to replace the quartet through the force of his own theory and attendant challenges to philosophical predecessors. On first blush, it seems that the "so-called elements" of Empedocles and other Presocratic thinkers—earth, air, fire, and water—do not turn out to be actual elements for Aristotle. As is seen here, this is not necessarily the case. Aristotle's positions and dispositions are nevertheless oppositional—both negatively in the sense of criticizing earlier speculative views and more positively in the sense of advancing a specific theory of contrariety, a disquisition on opposition.

Aristotle's philosophy of nature, as noted, is one of his most significant contributions, and it is treated in, among other texts, his physics—part of the triumvirate of theoretical sciences along with mathematics and metaphysics. There and elsewhere, he expounds a conception of nature that is processual and developmental rather than static and mechanical, as well as one that is intelligible rather than ineffable or unknowable. Aristotle clearly does not view reality as singular, unchanging, and indivisible because that would be tantamount to the destruction of natural philosophy, which is predicated on phenomenal change. And his broader solution to elemental challenges involves the development of a perspective that characterizes *physis* (nature) in terms of being an internal source of both change and stability in substances.[7] As Karl Jaspers has declaimed, "the soul of a landscape, the spirits of the elements, the genius of every place will be revealed to a loving view of nature."[8] Even if it is debatable whether Aristotle's outlook is "loving," there is little doubt that it is consistently attentive, keenly insightful and deeply respectful of organic processes in such a way as to light up the significance of the elemental world and environmental place.

We will take up Aristotle's multiple views of the elements and attempt to link, reconcile and unify them. In addition to identifying and investigating four main aspects of his four-element perspective, which itself appears in four separate accounts, we will contextualize, interpret, and examine Aristotle's positions on generation, the process of elemental transformation, and the status of a fifth element, prime matter, and the soul. In doing so, we will see that earth, water, air, and fire can be construed reasonably as fundamental and primary components of his physical system, despite some evidence to the contrary. In this chapter, we will discover how Aristotle's elemental theory is relevant to addressing environmental issues and problems related to inhabitation, dwelling, and the home by exploring in particular his deep engagement with the subject of natural place. The ensuing chapter shows that Aristotle's emphasis on physical contact and bodily touch, organic unity, geocentricity, and philosophical naturalism is valuable concomitantly for ecological thought and action.

A Dictionary of Elemental Definitions

In the first-known philosophical lexicon in Western history, Book Delta of the *Metaphysics*, Aristotle sets forth several definitions of *stoicheion* (element), providing us with a starting point for our investigation and a set of rungs to help assemble the scaffold of his theory or theories. Aristotle is methodologically more systematic than his predecessors in treating the elements, and this fact is evident in his attempts to define the *stoicheia*. For the most part, Aristotle's use of the term is stripped of metaphorical dimensions that were present in the earliest Greek usage. He identifies "element" first as "the primary component immanent in a thing, and indivisible in kind into other kinds" (1014 a26–27). We should note here the notions of (a) primary (b) immanence (c) indivisibility, and (d) kind (as opposed to quantity) that are brought out in this definition. In one sense, elements are, quite simply, those things that are fundamental, most basic, or elementary. For example, the elements of speech are the parts into which it can be divided ultimately such that these parts are no longer divisible into other speech that is different in kind. In illustrating this definition, Aristotle draws implicitly on two meanings of *stoicheia* (evident in Plato) when he resorts to a comparison via simile of the elements understood as components of speech (i.e., letters) with the elements construed in a material sense. Although this analogy holds, we should not consider the elements of physical things such as bodies to be linguistic elements. In this regard, we must speak of elements of something, not elements in themselves—that is, elements *simpliciter*.

Aristotle offers in the same work a second definition of *stoicheion* that stresses (e) smallness (f) simplicity, and (g) universality as belonging to the notion. This meaning is spoken of in terms of a transference and application of the initial definition such that it becomes useful for multiple purposes. The implication is that this understanding is more popular and common, as well as the source of the idea that the elements are the most universal of things because each is singular and simple, present in a plenitude of things. Such unity, Aristotle suggests, is what some earlier philosophers considered to be first principles. In any event, the idea of an immanent first component is part and parcel to all these meanings of element.

Aristotle also characterizes the elements as primary constituents of bodies in *De Caelo* (*Peri Ouranous* in Greek). An element is "a body into which other bodies may be analyzed (*diaipeitai*), present in them potentially or actually . . . and not itself divisible (*adiaipeton*) into bodies different in form (*to eidei*)" (302a16–18). This definition is significant because it calls attention to the fact that elements are simple bodies—as they are for Plato—and it reiterates their indivisibility. Aristotle concludes that such bodies must exist because, for example, fire and earth are potentially present in bodies such as wood and flesh given that they are seemingly exuded from them. He maintains, too, in the *Metaphysics*, that "we give the name of 'elements' to those geometrical propositions, the proofs of which are implied in the proofs of the others," adding that "both those who say there are several elements of corporeal things and those who say there is one, say the parts of which bodies are compounded and consist are principles" (998a25ff). In this last definition, elements are understood as primary propositions from which other propositions can be derived. We can recognize this sense of the term as it is later employed in the third and fourth century B.C.E. by Euclid, who refers to theorems used to solve all geometric problems, as the "elements" of geometry.[9] Euclid's *Elements* is the first major Greek mathematical text to survive, and many of his postulates find earlier parallels and comparable treatments in Aristotle's writings, leading us to see the lasting significance of Aristotle's elemental definitions, especially his definitions of the elements.[10] All of Aristotle's definitions are similar in kind and mutually reinforcing, and they provide the basis for his full-fledged view of earth, water, air, and fire. Elements, then, cannot be further divided; they are not composites but rather decidedly simple bodies.

The Ancient Generation Gap

Having clarified the linguistic sense and philosophical scope of *stoicheion*, we now take up summarily, and very briefly, the problem of whether the elements are generated along with the related issue whether they are singular or plural. Aristotle agrees with Empedocles that there are but four elements, though he qualifies this claim to be inclusive only of the terrestrial sphere because he will eventually introduce a fifth nonterrestrial element. Basically, he argues in *De Caelo* that the elements cannot be infinite in number because that would misapprehend the very concept of an element, which is indivisible into bodies of different form. Aristotle also criticizes the position that the *stoicheia* can be reduced to one and in the process distinguishes his own view sharply from those who adhere to forms of monism, likely, although not explicitly, referring to Thales (water), Anaximenes (air), Heraclitus (fire), and possibly Anaximander (an infinite body that embraces the heavens).[11] In developing this critique, Aristotle distances his own view from all strictly quantitative accounts of the elements, preparing the ground for a more qualitative stoicheiology and a reinvigoration but complete transformation of Empedocles' perspective. His primary objection to monistic theories rests on the argument that single element views admit of only one natural movement that is the same for each body, a position that belies the plurality of natural movements he establishes elsewhere. In deploying natural motion as a philosophical trump card and fundamental criterion, we see the central role it plays in his elemental framework.

While Aristotle argues initially against the acceptance of single-element theories on the one hand and infinite-element views on the other hand, it should be apparent that a vast range of options exists between these extremes. Although he proves to be a traditionalist in subscribing to a fourfold of simple bodies, two questions can be raised. First, why does he accept the classic tetrad of fire, air, water, and earth? And, second, does this number, along with the associated explanation of the four elements, reflect our experiences of and the divisions within the lifeworld? With regard to the latter question, we postpone a response until after examining Aristotle's notions of natural place and motion, which provide keys to a reply. The answer to the first question is ultimately to be found elsewhere in his theory of contrariety, which is an extension and development of earlier Milesian and mythological views and a matter to be examined later. However, a major clue as to their nature and number is provided in his response to the issue of whether the elements are eternal or subject to a coming-to-be and perishing, or a "generation" and "corruption" as it were. Presented as a provocative choice, this question also concerns a decision whether to opt in an Empedoclean or Platonic direction. In order to get to the heart of Aristotle's perspective and to concentrate on the features that are most relevant to our investigation, we forego, however, an extended analysis of his challenges to earlier views, especially because others have conducted such an investigation at length.[12] Nevertheless, several crucial points are briefly in order.

Unlike Empedocles' *rhizomata*, Aristotle's four sublunary elements are neither divine nor eternal. Aristotle argues that Empedocles' assumption that they are ungenerated and indestructible is misguided because observation teaches that, for example, water changes to air and fire is extinguished when it is quenched or dies out. And on this point he appears to be correct. The elements, in short, are generated out of one another, as they had been in a very different manner in Plato's *Timaeus*.[13] After acknowledging that they are subject to a coming-to-be and passing-away, the question arises as to whether they derive from something corporeal or incorporeal and, if they are generated from a body, whether they come from one another or something else entirely. Not surprisingly, Aristotle concludes that the elements cannot be generated out of anything other than themselves—either corporeal or incorporeal. The reasoning is that a theory that generated them from something incorporeal would require a void that itself is extra-corporeal. This is so because if the void were a body, we would be faced with the problem of two bodies occupying the same place at the same time—a nonpossibility given Aristotle's understanding of place and time.[14] Likewise, the elements are not generated out of another body because such an entity would exist distinctly apart from the elements themselves and be prior to them.[15]

By holding that the elements are generated, Aristotle distances his view from Empedocles but in rejecting geometrical forms of generation from something more "elemental" than the four elements, he separates himself from Plato as well. He criticizes Plato's attempt to give a determinate shape to each element even though he agrees ostensibly with Plato that earth, water, air, and fire are not completely unchanging.[16] Like Plato, Aristotle believes there is a quantitative factor involved in the transformation of the elements, being aware that air, for example, occupies more space than the water that evaporates into it, but he does not try to provide a mathematics for his system or formulate ratios and proportionalities of change. His own theory is again decidedly more qualitative than Plato's largely quantitative framework. We can conclude, then, that Aristotle does not base his theory of the elements on shape but rather something else, differentia that concern the property, function, and power of natural bodies.

In sum, Aristotle finds the Presocratic theories of the "so-called elements" and Empedocles' position on the *rhizomata* in particular inadequate because they fail to provide for the generation of the elements in a proper manner, or they identify either too few primary elements in the cases of Thales, Anaximenes, and Heraclitus, or too many in the case of the Atomists.[17] Admittedly, Aristotle is often more occupied with finding anticipations of own theory in the Presocratics than exploring this philosophy on its terms. He is not attentive sufficiently to the earlier stress on the seeming permanence of the elements and the denial of coming-to-be characteristic of the post-Parmenidean pluralists. Aristotle, instead, ostensibly claims that physical change presupposes a material substratum (*hypokeimenon*) that persists through change, which is considered to be the absence of some property from a substratum. He offers powerful challenges to the Empedoclean perspective and original re-readings or creative mis-readings of the Presocratics and Plato even if he does not always interpret these fragments and frameworks generously or accurately.

Aristotle's own account of the four elements is comprised of and premised on four basic and interrelated components:

1. A theory of heaviness and lightness.
2. A theory of natural motion.
3. A theory of natural place.
4. A theory of contrariety, specifically the oppositions of cold–hot and dry–wet.

Although we distill these notions from his works and treat them at times separately, it must be borne in mind that they coexist and cooperate so as to form a more coherent whole. Aristotle himself recognizes, for example, that a consideration of the heavy and the light is a part of a theory of movement and seems to indicate a manner in which weight and lightness are like the pairs of opposites, cold and hot. Similarly, his doctrine of place is imbricated intimately with his view of natural motion because the four elemental bodies are understood with respect to their tendencies to find or move toward their natural positions in the universe. In fact, we can pinpoint in embryonic form three of the four major parts of his more comprehensive perspective on the four elements in one short Aristotelian argument: "If [a] body possesses *weight and lightness*, it will be one of the elements; and if it has no *tendency to movement*, it will be an immovable or mathematical entity, and therefore not *in a place* at all" (305a25, italics added). Only the idea of contrariety—specifically the oppositions of cold and hot, and wet and dry—is absent in this remark, the other primary component to his stoicheiology. We turn first to look at his theory of weight.

Pondering Weight

In *The Unbearable Lightness of Being*, Milan Kundera claims that the opposition of weight and lightness is the most mysterious and ambiguous of all dualities.[18] This is so because although heavy burdens threaten to crush us, at the same time and in proportion to their heaviness they bring us closer to the earth, making our lives more tangible and real. Conversely, the absence of weighty problems enables us to be free, to be lighter than air so to speak, making us at once less real and our actions less significant. The perplexity arises because it is not clear which way we should choose and in which direction we should live. In other words, as Kundera asks, is lightness or heaviness preferable? From its outset, philosophy has *pondered* and—as the word itself suggests in its etymology from *pondus*—*weighed in* on this issue as well. Weight or heaviness has connoted depth, seriousness, and *gravitas*—a secure foundation, a way to ballast claims, a means of anchoring the eternal. At the same time, there has been an equally strong penchant (from *pendere*, to weigh) for philosophers to seek the solace of the heights, a countervailing tendency to flee to the heavens and the pure ether of independence. Parmenides, who divided things into a series of oppositions, opted in the end to view lightness as positive and heaviness as negative. Nietzsche later reconfigures this question in posing to us the problem of eternal return, what he identifies as the heaviest weight (*das schwerste Gewicht*) and burden of all. But he too seeks to slay the spirit of gravity, to find levity and to dance footloose and free in the land of the downcast.

In Aristotle, we can discern the paradigmatic philosopher of balance and even-handedness, the judicious weigher of competing claims, who is symbolized in Raphael's painting, "The School of Athens," with his hand outstretched *into* the world in juxtaposition to Plato, who gestures upward, *out* of the world. We find both movements manifested, an acceptance of the necessity of weight and lightness—what amounts to as perhaps the most primitive properties of natural bodies—along with the corresponding natural movements with which they are associated. More particularly, with regard to the sublunary bodies, Aristotle subscribes to a view of absolute weight and lightness, a position that stands in contrast to one that sees terms as relative or relational.[19] Aristotle admits, too, of the use of the distinctions up and down and their application to the world *in toto*.[20] For Aristotle, because the universe has an extremity and a center, there must be both an up and a down. The whole—whose extremity is commonly termed "the above"—is such as to be formed of hemispheres, but it must be recognized, as common usage is given to forget, that in addition to the hemisphere over us another exists, formed on this same pattern so that the center is below and the extremity always above.

Heavy and light, then, are understood as possessing a power of being moved naturally in a particular way. It could, in fact, be said that lightness and heaviness serve to mediate natural movements. The true meaning of light and heavy concerns motion, and these terms cannot be grasped adequately without reference to it. For Aristotle, heaviness and lightness are the tendencies of a body to transit either upward or downward. And by this he means there are some things with a constant nature of movement toward the center and other things with a constant movement away from the center. Absolute lightness means that an object or a body moves upward or toward the extremity while absolute lightness implies that an object or a body moves downward or toward the center. To speak properly of the relatively light, however, Aristotle's theory requires the existence of two bodies—both with weight and equal with respect to bulk—such that one moves more quickly downward.

Aristotle's view that all sublunary bodies have the tendency to move either to the center of the cosmos or toward its circumference is premised on two claims. First, certain types of matter tend to rise or fall in other types of matter despite variations in their relative bulk. Second, a greater amount of matter of one kind displays its character more fully than a smaller amount. Thus, it would be heavier if the type were heavy and lighter if it were light. After reviewing and rejecting previous theories, Aristotle's proffered solution is to recognize qualitatively different types of matter. If there exists only one type of matter, there is no possibility for absolute heaviness or lightness. Similarly, if there is only one type of matter along with its contrary, there can be no relative lightness or heaviness.[21]

The first definitions of "heavy" and "light" are given in *De Caelo* in terms of that which moves naturally toward the center and that which moves naturally away from the center. The purpose of this preliminary introduction of concepts becomes more evident when we consider the subject being treated. *Aether* is an exception to the general rule that all bodies possess weight, and Aristotle speaks of this phenomenon partly by way of an assumption and partly by way of proof.

All things that move down or up can be said to possess heaviness or lightness, but a body that moves circularly does not (and cannot) possess either heaviness or lightness since it cannot naturally move toward or away from the center. We examine the status of *aether* in more detail later, but it is important to note that it lies outside of the sublunary framework in part because it fails to meet the first criterion of sublunary bodies: the possession of weight.

Aristotle's theory of weight and lightness does not seem to comprehend explicitly the notion of mass, understood as the property of physical bodies and a measure of their inertia.[22] Mass is now construed as a measurement of the amount of matter that a body contains, giving it weight in a gravitational field. In modern physics, mass is one of the basic quantities upon which physical measurements are made in addition to time and length. By fashioning a place for lightness and heaviness and the vertical (up and down) kinds of movement associated with them, however, Aristotle provides for a mode of world-orientation, a way of situating things relative to one another, and a manner for understanding natural place. Augustine of Hippo, who posits that "my weight is my love," later articulates a modified Aristotelian view of weight and place in terms of *pondus amoris* in which things tend upward or downward to their domiciles or proper elements because the weight of their love propels them there. As Augustine puts it in his *Confessions*, "A body tends to go of its own weight to its own place, not necessarily downward toward the bottom, but to its own place."[23] In such remarks, we observe the considerable influence Aristotle's ideas exercise in intellectual history.

The Place of the Elements

For Aristotle, then, the differentia of the elements is not primarily shape or composition but their motion and tendency to move toward a particular location. What distinguishes the elements depends upon differences in the various kinds of movements. And the tendency of a body to move upward or downward is tied to the apparent fact that each element has its own proper place. Aristotle offers, in effect, a *place-based* view of the elements. Place (*topos*) is defined in his treatise on the heavens as "the boundary of that which contains it" (310b8)—place being like a pail as he will argue in the *Physics*—and it is to its like to which a body returns when it moves to its proper place. For example, earth moves naturally to the center and fire to the circumference. This distinction, too, depends more basically on his preceding but complementary argument that all bodies possess either weight or lightness. What is light moves upward and outward, whereas what is heavy moves downward and toward the center. Aristotle, in fact, provides us with a first and tentative elemental axiom by arguing that if a simple body resides in a place (*en topo*) and is locatable somewhere, it will necessarily be an element.[24]

If, on the other hand, such a body is not in a place, nothing can derive from it since coming into being (generation) and that out of which (*ex hou*) something comes are joined together.

The tendency of things to rise or fall is a *natural tendency*. It is, we could say, an internal principle of the element, apparently not dependent on external agency. As Aristotle writes, "the movement of each body to its own place is motion to its own form," (310a33) a notion that finds an inexact analogue in the earliest philosophies in the proposition that "like moves to like."[25] Thus, the natural position of earth lies at the center of the universe, and it will not rest until it arrives there.[26] Fire naturally moves upward. Water and air, by contrast, have a double potentiality, just as the human body, for example, can be either healthy or ill. Air will tend to rise in water or earth and tend to sink when beneath fire. Water will tend to rise in earth but sink when below air or fire.

From an Aristotelian perspective, these local motions are analogous to other types of change and motion in the sense that they are an actualization of potentiality. Aristotle distinguishes three kinds of motion involving change of size, form, and place, and in each case change occurs from contrary to contrary (opposite to opposite) or to intermediate states. With locomotion, there is not a fortuitous relationship between mover and moved (object). Instead, as a general rule, when similar and simple (i.e., undifferentiated) bodies are moved with the same motion, the place to which any single part moves naturally will be as well the place of the whole. Again, this has as much to do with Aristotle's conception of place as it does his conception of motion. The boundary of a place functions like the form for what it contains, and so it is to their "like" (in the sense of whatever they are given form by) that bodies move when they go to their own respective places, and adjacent bodies will share such a "likeness."

Furthermore, in this context, the relation of every outer body to that which is contained inside it is a form–matter relation. This enables Aristotle to establish that the consecutive members of his elemental series are "like" (given form by) each other—water is like air and air is like fire—so that the elements can be converted (or transformed) between intermediate bodies but not between intermediates and extremes. For example, if we say that water is like air, we can say as well that air is like water, but we cannot conclude (i.e., move) from the fact of water being like earth to the claim that earth is like water. What Aristotle seems to mean is that the extreme elements of earth and fire obtain their form from the boundary (*peras*) in which they are enclosed. Thus, when they move to their proper (i.e., natural) places, it is as if they are moving to their "like." As for the intermediate elements—water and air—these simple bodies take their form from contiguity with the extreme elements rather than directly from a *peras*. In short, circumference and center are presented as the formative elements, a position and interpretation that exists somewhat uncomfortably with Aristotle's claims about the privilege of *aether* earlier in *De Caelo* and his treatment of fire in *Generation and Corruption*, where he holds that "fire alone—or more than all the rest—is akin to the 'form' because it tends by nature to be borne towards the limit" (335a18ff).

Unlike other bodies, the light and the heavy—being bodies that have only locomotion—appear to possess the cause of their motion within themselves. They do not seem to require external stimuli. This is so because their matter is "nearest to being," by which Aristotle means they are more fully formed than other bodies. Locomotion pertains only to bodies that are isolated from others and, among the kinds of movement Aristotle distinguishes, it is generated last and hence will be first in (or closest to) the *ordo essendi*. Becoming ceases by reaching a terminus and goal, and in that location an element has being. It passes from a potentiality to an actuality in the multiple senses of quality, quantity, and place—three of Aristotle's most significant categories. For example, air that is generated from water (air being light and water being heavy) moves to the upper region. Once there, it now "is" and can no longer be described as "becoming." More generally, then, the elements will move toward their natural places unless something interferes, hinders or otherwise prevents them from so doing. But in a strict sense, there is an "external" source or cause of all motion including the four elements because something either takes away the hindrance to their natural motion or there is a material or surface off which they rebound—what Aristotle terms an *accidental cause* in the *Physics*—or some agent that initially gives things lightness or heaviness—what he calls an *essential cause* in the same work.[27]

Having looked earlier at Aristotle's theory of the heavy and the light and introduced his perspective on place and motion, we are ready to see how the properties of the four elements more fully link up. Fire and earth are absolutely light and heavy, respectively. Nothing rises above fire or sinks below earth. As long as there is no external hindrance, fire in any quantity will move upward while earth will move downward. As intermediaries, air and water combine the qualities of heaviness and lightness. They are only relatively light or heavy. In some bodies they rise; in others they fall. Both air and water are lighter than earth since in any amount they come to the surface of this element, while both are heavier than fire since a portion of either one drops to the bottom of fire. Relative to (i.e., in comparison with) each another, one (water) has absolute weight, whereas the other (air) has absolute lightness. This is so because air comes to the surface of water, and water falls to the bottom of air.

In addition to the four distinct, unadulterated simple bodies or elements, there exist composite bodies, which possess characteristics of both the heavy and the light. Their attributes and identity are due to differences in their noncompounded parts. Thus, one part will *preponderate*—or literally weigh down and outweigh others—and hence predominate, so that these bodies will be light or heavy according to the elements they contain. From this fact, we can conclude following Aristotle's earlier definition of *stoicheion* that one need only speak of the elements—the most simple parts and primary bodies—because all bodies depend on these most basic units. One does not, in other words, need to give a separate account of composites if one has provided an adequate explanation of simple bodies. It is due to differences in the properties of the elementary bodies that one can determine whether any particular body can be regarded as in one place light and another place heavy. Each of the elements has weight with the exception of fire, which possesses absolute lightness. As evidence for this point, Aristotle adduces the phenomenon of a bladder that, when inflated with air, weighs more than when it is empty. By contrast, earth does not possess any lightness because it always sinks to the bottom and in the process moves to the center.

As suggested previously, Aristotle's theory of form and matter comes into play in his theory of the elements. What he attempts to do is to relate the antithesis of light and heavy with the ostensible antithesis of form and matter. Lightness is most akin to form, whereas heaviness is most like matter. Put differently, in all categories, the continent (the container or receptacle which restricts and limit) relates to form and the contained (what lies circumscribed and within) concerns matter. There is, then, a further spatial distinction at work in Aristotle's stoicheiology. The surrounding "above" is determinate; the surrounded "below" is material. Matter, however, is both potentially light and heavy. It is decidedly the same matter in the two cases, but there is a logical distinction in operation—a discrepancy we might say in being—just as there exists a difference between a body that is healthy and the same body that is diseased. The two potentialities are distinct, just as are the actualities. Following Aristotle's more general analysis of matter and form, we can conclude that such a distinction is possible because of the indeterminacy of matter.

At the center of the Aristotelian cosmos is the earth since the center of a rotating body must be at rest. However, if there is earth, there must also be fire—which naturally moves upward—given that fire is the contrary of earth—which naturally moves downward. Fire, moreover, is prior in nature to earth because heat is the form and coldness merely a privation of this form. The intermediaries between fire and earth are air and water, and these intermediaries come into being and pass away because contraries are prone toward destruction of one another.

In Aristotle's sublunary theory of the elements, the types of matter must be as numerous as the kinds of bodies that exist. Because there are four simple bodies—fire, air, earth, and water—four kinds of matter must exist corresponding to these bodies. This is so because there must be manifested the four potentialities exhibited by the elements: two absolute and two relative, with respect to heaviness and lightness. If there were only a single matter for all things (such as a void or Plato's triangles), everything would have only one motion—either upward or downward—because Aristotle holds firmly to the notion that single element views allow for only one natural movement, a point he has established earlier. Thus, there would be lacking either an absolutely light body (which moves uniformly upward) or an absolutely heavy body (which moves uniformly downward). Furthermore, in certain instances, we would witness a phenomenon contrary to experience and observation of one of the intermediate bodies, air or water, moving more quickly downward than earth because in very large quantities it would possess a greater amount of material (e.g., triangles or particles) than a small quantity of earth. If, however, there are only two kinds of matter presupposed such as the void and the plenum, then the intermediary bodies cannot be adequately described in terms of their natural motions—even if uniform upward and downward motions could be provided for—because we will encounter the same problem just described. Nevertheless, in another sense, Aristotle remarks in passing and without further elaboration that there must also be a "common matter" for all of these bodies, a requirement necessitated by the fact that unlike Empedocles' *rhizomata*, the elements pass into one another; they are generated and perishable. Aristotle develops this schema of change in *On Generation and Corruption* and the *Meteorology*, where he provides an account of contrariety and elemental transformation, which is examined at later junctures.

The Elements of Place

For Aristotle, to be is to be somewhere, to be emplaced or seeking to return to one's natural place (*topos oikeios*), as it could be said of water qua rain. Everything has its proper place and is part of a broader, more encompassing "common place" (*topos koinos*)—wherein all bodies exist—afforded by the heavens, and one that he distinguishes from "special place" (*topos idios*), wherein a body first exists. Aristotle particularizes and further naturalizes the conception of place (*chora*) forged by Plato, whose view he challenges even as he acknowledges that among earlier thinkers, Plato alone sought to articulate *what* place is. The distinct nature of each element links it to the organization of the universe as a whole, which does not have a place itself because it is the whole and hence nowhere.[28]

Although Aristotle's theory of *natural place* is located in *De Caelo*, his account of place proper resides in the remarkable fourth book of the *Physics*, where he proceeds as both physicist and proto-phenomenologist. There are four topological possibilities: It can be form, matter, the interval between the extremities, or the extremities themselves. Place is not *form* because, although form like place is a boundary or limit (*peras*), the form of a thing is its boundary, whereas place is the boundary of the body that serves as a container. Despite appearances, place is not *matter* because the matter of a thing is not separable from the thing or able to contain it, whereas the place of a thing is separable and containing of the thing in question. Place is also not the *interval* between extremities because the interval does not exist on its own as a distinct entity but is an accident of bodies that in turn fill a container. Place, then, is the limit of the surrounding or containing body (*to peras tou periechontos*). And this boundary is determined by the point of contact (the site of touch) between containing body and contained body, which is able to move via locomotion; that is, through motion from place to place.[29]

Place seems difficult to comprehend because matter and form occur along with it, although it appears as if there is an interval that is distinct from movable bodies. Place, however, can be differentiated from these candidates. Instead of being like a boat on a river, which changes its location, Aristotle suggests that place is more like the river *in toto* that as a whole is not moved. Thus, we can add to the previous definition the qualifications that the boundary or limit is both innermost and motionless. "Being-in" a place necessarily implies that something is outside and other than the place. Aristotle distinguishes eight senses of one thing being in another, but only in the strictest sense is a thing "in" a vessel and thereby "in place." Place, however, is not "in" things because that would mean that place would be "in" a place, too. Instead, place is somewhere but in the sense that the limit resides in the limited not in the manner of something being in a place. We can also say that which has independent existence as an object will move *in* a circumambient place, whereas that which exists as part of an object will move *with* the object that surrounds it.

With respect to the four elements more particularly, place itself is not an element or composed of elements because although it possesses size, it is not a body, unlike the *stoicheia* (elements). All places, however, provide for a distinction between up and down, and all of the simple bodies will be carried naturally to their respective places, where they come to rest. This, in turn, allows Aristotle to speak of a place itself as being either up or down. Because place is relative to a system of movable bodies, we can say as well, for example, that earth lies in water or that water is in air. Each place has a "distinct potency" and its own directionality and dimensionality: right–left, up–down, ahead–behind, and so forth. Places are abiding, admitting us again and again even as they alter us. They are at once very *commonplace and yet extremely extraordinary.*

What is the relation of the physical and near-phenomenological account in the *Physics* to the more cosmological perspective in *De Caelo*? There is, it seems, not so much an outright contradiction in Aristotle's two views—which are not explicitly connected—as an uneasy tension that exists between them. The *Physics* tacitly affirms that objects (and elements) can be located anywhere because they are able to move or be moved about, whereas place is cast as a container or pail that is nonetheless nonportable (i.e., stationary). Place is defined in relation to bodies and premised on their movement from location to location, but it does not account for the theory that the simple bodies will tend toward their natural locations (not just move anywhere), as Aristotle holds in *De Caelo*. In this latter work, natural place is considered something more than just the "immediate unmoved limit of the surrounding body," even if his doctrine of natural place is compatible with this definition. Here, a close and essential connection exists between a body and its proper place. In the *Physics*, however, Aristotle does not argue that the *physis* (nature) of an element involves its movement to a given region. At the end of the account of place, he does admit that it is reasonable to believe that each of the simple bodies (elements) will be carried to its own place and remain there naturally, but by this point he has not delivered on the implicit promissory note nor explored the supposed proof of place provided by the locomotion of earth, water, air, and fire that he mentions at the beginning of the *Physics*.

Aristotle's theory of place contrasts with the view in the *Timaeus*, where Plato moves increasingly from an account of space to an exploration of place, and the places of the elements. Aristotle's disagreement centers on the relatively specious claim that Plato conflates matter with space (or place). For Aristotle, matter "replaces" the Receptacle (*hypodoche*) and in the process, he recasts Plato's idea in terms of it—a kind of *clinamen* or "misprison" to use Harold Bloom's phrase to describe a strong misreading of a predecessor.[30] Matter (*hyle*) and place overlap in Aristotle's account insofar as place is occupied by an object that reaches to the boundary of that place, but a substratum is not subsumed to place since body and place are separable. As indicated earlier, objects are movable, and *topos* does not belong to them in the same way as their materiality. In other words, for Aristotle matter and place are distinct. Place also does not contribute directly to an object's ontology or genesis. That is matter's task. Despite this important difference, Aristotle's assertion in *De Caelo* shares with Plato's *Timaeus* the idea that each of the four elements has a tendency to reside in a particular and proper place. Aristotle recognizes that Plato alone sought to discover what place is, but he is emboldened enough to still claim that he has "inherited nothing from previous thinkers" (207a35). This view is no doubt hyperbolic, but in the end we must give Aristotle a wealth of credit for developing a novel and influential position on place, a subject we will continue to consider for its environmental dimensions.

Homecoming and Inhabitation

If we step back and look at the broader Aristotelian perspective, we discover that the elements help provide for the definition and limits of place (*topos*). Earth moves downward to the bottom limit (center) while fire moves upward to the outer limit (circumference). Place, in turn, is "home" for the four elements, which are constantly seeking their natural locations, and it is further connected with the natural motions of the simple bodies, which are bound inextricably with their particular regions. *Topos*, then, is "elemental" in two senses: first as delimited cosmologically by the four simple bodies and their respective motions and, second, because to be is to be *somewhere* for Aristotle. Hence, place is "elementary" to all things, as it was for Plato, who offered a kind of elemental and ecological maxim with regard to it in the *Timaeus*: "anything that is must be in some place [*topos*] and occupy some room [*chora*], and that what is not somewhere in earth or heaven is nothing" (52b). "Where-ness" (or place) is, in fact, one of Aristotle's ten basic modes in which being is manifested in the world, as he posits in the *Categories*.

In the *Physics*, too, the elements are supposed to confirm the existence of place because they can be *re-placed*. What formerly contained water, for example, can in turn contain earth or air. Having another elemental body in this same place, the place will appear as different. Thus, place itself is distinct from both the elemental body that passed into it and the elemental body that passed out of it. But, according to Aristotle, the elements should provide an argument for the reality of place itself. "The typical locomotions of the elementary natural bodies—namely, fire, earth, and the like—show not only that place is something, but also that it exerts a certain power [*echei tina dynamin*]" (208b8ff). Aristotle remarkably suggests an elemental "replacement argument" to confirm the very existence of place itself, just as he deploys in a more complete way a "substitution argument" to show the mechanism of elemental transformation—each of contrary qualities *replacing* another so as to explain change. Furthermore, all things have a place in the cosmos except the cosmos itself (since it is not relative to anything else and thus without *topos*), and the most universal form of motion—which applies to the four simple bodies—as it turns out is motion in place (*phora*). In this manner, Aristotle magisterially makes place integral to his account of the elements.

In seeking their natural places, the elements are engaged in a kind of *homecoming* and thus in a form of their own "voluntary" or self-driven *domestication*. Prior to their arrival, they are "alienated" in a sense from their home-places. Their "proper places" are both types and parts of a broader system of places in which they are nested when at rest, one determined vis-à-vis a given system of natural bodies. Such places are not simply defined in relation to human bodies but instead can be seen as separate from us. "Up" and "down" are not just any directions, but where light (fiery) and heavy (earthy) bodies are moved respectively. This self-domestication of the elements with regard to place is then from our vantage something of a resolution or between-state of the subjective and objective. While other than human subjects, elemental places are nevertheless different as well from the objective determinations of mathematical position: "though they [mathematical objects] have no real place, they nevertheless, in respect of their position relatively to us, have a right and left as attributes ascribed to them only in consequence of their relative position, not having by nature these various characteristics" (208b23ff).

Place construed as container (*periechon*) implies boundaries and limits; what is contained must necessarily be circumscribed and de-limited. The recognition of limits is vital to environmental thought in the notions of ecological scale, population, and resource constraints, and the carrying capacity of land—what it can reasonably sustain and comfortably support.[31] In acknowledging limits as immanent and endemic to place itself, as there *ab initio*, rather than imposed from the outside or superimposed from above, Aristotle's conception of *topos* provides us with a theoretical model on which to build. He is indeed correct to counsel that "a student of nature must have knowledge of place" (208a27). To be emplaced is in some sense to be surrounded, to be ensconced in one's immediate surroundings. " 'Around here,' where we live, is a circular notion, embracing and radiating from the specific *place* where generalizations about land, landscape, and nature come home to roots," observes Lucy Lippard. By contrast, " 'Out there' is a line of sight, the view, a metaphor of linear time."[32] In this regard, Aristotle does not allow for a place without bodies. All places are inhabited corporally, although place is not a body itself even if it is three-dimensional (like bodies), having features of breadth, length, and depth in addition to surface. In acknowledging such dimensions of containment, Aristotle seems to imply rightly that places are experienced from the inside—from within, as intimate *inscapes* we might say—as opposed to from outside, like landscapes, which are often perceived at a distant, from afar. They are "not down in any map; true places never are," Herman Melville provocatively points out in *Moby Dick*.[33]

Containers and vessels are characterized by their ability to hold and carry what lies inside them. Places similarly shelter and retain. They possess perimeters—frequently protective edges—lines of demarcation mappable as, for example, topographical features such as watersheds, hills and valleys, or forest edges. But unlike vessels, places in Aristotle's view cannot be transported or trans-placed. They are immovable and ultimately unchangeable because place is "the first unchangeable limit (*peras*) of that which surrounds" (212a20). Here, it is helpful to keep in mind that Aristotle focuses on natural place rather than built or human *topoi*, which in both theory and practice can sometimes be moved and altered. While his physical account is divested largely of notions of the political (even if place itself exhibits power) and how places can be produced or constructed via architecture, cultural needs or human fiat, Aristotle's *Politics* does provide an analysis of the *polis* as a civic gathering place, a locus for public appearance.

If our ecological difficulties are connected to our relation with the elements, they are also inextricably tied to place and, more particularly, to the increasing disregard, loss, and simplification of natural and social locales. In its most basic form, what we might term *place alienation* involves a marked loss of physical or psychological contact with a given abode, niche, or location.[34] For the elements—to invoke an Aristotelian perspective—this is tantamount to having their transformational cycles significantly disrupted, obstructed or changed so that their relation with their "homes" (i.e., their kinds) is altered drastically. Where, for example, the earth is widely cloaked by concrete or denuded of native vegetation; where the air is befouled with exhaust, smog, factory smoke, and particulate matter; and where the water is contaminated with petrochemicals and agricultural runoff, elemental contact—between both the entities themselves and between us and the elemental masses—is greatly reduced, mediated, and masked. This, in turn, often interferes with material cycles and recycling. Elemental change slows (as when stagnant waters form) or quickens (as with topsoil erosion). It is no longer regular or self-regulating, as most mature ecological systems tend to be over the long run.[35] The elements may be unable to return to their home-places or they may be trapped "in place" with pollutants or other human-made compounds and thus unable to separate and circulate so as to "purify" themselves and their places, as water does in aquifers.

Even if we grant the very contestable Aristotelian claim that "place is not destroyed when what is in it is destroyed" (209a1), our all-too-human relation with it can be changed dramatically and even traumatically. When an old tree or hilly knoll is removed, when a stream dries up or is re-routed, or when the night sky is lit up by street lights, neon signs, and pulsing advertisements so as to white-out the stars, moon, and planets, the *topos* and the *cosmos*—the *topocosm*—will both seem to have been reconfigured.[36] One can easily experience a form of anomie and disorientation with this sudden loss or disruption. Given the close alliance of places and persons, place alienation manifests itself with a double-directionality, as Edward Casey observes: "I from it, it from me" such that one might feel uncannily "beside oneself."[37] Places can possibly become ill, even sick, when they are not well cared for, resulting in a *topo-clasm*, a destruction of place or an "ecotastrophe"—an ecological catastrophe.[38]

The deep connection between place and home is evident in Aristotle's treatment of the elements. The economy (the *nomos* of the *oikos*) of the elements is bound closely to the ecology (the *logos* of *oikos*) of air, earth, fire, and water because both are defined in relation to the domestic household—the hold of the home. If, as Aristotle says, "the potency of place [is] marvelous" (208b34), we can presume that part of this force is the native attraction, indeed magnetism, a location exercises on us and other beings. *Who* we are—our identity—is related deeply to *where* we are, and just as Aristotle's simple bodies or elements are driven to return to their homes—akin to salmon swimming to their spawning grounds—we retain place as memory in our own bodies and minds. Like Aristotle's elements, we are not only lured to a home-place, but when we are drawn out and away from it so as to gain perspective and to circulate in the economy and ecology of places, we often carry the physical and psychological orientation that a location has provided us.

This typically occurs via the prompts of recollection, the seductions of nostalgia, the beckoning of wishes, and the force of habit, all of which can confabulate and conspire with the sensuous imperatives—the pushes and pulls—of the surrounding habitat itself so as to allow us to comfortably reside in or seek our "element." As Lippard writes, "Place for me is the locus of desire . . . I fall for (or into) places faster and less conditionally than I do for people."[39] Places not only display breadth but as "containers" they bear depth; they manifest not just a horizontal extension but reveal a vertical intensity. They exhibit layers of philosophical, geographical, and ecological meaning that we memorialize or mine in journeying away from them or that we exhume and exfoliate in homecoming—in our inveterate attempts to re-domesticate ourselves and to locate a center, an *axis mundi*.

One viable response to ecological problems, then, is to "reinhabit" place as home, to come to know and to experience it in all its plenitude and, as Aristotle tells us, its power. Reinhabiting natural place necessarily involves re-establishing elemental contact. It implies, for example, observing where one's water comes from and goes to, knowing the carrying capacities and limits of the subtending earth, attending to the climate and weather patterns or one's breathing in the case of air, and consciously understanding, regulating and tempering our use technology (e.g., fire-arms) or even a campfire flame itself in the instance of fire. Re-inhabitation—inhabiting again even if it is the first time for us individually but the second or more iteration for the injured or disrupted habitat—requires an ecological *habitus*, the dispositional result of a repeated habit (what Aristotle calls *hexis*) or set of habits. It means trying to be "native to a place" through awareness of ecological dynamics that function within it and seeking active membership in a biotic community.[40] "To know the spirit of place," Gary Snyder elegantly advises, "is to realize that you are a part of a part and that the whole is made of parts, each of which is whole. You start with the part you are whole in."[41]

Like Aristotle, bioregionalism—a recent entrant into ecological discourse—stresses the importance of geographical regions that provide placial frameworks for situating and relating human communities within the encompassing natural world. In this sense, bioregions—literally "life places"—serve ideally in effect as both environmental *place-holders* and cultural *life-preservers*. Bioregions are areas defined by their life forms, biota, and topography as opposed to human conventions or political decisions, but they are distinguished with greater particularity than Aristotle's elemental places because they are delimited by soils, flora, climate, water, landforms, and fauna and can be further divided into eco-regions, geo-regions, and morpho-regions that fit into each other like Chinese boxes. Such areas may be as vast as the Ozark Plateau or Sonoran Desert, which covers about 100,000 square miles, or as specific as the Connecticut River Basin. Using this understanding of bioregions as a starting point, we could outline conceivably a paradigm and project with respect to the economy, forms of political organization, and the rest of society. According to its proponents, communities based on these territories would encourage a deeper respect for the earth and its inhabitants.[42] Bioregions, then, are a geographical and biological concept with political import. Both communitarian and liberal bioregionalists make a strong—albeit problematic case—for a new environmental and political paradigm involving local self-sufficiency and mutual aid that in some ways tacitly draws on but further naturalizes and expands a notion of the Aristotelian *polis* (civic community).[43]

Aristotle's theory is admittedly not without some difficulties.[44] One dimension absent from his account is recognition of the role of gender in the constitution of place. As Luce Irigaray argues very elliptically, there is a failure to engage the feminine insofar as a hard, closed, solid, more objective and male conception of *topos* predominates, one which ignores or effaces a softer, open, fluid, more subjective and permeable notion of place. Focusing on sexual difference, the corporeal, and particularly the female body conceived as vessel, envelope or container, she asks, "As for woman, she is place. Does she have to locate herself in bigger and bigger places? But also to find, situate, in herself, the place that she is."[45] Irigaray thus discovers a redoubled notion of bodily place as both mother (our first home) and woman, who is commonly "assigned to be place without occupying a place."[46] Her interpretation, in effect, finds the Aristotelian pail of place to be somewhat porous (or at least leaky) upon closer inspection, and in the process challenges us to rethink topology in terms of gendered bodies.

Still, Aristotle's place-based perspective was so powerful that it held sway for two thousands years until it was displaced by Newton's notion of universal gravitation, which does not strictly explain an experience or locate a force that can be seen, heard or touched—like elemental things—but rather states its effects. Theodore Roszak has asked in this regard why this physical law was discovered so late in history when it seems to us such an inescapable and apparent idea. He claims that for nonscientific cultures the role we allot for the physics of gravitation was occupied by a spiritual sense of "fallenness," a loss of a kind of "visionary levity" that retained moral and mythological dimensions. In this view, gravity—arguably the key concept of the scientific revolution—"becomes an important and isolated concept only after weightiness (fallenness) begins to seem like an irresistible fact of life needing to be accounted for." With the Newtonian theory of gravity, the West is at the outset of "a natural philosophy grounded in alienation" as measured by the way our cultural symbols are divested largely of transcendent energy.[47] Although this position may oversimplify the case, it does provocatively contrast a modern orientation with a premodern sensibility, and it indirectly underscores the force of Aristotle's earlier and enduring exposition of *topos*. Having investigated the place of the elements and the elements of place, along with Aristotle's positions on elemental generation, movement and weight, we are now poised to explore more fully the economy and ecology of earth, air, fire, and water.

Interstice: Heat and Cold

Do not all charms fly / At the mere touch of cold philosophy?

—John Keats, "Lamia"

That the glass would melt in heat, / That the water would freeze in cold, / Shows that this object is merely a state, / One of many, between two poles.

—Wallace Stevens, "The Glass of Water"

Hand a stranger a glass of cold water and when someone asks her a few minutes later what she thought of you, she will likely associate subconsciously the coldness with your personality. Touch an individual warmly on the shoulder, and he will probably transfer this warmth to your person and think of you in a more positive light. The poles of hot and cold along with the many gradations in-between—from tepid and temperate to cool and chilly—establish regulative limits for our corporeal experiences, and they impact profoundly all living beings on the planet as well as the particular physical states and composition of earth, water, and air. More often than we realize, heat and cold affect our choices regarding shelter, diet, and clothing; they alter our moods and outlooks on the world; and they influence an extensive gamut of practical decisions from vacation plans to battle strategies.

Hot and cold, of course, often involve relative assessments and qualitative judgments about the environment. That is, with the exception of clearly identifiable freezing and boiling points for chemical substances and solutions, they are frequently perceived as subjective states. Cold soup, bathwater, or wind for some of us might be felt as lukewarm, or at least tolerable, to others. Cold objects, too, tend to feel heavier to us than hot ones even when they are of the same weight. Still, we are "warm-blooded" animals—more exactly, homeotherms because we keep our temperatures stable through metabolic adjustments—and so tend to connect heat with affirmative feelings as when we are drawn to "warm-hearted" individuals with "constant" character traits. To most people, cold-blooded connotes insensitivity or unconcern, even cut-throatedness. Like other creatures, then, we possess prejudices of the body, biological dispositions, or orientations that congeal or quicken over time into *temperaments* such as "cool" or "hot-headed" demeanors—internal qualities that are exhibited outwardly and that are akin to external *temperature* variations.

Warm-blooded beings are able to survive precipitous drops in outside temperature for short periods, but because their resilience is usually purchased at the cost of burning body fat or by shivering, intense expenditures of energy may be required. As a consequence, some animals like birds may lose up to a third of their weight over the course of a night, and others might need up to ten times as much food as "cold-blooded" organisms, who are better able to withstand famine or to endure sparse surroundings. Cold-blooded creatures—more accurately, exotherms—maintain their body temperatures and heat (*therm*) from the outside (*exo*), deriving warmth from the sun, moving air, or flowing water. Termites, for example, position their mounds on a north–south axis so as to capitalize on heat absorption during the early and late hours of the day and to minimize it around noontime, keeping their homes close to a comfortable 86°F. Some animals have internal temperatures that are actually in sync with their immediate environs. Accordingly, lizards and snakes sun themselves on stones; desert dwellers burrow deeply underground during the unbearable heat of the afternoon; and fish ascend or descend in water to find appropriate temperature zones.

Heat and cold are thus elemental because they greatly condition the environmental "plasma" in which we dwell and through which we evolve and move: the media of air, water, and land that constitute an ambient setting or stage for ecological change, geological processes, and cultural life. "Sultriness or aridity extends space about us," notes Alphonso Lingis. "The cold is an unbounded zone open about our mobile body; the torrid expanse spreads amorphous directions for languid movement."[1] Such influence originates with the oldest and most complex story of them all: the beginning of the universe in that tremendous burst or "bang" of immense temperature and dense energy, the great "fireball" of heat and light that expanded into observed space-time. Recently, in fact, physicists have discovered a cosmological "cold spot" in the universe's radiation—the heat glow that remains after the cosmos was born—that may be a relic or glitch of that first magnificent moment some fourteen billion years ago.

Since the time of our own late arrival into this unfolding play of elemental polarities, heat and cold have continued to regulate the world we inhabit like a grand, if autonomous, thermostat, especially by way of the sense of touch, as we respond and adjust to fluctuations in their intensities and oscillations of degree. Long ago, Greek and Roman physicians believed that body heat originated from an interior fire located in the left ventricle of the heart. Later, in the early 1800s, Daniel Fahrenheit created a scale to measure heat gradients with the mercury thermometer. And now, we tend to view heat in terms of moving particles, such that the faster they are in motion, the hotter is a substance. Currently, there is some cause to believe that the universe will eventually end in a "heat death" following the second law of thermodynamics, which provides for increasing entropy within a physical system, so that the temperature of the cosmos—which has been steadily cooling since its inception—will approach absolute zero: about negative 459°F, when all motion ceases. An alternative but related theory with the same chilly outcome holds for the notion of a "big freeze" or "cold death" of the universe (assumed to be flat or hyperbolic in shape), whereby through ongoing expansion and loss of free energy it becomes too cold to maintain any kind of possible life.[2] "What then was life?," inquires novelist Thomas Mann. He answers: "It was warmth, the warmth generated by a form-preserving insubstantiality, a fever of matter, which accompanied the process of ceaseless decay and repair."[3]

Ancient philosophical and religious thought took an early interest in these primordial conditions and qualities, now largely delegated to the province of science. In the *Bhagavad Gita*, Krishna pointed to their transitory aspects: "Contacts with matter make us feel / heat and cold, pleasure and pain. / Arjuna, you must learn to endure fleeting things—they come and go!"[4] Bound naturally with this intrigue was the practical necessity of staying warm or fending off insufferable excesses of temperature. In proposing fire as the universal *logos*, Heraclitus gestured not only toward the significance of light—all heated matter produces some kind of glow—but to the fundamental force of warmth in the world and indirectly to the primitive fear of its growth and usurping dominance (e.g., the hell of a massive conflagration, holocaust, or world war) or to its dramatic disappearance (e.g., the arrival of nuclear winter or return to an ice age). Joseph Campbell aptly recollects well-springs of our emotional responses to cold and heat in speculating that "when that protohuman troglodyte Sinanthropus, in his dismal cave, responded to the fascination of fire, it was to the apparition of a power that was already present and operative in his own body: heat, temperature, oxidation; as also in the volcanic earth, in Jupiter, and in the sun."[5]

The four seasons embody and represent a terrestrial scale of temperature ranges. Although some cultures and geographic locales distinguish just a wet (or rainy) and dry season, those living in temperate areas commonly link heat with summer and cold with winter and then tend to see the intermediary seasons in terms of deviations from these poles. Heat—or its relative absence—becomes both a catalyst for and expression of climactic change. On first blush, then, heat and cold appear as if opposites. The former expands substances; the latter contracts them. But heat and cold are related more closely than is initially apparent, bound as they are through the common concept of temperature, which is a physical property of most systems. Deserts, for example, are places of extreme heat; however, when the sun dips below the horizon at night they can become bone-chillingly cold. The human body is capable of withstanding a fair range of such temperature changes, but heat and cold establish baselines for our beings. If our internal temperature varies much from 98.6°F, we will encounter major medical troubles ranging from fever, breathlessness, fainting, or shock at the hot end of the spectrum to hypothermia, hallucinations, heart rhythm problems, and comatose at the cold end before death sets in. The skin starts to tingle, ache, and burn when it hits a temperature of 68°F. Below 50°F, it grows numb and then freezes when it registers a temperature of 27°F. Externally, temperature extremes have been recorded from 134°F in Death Valley, California to −128°F in Antarctica, although hotter conditions have occurred temporarily within forest fires or near the explosions of atomic bombs and much lower temperatures have been generated through the use of cryo-coolers—devices that obtain cryogenic temperatures—in the laboratory.

Emerson conveys the ability of heat to insinuate itself into the warp and weft of our lives. "Hither rolls the storm of heat; / I feel its finer billows beat / Like a sea which me infolds; / Heat with viewless fingers moulds, / Swells, and mellows, and matures, / Paints, and flavors, and allures."[6] In Sanskrit, *tápas* means "heat," and within Hinduism, it suggests spiritual austerity but also the warm ecstasy of a yogin or *tāpasá*, a practitioner of *tápas*. In the discipline of yoga, *tápas* is viewed as a vital energy of concentrated effort that unfolds with time toward enlightenment and physical purification. It is considered one of the Niyamas or observances of self-control advocated by Patanjaili in the ancient yoga sutras. Through *tápas*, a yogi is supposed to be able to "burn off" and hence halt the accumulation of negative energy, thereby opening an avenue for spiritual development. Bikram or "hot yoga" in particular ratchets up the heat in a room to 105°F or more to encourage these actions.

"Everything living has soul," hypothesizes Aristotle, and it "cannot exist without the presence of natural heat."[7] In heightened temperatures, however, mammals withdrawal to the shade or subsurface; flowers fold up; and birds go silent. The world seems to slow down or even stop in order to conserve energy and preserve vitality. Of a hot day in the desert, Edward Abbey writes, "The inside of the trailer is like the inside of a kiln, a fierce dry heat that warps the loose linoleum on the floor, turns an exposed slice of bread into something like toast within half an hour, makes my papers crackle like parchment."[8] In these circumstances, sweating is our first line of response and thereby a form of corporeal air conditioning, a process that allows the body to breathe. Although many organisms seek to escape the intensity of heat, some creatures like tics organize their worlds around detecting and delighting in it. Heat is the lure—as smell is for us—that leads them to sustenance on the back of a passing deer or dog. Cats, snakes, and lions, among many other animals, will bask in patches of warm light for endless hours during a frosty winter day, engaging in the kind of sun worship that we humans have entertained for millennia.

Most basically, heat is a form of energy—what Blake calls "Eternal Delight"—and one of only two ways that such energy can be transmitted into or out of a system (the other is through work). These transferences between objects occur by way of conduction, convection, or radiation. Like water, which flows of its own accord from high to low locations, heat moves from sites of greater to lesser temperature. On a much broader scale, global climate change is largely a function of increased heat brought about by the burning of fossil fuels. We're warming up the planet at an alarming speed, covering it with a blanket of anthropogenic gases and trapping in the heat like a gigantic greenhouse. In the past century, we've raised the average temperature on the surface of the planet by about a full degree, and the predictions ranging from 2.5- to 10.5-degree increases by 2100 bode very dangerous. As a result of this warming, the oceans are becoming heat sinks; glacial ice is melting; permafrost is thawing; and weather conditions are more intense and unpredictable. These and other changes have had an adverse affect on the habitats, microclimates, and lives of many organisms, including we humans. In the yin and yang of hot and cold, we've moved too far toward one pole and thus need to "cool it" before we are consumed in an oven of our own making.

While Western philosophy commences in the warmer climes of the Mediterranean, it develops some its loftiest heights and greatest depths in the cooler regions of northern Europe, where thinkers are driven indoors and the focus of thought is eventually directed inward, away from the intoxicating wonder inspired by fire, ice, water, light, stone, and night. Cold domesticates us, sends us inside in search of the creature comforts of the hearth and human-generated illumination. Coldness, however, seems not just to be the absence of heat; it appears to possess a palpable reality of its own. It invades and numbs the body. The Koyukon people of northern Alaska go so far as to view the cold as a conscious entity possessing "a potent and irritable spirit" and thus admonish their children to refer to it with care unless they want to bring on its "frigid wrath."[9] In his poem, "The Snow Man," Wallace Stevens points in a parallel vein to the difficulty of embracing the chilly world with ease and grace. "One must have a mind of winter. . . . And have been cold a long time / To behold the junipers shagged with ice . . . and not to think / Of any misery in the sound of the wind . . . Which is the sound of the land."[10]

When I wrestled competitively, I would often wear a hat indoors and keep my hands in my pockets because I was trying to preserve what little remained of the heat in my body's furnace, having lost most of the fat on my frame in practice sessions that burned vast quantities of calories in an extremely hot room. I recall thinking that if hell exists, it must surely be cold rather than hot. Although it is said by experienced outdoor folk that a person who freezes should not be pronounced dead and departed until the body is again warm because he or she might be reanimated, deep cold provides us with a glimpse of our temperature at death and that may be a major reason we find it something to be avoided. We gain an inkling of this inevitable condition during sleep—what Shakespeare styles as that "little death"—when our body temperature plummets and we become more corpse-like.

We are especially vulnerable to cold on our extremities, particularly the face, feet, and hands. Warmth seems to seek a residence deeper within our skin and bodies, probably as a way to guard and insulate our vital organs. Shivering both expresses the experience of cold and simultaneously generates warmth. Cause and effect are concurrent. A shivering reflex occurs in the muscles around key organs, which start to quake in tiny movements so as to spawn warmth through physical activity. Surviving extreme cold is an exercise in technical ingenuity as well as creative panache. Fish go into suspended animation; penguins huddle together in groups; humans fashion clothing as a kind of second skin given that we are largely lacking the furry coats owned by many mammals. Jack London's short story, "To Build a Fire," tells the memorable tale of a man traveling through the remote territory of the Yukon in Canada when it is 75°F below zero, so cold that spittle freezes even before it reaches the earth. In order to survive, the narrator considers killing his own dog after his fire is snuffed out by snow cascading off an overhanging tree. Fortunately for the dog and less fortunately for him, the man's fingers are too cold to brandish a knife. The man perishes and the dog scampers off.

While searching for the endangered and rapidly disappearing season of winter in a warmed-up world, writer Gretel Ehrlich explored some of the nuances of the cold. As she ambled across the landscape in northern Greenland, she meditated on the possibility that there are notes of music lying dormant within the frozen ground itself. With each step she took, an effervescence of sound and song seemed to break forth. "The earth was a piano and my feet were searching for chords," she exclaims.[11] As suggested earlier, heat and cold are such elemental phenomena that they are transferred easily into other realms or transformed into literary tropes and cultural metaphors. Currently, there is talk of the emergence of a new "cold rush" that will exploit the Arctic and Antarctic for natural resources. We tend to divide colors into warm and cool, and subsequent to Marshall McLuhan's groundbreaking theories, we identify technological media as either "hot" (e.g., newspapers and the printed word, which require active engagement) or "cool" (e.g., television, which is more passive). All sorts of unconscious associations are attached to the sustaining fire of food (as well as to the substantive food fed to fire) depending on whether it is burning, lukewarm, raw or frozen, along with its calorie (i.e., quantity of heat) content. As Bachelard observes in his "psychoanalysis" of fire, "One could seek out the origin of all the metaphors which have led to the classification of foods in accordance with their *heat*, their *coldness*, their *dry heat*, their *wet heat*, their *cooling virtue*." In his view, one could even demonstrate "that the scientific study of alimentary values is distorted by prejudices formed by fleeting and trivial first impressions."[12]

Contrary to common perception, heat and cold are not always something to flee or to be rescued from. They make us susceptible in the flesh, but they can also strengthen us in character—protracted dealings with winter often build resilience and facilitate reflection—raising our thresholds of pain or empathy and contributing to our capacity to appreciate elemental change. Extreme heat and cold slow down our fast-paced lives a notch or two, prompting us to take notice of contingencies in our existence and pay attention to the vulnerability of our bodies. By contrast, air conditioning encourages us to languish indoors and to ignore the world-wild-web of other-than-human relationships. There are healthy and sustainable ways to relieve heat and cold without banishing them from everyday experience. Some spices, for example, appear to allow the body to sweat and expunge toxins, cooling it down along the way. Tapping the earth's geothermal energy or trapping solar light and tricking it through the alchemy of modern technology to emerge magically as heat or coolant represents another viable environmentally friendly path. "Between melting and freezing / The soul's sap quivers," says T. S. Eliot.[13] In this trembling, this ongoing attempt to render ourselves more comfortable, we might be made more mindfully and ecologically aware.

6

The Economy and Ecology of the Aristotelian Elements

Without Contraries is no progression.
                            —William Blake, *The Marriage of Heaven and Hell*

How does a part of the world leave the world? How can wetness leave water?
                            —Rumi, "Enough Words?"

Hot, cold, wet and dry, four champions fierce, Strive here for Mast'ry, and to Battle bring.
                            —Milton, *Paradise Lost*

Hot, Cold, Wet, and Dry

We have seen how place is integral—indeed essential and indispensable—to understanding the natural household, the human home, and the nonhuman environment, and how it figures in and configures prominently the Aristotelian perspective of the physical world. In order to deepen our analysis and more completely reconstruct and examine Aristotle's theory of the elements, we now explore the roles and status of the contraries—hot, cold, wet, and dry—as well as elemental conversion, the compound bodies that arise from the elements, the curious matter of "prime matter," and the whereabouts and meaning of a fifth element (*aether* or ether) introduced into the philosophical picture. In the process, we underscore the vital significance of elemental contact and bodily touch in linking us to our ambient surroundings and tethering Aristotle's disparate views together. Finally, we look at the relation of the *psyche* (soul) to the external world and the additional ways in which the four elements are relevant to ecological thought.

First, however, we turn to *On Generation and Corruption*, where Aristotle fashions an account of contrariety, advances an argument concerning elemental transformation and investigates the "so-called 'elements' of bodies." In this treatise, the true elements seem suddenly and *prima facie* not to be earth, air, fire, and water as concrete entities, but rather Milton's "four champions fierce": the pair of physical opposites—hot (*thermon*) and cold (*psychron*), wet (*hygron*) and dry (*xeron*)—which Presocratic cosmologies characterized frequently in the metaphorical terms of angry warriors at battle. Hot and wet form air; hot and dry constitute fire; dry and cold create earth; and cold and wet give birth to water. Each element thereby has two defining characteristics. Aristotle most commonly refers to the hot, cold, wet, and dry as "contraries" (*ta enantia*), but he uses the term *differentiae* (*diaphorai*), too. The contraries themselves are referred to as *principles* (*archai*)[1] and *forms* (*eide*), whereas the *Meteorology* describes cold as like a *material factor* and dry and wet as passive *matter* (*hyle*).[2] In speaking of the characteristics that relate to one another in a pair of elements, Aristotle also employs the expressions *corresponding factors, tallies,* or *counterparts* (*symbola*).

In the Aristotelian worldview, touch is primary and primordial. The main contraries must be tangible because touch is the only quality common to all perceptible things. In fact, perceptible bodies are equivalent with tangible bodies, a point we argue proves to be an important tie between his ostensibly unconnected accounts of the elements. Aristotle thus asserts in *De Anima* that the sense of touch is able to exist apart from other senses but that these senses cannot exist apart from it. Touch is the distinguishing quality of bodies qua bodies that are tangible, a position that in effect transfers "touch" to "tangibility." Moreover, touch is the only sense that all animals possess. And from the claim that touch can exist separately from other senses (but not vice-versa), Aristotle concludes that the qualities sensed by touch are the distinguishing characteristics of a body as body. We can see, then, that it is by way of a tangible contrary that Aristotle is able to differentiate the four primary bodies. For this reason, he does not choose contraries such as sweetness and bitterness or whiteness and blackness as his elements or, more precisely, so-called elements. They are nontangible contrarieties, even if they are still perceptible ones.

To this point, however, Aristotle has not established why the contraries of hot and cold and wet and dry are the true qualities of elements. There are other candidates that must first be eliminated. We have found only that the contraries must be tangible. In addition to hot–cold and wet–dry, the contraries that are correlative to touch include the hard and soft, the heavy and light, the rough and smooth, the viscous and brittle, and the coarse and fine. In order to proceed, Aristotle needs to develop and deploy some further criteria. The first such criterion and approach involves whether a tangible quality is capable of acting on or being acted on by others. What Aristotle appears to be seeking are simple bodies that can enter into mixtures, which are formed through mutual interactions of their components. In his schema of contraries, each simple body has a quality in common with two physical properties, and these properties are reciprocally active and susceptible. The heavy and the light, to which Aristotle attaches great general significance as we saw earlier, are hereby vanquished because they are neither active nor susceptible, although he does not produce an argument for this position. It is quite likely, however, that he holds this view because through contact heaviness and lightness are not transmitted from one body to another.[3] Hot and cold, however, imply the power to act—and hence are active—whereas dry and wet entail susceptibility, suggesting receptivity and even passivity. Both hot and cold associate things of the same type, although cold has the additional power of associating heterogeneous entities. The wet is easily adaptable in shape and not determinable by its own limits, whereas the dry is the reverse of this: not readily shaped but determinable by its own limits.

Aristotle's second tact is to show that the remaining tangible contraries are explainable (i.e., reducible) to other qualities, specifically to the four terms of hot, cold, wet, and dry, which are embedded in the contraries. These four do not in turn allow for further reduction and so prove tobe the most "elementary qualities."[4] In undertaking this reduction, however, Aristotle only relies on the pair, wet and dry, failing to provide a role for hot and cold. The tangible differences such as hard and soft, fine and course, viscous and brittle, and the rest all can be derived from the wet and the dry. To take one example, the brittle is derivable from the dry because what is brittle is completely dry—so much so that solidification is due to the entire absence of moisture[5]—whereas the viscous is derivable from the wet because viscosity in the case of oil, for example, is a kind of modified wetness. In neither case can we derive either the dry from the brittle or the wet from the viscous. It appears as if the viscous is not only of (belonging to) the wet and the brittle of the dry but that the former terms are of the latter as a species–genus relation.[6]

In the theory advanced in *De Caelo*, Aristotle established a definitive series of likenesses between earth, water, air, and fire. This view comes into play again in *On Generation and Corruption* so that a relation can be converted between intermediaries (air and water being most like blends) but not extremes (earth and fire being more pure). From absolute heavy to absolute light, this series was: earth–water–air–fire. Earth and water, possessing the property of weight, move downward (toward the center), whereas air and fire rise (move toward the limit) as a result of the attribute of lightness. Aristotle implicitly draws on this perspective, underscoring what amounts to as a regionalization of the simple bodies—that is, their movement to specific natural locations. The primary *topoi* are still the center (*kato*) and periphery (*ano*) of the sublunary realm, the places where the elemental bodies are headed as they move "homeward."

It might appear, as some commentators believe, that due to Aristotle's reliance on the notion of the contraries, the bodies of fire, air, water, and earth do not in the end turn out to be truly simple. In fact, Aristotle himself sometimes seems to say as much. According to this interpretation, the elements are instead blends, at least blends of the contraries. They would thus be analogous to simple bodies but not equivalent with them. In support of this view, one could point to the fact that on one occasion Aristotle refers to the simple body that corresponds to fire as the "such-as-fire" rather than fire itself (330b24). The hot–dry combination, he suggests, is not the same as fire, but it does have a fiery character and is the simple body, of which fire is something like a modified form we might say. In this sense, fire could be described as an excess of heat just as ice could be described as an excess of cold such that fire or ice are an extreme or exaggeration of the truly simple bodies which they resemble—in the sense that their quality *par excellence* (hot in the case of fire, cold in the case of water) is magnified or intensified. It is perhaps for this reason that Aristotle does not allow fire and ice to participate in the generation of living entities despite the fact that the simple bodies composed of the combinations of hot and dry or cold and wet do provide for the constitution of compound bodies (*homoiomeries*).

If we follow out this line of thought, Aristotle's recharacterization of the elements as "so-called" elements and his redescription of these "elements" in terms of a likeness to simple bodies—rather than the simple bodies themselves—is similar in some respects to Plato's own reappraisal of the *stoicheia* in terms of their qualities and geometric properties. One major problem with this interpretation, however, is that Aristotle's contraries are not material entities; they do not exist independently; and by and large they are no longer described as "powers."[7] They are always linked with a substratum, being factors that allow the substratum to come into being. As Aristotle argues in the *Physics*, "we do not find that the contraries constitute the *substance* of any thing" (189a29–30). Moreover, as we saw earlier, earth, water, air, and fire are described repeatedly as simple bodies, and being elements, they are indivisible, universal, and primary.

It needs to be observed, too, that the Greek words, *hygron* and *xeron*, have a wider meaning than the English terms *wet* and *dry* since *hygron* can refer to liquids and gases, whereas *xeron* refers especially, but not exclusively, to solids.[8] The option of rendering the Greek terms into *fluid* and *solid* is problematic because although fluid can refer to both water and air, solid is patently inapplicable to fire, which has flames that are conceivably dry. Aristotle appears to acknowledge that his own theory permits a wider rather than a narrower use of these terms. He distinguishes by degree dampness from wetness—both of which are opposed to dryness—noting that the damp has an alien wetness on its surface (as perhaps on a sponge) in contrast to something that is sodden to the core.[9] Despite these terminological difficulties, Aristotle's explanation of the elements as entailing pairs of contraries seems initially plausible, although it probably works less well with air than other simple bodies because air is not necessarily either hot or completely wet. For example, as I sit in early evening on my parent's patio in northeastern Pennsylvania next to a series of gardens that are visited by hummingbirds, honey bees, and Baltimore Orioles, I can sense the air turning colder while maintaining its near absence of humidity from earlier in the day. Air, in fact, often is a problem in many of the ancient theories, and in noting that it is akin to an "aqueous vapor," Aristotle might recognize some of its transitory properties.[10] Finally, we may raise the question of whether wetness and dryness are tangible qualities in the very strictest sense because although they are discoverable through touch, it is possible to determine that something is wet by sight, as through the movement of waves of water or via a reflection in and sheen off a liquid body. In any event, the case is not as clear with these qualities as it is with hotness and coldness.[11]

Converting the Contraries

Unlike Plato's truncated scheme in which earth is the odd element out, Aristotle allows for all the simple bodies to be changed into one another. He has established that in contrast to Empedocles' eternal "elements" (*rhizomata*), earth, water, air, and fire are subject to a coming-to-be or generation and that this process is reversible. Although Aristotle places much greater faith in the reliability of our senses than Plato, he concurs with him that the elements are transformable. Aristotle can make this conclusion for two reasons: first, because generation, unlike alteration, involves a change of contraries either into or out of one another and, second, because all the elements have a contrary in their interactions with other elements because their defining qualities are themselves contraries.

As stipulated earlier, fire is hot and dry; air is hot and wet; water is cold and wet; and earth is cold and dry. Because they are four in number, each element is characterized *par excellence* by one quality: earth by dry (not cold), water by cold (rather than by wet/moist), air by wet/moist (as opposed to hot), and fire by hot (instead of dry). Furthermore, in the Aristotelian framework, fire and water are contraries as are earth and water because the qualities that constitute the opposing terms are themselves contrary. Strictly speaking, then, Aristotle has defined earth, water, air, and fire twice over by the contraries of hot, cold, wet, and dry: first in terms of distinct pairs (e.g., fire as hot and dry) and second as marked by a single contrary in a unique manner (e.g., fire as most fully hot rather than dry) such that earth, water, air, and fire are counterposed as contraries: earth–air and water–fire. Thus, in some elemental combinations there are two (or both) qualities that are contrary, as in the cases of fire and water, whereas in the remaining elemental combinations, there is one (and only one) quality that is contrary, as in the case of water and air. These additions lend Aristotle's theory a further elegance, neatness, and completeness, and they facilitate the description of the transformational mechanisms. It is, however, a bit of a perplexity and problem that water is *par excellence* cold rather than wet, but again this attribution might be due more to a difficulty in treating air (as opposed to water) because in order to distribute all of the four contraries, Aristotle must make air hot.

We can distinguish four kinds of possible elemental transformation. There are six hypothetical combinations of the contraries or, as Aristotle says, "yokings" (*syzeuxeis*), although only four actually turn out to be possible. Two of the conceivable forms of transformation are to be discounted and disallowed because they involve a contrary being yoked with its own contrary, as for example, when wet is linked with dry or cold is linked with hot. Such a combination produces an impossibility—an "impossible object" so to speak—and a contradiction to use Aristotle's own terms, such that A and not-A are asserted at the same time. What results are four combinations of cold–wet, cold–dry, hot–dry, and hot–wet, each of which distinguishes one element or simple body. Although all the elements are capable of change, the elemental transformations, nevertheless, differ according to two factors: speed and facility. Accordingly, we can characterize the Aristotelian transformational scheme in the four ways that follow here.[12]

Rapid Reversible Transformation

One process of conversion is rapid and easy between those elements with "interchangeable complementary factors," as Aristotle calls them. This is so because there is only one factor that must change. It is, moreover, cyclical (i.e., reversible) because this method of transformation is simplest and easiest where there are consecutive elements that share such factors. Thus, the transformation of fire into air occurs more quickly than the change of air into earth. Fire, as we observed previously, is a combination of hot and dry, whereas air is hot and wet, so that air will result if the dry is "overpowered" (*kratethe*) by the wet.[13] The key to this process is thus the corresponding factors (*symbola*) that are at work in the elemental interchange. The cyclicality of the elemental conversions—their natural consecutive series—also follows the order they have been accorded in the vertical cosmological scheme in *De Caelo* so that earth is transformed into water, water into air, and air into fire, along with the reverse of this order.

Slow Reversible Transformation

A second kind of transformation takes place between those elements without interchangeable corresponding factors. This change occurs more slowly than the first process because there are more qualities that must change. The transition of fire into water or earth into air, for example, is more difficult than the transition of fire into air or earth into water. In the instance of a change of earth into air, both the cold and the dry must pass away. The process is also reversible, as in the first type of transformation. Thus, the second type of change differs from the first primarily in the length of time the conversion requires.

Rapid Irreversible Transformation

A third kind of transformation is rapid like the first form but differs from the first two processes in that it is not reversible. It also involves more elements, and it occurs more easily than the second method. In this case, two nonadjacent (i.e., nonconsecutive) elements are transformed into a third one. One factor from each of two elements perishes. For example, fire and water together result in either earth or air while air and earth together eventuate in either fire or water. How, one might ask, is it determined whether the combination of two elements (say fire and water) produces one (e.g., earth) or another (e.g., air)? The answer that the Aristotelian scheme provides depends on which qualities the two combining elements lose. If the cold of the water and the dry of the fire pass away, air will result since hot and wet remain. If the wet of the water and the hot of the fire pass away, earth will be produced since cold and dry remain.

Impossible Transformation

Finally, Aristotle identifies but excludes a fourth kind of transformation, one that involves two elements that are in consecutive order (i.e., adjacent) in the cosmological schema he established in *De Caelo* proceeding from heaviest to lightest: earth–water–air–fire. The rationale for this exclusion is that the qualities that remain in a third pair will be either identical or contrary, and it is not possible to form a simple body from such combinations. Thus, if earth and water combine, they will not produce either air or fire because if the dry of earth and the wet of water perish, we are left with a cold–cold combination—an identity—although if the cold of earth and the cold of water perish, we are left with a dry–wet yoking—a contrary. All consecutive elements possess an identical and a contrary quality. And it must follow that when a consecutive element is converted into another, the transformation concerns a single quality, whereas when two elements are converted into a third, more than a single quality has perished.

From here, we can turn briefly to a pair of supplementary speculations concerning the status of the elements and their transformation, each of which is enlisted to support the Aristotelian framework. Having developed his conversion scheme, Aristotle is concerned to show as well that one independent element cannot be the source of all the others. Change, he has argued, must always be into a contrary. Aristotle's position is that if all the elements were singular (only one true element, whether fire, earth, air or water) there would be alteration but not generation. In his view, none of the earlier theorists had actually thought that one element could persist as two (e.g., water and air) at the exact same time. Therefore, one must posit a distinguishing quality of some sort—a contrariety—that will belong to another element. If we assume Thales' water as an example of a universal substratum, in order to produce fire we need to find a contrary of heat, but this contrary will not belong to water because it cannot be said that fire is simply "hot water." Such a change again would only be alteration. In Aristotle's view, this holds not only for earth, water, air, and fire but for anything that one might conceive as "intermediate" between these four. In fact, intermediates do not really exist alone in the manner of lacking all qualities because every pair of contrary yokings has a privation in the way that cold is a privation of heat, or dry is a privation of wet.

Compounding the Quartet

Before engaging several difficulties with and controversies concerning Aristotle's theory of the elements, we need to sketch out the manner in which compound bodies (*homoiomeries*) can be formed of the simple bodies.[14] As Aristotle observes, this problem exists not only for those who do not acknowledge a coming-to-be of earth, water, air, and fire, but it is a serious issue for those like himself who generate the elements out of each other. It is one matter to explain the coming-to-be of water out of earth or air out of water, bodies that possess common contraries in the Aristotelian perspective at least, but one still is faced with the task of generating compounds such as bone and flesh.[15]

Aristotle's response is twofold. First, he puts to use a conceptual distinction in a new manner. To this point, he has only defended a nonrelational schema for the contraries. Hot, cold, wet, and dry have been understood in an absolute sense, as were heavy and light. Each of the contrary qualities provided differentiae for the four elements. Aristotle now recognizes that the scaled terms of wetter, drier, colder, and hotter, but he does not abandon absolute references. He achieves this by turning to the actuality–potentiality distinction so as to have it both ways.[16] What is hotter than water but colder than air possesses heat and cold in potentiality rather than in actuality. A change from what is hot, for example, now does not necessarily have to be to what is cold, but it could be to what is merely less-than-hot.

Aristotle gave us a different account of mixture in the first book of *On Generation and Corruption*, such that the combination of water and air, for example, would produce something neither cold nor hot in actuality. Now, he provides for the possibility of qualities existing in a relational manner and invokes the earlier explanation as well. A so-called "hot–cold" or "cold–hot" combination as we might say—one that exists between the completely hot and the completely cold—is either potentially more cold than hot or more hot than cold, or even in potentiality as much one as the other. This conception of potentiality is different from the one he employs in the transformational scheme and elsewhere.[17] It does not function in the way that matter exists *in potentia*. This fact is evident when he speaks of something as being doubly or triply as hot potentially as it is cold or he argues that when either cold or hot are fully real (in actuality) *simpliciter*, the other exists in a condition of potentiality. What is hot potentially turns out not to be hot at all in the *simpliciter* sense because it is actually cold. Again, the relevant issue here is that in the case of compounds, the contrary qualities (e.g., hot and cold) of earth, water, air, and fire exist in potentiality but not in the sense that they do with regard to prime matter (to be discussed later). Flesh or bone, for example, are potentially hot in a manner that provides for some real heat, while prime matter (if it is a coherent notion) is "potentially" hot in a way that does not allow for real heat (i.e., denies it).[18]

Aristotle's second response to the problem is to speak of the contraries as "suffering action" and thus to recall the account of action and passion advanced earlier in the treatise. The contraries, he argues, must be balanced equally with one another. Otherwise, without such equality, a generation of one element into another will take place because one contrary, as we showed earlier, will "overpower" another. Aristotle has made this point earlier, but he now adds the qualification that equality in an absolute sense is unnecessary. He allows instead for a middle range or stretch of equilibrium (as opposed to a point), a state of more-or-less equality to preside. This relaxation of requirements admits the possibility of internal variation in the mixture or compound. Indeed, the range of "equality" seems to be rather large because he has claimed earlier that a compound can be two or three times as hot potentially as cold, although he precludes great inequality, as when a drop of wine is combined with ten thousand gallons of water. In any event, the slightly different proportions in the mixture will determine whether the result is one compound such as flesh or another such as bone.

All of Aristotle's compound bodies are composed of each of the four simple bodies, thus providing us with a world of elemental objects. They must, first, contain earth because earth is the predominant element in the sublunary region, where they alone are to be found. Here, Aristotle relies on his theory of natural place that suggests that the location of all compound bodies is on the earth, although it is not clear why other mixed bodies such as aquatic plants and animals do not have a home in the water. Compound bodies, secondly, must all possess water because compounds have a definite outline, and water of all the elements is most easily adaptable in shape, a view evidenced in his theory of contraries. Water is, in short, the most readily bounded. Furthermore, earth possesses no capacity to cohere without the presence of moisture (wetness), which holds things together. On this point, it seems, however, that Aristotle has conflated wetness and water. According to his theory of contraries, wetness characterizes air as well and, more importantly, it is the differentia of air. Water consists of cold and wet qualities but is cold *par excellence*.[19]

Aristotle's argument for the presence of air and fire—the remaining two simple bodies—develops at first as we might expect, but on second glance it is slightly more complicated. The elements of air and fire are the contraries of earth and water respectively and thereby necessarily implied by the existence of the latter two. Thus, all compound bodies will contain all the simple bodies. Aristotle, however, adds a caveat: namely, the proviso insofar as a substance can be said to have a contrary, presumably because he denies elsewhere that substances possess contraries.[20] He then proceeds to claim that the generation of compounds is based on contrary constituents and that in all compound bodies earth (dry and cold) and water (cold and wet) must be present, suggesting in the latter instance that generation of compounds is actually possible from constituents that are not contraries.[21]

Prime Matter: A Persisting Problem

Although clearly original and powerful as an elemental theory, there are nevertheless questions and controversies with Aristotle's view that have been left unaddressed or unsatisfactorily explained. Having investigated the transformation of the elements, we are presently in a place to consider the Aristotelian problem of prime matter (*prote hyle* in Greek or *prima materia* in Latin), a notion that has generated a substantial amount of debate among scholars and commentators.[22] The traditional position on this concept is that in Aristotle's transformational theory, when one element changes into another, some kind of underlying matter loses one of its qualities but gains another. For example, when earth changes into water, there occurs a loss of the quality of dryness and the acquisition of the quality of wetness. Prime matter is that which persists through this change. But prime matter is neither perceptible nor actual, and what endures is neither water nor air. In the example just given, it is both of these elements potentially and, in fact, all things potentially. Prime matter is not corporeal, and it cannot be subsumed under any of the Aristotelian categories such as quality, quantity, relation, or substance.[23] Rather, it is indeterminate and impossible to isolate. In being "potentially alone," it has the capacity to receive form and then to emerge in such a way that perception permits us to experience the elements.

The problem of prime matter is a pivot point for the issue concerning the status of the elements in the Aristotelian framework. If there is something more primary or ultimate than the elements, then earth, water, air, and fire will be relegated to a secondary status at best. If, by contrast, there is enough reason to doubt Aristotle's commitment to prime matter or prime matter's claim to materiality, then perhaps the elements can be rescued from a further attenuation and displacement. Aristotle himself might even provide us with the armature and apparatus to undertake a resuscitation of the elements. In a sense, the "matter" of prime matter (along with other elemental problems) positions us on an apparent precipice between a choice for a kind of "reduction" (*à la* Plato) of the elements to something more basic or a "defense" (*à la* Empedocles) of the primacy and place of earth, water, air, and fire as fundamental bodies. We examine briefly both possibilities and argue that a viable case can be made if not so much "against" prime matter as "for" the four elements. Additionally, we suggest that even if one opts for the coherence of prime matter, the possibility still is open to attributing a comparably strong—if not primary—status to one of the elements themselves: the receptive and embracing earth. Should the notion of prime matter itself turn out to be questionable, not fully defensible, incoherent, or un-Aristotelian, then the elements may be "saved" for future environmental or theoretical work.

Matter and the material cause are undoubtedly two of the most complex and controversial concepts in Aristotle's philosophy. In fact, it could be said that the material cause is Aristotle's most significant contribution to his original theory of fourfold causality given that the other three—the formal, moving, and final causes—are no doubt present to one degree or another in earlier philosophers.[24] Curiously, however, Aristotle deploys his notion of the material cause as a challenge to his Presocratic (or Pre-Platonic) predecessors, claiming that *they* had in fact seen their way through to it but had reduced the other causes to this one alone.[25] In any event, at the top of the Aristotelian universe is an idea of God, who is both pure form and pure actuality, and who as prime mover inspires but does not directly cause activity in the world or create the world itself.[26] If we follow the main currents of the philosophical tradition, counterposed directly to God and lying at the bottom of the Aristotelian worldview is prime matter because it is thought in contrast to be pure matter and pure potentiality. Betwixt and between the extremes, matter and form—along with potentiality and actuality—combine so as to constitute from top (hence, closest to the divine, eternal, and pure form) to bottom (hence, closest to the profane, fleeting, and pure matter) the remaining existents: celestial bodies, humans, animals, plants, simple things, and then the four elements. For example, as Aristotle argues in *On the Generation of Animals*, animal bodies are composed of matter as nonhomogeneous parts, which in turn consist of homogeneous matter, which is finally made up of the four elements. In a few brash brush strokes, this is an encapsulation of a much bigger picture in which the problem of matter is situated, including the conundrum of primate matter.

The Case for Prime Matter

At the outset of Book II of *On Generation and Corruption*, Aristotle writes:

> Our own doctrine is that although there is a matter of the perceptible bodies (a matter out of which the so-called "elements" come-to-be), it has no separate existence, but is always bound up with a contrariety. A more precise account of these presuppositions has been given in another work: we must, however, give a detailed explanation of the primary bodies as well, since they too are similarly derived from the matter. We must reckon as an "originative source" [*arche*] and as

"primary" the matter which underlies, though it is inseparable from, the contrary qualities: for "the hot" is not matter for "the cold" nor "the cold" for "the hot," but the *substratum* is matter for them both. We therefore have to recognize three "originative sources": *firstly* that which is potentially perceptible body, *secondly* the contrarieties (I mean, e.g., heat and cold), and *thirdly* Fire, Water, and the like. *Only* "thirdly," however: for these bodies change into one another . . . whereas the contrarieties do not change. (329a24–b2)

This remark is reproduced at length because it is one of the most succinct formulations we can find on the issue in question and because it seems to make relatively clear that Aristotle does propound some kind of notion of prime matter in relation to the elements. Two preliminary points regarding this extended claim need to be made. First, the position advanced is in contrast to Plato's view in the *Timaeus*, which Aristotle has earlier examined and rejected. Aristotle has found Plato's account to be too imprecise because it does not distinguish between two very different roles of Plato's Receptacle that are ultimately incompatible: as (a) container and hence separable from the "elements" and as (b) material or substratum for the "elements" and hence inseparable. Adding to this difficulty is Plato's failure to put to use the Receptacle in an explanation of generation and corruption. Plato and Aristotle agree that the elements are capable of transformation, but in Aristotle's view, Plato's transformation occurs entirely via the mechanics of his geometry in which triangles are reconfigured to form solid figures. Second, when Aristotle notes that he has treated this subject in greater depth, he is likely referring to the *Physics* (Bk. I.6–9). There, after concluding that the first principles of nature must be contraries, Aristotle examines the nature and number of such principles, speaks of complex and simple bodies, and considers the question of substrata.

Turning to the quote, it appears reasonable to read it as claiming that the most simple perceptible or sensible bodies (i.e., earth, water, air, and fire) are not to be construed as the ultimate kind of matter. Rather, there is something that acts in the role as their matter, and this something is *potentially* a sensible body. Furthermore, this something does not exist by itself (*alla tauten ou choristen*), a point that seems to reiterate Aristotle's earlier claim that it is "better to suppose that in all instances of coming-to-be the matter is inseparable, being numerically identical and one with the 'containing' body, though isolable from it by definition" (320b12ff). Aristotle thus rejects the notion that matter can exist independently, in separation from those forms that provide it with actuality. In other words, matter must always be *of something*, as in the matter of earth or water or air. As the first passage implies, however, the elements not only seem to take a second seat to prime matter—which becomes now the true first principle—but also to the contraries as well since the so-called elements change into one another while the contraries do not.

This position finds ostensible support in a number of other passages. Aristotle looks, for example, at the matter of earth and fire and inquires as to whether and how they might be of the same or different matter (and being) given that they are transformed from one another but nevertheless composed of different configurations of the contraries.[27] (Recall: earth is cold and dry; fire is hot and dry.) The next passage suggests an answer: "Perhaps the solution is that their matter is in one sense the same but in another sense different" (319b3–4). That is, they may share something that underlies them *as* the underlying, whereas their actual being may be different. Thus, the prime matter of earth and fire would be one and the same, although fire—as the matter from which earth can come-to-be—is the matter of earth and is different from the matter of fire—that is, earth as that from which fire comes-to-be. Stated a bit differently, there exists a sense in which prime matter is different from any one of the elements but another sense in which it is the same as any one of the elements.

Aristotle, too, writes, "matter, in the most proper sense of the term, is to be identified with the *substratum* [*hypokeimenon*] which is receptive of coming-to-be and passing-away: but the *substratum* of the remaining kinds of change is also, in a certain sense, 'matter,' because all these *substrata* are receptive of 'contrarieties' of some kind" (320a3–6). Here, Aristotle seems to efface a distinction between what *underlies* the process of change and what *endures* throughout the process, indicating that the substrata is receptive of both generation and corruption and receptive of contraries. To be receptive of contraries thus implies that there is something that remains during a transformation. Contrary to the view that when earth changes to water there is nothing substantial that remains the same (only the quality of "cold"), this passage ventures to suggest otherwise. And one could enlist additional remarks of the type identified earlier in an effort to vindicate prime matter as well.[28]

If we opt for this avenue of interpretation—namely to defend prime matter—the question remains how we should think more particularly of this matter that refuses at length to materialize, even in a clearly perceptible manner within Aristotle's own text. One is inclined to say that it almost seems to be "corrupted" in the very act of its own "generation" and near appearance. Might prime matter be akin in this regard to one (or all) of the four elements, whose status is similarly suspended by scare quotes—"the elements"—that regularly enclose and suspend Aristotle's *stoicheia* like protective frames and that are perpetually prefaced by the "so-called" cognomen? The possibility of prime matter being simply one among the other three elements seems foreclosed to us from the outset given Aristotle's earlier assaults on the attempts to reduce the number of elements to one, but on further investigation this idea might not appear quite as absurd as it initially sounds.

Aristotle actually considers the possibility in the *Metaphysics* that fire could be prime matter, an example of what he terms via a new coinage the "that-en" (*ekeininos*)—to illustrate his point that something made from, for example, wood is called "wood-en" rather than "wood"—but rejects this elemental candidate quite summarily.[29] In the *Physics,* however, he points out that prime matter cannot be known except by way of analogy, a claim that is echoed more strongly in the *Metaphysics* by his position that matter in and of itself is unknowable. As it turns out, when it does momentarily turn up, prime matter is festooned by and laden with attributes of negation. It is not perceptible, not corporeal, not determinate, not actual, and not isolatable, a description *via negativa* that recalls for us Plato's own *chora,* famous for its evasive invisibility and amorphousness. Prime matter, then, does seem to have certain similarities to Plato's Receptacle, even if Aristotle rejects the Platonic notion of space/place in several texts.[30]

Is prime matter an analogue to Plato's primal mother or "nurse," which Plato describes—and Aristotle acknowledges elsewhere—as being like the earth?[31] And could Aristotle be subtly or unconsciously intimating the primacy of earth itself in the decidedly *terrestrial* sphere of elemental transformation? Aristotle refers at numerous points in his corpus to a philosopher who claims that earth is the most fundamental material substance, but this philosopher is left unnamed and scholars have been confounded as to who Aristotle might have in mind. Would it be too much of a stretch of the imagination to think it could be Aristotle himself?[32]

Perhaps more pointedly, prime matter must be something not only underlying like earth but also essentially receptive. Earth, as Aristotle characterizes it, is cold and dry, qualities that at least to the modern mind strike us as being more passive and "negative" than do hot and wet in the sense that they are given to receive, to wait for, or to be defined by an opposing "positive" quality. As we saw in the theory of contraries, however, Aristotle considers cold and hot to be active qualities and wet and dry to be susceptible or passive qualities. Thus, because of the ability of cold to associate the homogeneous and heterogeneous alike, it appears that earth would still possess an active "tally," making it very unlike the inertness of prime matter. But there is a potential avenue out of this apparent dead end because Aristotle admits, too, that cold can be a deprivation and so less real than the hot, which involves positive predication. In certain rough ways, then, the cold–dry combination might be construed as being both like *chora* (the all-receiving) and prime matter (the pan-potential). Furthermore, Aristotle describes earth as the predominating element in the sublunary area; it is the natural place for all compound bodies, serving as their support and bearer.

Even if it is not equivalent with prime matter (and there is probably too much countervailing evidence to presume it so), earth might still be a semi-privileged body in Aristotle's theory of the elements, just as it is for Plato in the *Timaeus.* A potential mitigating factor for this proposal is Aristotle's passing criticism in *De Caelo* of the prioritizing of earth by Plato in the generation and transformation of the elements. Still, although Aristotle's first body is *aether* (the fifth element), earth functions as a foundation in the sublunary region due its solidity and place, given as it is to "move"—however little much it does—toward center-stage. This point is in accordance as well with Aristotle's more general geocentricity, on which we elaborate later. Nonetheless, it must be admitted that earth is not itself the *arche*, the one material and governing source, beginning, and principle. Such a position would not be in keeping with the rest of Aristotle's work, particularly his theory of transformation and his critique of monistic theories.

Shielding the Elements

How might we undertake a defense of the ultimate primacy of the simple bodies of earth, water, air, and fire given the ostensible preponderance of textual support for prime matter and its ongoing maintenance within the philosophical tradition? Are the elements generated from a prior substratum or from each other? Or can we have it both ways? One thing is very clear from Aristotle's perspective. The analysis must terminate at some point since he rejects repeatedly the notion of infinite regress. Beyond this fact, it is necessary to point out that in several crucial places in which we might expect him to invoke the idea of prime matter, Aristotle is strangely silent on the topic. Although he provides for a particular account of the prime mover as pure actuality, Aristotle fails to offer a comparable treatment of prime matter as pure potentiality, and he often refers to *prote hyle* as a first matter in relation to composites. In fact, it often seems as if the "first matter" (*prote hyle*) is the *last matter* (subject) into which Aristotle wants to conduct a thorough inquiry.

In the opening pages of *On Generation and Corruption*, Aristotle explicitly challenges thinkers who generate everything from one thing because they make the mistake of confusing coming-to-be (a change in substance) with alteration (a change in property or quality whereby the substance remains the same). He is also clear that he understands the monists' "matter" as that from which things are generated, and he proceeds to equate this with a substratum that "always remains identical and one" (314b3). Generation and alteration thus appear as the two species of change in question, and the alternatives seem to be either that the substratum persists or that nothing persists through the change of which the term of the change is an accident or affection. The question thereby arises, how does prime matter fit in because it is supposed to be what continues through substantial change; that is, generation and corruption? For Aristotle, alteration involves *perceptible* persistence of a substratum, whereas prime matter (if in fact Aristotle subscribes fully to this idea) would be the *imperceptible* persistence of a substratum. Thus, at the very outset of the work presumed to advance the notion of prime matter, we find Aristotle erecting barriers to its potential development and deployment in an intelligible and coherent manner.

Aristotle clearly argues in *De Caelo* that the elements do not either come-to-be from what is incorporeal or from corporeal entities other than the elements themselves. This argument appears to rule out prime matter, which is not a bodily entity. Simple bodies consist of a combination of matter and form, but prime matter is thought to be in some sense beyond the corporeal elements as a pure potentiality. Aristotle, however, denies that the elements can come about via something noncorporeal because that would require the existence of an extracorporeal void, a notion he rejects in the *Physics*. In this section on generation, Aristotle is therefore able to conclude, "the only remaining alternative is that they [the elements] are generated from one another" (305a34).

The conspicuous absence of recourse to prime matter in the transformational schema of the elements is most telling.[33] Here, of all places, we would expect Aristotle to explicitly invoke the notion of prime matter if he held firmly to it since it would help to account for the means and mechanics of elemental change. Without the unwarranted necessity of assuming it to exist as a kind of haunting ghost-like presence throughout this process, one can more adequately explain elemental conversions by reference to the contraries. Moreover, if we did presuppose the tacit existence of prime matter, further unexplained difficulties are generated. Do we have a slight textual rationale, nevertheless, for granting the benefit of the doubt to the "friends" of prime matter? In the supplementary comments to his theory of transformation, Aristotle makes two remarks that might be so interpreted as friendly to prime matter. First, in his reconsideration of whether the elements are a "matter" (Aristotle deploys assertions here) of which natural bodies consist and his concomitant re-examination of the number of elements, he concludes, "Both Fire and Air, therefore, will be something else which is the same; i.e. there will be some 'matter,' other than either, common to both" (332a17ff). Because the argument that leads him to this conclusion applies as well to all elements, he takes it that there is no single element out of which all come-to-be. Later in this section, he observes of "matter" (again in quotes) that it is "the 'mean' between the two contraries, and matter is imperceptible and inseparable from them" (332a35ff). Both quotes could be construed in terms of potential support for prime matter, or perhaps more accurately, "common matter."

Proceeding, then, to the difficulty given this somewhat generous assumption, we should note that in the kind of change that we have termed *slow reversible transformation* the conversion process between elements is more difficult and time-consuming than the first, which we have called *rapid reversible transformation*. As we have interpreted these changes, this difference in time concerns the fact that in the second kind of transformation there are more *symbola* that must change than in the first since the elements in question are nonconsecutive (e.g., fire changing into water), whereas in the first mechanism they are consecutive (e.g., fire changing into air). Now, if we grant the functioning place of prime matter in this process, why would there be such differences in time? If the underlying, imperceptible matter is one prime matter, it would seem that more than one change could occur at a time, as when the hot sun bakes moist, white skin, turning it not only dry but also red at same time.

It must be further emphasized that Aristotle's elements are simple bodies, which are not reducible to something further. As indicated by his definitions, elements are bodies that are primary components of a thing. They are indivisible (*adiaipeton*), small, simple, and universal components. They are not compounds or composites, although they can form compounds. Otherwise, they could be made from more simple bodies. The elements instead are the simplest and most ultimate "stuff." Why? Because they can be produced from one another and do not need a primary matter, whose coherence (even if a commitment to it is assumed) is extremely open to question and criticism. That they are the simplest and most singular bodies is also shown by Aristotle's theory of motion, which admits of only specific types of movement to which these bodies correspond.

Finally, we must return to the issue of the status of contraries. Aristotle argues in the *Physics* that the contraries *themselves* do not change into each other and suggests in *On Generation and Corruption* that they are somehow second in stature to an underlying matter. As we discovered earlier, many of the Presocratics characterized the opposites as engaged in battle, and although Aristotle does his best to vanquish the vestiges of metaphor, he still speaks of the contraries in terms of one being "overpowered" (*kratethe*) by another, invoking the remains of warrior images in his "construction" of the elements. This leaves him with two options: either the "defeated" quality must "retreat" to somewhere else such as a place or element where it can find its kind, or it must die and "perish" in the agonistic field of change, to continue the metaphor. Aristotle does not choose the former option, though it was available to him as a model in Plato's *Phaedo*.[34] Instead, he suggests that one of contraries perishes. How might we interpret this position without either reifying the contraries or referring to prime matter? The most plausible way is to regard the loss of a quality as the loss of an essential attribute of one of the elements that then ceases-to-be (i.e., is corrupted) as a whole. For example, when the dry of earth perishes, Aristotle means that it loses a quality that made it be what-it-is, in this case a quality *par excellence*. As water comes-to-be in the transformation from earth, wetness persists qua quality in the resulting element. Something is no longer dry and that something is or, more accurately, *was* earth.[35]

To sum up, then, there are sufficient reasons to doubt the adequacy of prime matter or Aristotle's unwavering commitment to it given conflicting textual evidence and the lack of a clear and distinct account in any particular location. Furthermore, there are ways of providing for a defense of the primacy of the four elements themselves as simple bodies. A somewhat different challenge to the status of earth, water, air, and fire is provided in the form of a fifth element and first body that Aristotle introduces in *De Caelo* in that it lies outside of the natural, "restricted" economy of the lower four. It is to this element that we now turn.

Extra Terrestrials: The Fifth Element

The Aristotelian universe is rent in two divisions: a lower or sublunary region that extends downward from the moon and reaches to the center of the earth and an upper region that spans from the moon outward to a sphere of fixed stars. Earth, water, air, and fire reside solely in the sublunary region, where they undergo their reciprocal transformations. Therein lie the natural places, natural motions, distinct aspects of weight, and play of the contraries that we have examined thus far. The four elements in the lower cosmic region follow physical "laws" and there is an abundance of frenetic activity and change here: generation and corruption, growth and alteration, contact and oppositional clashing. The upper region, by contrast, is far more regular and orderly. The celestial bodies and the heavenly spheres in which they are contained are also composed of *aether*, a fifth element with movements and characteristics very different from the canonical four.

Aristotle introduces the fifth element, *aether*, in large part in order to satisfy his theory of motion. As noted, the heavenly bodies are said to be composed of this element. Because the activity of Aristotle's God is eternal, so must be the movements of the heaven (sky), which is divine and thus a rotating sphere. Similarly, the movement of *aether* is circular in contrast to the straight lines of the sublunary or terrestrial elements, and this circular movement has no contrary. Aristotle's approach here is to argue, first, that all natural bodies and magnitudes have the capacity for locomotion (i.e., movement in place) and that such motion must either be in a straight line or circular because these are the only existing simple magnitudes. Circular motion consists in revolution about a center, whereas motion in straight lines is either upward, hence away from the center, or downward, hence toward the center. Given the existence of simple bodies whose movement is in their own *physis* (nature), there will be simple movements (of which circular motion is an example) corresponding to such bodies so that some bodies will have by nature a circular motion. Admitting the existence of unnatural movement (e.g., through constraint), Aristotle proceeds to deduce the existence of a body whose circular motion is natural to it by arguing, among other ways, that it would be astonishing and inconceivable that a bodily movement that is continuous and eternal could be contrary to nature. For Aristotle, the circle is the perfect figure. Circular motion, too, is primary and prior to upward and downward motions, and so a body to which it belongs is naturally prior to other bodies.

From these considerations of motion, he affirms the existence of a body different and separate from those on earth, one whose "superior glory of its nature is proportionate to its distance from this world of ours" (269b17). This remark seems to recognize as well to one degree or another Aristotle's awareness of the vast regions of what we now call "outer space," providing him with some empirical grounds for holding to the doctrine in addition to the more theoretical arguments that he has advanced. In line with the Aristotelian account of the sublunary elements, it would appear that such a great expanse could not be filled with air or fire—the two elements that move naturally toward the outer limit—given that there must be a rough equilibrium between the contraries. The enormous amount of heat that would be required to occupy the celestial realm with either air (hot and wet) or fire (hot and dry) would be such as to greatly "overpower" the other elements, especially earth, thereby disturbing the terrestrial balance and perhaps the sublunary region itself. Thus, in Aristotle's perspective, it makes further sense for the heavenly area not to be distinguished by contrary qualities.

Additionally, Aristotle argues that *aether* is free from alteration and decay; exempt from changes in size and quantity; and singular in nature. That is, there cannot be more than one heaven. *Aether* does not possess either heaviness or lightness because these terms attach only to bodies with movements either up or down, and *aether* does not move in a straight line toward or away from a center. It is not even capable of forced movement in straight lines (i.e., unnaturally) because if its unnatural movement were upward, then its natural movement would be downward (given that with opposite movements such contrary direction and hence *physis* is implied), and vice-versa. Similarly, this primary body is neither generated nor destroyed because coming-to-be and passing-away occur via a contrary, as Aristotle argues in the *Physics*. Circular motion has no contrary and hence is incapable of decay or genesis. That *aether* has no contrary is a thesis to which Aristotle subscribes for two related reasons. First, the circular can be opposed to the straight line, allowing for two kinds of rectilinear motion that are contrasted with one another because of their relation to the respective and different places, up and down. Second, circular routes that pass through two exact same points number in the infinite whereas a rectilinear path is singular (e.g., A to B and back).

Aristotle himself speculates that the word "*aether*" derives from *aei thein*, meaning to "run always" or eternity,[36] although *aether* may be a literary creation formed by analogy with *aer* and not part of spoken language.[37] His arguments for the existence of *aether* appeal not only to natural motion and etymology,[38] but also to the traditional Greek belief that the gods dwell in the highest part of the sky.[39] In this respect, Aristotle believes that his theory is confirmed by and confirming of experience. This claim is a dubious one philosophically speaking, although it does reveal the enduring strength of religious and mythological convictions. Aristotle is on better but still weak and ultimately spurious grounds when he appeals finally to the evidence garnered through the senses and the supposed fact that no change seems ever to have occurred in the outermost heavens.

A number of difficulties in Aristotle's account of the elements arise because of the introduction and treatment of a fifth element. Perhaps most importantly, Aristotle does not provide an adequate explanation of the relation between the sublunary and celestial regions. The location of the fifth element begins where the four lower elements leave off at the level of the moon, and whereas earth, water, air, and fire naturally rise or fall, *aether* has a circular motion. The sublunary elements undergo constant change and their movements can be "enforced" or "unnatural" as, for example, when a rock—which has a natural motion and place in earth that is downward and below—is thrown upward in the air. The movement of *aether*, by contrast, is eternal and cannot be driven in an unnatural direction by external forces. How then is the joint between these two very different realms characterized? How could the fifth element convey movement to the other four without itself being affected in turn? The sun, Aristotle correctly recognizes, is responsible for changes in temperature and differences in the seasons, affecting conditions in the sublunary realm. But it is not the lower-most celestial body because it exists above the moon.

There is the further question of how and why celestial bodies such as stars give off light or, in the instance of the sun, emit heat. Because *aether* is not composed of the four contrary qualities, these bodies cannot themselves be hot. Aristotle appears to offer a hesitant but unsatisfactory response to this problem when he suggests that heavenly bodies produce heat and light through the friction of their movements without themselves becoming hot.[40] On a different but related note, we might ask if this problem of the relationship of the cosmological regions is similar to the contemporary question of where the earth's atmosphere (or earth itself) ends and "outer space" begins? By introducing a fifth element beyond the upper limit of fire, Aristotle does not necessarily expose the "natural economy" and cyclical ecology of the four elements to another dimension, but he inadvertently opens up, if not a Pandora's box of problems, then a host of new, unresolved questions. The status of *aether* in the Aristotelian scheme is in many regards a bit perplexing since it is not strictly comparable to the other four elements and seems, at times, to function like the Receptacle of Plato's *Timaeus*; that is, as the place of places. Nevertheless, for Aristotle, *aether*—the fifth element—remains what he terms the first or primary body.[41]

Elemental Contact: Beholding Tangible Bodies

Earlier, we alluded to the importance that touch and contact might play as connecting threads in Aristotle's multiple accounts of the elements. We now elaborate on this claim and then show the significance of being *in touch with the elements* in terms of ecological perception and bodily belonging to place. In *On Generation and Corruption,* Aristotle sought to discover the principles of perceptible bodies and specifically *tangible* bodies. All instances of tangible qualities can exist on a continuum with two opposing extremes such as rough and smooth, coarse and fine, or hard and soft. Some of these contrary states, however, are derivable from other more basic ones, and these turn out to be the pairings of hot–cold and dry–wet, providing us with four possible combinations of pairs to which correspond the four simple bodies of earth, water, air, and fire. In conceiving the problem in terms of providing an account of the sensible qualities of tangible objects, Aristotle commits himself from the outset, and in the process, to a qualitative theory of the elements, ruling out any further likelihood of a "reduction" of the elements to quantitative properties or differentiae, as Plato and the Atomists had attempted.

Contact also provides a link between the accounts in *On Generation and Corruption* and *De Anima* and proves to be central in Aristotle's theory of the elements more generally. In the former work, Aristotle is compelled to undertake an investigation of "contact," which is necessitated by the notions of "action–passion" (acting and suffering action) and "combination." More broadly, contact proves useful and, indeed, essential to his theory because it is not possible to consider the role of the elements in generation and corruption without first exploring what it means for entities to mix with, act upon or, alternatively, be affected by each other. What comes-to-be, he argues, is formed of particular material constituents and through combination, which in turn implies action and passion. Neither action nor passion, however, can occur between things that are not in touch with one another, nor can things combine without contact. Stated more precisely, things that combine must be capable of reciprocal contact, and, where there are two things such that one "acts" while the remaining one "suffers action," there must be contact as well.

Aristotle deftly distinguishes and deploys several meanings of "contact," building up a skeletal definition in the *Physics*. There, contact is spoken of as occurring when two things have extremes that are together. In *On Generation and Corruption*, the first sense of the term applies to things that can be said to have a position. Position, however, can only belong to that which also occupies place.[42] It is only this meaning—which involves place—that is the proper sense of contact. Thus, Aristotle enlarges the definition given in the *Physics* to state that all things that are discontinuous objects and that possess size and position, as well as having their extremes together, will be in contact with each other. From here, it is but a short step to his theory of natural place. For Aristotle, as we have seen, a primary differentiation of place is above and below, and so two things that are in contact with one another will possess either lightness or heaviness or, more accurately, either one or both of them will do so. Further, such things in contact with one another will be able to move or be moved by the other. We can reach this conclusion because heavy and light things are able to act or suffer action. They move naturally to either the center or circumference in the sublunary sphere.

A secondary sense of "contact" can be attributed nevertheless to mathematical objects, which Aristotle suggests can occupy place as well. Because this idea is not elaborated on, we can only conjecture that he might mean that insofar as they are abstracted from sensible physical objects, which in turn occupy a location, they have some sense of place or, alternatively, that they are located mentally in some kind of imaginary place (or space). We can identify an additional form of contact as that which moves but is not itself reciprocally moved and is without acting or being acted on. Again, Aristotle is not specific or clear, but he seems to have in mind the kind of relation that exists between the outer heaven and the neighboring celestial sphere. In this last kind of contact, bodies will touch without also being touched. As should be evident from the treatment of the four elements and *aether*, this kind of contact is not possible in the sublunary realm, where, for example, a body of earth clearly touches water, and water reciprocally touches earth.

Given such distinctions, Aristotle is able to differentiate "contact in general"—in which a relation exists between two positioned things whereby one is capable of imparting motion and the other is capable of being moved—from "reciprocal contact," which involves a relation between two things, whereby one is capable of imparting motion and the other is capable of being moved in such a manner that we can attribute action and passion to these entities.[43] Thus, for Aristotle, the relation between mover and moved is not univocal. One kind of "mover" can move other things without itself being moved, while a second kind can only move other things by being moved itself. This distinction corresponds within Aristotle's work to a similar distinction internal to acting itself because movers can be characterized as in some sense acting, and acting things as giving motion to something. A difference between the two notions, however, lies in the broader scope that "imparting motion" has than "acting." In any case, things that are given to cause motion, in one significant sense, can be said to touch those things that they move. The exception of the outer heaven "touching" the celestial sphere next to it is, Aristotle suggests, a bit like a person who "touches" others by causing them to experience grief or happiness but who is not "touched" back by them.

The subject of touch is considered in *De Anima* in relation to the order of living beings, to the other four senses of taste, smell, hearing, and vision, and to the four elements. As pointed out in our discussion of contraries, Aristotle argues that no sense can be found separately from touch but that touch can be found by itself. Thus, touch can be said to be the most primary and basic sense for Aristotle. This claim is confirmed for him empirically by the fact that all animals possess the sense of touch and yet many do not have smell, sight, taste, or hearing. Moreover, all animals possess a sense for food, which consists of the contrary qualities of wet and dry, hot and cold—the relevant *symbola* of the four elements—and these are the qualities that touch apprehends. More specifically, hunger and thirst are two forms of desire: hunger for what is hot and dry and thirst for what is cold and wet.

Aristotle returns to this topic so as to examine in greater detail the nature of each individual sense, exploring in turn sight, hearing, smell, taste, and finally touch. As with the other senses, he is concerned to know what the organ is for touch, and in this analysis, touch and tangibility are used as related and nearly interchangeable terms. Two possible candidates present themselves: the organ sought is either flesh or some homologous substance in the case of certain animals, or it is something that lies further inward so that flesh is not the organ but the medium of touch. Whereas the accepted view holds that the other senses have fields that are determined by the interval that exists between one pair of contraries, the field for touch in Aristotle's view has two pairs. This apparent discrepancy creates a problem for his analysis. In the case of sight, it is commonly thought to be black and white; with hearing, it is acute and grave; and in the instance of taste, it is bitter and sweet.[44] This difficulty is partially resolved by Aristotle in his observation and claim that the other senses do in fact have more than one pair of contraries, despite the common view to the contrary. Sound, for example, relies on the loud and soft as well as the grave and acute. Similarly, in the case of touch, we find the contraries of hot–cold, dry–wet, and hard–soft, among others elliptically unstated. Presumably, Aristotle also has in mind those other contraries he enumerated in *On Generation and Corruption* in connection with his consideration of the basic tangible contraries: heavy and light, rough and smooth, viscous and brittle, and course and fine. The problem nevertheless persists because in the case of touch a single subject cannot be readily discovered as underlying the contraries, one that corresponds with sound in the instance of hearing. The matter is also not resolvable in the direction of the position that the organ of touch is outward, hence epidermal, because the mere fact alone that an object touching the flesh is perceived by us is insufficient to adduce this conclusion, a view Aristotle reaches through a thought experiment that imagines a membrane stretched across or growing on one's skin.

Aristotle's inclination, approach, and answer are to find some naturally attached "medium" such as flesh in order to solve this dilemma. Flesh presents the best possibility because all living bodies must be solid and so composed of earth (along with other elements), thus ruling out water and air as individual candidates. In Aristotle's perspective, flesh in fact tends to be composed of a combination of earth, water, and air.[45] Therefore, the body sought will be naturally attached to a living organism, as is the case with flesh (or its analogue) among humans and other animals. And the tactile qualities that are transmitted through flesh will be manifold rather than singular, as is evident when we touch an object with the tongue, sensing not only tangible qualities but ones related to flavor as well. Touch and taste, however, cannot be equated in the Aristotelian sensory framework because they are not always found together in the same part of the body, as they are in the case of the tongue, despite the fact that earlier in *De Anima* Aristotle establishes that what is tasted must be a tangible entity.[46]

Having offered a preliminary answer to this initial question, Aristotle proceeds to consider the problem of whether perception of all objects occurs in the same manner. Do taste and touch, for example—which involve contact with their objects—take place in the same way as sight, hearing, or smell? The answer Aristotle provides is both affirmative and negative. On the affirmative side of the response, he endeavors to hold that all objects of perception, including those of taste and touch, are perceived through a *medium*. This occurs whether or not we are aware of it. In the case of the thought experiment given earlier, it is implied that we would not likely be cognizant of the fact that a membrane attached to the flesh is still a medium. Similarly, Aristotle argues that in water or air, two bodies do not literally touch one another because a third body (either the water or air) is interposed between them. In the case of water, for example, their contacting surfaces are not dry, as needs be for bodily touch. But this is not immediately evident to us because, as Aristotle suggests, we live in air and so being like water animals who do not know that "touching" objects have wet surfaces, we are usually not fully aware of the element (be it water or air) in which we immersed.

Because everything is perceived through a medium, Aristotle still maintains that the objects of hearing, sight, and smell are perceived over a *greater distance* than in the cases of touch and taste, and this constitutes one of the fundamental differences (and the negative side of his response) between touch (and taste) and the other senses. A further difference is that with sight and hearing, the medium has particular effects on us—in this way enabling us to perceive—whereas with touch, we are not so much influenced *by* the medium as affected *along with* it. It is, to use Aristotle's helpful analogy, a bit like a man who is struck through his shield such that the blow to his person and the protective metal are contemporaneous rather than consecutive. These differences between touch and the other senses allow Aristotle to determine that flesh is not an organ per se—which he defines later in terms of that in which the power of sensing ultimately resides (i.e., of receiving the sensible forms of objects but not their matter).[47] Rather, flesh is the medium of touch. The additional difference is important and amounts to the claim that in the case of smell, sight, and hearing—what we might now term the more distal as opposed to proximate senses—we obtain no perception of an object when it is placed directly upon the organ in question (e.g., a Susan B. Anthony dollar coin on the eye), but when an object (e.g., the same coin) is placed on the flesh, it is perceived. For Aristotle, the tongue and the flesh are relatable to the true organs of taste and touch in a manner analogous to the relation of air and water to the organs of sight, smell, and hearing. This being the case (or so he holds), Aristotle believes he can show that the ability to perceive tangible qualities lies inside the body rather than in the flesh.

If flesh is the medium, what then for Aristotle are the objects of touch, the true organ of perception, and the more exact mode and manner in which this perception takes place? As should be evident from the examination of the four elements, the objects of touch are those distinct qualities of body qua body that distinguish earth, water, air, and fire: namely, the hot, the cold, the dry, and the wet.[48] But here we need to be a bit careful with language. The objects of touch are not only the tangible but also the "intangible," where intangible is understood in the case of air as the possession in a very small degree of a tangible quality or, alternatively, the possession of such a quality in an extreme degree, as with destructive things, presumably like fire. The organ of perception, however, is not flesh but touch itself, which is the part of the body where the sense of touch is seated. It is, to use familiar Aristotelian language, that part that corresponds in a potential way to what its object is in an actual way. Stated somewhat differently, the organ of touch is *actually neither* of the contrary qualities (e.g., hot or cold) but *potentially either* of them.

Finally, touch is, moreover, a *mean* between two opposing qualities, and these qualities are what determine the field of the tactile sense. As a mean, touch provides us with the ability to discern objects since what lies in the middle is fitted to do so, being relative to extremes and able to put itself in the place or position of another. Aristotle's mean, however, unlike the role of the mean (qua *arete*, meaning virtue or excellence) in his *Nicomachean Ethics*, does not appear exactly suited to discern its own position (the middle) because it cannot perceive objects that are equally cold and hot for example.[49] For Aristotle, perception works on a model of necessary excess, so that what we perceive must possess one of the sensible and tangible qualities in a measure that exceeds a neutral condition.[50] We now take up more directly the environmental significance of cultivating contact and touch with the ambient elements, a theme to which we return in the eighth chapter.

In Touch With the Environment

We have stressed the significance of elemental contact and bodily touch in Aristotle's theory, particularly their centrality to tethering together the varied accounts, to connecting the elements with one another, and to tying the elements to the flesh of human and other-than-human bodies. In Greek, *haptein* has a wider sense than "to grasp" in English, connoting not only clutching but holding what exceeds the grip of the hands so as to encompass the whole body. It suggests fastening, clasping, laying hold of, linking, and touching, as when individuals embrace in a sexual or sensual manner or wrestlers grapple with each other. Touch is the mode in which we most completely *com-prehend*—literally grasp with or hold together in the sense of jointly—our environing world and its particular places. In grasping and *be-holding* place, we come to know and inhabit the ambient earth or air or water, along with elemental forces or objects, as opposed to understanding intellectually an abstract and elusory "nature." When we step into a new place, we become an elemental ingredient in the habitat and its ever-evolving hybridity because there is a bodily belonging to it, as Aristotle recognized. Place becomes an extension of the self-dispersing body, and via our legwork, we are propelled through it: from a near-sphere to the far-away; from here to there.

Touch often is more suited than sight to such elemental enterprises because of, on the one hand, the palpability, weight, and textures of earth and, on the other hand, the transparency of water or the invisibility of air, properties that are either difficult or impossible to perceive with our eyes.[51] Aristotle privileges sight in the *Metaphysics*, but in *De Anima* touch comes to the philosophical fore with the appearance of the four elements. In the work of Parmenides and Plato, Western thought reached an abstract and a-topic apogee where not only being and becoming were mutually exclusive, but sense perception was denied contact with lived reality. Aristotle rectifies this situation. Sight is by no means excluded from the perceptual process involving elemental things as it is reoriented from a privileged position. As Merleau-Ponty suggests, "Things attract my look, my *gaze caresses* . . . things, it exposes their contours and their reliefs, between it and them we catch sight of a *complicity*."[52] Caressing complicity here is key, especially given that, as we shall see, Merleau-Ponty astutely characterizes the flesh as the formative medium of subject and object—the bond between body and world—speaking of it as specifically comparable to the elements of the Presocratics and, we may add, Aristotle.

Touch attests to an object-bound, if not "objective," world that lies outside our selves but not beyond our reach. At the same time, given "it interests the not-me more than any other sense," touch necessitates a powerful subjectivity. When we feel an objective entity beyond the circumscribed boundaries of our bodies, we simultaneously experience self and other.[53] In this regard, the haptic sense is a perceptual system through which humans and nonhuman animals quite literally remain in touch with their surroundings.[54] Haptic experience involves "feelings of rhythm, of hard and soft edges, of huge and tiny *elements*, of openings and closures, and a myriad of landmarks and directions" that together constitute human identity.[55] Such views are echoed by others who have made the elements (or the elemental) central to their work and who provide in effect a form of relational knowing, a kind of "epistemology of contact."[56] Bachelard's remark, "Sometimes when I touch things, I dream of an element," is emblematic. Thoreau as well found a sinuous thread connecting the elemental world with human identity and geographical locale: "Think of our life in nature—daily to be shown matter, to come in contact with it,—rocks, trees, wind on our cheeks! the solid earth! the actual world! the common sense! Contact! Contact! Who are we? where are we?"

Place, as Aristotle points out, is "something important and hard to grasp" (212a8), but it is nevertheless something eventually *grasped*—through elemental touch and bodily contact. The somatic is arguably most deeply rooted in touch, and it is significant that Aristotle emphasizes the elements in their tangibility. Touch structures our world, and it differs from other senses in that our body and the bodies we are touching are joined; they are co-present. In order to understand the environment, we must be continually and viscerally affected by the ambient elements—despite their increasing domestication and technological mediation—and, when possible, share this contact with others through common practices and living stories.[57]

The Soul and the External World

Wallace Stevens has remarked cryptically, but provocatively, that "the soul . . . is composed of the external world."[58] Given Aristotle's abiding naturalism and his recurring interest in the *psyche* (soul) and matters psychological, one might wonder whether he would endorse or balk at the poet's claim. How does Aristotle construe the soul, and what is its relation, if any, to the natural world and the elements? Does he embrace a thorough "de-souling" of the elements or advocate an extirpation of the elements from the soul? To address these issues, we must turn to a new text and, more specifically, his claim that the "soul is all things."

The question whether the soul (*psyche*) is composed of elements or, alternatively, is one of the elements itself is raised initially in On Generation and Corruption. The matter is consigned, however, to another investigation: namely, De Anima (*On the Soul*). As in most of his treatises, Aristotle is concerned not only to develop and defend his own positions and dispositions but also to reveal the inadequacy of other philosophical views, if only to improve on or supersede them. Thus, part of the inquiry entails a critique of the theories of Empedocles and Plato, the two figures in addition to the Atomists whom we have singled out as providing the most original and penetrating early perspectives of the elements.[59] Aristotle argues that those thinkers who define the soul in terms of its capacity for knowing generally characterize it either as an element or as being formed out of elements. This is so because they rely on a theory of perception grounded in the notion that "like knows like." In maintaining that the soul consists of elements, they identify it with all that the soul is able to comprehend. The soul, moreover, tends to be marked by sensation, movement, and noncorporeality, and so like the elements it was believed that one could follow it back to an origin or governing principle (*arche*). In this regard, each of the elements found an advocate with the exception of earth. Diogenes, for example, claims that soul is of air because air is the finest of the elements and a first principle; Heraclitus identifies it with fire and warm exhalation; and Thales connects it with water. Empedocles and Plato fashion the soul, too, from elements based on the idea that like is known by like.

Aristotle, by contrast, treats soul as "the first actuality of a natural body which has organs" (412b5), although this definition is only one among at least four that he offers. Prior to this point he sets forth two others, and subsequently he advances a fourth that adds a causal dimension to the conception. The first three are more strictly generic "formulae" or nominal stipulations, whereas the fourth is most properly a robust definition. This approach is emblematic of a larger methodology that proceeds step by step, building on earlier formulations, clarifying, and honing to precision a new view. At each step, we advance closer to the "whatness" of the soul and to attainment of knowledge that is "noble and honorable" (402a1).

The importance of this formula is fourfold. First, it permits us to see the internal relations of three souls—plant, animal, and human—that Aristotle analyzes. Second, it is revealing of a broader area of psychology that Aristotle explores, and perhaps even a kind of phenomenological psychology. It is this perspective that shows the three souls are related organically or serially rather than being distinct or hierarchically ordered, and it hints at a grander environmental worldview, as when he says that "soul is in all things." Third, the definition entails necessarily a unity of body and soul, or at least rules out from the start certain types of dualistic thinking that have prevailed in philosophical thought from Plato, where the body (*soma*) is a prison or tomb (*sema*) for the soul, to Descartes, where the soul is distinct and prior to matter, and the body is dispensable. The body and soul in Aristotle's conception are integrated *ab initio* because of the intimate relation between form and matter. The body holds the potentiality of the soul and, moreover, it is beneficial for the soul to be united with it. Finally, the study and hence definition of the soul contributes to "every kind of truth" (402a5) and especially to an understanding of nature. The inquiry into the soul allows us to differentiate in the process the methods of the various sciences. Knowledge of the soul's "whatness" in turn will be useful to an investigation into the causes of its attributes, and Aristotle's definition is, in any case, the culmination or *entelechy* (realization) of this protracted process.

Like the soul, bodies are also substances, and natural bodies, of which the soul is a form (*eidos*), can be subdivided into the living and nonliving. The distinguishing criteria in this regard are the capacities for self-nourishment and growth and the fact of bodily decay over time, thereby ruling out some inanimate bodies like corpses, rocks, or bodies of water.[60] The soul is not strictly a body but rather the actuality of a body. This appears to be the case because the body is not life itself but what possesses life. It is matter for the soul just as the soul is form to the body.[61] Soul, in any event, is the vital principle, the "animator" in all living things and hence must belong to natural bodies.

From these distinctions, we arrive at a preliminary formula of the soul as "a substance as the form of a natural body potential with life" (412a20) and, more particularly, substance as actuality. Soul, therefore, is an actuality of a natural body. Two effects of this view are that it allows for the inclusion of plants as well as animals to be possessors of soul and that it circumvents, as noted, the possibility of a dualism right from the start by investing or embodying the soul. From this understanding, we move to another one that establishes that in the order of actualities, of which there are two, the soul is first and that the bodies of which he speaks have organs (again, these include plants, though their "parts" are simple). And finally, we come via the first two formulations to a common notion applicable to all souls, to the universal what-ness of the investigation—namely, "the first actuality of a natural body which has organs."

The relationship of soul to body, then, is one of intimate inseparability, even when or if the parts can be divided. The soul is the fulfillment (*entelechy*) of the body, which in turn exists as a potentiality for the soul. And this potentiality for life already possesses soul. Aristotle is not advancing an epiphenomenal view. The body is ensouled; the soul is embodied. Following these developments, there is a last reformulation and an arrival via redaction at a new definition, which takes us beyond the first three. Here the soul is spoken of in terms of being the principle of its functions and identified by its powers of nutrition, sensation, thinking, and ability to produce motion.

Aristotle maintains: "the soul is all things, but in a certain sense, for things are either sensible or intelligible, and in a certain sense, knowledge is the objects known while sensation is the sensible objects" (431b20ff). With this proposition, we return to the distinction between actuality and potentiality, and we find a soul now embodied not simply in a definition but in a cosmos, in "all things" sensible and intelligible. Aristotle's summation also leads us back to a passage, where he argues that the process of thought is continuous rather than circular because it culminates in a definition, an end, or *telos*. "Thinking is [the same as] the concepts," and they are one or "oned" by virtue of the fact that they are in succession (407a7ff). Thinking is a "coming to a rest or a standstill" or we would be thrown into an infinite regress in which the intellect thinks the same thoughts over and over. Thus, the "identity" of thought with its objects—or, analogously, sensation with its objects—is more a termination than a strict equivalency. The "in a certain sense" he invokes is a qualification of this ostensibly identitarian moment.

In another sense, the "in a certain sense," the hesitancy or the caveat about the sensible and intelligible, can be looked at through the lens of actuality and potentiality, for it is the actual that is given a primacy in his account and so the soul is all things, but all things in their realization and fulfillment. "Sensation" and "sensible objects" have two meanings—in potency and actuality—and it is in the actualization of a sensation that the actualization of the object occurs. Stated differently, it is the *activities* of the sensible object and the sensation that are the same, even if their essence is different. They are united or "oned" in the very act of tasting, smelling, hearing, or seeing. Sensation senses or "perceives" that it senses because if it did not we would be led into accepting an untenable position that an infinite number of senses exist or that the eye, for instance, can sense that the ear senses its sensible objects.

Similarly, actual knowledge is the same as the thing known and not potential knowledge, which is prior in time for individuals but not for a whole. It is intellect in its actuality, in its thinking, which is the objects it thinks. And these objects can either be undivided or a composition. Prior to thinking, the intellect is "none of the things" (429a24) as actuality—it is actually no-thing, except a capacity in potency. The intellect is primarily passive but able to receive the form of the intelligible just as sensation receives the form of the sensible. In other words, the things or objects of the intellect, and by extension, the things of the soul are not the "things themselves." They are not the four elements, for that would imply that stone, sky, and sea, for example, reside literally in the soul; rather, they are the forms (understandable aspects) of such things.

Here, however, a difference exists between the sensible and intelligible given that a sense loses some of its sensing power when acted upon by a strong object (e.g., the pungent smell of skunk spray), whereas the intellect can comprehend even more intelligent objects after being acted on by a highly intelligent one.[62] Aristotle resorts finally to analogy to clarify his qualified identity because one must understand through images, which are the "sense impressions" of a thinking soul, and holds that the soul is like an arm of a human. Just as the arm is "an instrument of instruments," the intellect is "a form of forms" and the sensing faculty is a "form of sensible objects" (432a1ff). With this analogy the soul is returned, in a sense, to the body.

In speaking about the soul as being in some way synonymous with "all things" Aristotle makes it co-extensive with life itself and with the realm of nature (*physis*) because the things of which he speaks include both the sensible and intelligible. Unlike many of the Presocratics, he stops short of embracing panpsychism, where all matter is invested with mind (or soul) given that he posits an important—and perhaps overly sharp—distinction between living and nonliving entities in terms of their degree of organization.[63] Nevertheless, there is not a radical divorcing of the soul (or mind) from nature, just as there is not a sharp cleavage between the soul and the body.

Aristotle is thereby able to complete a definition of soul he inaugurates much earlier. Where the soul was once "moved" in a sense so that we could see its sundry functions and dimensions, we are now brought to a resting point where sensation and its objects on the one hand and knowledge and its objects on the other hand are united. From a former, more theoretical standpoint, we have moved to a type of practical thinking that has reached its limits in the known and knowable universe. With one major exception—in addition to the movement from a hylozoist to a hylomorphic model—Aristotle offers a plausible and *naturalistic* account of the soul.[64] He avoids the difficulties that Plato encounters when the latter argues for an immortal and distinctly human soul and sharply separates the natural world and body from the soul. The soul is not imprisoned in the body but very much a part of it. Wise persons do not try to escape the soul, merely purify it of baleful bodily influences, or simply care for it as a preparation for death, as Plato claims. Rather, we should try to understand it and to see it as one of the many kindred souls who exist in the environing world. Aristotle's deep interest in and knowledge of natural processes causes him to construct an understanding of soul that is inclusive of all living beings, even if he does not animate fully "the elemental" or what we call the "inorganic."[65] Like other living beings, we are a unity of body and soul as one person. Aristotle's senses of the soul arrive through the sensing and embodied individual so as to make a plausible philosophical and psychological sense.

Aristotle and Ecology

In the process of our reconstruction and examination of this philosophical framework for fire, air, earth, and water, we have developed along the way numerous points of ecological interest, focusing particularly on Aristotle's idea of natural place. We close by indicating several further ways in which Aristotle's views speak potentially to environmental concerns by elaborating on his understanding of the elements, egocentricity, and philosophical naturalism. Once again—and as with Empedocles and Plato—we are not claiming that Aristotle is an "environmentalist" in the modern and current sense of the term but rather exploring how his work has possible implications and insights for better understanding and responding to our own predicaments.

Elements as Ultimate

It is first necessary to underscore and to reiterate the central role of the elements themselves in Aristotle's physics and philosophy. As we have argued, earth, air, fire, and water can be interpreted reasonably as the most basic "stuff" of the Aristotelian framework, even if they are composed of contrary qualities. Out of these simple bodies, all other things are composed. Prime matter might have an anxious and inarticulate status but as "pure potentiality" it is neither coherent nor ultimate. Unlike Plato's elements, earth, water, air, and fire are not reducible to something prior and more elemental. In contrast to the positions of Plato and the Atomists who espouse more quantitative frameworks, and similar to the view of Empedocles in at least this respect, Aristotle's perspective on the elements is qualitative. By his own understanding of the term in the *Categories*, "quality" can refer to four different kinds of things: habits or dispositions; capacities; affective relations; and shape. In this sense, Aristotle's elements have affective qualities in that heat and cold, for example, are capable of producing "affections," as when heat affects the sense of touch.

Looking back at the four major elemental Greek theories—if we add the Atomists to the mix of Empedocles, Plato, and Aristotle and rightly recognize their "element" as the atom—we can see a distinct transition of the elements of fire, air, water, and earth in terms of their overall characteristics and status with regard to change.[66] For Empedocles, the first of those who identify and explain all things in terms of an elemental fourfold, the *rhizomata* are qualitative and eternal (unchanging). For the subsequent and second group of Atomists (especially Leucippus and Democritus), the most basic elements (atoms) of the cosmos are still eternal (unchanging), but they are now conceived in quantitative terms. Plato, in a third turn, introduces a method of change for the elements but keeps the quantitative dimensions to their conception and construction, using as we saw the insights of geometry to explain their manner of transformation. Finally, Aristotle, returns full circle to a qualitative view of the elements but retains a transformational schema that allows the elements to change and stresses the loss or addition of a contrary quality. In an elegant way, then, this last theory closes the economy and ecology of the four. We *circle the elemental square*, reuse and hence recycle the *stoicheia*, having visited the four possible modalities and frameworks with respect to quality and quantity on the one hand and eternity and change on the other. With each new transition in the theories from Empedocles to the Atomists, from the Atomists to Plato, and from Plato to Aristotle, one of the old characteristics has been maintained and one has been abandoned, providing both a form of continuity and change, just as this schema functioned in Aristotle's sublunary realm with regard to contrary qualities.

Geocentrism

Aristotle's philosophical framework is marked clearly by a strong measure of organic unity and internal cohesion. Everything is seeking to realize itself in its form and to perform its function. There is a general priority of whole to part, a dimension evident even in his *Politics*. Individual entities matter, but what counts even more is the survival of a species (*eidos*), a point that accords with recent thinking about ecological stability. The natural world is a system of interacting elements. As Aristotle holds in the *Metaphysics*, "Observation shows that nature is not episodic, like a bad tragedy" (1090b19–20). The sublunary realm is, despite appearances, relatively orderly and comprehensible, and the economy of the elements is illustrative of this point. Aristotle's description of the cycling and recycling of water, for example, resembles the flows of hydrological cycles as they are understood today. In the *Meteorology*—a work that takes up the elements as well—Aristotle reveals an awareness of the earth's capacity for change over time.[67]

Aristotle's perspective is broadly geocentric, earth-centered—thus providing a healthy counterpoise to and ballast for the particularities of place, and the tight container model of *topos*. It is rooted in a deep commitment to the "this-worldly" and to causal explanation within a naturalistic framework. As suggested earlier, the role of earth is in certain respects slightly exceptional, vaguely akin to the status of prime matter, if this notion is assumed to be coherent. Aristotle's geocentricity develops in a way that liberates it from a solely local interpretation and overly narrow "lococentrism," perhaps making it in the process more a "glocal" (global and local) outlook we might say. As Frederick Woodbridge argues, Aristotle characterizes it vis-à-vis "the idea of relative locality generalized" and objects to a view of a "multiplicity of local systems on observational and dialectical grounds."[68] In this sense, there is a kind of complex "holism" and "organicism" inherent in his work that still acknowledges the vital role of parts, individuals and contexts. Organic nature is ultimately dependent on a Prime Mover but more proximately it is affected by the action of the sun, which is responsible for the cycle of the seasons. The fifth element, although a first body, does not open up and disturb the general equilibrium and order of the terrestrial economy, and it is not the place for human activity and dwelling, even if we now launch flights and satellites into space.[69]

Philosophical Naturalism

What is the relation of the elements to Aristotle's understanding of nature, and does *physis* begin to supersede and replace the *stoicheia* as an explanatory framework?[70] Although these issues cannot be addressed adequately here, a few general remarks are in order. *Physis* is translated typically into English as "nature" and is connected with Greek words meaning "plant," "offspring," and "to make grow" and so suggests the notion of being alive. But the root of the word is also a cognate with Latin, Sanskrit, and English words meaning "be" or, more broadly, "being-ness"—the essential nature of a thing.[71] In the *Metaphysics*, Aristotle distinguishes at least five different senses of the term *physis* that relate to generation, the inner essence from which something starts to grow, the source of motion in natural things, the fundamental material of which an artifact is composed, and the primary being of natural entities. Finally, he offers an inclusive definition of the concept in its first and chief meaning as the primary being of things that possess in themselves a source of their own movement. Following Aristotle, *physis* is used primarily as "beingness," especially of those things that grow. But it is often used by extension as well with reference to things that change and taken as a source of such change, movement or growth. In a nutshell, this is the background for later thinkers who come to contemplate the natural world.[72]

The elements clearly exist by nature (*ta physei*) since they have in themselves a principle of rest and movement (*kinesis*), and this distinguishes them from products of art (*techne*). Aristotle, however, understands movement in a broad sense to include three kinds: quantitative (growth), qualitative (alteration), and placial (location). He repeatedly defines the motions of natural bodies through a tendency (*horme*) to change in a particular manner. In construing *physis* in terms of an internal source of movement, Aristotle's bold and new conception of nature assumes and then supplants the role and status of soul (*psyche*) in Plato's philosophical framework. Physical entities, including the four elements, no longer require soul in order to move because they possess the immanent power of motion. Nature, though, is not alive in all its parts. Although Aristotle maintains that the capacity for self-motion is peculiar to living beings and a hallmark of life itself, the four elements are excluded from the possession of *psyche* and life, and there is an attendant loss of the hylozoism and panpsychism evident in earlier Greek thought.[73]

Recently, Aristotle's views have been adopted and adapted by a number of environmental philosophers who point to the possibilities of an environmental virtue ethic or develop connections between modern ecological concepts such as biocentrism, ecosystem, or biophilia on the one hand and Aristotelian notions such as *telos* (goal or purpose), *ergon* (function), and *eudaimonia* (well-being) on the other hand.[74] Social ecology, in particular, emphasizes the graded emergence of mind from the natural world, the continuities between first (biological) and second (cultural) nature along with their possible synthesis into an ecological society, and the power of dialectical and organismic traditions that derive from Aristotle. Social ecologists such as Murray Bookchin maintain that we can find an evolving ground for ethics and freedom in nature, which in their view develops dialectically and with directionality toward ecological notions of complexity, spontaneity, unity-in-diversity, and complementarity. Bookchin's notion of "dialectical naturalism" is an effort to ecologize the dialectic and to anchor ethical judgment in a natural ontology and causality that maintains close ties to Aristotle. He has propounded a sophisticated theory of the historical relation of the *idea* of the domination of nature to the domination of humans by one another. In so doing, Bookchin lays an original focus on hierarchy (as opposed to class), freedom (not only justice), the insights of organic cultures and the anarchist tradition, as well as the reconstructive and integrative contributions of the science of ecology in order to develop social ecology.[75]

Although Bookchin, Hans Jonas, and Ernst Bloch have developed Aristotle's naturalism in environmental directions, there are nevertheless grounds for proceeding with caution because of the controversial roles of functionalism, teleology, and naturalistic ethics within philosophical and ecological discourse.[76] In returning to ancient Greek thought, we admittedly encounter difficulties in relating contemporary ecological concepts to other eras. We have sought to scrutinize Aristotle's philosophical and geographical orientation, his approaches toward the elements and physical surroundings, and his sense of and sensibility about place—rather than a more restricted notion of scientific accuracy—and to consider the relevance, influence, insights, and shortfalls of this thinking for present-day problems. It should be clear that an Aristotelian perspective on the perennial elements still speaks 2,500 years later to emerging and evolving environmental concerns and remains relevant today.

Having completed our analysis of ancient *elemental theories*, we are ready to explore the nature and meanings of *elemental worlds* and move toward a more direct engagement with palpable or practical perspectives on earth, air, fire, water, and related topics. In successive chapters, we discuss the dynamic process and implications of domesticating the elements within the human household, especially efforts to capture, channel or control water. We then examine the return and recovery of the elemental in recent Continental philosophy by focusing on the ways that the landscape, the body, poetics, dwelling, gender, and perception may help to refresh and rejuvenate our language about and experiences of the environment. Finally, we investigate some approaches through which we might better appreciate, value, and protect elemental regions, forces, and phenomena by considering the possible contributions of environmental aesthetics, ethics, and public policy.

Interstice: Light and Shadow

More light, more light.

—Goethe, dying words

Look round and round upon this bare bleak plain, and see even here, upon a winter's day, how beautiful the shadows are! Alas! it is the nature of their kind to be so. The loveliest things in life, Tom, are but shadows; and they come and go, and change and fade away, as rapidly as these!

—Charles Dickens, *Martin Chuzzlewit*

In the beginning, there was darkness. Light entered this undifferentiated night to dramatically dethrone and substantially transform a preexisting uniformity and primordial unity. Shadows, in turn, are offspring of luminosity, kindred alter egos to sensuous things, stalking silhouettes but loyal companions of material objects. Together, light and shadow conspire to disclose a lush palette of phenomena, to promote biological growth and provide organisms with a cool respite, to encourage the interplay of notions of presence and absence, and to make possible the beautiful nuances belonging to aesthetic expression in painting, drawing, and photography. They are both essential, if often overlooked, ingredients of the elemental world.

In its origins and metaphysical history, Western thought is married profoundly with the language of light. Seeing is made synonymous with believing; brightness connotes intelligence; sight is said to be indispensable to insight. Plato famously places light at the epicenter of a conception of enlightenment in his Allegory of the Cave. Light, he maintains, is a prerequisite to the discovery of truth. To this end, the imprisoned souls in his myth make a series of turns from the darkness of dogma and *doxa* (opinion) to the illumination provided by a recessed fire, finding their way with intellectual inquisitiveness and philosophical persistence to the radiance of the sun, Plato's simile for goodness, beauty, and transcendental reality. Descartes likewise extols the very epistemological clarity of light and vision, which are supposed to guide us away from error and falsity. One can almost imagine his epiphanies as he meditates before a candle in the dark. And, more recently, Heidegger resurrects the ancient Greek notion of *aletheia* or truth as unconcealedness, that which is revealed and brought to light. In what could be a distillation of many of the predominant perspectives, Hans Blumenberg writes: "Light is intrusive; in its abundance, it creates the overwhelming, conspicuous clarity with which the true 'comes forth.'" From such a vantage point, it generates space and makes possible orientation in the physical environment along with the serene contemplation that gives rises to theory—the light of the mind. Light, then, is a "gift that makes no demands, the illumination capable of conquering without force."[1]

With few exceptions, the world's major religions have embraced and embedded light deeply within their frameworks. In ancient Egypt, the eye of the sun god Ra lit up the cosmos. In the *Bhagavad Gita*, Hinduism's most popular work, we find the avatar of Krishna—a hierophany of the god Vishnu and a manifestation of the all-encompassing Brahman—represented through superabundant radiance: "If the light of a thousand suns / were to rise in the sky at once, / it would be like the light / of that great spirit."[2] Other faiths take similar inspiration. Zoroastrians typically pray in front of fire and worship Ahura Mazda, a deity of goodness and light. Buddhist's counsel: "Be a lamp unto yourself." The Old Testament generates elemental light through divine command: *Fiat lux*. "Let there be light," heralds "Genesis" before it is deemed wonderful and as it is divided sharply from darkness.[3] With the emergence of Christianity, the Lord is portrayed as "the light of this world" as well as "the truth, the light and the way." Illumination is also conducted inward so as to be accessible through the hearts of believers. Christian scholars, in fact, labored to draw a distinction within light itself, separating *lux* from *lumen*, where *lux* is the being of light and its "spiritual" reality while *lumen* is the "body" of light and the material means through which it acquires presence.[4] And so the story of light's revelation issues forward and develops in intricate manners.

Light allows phenomena to appear but it does not arrive on the perceptual scene itself in quite the same way. In a broad sense, it is the grand stage wherein and through which the natural world unfolds and presents itself in all its pageantry rather being a mere constituent part of the cosmic drama. Nonetheless, light stealthfully eludes our discerning grasp, racing along at a speed of 186,000 miles per second, millions of times faster than a lumbering pedestrian or plodding automobile. In the vernacular of physics, light is electromagnetic radiation possessing a wavelength that is visible to the animal eye. Displaying properties of both particles and waves, it exhibits several elementary facets, including intensity (or brightness), polarization (the vibration angle), and frequency (which is perceived by us as color). Just as we more routinely discriminate artificial from natural light, we can distinguish radiant light from ambient light. Radiant light *causes* illumination through reverberation between disparate surfaces or between sky and earth; it departs from a given source as a form of energy; and it consists of a set of infinite rays without a structure. By contrast, ambient light is an *effect* of illumination; it gathers at the locus of observation as a kind of information; and it has a structure that is able to delineate an *Umwelt* or environment. James J. Gibson characterizes the phenomenal distinction this way: "Radiant light from a point source is not different in different directions; ambient light at a point is different in different directions . . . Radiant light is propagated; ambient light is not."[5]

Ecologically, light is a fundament of life. Photosynthesis—literally, "putting together with light"—is the quiet means through which plants convert sunlight, along with water and carbon dioxide, into sugars. Although it is easy to overlook, the entire economy depends on this ancient process because fossil fuels are the remains of millions of years of compressed organic matter, which was earlier nurtured and grown by the labor of light. Our solitary star, the sun, is this all-important source of energy and radiance, emitting its rays from a distance that demands eight minutes to arrive to our waiting bodies. With the sun's aid, we can, in turn, peer with the power of our own unaided eyes—small solar collectors—2.5 million light years away to the Andromeda galaxy and beyond so as to gaze on entities that have long since expended their candle power and capacities to shine. No wonder Milton waxed, "Thou Sun, of this great World both Eye and Soul."[6]

Our eyes gather light by way of a complex process fine-tuned through thousands of years of adaptive evolution, likely beginning with photoreceptor proteins or "eyespots" in single-celled organisms that could distinguish darkness from light but could not see the surrounding world. Goethe posited that our eyes owe their very existence to light itself, having been summoned forth by the power of sun with which they are reciprocally linked. Empedocles, however, was the first thinker to offer a primitive theory of sight, suggesting poetically that the goddess Aphrodite constructs our eyes through love from the four classical elements of earth, air, fire, and water to form a lantern, whereby "one vision of two eyes is born."[7] He advances the idea that objects send out rays that are detected by counterpart beams emanating like fire from the eye itself, which reaches out to touch the surrounding world. Plato extends the metaphoric power of light. "The mind's eye begins to see clearly when the outer eyes grow dim," he hypothesizes.[8] Theory (from *theoria*) thus comes to signify a sense of beholding, taking in, and comprehending with the contemplative and interiorized eye. Aristotle speaks subsequently of light as actualization of what is potentially transparent. Descartes explains it mechanically in terms of movement through a plenum, using an analogy with sound waves and anticipating the wave theory of light. And the attempt to understand this curious phenomenon continues through the science of Faraday, Maxwell, and Einstein.

Although most of us now saunter the narrow aisles of grocery stores in search of packaged or previously prepared food rather than stalk wild beasts or edible plants in the forests and open fields, we still scan the lighted horizon with discerning glances, noticing signs of danger, sites of refuge, sources of sustenance, and outcroppings of beauty, disease, and death. Whether we take conscious heed or not, our eyes revel in and adjust to a wide range of radiance. During the brief period when the sun is first rising or finally setting, we might observe a diffuse yellow light wash over the streets, poke an angled path through trees and glisten softly on the water and earth, coating the landscape in a warm hue. In this "golden hour," which photographers relish because the low glow of the sun intensifies color, it is especially enjoyable to be outdoors biking, hiking, or walking. *L'heure bleue*—known as "gloaming" in northern latitudes—is another remarkable manifestation of bluish illumination occurring between the hour of waning darkness and waxing light that vie and play with one another at a time of the day when the scent of flowers is also at its peak. On rare occasions, keen eyes might even detect the appearance of a green flash or ray—the yellow mixing with the blue—on the horizon spawned by light refracted in the atmosphere or on water. In such moments, we are rewarded with Zen telegrams from the unknown, prizes for putting ourselves "out there" on a brightened stage.

Color is light's mesmerizing garb, its peculiar way alighting or, we could say, lighting up itself. As an observer-dependent and secondary property, color is what is reflected back from an object to our gaze. It is, in a sense, what a thing wears but also casts off luxuriously to the admiring world. Appearing to arrive to the eye on invisible tendrils, color is the bait that many flowers deploy to catch an insect's eye and what we humans might spike our hair with to attract a mate. Birds mark territory or issue warnings with the distinct colors of their bodies. Other animals such as the pipefish, which stands on its nose to blend in like a blade of sea grass, camouflage themselves this way. Colors generate or express a vast array of emotions and even serve to stand in for these states, as in blue (sadness), green (envy), yellow (cowardice), and red (anger). "Colors are the deeds of light, what it does and what it endures," said Goethe, who developed his own influential account of the phenomena as well as explanations for colored shadows and refraction.[9] In contrast to Newton's earlier hypothesis, Goethe thought that color should best be understood as having experiential origins. In this view, light and darkness are reciprocally and dynamically involved, and their taut relation is resolved dialectically through the ur-phenomenon of color. Darkness, then, is not the lack of light, as Newton held, but rather polar to and interacting with it. "The blue of the sky reveals to us the basic law of color," Goethe remarked. "Search nothing beyond the phenomena, they themselves are the theory."[10]

With these words before us, the Northern Lights may be seen as one of the natural world's most extravagant spectacles, a way of shouting "look" to us and of intoxicating our eyes with amazing green and red glows. So powerful are these shows of luminosity—which are produced by the collision of charged particles in the magnetosphere with molecules in the atmosphere—that many cultures have fashioned myths or stories to explain and share the phenomenon. The Finns spoke in their legends of the lights as "fox fires" produced by sparks emitted from the tails of these sly creatures. The Scots saw them as merry dancers. The Algonquin considered them to be ancestors rejoicing around a fire. And the Inuit have linked the lights with the souls of their dead, who are playing a game in the heavens with a ball that we see as the Aurora, or alternatively associated the illumination with the recreation of children not yet born or with torches wielded by the deceased so as to assist their living kin during a hunt. The first time I witnessed the Aurora Borealis was not inside the Arctic Circle but at a much lower latitude in Oberlin, Ohio, where they materialized in the evening sky late one summer as shimmering columns and gossamer drapes—"chasms, trenches and blood red colors" to use Aristotle's bold characterization—while a group of us played volleyball at an outdoor wedding reception. At such times, we may fumble blindly for a language adequate to the dance of nature's prolific hues, shadings, and tints because there is often not a varied enough vocabulary in the palette of our minds to express the expansive range of light's bedazzled domain. Barry Lopez, however, fittingly envisions the Northern Lights in terms of watching "graceful, inward-turning, and protracted" Tai Chi exercises and as a "weightless curtain of silk, hanging down straight and rippling in the night air," one opening up the viewer emotionally and aesthetically to a diffident but beautiful third dimension.[11] As if to help out with the problems of phenomenological and poetic description, the four canonical elements each seem to adopt and offer up a smaller color set themselves from which we might learn to borrow: the blues and blacks of water, the reds and oranges of fire, the browns and greens of earth, and the azures and milky whites of air.

Light is so intrinsic to our lifeworld that it is typically taken for granted. Its sudden disappearance or removal is deeply disorienting. For one winter day, I led my friend Nasha blindfolded around the university town of Tübingen, Germany where we both studied so that she could better understand and empathize with the world of her blind friend. As the day developed, she learned more and more to rely on her other senses, but felt that something absolutely essential to her reality was missing. Even the blind need to experience light on their retinas in order to trigger and massage circadian rhythms or to help them avoid depression, which can derive easily from light deprivation. But we can be blinded by light as well as darkness. When some persons who have been without vision since birth are given the gift of sight after cataract surgery, they experience the world as oppressive and cannot conceive of space or depth in its full dimensionality. Patches of color disturb them; forms previously known only through touch or taste confuse them. The overwhelming brightness of the world leads many of them to long again for the dark they have learned to navigate.[12]

Of late, phenomenologists, post-structuralists, and feminists have advanced trenchant critiques of the privileging of vision and ocular-centrism, contesting the way we are beholden to an appropriating gaze and the ability of sight to suffocate other senses or to ignore shades and subtleties of meaning by becoming the dominant model of perception.[13] They have also articulated new views of light and sight. Merleau-Ponty, who characterizes vision in terms of a chiasm or nexus with the environment thus proclaims: "To see is to enter a universe of beings which *display themselves*, and they would not do this if they could not be hidden behind each other or behind me. In other words: to look at an object is to inhabit it."[14] Foucault diagnoses and challenges the way that vision has been channeled into disciplinary techniques and practices to become a mechanism of social power and control. We watch others; we watch ourselves; and institutions watch us. Vision, in brief, is transformed into monitoring, surveillance, and oversight—in a word, *supervision*.[15] Through the figure of Zarathustra, Nietzsche goes as far to surrender his own ability to illuminate a path for others. "For these men of today I do not wish to be *light*, or to be called light," he says. "*These* I wish to blind. Lightning of my wisdom! Put out their eyes."[16] In the stead of the eyes and the imperial sight of the abstract mind, Nietzsche draws attention to other forms of knowing through the more marginalized ears, nose, and visceral body.

In comparison with light, shadows seem to be gravity-ballasted clouds—insubstantial and immaterial shapes yielding a reservoir of darkness rather than a reserve of water. They add depth, relief, and distinction to our perceptual fields, providing us with a "negative ontology."[17] Shadows possess either an umbra—a dark inner area in which light is fully occluded—or a penumbra, an outer area where light is not wholly blocked because it arrives from a nonpoint source. Penumbra and umbra may coexist, as in the play of shadows generated by a chandelier on the ceiling. Shadows, too, will take on color through the influence of white light, and they can appear to be blue when they are illuminated by the overarching sky.

If light has been celebrated within philosophy, shadows have been relegated for the most part to the dark periphery of thought. They have been subordinated by a prevailing luminocentrism. While night is often disparaged, demonized, or perceived as a condition to be vanquished, shadows are alternately ignored, presented as pale vestiges of darkness, or seen as encumbrances to light. Plato, for example, refers to shadows (*skias*) as semblances and phantasms (*phantasmata*) lacking in reality, so distant from the realm of truth (*aletheia*) that they are beneath mere images in importance. Shakespeare even tells us that "life is but a walking shadow," a story that ultimately means nothing. As a consequence of the questioning of the hypnotic attention to light, however, the shadow is perhaps no longer so marginalized philosophically or culturally as it once was. Heidegger thus observes: "Everyday opinion sees in the shadow only the lack of light, if not light's complete denial. In truth, however, the shadow is a manifest, though impenetrable, testimony to the concealed emitting of light."[18] Levinas, in turn, presents the shadow as an enabling phenomenon, permitting "us to situate the economy of resemblance within the general economy of being." Unlike philosophical criticism, which operates through concepts, art "lets go of the prey for the shadow."[19] And David Michael Levin proposes that shadows render "visible our mortal inherence, our fatal investment, in the natural elements, foreshadowing the conditional term of our visibility in unified, coherent corporeal form." In this way, they become "signatures of time" and "time's way of playing with us."[20] Finally, Junichiro Tanizaki extols the lovely nuances, the rich subtleties and sense of understatement conveyed by shadows and shaded phenomena ranging from cloudy crystals, grains of aged wood, lacquerware, and gold embroidery to objects softly illuminated by candlelight or the interiors of brothels and bathrooms in his *In Praise of Shadows*, a short meditative work of Japanese aesthetics.

Pliny the Elder gestures to the notion that both painting and sculpture find their earliest origins in very primitive representation, specifically the tracing of a human shadow. He recounts the tale of a potter named Butades who lives in Corinth and whose daughter grows smitten with a young man about to travel far away. Before his departure, the daughter draws an outline of the shadow of her beloved's face on the wall, and Butades models this countenance in clay prior to baking it in the fire with his tiles. He casts (or shapes) the shadows, we might say, that have been cast (or hurled) themselves by the ballet of light. Eventually, so a version of the story goes, this likeness—this shadow of a shadow—winds up in the Shrine of the Nymphs.

We can only speculate as to the reasons for the initial representation in this story: the projection as stand-in for an absent figure, the desire for a surrogate lover, the need of a mnemonic to summon up a missing body, or simply the primitive fascination with the play of lines, shapes, and shades in a silhouette. Art, of course, expands beyond this first stage, filling in the shadow with color, distinguishing light from shade and experimenting with form.[21] Bridging the realms of blackness and illumination, sixteenth-century painters like Baglione and Caravaggio develop and starkly explore *chiaroscuro*—the subtle use of shading and light for dramatic effect also known as "claire-obscure"—some employing a style called *tenebroso* (Italian for "murky") by using violent juxtapositions of darkness and light. With time, the shadow of a human is even portrayed as the soul's true essence so that one notable writer in the eighteenth century is able to proclaim, "Physiogamy has no greater, more incontrovertible certainty of the truth of its object than that imparted by shade."[22]

"Shadows are in reality, when the sun is shining, the most conspicuous thing in a landscape, next to the highest lights," art critic John Ruskin points out.[23] They sashay in and out of pools of light, thickening our vision, extending the reach of objects. Night might even be viewed as a world of silky silhouettes, Diane Ackerman reminds us. "The only shadows we see at night are cast by the moonlight, or by artificial light, but night itself is a shadow."[24] The shadow, however, passes from material image to robust metaphor in theoretical psychology, where it is suggests the ambiguities of the human psyche. "Everyone carries a shadow, and the less it is embodied in the individual's conscious life, the blacker and denser it is," posits Jung.[25] "Taking it in its deepest sense, the shadow is the invisible saurian tail that man still drags behind him. Carefully amputated, it becomes the healing serpent of the mysteries. Only monkeys parade with it."[26] Confronting our own shadows—the repressed sides of our characters—then may be vital to enjoying the clarifying light of vision and day, especially because few of us are able to outrun or escape them with ease.

As for less figurative shadows, many of us enjoy basking in their shifting nuances. On occasion, the artist Andy Goldsworthy stands in a frost-laden field. While the sun slowly bakes away the moisture languishing on the ground, a distinct human shadow of ice crystals is tattooed upon the earth before him. As one who is intimately familiar with the elemental world, Goldsworthy creates by patiently tarrying with time—waiting while his father recovers from an illness inside the house or a farmer tills a plot of soil in the distance—letting the sun perform its silent labor, actively "doing nothing" (like the Taoist's practice of *wei wu wei*) to passively generate the shadowy remains of his figure. The warm light subtracts exposed water while the darkened earth temporarily embraces it and imperceptibly a work accrues that will be swallowed eventually by the sun. At other times, Goldsworthy summons a shadow to materialize by lying down on clay, dirt, or gravel as the rain beats on his supine and outstretched body so that a dry spot leaves a colored mark. As John Locke once observed, "The picture of a shadow is a positive thing," an idea Goldsworthy seems to understand.[27] Absence, in other words, dialectically begets a kind of complex presence.

Inside a great vaulted hall of the Tate Modern museum in London, Olafur Eliasson created a magnificent artificial sun—out of yellow lights positioned behind a large screen and beneath a mirrored ceiling—in order to explore the effects of light and weather on human moods and emotions. Curiously, many visitors to the exhibition seemed to enjoy sunbathing, picnicking, and exhibiting themselves, luxuriating in the human-generated solar stand-in as opposed to reveling in the real one outside and so extending the ancient practice of sun worship. Dennis Oppenheim has used light and shade to similar interesting effects. In 1970, he lay without a shirt for five hours in the hot sun, placing an open book on his chest so as to let his body be emblazoned with an outline of the text. Oppenheim imagines the photographed piece, entitled "Reading Position for Second Degree Burn," as having its roots in a notion of changing colors. His sunbaked skin becomes the pigment for a solar "self-portrait." After the events of 9/11, the city of New York projected shafts of vertical light thousands of feet into the air where formerly stood the Twin Towers. The lights built a shadowy presence of these vanished structures and generated an effect that was both memorializing and haunting. One August, I had the opportunity myself to explore the penumbral realm by participating in the International Shadow Project with a group of artists and activists who mark the anniversary of the bombing of Hiroshima and Nagasaki. In the middle of night, we whitewashed shadows of human and nonhuman figures on sidewalks and walls throughout Washington, DC to convey a sense of how thousands of Japanese citizens were incinerated in an immense explosion of elemental fire, heat, and light.

Generating widespread astonishment and, understandably, some discomfort, physicists have succeeded recently in slowing and then halting momentarily the very flow of light itself for several hundred-thousandths of a second in the laboratory. By stilling a light pulse without divesting it of all its energy, researchers believe that powerful quantum computers might be created and new methods devised so as to communicate over long distances, employing light as a conduit for information. Using fishnet structures and minute wires, scientists have also discovered ways to bend light in a backward direction, something that does not occur in the natural world. They hope this technology will enable others to develop invisibility cloaks or microscopes that gaze more deeply into living cells. For several decades, we have been harnessing and harvesting light in the form of solar energy, a key to addressing our vexing energy problems. The emerging prospect of mimicking the manner in which the leaves of trees convert light to food is extremely intriguing, and with this goal in mind ecological engineers are laboring to design solar cells on the molecular scale that could turn the quicksilver of light into the gold of electricity, tapping into an omnipresent but underused resource. And because light, like wind, actually presses upon objects in its path as photons strike entities and transfer momentum to them, this empirical fact raises other enticing possibilities such as creating solar sails that could accelerate the speed of vessels moving in outer space.

Occupying the elemental realms of air and fire, the silent legerdemain of light is what opens up and exposes the world to our hungry senses. It is perhaps the universe's most basic medium. And it appears increasingly as if our own future—along with the fate of shadows and other phenomena—is bound closely with its flickering fortune.

— Part III —

Elemental Worlds

— 7 —

Domestication of the Elements

I see water, I see fire and air and earth and all their mixtures coming to corruption, having little endurance; and yet these things were created, so that, if what was said is true, they should be secure from corruption.

—Dante, *Paradiso*, Canto VII

Nature is a hard taskmaster. It is the hammer and the anvil, crushing individuality. Perfect freedom would be to die by earth, air, water and fire.

—Camille Paglia, *Sexual Personae*

Deep down, we never really thought we could [change nature]: it was too big and too old; its forces—the wind, the rain, the sun—were too strong, too elemental.

—Bill McKibben, *The End of Nature*

Outside-In

The capture and creative use of fire is undoubtedly one of the most significant historical events, as well as ongoing actions, to impact and transform the natural and built worlds. No other species actively employs this element to its advantage in quite the same way as humans. In taming the flame and interiorizing it within our households and communities, we domesticated ourselves, birthing in the process agriculture, the mechanical arts, new energy sources, weapons of war, and eventually the whole ensemble of modern technology from computers to genetic engineering. Of fire, Stephen Pyne observes:

> Once tamed, it had to be fed, housed, cared for, and bred. It could no longer range for its own food, or be left to fend for itself in the elements. It had to be tended. Its reproduction, too, could be guided into select "breeds"—fire for cooking, fire for ceramics, fire for heating, lighting, hardening; fire for hunting, farming, herding, clearing the land.[1]

Anthropogenic fire, in turn, shunted nature's flame to the margins, and this process perpetuated and reinforced itself. Burning reshaped the landscape and altered fuel sources so as to limit human contact with wildfire while further encouraging the spread of domesticated fire.

Earlier, we reflected on some of the environmental expressions and philosophical implications of wild, feral, and vestal fire. We also showed how the elements undergo more generally a form of domestication in the theoretical works and surviving fragments of the first natural philosophers. "In the realm of the material imagination," Bachelard notes, "every union is a marriage, and there is no marriage *à trios*."[2] The elements are thus occasionally united as pairs, as in the wedding of feminine earth with masculine sky. Their interactions are described regularly, too, through domestic and familial language when they are introduced into and socialized within the human sphere. In Plato's *Timaeus*, earth, fire, air, and water are the offspring of cosmological generation and come to be housed and domesticated within an encompassing environmental matrix. In Aristotle's treatment, the elements are likewise involved in a homecoming and self-domestication as they journey to their "natural places" within a broader cyclical economy and ecology.

We now turn to examine the domestication of the elements more directly by focusing on water—fire's ostensible antagonist—so as to further illustrate this idea. We then discuss briefly the notions of earth alienation and the eclipse of the atmosphere as related examples of domestication before concluding with the question whether there has been an historical closing or end of the classical elements.

As with air, fire, and earth, water passes through the modern house and home, the human *domus*, where it is domesticated technologically in pipes and plumbing, bottles and baths, drains and dehumidifiers, showers and sinks, or refrigeration and radiators. In this sense, it is brought *outside-in*, its meanings—along with its volume and appearance—defined or demarcated in the process. Such filtering occurs practically but it can also take place epistemologically and linguistically, as when we fashion a nomenclature for the many phenomenal forms of the fluid—rain, sleet, snow, ice, hail, aquifer, ocean, lake, stream, and so forth—or attribute different names to types of drinking water. Thus, the poet Wislawa Szymborska writes, "There are not enough mouths to utter / all your fleeting names, O water. . . . Whenever wherever whatever has happened / is written on waters."[3]

Water, however, like air, often is still thought to be independent for the most part of human transformation and highly resistant to technical modification because of its unpredictable movement, deceptive strength, wide availability, or distinct chemical structure. Contrary to this image, we consider some of the myriad ways in which water is mediated—especially through technology—so that our encounters and experiences with this transparent medium and essential substance are altered profoundly by the means, techniques, and instruments we select to engage it. In looking at varied attempts to understand or respond to water's elusive properties and powers, we see how it is revealed, concealed, or transfigured through, first, aesthetic preferences and technologies of the landscape; second, waterways and waterworks that function as a kind of social and cultural channeling; and third, practices of purification that serve as a form of mediation in the instance of bottled water.

Domestication is a process that captures, interiorizes, and changes formerly unbridled fluids. The domestication of water helps us to better apprehend our relations with both the environment and technology because an enormous amount of water that we now consume or contemplate is neither thoroughly "natural" nor entirely "artificial" in the traditional senses of these terms. Rather, water is filtered frequently through a vast technological nexus that not only redirects its force and flow but also modifies or multiplies its meanings. Along the way, it is domesticated rather than dominated or released into an unadulterated presence. What are the philosophical, practical, and policy implications of such enterprises? Can or should we preserve water in a pristine state? Do we need to commodify or technologize water further in order to protect it and sustain us? What does the management of water reveal about contested issues such as pollution, wilderness preservation, and landscape restoration? Before it is possible to address these sorts of issues, it is necessary to reflect further on our evolving relationships with water and some of the technological dimensions of water use, especially their points of confluence.

Plumbing Philosophy

For multiple reasons, the notion and practice of domestication provides a more coherent theoretical and explanatory environmental model for our interactions with water and other environmental elements than the prevailing perspective associated with the "domination of nature," an idea advanced by the Frankfurt School and common today in much environmental discourse. Domination of nature—whether spoken of as conquest, mastery, or subjugation—is coupled in turn with a conception of liberation. Domination, however, is arguably a social category, and it is therefore problematic to conceive of a direct or successful effort in this regard, just as it can be misleading to advocate submission to unyielding "laws of nature," which are then applied to or read back into the social realm. Domination of nature is largely ideological; it is a motivating *idea*, ideal or goal that cannot be realized. As Hegel expresses it one way, "Nature itself, as it is in its universality, cannot be mastered."[4]

Water, then, is not dominated or, alternatively, liberated into a pure immediacy. Its course might be modified, channeled, or redirected. Its containers might be opened, enlarged, or reconfigured. But it is not oppressed, exploited, or emancipated in the manner of human persons. There are bidirectional and bivalent influences at work as well; water impacts us in significant ways even as we seek to domesticate it. We impose values on the fluid or read norms off of it—purity, cleanliness, wholeness, or rebirth (as in baptism)—in part because it seems to serve as a receptive liquid screen on which we project wishes that are often more stable and starkly colored. At the same time, water also carries and conducts values to us, as in the language we use and associate with it—currents, flows, floods, streams of consciousness, and so forth. And yet there are constraints in and limits to this process, for water seeks its own earthward or air-bound courses, follows indeterminate paths or its own tendencies, and disappears or descends in unexpected ways and at surprising times.

Here a rough analogy exists with the domestication of nonhumans, given that some animals such as dogs or commensal mice appear to "choose" us or adapt to our domestic worlds as much as, or even more than, we consciously select them.[5] Domestication shares an etymological root with "domination," and hence implies control, but it is also cognate with *domus* (house or home), thus rendering something very particular—in the present case water—known and relatively familiar on an everyday basis. Having these dual dimensions, domestication often is an ambiguous process and ambivalent prospect. It can generate both separation and sympathy, both isolation and inclusion, or both "dominance and affection."[6] It has helped to shift the focus of our attention from the surrounding world to a more hermetic, less environmentally attuned, and communally aware sense of self, but it has opened up inadvertently new realms at the same time, a recognition of which may help us to resist the further attenuation of perceptual experience or ecological complexity. Domestication, therefore, is not an ecological "original sin" (an analogue to Critical Theory's use of domination or some Marxist views of property), but neither should it be portrayed as a straightforward "natural" process that might serve to justify any and all relations we have with the environment or a newly "deconstructed" nature.

Because it concerns distinct entities (e.g., animals, earth, fluids, or fire), domestication is a decidedly less abstract practice and idea than the so-called domination of "nature." Typically, given that domestication involves walls—as in those of a well, house, fire pit, or barn—it raises questions about the meanings, limits, and porosity of interiors and exteriors, insides and outsides, and conceptions of inclusion and exclusion with respect to the environment. Anthropologist Peter Wilson argues accurately that "domesticated society is founded on and dominated by the elementary and original structure, the building, which serves not just as shelter but as diagram and, more generally, as the source of metaphors of structure that make possible the social construction and reconstruction of reality."[7] In this sense, the domestication of animals, plants, or elements is bound closely with—perhaps even preceded by—the domestication of human beings, a major event in the evolution of hominids. In fact, Aristotle's student, Theophrastus, goes so far as to assert with understandable hyperbole, "It is mankind, alone among all living beings, to which the term 'domesticated' is perhaps strictly appropriate."[8] In any event, spatial privacy is likely a consequence of—rather than catalyst for—human domestication, coming into existence with the erection of physical barriers that enhance opportunities for concerted concentration and interior creative expression (reading, thinking, painting, praying, writing, etc.) but complicate communication between people as well as distance us from interaction with the natural environment.[9] Such barriers can encourage forms of mediation or exclusion, buffering and insulating domestic denizens from elemental smells, sights, and sounds. The walls of the house thereby literally generate and govern an opposition between the public and private spheres, a distinction that operates pivotally in social and political theory.

As noted, animality is a constructive concept through which to view the biological embodiment of the elements as well as to observe their domestication. With the exception of fire, which nevertheless resides in humans and other mammals metaphorically as vital "animal heat," earth, air, and water are frequently teeming with living creatures. Until fairly recently, it has been very difficult to corral a wild river, to cordon off or conquer a rocky wilderness region, or to capture and control capricious winds. One way these kinds of enterprises have been carried out—even if indirectly or unintentionally—has been by theoretically or actually yoking animals that inhabit these elemental realms. Organism and environment—animal and ambient element as it were—form a material nexus, an intersection and interdependency of biomass and phenomenal field, especially where there is a porous complicity of "container" and "contained" in these places. In other words, fish and water; bird and air; or mole and earth are bound together closely by and through an encompassing medium that they often co-constitute or co-occupy. Aristotle, in fact, classifies animals with a broad and simple taxonomy that is based on three elemental differentiae, including the terrestrial, the aquatic, and the flying. Plato, too, sews the heavens with animal forms from the zodiac in a more mythological section of his elemental dialogue, the *Timaeus*. The zodiac—from the Greek, *zodiakos*, meaning "circle of animals"—and the nonhuman constellations found in the nebulous night sky, in fact, allow us to view a bestiary of creatures on a daily basis and not only to potentially "domesticate" their symbolic appearances but in the process to organize and know a complex elemental sphere through our cultural and psychological projections.

The concept of domestication allows us as well to potentially take into critical account the role of gender dynamics when we assess our relations with the natural world and human technology.[10] Water has been conceived commonly in feminine terms—typecast so to speak as receptive, fluid, and passive, even if powerfully so. As we saw earlier, this view is evident in Taoism, where we find the idea that "nothing in the world / is as soft and yielding as water / yet for dissolving the hard and inflexible, / nothing can surpass it."[11] Women, in turn, often have been associated closely with earthly processes, including the flows of various fluids.[12] The familial household—the primary seat of domestication—has been assigned as the traditional sphere of women in most cultures. As could be expected, the task falls to girls or their mothers in these societies to cook, clean, and care for children, domestic concerns that involve ongoing water use. In the developing world, too, if men might typically dig and build wells, women are regularly consigned to carry water long distances back home.[13]

The links between gender, water, and domestication rise to the fore in many historical eras, as in late nineteenth-century Europe when female nudity was connected as a cultural symbol to tap water in the bathroom. As Ivan Illich has shown, the closeness of the naked body and soapy suds in the bath tended to domesticate both human flesh and water. "Water became that stuff that circulates through indoor plumbing, and the nude became the symbol of a new fantasy of sexual intimacy defined by the newly created domestic sphere."[14] This point can be grasped by observing the paintings from the time in which the image of woman was joined with that of urban water in bathing instead of presenting her in more religious and mythological settings. As examples, we find Ingres' Turkish bath scenes or Degas' tubs and basins that he used to frame and exhibit his subjects. In a domestic setting, the natural beauty of the water is secured—and distanced from being viewed as "recycled toilet flush"—while the cultivated beauty of the woman is underscored and heightened. In multiple and varied ways, then, water—like fire, air, and water—is channeled into the domestic sphere, where it assumes novel and ever-changing relations with a populace that has through habit come to project a wealth of meanings onto this elemental medium. And domestication becomes not only a biological or historical process but serves as an apt idea, metaphor or trope when applied to other aspects of human culture.

Watercraft and Landscape Aesthetics

Landscape is as much a cultural entity as it is a strictly natural phenomenon, and as a result it is inseparable from the methods and artifacts humans use to sculpt earth and corral water. It may be thought of as a composition of human-made or anthropogenically altered places that function as the background or infrastructure for societies.[15] In other words, we should view the "fire" of technology as integral to rather than alien from landscapes, including what we might call "waterscapes." Stated even more forcefully—and perhaps too strongly—by historian Simon Schama: "Landscapes are culture before they are nature; constructs of the imagination projected onto wood, water and rock."[16] The Netherlands, for example, is able to exist only because of a complex technical system of canals, dikes, and pumping stations. It is as much a combined elemental "waterwork" and "earthwork" as it is a sovereign country in the European Union (EU). Dutch engineers have so modified the course of rivers and streams that it is hard to tell what originates with humans and what is the result of the force of unbridled or undirected water. Californians, too, have spent billions of dollars diverting rivers, occasionally pumping them over a water basin or continental divide to create a cultivated place which otherwise could not flourish. Let us look a bit more closely, although briefly, at five cases of the technologizing—and hence domestication—of water and waterways within the context of broader landscapes in order to illustrate some of the aesthetic issues related to water and what we may term *watercraft*.

Niagara Falls is one instance of the conflux or even conflation of watercourse, land mass, and "technoscape"—having once been redesigned, completely de-watered (stopped), and engineered by architects so that the river flow, fluid direction, erosion rates, and scenic views could be regulated by humans. As Anne Spirn succinctly puts it, "Niagara Falls is shaped by water flowing, rocks falling, and trees growing, by artists and tourists, by journalists and landscape architects, by engineers and works who divert the water." As both a technological construction and an other-than-human phenomenon, it is a product and ongoing process involving not just the law of gravity but bearing the influence of "paintings and postcards, memory and myth."[17] Understandably, there exist differing views of the Falls in terms of whether it should be an historical monument, a grand spectacle, or a recurring event. The conflict and tension between perceptions of Niagara Falls as a scenic landmark and source of power also mirror in many respects a split within the American environmental movement that goes back to the battles between conservationists such as Gifford Pinchot and preservationists like John Muir. And the discussion of how to restore the "vanished beauty" of the waterscape has involved a wide range of commercial, hydrological, and especially aesthetic issues, including water use, tourism, and technical patterns of flow and erosion.

David Rothenberg illustrates the complexity of the relationship between water and technology through his own encounter with Niagara Falls. Donning plastic raingear, he descends by way of an elevator into the human-made tunnels beneath the Falls in order to experience the full force of the hidden technology and the seemingly raw power of the roaring water. Reflecting on his gaze into the magnificent abyss of cascading fluid from within the landmark, Rothenberg writes, "It does not look like water, or even feel like water. Most present is the tremendous rumble, a roar of flowing Earth. This precedes all other perception." His observations continue:

> It is nature, not art, which is apprehended through the white fury at the end of the soaked shaft. But it is only the artificial pathway, cut and blast into the core of the rock, which makes this experience possible. A violent, rough course of dynamite and explosions made this route into the heart of Niagara. Once inside, we are able to perceive an unceasing force beyond our power to create. . . . It is does not seem to matter that the entire flow of the water is regulated and controlled.[18]

Rothenberg confesses that whenever he now sees water he thinks of it differently, having been brought "closer to nature" through technology; however, he does not indicate clearly if this new proximity is epistemological or physical, or both.[19] Nevertheless, the story does underscore a significant way that the meanings of water are crafted, perceived, or dramatically altered by the given technologies in operation.[20]

"Fallingwater," Frank Lloyd Wright's most famous legacy, is a second example of the intersection and merging of the world of human artifacts and technology with the ostensibly natural realm of water. Built in western Pennsylvania, the house is cantilevered dramatically over Bear Run. Sewn into a wooded setting, it is tethered to a waterfall and anchored aesthetically and structurally with the rock ledges below. Here beauty is found at the confluence of stone and water—building and stream—where we see the congress of stability and habitability of the architecture on the one hand with the flux of the moving fluid on the other hand. At "Fallingwater," we witness the captured moment and continuous momentum of domestication in which the meaning of the stream is suddenly and spectacularly redefined in its arranged marriage to Wright's home. Water not only rushes around and under the structure—as the other-than-human realm fills the dwelling unit with the sounds of the stream and visually registers its movements through expansive glass panels—but via steps unfolding from inside the living room and the hold of the house—one is able to descend to and into the bubbling brook.[21]

A third example is drawn from the work of Martin Heidegger—who is examined more fully in the next chapter—and his phenomenological description of a hydroelectric plant placed into the Rhine River. In Heidegger's treatment of modern technology, the hydroelectric plant transforms the river into a mere supply of waterpower. The Rhine is no longer a true river in the landscape except as "an object on call for inspection by a tour group ordered there by the vacation industry."[22] And this in the end is a kind of "monstrousness" that he finds intolerable. To the extent that this technology reveals the water, it is as "unlocking, storing, distributing, and switching." "Everything," Heidegger argues, "is ordered to stand by, to be immediately at hand" such that the natural world and the river in particular become "standing reserve" (*Bestand*) to be exploited.[23] At operation here in the focus upon technology by way of its relation to water is a sharp contrast that Heidegger develops more fully in other works between *poiesis* (poetic making) and *Gestell* ("enframing") such that the former is typically given privilege over the latter. That is, the artwork and aesthetics are set over and prioritized above the "waterwork" and technology. By way of contrast, Heidegger extols a wooden bridge and elsewhere celebrates a stone bridge that spans a stream as positive examples of human artifacts because they unite the water with the earth and sky while respecting their individual differences and elemental natures.[24] In both instances, the meaning of water is established ultimately by and through the kinds of construction built over or within it, including the aesthetic dimensions of the particular technological materials and processes employed.

Fountains are a fourth aesthetic mode of water domestication. To put it briefly, water is pumped, piped, and lastly plumed through a technological infrastructure into the public sphere in order to be revealed artfully in terms of an orchestration and display of power, beauty, or property. Ivan Illich remarks thoughtfully on this phenomenon in one cultural context:

> Rome's glory was the ostentatious domestication of Mnemosyne [the muse of memory] both through the codification of public memories in Roman law and through the piping of city water. Roman architects picked up a source in the mountains, channeled the water unmingled into the city, and chose for each one of the waters the stories it should tell in the city. . . . The artist used the water to give sparkle to the titrons and nymphs of his invention, and the Senate chose the street crossing to exhibit its power over that water flow.[25]

Other societies, of course, have displayed piped water, but they have not generally put it to use for the same amalgam of aesthetic and political purposes as ancient Rome, even if the waters have been invested routinely with signs of social significance. In the United States, for example, the fountains we find in arid environments and specifically in desert locales like Las Vegas are more likely to deploy water to enact luxurious displays of affluence and excess, flaunting the precious fluid as a symbol of over-the-top expenditure.

A final exemplary instance of landscape aesthetics involving water technologies arises in Denmark. There, a staggering ninety percent of rivers and streams have been "de-meandered," or straightened. This practice, which also occurs in other parts on the world, is driven by the need to drain fields and to deliver water or remove waste as efficiently and inexpensively as possible.[26] In recent years, however, there have been repeated public calls for "re-meandering" waterways from the Danish Skjern River to the Los Angeles River. Such cases point to the difficulties of separating clearly the physical, cultural and technological realms when we transform, restore, or interact with ecological processes. Why, we might ask, do so many of us share affinities with or nostalgia for meandering water? The un-straightening of the Skjern, which was de-meandered three decades ago, is apparently being sought by Scandinavians for a number of overlapping reasons, including as a benefit to animals; for the sake of water purity; and in the noble name of "nature." Action may also be necessary for the protection of surrounding agricultural systems, which need to be maintained and managed continually by human communities. Beneath all this discussion, however, the most compelling force at work might be that most humans simply prefer the aesthetic appearance of a wandering river or a wiggling stream to a linear flow. There may in fact be something within our learned or acquired perceptual sensibilities that loves the serpentine, or meandering movement of fluids, perhaps originating with a form of "biophilia" that emerged from our evolutionary past as we humans lived near flowing waters over many millennia.[27] Nature, it seems, abhors a straight line—in addition to a vacuum, as Aristotle once observed—if we may speak a bit anthropomorphically.[28]

What can we gather from these examples? First, many different forms of the art of watercraft emerge as we engage in a domestic "dialogue" and cultural "conversation" with the fluid. Water continually shapes, "scapes," and sculpts our sense of place through the force of its flows, and we respond in turn by channeling, corralling, or containing it in turbines, pipes, and trenches. Second, aesthetic issues are central factors in most hydrological projects even when they are not distinctly articulated as such. Like other values—ethical, political, and religious—they work in powerfully conscious and unconscious ways, such that beauty can even rival, complement or complete a sense of ethical duty when individuals seek to protect a particular ecosystem or environment. Third, engineering marvels and massive feats involving water such as Niagara Falls, Hoover Dam, the Golden Gate Bridge, and the Three Gorges Dam in China testify to the appearance of a "technological sublime," which either coexists or competes with conceptions of a natural sublime as well as more traditional notions of beauty, in human constructions that astound or awe our aesthetic sensibilities. David Nye notes accurately "great works of architecture and engineering, like mountains, vast waterfalls, and canyons" are often able to "leave a visitor dumbfounded, amazed, and deeply impressed either by natural forces or by human's ingenuity in overcoming them."[29] As he speculates, this was likely the case when, for example, ancient writers celebrated aqueducts and other large engineered structures in similar language.

Finally, we need to remain attentive to what is concealed or revealed in the use of water for aesthetic purposes and other goals. Simple appeals to purity and being "closer to nature" are not always illuminating or helpful, and they can in fact be obfuscating or dangerous. Political theorist Langdon Winner seems to recognize this point when he advocates skepticism toward the concept of nature as a criterion for technological critique. However, Winner nearly valorizes or privileges the abstract notion himself through a representative and embodiment of the biological world in a large gray whale who emerges from the ocean to meet and symbolically confront the Diablo Canyon nuclear reactor that Winner seeks to challenge. As a kind of elemental force and seemingly unassailable ambassador of the watery depths who leaves him in an "overpowering silence," the whale suggests to us that it is ever-tempting to invoke "nature" as a singular norm or unquestioned standard for assessing hydrological (and other) technologies, even when this approach may not be warranted because of the complex, multiple, and contested meanings of the term.[30]

From Waterways to Waterworks

"We took a pristine river and we turned it into a working river—a machine. It is a damn fine machine," proclaims Al Wright of the Pacific Northwest Utilities Conference Committee.[31] In this remark and the processes associated with the

Columbia River in the northwestern United States and southwestern Canada, we can observe the protracted transformation and taming of a wild waterway into a technological waterwork. We also can witness how human labor and knowledge of the physical world are intertwined deeply so that the result is what historian Richard White styles an "organic machine."[32] Through an extended cultural and historical analysis, White shows that the Columbia River is a system of energy that retains its other-than-human qualities even as it is greatly modified by human actions. He argues that nature is both a cultural notion and a set of forces exterior to us—one not completely contained by cultural constructions—and that it also must be placed into the context of history. "Nature," he writes, "is salmon swimming, the river flowing, and, I would add, humans fishing."[33]

White investigates the relationship between human history and natural history and in the process the connections between the technological and nonhuman worlds. He reveals how work—which he does not distinguish from labor—and our technological artifacts link us "for better or worse" to the natural environment.[34] In particular, White explores a seeming "piece of ghost technology" in the river dams along with salmon that navigate the river as an emissary and emblem of the physical world. Making a case for impurity and the blurring of boundaries and borders, he suggests that we should seek the "natural" in dams and see the "unnatural" in salmon, although he still appears to subscribe to a fairly traditional notion of nature in his analysis. Along the way, White uncovers a close relation between the work, energy, and action of the river and that of humans.[35] In the case of the Columbia River, and by extrapolation other water systems, local people acquire knowledge of a river through the work of trading, transportation, dam building, and fishing. "Dams, hatcheries, channels, pumps, cities, and ranches are all products of human work, and it is our labor that ultimately links us to the river. Our labor, our energy, is the nature in us. And we harness it, just as we harness nature, to social purposes." In White's view, normative calls for a "return to nature" amount to "posturing" and are akin to a "religious ritual and a pledge to sin no more promises to restore purity."[36]

In brief, White illustrates how technology has long been applied to rivers through canoes, dipping nets, and sailing vessels. In more recent historical periods, machines such as steamships, mills. and hydroelectric power have increasingly mediated our relationship to water. For the gillnetters, their labor often "naturalized" them in both senses of the term. "To watch gillnetters at work was to witness an elaborately choreographed dance of fish, river, and men. The habits of fish, the hydraulics of the river, and the organized labor of men all intersected. Labor and nature merged. No element, no movement could be separated from the other; each, to some degree shaped the other."[37] Irrigation farmers, too, removed water from the river but also established control of waterways, building as well "artificial" streams to hold what they took. Dams now rely on the flow of the Columbia to move turbines; however the building of reservoirs in turn effects the movement of the river itself, making still water from flowing fluids and deep water from shallow water. The organic and the mechanical, in short, are completely melded and merged, as technology critic Lewis Mumford had hoped when he spoke optimistically—and perhaps a bit naively—of hydroelectricity as the freeing of both nature and human labor and envisioned a Neolithic world of organic machines and ecological harmony.[38]

It is significant that White characterizes the river as an "organic machine" and not just a machine per se. "The Columbia," he asserts, "has become an organic machine which human beings *marriage* without fully understanding what they have created. The organic machine has, in turn, spawned a virtual river whose life influences the actual Columbia."[39] White is right to point out that machines can be *physically* disassembled and moved from location to location, unlike the river, which nevertheless has been *conceptually* taken apart. Such an approach to technology is interestingly similar to Langdon Winner's suggestive notion of "epistemological luddism," which advocates an active dissection or dismantling of new technologies—either materially or figuratively—in order to better understand their possible impacts, workings, and effects.[40]

By viewing the Columbia as a machine, the river has been transformed into separate spheres, functions, and parts. "Fishermen see habitat. Irrigators see water. Power managers, utility operators, and those who run aluminum factories see reservoirs necessary to turn turbines. Barge owners see channels with certain depths of water. Environmentalists see brief stretches of free-flowing water." White concludes: "All stake a social claim to their part of the machine. None of them are concerned with the river as a whole."[41] This division does not in the last analysis work, however, because the river is still linked to greater organic cycles outside of human control. The river, in other words, has its own life and purposes. It is, according to White, forever changing, mocking our attempts to rein it in. The complex and unanswered question arises if it can be viewed and treated once again as a whole, or whether this goal is a fiction and impossibility. Can we put Humpty Dumpty back together again—perceive it as an integrated whole? This might be asking for too much. White's diagnosis reveals our failed relationship with water and the surrounding environment. He asserts that we have neither killed nor raped the river, pointing out correctly that these metaphors are inadequate. It is more like a *failed marriage*—an analogy that "for better or worse" (as we say in these domestic agreements) underscores again the notion and role of domestication in our interactions with water and the elements. In White's perspective, we have gone far past the commodification of the river because it is now partly a human creation where the physical locale of the waterway—or water-work as it were—is dramatically rearranged.[42]

In the end, White's exploration and theory invites a less contemplative and more active (but still relatively respectful) connection with the physical environment, one that we have been terming *domestication*. Here we also see a potential bridge to the claims of environmental philosophers and technology critics who stress the notions of labor and work in understanding the ever-changing relations to our surroundings.[43] From this vantage point, activities ranging from fishing and gardening to building and sailing help us to grasp the ambient elements and elemental nature when we actively engage in them. Put briefly, the human hand—and its prosthetic extension in the fire of technology—is involved deeply in the mediation and transformation of water as we mix our bodily labor with the world around us.

Bottled Water

One of the newest American "necessities" or, alternatively, fads and perhaps even fetishes is bottled water. In this quickly growing phenomenon, water is domesticated minimally in the sense that it is captured from the hydrological and meteorological cycles—its flow arrested—before it is contained, "purified," and finally refrigerated or consumed in the human household, the encompassing site of domestication. In the process, water is to one degree or another altered, its meaning changed as our connection with it is mediated and the essential substance of life is marketed and sold like other goods. In the last decade, the per capita consumption of bottled water has more than doubled in the United States, and more than half of all Americans now drink it. In 2002, U.S. consumers spent more than seven billion dollars on this product alone, and that figure has been rising nearly ten percent each year to an estimated eleven billion dollars in 2006.[44]

Bottled water has acquired a high-tech appeal in the financial world as investors are rapidly buying up land for purposes of filtering, processing, and transporting the fluid. Corporations such as Coca-Cola, Pepsi, Chlorox Bleach, and Bechtel are currently joining the international rush to privatize and commodify water through political battles, pipelines, and bottling technology, developments that confirm the adage that "water flows uphill towards money."[45] Costing as much as $4.50 to $7 per gallon, bottled water is now more expensive per volume than milk, oil, soda, and gas, and about five hundred to one thousand times more expensive than tap water. Coca-Cola has encouraged and capitalized on these trends with a campaign against offering tap water in restaurants designed to promote Dasani, its entrant into the water wars.[46] There are even "water bars" emerging in some major cities, and many restaurants and stores regularly display water bottles from Europe as if they were filled with wine. The use of polyethylene terephthalate (PET) and associated technological developments clearly have been integral in facilitating these commercial and social changes given that PET is transparent, light, and flexible, thus permitting portability and disposability. This practice of economic enclosure follows the earlier historical cordoning, parceling, and packaging of earth for sale as well as the domestication and commercialization of fire. It sets the precedent, too, for buying, owning, and selling air rights or air access, something that is foreshadowed by the appearance of "oxygen bars," where one receives "hits" of scented forty percent oxygen (above the twenty-one percent we normally take in) delivered through masks, supposedly to ease stress and help allergies, headaches, and hangovers.[47]

In terms of the geological and technological filtering processes, about seventy-five percent of U.S. tap water historically has come from the surface water of streams, lakes, and rivers, and these sources have been vulnerable to different forms of contamination. By contrast, ground water is relatively free of pathogens if it journeys through clean routes. In Italy and France—the leading exporters—all bottled water derives from underground origins. Filtering occurs via the layers of rock and sand through which rain and melting snow transit, thereby "purifying" the water of microbial and chemical elements that might threaten its integrity for drinking. In the process, it acquires a "fingerprint" or defining signature—a tattooed mark so to speak of its mediation—through the mineral traces that give it character and taste, and it can remain in transit for several years in the earth before finally being bottled. The EU sets standards for mineral water, so that it must be free of particular microbiological and chemical components, bottled at the source, and untreated in any significant technological manner.[48]

By contrast, American "spring water" is required to begin underground and move of its own accord to the surface, although bottlers can add carbon dioxide to it. "Mineral water" is defined similarly, but it also must possess a specified but relatively small level of dissolved minerals. And "purified drinking water" is bottled water treated by a technical process (deionization, reverse osmosis, or distillation), although companies do not need to name the water source, which can even be municipal tap water. In the United States, spring water often is used as an interchangeable term with *artesian water*—from wells where the pressure is high enough to push water to the surface. In short, we can observe an extensive taxonomy and nomenclature emerging with the proliferation of technologically processed and purified bottled water that suggests the fluid is not an objective or singular thing-in-itself, but a physically and culturally mediated product—a conceptually contested substance with a plurality of forms and social associations involving status, health, safety, and a desire for the pristine.

In Europe, moreover, mineral water is widely considered "a living thing" and access to it is a guaranteed right in some countries. In Italy, the government leases privileges to bottle water and requires companies to supply taps where all citizens can fill their own containers. In both Italy and France, bottlers must show that the water has health-promoting qualities before it can be sold as mineral water. In an age of terrorism and geographical transience, Americans appear increasingly more concerned with safety and portability than with taste such that it is common to see a guarantee of "purity" on container labels. Despite such fears, which seem to drive much consumption, a study by the National Resources Defense Council has shown that bottled water is no safer than ordinary tap water and that weak or Byzantine-like governmental regulations can even make it an inferior product.[49]

Should, then, bottled water be considered natural, technological, or a hybrid entity? Put differently, is "denatured" domesticated water thus artificial or, alternatively, is "technological" water still natural? The lines between these distinctions and realms have indeed become murky and "impure." Some bottlers currently purify tap water and then add (we could say "adulterate" it with) calcium, bicarbonates, and magnesium for flavor—making it a kind of technological "designer water." One can now even find caffeinated, vitamin-enriched, and strawberry- or lemon-flavored brands. Most experts who work with mineral water seem to believe, however, that particular types of water cannot be duplicated in a laboratory, and that a key, missing ingredient may be the occurrence of microflora, which only is found in the biological world. In the purification process, therefore, it is not even completely clear what we are necessarily losing or gaining with filtration. As one might expect, the U.S. Food and Drug Administration (FDA) does not help much with these questions because it does not provide exact definitions of the categories in question. A great deal of American bottled water is little other than treated tap water sold as "drinking water," which the FDA also has not clearly defined. A business simply needs to treat the water according to a given technological standard of purity, such as reverse osmosis or deionization, which strips it of identifying characteristics.[50] This process, in other words, eliminates the water's "fingerprint," excising its taste. However, when water from different springs is sold under the same brand name, we are not given either a unique character and taste or a sense of its place and point of origin—important ecological considerations to be sure.

Both water purification and water pollution are physical phenomena—capable of measurement, testing, and technological treatment—but they also are philosophical problems because they necessitate an inquiry into matters related to ideals or degrees of cleanliness, contamination, and adulteration—notions that are deeply tied with their conceptual opposites. The filtration of water is manifestly an expensive process, and it is often the most viable way to get rid of cryptosporidium, giarida, and other pathogens not treatable by chlorine. Many inexpensive home-filtration systems can eliminate chlorine and lead while slightly more expensive filters are able to remove pathogens, thus providing a practical alternative to bottled water. It is important to keep in mind that the chemistry of groundwater is increasingly being altered by anthropogenic pollution. In recent years, dissolved "additives" have risen by ten percent and by as much as one third in terms of sodium, chlorine, salt. and sulfate. Leachates from herbicides, pesticides, fertilizer, radioactive traces, and toxic chemicals have been discovered throughout the water world, and the problem is exacerbated in the United States as a result of the flourishing chemical industry.[51] Bottled water poses a great penalty and huge ecological footprint on the environment because of the 1.5 million tons of plastic used annually to make containers that often are disposed of in nonrenewable ways—less than twenty-five percent of them are recycled—and requiring up to one thousand years to biodegrade. The Earth Policy Institute estimates that 1.5 million barrels of oil are expended to produce the water bottles used by Americans every year, an amount that could fuel one hundred thousand automobiles.[52] And the Pacific Institute calculates that the energy needed to manufacture the plastic, fill and transport the water, and treat the waste of each bottle is equivalent to filling it up one quarter of the way with oil.[53] The carbon emissions released in the transportation of twenty-two million tons of the liquid from one country to another each year and the increased demand placed on already over-taxed local aquifers are of ecological concern as well. The "revenge effect" and ironic result is that the security of common water resources can be compromised precisely because many people are seeking the supposed safety of bottled water.[54]

In bottling and hence domesticating water through technological processes we are, it appears, redoubling water's endemic (i.e., "natural") ambiguities, anomalies, and paradoxes. Water is necessary to life but not necessarily alive, seemingly shapeless but able to assume the shape of other things, and absent a given rhythm but capable of grounding the rhythmic flows of the body, tides, weather, and seasons. Through its domestication, a great deal of water is now a hybrid product—both natural and technological, purified but still not perfectly pure. As Illich points out: "Water throughout history has been perceived as the stuff which radiates purity: H_2O is the new stuff, on whose purification human survival now depends." He adds: "The transformation of H_2O into a cleaning fluid was complete. In the imagination of the twentieth century, water lost both its power to communicate by touch, its deep-seated purity and its mystical power to wash off spiritual blemish."[55] Even if this remark overstates the case, it is certain our bottle-toting citizenry no longer interact with or conceive of water in quite the same way as past generations.

Fire and Water

Illich ends his book, *H_2O and the Waters of Forgetfulness*, with the stark assertion that "H_2O is a social creation of modern times, a resource that is scarce and that calls for technical management. It is an observed fluid that has lost the ability to mirror the water of dreams. The city child has no opportunities to come in touch with living water."[56] Michael Oakeshott echoes this opposition of water and H_2O when he holds that "the word 'water' stands for practical image; but a scientist does not first perceive 'water' and then resolve it into H_2O: *scientia* begins only when 'water' has been left behind." Moreover, "To speak of H_2O as 'the chemical formula for water' is to speak in a confused manner: H_2O is a symbol the rules of whose behavior are wholly different from those which govern the symbol 'water.'"[57] In such claims, we find the perception and concern that the power of water has been diluted, so to speak, by the omnipresence and force of modern technology. In a sense, it has been cleaved into two separate substances—a primordial or archetypal fluid and a technological or commercial chemical. At the same time, if pollution like domestication is philosophically a kind of "inside-out" problem—in that we are not respecting what is perceived to be outside the scope of a particular conception of one's home or place—then in domesticating water, we are provided with the opportunity not just of bringing it to our bodies (via pipes and bottles) or onto our agricultural fields (via irrigation) but also of keeping it actively in mind as it enters the human household.

We have seen how water is domesticated and mediated increasingly by technological developments and how this elemental substance is revealed, concealed, or changed in significance by this process. We have looked at cases from philosophy (Thales in Chapter two), commerce (bottled water), landscape technologies and aesthetics (e.g., Niagara Falls and de-meandered rivers), and human labor (the Columbia River). Like the liquid itself, the meanings of water are ever-evolving as the forms of mediation are altered. It surely behooves us to remain attuned to the kinds of actual and theoretical filtering that occur with complex or hidden technologies because the possibility perpetually exists for a kind "reverse adaptation" to set in, whereby desirable social ends and goals (e.g., clean drinking water) are adjusted and reformulated to meet the available technical means chosen (e.g., water in plastic bottles) so we are left with a diminished result, a mal-distributed resource, or an unintended consequence.[58] When the "fire" of technology meets the "watery" flux of nature, we often find ourselves situated in—or moving between—Earth's given waterways and more human-generated waterworks. And if it is true that we have "transmogrified water into a fluid with which archetypal waters cannot be mixed," then we must certainly seek to better understand these cultural and technological fluid dynamics in order to best meet our social, ecological, and bodily needs.[59] We transition now from the domestication of water to consider very cursorily the interrelated transformations of the atmospheric air and the underlying earth.

Eclipse of the Atmosphere

Contrary to the popular expression, *the sky is no longer the limit*. In terms of optical perception and environmental orientation, the blue sky has been an invariant feature of the terrestrial horizon since time immemorial, separating clarity from opacity, and transparency from occlusion. Paul Virilio, however, warns that we are now proliferating a novel form of pollution—one he calls "dromospheric"—characterized by the loss of elemental depth and worldly dimension. Through the widespread introduction of virtual technologies and anticipated earlier by the inauguration of flight at Kitty Hawk and then the earthly escape missions of Apollo 11 (to the moon) and Pioneer 10 (the first human object to depart the solar system), we are *falling upwards* at break-neck speed, spinning in "reverse vertigo" as we liberate ourselves from gravity. "Contamination," Virilio avers, "has in fact spread further than the elements, natural substances, air, water, fauna, and flora it attacks—as far as the space-time of our planet."⁶⁰ To wit, the sky (or, minimally, a notion of it) may in some sense be disappearing and with it our distinctly geographic understandings of place—including relief, depth, volume, weight, and both an apparent and deep horizon—as anthropocentrism and geocentrism give way to a kind of "luminocentrism" built around speed, tele-presence, cyberspace, time-light, and a new trans-apparent horizon provided by the rectangular screens of TVs and computers.⁶¹

At the same time that we are breaching a perceptual and conceptual hole above us—an opening on high—it appears that the airy lower canopy of the *sky is falling* as well because of human activity. There is an old saying, sometimes attributed to Mark Twain, that everyone talks about the weather, but no one does anything about it. This is no more the case. In the last hundred years, not only have we altered in dramatic ways the chemical composition of the atmosphere, lit up the night sky, and lanced a large cavity in the ozone, but we have radically changed global weather patterns, too, by emitting industrial pollutants into the already saturated air. In "The Bering Bridge," writer and theoretical chemist Roald Hoffman laments: "The old men say / the sky was once so close / that if you shot an arrow up / it would bounce back at you" but later adds, "then the redwoods came . . . and / they jacked up the sky, / and then men with balloons and telescopes / pushed it back further." Airplanes and moonwalks, in turn, followed and further expanded the sky. In the last line of the poem, however, Hoffman depicts the return of a lower ceiling of air when he observes, "I see smog, the sky coming back down over California."⁶² Such is the cost it would seem of human progress.

With the "pollution of distances"—to use Virilio's phrase—the sky appears less like an ornate vaulted dome where the stars blink and shine and more like a flattened electronic screen on which we project anthropogenic lights and advertisements. It seems at times, in fact, to be a domesticated field where fabricated objects compete for supremacy or space. Indeed, with more than ten thousand man-made entities greater in size than a softball currently orbiting the planet, it will soon sound reasonable to demand stop signs and traffic signals to regulate the circulating commerce. Safe inside our domestic spheres, we regulate the temperature and humidity of the air around us from easy chairs and tune into a cable television network devoted entirely to tracking storms, sunspots, hurricanes, and rainfall amounts rather than peering through the erstwhile "24-hour weather channel"—the house window—or listening to and becoming literate with elemental processes.

With the conquest of a once relatively undomesticated atmosphere, too, the cultivated earth below, in turn, increasingly resembles either an extended basement floor when viewed from the heights of a plane or perhaps the "blandscape" of a computer chip—one increasingly made more uniform in composition and appearance by global monoculturing. As a consequence, we are much more likely to become mere sedentary citizens focused obsessively on technological control of our proximate environments. We transition next to examine this transformation of earth a bit more fully.

Escape from Earth

Earth alienation—a phenomenon first identified by political theorist Hannah Arendt—is a similar and related process to the eclipse of the atmosphere whereby the taking-hold and transformation of the Earth through modern geographic explorations, political expropriations, technological inventions, and then later flight into space have resulted, ironically, in a collapsing of spatial distances, a shrinkage of public places, and an estrangement from the planet.[63] Earth alienation is symbolized by the launching in 1957 of a satellite into outer space—an occurrence "second in importance to no other, not even to the splitting of the atom"—and stands in contrast, though not complete opposition, to *world alienation*, which involves the ongoing loss of a secure home in the world for many groups of people as well as the increasing abolition of otherness.[64] For Arendt, it originates with events in the sixteenth and seventeenth centuries, including, first, the discovery of America and the mapping and charting of the Earth; second, the Reformation, during which land was confiscated and millions of people were uprooted from their homes; third, the invention of the telescope, which encouraged a departure into space and a new universal relation to the cosmos; and finally, the triumph of Cartesian doubt—*De omnibus dubitandum*—and geometry, which freed humans from geocentric notions of space.

These developments facilitated the tendency to escape Earth-bound inhabitancy and carried the unpredictability and irreversibility of human actions into the natural world. The transition from natural to universal science and the location of an Archimedean point within the human mind, where it can be held or circulated about, also lies at the center of the notion of Earth alienation. The process that has permitted us to alter the natural world from outside the Earth, to create chemical elements not found on the planet, to manufacture life in a laboratory, to destroy it with atomic weapons, to reach speeds near to that of light or, alternatively, to freeze the flow of light itself are responsible, in this view, for alienating us so deeply from our given home. The airplane, too, is an emblem of the loss of an earthly bond attained by generating a *vertical* distance between humans and the terrestrial ground, where formerly *horizontal* distance was the norm. From an Arendtian perspective, however, the most significant change for the human condition would involve an "emigration of men from the earth to some other planet," a distinct possibility as we quickly expend the Earth's nonrenewable resources, overpopulate the land, and probe outer space for military, economic, or scientific purposes.[65] Arendt even goes as far to claim that the Earth has become, in some sense, dispensable: "we have found a way," she says, "to act on the earth and within terrestrial nature as though we dispose of it from outside, from the Archimedean point."[66]

If Earth alienation is initiated with the telescope and symbolized by the satellite, it is perhaps now embodied visually by the photographic image of the planet captured from an extra-terrestrial position. Although this representation enables us to see the Earth as a bounded blue sphere from a "god's eye view" in outer space or to perceive it potentially as a unique, vulnerable or even living entity worthy of our collective concern, it also may encourage us to view it as "a small, comprehensible, manageable icon—an easily manipulable token Earth that we can use to replace the unfathomably immense and overwhelmingly complex reality of the world which surrounds us."[67] "I was worried when I saw pictures coming from the moon to the earth," Heidegger remarked shortly before his death. "The uprooting of man has already taken place. . . . This is no longer the earth on which man lives."[68] Such photos, moreover, could be exemplars of what Merleau-Ponty calls "high altitude thinking" that, in the words of Michael Zimmerman, "conceives of itself as pure spirit rising above the natural world" and in which "we see Earth reflected in the rearview mirror of the spaceship taking us away from our home in order to conquer the universe."[69]

The *over-domestication* of the Earth is no doubt responsible in part for the increasing interest in fleeing or flying from it. As biologist Lewis Thomas has warned, "We are beginning to treat the earth as a sort of domesticated house pet, living in an environment invented by us, part kitchen garden, part park, part zoo."[70] Animal domestication in the United States for example, has been responsible for marked changes on the physical landscape since the arrival of early colonists in "the seeming endless miles of fences, the silenced voices of vanished wolves, the system of country roads."[71] Domesticated livestock have contributed to the decline of old growth forests and the destruction of native plant species through overgrazing, which result in a decrease in native perennial grasses and a loss in the density of vegetation. These effects have adverse impacts on soil—lost through erosion at a rate of roughly two billion tons each year in this country—which then reinforces the negative effects on biota. Grazing leads to decreased aeration of soils, increased runoff, and water accumulation on the surface of land.[72] The result is desertification—loss of the Earth's topsoil—a process that is occurring in some dry regions at a much faster than the speed of soil accretion, which can require up to twenty-five years to form half an inch of new matter. Coupled with these changes is deforestation, which has destroyed half of the rain forests of Central America and which is due greatly to cattle raised for the hamburger market. With the rise of biotechnology and the manipulation of DNA, we are perhaps witnessing, too, the *domestication of the gene*, what Neil Evernden calls "the final assault on the wildness of life." Exercising this capacity "exterminates wildness at the source and places all life within the domain of human willing." The Earth is "domesticated in body, in concept, and, finally, one must say, in spirit."[73]

The reach and impact of domestication on the contemporary environment, then, is clearly vast and growing. A scientific study of "domesticated nature" sponsored in 2007 by the Nature Conservancy showed that as of 1995 only seventeen percent of the world's land has not been influenced directly by humans through, for example, roads, agriculture, or artificial lighting—an enormous ecological footprint. The amount of water, too, now held behind dams is six times greater than the quantity flowing freely in rivers, and approximately half of the Earth's surface area has been converted to cropland or grazing regions. The study concludes that although the net benefits to humans have been positive in terms of productivity, safety, commerce, and convenience, there are few, if any, uniquely pristine places remaining on the planet. Given these circumstances, the authors nevertheless suggest that the goal of conservation policy should no longer be to preserve "the wild" but instead to domesticate the natural world with greater wisdom so as to better balance tradeoffs among ecosystem services.[74]

Is there a viable way of remaining "faithful to the Earth," to use Nietzsche's admonition? Optimistically, a practical combination of coherent ecological philosophy and sound environmental policy can help guide the unbridled flight of thought and the tempting thought of flight gently *back down to Earth* without cordoning them there unconditionally. After all, "the earth," Hegel reminds us, "is not the physical center of the world, but it is the metaphysical center."[75] Virilio wisely identifies the need for a *gray ecology* that would supplement, although not supplant, a traditional emphasis on *green ecology* by shifting some attention to the depreciation of the depth field of the land- and sky-scapes and presumably focus more on the urban, suburban, and industrial worlds.[76] Arendt argues, too, that we need to acknowledge limits in our quest for knowledge and that a more geocentric worldview may re-emerge once these constraints are accepted. She recommends that we recover the Earth—which is part of the "very quintessence" of the human condition—as our true home and begin to realize that mortality is a fundamental condition of scientific research. Throughout her work, she offers challenges to unchecked consumption, industrialism, capitalism, and productivism that are often consistent with, although not motivated by, a critical vision of a more ecological world. Consumer society, she wisely foresaw, is complicit with an economy of waste, "in which things must be almost as quickly devoured and discarded as they have appeared."[77] These kinds of critiques and suggestions are, to be sure, constructive starts on complex issues; however, as we see later, there is much more that can be said about and done on behalf of the air, water, and earth in order to protect the respective "breath," "blood," and "body" of the planet.

End of the Elements?

Like plants and animals, ideas and relationships also might become threatened or even go extinct. Perhaps we have underestimated our power over elemental forces. Speaking of global climate change wrought largely through effluences into the air and atmosphere, Bill McKibben argues in his influential work, *The End of Nature*, that although we have not yet halted the fall of rain or curtailed the arrival of sunlight, we have altered greatly their intensity through anthropogenic activities. In his view, the very *meaning* of rain, wind, and sun have changed as we have rapidly and wantonly transfigured the planet. "Yes, the wind still blows—but no longer from some other sphere, some inhuman place."[78] Whether the wind once did blow from a wholly independent realm and whether that is valuable or even necessary in order to have a meaningful world is certainly contestable. What is not debatable is the fact that the rate at which we are modifying the elemental environment is accelerating more and more quickly, and that such quantitative changes translate eventually into qualitative transformations, like a tsunami wave arriving from oceanic depths onto the shallow shoreline. While admirably and intelligently calling attention to human-generated climate problems before they were recognized widely, McKibben conflates and confuses the *idea* of the end of independent nature (a theoretical change and subjective loss) with the *actual* end of nature itself (a material change and objective impossibility) and also vacillates or equivocates in his claims, asserting that both nature is still *ending* and that it has in fact already *ended*. Nevertheless, such a perspective highlights the vital importance of the notion of meaning—cognitive and affective—that arises from and through our unfolding connections with other-than-human processes and phenomena, including the ambient air, water, or earth.[79]

As our interactions with the planet become regularly mediated by advanced technology, then, we find through critical reflection that artifacts increasingly condition, regulate, or intercede on our physical, psychological, and philosophical relationships with the environment. Air conditioning, electric lights, asphalt, gas and oil heating, cell phones, televisions, and indoor plumbing all clearly provide creature comforts and conveniences, but they also can crowd our worlds unnecessarily at times with distractions, distortions, and dangers arising from energy consumption, system failure, or psychological and physical distance. The impact of high technology on ecological perception is illustrated dramatically by astronaut John Glenn's flight into space aboard Friendship 7 in 1962. As Langdon Winner recounts the story:

> Glenn noticed something odd. His view of the planet was virtually unique in human experience. . . . Yet as he watched the continents and oceans moving beneath him, Glenn began to feel that he had seen it all before. Months of simulated space shots in sophisticated training machines and centrifuges had affected his ability to respond. In the words of chronicler Tom Wolfe, "The world demanded awe, because this was a voyage through the stars. But he couldn't feel it."[80]

In distancing ourselves from elemental surroundings, we may lose both literal and figurative touch with the environment in which we evolved and on which we deeply depend. To be out of touch with the elements is not to actively know and appreciate them, even when contact greatly alters their form or appearance.

These transformations, of course, did not occur in a vacuum or all at once. They are the culmination of protracted historical processes and philosophical paradigm shifts. Here, we should acknowledge that conceptual hierarchies and oppositions were being asserted and established quite early on in the development of thinking about the elements and natural world. Critical theorists Horkheimer and Adorno argue that:

> The categories by which Western philosophy defined its everlasting natural order marked the spots once occupied by Oncus and Persephone, Ariadne and Nereus. The Presocratic cosmologies preserve the moment of transition. The moist, the indivisible, air, and fire, which they hold to be the primal matter of nature, are already rationalizations of the mythic mode of apprehension. Just as the images of generation from water and earth, which came from the Nile to the Greeks, became here hylozoistic principles, or elements, so all the equivocal multitude of mythical demons were intellectualized in the pure form of ontological essences.[81]

In this sense, an early form of domestication appears to involve a drive toward classification and rationalization. Such a claim is surely putting the case a bit strongly, but it makes a point *in extremis*. More broadly, we must recognize these changes in their cultural context and realize that a long temporal perspective on the elements and natural world can contribute to an understanding of our present-day situation and predicaments.

If we break the story—or history—of the elements into four periods, an extremely brief outline might proceed along the following lines. First, earth, fire, air, and water appear in the mythic and religious perspectives of the ancient Chinese, Hindu, Persian, Greek, American Indian, and other indigenous cultures, especially in creation accounts where one or more of the four (and sometimes five) assume centrality. The elements typically arise in one of several ways: through a cosmogonic separation of an earthy below from an airy above, a development of living forms in primeval waters, an emergence of humans from the dust or dirt of earth, an inspiring soul-birthing breath, or a theft of fire from divinities. In a second and largely Greek phase, which we have explored in some depth, they are incorporated into more rational frameworks by Presocratic thinkers—especially Thales, Anaximenes, Heraclitus, and Empedocles—before being taken up by Plato and Aristotle within the contexts of physics, philosophy, and cosmology.

In an expansive third stage commencing with Aristotle's death and continuing through the Middle Ages into modernity, earth, air, fire, and water are displaced or diminished in major ways as explanatory phenomena. Where they do persist in alchemical treatises or speculative works by Neo-Platonists, the elements are divided frequently into active and passive kinds, with fire and air often construed as the former, and water or earth represented as the latter. Lucretius still testifies to their legacy when he styles them as *maxima membra mundi*, the great limbs of the world.[82] In fact, until the early seventeenth century, the French parliament arrested "heretics" who advocated five (as opposed to four) element theories, thereby underscoring Aristotle's lasting influence, which was linked closely with the authority of both the church and the state.[83] Nonetheless, the gradual departure of the elements is due in part to the ascendancy of notions of space and time over natural place with which the elements had been bound initially and also to more encompassing philosophical, cultural, and technological changes that eventuate in a new worldview during the Scientific Revolution. Poet John Donne captures a sense of these transitions in "An Anatomy of the World" when he writes in 1611:

> [the] new Philosophy calls all in doubt, / The element of fire is quite put out; / The sun is lost, and the earth, and no man's wit / Can well direct him where to look for it. / And freely men confess that this world's spent, / When in the planets, and the firmament / They seek so many new; then see that this / Is crumbled out again to his atomies. / 'Tis all in pieces, all coherence gone; / All just supply, and all relation.[84]

More basically, the notion of the four elements is subjected to intense scrutiny by influential chemists in the seventeenth and eighteenth centuries, and as a result earth, air, fire, and water come to be viewed as compounds rather than indivisible entities (a development discussed in Chapter two). As Robert Boyle remarks in *The Skeptical Chymist*, "if I would now deal rigidly with my adversary, I might here make a great question of the very way of probation which he and others employ, without the least scruple, to evince that the bodies commonly called mixt are made up of earth, air, water, and fire, which they are pleased also to call elements."[85]

At the same time, when the elements are invoked, it is often under the guise of an attempt to control them for strictly anthropocentric ends. Descartes thus recommends methods of "knowing the force and actions of fire, water, air" in order to "make ourselves, as it were, masters and possessors of nature."[86] With the rise of mercantilism and free-market capitalism, domestication is expressed increasingly as commodification when elemental places or phenomena are transformed into mere property relations. Marx himself—who characterizes nature as "man's inorganic body"—seems to have recognized this fact, lamenting critically, "Even the need for fresh air ceases to be a need for the worker. Man reverts once more to living in a cave, but the cave is now polluted." He adds: "Light, air, etc.—the simple animal cleanliness—ceases to be a need for man. Dirt—this pollution and putrefacation of man, the sewage (this word is to be understood in its literal sense) of civilization—becomes an element of life for him."[87] In Marx's era, the famous but perhaps apocryphal letter allegedly sent in 1854 from Chief Seattle to President Franklin Pierce, who was interested in purchasing land from American Indians, protests as well the very idea of unrestrained ownership over

the elemental commons. However genuine the epistle may be, it inquires simply but provocatively: "How is it possible to buy or sell the sky or the warmth of the earth? . . . As we do not own the freshness of the air and the brightness of the water, how could they be bought?"[88]

Before turning to more contemporary outcroppings of the elements and elemental phenomena within Continental philosophy in a fourth theoretical phase, a few final remarks on their status subsequent to Aristotle are in order. There is not presently an opportunity to provide a full accounting for and analysis of the changing roles, slow displacement, and near disappearance of earth, water, air, fire, and *aether* from philosophical thought. Nonetheless, we may cull several examples of exceptional thinkers who find a place for the elements within their perspectives and indicate very cursorily their respective orientations. As suggested earlier, Plato's theory of the elements has returned to favor in slightly different guise within theoretical physics, and the frameworks of Empedocles and Aristotle are still very relevant to environmental thinking. At some later time, one or more of the following views might come to exercise intellectual or cultural influence in unexpected ways, and so it is important to remain aware of these ideas.

The Stoics

Like Heraclitus, the early Stoics such as Zeno of Citium, Cleanthes, and Chrysippus take fire to be the universal "stuff." They conceive God as an active immanent fire and responsible as well for the four elements that compose the material world. Fire (hot) and air (cold) are active elements, whereas water (wet) and earth (dry) are passive elements. The elements issue from God and return to him in a universal conflagration (*ekpurosis*). The body of the world is developed from fiery vapor, which becomes air then water and earth. Through this *ekpurosis*, new worlds are repeatedly created and destroyed. The Stoics, too, develop an ethic of living according to both surrounding nature (*physis*) and human nature (reason)—which in many ways amount to the same thing—because in their view these "laws" govern the universe. From a Stoic perspective, *nous* (mind) is present in all living things, and like Aristotle's perspective, the Stoic physics is qualitative. Where the Stoics differ from earlier views is their idea of *pneuma* (vital spirit or breath), which consists of fire and air. Being an active principle, it pervades all existing things, causing them to cohere. *Pneuma* is a dynamic force inherent in the universe that allows multiple levels of unification, where there is common affinity or *sympatheia* at work between parts.[89]

Paracelsus

In the sixteenth century, Paracelsus advances his theory of four elements as active forces in *Archidoxis* and *The Philosophy Addressed to the Athenians*. In the former work, each of the elements can exist in any given object, however one of them will attain to perfection as a "ruling power." The three remaining entities, in fact, are too imperfect even to be called "elements." In the latter work, the four elements are represented as spiritual and self-active forces that possess an *archeus*, a dense vital feature that guides their development over time. The elements are generated from a *mysterium magnum* (literally, "great mystery") and eventually return to it. Each element constitutes a world, and the four worlds evolve independently. From water as matrix come fish, marine plants, coral, and the like; from the earth, the world of stones, seeds, sands, and humans arrive. Each of the four worlds, although evolving separately, is formed through a mutual consensus with the others. Humans are but one among numerous beings and, more particularly, we are a microcosm, a meeting point of three different realms. Through the visible body humans take part in the terrestrial world (the world of elements), through an astral body we participate in the sidereal place, and through an immortal soul we belong to the divine world.

Paracelsus modifies an Empedoclean understanding, one that is essentially holistic in its tenets. "That philosophy then is foolish and vain which leads us to assign all happiness and eternity to our element alone, that is, the earth, and that is a fool's maxim which boasts that we are the noblest creatures. There are many worlds and we are not the only beings in the world."[90] Paracelsus' philosophy of nature becomes associated with pantheism and revolutionary political ideas that were radically libertarian in spirit. He stresses the freedom of common people to study nature as a self-activating world, and his ideas are adopted as part of the social philosophy of groups such as the Diggers, who seized common land in order to establish egalitarian and utopian communal societies.[91]

Hegel

In his *Philosophy of Nature*, Hegel defends as well the elementary status of earth, air, fire, and water as against substances like oxygen and carbon, which are but "sides" of the aforementioned, and he proceeds to characterize their meteorological interactions and the dialectic in which they are engaged.[92] He agrees with the ancient Greeks that the elements are four in number, but he emphasizes other dimensions of the canonical tetrad. Briefly, air is the element of negative universality (unlike the medium of light in that it is heavy), fire is the element of negative universality that consumes and destroys, water is the element of passive neutrality, and earth is the element of individual determinateness and developed difference. Fire and water are elements of opposition: Fire is an "active being-for-other," whereas water is a "passive being-for-other." Hegel makes a distinction between elements as defined in their simplicity by chemistry (which destroys their individuality) and the idea of a physical element as real and universal matter. In the *Phenomenology of Spirit*, he also maintains that nature manifests itself in the four elements. "Air is the enduring, purely universal, and transparent element; Water, the element that is perpetually sacrificed; Fire, the unity which energizes them into opposition; lastly, Earth, which is the firm and solid knot of this articulated whole, the *subject* of these elements and of their process, that from which they start and to which they return."[93] Like a number of other thinkers from Plato to Merleau-Ponty, Hegel underscores the special role of the Earth as a whole, which as "universal individual," preserves existing differences within itself. In one sense at least, he returns us to a philosophical understanding that acknowledges that qualitative changes occur between the elements, as when water becomes vapor and finally air. In this regard, Hegel contributes to the notion of the four elements as the "elevation of sensuous ideas into thought."[94]

Fortunately, the story does not end with the attenuated demise and disappearance of the elements. As is soon seen—and here developments are for the most part unrecognized—they begin a transformed comeback with the concurrent breakdown of ecological processes in the twentieth century. When the elements begin to resurface within phenomenology, literature, and post-structuralist thought, they open up a host of new philosophical, cultural, and environmental possibilities. It is to this recent work that we shortly turn.

Interstice: Night

> Where is the philosopher who will give us the metaphysics of the night, the metaphysics of the human night?
>
> —Gaston Bachelard, *The Poetics of Reverie*

> Press close, bare-bosomed Night! Press close, magnetic, nourishing Night! / Night of south winds! Night of the large, few stars! / Still, nodding Night! Mad, naked, Summer Night!
>
> —Walt Whitman, *Leaves of Grass*

I woke up suddenly in a cold sweat on the cement floor of a dank basement in an old Victorian house in Minneapolis. Bathed in utter blackness and drowning in the impenetrable depth of night, I was sequestered deep inside something without an apparent outside. Palpable fear and panic set in. I was disoriented, lost even to myself, unsure if I was truly alive and yet so nervously awake as to be able to conclude with implacable logic that I could not possibly be dead. Tripping over sleeping bodies strewn pell-mell before me, I felt my way with the eyes of my feet to a set of stairs, where I extricated myself awkwardly from this abyss and emerged into a less tangible darkness, one which revealed me again to the scrutiny and certitude of my own gaze.

"Night is *made of night*," observes Bachelard.[1] As an ethereal, insubstantial "substance" lit up by itself, night might be apprehended fully only by a highly developed material imagination. Night papers over details and sharp distinctions, enveloping and enshrouding those who enter into its midst and seeming to play a kind of hide-and-go-seek with itself. "Night, the female, / Obscure, / Fragrant and supple, / Conceals herself," says Wallace Stevens.[2] But darkness is not always such a black-and-white affair. It is more typically a phenomenon distinguished by degrees, ranging from the dimming light of day to that of "starlings blotting out the sunset or black ants storming a dead opossum"—to use the imagery of a contemporary novelist—a chasm so rich it consumes our very bearings.[3] Thus, we might speak preferably of qualitatively different kinds of night and characterize it in terms of shades, textures, tones, tints, or tiers. These intricacies are hinted at through the prism of language. In German, for example, there are several different words for darkness, including *das Dunkel* (the dark), *die Finsternis* (suggestive of complete and ominous darkness), and *die Dunkelheit* (where vision is clouded or obscured). "The imagination," Bachelard hypothesizes, "commonly accepts dreams of an active night, a penetrating night, an insinuating night, or of a night that invades the substance of things."[4] Dusk and twilight are not simply transitional realms between the luster of day and the opaqueness of night but atmospheric conditions with their own character. Of evening, Rilke writes, "The sky puts on the darkening blue coat / held for it by the row of ancient trees; / you watch: and the lands grow distant in your sight, / one journeying to the heaven, one that falls; / and leave you, not at home in either one."[5] Strolling through a stand of trees by moonlight, awakening from slumber in a strange bed, rushing for shelter during a lightning storm, or moving between rooms in a poorly lit house, we may step into and out of many forms of the flickering presence of night while our ears and touch compensate for our slowly adjusting eyes and mind.

Positioned in a metaphoric way between the withdrawn glow of fire in the form of the sun and the concealed but light-squelching earth in the form of the land, night belongs most basically, however, to the realm of elemental air. Here, it assumes a shapeless shape, obliterating horizons, softening sharp edges, colonizing once familiar spaces, and blooming into an ambient or encompassing event as opposed to an isolated entity. In the words of Alphonso Lingis, "It extends a duration which moves without breaking up into moments." It arrives "incessantly in a presence which does not mark a residue as past nor outline a different presence to come."[6] In dialogue with all four of the classical elements, night exhibits a special relation to liquidity as well. As Bachelard puts it, night "penetrates the waters, dims the depths of the lake, saturates the pool."[7] Swimming or being at sea very late in the evening, in fact, redoubles and intensifies the experience of the nocturnal deep, subsuming us at once from above and below. Thus, when Pip goes overboard in Melville's *Moby Dick*, he becomes invisible three times over in the omnivorous dark, as the crew looks for a Black boy in a black sea in the very blackness of night. As night dematerializes completely into a mythic realm, it thoroughly devours and digests elemental earth, water, and air, having already snuffed out the bright light of fire. For the dreamer, especially, nights do not possess a history and hence lack a future because they are ostensibly unconnected with one another. "The night dream does not belong to us," declares Bachelard. "It is an abductor, the most disconcerting of abductors: it abducts our being from us."[8] Of the night, psychologist Erich Neumann proclaims it is "the Great Round, a unity of underworld, night sea, and night sky encompassing all living things."[9]

Following the lead of Bachelard, we can distinguish two phenomenal forms of space as the intimate and the exterior. Night appears to chiasmatically conjoin and perceptually fuse—indeed serenely confuse—these two conceptions and realms. It quietly conducts an indistinct "there" to right "here"—to the near-sphere—while casting our more proximate "here" into an immeasurable and occluded "there" . . . over there, somewhere beyond our reach or outside the scope (or telescope) of apprehension. The once apparent horizon crafted by the intersection of earth and sky, or sea and sky, shimmers, fades, and blurs as it is swallowed in the dark. When the night slowly tiptoes in like an encroaching fog or closes upon us more assiduously as it does during an unexpected evening storm or electrical outage, it generates a cloistered sense of space around objects while at once opening up an expansive atmosphere of depth, an "intimate immensity," we might say, using Bachelard's suggestive and near oxymoronic words. Such an affective magnitude, though, may belong more to the rubric of the imaginative daydream than to the categories of discursive thought. Nevertheless, this is phenomenology minus phenomena, insofar as capacious nocturnal space is quality sans substance, not an entity per se but also not quite nothingness. More paradoxically put, it is a nothing (or no thing) that is exquisitely real, even *de-light-ful*, though largely divested of light itself.

From a Levinasian perspective, the night comes close to the experience of the *there is* [*il y a*], of being in general, that "impersonal, anonymous, yet inextinguishable 'consummation' of being, which murmurs in the depths of nothingness itself."[10] During its reign, darkness rules with a queer kind of stifling presence, although we are not engaging with much of anything. Nor are we dealing with pure nothingness. This "universal absence" is actually "an absolutely unavoidable presence." Darkness fills nocturnal space, but it is replete with the "nothingness of everything." And this silent or mute experience can give rise equally to feelings of tranquility or to menacing insecurity, even horror, since "nothing approaches, nothing comes, nothing threatens."[11] No determinate being alights, only an insubstantial ambience of presence that is capable of generating a fear far different from Heideggerian anxiety, which as being-toward-death can at least be understood potentially.

Van Gogh, whose "Starry Night" is rife with swirling clouds, blazing stars, and a cresset moon, felt the night to be more richly hued and more vibrantly alive than the day. In works like "Café Terrace at Night" and "Starry Night Over Rhone," he reveals the night sky and the effects of nocturnal light on water, stone, and air. In a letter to his sister, he beams with enthusiasm for his approach to painting as shown in "Café Terrace":

> Here you have a night painting without black, with nothing but beautiful blue and violet and green and in this surrounding the illuminated area colours itself sulfur pale yellow and citron green. It amuses me enormously to paint the night right on the spot. Normally, one draws and paints the painting during the daytime after the sketch. But I like to paint the thing immediately . . . it is the only way to get away from our conventional night with poor pale whitish light, while even

a simple candle already provides us with the richest of yellows and oranges.[12]

Indeed, artists might follow Van Gogh's lead to consider portraying the night *during* the night if they seek to better understand it and the very nature of light itself. Sandy Gellis has attempted such a task from inside an airplane with nocturnal depictions of the earth that probe the nuances of nightscapes, including "Night Views over Land from Seat 8A," a work that belongs to her elemental "Earth, Air and Water Studies." By contrast, Fuseli's painting, "The Nightmare," shows the richness of a benighted setting through a haunting horse (i.e., mare) who pokes his head between the curtains in the dark to unite fear, sexuality, and night together for one brief visceral moment, shocking the sobering daylight out of us, one might say. And Rembrandt likewise explores brilliantly this dynamic interplay of light, apparent night, and shadow in his famous "Nightwatch," even though the picture is actually and ironically of a day scene. Photography—literally "writing with light"—is another aesthetic means to document the night, though one must take care not to unduly compromise the peace of eventide or the uncanny charms that may emerge in this world. Of the Parisian night, which photographers like Brassaï have masterfully captured, Julian Green comments elegantly:

> In all great cities there are zones which reveal their true character only after dusk. By day they wear a mask, assume a look of amiable good-fellowship that hoodwinks even the astute. . . . But when the nightmists rise, such places wake to life that is a parody of death; the smiling banks turn livid, dark surfaces grow pale and flicker with funereal gleams, coming with evil glee into their own again. It is the street-lamp that works the transformation. Under the first ray of this nocturnal sun, the nightscape dons its panoply of shadows and a malefic alchemy transforms the textures of the visible world. The smooth, sleek trunks of the plane-trees seem suddenly transformed to leprous stone, the cobbled pavement grows darkly mottled like the skin of a drowned man, even the river-water burns with a metallic sheen. There is nothing that does not take on a life-forsaken aspect, sloughing off the honest form it had by daylight. . . . [I]t is as if the stage were set in preparation for some furtive drama. Under the broken gleams of the lamplight buffeted by the wind, amid the odour of death that hovers on the water, this dark domain of silence and the rats is hospitable only to the thief counting his plunder.[13]

The passage from evening to night is the time for philosophy when, as Hegel noticed, the Owl of Minerva takes flight. Introspection blossoms; mental acuity is sharpened; the senses are heightened and abandon their defenses; meditation is made possible.[14] The emerging darkness is restorative, conducive to wonder, even poetic. Before philosophic thought fully flourishes in Greece, night plays a small but significant role in ancient cosmogonies. In Hesiod's dramatic *Theogony*, which sets forth an eighth-century B.C.E. myth of the birth of the world and gods, Night comes into existence from Chaos—the gap between earth and sky—along with Erebos (Darkness), and in turn it parents Hermia (Day) and Aether (bright upper air). But night is often marked with negative associations in early western thought. "The fearsome home of dismal Night [is] / Hidden in dark blue clouds," warns Hesiod, adding "deadly Night . . . brings Sleep, / Brother of Death."[15] Homer likewise speaks of Night as "subduer of gods and men" while Parmenides' draws a sharp division between the Way of Truth (the realm of light) and the Way of Mortal Opinions (the realm of "ignorant night"), which does not really exist ontologically since it concerns what-is-not. In generating this distinction, Parmenides identifies in the process for the first time two distinct "elements" and forms of "matter" with unique attributes: Fire that is light, bright, hot, and dry, and night that is dense, dark, heavy, cold, and wet.[16]

Eastern thought, however, provides a more robust place for the night than the West, which has been beholden to the revelatory power of bright images and a menu of metaphors linking light and truth. In China, Taoism celebrates the mystery and manifestations arising from blackness as a basis for enlightenment: "Darkness within darkness. / The gateway to all understanding." "Know the white, / yet keep to the black," suggests the *Tao Te Ching*.[17] In India, the ancient *Rig Veda* announces in a creation myth that "darkness was hidden by darkness in the beginning; with no distinguishing sign." In the same Sanskrit text, a hymn is dedicated to the goddess of Night, who is sister of Dawn and, interestingly, also a bright deity. The immortal Night—"palpable, black, and painted"—fills the great space between earth and sky.[18] In these and other ways, we acquire wisdom by accepting and understanding that which is normally occluded or withheld from us. "Philosophy needs to recover the darkness that comes not as a menacing stranger but as a gift of the night, the time of philosophizing," Erazim Kohák rightly notes.[19]

Being broad of breast and back, all-inclusive in its coverage, and relentlessly reliable in arriving, night does not discriminate geographically or biologically. Hence, the sun's daily disappearance not only affects our own lives but the behavior, morphology, and physiology of nonhuman organisms as well. Although most creatures sleep at night, moths, raccoons, crickets, badgers, skunks, and desert-dwelling animals are extremely active, confirming the poetic point that "night hath a thousand eyes." Crepuscular beings know and occupy a world little of us comprehend. Every night, twenty million female Mexican free-tailed bats depart from the recesses of Bracken Cave outside of San Antonio, Texas in a dark cloud that continues to unfurl across the landscape for five unending hours. In search of food, they leave their offspring inside the cave and ride winds up to a height of ten-thousand feet before returning to find and nourish their young, accomplishing the complex operations of navigation, predation and feeding all in the blackness of night.[20] Plants also have evolved to function and flourish in periods without sunlight. Some keep their stomata shut during daylight—thus preventing loss of precious water—because they have adapted to keep carbon dioxide as an organic acid in their tissues at night and then to use it in the day for carbohydrate synthesis.

In contrast to the centuries of cultural life when people worked and repaired to rest with the rhythms of the heavens, night is now routinely so illuminated by artificial lighting that in many locales across the United States as few as ten percent of the population is able to observe the twenty-five hundred stars that are visible under normal weather conditions. Nature writer Henry Beston wonders whether our fascination with or addiction to electrical lights has driven the beauty of night back to the oceans and woods and is a symptom of a deeper dread of this primordial sphere. "Primitive folk, gathering at a cave mouth round a fire, do not fear night; they fear, rather, the energies and creatures to whom night gives power; we of the age of machines, having delivered ourselves of nocturnal enemies, now have a dislike of night itself."[21] Whatever truth there is to this claim, nonhuman creatures clearly can become lost or die violent deaths as they attempt to navigate through the built world because of light pollution. Sea turtle hatchlings will continue on their course toward water even if they pursue a light to an abandoned fire that consumes them alive. Birds may begin singing oddly late at night when streetlights are turned on. Human-generated light also affects the ability of migrating birds to navigate because many fly at night, relying on constellations for orientation. Bright lights influence detrimentally their steering, and consequently many thousands crash into windows each year. Fifty thousand birds, in fact, were once killed when they followed a light beam directly into the ground at Warner Robins Air Force Base in Georgia.[22]

By comparison, night invites immersion and participation. It provides voluptuous depth by deleting distance, or at least depriving us of the visual experience of it. While day is beautiful, night is sublime. Or so Kant insisted. The former can "charm" us, but the latter has the capacity to "move" us.[23] Where light clarifies, darkness welcomes ambiguity. Where the day differentiates, night absorbs. Our bodies seem more dispersed and fluid, less discrete and tightly bound, in the ink of midnight. A lantern or flashlight casting its rays into the night serves to illuminate a path but also to separate and isolate us from the embracing dark, calling attention to our individuated or atomized selves. Exploring the dark is a tricky task. By its very nature, light destroys the relative monism of night—as sound disrupts the repose of silence—and ushers one back to the glare of day. Candles, torches, and headlights may open a small portal into the dark—they chisel a tiny window in the hazy wall of night—but, take heed, it is usually advisable to set these appurtenances aside in order to acquire the appropriate kind of vision. In his "Sonnet to Darkness," Michelangelo notes, "Any place that's closed, or any room / that solid walls shut in on every side / gives shelter to the night when daylight comes, / defends her from the sun's ferocious play. / Fire and flame can drive her from her home / and every day she's hunted by the sun, / but even little lights can stain her beauty; / a firefly or two and it is gone."[24] And Shakespeare writes: "Dark night, that from the eye his function takes, / The ear more quick of apprehension makes; / Wherein it doth impair the seeing sense, / It pays the hearing double recompense."[25] With the spirit of these words from *A Midsummer Night's Dream* in mind, I've imagined holding a dinner or party entirely in the dark in order to displace attention away from the gaze of the eyes and to draw it toward the tactile and auditory senses, permitting guests perhaps to know one another in new, more sensual manners.

"Most glorious night! / Thou wert not sent for slumber!," Lord Byron proclaims in "Childe Harold." To night belongs the intoxicating gift of the unconscious—maybe even the wilderness of a collective unconscious—and the possibilities of transgression, lucid dreaming, libidinal desire, romance, and crime. Events unfold under the carapace of darkness that would never show themselves in daylight. Here, we should remember, is where the figures of Hermes, Dionysus and Orpheus reside. David Michael Levin observes:

> The vision of the night draws its strength, not from duality, but from the *integration* of subject and object, the *dissolution* of the ego's defensive boundaries, the *questionableness* of daytime certainties. The night questions our "presence," our self-mastery, our self-possession: we lose our footing, we go astray; . . . our eyes play tricks on us, we see things that "are not there," and we fail to see "the things that are." We encounter our own projections: we *could* go mad.[26]

The cloak of night facilitates, too, the dormant art of getting lost, of wandering off the map—or mapquest.com—without a clear sense of direction but likely discovering new worlds in the process, a fortuitous feat that is becoming ever more difficult in an era of cell phones, global positioning satellites, and computer connectivity. In my days of scouting, our troop leader would reward teenage horseplay at winter camp with long penitent walks into the cavern of night, often becoming lost himself in the woods and fields or on desolate back roads. As an exhausted group, we eventually stumbled our way back to the warmth of the cabin many hours later through happenstance or by dawn's light, usually with a story or two to tell about actual or imagined confrontations with threatening creatures lurking in the shadows of the dark.

Although night is conducive to sleep, our bodies and minds may resist at times. Stricken with a bout of insomnia, I once remained awake continuously for an entire week. Not a single wink of sleep passed my way. Day became a hallucinogenic horror. Darkness and light both were nightmarish. "Insomnia is a wakefulness that suffers from not being able to awaken, to be born," observes

Lingis.²⁷ In fruitless attempts to sleep, I tried everything from medicinal teas to alcohol and incessant exercise, but day was still a constant torment and the calm of night did not arrive until I collapsed unknowingly into its embrace after seven or eight days.

Normally, the day drifts into the dark protractedly, but on occasion, we are witness to an abrupt and Promethean theft of light and the immediate arrival of a temporary but terrifying night. At such unexpected times, the world seems to be hushed by a giant hand that plucks the sun from the broad face of the sky, like a velvet glove removing the eye of a cyclops. Total solar eclipses—which take place when the moon moves between the sun and earth, completely obscuring the view of our closest star—have been known to be exceptionally frightening events, especially when the sun vanishes in the middle of day and the heavens darken in a brief few minutes. The resulting sky, shaded lunar outline, and faint corona of the sun, however, are extremely spectacular to behold, and they can be accompanied now and again by faint solar flares. Herodotus reports that Thales—widely considered to be the West's first philosopher—predicted an eclipse during a war between the Lydians and Medians and that soldiers from both armies laid down their weapons and agreed on a peace as a consequence. Sudden electrical blackouts are capable of creating similar oscillating waves of panic, awe, and quiet calm as communities respond to darkness in unfamiliar ways. Before they went extinct, great flocks of passenger pigeons could also blacken out a blue sky without warning as they flew en masse across the landscape in swaths up to forty miles long, providing opportunities for enterprising individuals to swat them to the ground from rooftops in order to make pigeon pies. And, finally, by way of a much slower pace, day is increasingly benighted by smog in urban areas like Los Angeles and Mexico City for up to two months each year, causing a low-grade anthropogenic night and translucent haze to come into existence.

Nights are generally shorter than days in most geographical areas because the sun is an arc rather than a point, and so it throws a "shadow" of illumination extended in time on the planet. The Earth's atmosphere, moreover, refracts sunlight, which will still reach the ground when the sun is actually below the horizon. Inside polar regions, however, we find continuous daylight in parts of the summer followed by unceasing night in winter. Such periods of prolonged darkness can alter the circadian rhythms of inhabitants, greatly upsetting their sleeping and working patterns. Still, like complete silence, unadulterated darkness is rare, if not nearly impossible, to find. Beston speculates that the closest approximation to it within the natural world might be "the gloom of the forest country buried in night and cloud."²⁸ Surely, however, coal miners sequestered deep inside the Earth must know—and maybe even grow to tolerate or appreciate—something of this profound opacity.

The night, then, is much more than a *tabula rasa* given that it is usually populated with a frenzy of subtle movements, a low-level percussive buzz, the rattle and hum of aerial and terrestrial activity, and even intermittent illumination, as when fireflies glow on its sensuous skin or the "living light" and "wet fire" of glow-in-the-dark phosphorescence smolders and rolls onto the beach from the sea, sometimes invading and lighting up the bodies of sand fleas. If night is an elemental absence, therefore, it is surely a fecund or pregnant negativity. Even if, as Manet declaimed, "black is not a color"—since it absorbs all color and reflects none—the night is still a kind of primordial paste that retains the capacity to paint the atmosphere and mood of a situation in poignant ways. "Black seems to make a colour cloudy, but darkness doesn't," avers Wittgenstein in making a helpful distinction. "A ruby could thus keep getting darker without ever becoming cloudy; but if it became blackish red, it would become cloudy."[29]

In the end, however it is conceptually sliced, elemental night bleeds, bends, and blurs into a trope for finality and death, that great vanquisher of time, as we pass from a notion of physical to metaphysical darkness. In dedicating a series of poems as "Hymns to the Night," Novalis investigates the romantic dimensions of this association. "Are you teasing us, dark Night? What're you holding under your cloak, that grabs so unseen at my soul?," he inquires. In search of an answer, Novalis proceeds to speak about the way unremitting night humanizes us and offers us potentially a "mighty womb of revelations" along with a sizable coffin and ultimate resting place.[30] When Victor Hugo lay dying, he reportedly whispered in his last breaths, "I see black light." As night waxes further across the cosmos, it becomes attenuated, less tangible, more abstract space until at length it dematerializes seemingly into the nothingness of everything—that close kin of an elastic infinity. Diane Ackerman ruminates:

> What we call "night" is the time we spend facing the secret reaches of space, where other solar systems and, perhaps, other planetarians dwell. Don't think of night as the absence of day; think of it as a kind of freedom. Turned away from our sun, we see the dawning of far-flung galaxies. We are no longer sun-blind to the star-coated universe we inhabit. The endless black . . . seems to stretch forever between the stars and even backward in time to the Big Bang.[31]

Night undoubtedly possesses a sequestered reality and richness. Excavating the modes and many degrees of darkness is vital to acquiring ecological wisdom and to learning how to better perceive the world around us. Knowledge of the night enables us to develop a more robust framework of vision that encompasses both bodily sight and an expansive sense of "seeing as"—that is, aesthetic apprehension and interpretation of the ambient environment through the mind's eye. The night and its multiple manifestations—from silken shadows cast by thunderclouds crawling across a verdurous landscape to the last blinking traces of twilight in the city square or the near-incomprehensible and supremely distant black haze of outer space—cannot be captured fully or conveyed solely through philosophical analysis or scientific theory. Darkness, likewise, cannot be reduced to a lack of light or portrayed adequately in terms of the seductions of pure emptiness. It can, however, be evoked, experienced, and transfigured creatively through the medium of poetic and phenomenological language, artistic representation, and, most significantly, explorations by those emboldened enough to venture regularly into its embrace. Understanding the dialectical dance of illumination with darkness invigorates both our encounters with the unfamiliar recesses of wilderness and the more familiar brightness of urban streets, both the confusion brought by dreaming sleep and the seeming clarity afforded by the subsequent day. As to whether we do or "do not go gentle into that good night," following the counsel of Dylan Thomas, the choice may be best left to each one of us. Then again, the night may have something to say about that, too.

— 8 —

In Touch With the Sensuous World

The Reclamation of the Elemental in Continental Philosophy

> The eyes of fire, the nostrils of air, the mouth of water, the beard of earth.
> —William Blake, *The Marriage of Heaven and Hell*

> Why not still proceed over the untamed yet obedient element?
> —Mary Shelley, *Frankenstein*

> Elements are the glue of the world, the vicarious cause that holds reality together, the trade secret of the carpentry of things.
> —Graham Harman, *Guerrilla Metaphysics*

> I came closer to living then than at any other time in my life because I was close to elemental things.
> —Ansel Adams, Letter on his time in Yosemite

With the growing recognition of the widespread disturbance and disruption of the environment, the notion of the elements that first appeared in Presocratic thought as Thales' water, Anaximenes' air, Heraclitus' fire, and Empedocles' *rhizomata* have resurfaced in transfigured form and returned quietly to the philosophical fore. Continental philosophy of the twentieth and twenty-first century has begun, in fact, to critically explore and creatively embrace the biological and built worlds with a new language and fresh perspective.[1] In the process, the recent re-emergence of what we may identify as "elemental philosophy"—the elements in effect having become adjectival—provides the potential to help transform contemporary environmental discourse and address ecological dilemmas.

We have examined previously the role of bodily touch and physical contact and advanced the idea that due to their domestication and technological mediation we have lost, forgotten, or misplaced significant epistemological, ontological, and cultural connections with water, air, earth, and fire, even if they are not necessarily encountered with unencumbered immediacy. For a number of ancient Greek thinkers, touch plays a central role in their frameworks. In general, they stress important elemental links between the physical, psychological, and philosophical dimensions of the environment. In Aristotle's theory, for example, we saw how contact provides a hidden and binding thread through his various accounts and allows us to apprehend and indeed *grasp* a deep sense of place.

We now consider a few additional ways that new ecological, experiential, and philosophical relationships with the elements or elemental phenomena might be forged by pointing to routes that encourage us to be in better touch and closer contact with the ambient air, water, earth, and fire. Each of the thinkers to whom we presently transition works to find or fashion a vocabulary or voice—frequently through the field of phenomenology—in which to express our changing relations to the natural world and the encompassing environment. Rather than interrogating an abstract, elusive, and often overdetermined concept of nature, they generally investigate instead the appearance and showing of the elemental. This Continental thought assists us in generating an alternative kind of environmental sensibility that is attuned to other-than-human realms, as well as our built surroundings. By attending to the avenues these philosophers open up, we might, in turn, form practices and perspectives that enable us to better protect the places we inhabit.

We spoke of Deleuze and Guattari's rhizomes as a creative extension and pragmatic reworking of Empedocles' *rhizomata*. We also brought the philosophy of Husserl, Whitehead, and, to a lesser extent, Derrida, Arendt, and Virilio to bear on our discussion of the elements. Through Gaston Bachelard's archetypal reanimation of earth, air, fire, and water, we now explore the ontological and material aspects of an elemental poetics and reverie. By way of Martin Heidegger's notion of a fourfold, we examine the significance of dwelling and its connection to understanding our place on and within the earth. Via an invocation of Maurice Merleau-Ponty's late work, we touch on the notion of the flesh as a form of corporeal re-*membering* of the enveloping elements. We also take up Luce Irigaray's focus on elemental passions, the air and the gendered body in relation to the classical tetrad. The composite world of natural things and the elemental demands or imperatives they exercise on us necessitates, too, an encounter with the ideas of Emmanuel Levinas and Alphonso Lingis, who both meditate on the meanings of exteriority, elemental sensibilities, and our sensuous surroundings. Finally, as the human mind engages the impersonal forces and natural phenomena that encapsulate us, the insights of Edward Casey and John Sallis provide valuable philosophical suggestions for navigating the elemental landscape and developing the elemental imagination, two integral aspects to a robust environmental aesthetics. Together, these thinkers further facilitate a slow shift from a restricted emphasis on the classical elements of earth, air, fire, and water to an enlarged dialogue with the elemental world.

Elemental Reveries: Bachelard's Poetics

The most creative articulation and sustained investigation of the elements in the twentieth century occurs in the work of French writer Gaston Bachelard when phenomenological concerns meet poetic thought. Bachelard, who was trained in physics, chemistry, and the philosophy of science, dedicates a series of books to surveying each of the four elements in studies involving alchemical symbols, literary criticism, psychoanalysis, scientific history, dream images, and various other forms of reverie. In works ranging in name from *Water and Dreams* and *The Psychoanalysis of Fire* to *Earth and Reveries of Will* and *Air and Dreams*, Bachelard turns to images of matter and the "things themselves"—as Husserl puts it—in order to illustrate the importance of the material imagination and to study "direct ontology" as well as the role of myth and metaphor in philosophy.

Earth, water, air, and fire are capable of revealing and releasing our imaginations, and Bachelard seeks to explore an image—which can serve as the condensation of an entire mind—without reducing it simply to a cause. The elements, which tend either toward material or dynamic poles, resemble Jungian archetypes and exhibit unconscious and subjective dimensions. "Sometimes even when I touch things I still dream of an element," remarks Bachelard.[2] Although speaking at times of a "law" of the four elements, he acknowledges that composite images exist even though they point to a more pure line of filiation, a kind of primal matter. For Bachelard, science and poetry emerge from the same deep source but develop along different axes. Science, however, tries to eliminate or bypass the force of metaphors, which persist nevertheless, and philosophy can only hope to make science and poetry complementary and bring them together as but two contraries.[3]

Our "hunger for images" leads Bachelard to undertake a poetics, phenomenology, and psychoanalysis of the elements. Like the phenomenologist, he admonishes us to set aside our naive belief that objects exist apart from consciousness of them. He strives, however, for an expanded sense of phenomenology, hoping to "reverberate" images, remaining amenable to an "animalized" phenomenology so as to read in new ways, and believing that both poets and painters are preternatural phenomenologists. Like the poet, he explores symbols, images, reverie, and the limits of language, but, as Colette Gaudin has argued, he refuses the enticements of a "Romantic metaphysics that would turn the imagining subject into a mouthpiece for a transcendent being." Thus, the question, "who speaks, the dreamer or the world?," remains unresolved.[4] Like the psychoanalyst, he is interested in desire, dreams, and the unconscious but as Jean-François Lyotard has observed, his recourse to the field concerns word play or what he calls "usurpation." He places nature as well as culture on the couch and performs "psychoanalysis without a patient," to use James Hillman's phrase. One passage—cited earlier but worth repeating in part—captures the connection Bachelard's perspective keeps quietly to the Presocratics and provides a sense of the overall orientation of his work: "In order for a reverie to continue with enough persistence to produce a written work... it must find its *matter*; a material element must give the reverie its own substance, its own law, its specific poetics."[5] As suggested previously, such is the case with the first Western philosophers, who provide thought with pathways through powerful material images: the meditative rhythms of water, the capricious currents of air, the guiding lines of the earth, and the catalytic flames of fire.

Water—Western philosophy's first element—causes us quite naturally to "reflect" and indeed to dream since it inhabits our very eyes. In Bachelard's psycho-physics and psycho-chemistry, it is more transitory, feminine, receptive, and uniform than the other elements. Water illustrates a kind of Heracliteanism, a philosophy of flux and flow. It offers, however, both a concrete and complete ontological or aesthetic viewpoint. Although aquatic poets tend to participate to a lesser degree than earth or fire poets in the watery reality of nature, one still needs to acknowledge the intimacy, depth, and even density of this fluid. "Water always flows, always falls, always ends in horizontal death" even if the smallest detail of color or odor in the liquid can register itself as a symbol for the absorbent mind.[6]

Bachelard admits that within matter contradictions do exist, but they are more likely to be dreamed than perceived. They are akin to "imagined images" or "sublimated archetypes" that go beyond or "sing reality." We are, then, able to distinguish poets of water from one another. Edgar Allan Poe, for example, is a poet of thick, heavy, or dormant water, whereas Algernon Charles Swineburne is an investigator of more fluid and dynamic water.[7] Each strong poet—to use Harold Bloom's phrase—follows the course of an element or material image in his or her language, and each of the four elements has its disciple who creates a framework of "poetic faithfulness." Alternatively, for a philosopher such as Heraclitus, who invokes the force of fire, death is tantamount to water itself.[8] Bachelard examines the aesthetics and psychology of clear water, running water, deep and dead water, maternal water, pure water (i.e., its "morality"), and violent or "muscular" water as he moves deftly between the playful surface and the profound depths of material imagination, and transits across poetic and metapoetic levels of reverie. Along the way, he identifies a Charon complex and an Ophelia complex. Bachelard, too, probes the ways in which water is able to combine via a kind of domestic "marriage" with other elements to form imaginative material compounds, and he shows the connections between the voices of water and the language of humans.

Bachelard proclaims with verve: "Tell me which infinity attracts you, and I will know the meaning of your world. Is it the infinity of the sea, or the sky, or the depths of the earth, or the one found in the pyre?"[9] Arguably, he may carry this classification scheme a step too far toward exclusivity: "He who listens to the stream cannot be expected to understand the one who hears the singing of the flame."[10] Bachelard shows, in any event, the close relation that exists between the materiality of things and the near palpability of words so that, for example, the language of water retains "the lesson of the stream."[11] Indeed, water itself is said both to see and to dream, an image he explores when considering bodies of water as eyes of the earth, an idea we also find in the writings of Thoreau.

Bachelard takes up, in turn, the image of the burning, transfiguring, paradoxical, and perishing flame that has occupied the human imagination from the myth of Prometheus, the philosophy of Heraclitus, and the religious imagery of Zoroastrianism to the arsonist's sexual fantasies, the alcoholic's "fire water," and the fire power inherent in the technology of warfare or modern holocausts. He reveals the hypnotic effect that fire exercises on the mind, thus making the contemplative or pensive figure suitable for psychoanalytic investigation. Consequentially, fire is as much a social as a natural reality. It is both universal and intimate such that it "smolders in a soul more surely than it does under ashes." "It rises from the depths of the substance and offers itself with the warmth of love. Or it can go back down into the substance and hide there, latent and pent-up, like hate and vengeance."[12] Unlike other phenomena, we can predicate the values of both good and evil to fire because it is capable seemingly of contradicting itself.

Bachelard diagnoses briefly a variety of perennial "complexes" (or myths) associated with fire, including those named after Prometheus (fire and respect), the poet Novalis (fire and prehistory), the writer E.T.A. Hoffman (spontaneous combustion) and one that he terms the "Empedocles complex," the destruction of the human soul and the world by fire. Fire reveals a desire for change, a drive to accelerate the flow of time, even so as to carry all of life to an end or hereafter.[13] As represented by Hölderlin and the poetic tradition, Empedocles plunges to his fiery death in Mount Etna as a leap of faith, which is thought to testify to the power of his wisdom. But if the entranced individual hears and then heeds the call of the funereal flame, the destruction is also a beckoning toward possible renewal. Bachelard notes that during his work on the psychoanalysis of fire, he learned that all images of interior fire—hidden, smoldering, and unseen fire; that is fire which necessitates metaphor—are also images of life.[14] The flame—that "stem of fire"—is a vertical axis of reverie: "To play with being and non-being, starting from a trifle, from a flame—perhaps merely an imagined flame—is for a philosopher a beautiful instance of illustrated metaphysics."[15]

The element of air, Anaximenes' beginning point, also occupies Bachelard's critical faculties. Air is, in one sense, extremely attenuated matter, but it is movement and metaphor more than materiality that interests Bachelard in his consideration of aerial images and the freedom they promise through both external and internal mobility. By way of the medium of air—that "hormone" of the imagination that enables us to grow psychologically—he examines flight and imaginary journeys, ascension, verticality and falling, the blue sky, constellations and clouds, wind and breath. Air has its own physical and imagined geography or, more accurately, aeolian regions, and Bachelard proceeds to drift, dock, decamp, and dream his way through these shifting and often indeterminate spheres and tiers. Hurricanes, for example, embody violent or wrathful air and display pure motion and "elemental fury," whereas clouds offer amorphous or "imaginary matter for a lazy modeler" and suggest "reverie without responsibility."[16] Nebula provide for constant change, adulterated as they are by both milk and cloud—think here of the Milky Way. Breath is the font of poetic inspiration and exuberance, the cauldron of rhythm that makes poetry a "pneumatic reality."[17] As in his other studies, Bachelard points us toward an active, dynamic relation with the elements—none are static or inert—that calls for engagement and participation in the natural world rather than disinterested contemplation or an impractical withdrawal from it. Here, for example, is the sky "waiting to be touched by a hand / Of fabulous childhood."[18]

Of particular interest to elemental thought is his reading of Nietzsche as the poet-philosopher of air *par excellence*. Although great writers call upon the images of all the elements, Nietzsche is the paradigmatic vertical poet, a figure of heights, summits, and ascensions. Bachelard rejects in turn the element of earth because Nietzsche's images are not wrought from clay, sponge, fields, or soft ground; the element of water, which is too servile; and the element of fire because, although existing in his work, it has a sudden but not substantial or subtending presence there. Instead, Nietzsche is the aerial poet because air is the very stuff of human freedom and the substance of great joy. It liberates us temporarily from a dependency on matter. Air is the element where one acts in the open, even when one is a predator. Bachelard's interpretation is borne out in part and could conceivably be bolstered further by references to Nietzsche's frequent references to scent and odors that he abjures; silence that he values and upholds; coolness that lends his thought a sublime indifference; height where he finds his notion of the eternal recurrence of the same; flight to which he aspires as respite from the crowd; and lightness that he advises us to cultivate in our quest to overcome and slay the spirit of gravity.[19]

Finally, Bachelard focuses on the elemental imagination of earth, devoting one part of a diptych study to introverted dimensions of depth and repose and the other to the extroverted aspects of human labor.[20] He stresses earth's dynamism and its creative potential, which is counterbalanced by an opposite telluric tendency toward destruction and the possibility of renewal. We need to remember that the earth bears us into the world but eventually buries us as well. We all possess imaginatively "a material image of *ideal earthen matter*, a perfect synthesis of yielding and resistance, a marvelous equilibrium of the forces of acceptance and of refusal."[21] From such a notion of balance, which we can internalize in our laboring hands, Bachelard shows we derive our instinctive or intuitional judgments with respect to something being either too hard or too soft.

Toward the goal of illuminating the many material and imagined forms of earth, Bachelard proceeds to examine literary and poetic encounters with rock, metal, minerals, mountains, crystals, and pearls. He also takes up the "psychology of gravity" in order to show the profound power of the terrestrial imagination and its relation to both falling and flight. The Atlas Complex thus represents a human striving to surmount the pull of gravity and to bear weight, as when climbers or hikers carry a heavy pack on a journey with an odd sort of pleasure. Images of earthen matter generate a muscular enjoyment when we choose to work with them, encouraging an active relation to the elemental world. Earth, more than the other three elements, nevertheless, resists the efforts of our hands and our will and becomes along the way an objective partner to human shaping, sculpting, smithing, metallurgy, or what we could call more generally terra-forming. At the same time, the terrestrial mind constructs a realm of images involving the deep interiority of things, which often serve like places of refuge as, for example, caves, houses, and wombs. Earth, in fact, is a kind of flesh that "responds muscle for muscle to humans who think of their lives as part of nature."[22] Here we see a hint of the implicit connections that arise between the body and the sensuous world and that are developed further by Merleau-Ponty and some eco-phenomenologists.

Bachelard delves, too, into the nuances of indeterminate earth and soft matter such as mud, which is painted by our imaginations as a primitive and originative stuff, a plastic and primordial substance. It is akin to paste, clay, dough, and molten metal. In this regard, a potential link can be made to fecal matter, an earthy and ecological substance that has often animated the human psyche. In dreaming of the hidden power of substances such as earth, which is projected into our unconscious, we conjure, according to Bachelard, our own secret being. Bachelard's study of terrestrial phenomena suggests, a depth psychology that can be traced eventually to Heraclitus, who teaches that the real constitution of things is given to concealment: "*physis kryptesthai philei.*"[23] Nature—especially the earth—loves to hide.

Bachelard's elemental explorations are germane, then, to a broad form of cultural ecology that unites the material and figurative realms. He invokes the idea of a botanical graft as a point of inquiry for his investigations, where culture marks itself—graft is from *graphein*, meaning to write—upon the natural world, serving as the place of intersection for the human and nonhuman, and thus acknowledging that organic metaphors (e.g., trees and roots) are always cut with social tools as well as being born of the imagination. His primary metaphor for the imagination is botanical—"imagination is a tree"—because it is able to conjoin the above (sky) and the below (earth) as well as the real and the dreamed.[24] It is an object of integration because it can be everywhere at once. Bachelard's arboreal image is expansive and inclusive of roots and boughs; it becomes the cosmological tree, the form that symbolizes the universe. The tie to the Empedoclean tradition of elemental thought becomes even more direct when he speaks of the contiguity and connection of trees with roots. A root is a mysterious, subterranean, and inverted tree.[25] At the boundary of the worlds of earth and air, the root—part serpent, part claw; part hair, part rock; part wood, part filament—moves sluggishly in two directions, depending on whether our dreams send it downward toward the dead or bend and bear it to the heavens.

There is some reason for believing, as critic Colette Gaudin does, that Bachelard favors the optimism of verticality (e.g., trees and flames), but this interpretation ignores the extent to which the tree is capable of becoming mobile and horizontal roots or, alternatively, roots blossoming into a tree. Both like and unlike the more *and* less "radical" understanding of rhizomes by Deleuze and Guattari—which are markedly distinct from the images of roots they criticize—Bachelard's botanical images of imagination partake to a degree in multiplicity and heterogeneity. "To participate through reveries in the text," he says, "we may replace the conjunction *or* with the conjunction *and*. The *or* departs from the fundamental laws of oneiric life. In the unconscious, *or* does not exist."[26] In these and other ways, Bachelard reveals that earth—like the remaining perennial elements—might fertilize our theories and thoughts, and nourish our dreams and desires. In creatively retrieving air, fire, water, and earth through the insights of phenomenology, psychoanalysis, and poetic criticism, Bachelard bequeaths them to us in fresh and startling perspectives that allow us to see each again as if for the initial time, in ways they might have first appeared to the Presocratics or may still alight in the world for an imaginative child playing in a sandbox, chasing gulls at the seashore, navigating a kite in a brisk wind, or poking a stick contemplatively in the embers of a campfire.

Elemental Dwelling: Heidegger's Fourfold

The elemental thought of ancient Greece is also transformed indirectly twenty-five hundred years hence in the later work of Martin Heidegger—particularly his essays, "Building Dwelling Thinking" and "The Thing"—into a fourfold or Quadrate. Heidegger's expression, *das Geviert*, is past participle of *vieren*, meaning literally "to four," and it maintains a close relation to poetic traditions, as do ideas of the perennial elements more generally. As a notion with implicit environmental dimensions or implications, it can assist in shedding some additional light on the philosophically sheltered elements and help to reveal the centrality of the practice of dwelling to our daily lives.

Part of the significance of Heidegger's conception of the fourfold lies in the ways in which *things* themselves can potentially call forth a world into being. In other words, it is not simply humans who are capable of disclosing or revealing an environment. Bridges, jugs, trees, and even shoes, for example, can also assemble a world around themselves. There is, as well, an element of spontaneous organization to this process (i.e., this "fouring" and "worlding").[27] That is, the world is in some sense self-organizing and capable of unfolding from itself. The fourfold, moreover, is characterized by unity-in-diversity or, to put differently, a wholeness through difference—a notion that suggests complementarity, participation, and differentiation but also ontological parity, again like Empedocles' "roots," each of which rules in turn. As in his most important philosophical contribution, *Being and Time*, there exists a unity of Being and world—that is, being-in-the-world and, we might add, being *on-the-earth*—as well as a unity of the four "elements" in the fourfold. In short, Heidegger shows the "simple oneness of the four" that occurs through dwelling. As he says, when we speak of one, we also speak tacitly of the other three. There is thus a presence in absence at work, too. "In saving the earth, in receiving the sky, in awaiting the divinities, in initiating mortals, dwelling occurs as the fourfold preservation of the fourfold."[28]

When we look at the individual "elements" of the fourfold, we find that earth, "the serving bearer," is often described like Heidegger's reading of the Greek conception of *physis* (nature), that is, as blossoming, growing, rising up, and issuing forth.[29] The earth is "self-dependent," "effortless and untiring," that which provides a shelter, anchor, and orientation for beings.[30] Sky, by contrast, is the "vaulting path" of the sun, the course of the moon, weather, and clouds. The divinities are "beckoning messengers" of a godhead, where deities appear or withdrawal. This "element" is perhaps the most difficult of the four to grasp in naturalistic terms but, among other things, it might be assimilated to the presence of value or meaning in the world insofar as the divinities are conceived as eternal and abiding. Mortals—the last stead in the Quadrate—are humans, or individuals who die. In one important sense, mortals are those whom Heidegger has fashioned as *Dasein*, his special term for human existence and "being there."

Heidegger holds that it is through the "round dance" of appropriation (*Ereignis*)—possibly his own version of Plato's *chora*-graphy—that we mortals bind ourselves to the world. In this view, when we invoke earth, sky, divinities, or mortals, respectively, we think of the other three, but we do not necessarily realize their unity, something that occurs only through inhabitation. Heidegger shows that we belong in the fourfold though dwelling, by which he also means preserving and sparing. First, mortals dwell insofar as we "save the earth," meaning to set it free into its own presencing. "To save" (*retten*) implies not only to rescue or conserve but also to preserve and protect, in short to "let be." It suggests a new comportment and sensibility to things such that as earthly inhabitants we become genuine caretakers. Heidegger thereby advances a forceful environmental position: "To save the earth is more than to exploit it or even wear it out. Saving the earth does not master the earth and does not subjugate it."[31]

Second, mortals dwell when we receive the sky as sky. Here Heidegger suggests that we leave the sun, stars, and moon to their journeys and allow the seasons to their respective blessings or inclemency. In other words, we should not seek recklessly to turn night into day, for example. However, from emerging plans for the "greening" of Mars at the arguably more benign end of the spectrum to polluting the atmosphere and damaging the ozone layer at the other dangerous end, we do not appear to be heeding such philosophical or environmental advice. Most of us are, in short, insulated and sheltered from wind, rain, night, and snow to such an extent that they cannot appear to us in their own modes of existence or peculiar "presencing" but only as potential use objects, energy sources, or mere encumbrances and inconveniences.[32]

Third, mortals dwell in awaiting the divinities as divinities. Here Heidegger seems to recommend listening and patience, attending to what is truly valuable (or perhaps even sacred if we use a religious vernacular) in the physical world in its own manifestation, or hierophany. But, he implies, we must wait for signs of such appearances and respect indications of their absence. Given, as it seems, that we have increasingly fewer common cultural stories, dances, and songs to guide us to special dwelling places in the landscape or bind us to the earth, such perseverance and attentiveness may be all the more important. Heidegger suggests, moreover, that we should not attempt to make "gods" of ourselves as is almost possible today with, for example, the advent of trans-species genetic engineering or worship idols as we are given to do in our predominant social relationship to high technology.[33]

Finally, mortals dwell in that we initiate our own nature—our mortality—which means being capable and presumably cognizant of death as death. Here, the "good death" of which Heidegger speaks stands in contrast with the existential anxiety that imbues it in *Being and Time*. Death is central to our very self-understanding and to a robust apprehension of Being. Death is our ultimate limit and, moreover, it is related intimately to the Heideggerian conception of care (*Sorge*), which is potentially applicable to environment concerns. In Heidegger's thought, however, death is almost always associated with particular individuals, single isolated *Dasein*, for it is presented as an inescapable, looming fact that each of us must face alone. Death, in this depiction, seems to separate humans rather than to bind us together or tether us closely to the land, place, and earth.

But if death is something toward which we invariably experience dread *individually*, it is reasonable to suggest that the possibility of the death of the entire human community, animal species, or even the animate earth itself should quite rightly induce an analogous but *collective* anxiety, a deep expression of ecological care and concern. Such a realization might lead us not so much to face our singular deaths resolutely, as Heidegger counsels, but to face and face-off with the very forces that threaten us, the earth and its inhabitants with a final ending, which would really amount to an *end to birth*.[34] Through threats of ecological and social collapse raised by climate change, resource depletion, proliferation of unbridled technology, and simplification of the natural world, it is just this very event, or series of events, with which we may be confronted. We humans are the very source and cause of an ongoing massive planetary extinction that may decimate a quarter or more of all species in the next fifty years because of anthropogenic habitat destruction, invasive species transport, pollution, overconsumption of natural resources, and human overpopulation.[35] Our own lives, however, are not divorced from these deaths, and by ignoring this fact, we continue to dwell unrealistically or "inauthentically" to use Heideggerian language.[36] While acknowledging that Heidegger does not include nonhuman animals (or plants) within his conception of mortality because they only "perish" rather than being conscious of death as such, humans nonetheless are only one entity in the fourfold and the last at that.[37]

Dwelling, in sum, is what Heidegger styles as the fourfold preservation of the fourfold. As a form of preservation, dwelling can be interpreted as bringing the inhabited Earth under our watchful care. This idea gestures toward the practice of stewarding the planet—a notion that he calls "shepherding" elsewhere—and it shares some affinities with the Christian and Judaic traditions insofar as they recognize and respond to environmental issues.[38] As such, it reveals a tension within Heidegger's thought between a biocentric disposition (letting beings or things be) and a more anthropocentric disposition (tending, caring for, and shepherding the Earth). In either case, the fourfold remains present because dwelling is always a "staying with" things. Dwelling is the singular way that the fourfold can be brought into its unity. It is only when the things themselves qua things are left to be in their presencing that the fourfold is attained. In terms of a more exact comparison with the classical theory of the elements, there is ostensibly a rough correlation between ancient Greek notions of earth and air on the one hand and Heidegger's view of earth and sky on the other hand, and a less direct comparison between fire and the divinities. What appears to be missing is an analogue for water, although—as seen shortly—Irigaray argues that the absent element in Heidegger's thought is the invisible air.[39]

Heidegger's phenomenological description of a simple stone bridge serves as an illustrative example of a thing gathering in the fourfold and exhibits the way that building—which we might best think of as a gerund rather than a static noun—can belong ecologically to the practice of dwelling, even though he limits himself to building in the relatively narrow sense of construction. A stone bridge is similar to a Greek temple on the shore of the sea—which Heidegger describes in his "Origin of the Work of Art" essay—in terms of the way it assembles an elemental world, although it is unlike it in the sense that the art object and the use object have merged in the everyday world. However, a stone bridge is unlike a hydroelectric plant on a river—which he invokes in "The Question Concerning Technology"—because in the latter instance moving water is revealed as a merely a resource for human use. The bridge is, in short, an example of a built object but also for Heidegger an instantiation of good technology in that it coalesces a world and "lets things be."

For Heidegger, a bridge does not merely connect the opposing banks of the stream. Rather, the banks emerge only because of this overpass, which brings stream, bank, and land into each other's *neighborhood*—that is, it makes them "dwell near" to one another as this word suggests through its etymology. A bridge is able to gather the elemental fourfold in its own way, just like a jug of water resting on a table or a jar positioned on a hilltop might do in a different dwelling place, as in Wallace Stevens' poem, "Anecdote of the Jar."[40] It unites earth (the landscape or the stream that is left to run its course), sky (the clouds and weather), mortals (who come and go upon it), and divinities (who find a passage that crosses before them). In Heidegger's view, this congregation occurs whether or not we think of and give thanks for such presencing, as he plays on the linguistic and psychological threads through thinking and thanking.

What is lacking in this description of the bridge—in addition to an explicit connection with the elemental waters and the fire of technology used to forge the foundation—and absent more generally from his thinking of things, is a recognition of the power and hence politics that inhere in or at least surround most artifacts. What is it about a viaduct or a stone bridge in particular, we should ask, that is vastly different from the way a nuclear power plant lying on the shores of Lake Erie, for example, sets up or gathers in a surrounding world?[41] And how should we attempt to reconcile Heidegger's notion of a fourfold with his position articulated in other writings that our destiny is bound up with the unfolding of modern technology, which "devours the earth"?[42] These matters, in short, point to a complex problematic involving the politics of technology and its relation with environmental and elemental issues.

As to the latter question, the elemental fourfold or *Geviert* seems to find its antipode or perhaps deprivation in Heidegger's notion of *Gestell*. In everyday German, *das Gestell* signifies a skeleton or framework, and it is usually translated as "enframing."[43] In Heidegger's particular usage, it gathers together the family of verbs associated with *stellen* (to place or set) such as *bestellen* (to order or command), *verstellen* (to block or disguise), *herstellen* (to produce), *darstellen* (to represent or show), *vorstellen* (to introduce, represent or imagine), *sicherstellen* (to secure), and the like. Technology as *Gestell* assembles and orders a distinct social configuration in calling it forth. Enframing is thereby a mode of revealing but its rule is dangerous to the extent that the world is shown technologically as resource, or what he terms "standing reserve" (*Bestand*). "The earth now reveals itself as a coal mining district, the soil as a mineral desert." Nature comes to be understood as pure "presence at hand" (to use the phrasing of *Being and Time*), an object of knowledge or a great gas station to be tapped as a source of energy for industry.[44] When so understood, "the Nature which 'stirs and strives,' which assails us and enthralls us as landscape, remains hidden."[45] In brief, the elements of the fourfold cannot set themselves forth. They remain occluded, concealed, forgotten, or domesticated in a largely human setting.

Thus, the *Geviert–Gestell* contrast also characterizes a dramatic opposition that emerges between, on the one hand, the poetic, meditative, spontaneous, and natural and, on the other hand, the technological, calculative, utilitarian, and artificial. Like the elements, both notions—along with Heidegger's articulation of the historical emergence of a world-picture or *Weltbild*—acknowledge the primacy of a configuring frame and creative fourfold, even if *Geviert* and *Gestell* clearly possess very different relations to their mode of gathering and disclosure.[46] Heidegger, in effect, raises the possibility of thinking about, working toward or waiting for a period where we witness the difficult transition from the present age as enframed by the power of technology and represented as a picture—consider the omnipresent frames of televisions, cameras, and computers in everyday life—to one where we are able to dwell more poetically and sustainably.

Appropriately, Heidegger begins his philosophical questioning by returning to Aristotle's four causes (material, formal, moving, and final) as a way to shed light on technology represented as an instrumental means. In his view, the four causes are co-present and cooperative agents that are responsible for the existence of worldly things.[47] They bring something into appearance, set it forth into presencing (*An-wesen*), and thus are a form of *poiesis* (poetic creation). The four causes are portrayed as being "at play" in this bringing-forth (*Hervorbringen*), and their phenomenological description resembles Heidegger's understanding of *Geviert* in a number of ways, including their coresponsibility and mutual indebtedness; their belonging-togetherness; their relation to *poiesis* and *physis* (considered to be the highest form of *poiesis*); their fourfold nature; and their manner of occasioning and revealing. In all these dimensions, including the stress on ontological and material "play," we are called back creatively—if not critically—to the ancient Greek and perennial conceptions of the four elements.

Heidegger, in fact, returns again and again to "roots" in another sense in his recourse to etymology and in particular to ancient Greek root words, as he attempts to show the loss—one could say domestication—which has occurred through time and translation. "Roman thought," he maintains, "takes over the Greek words without a corresponding, equally authentic, experience of what they say, without the Greek word. The rootlessness of Western thought begins with this translation."[48] Here, within the realm of language—what Heidegger calls "the house of Being"—the elements understood as letters that form syllables, constitute words (Heidegger repeatedly separates and hyphenates words into their components), and eventually spell the environing world are placed under scrutiny, as they were in a different manner by Plato. Heidegger even posits that "the ultimate business of philosophy is to preserve the *force of the most elemental words*" in which being manifests itself.[49] A typical example of this etymological investigation occurs in the essay "Building Dwelling Thinking" and this chain of words (*Bauen Wohnen Denken*), which are linked by a lack of caesura. Heidegger suggests that a way of inhabiting the world and finding a home can be found or even heard in language itself when one proceeds to the root of things. To build is to dwell, and we are able to attain to dwelling only through building.[50] Heidegger then relates *bauen* (building), which he associates with the old English and high German word *buan*, meaning to dwell, and proposes that *bin* belongs to *bauen* such that one can say "Ich bin" (I am) and "Du bist" (you are) as "I dwell" and "you dwell." Dwelling, thereby, is considered the most elemental character of Being, and a deeper problem lies not simply with a lack of dwelling units and adequate housing but in our forgetting or failure to dwell deeply so as to experience place and the encompassing land fully.

Notions of roots and rootlessness and, correspondingly, home and homelessness, come to the fore with frequency in still another premonition in Heidegger's later thought, and these outcroppings often are linked with his sense of an ecological and technological crisis, although he does not designate it explicitly as such. In 1955, for example, at an address delivered in his hometown of Messkirch, he speaks of homeland and asks, "Does not the flourishing of any genuine work depend upon its roots in a native soil?"[51] Heidegger proceeds to assert that "the rootedness . . . of man is threatened today at its very core"[52] as he searches for a "ground and foundation" for a "new autochthony" (*Bodenständigkeit*).[53] In fact, quoting the poet Johann Peter Hebel, he suggests that humans are akin to botanical beings: "We are plants which—whether we like to admit it to ourselves or not—must with our roots rise out of the earth in order to bloom in the ether and to bear fruit."[54]

Heidegger is wrestling in this regard with the loss, forgetting or recession of ground as *Boden* (soil), *Heimat* (home), and *Ort* (place) and with the problem of grounding, as in philosophical *Grund* (ground), *Gründung* (foundation), *Ur-rund* (primal ground), and *Ab-grund* (abyss). In his *Introduction to Metaphysics*, as in *Being and Time*, he concerns himself with the most basic or fundamental question (*Grundfrage*), which deals itself with the nature and ground (*Grund*) of Being. In so doing, he repeatedly and persistently seeks to uncover and recover that which lies in depth, underlies all else or, in brief, is at the root and source of things. In attempting to bring this darkness to light, he is compelled to unearth and pile before us a mountain of words sharing the same root word, and in particular *Grund*. An example: "This question with its Why does not move on one level or surface only but penetrates the underlying ['*zu-grunde liegenden*'] realms to their ultimate reaches, to the limits; it is opposed to all surfaces and all shallowness and strives for the depth; as the widest question it is also of all deep questions the deepest."[55]

Heidegger's appeal to a *radical* solution (i.e., one that goes to the roots) is, of course, not immune to problems, especially the charge of nostalgia and a privileging or mythologizing of origins, which is apparent both in the ontological and existential dimensions of *Being and Time*.[56] Heidegger instructs us habitually to return, to go back, and to go home again in order to uncover the original or primordial (*ursprünglich*) "meaning of Being," which has been concealed by the tradition he hopes to dismantle and destroy. But in counseling a going under (to roots) as a going back (return) in this way, he implies that some original, unmediated, pure, or authentic experiences and meanings in fact exist, or at one time existed, a point that has been effectively contested by a host of recent thinkers and that we questioned earlier with regard to the elements and elemental roots (*rhizomata*) in particular.[57] His root metaphors, which often remain attached to a latent commitment to foundations, are evident in a range of works, including "What is Metaphysics"[58] (where he suggests that the discipline of philosophy is like a tree which grows from the main root of metaphysics and branches into the sciences); "Letter on Humanism"[59] (where he writes that "To speak in images it [the remembrance of Being] does not tear out the root of philosophy. It digs up the ground and plows the soil for it"); and *Being and Time*. He opens this last work by proclaiming:

> At the beginning of our investigation it is not possible to give a detailed account of the presuppositions and prejudices which are constantly *reimplanting* and fostering the belief that an inquiry into Being is unnecessary. They are *rooted* in ancient ontology itself, and it will not be possible to interpret that ontology adequately until the question of Being has been clarified and answered and taken as a clue—at least, if we are to have regard for the *soil* from which the basic ontological concepts developed.[60]

To his credit, Heidegger seeks to avoid foundational philosophy (*Ursprungphilosophie*) in his later thought even though root and tree metaphors still proliferate, and it is here that an eco-philosophical connection can most fully be made.[61] The quasi-elemental *Geviert*, as a unity with fourfold polyvalence, avoids grounding, explanation, and causality in any traditional sense. The world, in other words, is not based on a ground that is external to it, and no single "element" can provide such a foundation. The concealing-revealing *in* the world is a groundless ground because it is *of* this world. The fourfold is moreover—when represented as a pictogram whose center is Being and whose four corners or sides (earth, sky, gods, and mortals) are linked by lines passing through a midpoint—not a "crossing out" (*Durchstreichung*) as it is when he writes Being under erasure, but instead a relating, unifying "crossing through" (*Durchkreuzen*).[62]

Heidegger has been called the "metaphysician of ecologism"—an awkward phrase used by George Steiner—and there is some plausibility to this claim, for he offers a broad environmental *ethos* as opposed to a more narrow, humanistic ethic, speaks of "saving" the earth (meaning to free it into is own essence), challenges modern technology and science as stripping nature of its significance, and presents humans as shepherds or stewards of the earth, among other suggestive directions.[63] Recently, there have been attempts to develop a Heideggerian ecology and to associate Heidegger with the environmental philosophy and movement known as deep ecology.[64] Such work has proved to be productive, interesting, and often fruitful even if there are limitations to this application of ideas.[65] We have seen that Heidegger's thought is significant for its consideration of dwelling, inhabitation, and place—fundamental issues in environmental theory and practice—and the implicit link in his work between these subjects and the elements. In this regard, we routinely "take shelter from the elements" but generally fail to appreciate the full depth of dwelling and how dwelling-places are related to the surrounding air, water, earth, and enclosed fire. Therein lies one of the merits of recalling and reexamining the relatively sheltered tradition of the elemental world and the four elements themselves.

Elemental Flesh: Merleau-Ponty's Re-membering

In the late work of phenomenologist Maurice Merleau-Ponty, the notion of the elements also makes a cryptic return, once again in the form of surviving "fragments" of uncompleted writing—like the extant shards of the Presocratics—and in particular his working notes to *The Visible and the Invisible*. Merleau-Ponty points us indirectly toward the ancient Greeks, although he does not usually mention them individually by name. A suggestive notion in his philosophy is "the flesh" (*la chair*), a general name for Being and the bond between body and world. The flesh, however, should not be best thought of as matter, mind or either a physical or mental substance. In order to identify and speak of it more properly, Merleau-Ponty requires "the old term 'element'" as it was used in reference to air, water, fire, and earth—that is, as a "general thing, midway between a sort of incarnate principle that brings a style of being wherever there is a fragment of being."[66] In other words, flesh, which has no true philosophical name, is more like an " 'element' of Being." It is the medium of subjects and objects, as opposed to something atomic. Flesh is, in short, most like an element in that it serves as a "concrete emblem" of a way of being.[67]

Aristotle construed the four elements as sense-perceived contraries of the tactile class, and he argued that the medium of touch (*aphe*)—an intermediary between organ and object—is the flesh, as it had been for some of the later Presocratics and Plato.[68] This is so because bodies cannot act or be acted upon unless they are in contact with one another—literally in-touch. In Empedocles' sense perception theory, one also finds a meeting between an element within us and a similar element outside us in the physical environment. Thus, Merleau-Ponty's presentation of flesh in elemental terms is understandable, for he seeks as well a robust connection between the visible and invisible, endeavoring to express our living ties with the natural world.[69] In this regard, he points to the "forgetfulness of the earth"—as Heidegger explores the forgetting of being (*Seinsvergessenheit*)—which serves as the "ground" [*sol*] of human experience and the basis of spatiality and "homeland."[70]

Merleau-Ponty's "recycling" of the elements occurs appropriately enough in a series of unfinished philosophical remains such as the following:

> Perception is not first a perception of things, but a perception of *elements* (water, air . . .) of *rays of the world*, of things which are dimensions, which are worlds, I slip on these "elements" and here I am in the world, I slip from "subjective" to Being.

> For me they [Being and the imaginary] are "elements" (in Bachelard's sense), that is, not objects—but fields, subdued being, non-thetic being, being before being.
> I am visible from elsewhere, and if I and the cube are together caught up in one same "element" (should we say of seer, or of the visible?).
> [Y]ellow becomes a universe or an element.
> Thus the painting is a "world" by opposition to the unique and real world—In any case, it forms a world with all the other paintings—the same sensible elements signify something else there than in the prosaic world.⁷¹

The etymology of "member" derives from the Latin, *membrum*, and is akin to the Gothic *mimz* (flesh), the Greek *meninx* (membrane) and *meros* (thigh), and the Sanskrit *amsa* (flesh). In all these linguistic forms, the basic meaning is thus "flesh." Recalling, reanimating and re-*membering*—fleshing out again—the elements and the vital role they play in our lives and the lives of other beings, then, entails giving attention to the lived body in its flesh-bound forms. In a very deep sense, the environment—as Merleau-Ponty, some deep ecologists, and selected Eastern philosophers have skillfully shown—is bound closely with our living bodies and our changing identities.

Merleau-Ponty develops phenomenology in a different direction than had Heidegger, guiding it through and linking it with the body, which Descartes differentiated sharply from mental processes and thereby disparaged, and which Heidegger largely ignores or marginalizes. Merleau-Ponty begins with the fact that we discover ourselves as embodied creatures living in the midst of a changing world. One's self is not narrowly delimited by the boundaries of one's skin but is spread instead over a region—what Heidegger terms a *field of care*—that extends into the ambient environment as far as one's concerns stretch. In contrast to Descartes' withdrawal *from* the natural world in a near futile attempt to locate stability and certainty, phenomenology starts, as we noted earlier, *in* the world and consciousness is ever *of* the world, rather than a solitary mind. It thereby strives to bring worldly things to light and to allow them to be comprehended as directly as possible by avoiding unnecessary presuppositions, revisiting a world prior to knowledge but basic to it, and describing appearances with a rigorous methodology.

Merleau-Ponty elucidates a variety of concepts that might be employed potentially to further cultivate an ecological sensibility or to address philosophical *aporias* related to the environment, even if these ideas were not deliberately planned as such. He advances, for example, the notion of *phenomenal field*, a term that breaks down a stark dichotomy between earth and world—as found in Heidegger's work—and perhaps also the apparent opposition between nature and culture. A phenomenal field is pre-objective and resembles an atmosphere or *Gestalt*, while bearing similarities to the quasi-field theories of ecological science.[72] Likewise, *landscape* provides the "setting" for our lives and functions as a third term between earth and world, eventually replacing phenomenal field. Finally, Merleau-Ponty speaks of forms of *inhabitation* that allow for a place-based perspective, and he surmises about *transcendental geology*, a possible effort to surmount the difficulties inherent in an ontology or metaphysics of grounding.[73] Although remaining suggestive rather than fully articulated and "fleshed out," Merleau-Ponty's notion of the flesh and attendant ideas still help us to re-engage and re-imagine elemental philosophy in helpful ways.[74]

Elemental Sensibility: Levinas on Enjoyment

In his bellwether work, *Totality and Infinity*, Emmanuel Levinas explores the elements in relation to concepts such as sensibility, the domicile, physical things, and human enjoyment. In his view, we discover ourselves in a world of elements and alien objects that are other than ourselves but nevertheless not negations of us. We take pleasure in worldly things, which assume form within a milieu or medium such as air or earth through which we touch, recognize, and alter them. Levinas rightly identifies how an elemental medium is essential to the constitution of objects yet is able to maintain its own relative density, independence, and exteriority. It contains and envelops, although it is not contained or enveloped itself. An element is a quality sans substance, and for Levinas it seems to include phenomena and forces like the wind, sky, air, earth, and sea, which he characterizes as sufficient unto themselves. Unlike things, which might become property, the elemental is not possessed or capable of possession. Earth, light, and sea, for example, are no one's belongings. "The navigator who makes use of the sea and wind dominates these elements but does not thereby transform them into things. They retain the indetermination of elements despite the precision of the laws that govern them."[75] Elements do not possess forms that contain them; rather, they are content lacking form.

In one sense, an element might have a side or "face" such as the (sur)face of the water, the outer limit of a field, or the approaching edge of the wind. In this way, one might conceivably extend and creatively develop the broader Levinasian position that ethics arises in a response—and hence responsibility—to the alterity of the face, which also resists possession, so as to include not just human countenances and even animal faces but inhuman elements—their surfaces and fathomless recesses—as well.[76] In another sense, an element truly only possesses depth given that we are steeped within it. "I am always within the element," Levinas observes of his own bodily position.[77] This being-in-the-element involves an inward flow, a "movement of afflux without respite" because the anonymous element comes to us seemingly from nowhere, from that which is not substantial and underlying, separating us in the process from the infinite and thereby resembling the Presocratic *apeiron* or boundless.[78]

We "overcome the elements only by surmounting this interiority . . . by the domicile, which confers upon [us] an extraterritoriality."[79] We gain a "foothold in the elemental" by appropriating "a side" (or face) of it through human labor (which enables us to discover the world), transformations such as the cultivation of the land, fishing in the oceans, or cutting wood from a forest, actions that all relate back to the domicile or human household. We plunge into the elemental, then, from the home, which makes property and an inner life possible. Here, Levinas acknowledges the primacy of dwelling and inhabitation in relation to the elements as do Heidegger and Aristotle—what we have been exploring as domestication. In Levinas' characterization, the home is distanced physically from the anonymity of the elements—sea, earth, air, light, forest, air, and the like. Upon departing the *domus*, we are no longer in extended Cartesian space but instead "bathing" in an element or the elemental, which amounts to inhabiting the world as "inside-out."

John Sallis summarizes succinctly some of these key dimensions of Levinas' depiction of the elemental in noting:

1. It is a medium characterized by indeterminacy and lack of clear form.
2. In encounters with it one is immersed within something without true sides or intervals.
3. It arrives anonymously and seemingly from nowhere, manifesting no support from a substance.
4. It is marked by a strange kind of concealment that is revealing of absence and impersonal existence.
5. It has unfathomable depth.[80]

Levinas uses the language of sensibility in order to establish a meaningful relation to the elements. Through sensibility, which he describes as a moment of enjoyment rather than an instance of representation, things can return to their respective elemental qualities. Enjoyment is "in touch" as an affectivity and sentiment—rather than as intellection—with an "other" (or otherness) insofar as a future is suggested within that element. It is more accurate to say we live elements as sensible qualities—"the green of these leaves, the red of this sunset"—than we know them. Levinas writes: "This earth upon which I find myself and from which I welcome sensible objects or make my way to them suffices for me," adding "the earth which upholds me does so without my troubling myself about knowing what upholds the earth."[81]

Levinas is, in brief, content with his "corner of the world" and the horizon where he resides. He understands the mythical dimensions of the elements—which earlier gave rise to impersonal and faceless gods—but he seeks to provide them with a philosophical underpinning while recognizing that an elemental sensibility still confounds logical thought. Enjoying the elements and doing so without reference to their utility enables us to cultivate "an ultimate relation with the substantial plenitude of being, with its materiality" and to live life as play (as Plato advises) in what Levinas calls "the bowels of being," where the element reaches into an expansive existence, a robust "there is."[82]

Elemental Imperatives: Lingis and Our Sensuous Surroundings

Alphonso Lingis is a phenomenologist footloose in the ragged material field of social and ecological reality, exploring the realms of the elemental, the exotic, and the erotic in intriguing manners. As a protean and intrepid philosopher turned anthropologist and travel writer, he plunges us into the rapture of the watery deep; he leads us up into the majestic stone-carved heights of the Andes; and he hitches us to a journey through ice at the end of the earth in Antarctica. Along the way, Lingis telescopes his observant vision on embodiment, death, sensuality, extreme physical conditions, dangerous emotions associated with lust, violence and love, and the primitive power of animal faces. Merleau-Ponty's notion of flesh as element is here given a more fully carnal voice. Deleuze's nomadicism is provided a palpable form in the peripatetic reflections and figure of Lingis himself. Levinas' ethics are expressed in a novel idiom. And Nietzsche's libidinal energies and transgressive questions are unleashed in the wild world at large.

Building on and playing off the work of these thinkers, Lingis advances a new phenomenology of perception and provides a compelling place for the elemental realm within his account.[83] He shows astutely that perception is not simply a passive reaction or mechanical adjustment to our surroundings, nor is it merely a volitional and teleological act. Lingis reveals instead the manifold ways in which we respond to powerful directives and imperatives within the sensuous environment, including the pushes and pulls of the elements, as well as the night, human and nonhuman faces, material things, and alien spaces. As he discovers and exfoliates them, the elements are "sensuous realities" and depths absent boundaries and surfaces. To grasp them, we must recognize that we are truly *immersed* in the world—not just perched on an earthly plane—and hence saturated within a "beginningless, endless, and fathomless" tangible plenum. From its outset, life is enveloped in the superabundance of the elements, "in boundless light, in terrestrial warmth, in resonating depths."[84]

Lingis takes the next necessary step of locating a domestic place for the elements within everyday life, as do Aristotle, Bachelard, and Levinas. Home, although a "haven of serenity" is still "a condensation in the elements" rather than an insular shelter from them.[85] Work draws on the elements, which the hands grasp and shape. A perennial virtue such as courage is even depicted as "the strength of the heart that hears the advance of death as a summons to engulfment in the elements, to the horror of decomposition of a corpse, to extinction."[86]

Because the elements and the elemental evade traditional definition, Lingis initially courts an approach through the negative. The elements are not structures of intelligibility or perceptible dimensions, and their qualities cannot be reduced to properties of a substrate. They are not an abundance of singular things, a plethora of discrete objects, or a profusion of sense data that can be collected and interpreted. They are neither a means nor an intermediary. They are more accurately described in such terms as an "incessant oncoming" without an apparent source and a "voluptuous sensuality," or as "unfragmented and fathomless." The elements are mobile adjectives as opposed to static nouns, and in this regard they seem to share affinities with Delezue and Guattari's rhizomes.

Lingis' elements are clearly distinct from common material entities or "things," which tend to be more discrete and relocatable in space or place. That which provides no surface to grasp (as with light, air, heat, or night) and that which is not detachable (as with clouds or mountains) cannot be considered to be mere things. Instead, these phenomena are more like "ultra-things," or what Edward Casey terms "mega-things." They are less determinate. Here, Lingis introduces the notion of "levels" to his phenomenological analysis, suggesting a plurality of dimensions to the elemental world and offering a perspective that both Husserl and Heidegger failed to appreciate in viewing the environment in terms of a background and figure relation or as a field of things. Colors, for example, receive their curious characteristics from levels of light; sounds acquire their distinct dimensions from sonorous levels from which they depart. These levels and their attendant reliefs offer "directions of support" for sight, touch, and smell. They are relational as opposed to systematic, and they take shape in an elemental medium such as the earthy ground, air, night, light, or warmth. "To see the water, our eyes do not fix on where it is, do not fix on the pool; our look is led by the light which precedes it and guides it and is led by the water which makes visible the zigzags of the tiles and the sheets of light within it and sends flashing ripples across the screen of cypresses at the back of the garden."[87] Ultimately, then, it is an expression and perception of "style" that provides consistency and coherence to these elementary phenomena that captivate us. It is the particular and unique ways they unfold, endure, or perish that allow us to recognize and retain them, as when we encounter styles of bodily gestures, gaits, and postures in activities such as walking.

We encounter the elements by sensuous and often involuntary bodily movements within an encompassing medium:

> One finds the light by immersion, one is in atmosphere, in sonority, in redolence or in stench, in warmth or in cold. One feels the supporting element of the ground rising up within one's posture and

within one's orgasmic prostration and in one's sleep where dreams hover. The elements manifest themselves adverbially, qualifying our movements and our composure. Liquidity is there by giving play to the hand that is immersed in it, by yielding before and sustaining the thrust of the swimmer.[88]

Lingis beautifully enlarges the canonical conception of the four elements to include such phenomena as the cold, the dark, the oceanic, the terrestrial, the sustaining, the luminous, the lambent, the exultant, the gloom, and the savage. Like Levinas, he draws attention to affective aspects in our engagements with the elemental. "To be alive is to enjoy the light, enjoy the support of the ground, the open paths and the buoyancy of the air."[89] The elements are a "nourishing medium" for which we can even possess an appetite.

The elements, however, cannot be dominated or even fully domesticated. "One cannot make oneself something separate and consolidate oneself by appropriating the light, by making private property and depriving others of the atmosphere, by monopolizing the warmth, by expropriating the things distributed over the ground of their support."[90] Lingis advances a loose challenge to modern mega-technology in this regard, suggesting that humans often engage in a kind of ethical or aesthetic violence against them, as some of the early Greeks claimed. "Do we not find offensive the one who, when landscapes fade out before the epiphany of the cosmic light, puts shades over his eyes so that he can read his texts or decipher the alleged text of the spectacle of a world?," he asks. He observes: "We turn away, as from a disordered and distempered organism, from the one who pulls the blinds of his windows against the glory of high noon to crawl into his bed . . . only to offend the night with his fidgety agitations under the glare of incandescent wires." And he remarks: "Do we not avert our steps from the one whose ears are scabbed with a Walkman when the winter arrives tinkling in on snowflakes?"[91] Although it is not entirely clear whether we should best construe such comments as aesthetic judgments, personal opinions, or wistful moralisms, Lingis rejects the holism frequently found in environmental philosophy and phenomenology, refusing to assimilate the various directives to which we respond. In his view, freedom is found in sensual submission to the elements and other earthly things rather than in mastery of them. This delightful "obedience," in turn, provides an opportunity for one to become elemental, in Deleuze and Guattari's sense of becoming-other. "Is there not in the ground, dampness, atmosphere, and light in which we are immersed the imperative that life live in becoming support, becoming oceanic, becoming aerial."[92]

In *Foreign Bodies,* Lingis speaks of elemental bodies and the elemental as "the weight of the terrestrial, and rivers, and sun."[93] Inspired by Deleuze's encounter with the same story, he explores the role of the elemental in a reading of Michel Tournier's *Friday,* the retelling of Daniel Defoe's narrative of Robinson Crusoe on a deserted island. Like Bachelard, Lingis invokes the force and metaphors of an elemental poetics. He speaks, for example, of the voyage to a land "where terra firma is doubled by the objects situated on it and objectives sought on it, and doubled by the free elements—by light that does not elucidate or clarify, wind-intoned musicality without a text, sun that fecundates an inhuman progeny."[94] In his suggestive interpretation, there is another "elemental island" reached in bypassing a restrictive ontology based on an underlying substrate.[95] This leads Robinson to a region of "free elements" that emerge from an "elemental depth" and causes a doubling of his libidinal body. For months, Robinson passively contemplates the skies, the air, and the light until he is drawn into a voluptuous, promiscuous, and incestuous zone where sea and earth meet and commingle, where "elemental signs" appear, and where elemental forces beseech and beckon him until he descends into the maternal earth and responds sensually and erotically to a "tellurian causality."

Through his reading of the story, Lingis articulates the notion that there exists an imperative, prior to all formal, interior, and mental ones of which Kant speaks, and to which our sensibilities expose themselves. This imperative, originating from the exterior—rather than the inside and not limited to a human or divinity—is to an element such as earth or air or light or the flux in which sensory forces take shape. And such demands are taken in through our receptive bodies, though for instance the lungs that filter the wind and the muscles that engage the earth. As Lingis expresses it, "The sensuous involution in the elements makes our eyes luminous, our hands warm, our posture supportive, our voice voluble and spiritual and our face ardent."[96]

Elements and natural entities, then, can generate perceptual and ethical claims, as Lingis suggests. They summon or beguile us; they hypnotize and mesmerize us; they force us to recognize and respect something outside ourselves. I watch a red-tailed hawk swoop down from the autumn sky and pluck up a squirrel with her talons in the neighborhood cemetery, conjoining before my eyes in one entrancing moment sudden death with winged flight. I notice a red fox and her two cubs playing in a pool of light at the edge of campus, skirting in and out of the shadows in the late afternoon sun. I spy cockroaches storming a sidewalk grate in the middle of the night to devour a sandwich tossed wantonly on the earth. I stare fixedly at an opossum bearing his fanged teeth and holding his ground on the wooden deck behind my house. These phenomena take hold of me; they seize my attention and command my interest.

For Lingis, objects of the physical environment are not the result of activities of the human mind. Rather, in the words of Graham Harman, they are "tribes of omens always already set loose to practice their dark and noble crafts in the world. The autonomy of stars and coral reefs is *real* for Lingis, no less than the independence of electric eels, cinemas, sunflower fields, snowflakes, and molten ores buried deep in the moon."[97] As Harman observes, Lingis is by training a phenomenologist, but by temperament a cosmologist—and nearly an animist—who is

316 | Elemental Philosophy

"perhaps less attuned to the mannerisms of the human salon than Merleau-Ponty, but more alert to the chatterings of birds and the cracking of ice-shelves and the drifting of meteors in distant space."[98] To that extent, he is sure to continue illuminating and revealing the elemental world.

Elemental Passions: Irigaray on Breath and Body

French philosopher, psychologist. and feminist Luce Irigaray has authored a series of theoretical and personal books on the elements, including *The Forgetting of Air in Martin Heidegger*, *Elemental Passions*, and *Marine Lover of Friedrich Nietzsche*. In her view, the elements represent "natural matters" that originate our bodies and lives as well as the environment and "the flesh of our passions."[99] By investigating earth, fire, air, and water, Irigaray endeavors to provide a vocabulary for this matter and to explore the affects and affections associated with the elements. Although she focuses on gender issues and claims that nature is a "second mother" in a "sexed universe" that should be praised and sung rather than exploited, she warns against an anthropocentric appropriation of the elements because they begin outside our language.[100] The four elements—which she particularizes as "sea, sun, air, and earth"—are extra-linguistic phenomena, even if often filtered through masculine language.

Irigaray invokes the elements as an alternative way of describing the complexities of the human body and our feelings. The elements permit her, as Margaret Whitfield argues, "to speak of the female body, of its morphology, and of the erotic, while avoiding the dominant sexual metaphoricity which is scopic and organized around the male gaze; she can speak of it instead in terms of space and thresholds and fluids, fire and water, air and earth, without objectifying, hypostatizing, or essentializing it."[101] This vocabulary is not reducible quickly to either the male or female form, possessing instead a malleability and openness to individual and collective interpretation. Like Lingis, Irigaray attempts the risky turn to the primal roots of language in the sensuous world. "Whereas, Deleuze and Guattari find the more 'scientific' language drawn from other disciplines (intensities, fluxes, etc.) attractive, Irigaray uses more personable language of elements and corporeal feeling—she deliberatively turns to a more 'crude' and 'primitive' language associated with nature, magic, witchcraft, myth," observes Tasmin Lorraine.[102] In other words, Irigaray is receptive, like Bachelard, to the precognitive and intuitive realms, prioritizing elemental touch in the process.

Irigaray reveals in particular that air, especially bodily breath, is an invisible, unthought, or misconstrued presence within the Western philosophical tradition. In contrast to Heidegger, she maintains that our first home is not in language but within the ambient air—Anaximenes' first element—which she invokes in its many modalities, including that which surrounds and unites all bodies, that which carries the voice and call of the other, and that which grants us autonomy when we begin to breathe outside the mother. Irigaray rightly notes the Eastern philosophical connections with air when she points to the breathing practices in yoga and the example of Buddha, who teaches that one can experience a rebirth through breathing. And she goes as far as to maintain that people who love one another are attracted reciprocally through breath and air—one might reasonably say smell—which are beyond mere words.[103]

In a work and idiosyncratic dialogue she started a few days after his death in 1976, Irigaray focuses in particular on Heidegger, calling attention to what she claims is his forgetting of the encompassing air and those elements missing this type of density. This lack of awareness results in part from his being locked up in a "house of language" such that he is unable to see that a subject can be dual or dyadic (as in the maternal origin of the self) and not simply singular, a position that eventuates in his view that life finds its limit in death rather in a relationship with another. According to Irigaray, Heidegger rarely departs the ground, in both the sense of *logos* and earth, an interpretation that is bolstered and ballasted, we might add, by his frequent use of metaphors involving paths, soil, country roads, and the like. Thus, he never really leaves metaphysics, which is based in and on the solid and inscribed "neither on/in water, nor on/in air, nor on/in fire."[104] Irigaray in fact finds a long-enduring association between philosophical rationality and a "mechanics of solids" that tends to privilege the rigid, the bounded, the definite, and the clearly defined while denying or undervaluing the fluid, the permeable, and the porous as well as that which appears to be less tangible.[105] But it is precisely the air, this transparent and translucent medium—which seems to be imperceptible, impalpable, and unintelligible—that she finds at the "groundless foundation" of Western metaphysics, a true recognition of which would amount to a thorough ruination of it.

Irigaray inquires: "Is not air the whole of our habitation as mortals? Is there a dwelling more vast, more spacious, or even more generally peaceful that that of air? Can man live elsewhere than in air?" According to her, habitation is not truly possible in fire, earth, or water. "No other element can for him take the place of place. No other element carries with it—or lets itself be passed through by—light and shadow, voice or silence."[106] Air is space prior to all forms of localization. It is at once moving and immobile, permanent but ever fluid, while remaining constitutive in an original sense of the whole of the world. It is a difficult challenge, indeed, to think this "forgotten *material mediation* of the *logos*"[107] in contrast with other elements such as fire, which have been privileged in their manifestation—as in Heraclitus' cosmology—even when they depend, like fire, on air for their very appearance.[108] In Irigaray's view, it is such forgetting that facilitates human hegemony over the natural world. "Nature in its elemental multiplicity is already bowed to the autarchy of a power: *physis* already opened up by and for man in accordance with his needs, or desires, to appear."[109]

Irigaray proclaims that what the present era truly requires is a return to breathing, that "elementary and necessary reality of life."[110] From her perspective, we are spiritually in an "age of breath" because Christian, Hebraic, Islamic, and Far Eastern cultures all underscore the role of an animating and inspiring breath in their religions, and so these traditions could unite ideally in a "culture of the breath." Although this cultural diagnosis and prescription remains, in the end, rather vague, Irigaray does point to an often neglected but absolutely vital human activity and its place within the encompassing environment. She suggests, for example, that women possess an extra reserve of breath, which they practice during pregnancy and maternity and which they keep in order to share with another, whereas men tend to use their breath for building up their world and making objects. Breath, moreover, is what permits us to coexist and so is capable of being shared across and among diverse traditions, sexes, and peoples.

In *Marine Lover of Nietzsche*, Irigaray also advances the idea that it is the element of water that another famous Western thinker—in this case Nietzsche—most fears or forgets. In water, she discovers and articulates a complex affinity between the fluid and the feminine, which she uses to conduct an amorous confabulation with and critique of the German philosopher, who in one work specifically admonishes fidelity to the earth.[111] In a personal dialogue reminiscent of her posthumous conversation with Heidegger on air, she attempts to disrupt conventional discourse by writing in a poetic and lyrical style that blurs the lines between philosophy and fiction as well as theory and narrative. The elements, too, make another more veiled appearance in Irigaray's *Elemental Passions*, where she investigates the relationships between women and men through meditations on the senses and the elements by way of a series of love letters in which the identity and reality of the addressee are obscured. In these and other ways, Irigaray continues to probe and transform the ancient tradition of reflections on earth, water, air, and fire, calling the forgotten fourfold back to the philosophical forefront.

In a fashion similar in some respects to her French counterpart, philosopher, theologian, and radical feminist Mary Daly advocates "elemental feminist philosophy," by which she means a post-patriarchal consciousness that is attuned to what is wild in both the individual self and the encompassing natural surroundings. Combining a stinging, and at times hyperbolic, critique of male culture and theory with a celebration of primal forces in the elemental world, she generates an elaborate, often exotic, menu of archaic myths and alliterative, new metaphors so as to recommend the possibility of an "elemental participation in Be-ing" that is informed by intuitive and immediate "elemental knowing." Daly counsels women to connect creatively and corporally with the elements: the "sweet earth, wild winds, rich rain, warm sun."[112] In the process, she anticipates and gives voice to an early version of ecological feminism, extolling the virtues of biophilia, the value of the wild world and the merits of elemental life. Daly appeals to multiple senses of "element," including (a) the "physical" aspects, or what is simple, natural, primitive, fundamental, and earthy; (b) the "spiritual" sides of the term as it is used, for example, by the alchemist and philosopher, Paracelsus; and (c) the "metaphysical" dimensions involved with first principles or rudiments of things. She recognizes, too, the multivalent associations of the Greek, *stoicheion*—including letters of the alphabet, the deep realms of reality to which we are sensually tied, and the metaphoric extensions of the concept into human society.

It is particularly the last sense of the term through which Daly hitches the four classical elements to her distinct mythopoetic and feminist vision. Thus, she develops the links between fire and passion, air and breath, earth and healthy lust, and water and freedom of movement. Her elemental philosophy, although decidedly "of the world"—as she puts it—stands firmly and uncompromisingly against traditional religious references to the *stoicheia* (as in Biblical allusions to "elemental spirits"), opposed to what she calls the "modern technological war against the elements," and even counter to male writers who ostensibly embrace environmental thought (e.g., James Lovelock's "obscene" "lust for Gaia" or René Dubo's "wooing of the earth"). Her perspective shares much with Irigaray's view of the elements, especially in the experimentation with language and metaphor, the search for a primitive but powerful mode in which to express a feminist framework, and the critique of predominant forms of philosophical and political reason. Her more recent work, *Quintessence*, continues the invocation of elemental philosophy, gesturing to a fifth essence that she believes pervades the entire universe. This notion of quintessence harkens back, of course, to Aristotle's *aether* and represents Daly's most extravagant response to "the call of the wild," serving she hopes as a way to realize an "archaic future" that is ultimately about "elemental connectedness" in the world.[113]

Elemental Landscapes: Casey on Place

Phenomenologist Edward Casey has been instrumental in helping to restore the subject of place to the philosophical and ecological map. In a series of books that includes *Getting Back Into Place*; *The Fate of Place*; *Representing Place*; and *Earth-Mapping*, he advances the cogent claim and powerful case that ancient and contemporary encounters with *topos* (place) are vitally relevant to understanding inhabitation and our relationship with the environing world. Casey argues convincingly that place has been subordinated historically to notions of time, being, and space, and that this neglect has been detrimental not only to philosophical wisdom but also to our lived experience of the natural and built realms. As he observes, "where we are . . . has everything to do with what and who we are."[114] In this regard, Casey offers a rigorous topo-analysis—rather than merely a sympathetic topophilia (love of place)—as he unearths and explores a panoply of placial concepts such as site, position, region, location, limit, horizon, and home. "Place," as he expresses it tersely, "is the phenomenal particularization of 'being-in-the-world.'"[115]

In terms of his stance on wild places, Casey tills a middle ground between the positions of social constructivism and an ontologically independent nature-in-itself, invoking Charles Sanders Peirce's productive notion of "secondness" and a "refractory facticity set over against us" that "jabs you perpetually in the ribs" to defend his thesis.[116] In the process, he identifies and illuminates six related phenomena or "moments" of nature: the surrounding array, the sensuous surface, the ground, natural things, the vanishing arc, and the permeating atmosphere. Casey also gestures toward the notion of a place-based ethic, a kind of loco-centrism and eco-centrism that reveals the features of placescape, landscape, and wildscape. He rightfully observes that our obligations to other humans are in the end "to *people in places*, not to unplaced persons existing in a void," and ethically we cannot avoid the imperatives urged on us by place.[117]

In recent work, Casey locates a place for the elemental within landscape painting and photography. He uses an analysis of phenomenal elements—water, air, rock, and light—in order to understand placescapes and their pictorial representation. In keeping with the tradition of phenomenology, Casey construes the elements in terms of sensed aspects of the landscape rather than as scientific constituents. The elemental is that which is in a relatively pristine condition and so serves to bind together a physical area and link us deeply to a particular place. Elemental factors are, in short, the most qualitative dimensions of a represented region that provide both images and models for our placial and spatial orientation.

Casey uses the work of American painters to reveal the elemental landscape. Elemental light is the "great organizer" in the representation of place and the basis for perception of the atmosphere and air. It is the alchemical medium of illumination that at the same time changes what it conveys. It subtends place, distinguishes objects, and secures the things of the world in its bathing or clarifying presence. Painters such as Fritz Hugh Lane use it not just as a means to show the entities that occupy a place but to portray the power of light itself, to light up the lighting in effect. As Casey puts it, this difficult enterprise "not only makes visible *things in a place*, but also creates *places for things*."[118] By contrast, Frederick Edwin Church deploys light not to suffuse it over a scene but instead to diffuse and dissolve objects of their objectivity so as to change a natural place into a wild one—to literally *be-wilder order* in a landscape. Light thereby possesses the power to both animate and enliven the phenomenal elements in the world as well as to divest or transmute energies associated with the sea, sky, or earth.

Water, in turn, is allied closely in landscape art with the light that it reflects, absorbs, or exhibits. Lane's famous depictions of Norman's Woe cove, for example, anchor and hold the luminosity of the paintings. Bodies of water form containers for contemplation, reveal sites for the appearance of the sublime, or provide planes of placial giveness and perceptual stability. The plasticity of this element and its ability to take on the shape of its proximate surroundings can suggest depth and stillness beyond a tormented surface. Water is a middle field and medium between earth and sky. It becomes "the ultimate elemental mediatrix," the in-between and mediating place for elements.[119] As Casey suggests, water often constitutes a kind of active "interplace" and realm of elemental exchange, a point evident to Bachelard and Thoreau, who speaks of the lake as both the "earth's eye" and as "sky water."

Despite its pervasiveness in landscape painting, earth is commonly overlooked and underappreciated by art historians and critics. As Casey speculates, this may have to do with the fact that earth is more resistant to the force of light—and thus more opposed to displaying protean qualities—than other elements or features of a place. However, the role of earth in landscapes is both unique and primordial because it provides an unyielding and solid support for other many of a place. It is the "where-in" of the painting. Or as Casey remarks, earth is the "topic of topics" and the "matrix of matrices" that is "materially encompassing" with respect to its tendency to downward depth and "formally ordering" in terms of the way it provides a locus of orientation by way of the region.[120] In landscape pictures, earth is typically both underlying—beneath sky and water—and regionalizing in the sense of delimiting boundaries. In this way, it is capable of both *holding* place and *beholding* our aesthetic attention.

In Casey's view, elemental factors are expressed decidedly as forms of plenitude that fill up and complete a place in its given representation. "Light pervades, water reaches to the outermost limit of its container, and earth is a plenum of depth and region. Everywhere we encounter the fullness of the elemental."[121] Despite such robustness, the elements are at times "transplaced" to make room for a void so as to allow for the contemplative sublime or to effect a place for the transcendental, whether in Kantian or Emersonian guise. In evacuating water or earth or air, such a void still often retains a material presence, as in Lane's *The Western Shore with Norman's Woe*, where the watery cove is drained completely of content. Through the combination of the painter's brush and creative eye, the topography of a place is thereby able to speak "with the silence of its own voice from the void of its own place."[122] In expanding the scope of his concerns to include the elements and elemental realms, Casey continues to reveal his wisdom as *periegete*—a guide to place—both of particular and unique geographical locations as well as the philosophical and aesthetic placescape more generally.

Elemental Nature: Sallis on Imagination

Turning to the ancient Greeks and using the approaches and language of phenomenology, John Sallis has of late advanced a notion of "elemental nature" and with it the possibility of what he calls a "return of nature" that bears some striking similarities to and relevance for our present investigation of the elements.[123] In doing so, he highlights the faculty of imagination, which permits us potentially to understand earth, sky, fire, and water in new and transfigured ways. As Sallis puts it, in order for philosophical vision to sustain a required level of reflection, the philosopher, who typically withdraws from the world in order to know it, must "be brought back to a vision of self as situated amidst the elements, as engaged by force of necessity in comportment to the elements."[124] The return of the elements—both in the classical Greek sense we have been exploring and the manner in which they are used in common parlance (rain, snow, wind, lightning, etc.)—by way of recourse to nature also entails a turn to the sensible and sensuous as opposed to merely the intelligible realm.

Sallis warns these turnings and returnings can only be significant if we move away from a "determination of the elements as constituting the *from which* of composition" and instead focus on their manifestation, their self-showing, or in short *their appearance* as stone, cloud, sea, sun, sky, and the like.[125] Through an active remembrance of the insights of Greek thought, we can cultivate "solicitousness for elemental nature" and "practice a kind of receptive prospection capable of opening one's vision to the rare sight of the natural elements."[126] In this way, Sallis hopes we might rediscover an "exorbitant sense" of elements and in the process redetermine nature, or at least a sense of it.

In contrast with natural things, which are bounded by horizons, "elementals" are encompassing rather than encompassed, thus reinforcing a point Levinas and Lingis both make. Storm, sea, and sky reveal themselves in very distinct manners from things, and they manifest themselves differently from one another, even if elementals might intersect or overlap. The elemental is also impersonal and agentless, and to the extent that we are immersed and bathed within an element, we are unable to acquire a perspective on it so as to treat or use it as a thing or constellation of things. This inability to distance or shake oneself loose of an encompassing element is especially the case with sky and earth because of their near limitless depth and their role in delimiting the boundaries of our perceptual lives. In fact, Sallis goes as far as to speak of the elemental as "monstrous" because it exceeds natural things while still adhering to the realm of nature. In this sense, it is a form of "hypernature within nature" that tends to be displayed as indefinite or gigantic and at the same time strangely one-sided, as when wind and rain pass forcefully through a valley, confronting our senses as an advancing edge or retreating front. The elemental is, however, not a surface or a profile but instead reveals itself as an expanse with near fathomless depth, as we witness when a storm stealthfully withdraws.

Sallis finds the invocation of the elements by poets and writers such as Hölderlin, Shakespeare, and Schelling particularly revealing. In his view, we can reasonably refer to "elemental tragedy." In *King Lear*, for example, we discover the "fretful elements" (to use Shakespeare's words) in their monstrosity through the "deformity of nature and excess of nature" when Lear stands subsumed in a wild tempest with his Fool. Through the force of imagination and our sensuous encounters with such phenomena as thunderstorms—what Hölderlin calls "the fire of the sky"—we can be seized or surprised by the power and alterity of a raw and elemental nature. Such encounters might even link us up, as we saw with the Presocratics, to the realm of the mythical where Poseidon rules the seas or Zeus governs the skies. According to Sallis, we might speak, too, of "elemental time" because it is "borne and offered not only by things but also, above all, by the elementals." As Heidegger puts it, "Time first shows itself in the sky, that is, precisely there where one comes across it in directing oneself naturally *according to it*, so that time even becomes identified with the sky."[127] Time is "the element in which we exist," Joyce Carol Oates notes succinctly. As a primordial feature of the ever-changing world, "we are either borne along by it or drowned in it."[128]

Sallis is undoubtedly correct to call attention to the essential and constructive role of imagination in a consideration of the elemental. Imagination—construed in a sense that includes but surpasses intellectual activity and passes through the body and into the natural world—is arguably a necessary component of a robust environmental ethos and awareness because it allows us to engage empathetically the natural and built environments in ways that would have otherwise been foreclosed.[19] Sallis, however, tends to emphasize the liminal experiences and extraordinary or extreme senses of the elemental: their exorbitant and monstrous obtrusions into everyday life on relatively rare occasions. These outcroppings clearly can be cathartic, epiphanic, and awe-inspiring, but they are not our only or even our most common encounters with the elements or elemental, as earlier chapters have made clear. In this regard, his conception of elemental nature bears some resemblance to the notion of the sublime as it has been advanced and reconfigured by thinkers from Longinus through Burke and Kant. Although its history is complex, the sublime has come to mean, in part, the magnificent primal forces of both beauty and terror that lie outside the domesticated human sphere and that inspire mystery and awe, or at least recognition of radical nonhuman otherness.

Sallis' idea of "turning back" and returning (to) nature via "remembrances" or even philosophical "regressions" is nonetheless somewhat sketchy and potentially problematic.[130] At times, it begins to echo a Heideggerian nostalgia for lost or perhaps fictional origins as well as the attendant hope for the reappearance of the elements at some deferred future date. Although his account bears some of the mark and influence of Levinas and perhaps even Lingis in its phenomenological descriptions of depth, things, and surfaces in relation to the elemental, Sallis does differentiate his view on several counts from these thinkers.[131] And, like the contributions of other Continental theorists, his work helps to open up a constructive space within which we may creatively explore and critically engage the elements and elemental philosophy.[132]

From Elements to the Elemental

What, then, one might ask, ultimately are elements? Given that we have surveyed and scrutinized the evolving historical and philosophical features of this concept, posing the question in such a way probably frames the issue in a misleading manner. As Nietzsche points out aphoristically, "only that which has no history is definable."[133] Although elements are that which is fundamental, primary, and perhaps primordial to the landscape or human lifeworld, they are not in the end subsumable to unchanging things-in-themselves or reducible to something like chemical formulas. Thomas Sharp, the planner for the city of Oxford after World War II, once wrote that an "experience is elemental, beyond the power of words or photographs to describe."[134] There is, without doubt, a certain truth to this remark, but it overstates the ineffability of these phenomena and forces. Elements are indeed a somewhat labile and elastic notion, fraught with ragged edges and subject to a degree of physical, cultural, or epistemological shape-shifting, even if they are not wholly indeterminate or utterly unidentifiable entities.

Bachelard skillfully shows how the elements become material images tethered to our imaginations and how they grow into metaphors that govern the language of philosophical and poetic texts. Levinas is correct to point to the seeming depth and near fathomless dimensions of the elemental and our immersion within it, as well as to expand our categories and consciousness of what may count as an element. Merleau-Ponty suggestively reveals the elemental as formative "flesh" conjoining body and ambient world, whereas Casey exposes it adeptly through an exploration of phenomenal fields and places, especially in the realm of art. Lingis, in turn, rightly presents the elemental in terms of sensuous, mobile, and nourishing realities that exercise powerful directives upon all of us. In each of these characterizations, the elemental tends to serve as an enveloping or underlying medium and as an ecological matrix. Nature—if we choose to employ this contested concept—is often concretized and subsequently encountered in elemental ways while the elements are still quite "natural." But when earth, air, fire, and water—or heat, ice, light, night, and stone if we broaden the canon—enter more immediately into the human arena of culture or creative expression, "substance" is invariably reconstructed by our psyches so as to integrate and entwine us deeply with the existential and ontological paradoxes of the world. This is the insight Bachelard conveys when he observes: "One dreams in front of his fire, and the imagination discovers that the fire is the motive force for a world."[135]

In general, Continental philosophy has transitioned from a focus on distinct *elements* and theories of earth, air, fire, and water, as they were conceived or constructed in ancient Greek thought, to enlarged but still emerging accounts of *the elemental*. There is less emphasis now on cosmological speculation and more attention to aesthetic and affective details related to, for example, the body, place, or language. There is likewise less stress on the generation and internal coherency of particular interrelated elements and more concentration on their broad phenomenal appearances and forms. Nonetheless, the return and reclamation of an expanded sense of the elemental should not be construed as an attempt to locate a new metaphysical first principle, ultimate ground, or autonomous foundation on which to erect precarious philosophical frameworks or environmental edifices.

Perhaps Bachelard, whose work provides a bridge between ancient and contemporary thought, as well as a kind of Ariadne's thread through many mythological, literary, and philosophical perspectives on the elements, deserves a last provocative word on the subject. "Haven't the philosophers of antiquity," he asks rhetorically, "given us precise evidence of worlds substantialized by a cosmic substance?" He adds that such "were *the dreams of great thinkers*," and he is "astonished that historians of philosophy *think* these great cosmic images without ever *dreaming* them, without ever restoring to them their privilege of reverie." In this view, it is vital "to learn to dream again" in profound and original ways if we wish to keep alive these "audacious reveries."[136] That seems to provide a challenging goal as we continue to explore, elaborate on, and apply our understandings of these perennial ideas, images, and archetypes to the ever-changing and sensuous world encircling us.

Interstice: Space

The surface of the Earth is the shore of the cosmic ocean. From it we have learned most of what we know. Recently, we have waded a little out to sea, enough to dampen our toes or, at most, wet our ankles. The water seems inviting. The ocean calls. Some part of our being knows this is from where we came. We long to return.

—Carl Sagan, *Cosmos*

We came all this way to explore the moon, and the most important thing is that we discovered the earth.

—William Anders, astronaut, Apollo 8

In November 1961, a poem entitled "Space Prober" was inscribed on the instrument panel of a satellite launched from Cape Kennedy into the Earth's orbit. It read: "And now 'tis man who dares assault the sky . . . / And as we come to claim our promised place / Aim only to repay the good you gave / And warm with human love the chill of space."[1] Tethered by gravity at 600 miles altitude, this satellite will continue to circle the planet for 750 years before it either falls back to its terrestrial birthplace or is plucked from the heavens like a talisman by celestial navigators from another realm.

The dream of escaping the Earth and world of tellurian elements is a perennial one, embedded deeply within myth, story, religion, and the history of technology. Icarus flew too near the sun and paid the ultimate toll. The Presocratic philosopher Anaxagoras reputedly saw the very purpose of life as an investigation into the heavens. We read in the Book of Genesis, "let us build ourselves a city and a tower with its top in the heavens."[2] Leonardo da Vinci delighted in the idea of flying machines, including the hang glider and "airscrew," a prototype of the modern helicopter that would propel us high into the sky. Before planes, hot air balloons lifted humans several miles toward the elusive stars. Starting in the

1940s, photographs from cameras attached to rockets provided us with startling new perspectives of our aboriginal home, re-enchanting it temporarily as a consequence. Fifty years ago, Sputnik was sent ceremoniously into orbit and the Space Age was officially inaugurated. Shortly thereafter, cosmonauts followed by astronauts succeeded in breaking the bonds of gravity, the latter touching down on the lunar landscape. We are now exploring Mars, Saturn, and the vast reaches beyond these outposts. At the same time, private companies and subcultures are preparing for intra-galactic travel by projecting millionaires into the beyond or simulating space colonies in the desert. The cables that tie these intrepid "technomads" to mother ships might one day be considered embryonic umbilical cords, conduits between a human past and a post-human future.

Given that outer space is by its very nature extra-terrestrial—afar of the planetary pail where earth, air, fire, and water co-exist and intermix—it poses a special challenge for contemplating matters elemental. Kant understandably asks, "How is it that in this space here, we can make judgments that we know with apodictic certainty will be valid in that space, there?"[3] One line of response points to the continuity and similarities between these spheres. Things by this reckoning are not wholly and utterly different "out there," especially if space and time are *a priori* as Kant thought. The moon's matter is arguably akin to a second earth; the sun burns with primordial fire; water is locked up as interstellar ice or may lie dormant beneath the soil of other planets; and the medium of space almost seems to be a type of highly attenuated air. And yet in outer space, elemental activity is generally of a very different order. The energy of stars emanates from thermonuclear furnaces with interior temperatures reaching upwards of fifteen million degrees. Solar flares are more powerful than the greatest atomic blasts on Earth. Black holes warp the cloth of space and tug at the arrows of time. We are stepping without a reliable compass into an exotic terrain of anti-matter, leptons, wormholes, bosons, quarks, and hadrons. Even the names of such phenomena are foreign-sounding and discomfiting. Although the nascent field of astrobiology is searching diligently, there are no signs of life in view. This is not just nonhuman territory; it is extreme and inhuman compared with everything we have known.

Kant himself was fascinated by thorny quandaries involving the relation of inner and outer worlds, concluding his *Critique of Practical Reason* with the admission that "Two things fill the mind with ever new and increasing admiration and awe ... the starry heavens above and the moral law within me."[4] However these realms may be related, outer space is not simply an empty void or vacuum as is commonly thought, even if vast reaches appear to us as benighted because only a small percentage of the universe is luminous. Space contains a diverse montage of widely dispersed stars, nebulae, planets, comets, asteroids, meteors, and dust. And, more basically, it consists of low-density particles and especially hydrogen plasma, along with dark matter, dark energy, and electromagnetic radiation. By degrees, however, the blue of our planet's sky gives way to the relative black of the heavens.

Where the moment of transition occurs between the terrestrial and extra-terrestrial is subject to disagreement. One frequently used marker is the Kármán line, which begins one hundred kilometers above the surface of the Earth, separating the aeronautic from the astronautic region as the atmosphere thins.

More theoretically, the Copernican revolution ushered us from a geocentric to a heliocentric paradigm, but we no doubt are still wrestling with the implications of this seismic shift and epistemic rupture, which radically undermined and then reorganized existing scientific and philosophical verities. Our minds stretch to their ultimate limits in attempting to comprehend different scales of time and enormous distances. And as we peer *out into space* we look concurrently *back in time*. With the orbiting Hubble Telescope—a kind of elaborate time machine—we can observe light coming from stars billions of years ago, before the Earth itself existed. An ever-expanding universe—which is at least ninety-three billion light years wide—most likely means that distances between galaxies are growing (while the density of matter is decreasing) as opposed to matter progressing into a spatial void, as smoke might fill up an empty room. We can gain a small inkling of these unfathomable temporal and spatial spans by sauntering along the "Cosmic Pathway" in New York City's Hayden Planetarium, a scaled pedestrian walk that stretches from the gravitational singularity of the big bang until the present epoch. At the very terminus of the path, upon which every stride crosses seventy five million years, the entire period of human history is represented by the thin width of a single human hair embedded in a clear solid block!

As telescopes—our prosthetic and amplified eyes—wax in strength, the stars also seem to expand correspondingly in number. Galileo asserted enthusiastically that "the milky way itself, which with the aid of the spyglass, may be observed so well that all the disputes that for so many generations have vexed philosophers are destroyed by visible certainty, and we are liberated from wordy arguments."[5] Whereas prolix controversies have since multiplied rather than been laid to rest, constellations still offer us metaphysical consolation and geographic orientation. The mind discovers the bear, the bull, and the dog roaming in the nether worlds of a dark sky. We tame the wilderness of night through pointillist lights that crystallize into a bestiary of recognizable figures. "These constellations are all false," observes Bachelard, "but deliciously false!" He adds provocatively: "'Knowing' the constellations, naming them as in books, projecting a classroom map of the sky on the sky itself, is brutalizing our imaginary powers and depriving us of the benefits of the stars' oneirism."[6] Perhaps; but this is tricky turf or, we might say, astro-turf. Domesticating outer space with taxonomic schemes or technological machinery from Earth is a way of rendering it familiar and bringing it home metaphorically in manageably sized parcels, even though this enterprise might perform a disservice to the alterity of the cosmos as well as to the crucible of our imaginations. Rilke strikes a poetic note in proposing another perceptual option: "Often a star was waiting for you to notice it," he surmises.[7] In maintaining "the most incomprehensible thing about the universe is that it is comprehensible," Einstein singles out a crux in this dilemma and identifies in the process a tension that arises in overlapping scientific and philosophical magisteria between conceptions of chaos and cosmos; metaphysical order and ontological anarchy; epistemological certitude and confounding paradox.[8]

Space travel and space colonization raise incommodious questions about our place in the grand scheme of things. Techno-optimists and futurists tend to perceive these developments as inevitable and generally desirable. They view our destiny as hitched with otherworldly destinations. In *2001: A Space Odyssey*, Stanley Kubrick reincarnates an astronaut who floats in a kind of amniotic sack as a fetus while the earth remains in the perceivable but distant background, thereby suggesting the possible rebirth of humanity in the heavens. Flight into outer space dares to reset the very biological trajectory and historical understanding of our humanity as earthbound beings. Our brains, body posture, and identity evolved and were literally given shape in a weight-bearing world. In space, we move more tenuously, with less swagger and self-assurance—at least to date. Issues surrounding outer space often redound to questions about our own nature and the inner space of our minds and corporeal lives. Whither are we going, if anywhere in particular? The first astronauts actually fought to have apertures cut in the walls of their spacecraft in order to see where they were headed and from whence they came. So far, the rest of us here on Earth have had to be content with wielding telescopes and our imaginations in order to make sense of this recurrent conundrum. A haiku offers one tiny vantage with childlike simplicity: "A lovely thing to see: / through the paper window's hole, / the Galaxy."[9]

Like the aspiration of Hindus who seek to realize the identification of self with universe, *Atman* melded ontologically with *Brahman*, space exploration represents in one sense a grand technological and spiritual endeavor to wed humankind with the cosmos. What we may be courting or bargaining for, of course, remains opaque, or minimally unclear. The eerie silence of infinite spaces frightens many of us, as it once did Pascal. One thinks melancholically of David Bowie's "Major Tom" drifting about all alone in his "tin can" far above the planet. As an antidote for such *horror vaccui*, the astronomer Johannes Kepler suggested that we "create vessels and sails adjusted to the heavenly ether and there will be plenty of people unafraid of the empty wastes."[10] Both the possibility that we are alone and the plausible scenario that we are not may be deeply disorienting, even disconcerting. Entry into space teases us with the intriguing idea and opportunity for achieving a semblance of objective immortality. Since the Earth too will perish, colonizing, seeding, or terra-forming other planets in order to make their atmosphere or landscape more earth-like could be tantamount loosely to a "second genesis" project. Space travel might reasonably be the next step in our evolutionary advancement as we transition to "Humanity 2.0" or "robo-*sapiens*" or cybernetic organisms, or something of the sort. But it is easy to envision ignoble and even dark motives coming quickly into play: mining asteroid belts for metals; placing satellite eyes in the sky to watch over us; and extending or enhancing militaristic means and dreams.

To this point, the moon has served as a Janus-faced way station that permits us both to gaze further or step forward into the universe and to glance back and return humbly to our own cozier world. When astronauts first walked on the moon on July 20, 1969—"a different night from all other nights of the world" as an Italian poet put it—the Earth itself momentarily became a lunar satellite.[11] Orbiting above the planet, Neil Armstrong closed one eye and with his thumb canceled out entirely the Earth as if it were an ordinary postage stamp, commenting without words on its diminutive size and vulnerability. Like much travel, we come to understand more fully the lands we inhabit after we actually leave them. As to whether "the end of all our exploring / Will be to arrive where we started / And know the place for the first time" as T. S. Eliot believed, that is open to question.[12] Journeys to outer space invariably reshape the cultural meanings of the Earth. In the nineteenth century, a British historian and philosopher speculated optimistically, "Mankind will migrate into space, and will cross the airless Saharas which separate planet from planet and sun from sun. The Earth will become a Holy Land which will be visited by pilgrims from all the quarters of the Universe."[13] Time, one supposes, will eventually decide.

In great measure, philosophy begins and likely ends here—with a contemplative gaze directed toward the heavens—with innocent awe, unbounded curiosity, and healthy bewilderment. As the first serious thinkers looked closely into the terrestrial world, they turned as well to peek with equal interest outside of it. The very structure of time and space; the purpose or absurdity of existence; the dynamic relation of the many and the one; the meanings of home and human identity; and the nature of elemental reality were all opened up to meditation, conversation, and contestation. This is where thought itself takes flight as a form of wonder on the back of dozen different "hows" and a flowering of "whys." Creation myths, cosmogonies and cosmologies, have always offered up answers and explanations to these perennial questions. In one common story, the universe is a great egg that ranges from expansion to collapse; in another, it is the offspring of male and female gods; and in still another, it is fashioned from pre-existing material, like the corpse of a deity. The elemental accounts of the early philosophers enter the fray: Empedocles' cosmic cycling of *rhizomata* is followed by Plato's Demiurge and its creative matrix, which gives way to Aristotle's naturalistic framework, concentric celestial spheres, and the arrival of quintessential *aether*. From here the complex history courses through the work of Ptolemy, Copernicus, Newton, Descartes, and Einstein, and then grows out of theoretical models emphasizing variously expanding flat space; a static and steady-state perspective; kinematic expansion; and cosmic inflation, among others. As if to compound the increasing intricacy, some contemporary physicists and philosophers believe the cosmos may actually be one of many "multiverses"—to use a word coined by William James—that are essentially unrelated to each another, with the mind-numbing possibility that new universes are generated with each and every quantum measurement.

Perhaps high technology will facilitate a slow transition to a meaningful "cosmo-centrism"—if that notion proves coherent—although in the short run this is unlikely to occur except in the worldviews of the physicist turned mystic, the philosopher become poet, or the artist as shamanic astronaut. In part due to our biological inheritances and thousands of years of tribalism, we have not been very successful in cultivating an enlarged consciousness, an expansive sense of solidarity, or an inclusive conception of community, mind, and reality. At present, too, we are barely able to respect and protect local biota and ecosystems, let alone embrace the Earth as a whole or much beyond it. Before we try to act or "think cosmologically," we had better learn to "think globally" or even "think like a mountain," as Aldo Leopold advised. Nevertheless, some prophetic voices hold forth on the side of cautious hope, whether that assumes the shape of nonrational belief or a more intellectual vision. "It is the Infinite that is the source of abiding joy," counsels the Chandogya Upanishad, signaling us toward a greatly broadened view of the "indivisible unity" of elemental and extra-elemental things.[14] Here, we should remember—for better or for worse—that interest in space exploration from Kepler to Jules Verne and NASA has exhibited deeply religious longings, linked as it frequently is with ideas of ascension, escape from the body, transcendence, and eternal life.

Like the Nietzschean figure who bounds into the marketplace proclaiming the death of God only to be met with incredulous stares and complacent countenances, we might summon the courage and wherewithal to reflect in advance on whether in leaping boldly into space we are also inadvertently portending the demise of the Earth and thus falling skyward into a magnificent abyss or simply beginning to discover a genuine home in the universe. In "The End of the World," Archibald MacLeish proffers one kind of commentary and response: "There in the starless dark, the poise, the hover / There with vast wings across the canceled skies / There in the sudden blackness the black pall / Of nothing, nothing, nothing—nothing at all."[15] Until we find evidence to the contrary or locate another habitable abode in the Milky Way, it appears as if we still need to make this planet and the terrestrial elements that constitute it our haven, our harbor, and our home.

— 9 —

Revaluing Earth, Air, Fire, and Water

Elemental Beauty, Ecological Duty, and Environmental Policy

First use the fourfold spell . . . / Whoever ignores / The elements' cores / Their energy / And quality / Cannot command / In the spirit's land.

—Goethe, *Faust*

It [is] a question therefore of acquiring familiarity with the element, whereupon everything [will] take its course.

—Umberto Eco, *The Island of the Day Before*

"Excellent!," I [Watson] cried. "Elementary," said he [Holmes].

—Arthur Conan Doyle, "The Crooked Man"

We have explored and attempted to reanimate the earliest Western understandings of the elements and to suggest that environmental implications exist for a critical reclamation of such a perennial and pervasive idea. We have looked closely at ancient theories of earth, air, fire, and water, examined their domestication and transformation, and discussed the philosophical reappearance of elemental ideas within recent and contemporary thought. Through sustained and sustainable ecological practices along with a rekindled attentiveness to natural phenomena and the elemental imperatives they urge on us; by a vigilant remembering of the feral flesh and the passions of the lived body; via ongoing recollection of poetic and philosophical reverie; and a renewed focus on landscape, dwelling, and place, we may start to rediscover—even re-enchant and recover—an elemental connection with the natural world and earth, fire, air, and water more particularly. In so doing, we might find once again like the early Greeks that the elements are also our letters, our *spell-binding* means of constructing and connecting with the cosmos. In such a way, we might eventually help to create a more livable environment and a more bountiful and ecological abode for the interactions of air, fire, earth, and water as well as the creatures that inhabit or rely on them. All of this suggests that we can transition toward an active ethical, aesthetic, and cultural relationship with the elements and that we can bring the elemental world to inform, guide, or challenge our existing philosophical or political frameworks. What could an elemental sensibility or ethos entail? How might steps be taken in this direction? Let us close our investigation with a few concluding thoughts about the relation of the elements and the elemental to environmental aesthetics, ethics, and policy in order to better appreciate, value, and defend the places, phenomena, and forces associated with earth, air, fire, and water.

Elemental Ethics

How and why does the elemental world matter, and what kind of value should it be accorded? We have already provided an analysis of the linkages among the elements and human identity, natural place, pollution, the body, landscape, language, and other subjects. Most fundamentally, cultivating an ecological sensibility involves first actively noticing and regularly exposing ourselves to air, earth, fire, water, night, ice, stone, and the like and allowing them, in turn, to take hold of us through an array of perceptual, aesthetic, or ethical imperatives. Despite their increasing mediation by human artifacts and our tendency to forget them, elemental forces still abound all around us, and even within us. A Zen parable is instructive: "It is too clear and so it is hard to see. / A dunce once searched for a fire with a lighted lantern. / Had he known what fire was, / He could have cooked his rice much sooner."[1] With respect to earth, several writers have likewise summoned us to reflect on the sensuous surface of the planet and to delve into its elemental depths: "From soil we come, and to the soil we bequeath our excrement and remains. And yet soil—its cultivation and our bondage to it—is remarkably absent from those things clarified by philosophy in our Western tradition." Toward this end, they have issued a call for a "philosophy of soil" that entails "a clear, disciplined analysis of that experience and memory of soil without which neither virtue nor some new kind of subsistence can be."[2] We might try, in other words, to open the domestic human household to the vast untamed realm both inside and outside of our own material or mental walls, a task and opportunity that points to the value of be-wildering—making wild—our conceptions of ontological, epistemological, and social order itself.

Once considered profoundly animate, social, and even divine—whether in the guise of localized bodies, purposeful forces, or powerful deities—the elements now strike us as largely impersonal, lifeless, and without agency. On first blush, they may appear to be too indifferent, remote, or inhospitable for many of us to connect with them in the kinds of ways we discover deep affinities with living beings. The elements and the elemental, however, merit recognition, respect, and an understanding of how reciprocal relationships already exist with them or can be forged to them. Historian Stephen Pyne has spoken in this regard of our synergistic and mutually advantageous alliance with fire, the preservation of which he finds to be our oldest ecological duty. Taking a cue from this kind of symbiotic relationship, we could recognize conceivably a figurative or even quasi-legal elemental "contract" with earth, water, and air as well so as to articulate and internalize mindfully our immediate or more mediated responsibilities toward them. Such a provocative thought, and one not without its share of conceptual or juridical difficulties (e.g., how would such an agreement be enforced or honored?) has been advanced very loosely with respect to the commons—"a contract people make with their local natural systems," as Gary Snyder puts it. The task, he suggests, is to usher the "world of 'common pool resources' into the Mind of the Commons" because "any resource on earth that is not nailed down will be seen as fair game to the timber buyers or petroleum geologists."[3] Michel Serres has even proposed establishing a "natural contract" with the entire planet along the lines of a human social contract.[4] Such suggestive ideas could be further particularized and fleshed-out to focus on key elemental places or regions as they are debated and discussed.

Within environmental ethics more properly, each of three major philosophical frameworks—anthropocentrism, biocentrism, and eco-centrism—can accommodate comfortably or defend theoretically a significant status for the elements. If one adopts an anthropocentric (human-centered) perspective, it is clear that the elements are allied intimately with our everyday needs related to breathing, shelter, cleanliness, nutrition, and warmth, and so it is incumbent on us not to misuse or pollute them unnecessarily. Our lives are utterly dependent on the ongoing existence of "natural capital": clean air, fresh water, arable earth, and nourishing fire that generates both heat and light as well as regenerates forests and the landscape through periodic burnings. An organism or species that continually destroys its proximate surroundings and the world in which it is embedded materially is surely engaging in a form of suicide and even "biocide" or "ecocide," and so there is due cause to value the elemental realm for homocentric reasons alone. Anthropocentric arguments related to environmental policy are often more persuasive to the public than other philosophical rationales, but appeals to human interests alone need to be made pragmatically and strategically without forfeiting respect and protection for the entities in question.[5]

Alternatively, there are indirect biocentric (life-centered) reasons to be concerned with the elements that are tied to the fact that water, air, and earth contain and sustain a vast plenum of flora and fauna. Indeed, their very chemical, biological, or geological composition is interdependent with and partially constituted by the physical bodies and activities—laboring, reproducing, eating, excreting—of microorganisms, bacteria, reptiles, fish, birds, and mammals of all stripes and types. Protecting individual animals or native species entails preserving their habitats, and this requires safeguarding specific places, sites, or spaces of water, air, and earth in their various forms. Even though the elements are not necessarily alive individually, a rich forest soil profile, a vibrant cross section of summer air or a soupy pond might be so teeming with organic activity as to be considered living or flourishing as a collective singular entity—a very differentiated whole—when viewed as a phenomenal field rather than a discrete point. Stated in other words, it is not easy or even ecologically sound to separate sharply water, air, and earth from their living inhabitants.

There are powerful eco-centric (place-centered) reasons, too, for focusing on the elements. Water, air, and earth create the very materiality of the landscape and literally configure the matrix we term *the environment*. Ice, stone, and dirt, for example, provide an undergirding base and earthen support, whereas wind, water, and fire serve as transformative agents and catalysts of ecological change. A placed-based ethic points to obligations to particular bodies of water, the ambient air around us, and the earth under foot but also more broadly to the value of land in an ecosystem or bioregion. Here the confluence and complex of the elements tends to possess systemic worth more so than instrumental or inherent value, which is usually thought to reside in individual parts or pieces of a whole. Food selections, building materials, energy options, and even reproductive choices are thereby embedded in and conditioned prescriptively by their contexts or the peculiar details of a given location rather than being universalizable.

The challenges posed by the elements and elemental forces to environmental ethics are similar to the dilemmas related to valuing non-living natural objects like national monuments (e.g., the Petrified Forest or the Grand Canyon) and earthworks such as Mount Rushmore, although they also raise new questions and quandaries to the extent the phenomena are relatively insubstantial or ostensibly immaterial, as is the case with air, light, outer space, and the night sky. One interesting and emerging case involves Antarctica, an area composed largely of great sheets and gorges of ice. In a sense, this continent is only a form of proto-earth (roughly two percent is land, mostly at the margins) that is absent many familiar or "higher" plants and animals, including human inhabitants, usually endemic to more complex ecosystems and commonly present in an eco-centric land ethic. Life exists here, but it is sparse and generally microscopic in size—the largest land-dwelling animal is a wingless midge, only one centimeter in length—and it mostly confined to the waters and coastal edges, which serve as nesting, feeding, and resting grounds. If a life-centered ethic is possible in Antarctica, it is, as Holmes Rolston points out, a "miniscule biocentrism." Rolston argues convincingly that ethical models and political frameworks employed on the other six continents do not really work in this barren realm—Antarctica is a unique socially constructed international "regime"—and that a moral perspective focused on conceiving the region as wilderness and in non-anthropocentric terms is promising. This is a terrain of extremities, where landscape exists that has not encountered rain in two million years and life presses against the limits of temperature, light, and biological sustenance. Although desolate ice, rock cliffs, dry valleys, and cleaving glaciers do not have interests per se, they might still have "site integrity" and possess special qualities worth preserving. Even if there may not be direct obligations to "natural givens" like clouds, waves, or tectonic plates, we might have duties, Rolston suggests, to "life support processes, the hydrology, the meteorology, vital to life."[6] Antarctica, Rolston concludes, should not be viewed as *res nullius, res communis,* or *res publica,* but rather *res naturalis*. In belonging to no one, it belongs to everyone—to all of us—and so could become "a pace setter for an ethic of the common heritage of humankind."[7]

Terra-forming or even "greening" the moon or Mars, both of which are lifeless masses of earthen material, presents another set of ethical problems. Can we do whatever we want there? Should we respect these elemental places for potential future life, however remote that possibility might be? Do we have any obligations to maintain lunar mountains or Martian rock formations? Like our dynamic relations more generally with water, stone, fire, sky, soil, or ice, such issues cannot always be resolved in the abstract. They require an awareness of political, historical, and contextual matters and willingness to compromise when ethics becomes practical or meets public policy. They entail as well the need to grapple with broader issues about what we should value as a culture or global community over the long term. Edward Abbey makes a point worth considering in this regard when a character in one of his novels says, "We'll work it out as we go along. Let our practice form our doctrine, thus assuring precise theoretical coherence."[8] In other words, patience and practicality combined with an approach that takes the elemental phenomena and "things themselves" seriously may prove to be of merit.

Theoretically, an ethic for the elements—and an elemental ethic—would be less abstract than general duties often proclaimed toward a vague conception of "nature." It might necessitate a more open attitude toward our surroundings, encouraging, when possible, exposure or even vulnerability to the wind, waters, rock, ice, heat, snow, and light without at the same time asking us to surrender unduly a semblance of safety. And it would involve a clearer recognition and appreciation of the tradeoffs we broker for when we choose to build and reside on flood plains, fault lines, beachfronts, or delicate ecotones so as to experience open skies, roiling waves, or aesthetically appealing landscape. As a result, such a perspective may offer us a broader sensitivity toward a very differentiated world that cuts across, transcends, or is potentially inclusive in a robust pluralistic way of the best dimensions and insights of anthropocentric, biocentric, and eco-centric frameworks and considers the merits and ideas of non-Western perspectives evident in Taoism, Hinduism, or Buddhism. It may turn out that such an outlook—an elemental sensibility in short—also proves to be multicentered, pragmatic, or even a-centered in orientation, but ethics, like organisms and ideas, is evolving and system-sensitive, and we cannot simply posit this outcome in advance.

One constructive way to merely begin thinking about our ethical relationship with the elemental world is through regular, reflective, and critical human ambulation, especially because walking is one of the most basic, everyday activities in which we engage. Furthermore, it is commonly oriented by and directed through the ambient earth, air, fire, and water. Our walks often originate from and return to the hearth (fire), the heart of the home. They are frequently guided by the ever-changing sky and atmosphere (air) and follow the paths, flows, and rhythms of a river or stream (water). And they are grounded and governed by the lay of the land and landscape (earth) along with the confluence of sky and earth in the horizon. This elemental fourfold continually circulates and is gathered or unified in the motion of the moving body. Thoreau thus waxes: "This is a delicious evening, when the whole body is one sense, and imbibes delight through every pore. I go and come with a strange liberty in Nature, a part of herself. As I walk along the stony shore of the pond in my shirt-sleeves, though it is cool as well as cloudy and windy, and I see nothing special to attract me, *all the elements are unusually congenial to me.*"⁹ Here we observe not only the embodied walker in the midst of the surrounding elements but also detect a porous and bivalent sense of "sympathy with intelligence," as Thoreau puts it, at work in the natural world, where the individual is watching, hearing, smelling, and touching the environment but also likely being watched, heard, sensed, and touched him or herself. In ways too varied to detail here, walking helps to elicit attention to place, encourage awareness of local issues and environmental problems, and better enable us to move from the experience of environmental beauty—as it is routinely felt during an outdoor amble—to a sense of ecological duty. It assists us potentially in cultivating responsible ecological citizens who might learn and exhibit environmental virtues such as moderation, simplicity, humility, care for surroundings, and kindness toward living beings.¹⁰

Elemental Aesthetics

As the activity of walking often attests, one of the most viscerally persuasive but intellectually underappreciated approaches to knowing and protecting the natural environment starts with or focuses upon its beauty—whether that is inherent or socially constituted—a point that likely was not lost to ancient philosophers. *Kosmos* (cosmos) is related to the active, transitive verb *kosmeo*, which means to arrange or set in order, so that it can be said for many of the early Greeks that the physical world of nature is brought by random forces, teleology, intelligence, or a mythic cosmogony into a harmonious arrangement, one that was considered widely to be both moral and beautiful cosmetically—a word akin to cosmos. For instance, in Plato's work, the ordered and adorned universe is assembled out of a primordial and bewildering disorder or chaos. In this regard, there is arguably even a beauty as well to many of the oldest elemental theories given their elegant simplicity, internal coherence, and quasi-scientific and philosophic insights. And, as we have seen, we are well advised to listen to this ancient wisdom although it may speak to us through a foreign language, another era, or a different set of concerns.

More recently, the notion of beauty has entered the discussion of ecological issues through the emerging field of environmental aesthetics, which seeks to examine and clarify ways of appreciating the biological, inorganic, and built worlds around us. In doing so, it addresses questions such as, "Is all (or only parts) of the natural world beautiful?" "What are the proper roles of science and art in landscape evaluation, design or preservation?" "What is the nature and aesthetic value of a soundscape?" "How do narrative and story telling figure in the beauty of natural realms?" As environmental aesthetics steps out of a long shadow cast by art-based theories, it holds forth the possibility of contributing to other debates as well, including those concerning restoration ecology, our obligations to the natural world, and the ontological or social status of nature.

Two broad and competing aesthetic frameworks tend to dominate the philosophical terrain. On the one hand, there is a "cognitivist" model that stresses the need for knowledge of science and natural history in order to appreciate fully and rationally forests, mountains, deserts, or seas and, on the other hand, there is an "engagement" model that emphasizes the necessity of active, somatic, and sensorial participation or immersion in the environment.[11] Although each of these views has its multiple merits, a middle syncretic path that critically embraces the best of both polar views is possible and perhaps ultimately preferable, one that accepts the value of the interrelated and dialectical roles in aesthetic experience and evaluation of both the body and mind, both emotion and reason, and both imagination and science.[12] We can without contradiction, it seems, intellectually investigate the meteorological or ecological aspects of rain, lightning, wildfire, or snowfall, for example, in order to deepen our appreciation of the natural world as well as at the same time be emotionally moved or creatively inspired by these phenomena. The vast scale and utter transience of weather activity—morphing cloud formations, approaching and retreating storm fronts, the ebb and flow of hydrological processes, fading and flickering patterns of light and shadow, and ever-changing colors of ocean and sky—present particular challenges for appreciating the elemental world through traditional art-based perspectives. This is especially true because there is not frequently a way to stabilize, freeze, or frame (i.e., delimit or bound) mercurial and often monumental elemental forces that can encompass one in their very midst while still doing justice to the phenomena in the way one might do so in a gallery or museum housing more static or stationary human creations.

In gauging its beauty, we should be careful, however, not to make the elemental world a mere means or raw material for artistic appropriation or aesthetic appreciation. As Holmes Rolston warns, "In the forest the elements are savage;

one is not dealing with art or artifact, nor even of artist, but one has penetrated to the archetypes."[13] Massive ice, intense heat or bone-chilling cold, voluminous rock, brilliant light or pitch darkness, and endless stretches of sand offer the possibility of a liminal—and often an extreme—aesthetic relative to most constructed and, especially, pastoral norms of beauty, particularly when they do not offer safe domestic havens for human or animal life. Beauty and terror may be more closely associated in these realms than we initially imagine. "Explorers of desert and ice may be said to be half in love with piercing beauty and half in love with death," speculates geographer Yi-Fu Tuan.[14] Waxing elemental, Edward Abbey remarks of the desert he inhabited that it is "naked, monolithic, austere, and unadorned as the sculpture of the moon," adding that it is "clean, pure, totally useless, quite unprofitable."[15] The elements and elemental often resist easy cooptation, and this fact likely contributes to their beauty and the sheer force they exercise on our senses and faculties, compelling us at times to stop and listen, turn our heads and gaze, reach out our hands so as to touch, or open our mouths in order to taste.

Several Continental theorists have helped of late to revive the consideration of the elements more directly by presenting them in fresh, although largely undeveloped, aesthetic perspectives. Jean Baudrillard, for example, has proposed seduction as a nondiacritical model for the interaction of the elements, in place of a view of the physical world premised on sharp contrasts and stark oppositions. He imagines a universe in which cold seduces hot, subject seduces object, and absence seduces presence, as well as the reverse of these movements. Baudrillard portrays seduction as pushing terms toward one another and uniting them at points of heightened energy and charm. Speaking broadly and without much textual or historical support, he claims that in ancient cosmogonies the elements do not enter into specific structural relations of classification such as air/earth or water/fire. Rather than being "distinctive" elements, they are more like "attractive" entities that seduce one another so that we can say water seduces fire or, alternatively, is seduced by it.[16] Despite the deficit of scholarly evidence and the sketchy and elliptical nature of his claims, the effect of this thought-provoking aesthetic thesis is to socialize the four elements and to present them through the lens of cultural mediation and cosmic play as do many of the ancient Greek thinkers.

By way of comparison, William Desmond depicts the world in terms of elemental indeterminacies of earth, fire, air, and water, characterizing these four as a "rapturous univocity" as opposed to a "universal homogeneity" and one that "corresponds to the lived immediacy of our being enveloped in the 'pure' stuff of being." In this sense, we stand in the thickened middle of a sensuous flux, at the juncture not only of materiality and imagination but at the conjuncture of an undomesticated primordial "plasma" of the four elements. For Desmond, the elemental and our "swoon" into it can be identified with a "primal aesthetic being there of the world."[17] From such a perspective, we can read Thales' water, Heraclitus' fire, or Anaximenes' air in metaphysical as well as cosmological terms, through *poiesis* (poetic making) as well as *logos* (reason) and philosophical language, and via their sensuous excesses in addition to their domesticated homogeneity, singularity, and mediation.

Beyond the path-breaking work of Bachelard on the poetics of earth, air, fire, and water, one effort to provide an aesthetic of the elements has been made by Hans-Erik Larsen, who uses a phenomenological and semiotic approach to describe the elemental world, particularly as it is depicted in the realm of art through paintings and literature. Larsen constructs a theory of the imaginary that presents the elements as material constituents that serve to generate a cognitive view of and structure for the surrounding world. He builds on Merleau-Ponty's notion of "prereflexive elements of content" and Michel Serres' emphasis on the power of "tactility and topology."[18] He also points to the significance of morphology in comprehending near and distant phenomena, which he expresses in terms of euphoric (positive) and dysphoric (negative) values. In the process, Larsen reveals the elements as "concrete, realistic, and substantial aesthetic materials" and "real macrophysical representations of the natural world."[19] Although his analysis is directed more toward the elements as represented rather than viscerally encountered, it offers a helpful framework for thinking through the dynamics of texts and paintings by Søren Kierkegaard, J.M.W. Turner, and Edward Hopper, among others.

In the young but vibrant field of environmental art, Andy Goldsworthy deserves special attention for using the material and media of rock, wood, water, soil, light, sand, shadows, and even air in startling but sometimes simple ways to fashion "earth works" that generate an original elemental aesthetic.[20] From exhumed stone in upstate New York, he builds a sinuous wall that wends and weaves through the woods, framing trees and disappearing into a body of water. In his native Scotland, he erects graceful, gravity-defying arches and delicately balanced cairns—egg-shaped pillars of rock that serve as place markers or memorials to the passage of time. He launches colorful leaves, which are tethered together to form beautiful snaking threads, into a flowing stream. He tosses snow or dirt into the sky so as to catch a whimsical wind and thereby form flickering spectral shapes. He employs roots, moss, sticks, wool, and branches to make new images in and on the earth. He painstakingly cobbles together tendrils of ice to create exquisite sculptures that glisten in the destructive rays of the sun. And he transports giant snowballs mysteriously into the city in summer to allow joyful crowds to watch them slowly vanish.

Goldsworthy often carries these sculptures to the precipice of collapse, the precarious point where a fragile work may revert back to the earth that sustains it. Such objects are temporary but profound constructions, shimmering and evanescent entities like the elemental world itself, which is likewise subject to the eroding effects of weather and time. Although he documents his work through photographic images, all of his creations embrace or acknowledge the deep reality of change, what Buddhist's call *anicca* (impermanence). They are transformed or consumed by water, fire, air, and earth—swept away by tides, melted by the sun, scattered by wind, or engulfed by vegetation. What we perceive is often but the beauty of vanishing traces and fading remains, "trace elements" one might say.

James Hatley, in fact, suggests that a notion of the trace may be one constructive means through which to view wilderness—and by extension Goldsworthy's art—in contrast to an aesthetic or ethic that focuses on a problematic conception of the pristine, untouched or pure, the kind of etiquette that counsels "leaving no trace" when one goes hiking or camping. "The very figure of the trace," he points out, "recalls humans traversing a terrain in search of innumerable spoor—the signs and tracks and droppings left behind by a diversity of creatures, as well as climactic and geological processes. In calling upon the trace, one remembers that to follow a trail upon the earth is to come upon innumerable variations of that trail, each offering its specific purview or hold on what is at issue in one's surroundings."[21] This idea of the trace resonates well with one that we find in the philosophy of Jacques Derrida, where it comes to mean that which a sign differs/defers from—his operative term is *différance*—what remains absent in a sign's presence after everything has seemingly been accounted for. Strictly speaking, however, the "trace itself does not exist" since in appearing it is effaced or erased.[22] "The trace is the intimate relation of the living present with its outside."[23] The "play of traces,"[24] to use Derrida's words, is one very simple way to describe how Goldsworthy works with materiality—through what is left over in time and place—in order to explore appearing and disappearing elemental phenomena and to heighten our appreciation of the flickering world.

Goldsworthy collaborates with the elements—rather than exercising mastery over them—as he works on what we might call *out-stallations* (as opposed to gallery installations) in order to reveal or frame rock, wood, ice, or water in fresh perspectives. Seeking an intimate, tactile engagement with the environment, he observes, "I must touch . . . I take nothing out with me in the way of tools, glue or rope, preferring to explore the natural bonds and tensions that exist within the earth."[25] Laboring with the elements is decidedly a "hands-on" enterprise for Goldsworthy. Indeed, in one piece, he holds his own hand against thin, spring ice to leave a haunting imprint and subtle signature of his presence. Even in extreme cold, he works with bare hands, noting that one does not normally greet another person while wearing gloves, and so he extends this respect to the elemental world as well when he "shakes hands" with it each day. In this sense, Goldsworthy's aesthetic approach is premised on an intimate two-way "dialogue" with the landscape—where there exists a kind of co-existence, communion, and perhaps even communication—that reveals a deep reverence for and celebration of the particularities of a given place so that the work grows, evolves, and ultimately perishes there. Although he puts rock, wood, and water to use, he minimizes, when possible, the impact of his interventions, rarely carving, cutting, or breaking objects, but choosing instead to let elemental materials reveal themselves in a new light or releasing their internal energies to the encompassing environment, employing time, and seasonal changes as handy tools.

Journeying through and residing in remote wilderness regions and off-the-map outposts over a span of seven years, Jay Griffiths has also explored the beauty of the elemental world with noteworthy attentiveness, exuberance, and courage, seeking "the will of the wild" and the ways it appears in "elemental vitality, in savage grace."[26] Organizing her travels around the fourfold of wild earth, wild air, wild fire, and wild water—which she splays open in order to add wild ice—Griffiths fraternizes with cannibals, confabulates with gypsies, learns from Amazonian shamans, and wanders the outback with Australian Aborigines. She lies naked, cold, and vulnerable in the Arctic snow, hunts magnificent ocean whales, hikes through the heat and desert sands, descends into the darkness of the sea, and disappears into the airy majestic heights of the mountains. Like Lingis, she longs "to live at the edge of the imperative, in the tender fury of the reckless moment" and to know the wild landscape so that through "knife-sharp necessity" she might "trust to the elements [her] elemental self."[27] Along the way, Griffiths voices an unbridled defense of elemental wildness and a passionate protest against the traps of domestication, maintaining boldly: "We may think we are domesticated but we are not. Feral in pheromone and intuition, feral in our sweat and fear, feral in tongue and language, feral in cunt and cock. This is the first command: to live in fealty to the feral angel."[28] As had the Presocratics, the Romantics, and some inspired phenomenologists before her, Griffiths sets forth her elemental experiences in vibrant poetic prose situated at the fertile intersections of science, myth, literature, and philosophy.

Goethe's literary, scientific, and philosophical work, which often is very phenomenological and participatory in its approach, is especially relevant to elemental aesthetics. Using Goethe's ideas, along with the thought of Bachelard and Rudolph Steiner, Nigel Hoffman presents the four elements as "modes of cognition"—dispositional, qualitative, and creative ways of perceiving the environing world.[29] More than mundane matter, the elements are *imaginal* phenomena that open up and reveal the landscape and human mind in fascinating new ways. Wedding art with organic science and building on the ancient principle evident in Empedocles that "like knows like," Hoffman shows in specific instances—through leaf shapes, flowers, musical scales, and the gestures of birds—how earth cognition entails physical and analytical thinking; how water cognition is imaginative, temporal, and sculptural in form; how air cognition is essentially inspirational and musical in nature; and how fire cognition is an intuitive and poetic kind of understanding. Hoffman then applies these elemental ideas to the Yabby Ponds, which lie north of Sydney, Australia, in order to disclose the dynamics of a particular place, including its geology, ecology, topography, and animal life. In such a way, he integrates and unites the four elements with art and a science of living forms.

There are significant outcroppings of the four elements, too, in poetry, drama, and literature that engage archetypal or perennial themes and that provide in the process potential clues to the meanings of these works. In *Antony and Cleopatra*, Shakespeare casts Cleopatra as commanding the three elements of air, water, and fire but excludes earth from her control. Lacking this necessary stead, which signifies order, realism, and stability, she tragically dooms Antony and herself. In essence, Cleopatra serves as a force of attraction for the elements like the role Empedocles allots to Aphrodite (*philia* or love).[30] In *Julius Caesar*, a celebration of the elements arises by way of Marc Antony's remark of Brutus, "The elements / So mixed in him, that Nature might stand up / And say to all the world, 'This was a man!' "[31] And in one sonnet, Shakespeare uses the relative heaviness of earth and water—"Receiving naught by elements so slow / But heavy tears, badges of either's woe"—to reveal deep melancholy at the absence of a lover. In the paired sonnet that follows, he summons the "quicker elements" of "slight air and purging fire" to symbolize respectively his thought and desire for the distant youth while recognizing that life is composed of all four.[32]

T. S. Eliot likewise uses the canonical fourfold to great effect. Each section of his poem, "Four Quartets," praises one of the elements: "Burnt Norton" (air), "East Coker" (earth), "Dry Salvages" (water), and "Little Gidding" (fire). The poem, in fact, opens with epigraphs from Heraclitus and then concludes, "We only live, only suspire / Consumed by either fire or fire."[33] Eliot's most well-known work, "The Wasteland," similarly invokes this organizing theme in each of its first four parts—"Burial of the Dead" (earth); "Game of Chess" (air); "Fire Sermon" (fire), and "Death by Water" (water)—while the fifth and final section, "What the Thunder Said," is likely a reference to the quintessence of *aether*.

Thoreau's aesthetic vision of the natural world is deeply elemental in its origins and conception as well. Thus, he writes: "He would be a poet who could impress the winds and streams into his service, to speak for him; who nailed words to their primitive senses . . . transplanted them to this page with earth adhering to their roots."[34] Like Bachelard, who proceeds more systematically to develop an elemental poetics, Gary Snyder—a contemporary nature writer and environmentalist with a Thoreauvian lineage—playfully partitions poets according to their imagistic and linguistic affinities with a particular element. Earth poets "write small poems" and "need help from no man" while air poets "play out the swiftest gales / and sometimes loll in the eddies." A fire poet, alternatively, can write when "fuel oil won't flow" and "burn at absolute zero" unlike the water poet who may leave "millions of tiny / different tracks / criss-crossing through the mud."[35] By contrast, playwright, poet, and actor Antonin Artaud summons the traditional fourfold so as to subject it to a radical aesthetic upheaval: "The fire in the water, / the air in the earth, / The water in the air / and the earth in the sea. / They are not yet insane enough, / They are not enough at each / other's throats, and the more furious, the more enraged, the nearer and / dearer they are."[36] And after linking Goethe's German version of Mephistopheles and *Geist* with fire, associating French poet Paul Claudel's *esprit* with water, and connecting the *espiritu* of Argentine writers—"children of the Pampas"—with earth, Richard Nirenberg even speculates on a possible, if very problematic, poetic relation between the elements and geographic place. He invites us to imagine an "extended research project on nations and their dominant spiritual element" that might help to explain "why nationalisms bloodily clash, and [how] we may even learn how to avoid future massacres."[37]

There is an "elemental sublime" that emerges in the work of writers and artists when earth, fire, air, or water gesture toward a sense of transfiguring, more-than-human awe. We see this, for example, in the depiction of the whirlwind out of which God manifests himself in the Book of Job; in the whirlpool of Edgar Allen Poe's story "Into the Maelstrom;" and in some of J.M.W. Turner's romantic landscape and seascape paintings. In more contemporary work, New York-based artist Heide Fasnacht draws luminous vapors of air, clouds of atoms, bodies of land, rainwater on windows, fireworks, geysers, and volcanoes to probe elemental themes and the phenomenology of perception.[38] The graphic images of Latvian-born American artist Vija Celmins, too, explore in great realistic specificity ocean surfaces, desolate desert floors, small stones, night skies, and distant galaxies to wonderfully evoke elemental realms. By focusing on the minutiae and microscopic detail of these placescapes and objects, however, her depictions tend to challenge or subvert romantic ideas of a natural sublime.[39] Aesthetic activity involving earth, air, fire, and water sometimes takes more mundane and ludic forms as well, bringing together productive work with possibilities for joy. Thus, writer Phillipe Soupalt unites the fourfold in his description: "The garden was enchanted. In their play [the children] harnessed the four elements, building canals, primitive ovens, windmills, and tunnels."[40]

Finally, the elements play a prominent role in the alchemical and astrological symbol systems of the Middle Ages and Renaissance.[41] Camille Paglia summarizes a common view within astrology when she distills their meaning as follows: "Fire is will, originality, boldness, the amoral life force. Air is language, wit, balance, humane perspective. Water is intuition, sympathy, deep feeling, mystical oneness, and prophecy. Earth is method, order, precision, realism, materialism."[42] Here it should also be noted that in chiromancy (or palmistry), the hand is sometimes divided into four types—practical (earth), intuitive (fire), sensitive (water), and intellectual (air). In all these ways and many more, the elements engage both the bodily senses and the imaginative and artistic mind to reveal novel ways of environmental perception.[43]

Environmental Action

One final portal through which to view the elements in evaluative ways and to respond more directly to ecological problems is the sphere of public policy. In this regard, the dilemma known as "the tragedy of the commons," which has focused since the late 1960s on issues related to open or limited-access natural resources, is a particularly helpful theoretical framework. As far back as 1625, legal theorist

Hugo Grotius proclaimed influentially: "For the magnitude of the sea is such, as to be sufficient for the use of all nations, to allow them without inconvenience and prejudice to each other the right of fishing, sailing or any other advantage which that element affords." "The same," he added, "may be said of air as common property, except that no one can use or enjoy it, without at the same time using the ground over which it passes or rests."[44] As an old Latin expression states it: *Cuius est solum, eius usque ad coelum* ("He who has property in the soil has the same up to the sky.") This kind of claim has since been made many times about the supposed unlimited carrying capacity and resource abundance of the planet, and it has been advanced more recently about outer space as well. First formulated by Garrett Hardin, the tragedy of the commons asserts that the commons and natural resources contained within them will be exploited, overused, and eventually eliminated when they are not either privatized (free-market responses) or owned and regulated by the government (socialist approaches). There is a deep discrepancy, in other words, between individual rationality (e.g., an incentive to add one more sheep to a common pasture) and collective rationality (e.g., the need to preserve the land and limit access) that can lead to environmental ruin when it is not balanced properly.

With regard to air, water, and earth, predicaments arise for existing commons due both to unbridled instances of "putting in" (pollution) and "taking out" (excessive extraction). Setting aside the many controversies surrounding the characterizations and possible ways out of the ostensible logic of this calamity, it is now patently evident that the atmospheric commons (e.g., climate, night sky, or silence), the oceanic commons (e.g., deep sea fish or water cleanliness), and the remaining terrestrial commons (e.g., genetic diversity or arctic ice and tundra) are under serious and sustained assault. The increasing privatization and commodification of water, air, and earth have not mitigated the problem but contributed instead to the enclosure and disappearance of shared domains. With respect to the "putting in" side of the tragedy, it may behoove us to think of pollution, in part, as an inside-out issue, whereby what is considered "outside" in the air and water or on earth—and hence susceptible to being despoiled or disrupted—is brought conceptually "inside" into an enlarged domestic arena where it can be cared for like other more human concerns or creations. We need, therefore, to devise more creative strategies, workable means, and sustainable ends to protect water, air, and soil by using both market and governmental mechanisms as well as approaches focused on individual conservation and reduced consumption. We close this study by suggesting a few broad environmental policy directions and recommendations related to the four elements.

Water

There are clearly ecological and political reasons to be active in addressing the current state of water in the world. A vast volume of water is no longer able to purge itself of industrial pollutants. As Alice Outwater points out, "By dredging, by damming, by channeling, by tampering with (and in some cases eliminating) the ecological niches where water cleans itself, we have simplified the pathways that water takes through the . . . landscape; and we have ended up with dirty water."[45] Water problems do not possess simple technological solutions, although there are without question emerging techniques and processes that can better assist us with matters related to distribution, filtering, and sanitation. The amount of water on the planet is finite, and the demand for fresh water is growing. We cannot make additional water even if we can desalinate it, often at great expense. We need to use less, conserve more, and to address population issues if we continue to use the same amount.

Global water problems necessitate both upstream and downstream solutions—more equitable uses in the former instance and more judicious development of resources in the latter case. With more than one billion people having no regular access to potable water and as many as three billion without reliable access to sanitation services, the expense of failing to provide water for these activities will far exceed the cost of doing so in terms of health care and social welfare. Water expert Peter Gleick recommends that the United Nations Educational, Scientific and Cultural Organization (UNESCO) adopt a human entitlement of fifty liters of water per person per day—which amounts to about five liters for drinking, twenty for sanitation, fifteen for bathing, and ten for cooking—a figure still greatly below the minimal average withdrawals per capita in most countries poor in water resources. And because water is a social good—a prerequisite for all rights we might say—we may eventually need to establish a "universal lifeline rate" for consumption so that water used above that point is priced much higher.[46]

In any case, we require innovative, fair, and practical water policies and solutions no matter which of the three major hydrological choices are selected: producing more potable water via desalination techniques (e.g., reverse osmosis and distillation); consuming less through conservation measures (e.g., new pricing systems, better management, wastewater reuse, technological developments); or using the same supply but with fewer people on the planet.[47] One new low-technological, minimal-cost development called "Watair" is inspired by spider webs and leaves that passively collect beads of dew and holds promise for obtaining water from the air in arid, remote, or polluted regions. Constructed as an inverted pyramid made from elastic canvas or recycled glass and metal, its panels capture at least forty-eight liters of water daily through gravity, which pulls moisture downward into tanks or bottles.[48] In agriculture, calibrated emitters that release dripping water directly to plant roots; consultants who provide advice to farmers about efficiency; and pricing structures that allow irrigation districts to sell back "saved" water have proved valuable in reducing waste. In buildings, "living machines" that use biomimetic techniques to treat and recycle wastewater offer viable solutions.[49] In and the around the home, individuals can contribute to reshaping policy and economic options by using low-flow faucets, toilets, and showerheads; washing clothes in horizontal axis machines; harvesting and reusing rain and gray water in tanks; and even transforming swimming pools into aquaculture ponds for raising fish. Finally, mulching in and around garden areas, watering during morning hours, and planting native flora that needs less water than non-native plants are steps in the right direction in terms of landscaping.[50]

Air

Public policy toward the air and atmosphere is also a paramount, if complex, concern. Currently, we measure air quality in the United States by levels of six common pollutants—carbon monoxide, sulfur dioxide, lead, particulate matter, ozone, and nitrogen dioxide—and over the twenty years ranging from 1979 to 1998, it improved significantly in most geographical areas. The Clean Air Act of 1970 was a major success in this regard, but like the Clean Water Act this legislation now appears addressed in part to the issues of an earlier era. We not only have pollution with which to contend but global warming, a greater and growing number of mobile sources generating emissions, and high incidences of medical problems related to air quality that tend to hit hardest on children, elderly persons, and those with allergies, asthma, or emphysema. "Global dimming," too, is an emerging phenomenon whereby less sunlight is arriving on the surface of the planet because of increased aerosol usage, carbon dioxide accumulation, cloud cover, and air contamination, and this in turn affects adversely ocean evaporation rates and agricultural productivity, especially light-loving plants such as tomatoes and peppers.[51]

With the air, transitional moves toward sustainability must vigilantly protect the "lungs" of the planet—the world's forests—through a focus on ecological technologies, the greening of architectural space, and the promotion of alternatives to fossil fuels in order to reduce the production or effects of greenhouse gases. Effective climate change policy is absolutely imperative. As a "third-generation" environmental problem, anthropogenic climate change is global, unpredictable, transboundary, and long-term in nature, and it presents especially complicated social and economic challenges given that greenhouse gases are emitted from many varied sources and we are all complicit in releasing them into the atmosphere. At the same time, the topic has low political salience for most Americans despite the fact that the United States contributes one fourth or more of all such gases to the world's air. Governmental approaches that stress voluntary responses by industry, tie political commitments to the actions of other nations, and use economic growth as a rationale for inaction or delay are insufficient and often retrogressive given the severity and scope of the crisis. What is needed is an international climate treaty with far-reaching but achievable goals, clear and enforceable regulations, and economic incentives and punishments for compliance and noncompliance respectively—a Kyoto Protocol with stronger teeth in effect.[52] Culturally, we should also seek an easily communicable symbol or recognizable image of atmospheric change that would help to bring home the palpable severity of the problem to millions of people, underscoring both the dangers and constructive hopes for concerted change.

The benefits of using air itself in the form of wind power to supplement or supplant nonrenewable resources are great. Potential wind energy is bountiful, clean, widely available, and decreasing rapidly in cost in many parts of the United States and world. Between one and three percent of the energy from the sun that reaches the planet is converted into wind energy, many more times than the amount that is transformed into biomass by plants through photosynthesis. Theoretically at least, long-term use of wind power could meet the world's current energy consumption levels, and while there are legitimate concerns about clearing trees to build wind farms and parks, the death of birds caught in turbines, and so-called "visual pollution," these are acceptable tradeoffs in terms of the overall ecological footprint of available technologies. Although presently a relatively small contribution to the energy grid in the United States—enough to power about a million and a half homes—wind farms are practical when the average speed of moving air, which travels faster at high altitudes, is ten miles per hour or more. Wind-powered generators now account for almost a quarter of electricity use in Denmark, and Germany harvests about a third of the world's total capacity. These are surely hopeful signs.[53]

There are other policy options available to us, too, for air-related issues. For example, the tradable permit system used for sulfur dioxide, which set targets for and limits on pollution for an industry or geographical area and allows companies to buy and sell rights to pollute, has been very successful in reducing emissions and could be applied to other noxious gases. Given the enormous volume of greenhouse gases that airplanes release, making ever-expanding air travel less harsh on the atmosphere through green taxes on tickets, greater support for public transportation, or alternative fuel sources is also an economic and political challenge worth pursuing. Similar dilemmas arise with air conditioning, which in the United States accounts for nearly one fifth of all kilowatt-hours and uses more electricity each year than the total consumption of India and Indonesia—the second and fourth most populated countries—combined. By encouraging economic development in and population shifts toward southern states, air conditioning has given rise to the so-called "frioconservatives" and may even have helped George W. Bush—no friend to the environment—to become president.[54] Of our "air-conditioned nightmare" (to use Henry Miller's phrase), Stan Cox speculates that if the units were once banned during wartime but later identified by many as a necessity in a period of wealth, we should not consider them now to be irreplaceable or inevitable. Indirectly, they may be numbing us to global climate change, maintaining our addiction to foreign oil and our support of repressive regimes with abundant supplies of the resource, and encouraging us to stay in our homes or in commercial spaces rather than connecting with a larger civic community and the outdoor environment. "In an era when air-conditioning systems are proliferating, heating up the planet and chilling the social and political climate, their most important feature has become the 'off' switch."[55] Failing that choice by individuals, public policy needs in the interim to raise energy-efficiency standards for the technology, engage in educational efforts to show the baleful effects of the luxury, and provide alternative, less energy-intensive cooling methods.

Earth

Much of the major legislation and policy concerning land use and pollution—including the Resource Conservation and Recovery Act, and the Comprehensive Environmental Response, Compensation and Liability Act known as "Superfund"—has focused on reducing the negative effects of unwanted waste. While this regulation is understandable, we need to move toward long-term strategies that create a no- or low-waste economy, which reconceives outputs (e.g., garbage, emissions, or by-products) as "wanted" inputs or even treats them as "food" (e.g., methane released from landfills as fuel) so as to close ecological loops rather than supporting linear and unsustainable cradle-to-grave models of production and consumption. Innovation must be supported with economic incentives or rewards through a green tax plan and "green accounting" that indicates the true price of goods and services, including the costs borne by the environment and humans due to "negative externalities" such as deforestation, disease, and pollution. Steps in the international arena that might serve as points of inspiration include an experiment in Kalundborg, Denmark, where a housing development and number of businesses have been collocated so that the so-called waste (e.g., steam, water, or gas) of one unit becomes a vital resource for another, and "take-back" laws in Germany that encourage or require producers of durable goods such as refrigerators, TVs, or washing machines to take back and reuse packaging or worn-out commodities.[56]

If we are going to be serious about achieving long-term sustainability and taking into consideration the survival and well-being of future generations, environmental policy toward the land and earth must involve as well a deep rethinking of transportation systems, agriculture, parks and the public domain, housing, suburban sprawl, and mining practices. Agricultural legislation and food policy, for example, have tended to treat living soil as lifeless dirt; to saturate plants with chemical pesticides and fertilizers that wind up through nonpoint runoff in our rivers, lakes, and eventually our bodily organs; to waste great amounts of water; and to support large-scale agribusiness, monocultures, and growing practices that necessitate long distance shipping, overgrazing, and unhealthy eating. A culture that values agriculture, and the soil on which it is based, would move in precisely the opposite direction. It would fashion a major place for organic farming, health, and nutrition concerns, energy conservation, just pricing procedures, and equitable

distribution to less affluent neighborhoods. Instead of an industrial top–down framework, where food travels on average up to fifteen hundred miles to reach one's plate, changes hands roughly a dozen times, requires ten calories of energy to produce one calorie of edible material, and mainly grows only seven crops, a green model would build upward from the earth to nurture more of the 200,000 species of wild plants on the planet and encourage alternative institutions and practices like farmers' markets, community-supported agriculture, sustainable gardens, and rooftop or urban soil plots.[57]

Fire

Finally, in terms of policy toward the "fire" that literally or metaphorically inhabits the furnaces, engines, fuel cells, and microprocessors of modern technology, a great deal could be said regarding energy choices, military firepower, or nascent biotechnology, and their effects on our surroundings. Although the elemental world is physically proximate, it is often concealed through human artifacts, techniques, and processes that have transfigured air, water, fire, and earth and brought us along the way both the bodily benefits and environmental burdens of air conditioning, bottled water, oil and gas heating, and asphalt roads, to mention but a few developments. As the world is remade through anthropocentric action, it may even be the case that the environment—and by extension environmental ethics—is becoming a prosthetic branch of technology. Unfortunately, there is very little public assessment or critique of technology prior to—or even following—its implementation or adoption. Perhaps we have been seduced unwittingly by the hypnotic force of fire and embraced a blind or dogmatic "technological fundamentalism," as Wendell Berry terms it, that views most all emerging technologies as facilitating progress or being socially progressive and hence immune to criticism.

The primary problem with our dependence on both the virtual and actual flame is that we have relied on fire technologies without using them, and hence organizing society, in a wise and ecological manner. Such a move toward sustainability must undoubtedly involve a widespread embrace of solar energy; the rapid ratification, enactment, and enforcement of a strong protocol on global warming and climate change; an active disengagement from an international dependency on oil, coal, and gas; the adoption of hydrogen fuel cells and alternative energy sources; the phasing out or substitution for petrochemicals and noxious fertilizers; and similar public policy measures. Restoring fire to ecosystems where it is lacking and needed is also a complex practical and theoretical endeavor as the realms of the "natural" and "artificial" become more deeply imbricated and the choice between wild natural fire and managed anthropogenic burning appears less clear. Like other forms of ecological restoration, this enterprise will involve learning by doing—trial and experiment—with the lessons of failure hopefully proving as instructive as the successes.

We can, then, work with and tap the elements in sustainable ways without exhausting them or completely despoiling the environment. Wind turbines (air), photovoltaic power from the sun (fire), hydrogen fuel cells and hydroponic growing practices (water), and geothermal energy and biomass (earth) all provide more ecological alternatives to our use of coal, gas, and oil. We have a very literal and physical task of cleaning up and protecting aquifers, rivers, and oceans; reducing lethal emissions and greenhouse gases in the air; slowing desertification and destruction of the land; and better managing fire in the forests. But we also need to view our actions and affairs more imaginatively: to perceive, for example, high technology, warfare, and the overreliance on fossil fuels as transformations and uses of fire.

Politically, the so-called Red and Blue state division in the United States might even be rooted in a more primordial distinction between the realms of earth and water. When one examines a map of voting behavior and political affiliations, it tends to separate in a very rough way between those populations tied more closely to the land in the midwest, south, and far west and those groups living near oceans, river systems, and lakes along the continental coasts and the Great Lakes region. Influenced, although by no means determined, by the solidity of the earth or the fluidity of water, individuals and communities often are by various degrees either accepting of or resistant to sudden or ongoing change brought about by storms, drought, floods, and other weather phenomena as well as the flowing movement of immigrants, travelers, trade goods, and cultural ideas. Farmers, for example, who are deeply dependent on the security and stability of the soil and the regularity of seasonal patterns may feel threatened by unpredictable changes generated by actions of the hydrological cycle, whereas others—sailors, merchants, artists, and academics, for example—may welcome the social, economic, or political opportunities afforded by the fluidity of water, which conducts new people, products, or possibilities to their setting.

Bewildering Order

It has been said, "The cygnet finds the water, but the man / Is born in ignorance of his element."[58] Perhaps so; but that does not mean we cannot locate a suitable medium or sustainable home in the world nor does it preclude the possibility that, unlike the cygnet, we might even discover something of value in all of the ambient elements. Both mundane and extraordinary encounters with elemental realms have enduring implications. They leave something of themselves on our imaginations and outlooks. Stone hardens our resolve. Clouds give us license to drift and to dream. Air conducts our voice; water channels our language; and each gives shape to our corporeal form. Ice and snow teach us about the transience of sensuous things. Heat and cold temper our characters and help forge our cultural identities and temperaments. Wood bequeaths us substance for creative hands. Light reveals and clarifies while night invites retreat and restorative rest. Fire magnifies the power of our muscles as it mocks and extinguishes human gestures pointed toward permanence. Space opens us to the infinity of natural wonders and possible worlds. And earth magisterially ballasts and balances of all this as a supportive body. In brief, elemental phenomena are basic to the shimmering fabric of the physical environment, which is wrought or displayed, in large measure, through their mesmerizing dance of appearance and disappearance. Stone, light, cloud, fire, ice, heat, air, and water exist, we may be tempted to say, as expressions of a kind of elemental or ontological *a priori*, a realm prior to but deeply present in our daily lives.

In "Toward a Theory of Weather," Goethe provocatively suggests the four elements can embody "willfulness itself" as they seek to "go their own wild and brutal way." In this view, "earth continually strives to seize the water and force it to solidify, annex it as earth, rock, or ice. With equal turbulence the water . . . hurl[s] the earth once more into its abyss, the earth it so reluctantly left behind. The air, supposedly an enlivening and protective friend, suddenly races down upon us as a storm to smash us and choke us. The fire relentlessly attacks everything in reach which is flammable or meltable." In other words, the elements also may appear as "colossal opponents" against which "we must forever do battle," and they might only be "overcome" by putting to use "the highest powers of the mind, by courage and cunning."[59] In a loose sense, we humans have become an odd kind of fifth element, an ultra-powerful force that is able to alter profoundly the make-up and meaning of land, sea, fire, and sky. We are acting on the natural world as if we reside outside it, located like the *aether* of the ancients in an autonomous sphere where—we seem to assume—there are few, if any, lasting consequences to our decisions.

Herein lies our challenge: to both acknowledge our immense capacities to change the local environment and planet as a whole but also to understand the ways we can rein ourselves in and act responsibly. As we have seen, "battling the elements" is not the only perspective open and available to us, even among a coterie of Romantic writers. In "A Defence of Poetry," Shelley concludes more reasonably that "the cultivation of those sciences which have enlarged the limits of the empire of man over the external world, has, for want of the poetical faculty, proportionally circumscribed those of the internal world; and man, having enslaved the elements, remains himself a slave."[60] In essence, this standpoint questions the deep philosophical and cultural assumption that we must remain perpetually "at two with nature," to use Woody Allen's humorous but insightful phrase.

Today, it seems as if the "four elements" are more likely to appear as the tetrad of concrete, smog, plastic, and silicon—along with the ether of cyberspace, if we add a quintessence or fifth matter—rather than earth, air, water, and fire, respectively, even as the chemical fourfold of hydrogen, carbon, nitrogen, and oxygen predominate in the universe as well as in organic compounds. However, we could also choose to interpret these recent cultural and commercial changes as a new challenge in the same way that the emerging field of green chemistry is working with the elements of the periodic table to create environmentally friendly compounds and biodegradable products.[61] And we could take inspiration from those environmentalists who are pushing in creative ways for a more hydrogen-based economy rather than a carbon-dependent one and pressing for a mixed-media strategies and task forces (multi-element approaches we might say) on pollution rather than focusing individually on one medium (element) because toxins trespass territories and change form via the agency of wind (air), rain (water), burial (earth), and combustion (fire).[62]

In the end, we need to view the four elements as interconnected, of course, because they do interact in both routine and complex ways through transport cycles, feedback loops, and unpredictable events. Fire transforms the earth and soil; land use affects air quality, which in turn can precipitate thunderstorms or acid rain; parched prairie grass encourages wild fire, and so forth. All of this impacts living organisms, including humans, directly and indirectly; hence the need for cross-media or "cross-elemental" perspectives. Although we have treated the four elements individually at points in this work, it is incumbent on us, when possible, to think about and experience them together without reducing their plurality to an undifferentiated unity. At the same time, it is important not to calcify the category of the four elements and essential to be receptive to the possibility that other very primordial or elemental aspects of the environment exist—whether they involve, for example, light, silence, heat, space, and time or appear in non-Greek and non-Western sources.

Speaking of an elemental desert structure known as Delicate Arch, Edward Abbey speculates that its value may lie "in the power of the odd and unexpected to startle the senses and surprise the mind out of their ruts of habit, to compel us into a reawakened awareness of the wonderful." As a "weird, lovely, fantastic object," it possesses "the curious ability to remind us—like rock and sunlight and wind and wilderness—that *out there* is a different world, older and greater and deeper by far than ours, a world which surrounds and sustains the little world of men as sea and sky surround and sustain a ship." It is what he calls the "shock of the real" that allows us to see again for a spell the way children perceive the universe as brimming with marvels.[63] Similarly, therein may lie some of the worth of elemental encounters: to remind us not only of our profound everyday interdependence with air, water, light, stone, ice, soil, fire, and the like but also their ability to guide—or jolt—us outside of ourselves (or our narrowed experiences of the self) for a time so as to appreciate and engage an ancient, sometimes strange but also strangely familiar, and certainly more capacious sphere that we cannot easily assimilate. Tom Robbins no doubt stretches credulity a bit too far when he declares, "The brown paper bag is the only thing civilized man has produced that does not seem out of place in nature."[64] But his provocative comment might be borne in part of the sense that in the elemental world we can conceivably discover a foreign or feral realm of being, a bewildered order, or a kind of chaotic cosmos—a *chaosmos*, to use James Joyce's term.

It must be acknowledged clearly that the modern scientific view of the elements has largely supplanted the philosophical, mythical, experiential, and poetic perspectives. We now know, for example, that the uneven heating of the earth produces winds. And yet, as writer Jan DeBlieu expresses it, "Somehow, out in the elements, the wisdom of science falls a bit short. It is easier to believe that wind is the roaring breath of a serpent who lives just over the horizon."[65] Our living and evolving world in all its complex and confusing order thus cannot be contained or fully explained by any one account, whatever its pretense to comprehensiveness or objectivity. In "The Four," D. H. Lawrence observes that if we use our senses as a gauge, the elements will always be four in name and number because these are "the elements of life, of poetry, and of perception." They are "the four Great Ones, the Four Roots, the First Four / of Fire and the Wet, Earth and the wide Air of the world." To locate other elements, "you must go to the laboratory / and hunt them down." By contrast, "the four we have always with us, they are our world" and, more exactly, "they have us with them."[66] Even if we have become animals absent well-defined niches, an uprooted and wandering gang of "natural aliens," "rogue primates" or incipient "robo-*sapiens*," that truth should not prevent us from experiencing and exploring the deep grasp that such a powerful idea holds on our philosophical, historical, and ecological imaginations.[67] With some patience, fortune, and persistence, we might be able to rediscover and recover a deeper and more lasting connection with the elemental world and in the process find our place—reside in our own element or elements—within the bewildered and bewildering beauty everywhere around us.

Notes

Preface

1. Annie Dillard, *Pilgrim at Tinker Creek* (New York: HarperCollins, 1999), p. 51.

Introduction

1. Henry Beston, *The Outermost House* (New York: Henry Holt, 1992), p. 10.
2. Mortimer J. Adler, *The Great Ideas: A Lexicon of Western Thought* (New York: MacMillan, 1952), pp. 177–84.
3. Alfred North Whitehead, *The Concept of Nature* (Cambridge, UK: Cambridge UP, 1920), p. 19.
4. Georg W. F. Hegel, *Philosophy of Nature*, ed., M. J. Petry, Vol. 2 of *Encyclopedia of the Philosophical Sciences* (London, UK: Unwin Brothers Limited, 1970), par. 281.
5. Georg F. Hegel, *Lectures on the History of Philosophy*, Vol. 1 (Lincoln: U of Nebraska P, 1995).
6. Heidegger performs something akin to this action with his arguably hypostasized term "Being" when he crosses it through, both marking it and, in effect, taking it away.
7. For a more complete examination of the notion of domestication, see David Macauley, "Be-wildering Order: On Finding a Home for Domestication and the Domesticated Other" in Roger Gottlieb, ed., *The Ecological Community* (New York: Routledge, 1997).
8. See David Macauley, "The Domestication of Water: Filtering Nature Through Technology," *Essays in Philosophy* 6.1 (2005).
9. Ivan Illich, *H_2O and the Waters of Forgetfulness* (Berkeley, CA: Heyday Books, 1985), p. 76.
10. Gary Paul Nabhan, *The Cultures of Habitat* (Washington, DC: Counterpoint, 1997), p. 319.
11. Quoted in Philip Ball, *Life's Matrix: A Biography of Water* (Berkeley: U of California P, 1999), p. 142.
12. Quoted in George Johnson, *Fire in the Mind: Science, Faith, and the Search for Order* (New York: Vintage, 1995), p. 71.
13. See Paul Davies, *The Cosmic Blueprint* (London, UK: Heinemann, 1987).
14. Primo Levi's meditation on some of the chemical elements is an exception to this general rule. See Levi, *The Periodic Table*, trans. Raymond Rosenthal (New York: Alfred A. Knopf, 1996).

15. See Ernst Cassirer, *The Philosophy of Symbolic Forms*, trans. Ralph Manheim (New Haven, CT: Yale UP, 1955).

16. John Rist, "Why Greek Philosophers Might Have Been Concerned About the Environment," in Laura Westra and Thomas M. Robinson, eds., *The Greeks and the Environment* (Lanham, MD: Rowman & Littlefield, 1997), p. 23.

Chapter 1: Philosophy's Forgotten Four

1. J. Donald Hughes, "Theophrastus as Ecologist," in *Theophrastean Studies*, Vol. 3, William Fortenbraugh ed., pp. 67–75 and Hughes, "Early Greek and Roman Environmentalists," in *Historical Ecology: Essays on Environment and Social Change*, ed., Lester J. Bilskz, pp. 44–59.

2. For further thoughts in this regard, see David Macauley, "Greening Philosophy and Democratizing Ecology" in David Macauley, ed., *Minding Nature: The Philosophers of Ecology* (New York: Guilford, 1996), pp. 1–23.

3. See Rainer Maria Rilke, *The Selected Poetry of Rainer Maria Rilke*, ed. and trans. Stephen Mitchell (New York: Vintage, 1984), pp. 385, 387, and 511. In "The Young Workman's Letter," he speculates: "This growing exploitation of life, isn't it a result of the centuries-long devaluation of the earthly? What a swindle to steal the images of earthly delight and sell them to heaven, behind our backs! The impoverished earth should long ago have called in all those loans . . . The proper use, that's the important thing. To take the earthly in our hands, properly, in a truly loving way, with awe" (p. 310).

4. This sense of the invisibility and mystery of earth is also suggested beautifully in e.e. cumming's poem, "O sweet spontaneous" in e.e. cummings, *100 Selected Poems* (New York: Grove Press, 1959), p. 6.

5. James Hillman, *Dream and the Underworld* (New York: Harper & Row, 1979), p. 37.

6. William Bryant Logan, *Dirt: The Ecstatic Skin of the Earth* (New York, NY: Riverhead Books, 1995), p. 95.

7. Yvonne Baskin, *The Work of Nature: How the Diversity of Life Sustains Us* (Washington, DC: Island Press, 1997) p. 10.

8. David R. Montgomery, *Dirt: The Erosion of Civilization* (Berkeley: U of California P, 2007).

9. William Bryant Logan, *Dirt*, op. cit., p. 11.

10. Gary Snyder, *Practice of the Wild* (San Francisco, CA: North Point Press, 1990), p. 128.

11. Charles Darwin, *The Formation of Vegetable Mould, Through the Action of Worms, With Observations on Their Habits*, quoted in Amy Stewart, *The Earth Moved: On the Remarkable Achievements of Earthworms* (Chapel Hill, NC: Algonquin Books, 2004), p. 1.

12. Michael Pollan, *Second Nature: A Gardener's Education* (New York: Delta, 1991).

13. Virginia Woolf, *The Waves*, quoted in Gaston Bachelard, *Earth and Reveries of Will*, trans. Kenneth Haltman (Dallas, TX: Dallas Institute Publications, 2002), pp. 56–57.

14. Basil Valentine, quoted in Fred Gettings, *The Book of the Hand* (London, UK: Paul Hamlyn, 1965), p. 43.

15. Logan, *Dirt,* op. cit. p. 37.
16. John Updike, "Ode to Fragmentation," *Paris Review* 94 (1984).
17. Pliny, quoted in Carolyn Merchant, *The Death of Nature* (New York: Harper & Row, 1980), p. 30. On the ethical constraints against "violence" to the earth, see pp. 29–41.
18. W.K.C. Guthrie, *The Greeks and their Gods* (Boston, MA: Beacon Press, 1995).
19. Thomas Moore, *Care of the Soul,* quoted in <http://www.worldandi.com/public/1992/july/bk2.efm>.
20. Seneca, quoted by International Lutheran Laymen's League, <http://www.1hm-eastern.district.org/bstudy03Call-Intro.html>.
21. Maurice Merleau-Ponty, *The Primacy of Perception* (Evanston, IL: Northwestern UP, 1964).
22. Gaston Bachelard, *Earth and Reveries of Will,* op. cit., p. 35.
23. Logan, *Dirt,* op cit., p. 75.
24. *Xenophanes: Fragments and Commentary,* in Arthur Fairbanks, ed. and trans., *The First Philosophers of Greece* (London, UK: K. Paul, Trench, Trubner, 1898), frag. 8.
25. Venerable Bede, quoted in Daniel J. Boorstin, *The Discoverers* (New York: Vintage, 1985), p. 92.
26. Homer, *The Homeric Hymns,* trans. Apostolos Athanassakis (Baltimore, MD: Johns Hopkins UP, 1976), pp. 67–68.
27. Plato, *Phaedo,* trans. Hugh Tredennick, in Edith Hamilton and Huntington Cairns, Eds., *The Collected Dialogues of Plato* (Princeton, NJ: Princeton UP, 1989), p. 91 (110b).
28. Plato, *Laws,* trans. Trevor Saunders (Harmondsworth, UK: Penguin, 1970), p. 208 (740a) and *Laws* in Edith Hamilton et al., *The Collected Dialogues of Plato,* op. cit., p. 1325.
29. Marge Piercy, "The Common Living Dirt," *Stone, Paper, Knife* (New York: Knopf, 1983), p. 123.
30. Edmund Husserl, "Foundational Investigations of the Phenomenological Origin of the Spaciality of Nature," *Husserl: Shorter Works,* Peter McCormick and Frederick Elliston, eds. (Notre Dame, IN: U of Notre Dame P, 1981).
31. Jacques Derrida, *Edmund Husserl's "Origin of Geometry:" An Introduction,* trans. John P. Leavey (Lincoln: U of Nebraska P, 1989), p. 81. "The question," Derrida writes, "is to exhume, to unearth, the Earth, to lay bare the primordial ground buried under the sedimentary deposits of scientific culture and objectivism" (Ibid., p. 84).
32. Maurice Merleau-Ponty, "Husserl et la notion de Nature," *Revue de Métaphysique et de Morale* (July–September, 1965) and *Themes from Lectures at the College de France, 1952–60,* trans. John O'Neill (Evanston, IL: Northwestern UP, 1970).
33. Gilles Deleuze and Félix Guattari, *A Thousand Plateaus,* trans. Brian Massumi (Minneapolis: U of Minnesota P, 1987), p. 40.
34. Ibid., pp. 338–39.
35. Stephen David Ross, "Biodiversity, Exuberance, and Abundance: Cherishing the Body of the Earth," in Bruce Folz and Robert Frodeman, eds., *Rethinking Nature: Essays in Environmental Philosophy* (Bloomington: Indiana UP, 2004).
36. John Sallis, "The Elemental Earth," in Folz and Frodeman, eds., *Rethinking Nature,* op. cit., p. 142.

37. Edward Casey, "Mapping the Earth in Works of Art," in Folz and Frodeman, eds., *Rethinking Nature*, op. cit., p. 263.

38. Antoine de Saint-Exupéry, quoted in Paul Virilio, *Open Sky*, trans. Julie Rose (London, UK: Verso, 1997), p. 118.

39. Robert Frost, "To Earthward" in *Poetry of Robert Frost: The Collected Poems* (New York: Henry Holt, 1979).

40. "Burial Hymn," *Rig Veda* 10.18.11, trans. Wendy D. O'Flaherty (London, UK: Penguin, 1981), p. 53.

41. See especially Martin Heidegger, "The Origin of the Work of Art" in *Poetry, Language, Thought*, op. cit., p. 47 and Heidegger, *Introduction to Metaphysics*, trans. Ralph Mannheim (New Haven, CT: Yale UP, 1959).

42. William Shakespeare, *Timon of Athens* (Oxford, UK: Oxford UP, 2004), Act IV, Scene 3.

43. Peter Sloterdijk, *Critique of Cynical Reason*, trans. Andreas Huyssen (Minneapolis: U of Minnesota P, 1988), p. 151.

44. Wislawa Szymborska, "Sky" in *View with a Grain of Sand: Selected Poems*, trans. Stanislaw Baranczak and Clare Cavanagh (New York: Harcourt Brace, 1995), p. 173.

45. Friedrich Nietzsche, *Thus Spoke Zarathustra*, trans. Walter Kaufmann (New York: Penguin, 1982), p. 13.

46. For a discussion of the phenomena of earth-alienation, see David Macauley, "Hannah Arendt and the Politics of Place: From Earth Alienation to *Oikos*" in David Macauley, ed., *Minding Nature*, op. cit., ch. 5.

47. Wallace Stevens, *Letters of Wallace Stevens* (Berkeley: U of California P, 1996), p. 73.

48. Aristophanes, *Clouds*, in G. Lowes Dickinson, *The Greek View of Life* (New York: Collier, 1961), p. 45.

49. Joe Sherman, *Gasp: The Swift and Terrible Beauty of Air* (Washington, DC: Shoemaker and Hoard, 2004), p. 3.

50. William Shakespeare, *Romeo and Juliet* (New York: Washington Square Press, 2004), Act 2, Scene 5, p. 105.

51. See Craig Stanford, *Upright: The Evolutionary Key to Becoming Human* (Boston, MA: Houghton Mifflin, 2003), pp. 52–53.

52. Sylvia Plath, *The Bell Jar* (New York: Harper Perennial, 2000), p. 199.

53. Foodsheds define and describe a geographical area in terms of the flow of food from the point where it is grown to the location where it is consumed. See J. Kloppenberg, J. Hendrickson, and G. W. Stevenson. "Coming in to the foodshed," *Agriculture and Human Values*, 13:3 (1996), pp. 33–41.

54. There are references to Okeanos in Homer's *Iliad* and *Odyssey* as well as in Herodotus. Some ancient Greeks believed for a time that Okeanos was the source of all existing things.

55. Gary Snyder, *The Practice of the Wild*, op. cit., p. 69.

56. Tom Jay, "The Salmon of the Heart," in Finn Wilcox and Jeremiah Gorsline, eds., *Working the Woods, Working the Sea* (Port Towsend, WA: Empty Bowl, 1986), p. 116.

57. Malcolm de Chazal, "Water Aphorisms" in David Rothenberg and Marta Ulvaeus, eds., *Writing on Water* (Cambridge, MA: MIT Press, 2002), p. 33.

58. Giambattista Vico, *The New Science of Giambattista Vico*, trans. Thomas G. Bergin and Max H. Fisch (Garden City, NY: Anchor Books, 1961), pp. 75–77 and 218–19.

59. Vico points out that the Romans employed *contemplari* as a verb to indicate the act of observing those parts of the sky from which auguries came or were taken. Such regions were referred to as *templa caeli* (temples of the sky). Plato uses the image of a stargazer in his *Republic*, too, to suggest that a captain of a ship (and by analogy a philosophical ruler) would be able to navigate (rule) by skillfully reading the skies, though others would view him as lost, without true bearings, or as having his head in the clouds.

60. Wislawa Szymborska, "Sky" in *View with a Grain of Sand*, op. cit., p. 173.

61. Rainer Maria Rilke, *Ahead of All Parting: The Selected Poetry and Prose of Rainer Maria Rilke* (New York: Modern Library, 1995), p. 191.

62. Edmond Vandercammen, quoted in Gaston Bachelard, *The Poetics of Reverie*, trans. Daniel Russell (Boston, MA: Beacon Press, 1971), p. 118.

63. John Ruskin, "Of Truth of Skies" in *Selected Writings* (Oxford, UK: Oxford UP, 2004), p. 9.

64. Peter Pesic, *Sky in a Bottle* (Cambridge, MA: MIT Press, 2005), pp. 3–4.

65. Johann W. von Goethe, *Theory of Colors*, quoted in Pesic, *Sky in a Bottle*, op. cit., p. 77.

66. See Diane Ackerman, *A Natural History of the Senses* (New York: Random House, 1990), pp. 235–36.

67. David Lukas, "Of Aerial Plankton and Aeolian Zones" in David Rothenberg and Wandee Pryor, eds., *Writing on Air* (Cambridge, MA: MIT Press, 2003), pp. 39–43.

68. To the extent to which the air is binding and enclosing, it is an enabling idea and force that points toward a form of nonduality or *advaita* for the Hindu, suggesting an ecological conception of the self in which humans and environment form an essential unity.

69. Robert Browning "An Epistle Containing the Strange Medical Experience of Karshish, the Arab Physician," line 6 in *The Poetical Works of Robert Browning*, Vol. 5, eds., Ian Jack and Robert Inglesfield (Oxford, UK: Oxford UP, 1995).

70. Luce Irigaray, *The Forgetting of Air in Martin Heidegger*, trans. Mary Beth Mader (Austin: U of Texas P, 1999), p. 9.

71. Brihadaranyaka Upanishad, quoted in *The Upanishads*, trans. Eknath Easwaran (Tomales, CA: Nilgiri Press, 2007), p. 306.

72. *The Bhagavad Gita*, trans. Barbara Stoler Miller (New York: Bantam Books, 1986), pp. 60–61.

73. See the Buddha's *Anapanasati Sutra* contained in Thich Nhat Hanh, *Breathe! You are Alive: Sutra on the Full Awareness of Breathing* (Berkeley, CA: Parallax Press, 1996), pp. 1–12.

74. Hippocrates, quoted in Carl Jung, *Psyche and Symbol*, ed., Violet S. de Laszlo (New York: Anchor Books, 1958), p. 251.

75. James H. Austin, *Zen and the Brain* (Cambridge, MA: MIT Press, 1999), p. 93.

76. Rumi, *The Essential Rumi*, trans. Coleman Barks (New York: HarperCollins, 2004, p. 32.

77. The likelihood of lightning igniting a forest fire increases by seventy percent for every one percent increase in oxygen concentration.

78. The oxygen content in chemical equilibrium but lifeless worlds such as Mars and Venus would be a mere trace presence.

79. Aristotle, *Aristotle on the Soul: Prava Naturalia, On Breath* (London, UK: Heinemann and Harvard UP, 1936), p. 489.

80. Jacques Derrida, *Dissemination*, trans. Barbara Johnson (Chicago, IL: U of Chicago P, 1981), p. 347. On the role of breath in theory, particularly in relation to theatre, see also Sreenath Nair, *Restoration of Breath: Consciousness and Performance* (Amsterdam: Rodopi, 2007).

81. Much of what survives and is known about Anaximenes' work exists via Theophrastus and Plutarch. Aristotle also comments upon Anaximenes, and an extensive doxographical remark is provided by Hippolytus in his *Refutation of All Heresies*, I, vii, 1–9.

82. Anaximenes seems to have been aware of temperature differentials in the air between keeping the mouth open and holding it is closed. Objects, too, seem to float on or through air, and Axaximenes appears to have believed that the earth, being flat, rides as a leaf on this element while celestial entities are also buoyed by and move on air. See Aristotle, *De Caelo* (294b13) in Richard McKeon, ed., *The Basic Works of Aristotle* (New York: Random House, 1942).

83. Diogenes of Apollonia later attributes intelligence to air in this association.

84. Breath and wind share a similar meaning. Anaximenes uses the word *pneuma*, usually translated as "breath." See Anaximenes, DK 13B2 in G. S. Kirk, J. E. Raven and M. Schofield, *The Presocratic Philosophers* (Cambridge, UK: Cambridge UP, 1983), pp. 158–59.

85. Anaximenes may not have used the word *kosmos* (cosmos) in the sense attributed to him by Aetius.

86. One of the decisive differences between the classical view of the elements as articulated by early Greek philosophers and the preclassical view as expressed in poems and mythology seems in fact to lie in the role allotted to *aer* (air). *Aer* is construed originally as neither a place or substance but a force or condition that makes things invisible. In contradistinction, *ouranos* (sky) is often used to designate all that exists above the head. It is the counterpart to earth and associated with the roof of world and Atlas' four posts, which support the weight of heaven, as in the Egyptian worldview. In Homer, too, *ouranos* is the place where stars are seen, while *aither* (*aether* or ether) is not a region or place but a condition of the sky (i.e., celestial light). A parallel, however, is eventually established between these terms (or elements), and *aither* is increasingly substituted for *ouranos*. See Charles Kahn, *Anaximander and the Origins of Greek Cosmology* (New York: Columbia UP, 1960).

87. Mircea Eliade, *The Sacred and the Profane*, trans. Willard R. Trask (New York: Harcourt Brace Jovanovich, 1959), p. 119.

88. Ralph Waldo Emerson, "Nature," in *The Portable Emerson*, ed., Carl Bode (New York: Penguin, 1946), op. cit., p. 20.

89. See James Lovelock, *Gaia: A New Look at Life* (Oxford, UK: Oxford UP, 1979). For some critical perspectives on the Gaia hypothesis, see Stephen Schneider and Penelope Boston, eds., *Scientists on Gaia* (Boston, MA: The MIT Press, 1991).

90. It is noteworthy that in the late eighteenth century, James Hutton, the father of modern geology, had proposed that the proper study of the earth was through the field of physiology—Lovelock now proposes geo-physiology—since the earth appears to exhibit features of being an organism. In facilitating an understanding of the planet, he compared the recent discovery by Harvey of the circulation of blood in the human body with the cycling of the elements.

91. Lovelock points to the planet's resiliency rather than to its fragility, minimizing

at times the possible effects on the long-term integrity of the earth by anthropogenic pollution or even nuclear war. Rather than taking an anthropocentric, biocentric, or eco-centric position, he views matters through the wide lens of geologic time.

92. Gregory Nagy, "As the World Runs out of Breath," in *Earth, Air, Fire, Water: Humanistic Studies of the Environment*, eds. Jill Conway et al. (Amherst: U of Massachusetts P, 1999).

93. Harold Fromm, "The Psychedelics of Pollution," in Rothenberg and Pryor, eds., *Writing on Air*, op. cit., pp. 9–10.

94. Joan Maloof, *Teaching the Trees: Lessons from the Forest* (Athens: U of Georgia P, 2007).

95. Ranier M. Rilke, "First Elegy," *The Selected Poetry of Rainer Maria Rilke*, op. cit., p. 151.

96. See Curt P. Richter, "The Discovery of Fire by Man—Its Effects on his 24-hour Clock and Intellectual and Cultural Revolution," *Johns Hopkins Medical Journal* 141 (1977), pp. 229–32.

97. Plato, *Protagoras* (321d) in *The Collected Dialogues of Plato*, op. cit.

98. See Charles H. Kahn, ed., *The Art and Thought of Heraclitus* (Cambridge, UK: Cambridge UP, 1979), fr. 37. Hereafter, the fragment references are given following the text and the translation refers to Kahn.

99. On plurisignation, see Philip Wheelwright, *The Burning Fountain: A Study in the Language of Symbolism* (Bloomington: Indiana UP, 1968), pp. 115–19.

100. Gaston Bachelard, *The Psychoanalysis of Fire*, trans. Alan C. M. Ross (Boston, MA: Beacon Press, 1964), p. 16.

101. See James Frazer, *The Golden Bough*, abridged version, ed., Theodor H. Gaster (New York: Mentor Books, 1964) and *Myths of the Origin of Fire* (London, UK: Macmillan, 1930).

102. On the role of fire in human history, see Lewis Mumford, *Technics and Human Development: The Myth of the Machine* (New York: Harcourt, Brace and World, 1966). See also the many works of Stephen Pyne, including *Fire in America* (Princeton, NJ: Princeton UP, 1982) and *World Fire: The Culture of Fire on Earth* (New York: Henry Holt, 1995).

103. See Henry David Thoreau, *Walden and Other Writings*, ed., Brooks Atkinson (New York: Modern Library, 1937).

104. Indeed, Plato's famous myth of the cave, where he locates a fire that casts long epistemological shadows, could be read in modern terms through the medium and metaphors of the television, especially the images, mediation and altered sense of reality it provides.

105. See, for example, Hazel Rossotti, *Fire* (Oxford, UK: Oxford UP, 1993), pp. 228–31.

106. Shepard Krech III, *The Ecological Indian* (New York: W.W. Norton, 1999).

107. Stephen J. Pyne, "Consumed by Either Fire or Fire: A Prolegomenon to Anthropogenic Fire" in Conway et al., eds., *Earth, Air, Fire and Water*, op. cit., p. 86. See also Pyne, *Fire: A Brief History* (Seattle: U of Washington P, 2001).

108. Stephen Pyne, *Fire: A Brief History*, op. cit., p. 24.

109. Stephen Pyne, "Consumed by Either Fire or Fire," op. cit., p. 79.

110. Stephen Pyne, *Vestal Fire* (Seattle: U of Washington P, 1997), p. 43.

111. Stephen Pyne, *Fire: A Brief History*, op. cit., p. 86.

112. Ibid., p. 138.

113. Stephen Pyne, *Fire: A Brief History*, op. cit., p. 154.
114. Ibid., p. 120.
115. Martin Heidegger, *Early Greek Thinking*, trans. David Farrell Krell and Frank A. Capuzzi (New York: Harper & Row, 1984), p. 103.
116. Ibid., p. 117.
117. Jacques Derrida, *Of Spirit: Heidegger and the Question*, trans. Geoffrey Bennington and Rachel Bowlby (Chicago, IL: U of Chicago P, 1989). Derrida also explores the place and play of fire in *Cinders*, a text that engages in a dialogue or, rather, interior monologue with his own writings, consuming them prior to a burning. "No cinder without fire," he proclaims, as he meditates on the meanings of the phrase, "Il y a là cendre" (there are cinders). Jacques Derrida, *Cinders*, trans. Ned Lukacher (Lincoln: U of Nebraska P, 1991).
118. See Jeremy Rifkin, *Algeny* (New York: Viking, 1983).
119. The earlier part of the quote from Blake speaks of a bodily connection of fire with the senses and faculties of sight, hearing and speaking as had Keats' remark (which noted the role of "touch"). Blake writes: "Unless the eye catch fire / The God will not be seen / Unless the ear catch fire / The God will not be heard / Unless the tongue catch fire / The God not be named / Unless the heart catch fire / The God will not be loved." See "Pentecost" in *William Blake: Selected Poetry*, ed., Michael Mason (Oxford, UK: Oxford UP, 1998).
120. Bachelard, *Psychoanalysis of Fire*, op. cit., p. 9.
121. See André Fraigneau, *Cocteau* (New York: Grove Press, 1961).
122. Robert Frost, "Fire and Ice" in *Robert Frost: Collected Poems, Prose and Plays*, ed., Richard Poirier and Mark Richardson (New York: Library of America, 1995), p. 204.
123. Aristotle, *Metaphysics* in McKeon, ed., *The Basic Works of Aristotle*, op cit., 983b6.
124. There are parallels between the primacy of water given in Thales' account and the Babylonian creation myth, the *Enuma Elish*, as well as similarities with other Egyptian conceptions.
125. The view regularly attributed to him that "all is water" or composed of water was probably Aristotelian in origin and also not wholly reliable. Anaximenes, however, claimed clearly that all things were composed of air.
126. Thales also maintained that seemingly inanimate things are in some manner alive and that the world is "full of gods." Quite astonishingly, Western philosophy thus begins—if we place faith in the tradition—with the *contemplation of water and rock* rather than a thought or another human mind or a god. Thales pondered a magnesium stone that revealed to him a world in which soul (*psyche*) is kinetic and the world is alive ("full of gods"). His apparent claim was that the loadstone possesses soul—which, whether associated with spinal fluid, breath or blood and later mind, was widely considered to be the source of life or consciousness—because it, the stone, literally moves iron. In other words, what possesses and manifests the capacity to move and change of its own accord is animated, alive.
127. Friedrich Nietzsche, *Philosophy in the Tragic Age of the Greeks*, trans. Marianne Cowan (Chicago, IL: Gateway, 1962), p. 39. According to Nietzsche, it is only the third reason that makes Thales the first Greek philosopher because in doing so he goes beyond empirical and scientific observation.
128. I have consulted several translations of this work, including *Tao Te Ching*, trans. Stephen Mitchell (New York: HarperCollins, 1988); *Tao Te Ching*, trans. D.C. Lau, (New

York: Penguin, 1963) and *The Way of Life*, trans. R. B. Blakney (New York: New American Library, 1955). See Chapters 8, 14, 15, and 78 for sources of the quotes.

129. See Theodor Schwenk, *Sensitive Chaos: The Creation of Flowing Forms in Water and Air*, trans. Olive Whicher and Johanna Wrigley (New York: Schocken, 1976).

130. Novalis, quoted in Ibid., p. 58.

131. Gary Snyder, *The Practice of the Wild*, op. cit., p. 29.

132. See, for example, Dogen, *Moon in a Dewdrop: Writings of Zen Master Dogen*, trans. Kazuaki Tanahashi (San Francisco, CA: North Point Press, 1985).

133. A more recent use of the element of water—particularly in the form of a river—as an image of and metaphor for life occurs in the literary and quasi-philosophical work of Herman Hesse's *Siddhartha*, trans. Hilda Rosner (New York: Bantam, 1951).

134. Arthur C. Clarke, quoted in James Lovelock, *Gaia: A New Look at Life*, op. cit., p. 84.

135. Perhaps for this reason, the image of the infant recurs in the *Tao Te Ching* and is associated with the notions of both "Tao" and "Po" (a term suggesting original nature).

136. The salinity of the oceans currently lies at 3.4 percent, and in order for life to survive it cannot exceed 6 percent. The faculty of sight also begins in the water, where early life forms develop skin patches that are able to sense light and to distinguish light and dark shapes and eventually directions, motions and sources of illumination.

137. Neil Shubin, *Your Inner Fish: A Journey Into the 3.5-Billion-Year History of the Human Body* (New York: Pantheon, 2008).

138. Victor Schauberger, for example, argues that water in its natural condition is alive because it reveals a vortex or spiraling motion not found in municipal or filtered water. See Victor Schauberger, *The Water Wizard: The Extraordinary Properties of Natural Water*, trans. Callum Coats (Bath, UK: Gateway Books, 1998).

139. Herman Melville, *Moby Dick* (London, UK: J. M. Dent, n.d.), p. 8.

140. Philip Ball, *Life's Matrix*, op. cit., p. 116.

141. See Mircea Eliade, ed., *From Primitives to Zen* (New York: Harper & Row, 1977), pp. 88–91.

142. "Creation Hymn," *Rig Veda*, 10.129, op. cit., p. 25.

143. *The Koran*, trans. N. J. Dawood (New York: Penguin, 1995), Sura 21.30, p. 229.

144. Mircea Eliade, *The Sacred and Profane*, op. cit., p. 130.

145. Bachelard, *Water and Dreams*, trans. Edith R. Farrell (Dallas, TX: Dallas Institute Publications, 1983), p. 165.

146. Ibid., p. 20.

147. Ibid., p. 99.

148. Ibid., p. 117.

149. Ibid., p. 118.

150. See Jacques Leslie, "Running Dry: What happens when the world no longer has enough freshwater?" *Harpers*, July 2000, pp. 37–52 and Marq De Villiers, *Water: The Fate of Our Most Precious Resource* (Boston, MA: Houghton Mifflin, 2000), p. 20.

151. Theodor Schwenk, *Sensitive Chaos*, op. cit., pp. 31–32.

152. John Ruskin, "Of Truth of Water," *Selected Writings*, op. cit., p. 6.

153. See Sidney Perkowitz, "The Rarest Element" in Rothenberg and Ulvaeus, eds., *Writing on Water*, op. cit.

154. Tom Robbins, *Even Cowgirls Get the Blues* (New York: Bantam, 1976), pp. 1–2. Compare Robbins' praise of water with Pliny the Elder's tribute to "the element that commands all others" in his encyclopedic survey of the natural world in the first century A.D. "Water engulfs lands, quenches flames, climbs aloft and lays claim even to the sky, and by a covering of clouds chokes the life-giving spirit that forces out thunderbolts, as the world wages war with itself. What could be more amazing than water standing in the sky?" Pliny the Elder, *Natural History: A Selection*, trans. John Healy (London: Penguin, 1990), p. 272.

155. Wislawa Szymborska "Water" in *View with a Grain of Sand*, op. cit., p. 29.

156. For a critical view of water wars see Aaron Wolf, " 'Water Wars' and Other Tales of Hydromythology" in *Whose Water Is It?*, ed., Bernadette McDonald and Douglas Jehl (Washington, DC: National Geographic, 2003), pp. 109–24. Wolf claims that there is a lack of evidence for such theories. He argues that historically there has been more cooperation than conflict over water resources and that the only true water war occurred 4,500 years ago between the states of Lagash and Umma in the Tigris-Euphrates Basin.

157. De Villiers, *Water*, op. cit., p. 12.

158. David Orr identifies the ways in which the unwise use of oil—in contrast with the wise use of water—has undermined our collective intelligence in terms of its effects on community cooperation, the landscape, specialization, urban sprawl, labor, and technology use. See Orr, *Earth in Mind* (Washington, DC: Island Press, 1994), pp. 54–59.

159. Norman Weinstein, "Water/Theos" in Rothenberg and Pryor, eds., *Writing on Water*, op. cit., pp. 273–78.

160. Ralph Waldo Emerson, "Nature," in *The Portable Emerson*, op. cit., pp. 12, 7.

Interstice: Stone

1. Wislawa Szymborska, "Conversation with a Stone" in *View With a Grain of Sand*, op. cit., pp. 30–32.

2. Georg W. F. Hegel, quoted in Jacques Derrida, *Dissemination*, op. cit., p. 172.

3. Theophrastus, *On Stones*, trans. Earle R. Caley and John C. Richards (Columbus: Ohio State UP, 1956).

4. Marcia Bjornerud, *Reading the Rocks: The Autobiography of the Earth* (Cambridge, MA: Westview Press, 2005), p. 5.

5. See Arnold Berleant, "The Soft Side of Stone: Notes for a Phenomenology of Stone," *Environmental Philosophy*, IV:1 and 2 (2007), pp. 49–57.

6. Psalm 18 and Matthew 16:18, *The Oxford Study Bible*, ed., M. Jack Suggs et al. (New York: Oxford UP, 1992), p. 1286.

7. Mircea Eliade, *The Sacred and Profane*, op. cit., p. 155.

8. Nathaniel Hawthorne, "Sketches from Memory": The Notch of the White Mountains, in *Mosses from an Old Manse* (New York: Modern Library, 2003), p. 334.

9. Robert Frost, "Mending Wall," in *Poetry of Robert Frost: The Collected Poems*, op. cit.

10. See Ric Burn's documentary, *Ansel Adams* (Sierra Club Productions and Steeplechase Films, 2003).

11. Michelangelo, quoted in Maria Fletcher Roscoe, *Vittoria Colonna: Her Life and Poems* (London, UK: MacMillan, 1868), p. 169.
12. Marcia Bjornerud, *Reading the Rocks*, op. cit., p. 33.
13. Edward Abbey, *Desert Solitaire* (New York: Ballantine, 1968), p. 71.
14. Gaston Bachelard, *Earth and Reveries of Will*, op. cit., p. 210.
15. Alphonso Lingis, *Abuses* (Berkeley: U of California P, 1994), p. 54.
16. See Marjorie Hope Nicolson, *Mountain Gloom and Mountain Glory* (Ithaca, NY: Cornell UP, 1959).
17. William Blake, *The Complete Poetry and Prose of William Blake*, ed. David V. Erdmann (Berkeley: U of California P, 1982), p. 511.
18. Friedrich Nietzsche, *Thus Spoke Zarathustra*, op. cit., p. 41.
19. Albert Camus, *The Myth of Sisyphus*, trans. Justin O'Brien (New York: Vintage, 1982), p. 89.
20. Bachelard, *Earth and Reveries of Will*, op. cit., pp. 149–50.
21. Jean Paul Sartre, *Being and Nothingness*, trans. Hazel E. Barnes (New York: Washington Square Press, 1966).
22. Jacques Derrida, *Of Spirit*, op. cit., p. 19.
23. John Sallis, *Stone* (Bloomington: Indiana UP, 1994).
24. Ranier Maria Rilke, "Archaic Torso of Apollo," *The Selected Poetry of Rainer Maria Rilke*, op. cit., p. 61.
25. Charles Simic, "Stone," *Dismantling the Silence* (New York: George Braziller, 1971), p. 59.
26. Dylan Thomas, *Collected Poems* (New York: New Directions, 1957), p. 52.

Chapter 2: The Topology of the Elemental Environment

1. See Francis Cornford, *From Religion to Philosophy: A Study in the Origins of Western Speculation* (New York: Harper & Row, 1957).
2. "Archetoplogy" combines the concepts of "archetype" and "topology" and is first used by Edward Casey in *Spirit and Soul* (Dallas, TX: Spring Publications, 1991), p. 291.
3. Martin Heidegger, *Being and Time*, trans. John Macquarrie and Edward Robinson (New York: Harper & Row, 1962), sect. 220, pp. 262. Heidegger adds that the goal is "to keep the common understanding from leveling them off to that unintelligibility which functions in turn as a source of pseudo-problems."
4. Walter Burkert, "STOIXEION: Eine semasiologische Studie," *Philologus* 103 (1959), pp. 167–97 and Geoffrey Lloyd and Nathan Sivin, *The Way and the Word: Science and Medicine in Early China and Greece* (New Haven, CT: Yale UP, 2002). Hermann Diehls notes that the plural is older than the singular. See his *Zur Geschichte des Begriffes Elementum bei Griechen und Römern* (Leipzig, Germany: B.G. Teubner Verlag, 1899).
5. For more on this phenomenon, see Anne Buttimer, "Nature, water symbols, and the human quest for wholeness," in David Seamon and Robert Mugerauer, eds., *Dwelling, Place and Environment* (New York: Columbia UP, 1985).
6. Ralph Waldo Emerson, *The Portable Emerson*, op. cit., pp. 19–21 (italics added).
7. The English language also possesses some of these elemental combinations (e.g., "fire-water" is alcohol).

8. See, for example, Nancilee Wycha, *Feng Shui* (Chicago, IL: Contemporary, 1996). In some respects, *feng shui* bears similarities in microcosm to the environmental movement of bioregionalism.

9. Interestingly, the notion and practice of *feng shui* agrees at a number of points with Plato's theory in the *Timeaus* where, for example, fire is accorded a triangular shape and earth is attributed a square shape.

10. Thus, fire is associated with the color of red; the figure of a triangle (given to less stability); material items such as kettles, tiles, and napkins (for their triangular shapes); uses such as warmth and cooking; the direction of south when one is in the northern hemisphere (and moving toward the tropics); and emotions that excite, incite, or ignite.

11. The character for mountain (*shan*) is particularly pictorial and one of the most widely written in the language. Ancient Chinese culture identified five sacred mountains, one each for the cardinal directions, including the center, on which temples were built. Landscape also is a classic subject for Chinese painting.

12. Wang Hsi Chih, quoted in Amaury de Riencourt, *The Soul of China* (New York: Harper & Row, 1990), pp. 6–7.

13. Nirenberg further argues: "From unbridled, overpowering natural forces to a mere exhalation: the taming, dematerializing trajectory doesn't end just here; the next and second step for the Spirit is to become a thoroughly undetectable ghost. Such a possibility existed always in *pneuma* no less in *Geist* and *spiritus*, all of which could denote, among other things, phantoms, revenants or apparitions, but this destiny, this parallel fate shared by the Spirit and the letter H, became fully realized in Latin, where H is but a soundless ghost." See Ricardo L. Nirenberg, "H" in *Exquisite Corpse* 44 (1993), pp. 10–12. See as well Nabokov's remark in his autobiographical *Speak, Memory*, where he writes of the phenomenon of synaesthesia and what he calls "colored hearing": "The long *a* of the English alphabet ... has for me the tint of weathered wood, but a French *a* evokes polished ebony. This black group also includes hard *g* (vulcanized rubber) and *r* (a sooty rag being ripped). Oatmeal *n*, noodle-limp *l*, and the ivory-backed hand mirror of *o* take care of the whites ... Passing on to the blue group, there is steely *x*, thundercloud *z*, and huckleberry *k*."

14. Max Horkheimer, *The Eclipse of Reason* (New York: Continuum, 1992), p. 101.

15. Carl Jung, "Approaching the Unconscious," in Jung, ed., *Man and His Symbols* (Garden City, NY: Doubleday, 1964), pp. 94–95.

16. See, for example, Clarence Glacken, *Traces on the Rhodian Shore: Nature and Culture in Western Thought from Ancient Times to the End of the Eighteenth Century* (Berkeley: U of California P, 1973).

17. Hesiod, *Theogony* and *Works and Days*, trans. Dorothea Wender (New York: Penguin, 1973).

18. Gilles Deleuze, *The Logic of Sense*, trans. Mark Lester and Charles Stivale (New York: Columbia UP, 1989), p. 127.

19. On Anaximander and maps, see Charles Kahn, *Anaximander and the Origins of Greek Cosmology*, op. cit., pp. 82–84.

20. On the notion of the horizon, see, for example, Edmund Husserl, *Ideas: General Introduction to Pure Phenomenology*, trans. W. R. Boyce Gibson (New York: Collier, 1962). For Heidegger's treatment of the horizon, especially in relation to time, see *Being and Time*, op cit., sect. 365.

21. On the relation of depth and place and the notion of "zonal place," see Edward S. Casey, " 'The Element of Voluminousness': Depth and Place Re-examined" in M. C. Dillon, ed., *Merleau-Ponty Vivant* (Albany: SUNY P, 1991), pp. 1–29.

22. Edward S. Casey, *Getting Back into Place* (Bloomington: U of Indiana P, 1993), pp. 61–62.

23. For further consideration of ecological optics, see James J. Gibson, *The Ecological Approach to Visual Perception* (Hillsdale, NJ: Lawrence Erlbaum, 1986), quote from p. 164.

24. Maurice Merleau-Ponty, *Phenomenology of Perception*, trans. Colin Smith (London. UK: Routledge & Kegan Paul, 1962), p. 68.

25. Ibid., p. 230.

26. Martin Heidegger, *Discourse on Thinking*, trans. John M. Anderson and E. Hans Freund (New York: Harper & Row, 1966), pp. 64–65.

27. On Derrida's notion of horizon, especially relative to Husserl, see Jacques Derrida, *Edmund Husserl's "Origin of Geometry,"* op. cit., pp. 80–83, 104–10, 114–16, 171–73 and 176–78.

28. Maurice Merleau-Ponty, *The Visible and Invisible*, ed. Claude Lefort, trans. Alphonso Lingis (Evanston, IL: Northwestern U, 1968), p. 149, translation altered.

29. Ralph Waldo Emerson, *The Portable Emerson*, op. cit., pp. 10–11, 228.

30. Aristotle, *De Caelo* (284b6ff) in *The Basic Works of Aristotle*, op. cit. Aristotle argues that motion proceeds from the right, privileging this direction as many cultures have done. There is a growing controversy in cosmology over whether an inherent directionality exists in the universe itself, one involving physical and philosophical issues such as the nature of up and down. See also G.E.R. Lloyd, "Right and Left in Greek Philosophy" in Lloyd, *Methods and Problems in Greek Science* (Cambridge, UK: Cambridge UP), pp. 27–48.

31. Henrik Ibsen, quoted in Nina Leen, *Women, Heroes and Frogs* (New York: W.W. Norton, 1970), no page.

32. In the nineteenth century, anthropologist Adolph Bastian used the term *Elementargedanken* (elementary ideas) to refer to perennial and recurrent motifs in human culture, influencing Jung's later theory of archetypes.

33. Carl Jung, "Mind and Earth" in *Complete Works* 10 (London, UK: Routledge & Kegan Paul, 1970), p. 31.

34. Carl Jung, *Psychology and Religion* (New Haven, CT: Yale UP, 1938), pp. 70–71.

35. In the Hermetic tradition, the natural order, too, is represented either as a cross with a center as the *quinta essentia* or it is depicted in concentric circles with fire as the outermost circle and earth as the center. For a consideration of Jung on the importance of fourfold-ness, see A. Plaut, "The Ungappable Bridge," *Journal of Analytical Psychology* 18 (1973).

36. Carl Jung, *Aion* (Princeton, NJ: Princeton UP, 1952), p. 242.

37. See Plato, *Theaetetus*, trans. F. M. Cornford in *The Collected Dialogues of Plato*, op. cit.

38. Gaston Bachelard, *The Poetics of Space*, trans. Maria Jolas (Boston, MA: Beacon Press, 1964), p. xxxiv.

39. Gaston Bachelard, *Water and Dreams*, op. cit., pp. 5–7.

40. We consider the appearances and uses of the elements in the arts in a later chapter.

41. Lucretius, *On the Nature of the Universe*, trans. R. E. Latham (New York: Penguin,
42. Aristotle, *Categoraiae*, trans. E. M. Edghill in *The Basic Works of Aristotle*, op. cit.
43. Aristotle, *De Interpretatione* in *The Basic Works of Aristotle*, op. cit.
44. See Aristotle, *Metaphysics* in *The Basic Works of Aristotle*, op. cit., 986b.
45. See the fragments of Leucippus and Democritus in G. S. Kirk et al., *The Presocratic Philosophers*, op. cit., pp. 402–33. See also D. J. Furley, *Two Studies in the Greek Atomists* (Princeton, NJ: Princeton UP, 1967).
46. See *Hippocratic Writings*, ed., G.E.R. Lloyd, trans. J. Chadwick and W. N. Mann et al. (New York: Penguin, 1983) which contains the work, *Airs, Waters, Places* and see *Ancient Medicine*, trans. W.H.S. Jones, Loeb Classical Library (Cambridge, MA: Harvard UP, 1948).
47. Plato, *Timaeus*, trans. Francis M. Cornford (New York: Macmillan, 1959), sect. 82a.
48. Jean Bodin, quoted by Clarence Glacken in *Traces of the Rhodian Shore*, op. cit., p. 439.
49. *Neikos* (strife) and *philia* (love) do play a significant role in Empedocles' cosmology, but they are not equivalent to the eternal *rhizomata*.
50. In this regard, it has even been argued that all lasting philosophies depend on one of four root metaphors. These have been identified as formism (the root metaphor of similarity or the identity of a single form out of multiplicities), mechanism (the root metaphor of material attraction and repulsion), organicism (the root metaphor of a dynamic and organic whole, as in Hegel), and contextualism (the root metaphor of a fleeting historical situation along with its biological tensions, as in Dewey). Stephen Pepper, *World Hypotheses: A Study in Evidence* (Berkeley, CA: U of California P, 1942). Pepper adds a fifth root metaphor, the purposive act, in a later work, *Concept and Quality: A World Hypothesis* (LaSalle, IL: Open Court, 1966).
51. The first true attempt to classify the elements was by the German chemist Johann Döbereiner in the mid-1820s. He observed triads of elements and found that in some of the trios the properties of the middle element were predictable relative to the properties of the other two elements. In this way, the elements were given an atomic weight.
52. As of the time of this writing, an element with the atomic number of 118 and temporarily named "Ununoctium" has been reputedly discovered, although not yet confirmed.
53. See Robert Boyle, *Skeptical Chymist* (Whitefish, MT: Kessinger, 1992). Boyle challenged the occult dimensions of alchemy (but not alchemy per se) and advocated a mechanistic theory of matter, defining elements as primitive bodies from which the panoply of other substances are composed.
54. Quoted in Mortimer Adler, *The Great Ideas*, op cit., pp. 180–81.
55. See J. R. Partington, *A Short History of Chemistry* (New York: Dover, 1989) and Philip Ball, *Life's Matrix*, op. cit. for further discussion of the elements in modern science.
56. Although this idea was accepted in France because of the influence of Lavoisier, it was still denounced in England and elsewhere. As late as the 1620s, however, France was still arresting "heretics" who challenged the authority of Aristotle by introducing, for example, five-element systems.

57. Paul Radin, *Primitive Man as Philosopher* (New York: Dover, 1957).

58. Tung Chung-shu, quoted in Chang Chung-yuan, *Creativity and Taoism: A Study of Chinese Philosophy, Art, and Poetry* (New York: Harper & Row, 1963), p. 139.

59. Ibid.

60. There is, by way of contrast, nothing of this kind of relation in Empedocles' philosophy. For further consideration of nature in China, see Joseph Needham, *Science and Civilization in China* (Cambridge, UK: Cambridge UP, 2006) and Yu-lan Fung and Derk Bodde, *A History of Chinese Philosophy*, 2 Vols. (Princeton, NJ: Princeton UP, 1983).

61. *Tao Te Ching*, trans. D. C. Lau, op. cit., p. 82. I have altered Lau's translation.

62. See Ip Po-Keung, "Taoism and Environmental Ethics," *Environmental Ethics* 5 (1983); Russell Goodman, "Taoism and Ecology," *Environmental Ethics* 2 (1980), pp. 73–80; Roger Ames, "Taoism and the Nature of Nature," *Environmental Ethics* 8 (1986), pp. 317–50; and R. P. Peerenboom, "Beyond Naturalism: A Reconstruction of Daoist Environmental Ethics," *Environmental Ethics* (Spring, 1991). One can find strong similarities between some of Empedocles' poetic positions on genesis and destruction, for example, and the work usually attributed to Lao Tzu. Moreover, the Greek and Taoist fourfolds are united in some sense in the later work of Martin Heidegger. (See Chapter Eight, this volume.)

63. Chandogya Upanishad Prapathaki VI in *Sacred Books of the East*, trans. F. Max Muller (Oxford, UK: Clarendon Press, 1879).

64. Taittiryiy Upanishad, 2-1 in *Eight Upanishads*, trans. Swami Gambhirandanda (Calcutta, India: Advaita Ashrama, 1977), p. 287.

65. K. L. Seshagiri Rao, "The Five Great Elements" in Christopher Chapple and Mary Tucker, eds., *Hinduism and Ecology* (Cambridge, MA: Harvard UP, 2000), pp. 23–38.

66. Maitri Upanishad in Sarvepalli Radhakrishnan and Charles Moore, eds., *A Sourcebook in Indian Philosophy* (Princeton, NJ: Princeton UP, 1957), p. 95.

67. Chandogya Upanishad in Patrick Olivelle, *Upanishads* (Oxford, UK: Oxford UP, 1996), 4.3.1–3.

68. See John Koller, *The Indian Way* (Upper Saddle River, NJ: Prentice Hall, 2006), pp. 61–63. Ultimately, it seems a direct or immediate identification of the Self (*Atman*) with the elements is not fully embraced in part because the Self disappears into the All (*Brahman*). As the Brihadaranyaka Upanishad puts it, "Separateness arises from identifying the Self with the body, which is made up of the elements; when this physical identification dissolves, there can be no more separate self." Forest Baird and Raeburne Heimbeck, eds., *Asian Philosophy* (Upper Saddle River, NJ: Prentice Hall, 2006), Chapter Two, 4.12, p. 10.

69. See K. L. Sheshagiri Rao, "The Five Great Elements" in Chapple and Tucker, eds., *Hinduism and Ecology*, op. cit. for thoughts on this possibility.

70. See *The Upanishads: Breath of the Eternal*, trans. Swami Prabharananda and F. Manchester (New York: Mentor Books, 1957), pp. 36ff. On Hinduism and the environment, see Christopher Key Chapple and Mary Evelyn Tucker, *Hinduism and Ecology*, op. cit.

71. "Hua-yen Sutra," *Dharma Rain: Sources of Buddhist Environmentalism*, eds., Stephanie Kaza and Kenneth Kraft (Boston, MA: Shambhala, 2000), pp. 49–50.

72. "The Parable of the Fire," in Mircea Eliade, ed., *From Primitives to Zen*, op. cit., pp. 576–77.

73. Omar Khayyám, *The Rubáiyát of Omar Khayyám*, trans. Peter Avery and John Heath-Stubbs (New York: Penguin, 1981), verse 29.

74. Ojai School in *Earth Prayers*, ed. Elizabeth Roberts and Elias Amidon (New York: HarperCollins, 1991), p. 345.

75. Mircea Eliade, *From Primitives to Zen*, op. cit., p. 135.

76. See Grenville Goodwin, *Myths and Tales of the White Mountain Apache* (Tucson: U of Arizona P, 1994), p. 1.

77. S. P. Smith, "Lore of the Whare-Wananga," *Memoirs of the Polynesian Society*, III, p. 105.

78. Ibid.

79. On the ecological dimensions of the Maori, see John Patterson, "Maori Environmental Virtues," *Environmental Ethics* 16.4 (1994), pp. 397–409.

80. *Enuma Elish*, trans. N. K. Sandars, *Poems of Heaven and Hell from Ancient Mesopotamia* (Baltimore, MD: Penguin, 1971).

81. "Genesis," *The Oxford Study Bible*, op. cit.

82. Francis of Assisi, "The Song of Brother Sun and All Creatures" in J. J. Clarke, *Voices of the Earth: An Anthology of Ideas and Arguments* (New York: George Braziller, 1994), pp. 59–60. See also Edward A. Armstrong, *St. Francis: Nature Mystic* (Berkeley: U of California P, 1973) for a relevant discussion.

83. Clarence Glacken, *Traces on the Rhodian Shore*, op. cit., p. 154.

84. Thomas Browne, *Sir Thomas Browne's Religio Medici*, ed. W. A. Greenhill (Kila, MT: Kessinger, 2003), Pt. II, sect. 11.

85. Vico adds, however, that the theological poets grasped very little of such intelligent "substances" so "that down to Homer's time they did not understand the human mind itself insofar as, by dint of reflection, it opposes the senses." See *The New Science of Giambattista Vico*, op. cit., pp. 213–14.

86. Recently, it has been claimed that a fifth distinct taste exists called "umami," a Japanese word meaning "meaty" or "savory." Although controversies about the taste (or flavoring) can be found, the taste is thought to apply to glutamates, which are common in meats, cheese, and mushrooms.

87. Euclid claims that a number is essentially an aggregate compound of units.

88. For further discussion of the number four and its relation to languages and history, see Karl Menninger, *Number Words and Number Symbols* (Cambridge, MA: MIT Press, 1969), esp. pages 22–26, 146–49, and 178–80 and Anne Marie Schimmel, *The Mystery of Numbers* (Oxford, UK: Oxford UP, 1993).

89. In modern Greek, a "square man" (*tetragonos aner*) is a good or righteous man. Thus, the Greek lyric poet Simonides remarks, "Hard is it on the one hand to become / A good man truly, hands and feet and mind / Foursquare, wrought without blame." Quoted in Plato, *Protagoras* (339b) in *The Collected Dialogues of Plato*, op. cit.

90. Plato, *Timaeus* (32c), op. cit. Aristotle concurs with this view in *De Caelo*, I.9.

91. See, for example, Frank Waters, *The Book of the Hopi* (New York: Ballantine, 1963) and Yi Fu Tuan, *Space and Place* (Minneapolis: U of Minnesota P, 1977).

92. Whereas some ancient Greek thinkers recognized four primary colors, only three (red, green, and blue) are now acknowledged.

93. This phrasing is quoted by both Porphyry and Iamblicus.

94. Aristotle, *Metaphysics* in *The Basic Works of Aristotle*, op. cit., 986a.

95. Tobias Dantzig, *Number: The Language of Science* (New York: Free Press, 1954), p. 42.

96. "Mandukya Upanishad," in Sarvepalli Radhakrishnan and Charles Moore, eds., *A Sourcebook in Indian Philosophy*, op. cit., p. 56.

97. See Martin Heidegger, *The Question Concerning Technology*, trans. William Lovitt (New York: Harper Torchbooks, 1977) and Jacques Derrida, *Truth in Painting*, trans. G. Bennington and I. McLeod (Chicago: U of Chicago P, 1987). We take up this subject more fully in Chapter Eight.

98. Derrida's "four-thought" and "four-play" occur in many texts, including his readings of Lautreamont, Hegel, Freud, Sollers, and Poe. Derrida's essay, "Dissemination" is the place or "square of writing" where he most explicitly (and illicitly) takes up this thematic. The text is itself divided into ten sections (a Pythagorean reference since 1 + 2 + 3 + 4 = 10) and a supernumerary (number XI) that disseminates and disassembles the fourth surface and opens up the whole work. See Jacques Derrida, *Dissemination*, op. cit.

99. Ibid., p. 307.

100. For a major work that helped to spark and define this debate, see Peter Berger and Thomas Luckmann, *The Social Construction of Reality* (Garden City, NY: Anchor Books, 1967).

101. Deep ecologists such as Bill Devall and George Sessions tend to fall into this camp. See their *Deep Ecology: Living as if Nature Mattered* (Salt Lake City, UT: Peregrine Smith Books 1985). Although emphasizing the social nature of ecology, Murray Bookchin stresses the reputed objectivity that inheres in or emerges from evolution. See Bookchin, *The Ecology of Freedom* (Palo Alto, CA: Chesire Books, 1982) and *The Philosophy of Social Ecology*, 2nd ed. (Montreal, Canada: Black Rose Books, 1995). On Bookchin's work, see David Macauley, "Evolution and Revolution: The Ecological Anarchism of Kropotkin and Bookchin," in Andrew Light, ed., *Social Ecology After Bookchin* (New York: Guilford, 1998).

102. See Neil Evernden, *The Social Creation of Nature* (Baltimore, MD: Johns Hopkins UP, 1992) and Steven Vogel, *Against Nature: The Concept of Nature in Critical Theory* (Albany: SUNY P, 1996).

103. For an overview of this debate, see Peter Dickens, *Reconstructing Nature: Alienation, Emancipation and the Division of Labour* (London, UK: Routledge, 1996), pp. 71–84.

104. F. M. Cornford provides the example of the Andamanese, who possess no separate word to designate fish, whom they refer to as "food," because this word expresses the basic function or role of fish in their social and economic world. Cornford, *From Religion to Philosophy*, op. cit.

105. See James Hillman, *Re-visioning Psychology* (New York: Colophon, 1975), pp. 11ff. for a discussion and defense of personifying and animism. He argues that "because personifying is an epistemology of the heart, a thought mode of feeling, we do wrong to judge it as inferior, archaic thinking appropriate only to those allowed emotive speech and affective logic—children, madmen, poets, and primitives" (p. 15).

106. James Clerk Maxwell, quoted in George Johnson, *Fire in the Mind: Science, Faith, and the Search for Order*, op. cit., p. 9.

107. Cicero, *De Natura Deorum*, trans. H. Rackham (Cambridge, MA: Harvard UP, 1951), II, p. 57.

108. Gaston Bachelard, *Water and Dreams*, op. cit., p. 135.

109. Quoted in W.K.C. Guthrie, *The Greeks and Their Gods*, op. cit., pp. 53–54.

110. Marriage quaternio typically involves a cross-cousin relationship such that there is a tie through both birth and marriage. See Carl Jung, *Alchemical Studies*, pp. 209–11, 226–65 and *Practice of Psychotherapy*, pp. 219–35 in *The Collected Works of C.G. Jung*, trans. R.F.C. Hull, Bollingen series (Princeton, NJ: Princeton UP, 1967).

111. See Peter Kingsley, *Ancient Philosophy, Mystery, and Magic* (Oxford, UK: Clarendon, 1995) for further consideration of this motif.

112. William Blake, "Marriage of Heaven and Hell" in *William Blake*, ed., J. Bronowski (New York: Penguin, 1958), pp. 93ff.

113. Plato, *Sophist* (242c–d) in *The Collected Dialogues of Plato*, op. cit.

114. In Aristotle's works, form and matter are separable theoretically but not in fact.

115. This debate takes multiple forms, including controversy over the role of altruism, the kinds and degrees of selfishness or sacrifice that exist, and the significance of mutual aid within human and animal societies.

116. On social ecology, see Murray Bookchin, especially *Ecology of Freedom*, op. cit.

117. F. M. Cornford, *From Religion to Philosophy*, op. cit.

118. Ibid., p. 63.

119. Cornford points out that the Dorians considered *kosmos* to be a political notion before it came to mean the universal order among philosophers, Ibid., p. 53.

120. For an article suspicious of these claims about Thales, see D. R. Dicks, "Thales," *Classical Quarterly* 9 (1959), pp. 294–309.

121. See Herodotus, *Histories* 1:75 in M.I. Finley, ed., *The Portable Greek Historians* (New York: Penguin, 1958).

122. Although generally an extremely reliable source on the Greeks, W.K.C. Guthrie, for example, may overstate the case in holding that "The environment of the Milesian philosophers, then, provided both the leisure of the stimulus for disinterested intellectual inquiry, and the dictum of Aristotle and Plato, that the source and spring of philosophy is wonder or curiosity, finds its justification. Tradition describes these men as practical, both active in political life and interested in technical progress; but it was curiosity, and no thought of mastering the forces of nature in the interests of human welfare or destruction, which led them to those first attempts at a grand simplification of natural phenomena which constitute their chief title to fame . . . Philosophy (including pure science) can only be hampered by utilitarian motives, since it demands a greater degree of abstraction from the world of immediate experience . . . Philosophy did not arise from a demand for the necessities or amenities of human life." See Guthrie, *History of Greek Philosophy*, Vol. 1 (Cambridge, UK: Cambridge UP, 1962), pp. 30–31.

123. The problem of how to categorize or characterize Empedocles' work plagues critical commentary about him, as is seen in the next chapter. He, too, was likely involved in a direct manner with practical problems and applications of his elemental knowledge.

124. The Halys River is now called the Kizil Irmak. It is more than 750 miles in length, and located in modern Turkey.

125. For a convincing argument on the likelihood of Thales' activity in this regard, see Mott T. Greene, *Natural Knowledge in Preclassical Antiquity* (Baltimore, MD: Johns Hopkins UP, 1992). Greene argues that because the "Halys is a very big river, and even with an army, digging a crescentic channel large enough to skirt an army encampment of many thousands would not have left enough time for a summer campaign. So Thales did the sensible thing. He found the dried-out channel of an oxbow lake. He moved the army within its radius. He had the army cut away at the silted-in entrances—first downward and then upstream. The river divided its flow and became fordable in both its parts" (p. 100).

126. Ibid., p. 105. Perhaps, then, we also need to begin to dispense with the hallowed image of the philosopher in his or her study, divorced from the natural and social world. Like Thales, we are often and already immersed in the encompassing elements. This thought is echoed by Henri Bergson, who remarked that philosophers "seem to philosophize as if they were sealed in the privacy of their own study and did not live on a planet surrounded by the vast organic world of animals, plants, insects and protozoa, with whom their life is linked within a single history." From William Barrett paraphrasing Henri Bergson in Barrett, *The Illusion of Technique* (Garden City, NY: Anchor Press, 1979), p. 365.

127. We take the word "meandering" from the Meander River, which Ovid celebrated. The serpentine, ribbon-like curves, which mark such water flows, make it amenable to the kind of engineering project that Thales may have undertaken. Although it was a different river, the Halys does meander substantially, following a sinuous course rather than a straight line.

128. See D. J. Furley, "Empedocles and the Clepsydra," *Journal of Hellenic Studies* 7 (1957), pp. 31–34.

129. Karl Wittfogel, *Oriental Despotism: A Comparative Study of Total Power* (New Haven, CT: Yale UP, 1957). On Wittfogel's place within critical theory, see Martin Jay, *The Dialectical Imagination* (Boston, MA: Little, Brown, 1973). For an application of Wittfogel's analysis to the Colorado River, see Donald Worster, "Water and the Flow of Power," *The Ecologist* 13 (1983), pp. 168–74.

Interstice: Wood

1. Ezra Pound, "The Tree," *Selected Poems of Ezra Pound* (New York: New Directions, 1957), p. 6.

2. The Ralph Waldo Emerson Society notes that this remark, widely attributed to Emerson, does not appear in any of his published writings.

3. Zen Buddhist koan, in *Two Zen Classics: Mumonkan and Hekiganroku*, trans. Katsuki Sekida (New York: Weatherhill, 1995), p. 110.

4. John Muir, *My First Summer in the Sierra* (Boston, MA: Houghton Mifflin, 1911), p. 196.

5. Robert Pogue Harrison, *Forests: The Shadow of Civilization* (Chicago: U of Chicago P), p. x.

6. Holmes Rolston, "The Aesthetic Experience of Forests," in Allen Carlson and Arnold Berleant, eds., *The Aesthetics of Natural Environments* (Toronto, Canada: Broadview Press, 2004), p. 188.

7. Gary Snyder, *The Practice of the Wild*, op. cit., p. 128.

8. Ibid., p. 138.

9. Alan Weisman, *The World Without Us* (New York: St. Martin's, 2007), p. 14.

10. Colin Tudge, *The Tree: A Natural History of What Trees Are, How They Live, and Why They Matter* (New York: Crown, 2005), p. xvii.

11. Ibid., p. xvi.

12. Michael Pollan, *Second Nature*, op. cit., p. 197.

13. See Janine Benyus, *Biomimicry* (New York: William Morrow, 1997).

14. François-René de Chateaubriand, quoted in Glenda Fauske, "Teaching about Trees and Forests," in *Tree Talk* (Dec. 2006, Vol. 2:5).

15. Gary Snyder, *The Practice of the Wild*, op. cit., p. 138.

Chapter 3: The Flowering of Ecological Roots: Empedocles' Elemental Thought

1. See, for example, Robert Sallares, *The Ecology of the Ancient Greek World* (Ithaca, NY: Cornell UP, 1991); Clarence Glacken, *Traces on the Rhodian Shore*, op. cit.; and the "Religions of the World and Ecology" series featuring volumes on Hinduism, Buddhism, Confucianism, and Christianity, edited by Mary Evelyn Tucker and John Grim (Cambridge, MA: Harvard UP).

2. I use *ecological sensibility* here in contradistinction with *environmental ethic*. John Rodman defines ecological sensibility as "a complex pattern of perceptions, attitudes, and judgments which, if fully developed, would constitute a disposition to appropriate conduct that would make talk of rights and duties unnecessary under normal conditions." John Rodman, "Ecological Sensibility" in Louis Pojman, ed., *Environmental Ethics: Readings in Theory and Application*, 2nd ed. (Belmont, CA: Wadsworth, 1998), p. 176.

3. For the original Greek, English translations, and valuable commentary, I have consulted M. R. Wright, *Empedocles: The Extant Fragments* (London, UK: Gerald Duckworth, 1995); William E. Leonard, trans., *The Fragments of Empedocles* (LaSalle, IL: Open Court, 1908); and Brad Inwood, *The Poem of Empedocles* (Toronto, Canada: U of Toronto P, 1992). I have also benefited from W.K.C. Guthrie, *A History of Greek Philosophy*, Vol. 2 (Cambridge, UK: Cambridge UP, 1965). For citations within the text, the fragment (fr.) numbers given refer to the traditional arrangement of Diels-Kranz in *Fragmente der Vorsakratiker*. The English translations, unless otherwise noted, are those of Leonard, who preserves much of Empedocles' poetic language.

4. Simone Weil, *The Need for Roots* (Boston, MA: Beacon, 1952), p. 43.

5. For challenges to Aristotle's interpretation, see Harold Cherniss, *Aristotle's Criticism of Presocratic Philosophy* (Baltimore, MD: John Hopkins UP, 1935) and Peter Kingsley, *Ancient Philosophy, Mystery and Magic*, op. cit.

6. See, for example, Gregory Vlastos, "Theology and Philosophy in Early Greek Thought," *Philosophical Quarterly* 2 (1952), pp. 97–123 and E. R. Dodds, *The Greeks and the Irrational* (Berkeley: U of California P, 1951).

7. See Nietzsche, *The Birth of Tragedy*, trans. Walter Kaufmann (New York: Vintage, 1967).

8. See, for example, Hermann Diels, "Über die Gedichte des Empedokles," in *Hermann Diels, Kleine Schriften*, ed., W. Burkert (Darmstadt, Germany: Wissenschaftliche Buchgesellschaaft, 1969) and J. Bidez, *Biographie d'Empedocle* (Ghent, Belgium: Clemm, 1894).

9. For example, the "golden age" of peace spoken of in the *Purifications*, is comparable to the precosmic stages of the Sphere in *On Nature* while the purified beings of the former work find a parallel in the reign of love in the latter work. I tend to agree with the positions expressed by Charles Kahn, "Religion and Natural Philosophy in Empedocles' Doctrine of the Soul," *Archiv für Geschichte der Philosophie* 42 (1960), pp. 3–35 and earlier

Ettore Bignone, *Empedocle: Studio Critico* (Turin, Italy: Bocca, 1916). As Cornford has written, "The first condition for an understanding of Empedocles is to banish the notion of a gulf between religious beliefs and scientific views. His work is a whole, in which religion, poetry, and philosophy are indissolubly united." F. M. Cornford, *Principium Sapientiae: A Study of the Origins of Greek Philosophical Thought*, ed., W.K.C. Guthrie (New York: Harper & Row, 1952), p. 121.

10. On the thought of Thales, Anaximenes and Heraclitus, see G. S. Kirk et al., *The Presocratic Philosophers*, op. cit.

11. Empedocles writes in hexameters. Because of his use of language and imagery, Aristotle styles him as the first rhetorician.

12. Some commentators, however, dismiss their relevance entirely. Thus, William Turner maintains that the "mythological names" Empedocles attributes to the *rhizomata* "have no particular philosophical value; they may be regarded as the accidents of poetical composition." William Turner, *History of Philosophy* (Boston, MA: Ginn, 1929), p. 59.

13. For a discussion of this problem, see Kingsley, op cit. In the extant fragments, Empedocles refers only once to the fourth root as *ouranos* (heaven) rather than *aither*. He does not generally use the term *aer* in this regard—as one of the four fundamental *rhizomata*—though he does employ it on several occasions in other capacities (e.g., fr. 78).

14. Aristotle confirms that Empedocles is the first philosopher to grant the four elements primacy, although *arche* is not used explicitly by Empedocles to characterize the *rhizomata*.

15. Aristotle, *On Generation and Corruption* (333b20) in *Basic Works of Aristotle*, op. cit.

16. We also encounter, for example, Hephaistos (who is associated with fire in fr. 96 and 98) along with multiple terms for earth (*gaia, chton, ge*) and water (*hudor, ombros, pontos, thalassa*).

17. Democritus depicted these four colors as key, and we also find a correlation of colors and elements in Chinese texts. The four main colors of the Greeks, of course, do not correspond exactly to our notion of primary colors.

18. See especially Plato's *Theaetetus* (201e), trans. F. M. Cornford in *The Collected Dialogues of Plato*, op. cit. and the discussion in the following chapter.

19. Gilles Deleuze and Félix Guattari, *A Thousand Plateaus*, op. cit., pp. 3–25.

20. See, for example, Aeschylus, *Seven Against Thebes*, trans. Anthony Hecht and Helen Bacon. (Oxford, UK: Oxford UP, 1991), line 413.

21. *Nous* (mind) has a place in this process of perception, but it cannot obtain certainty either. On the senses and sense-perception, see A. A. Long, "Thinking and Sense-Perception in Empedocles: Mysticism or Materialism?," *Classical Quarterly* 16 (1966), pp. 256–76.

22. We return to the subject of elemental touch in a consideration of Aristotle (Chapters Five and Six) and Merleau-Ponty (Chapter Eight).

23. Charles H. Kahn, *Anaximander and the Origins of Greek Cosmology*, op. cit.

24. Homer, *The Iliad*, trans. Richmond Lattimore (Chicago, IL: U of Chicago P, 1961), 15.189.

25. Empedocles' remark: "those things that are most apt to mix are alike" (fr. 22) associates love and likeness. The link between hate and difference is evident in his claim, "all through Wrath are split to shapes diverse" (fr. 21).

26. Most notably, Aristotle argues this point.

27. The first stage appears to begin with fragment 27; the second in fragment 31; and the final stage at fragment 35. The stages and exact nature of this process are subject to a great amount of debate. For one reconstruction, see D. O'Brien, *Empedocles' Cosmic Cycle* (Cambridge, UK: Cambridge UP, 1969).

28. An aside or an amputated footnote on this lack of feet in the unity: "Picasso says there are no feet in nature. . . . If reality is singular then there are no feet in nature, if plural, a great many. If the world is one (everything part of the same thing—called by Picasso nature) then nothing either begins or ends. Only when things take the shapes of *each*es, *every*s, *any*s, *either*s (have ends) do they have feet. Feet are attached to ends, by definition. Moreover, if everything is one, and has neither ends nor beginnings, then everything is a circle. A circle has neither a beginning nor an end. A circle has no feet. If we believe that nature is a circle, then we must also believe that there are no feet in nature." From Nathaniel West, *The Dream of Balso Snell* (New York: Avon, 1965), pp. 113–14.

29. Something similar to Empedocles' notion of the *Sphairos* (Sphere) seems to have been held by Xenophanes (the divine as sphere, which is all-seeing, all-hearing, and all-thinking) and Parmenides (the world as immobile sphere).

30. This could be the translation if we opt for an anthropomorphic or theriomorphic rendering, which Empedocles himself seems to resist.

31. This is a point for which Aristotle criticizes Empedocles. Following Husserl, however, one might interpret repetition not as redundancy and lack of rigor but as a mark of essence or the essential.

32. See, Nietzsche, *Thus Spoke Zarathustra* in *The Portable Nietzsche*, trans. Walter Kaufmann (New York: Viking, 1954). On Nietzsche and nature, see Max O. Hallman, "Nietzsche's Environmental Ethics," *Environmental Ethics* 13 (1991), pp. 99–125; Martin Drenthen, "The Paradox of Environmental Ethics: Nietzsche's View of Nature and the Wild," *Environmental Ethics* 21 (1999), 163–75; and Graham Parkes, "Nietzsche's Environmental Philosophy: A Trans-European Perspective," *Environmental Ethics* 27 (2005), pp. 77–91.

33. Mircea Eliade, *The Myth of Eternal Return* (Princeton, NJ: Princeton UP, 1974).

34. The *rhizomata* are *iso ponta* (all equal). In this regard, they are comparable to Parmenides' treatment of fire and night (fr. 9.4), which are considered *iso amphoteroi* (both equal).

35. In the *Purifications* (unlike *On Nature*) there does seem to be a semi-distinctive (although not privileged) role accorded to earth as "mother" (fr. 122) and "strange place" (fr. 118), a bit like the central role it plays in Hegel's *Philosophy of Nature*, Plato's *Timaeus*, and Heidegger's later work. It does not, however, rest entirely apart, as sole source of solidity or ground, as place of places, or as a kind of super-locater for the other elements.

36. See Aristotle's *Politics* for the Greek notion of citizenship and the notion of rule in turn.

37. See Diogenes Laertius, *Vitae Philosophorum*, ed., H. Long (Oxford, UK: Oxford UP, 1964), VIII, 63, DK 31A1.

38. *Dikaiosyne* (justice) is not used explicitly by Empedocles, although it is expressed indirectly when he speaks of a "broad oath" at work in the world (fr. 30).

39. Aetius (5.30) in *Doxographi Graeci*, ed., Hermann Diels (Berlin, 1879).

40. On the history of ecological concepts and the relation of modern ecology to philosophy and theoretical physics, see J. Baird Callicott, "The Metaphysical Implications

of Ecology," *Environmental Ethics* 8 (1986), pp. 301–16. In terms of the connection between the science of ecology and the philosophy of deep ecology, consult Frank B. Golley, "Deep Ecology from the Perspective of Ecological Science," *Environmental Ethics* 9 (1987), pp. 45–55. For a critique of the notion of balance, harmony and equilibrium states in ecosystems and nature, see Daniel Botkin, *Discordant Harmonies* (New York: Oxford UP, 1990).

41. For an elaboration of this perspective more generally in ancient Greek thought, see Gregory Vlastos, "Equality and Justice in Early Greek Cosmologies," in *Studies in Presocratic Philosophy*, Vol. 1, ed., D. J. Furley and Reginald E. Allen (New York: Routledge and Kegan Paul, 1970), p. 63.

42. Murray Bookchin, "Toward a Philosophy of Nature—The Bases for an Ecological Ethics" in Michael Tobias, ed. *Deep Ecology* (New York: Avant Books, 1985), p. 220.

43. See, for example, Paul Taylor, "Biocentrism"; Arne Naess, "Ecosophy T"; and Murray Bookchin, "Social Ecology Versus Deep Ecology" in Pojman, *Environmental Ethics*, op. cit. and Harold Wood, "Modern Pantheism as an Approach to Environmental Ethics," *Environmental Ethics* 7 (1985), pp. 151–63.

44. This position is somewhat simplified because Empedocles claims at one point that sight involves water as well. Perception is also explained in terms of his pore theory (via the similarity of pores), but it mainly relies on the attraction of like things. The idea seems to have been picked up in part by Plato in the *Timaeus*. Chapter Four discusses how Plato derives his elements—especially earth and fire—near the outset of the dialogue.

45. See Ernst Bloch, *Das Prinzip Hoffnung* (Frankfurt, Germany: Suhrkamp Verlag, 1967), Band III.

46. Although these biological extensions (feathers, hair, leaves, etc.) may not be alive in the same way as the organism or entity to which they belong, they are revealing as to the general question of what is alive. In Redwood tress, for example, less than three percent of the tree is actually alive and growing.

47. For a similar kind of problem, see the passage by Jorge Luis Borges quoted in Michel Foucault's *The Order of Things* (New York: Vintage, 1973) and my treatment of it in David Macauley, "Be-wildering Order: On Finding a Home for Domestication and the Domesticated Other," in Roger Gottlieb, ed., *The Ecological Community*, op. cit.

48. David Skrbina, *Panpsychism in the West* (Cambridge, MA: MIT Press, 2005), pp. 33. For a defense of panpsychism, see Freya Mathews, *For Love of Matter: A Contemporary Panpsychism* (Albany: SUNY P, 2003).

49. J. Baird Callicott, "Traditional American Indian and Western European Attitudes Toward Nature," *Environmental Ethics* 4 (1982), pp. 293–318.

50. David Skrbina, *Panpsychism in the West*, op. cit., p. 268.

51. For critical analysis of panpsychism, see Colin McGinn, *The Mysterious Flame: Conscious Minds in a Material World* (New York: Basic, 1999) and Thomas Nagel, *Mortal Questions* (Cambridge, UK: Cambridge UP, 1979).

52. Like his predecessor, Lucretius (100–55 B.C.E.) is able to forge a unique blend of philosophy, poetry, cosmology and natural science in his work, *De Rerum Natura*. He describes the elements as *maxima membra mundi*—"the great limbs of the world"—but still proceeds to advance a number of short arguments against the physical side of Empedocles' view, many of which reveal insufficient understanding of the cosmological dimensions. See Lucretius, *On the Nature of the Universe*, op. cit., I. 716ff.

53. For sources for these and other accounts, see Diogenes Laertius, op. cit., 8.70 and 8.60–61.

54. One might note the irony of the reputed causes of death of Presocratic thinkers, Thales, Heraclitus, and Empedocles. Thales, who gives primacy to water, is reported to have died of heat and thirst (i.e., lack of water), whereas Heraclitus, whose *logos* is connected to fire, is said to have contracted a fatal case of dropsy (too much water) and comes to be called "the weeping philosopher" by the Romans. Empedocles, as the story has it, is consumed by the volcano, which represents in a sense the interplay and cycling of all the elements.

55. J. Donald Hughes, "The View from Etna: A Search for Ancient Landscape Appreciation," *The Trumpeter* 4 (1987), p. 10.

56. For a relevant discussion of volcanoes by an ecological scientist interested in myth and metaphor, see Daniel Botkin, *Discordant Harmonies*, op. cit., pp. 91–93. Botkin notes that Athanasius Kircher, a seventeenth-century Jesuit and one of the first to descend into an active volcano and survive, described his journeys into Aetna and Vesuvius in elemental and poetic terms. Water and fire "sweetly conspire in mutual service, and with an inviolable friendship and wedlock" blend together their "several and distinct private lodgings" for the "good of the whole," a description reminiscent of Empedocles. See, too, Kircher's *Mundus Subterraneus* in XII *libros digestus,* (Amsterdam: Joannes Janssonius à Waesberge and Filios, 1678).

57. Gilles Deleuze, *Logic of Sense*, op. cit., p. 128.

58. See Mircea Eliade, *Shamanism* (Princeton, NJ: Princeton UP, 1964). For relevant discussions, see F. M. Cornford, *Principium Sapientiae*, op. cit.; E. R. Dodds, *The Greeks and the Irrational*, op. cit.; Peter Kingsley, *Ancient Philosophy, Mystery, and Magic*, op. cit.; James Frazer, *The Golden Bough*, op. cit.; and John Grim, *The Shaman: Patterns of Siberian and Ojibway Healing* (Norman: U of Oklahoma P, 1983).

59. Hermann Diels, "Über die Gedichte des Empedokles," op. cit.

60. Despite the deep involvement with and understanding of the natural world by shamans, there might still be a sense in which they and their successor, the priests, begin to increasingly erect hierarchical social boundaries of knowledge and power, to manipulate community relations, and to generalize in such a manner to help undermine older forms of animism. See Murray Bookchin, *The Ecology of Freedom*, op. cit., pp. 83–84, 91–93, and 100–01.

61. For a Native American story on this subject with environmental implications, see "The Woman Who Married A Bear" in Gary Snyder, *The Practice of the Wild*, op. cit., pp. 155–74.

62. "The notion of gravity—'weighed-downness'—comes into existence as a companion idea, almost by negative definition," Roszak argues. "Gravity is the shadow side of levity; in the shaman's experience, it becomes symbolic of what one feels when the soul drifts from the sense of buoyancy that keeps it close the sacred." Theodore Roszak, *Where the Wasteland Ends* (New York: Anchor Books, 1973), pp. 330–31.

63. Aristotle, *Physics* (198b29–33) in McKeon, ed., *The Basic Works of Aristotle*, op. cit.

64. See Aristotle's critique as well in *On Generation and Corruption* (333b15), *De Caelo* (300b25ff) and *Metaphysics* (1000b12) in McKeon, ed., *Basic Works of Aristotle*, op. cit.

65. Simplicius, *On Aristotle's Physics* (371.33). See Richard Sorabji, ed., *The Philosophy of the Commentators, 200–600 AD: A Sourcebook*, Vol. 2: Physics (Ithaca, NY: Cornell UP, 2005).

66. See also G. Rudberg, "Empedokles und Evolution," *Eranos* 50 (1952), pp. 23–30.

67. Empedocles, too, explains the structure of the eye analogically as a lantern and advances a remarkable early theory of perception based on it. See J. I. Beare, *Greek Theories of Elementary Cognition* (Oxford, UK: Clarendon, 1906).

68. Trees, Empedocles observed, obtain nourishment from the air through pores, an idea suggestive of modern thinking in botany (frs. 77–78).

69 See Ruth Harrison, *Animal Machines* (London, UK: Stuart, 1964); Peter Singer, *Animal Liberation* (New York: Avon, 1975); Tom Regan, *The Case for Animal Rights* (Berkeley: U of California P, 1983); and John Wynne-Tyson, *Food for A Future* (New York: Universe Books, 1979).

70. See Stanley and Roslind Godlovitch and John Harris, eds., *Animal, Men and Morals* (New York: Grove, 1972); Peter Singer, ed., *In Defense of Animals* (Oxford, UK and New York: Basil Blackwell, 1985; Steve Sapontzis, *Morals, Reason, and Animals* (Philadelphia, PA: Temple UP, 1987).

71. See, for example, Eugene Hargrove, *The Animal Rights/Environmental Ethics Debate: The Ecological Perspective* (Albany: SUNY P, 1992) and J. Baird Callicott, "Animal Liberation: A Triangular Affair," *Environmental Ethics* 2.4 (1980). For some of my own work in these areas, see David Macauley, "Political Animals: A Study of the Emerging Animal Rights Movement in the United States," *Between The Species: A Journal of Ethics* 3.2 to 4.2 (serialized in five parts from Spring 1987 to Spring 1988); Macauley, "Consuming Passions: An Intercourse on Animals and Food," *Lomakatsi* 3 (1988); Macauley, "Animals, Ecology and Anarchism," *Lomakatsi* 1–2 (serialized in two parts from Spring 1987 to Summer 1987); "The Animal Rights Movement: Pythagoras' Heirs or the New Luddites of the Left?," *William and Mary Magazine* (1986); and "Interview with Peter Singer," *The Animals' Agenda* (September 1987).

72. For a thorough and competent treatment of animal issues in ancient Greece, see Richard Sorabji, *Animal Minds and Human Morals: The Origins of the Western Debate* (Ithaca, NY: Cornell UP, 1993).

73 See, for example, Frans de Waal, *Good Natured: The Origins of Right and Wrong in Humans and Other Animals* (Cambridge, MA: Harvard UP, 1996) and Stephen Clark, *The Moral Status of Animals* (Oxford, UK: Clarendon Press, 1962).

74. See, for example, Kropotkin's works such as *Mutual Aid* (Boston: Extending Horizon Books, n.d.), originally published in 1902, and *Fields, Factories and Workshops Tomorrow*, ed. Colin Ward (New York: Harper & Row, 1974). See also David Macauley, "Evolution and Revolution: The Ecological Anarchism and Kropotkin and Bookchin" in Andrew Light, ed., *Social Ecology After Bookchin*, op. cit.

75. Haeckel's works include, *The Wonders of Life* (London: Watts, 1904), *The Riddle of the Universe* (New York: Harper & Row, 1900) and *Monism as Connecting Religion and Science* (London: A. and C. Black, 1894).

76. Carol Kaesuk Yoon, "Plants Found to Share Water with Neighbors," *New York Times*, Oct. 26, 1993, C1, 10. In the leaves and branches, at the other end of the roots—or the roots that rise into the sky—it is now recognized that some trees which are attacked by insects issue warnings by wafting airborne chemicals to neighboring trees, which subsequently increase their concentration of protective chemicals, making their foliage difficult or deadly to consume. See Shannon Brown Lee, "The Silent Battle," *Discover* (September 1983) and Ben Patrusky, "Plants on their own Behalf," *Mosaic* 14.2 (March/April 1983) for discussions of plant defensive and communication methods.

77. See as well, John Rodman, "The Other Side of Ecology in Ancient Greece," *Inquiry* 18 (1976), pp. 115–25 and Jim Cheney, "In the Shadow of Ancient Ruins: Hellenism and Gnosticism in Contemporary Environmental Ethics," *Environmental History Review* 15.2 (1991), pp. 31–54.

78. Neil Evernden, *The Natural Alien: Humankind and Environment* (Toronto, Canada: U of Toronto P, 1985), p. 40. Compare as well Martin Buber's description in *I and Thou* of a tree when he is "drawn into a relation and the tree ceases to be an It." These understandings stand in stark contrast to Sartre's encounter in *Nausea* with a tree and its roots: "So, I was in the park just now. The roots of the chestnut tree were sunk in the ground, just under my bench . . . I was sitting, stooping forward, head bowed, alone in front of this black, knotty mass, entirely beastly, which frightened me." *Nausea*, trans. Lloyd Alexander (New York: New Directions, 1964), pp. 126–27.

79. For a primer on ecology, see Michael Allaby, *Basics of Environmental Science* (London, UK: Routledge, 1996) or, for a more classic text, Eugene P. Odum, *Fundamentals or Ecology*, 3rd ed. (Philadelphia, PA: W.B. Saunders, 1971).

80. Gregory Vlastos, "Equality and Justice in Early Greek Cosmologies," in *Studies in Presocratic Philosophy*, op. cit., p. 56.

81. Donald Hughes, "The Environmental Ethics of the Pythagoreans," *Environmental Ethics* 3 (1980), p. 195.

82. Hwa Yol Jung, "The Orphic Voice and Ecology," *Environmental Ethics* 3 (1981), pp. 329–39.

83. "Da stieg ein Baum. O reine Übersteigung! / O Orpheus singt! O hoher Baum im Ohr! / Und alles schwieg. . . . / Tiere aus Stille drangen aus dem klaren / gelösten Wald von Lager und Genist." Rainer Maria Rilke, *The Sonnets to Orpheus*, sonnet I, i, in *The Selected Poetry of Rainer Maria Rilke*, op. cit. Note the linguistic resemblance of the "tall tree in the ear" to fr. 99 of Empedocles.

84. See Chapter Two for a discussion of the "construction" of the elements and Chapter Four for a consideration of their construction in Plato's philosophy.

85. On the importance of this last device—used for raising liquid from one vessel and releasing it into another vessel—in his account of respiration, see D. J. Furley, "Empedocles and the Clepsydra," *Journal of Hellenic Studies*, op. cit., pp. 31–34.

86. In fr. 8 and 9 by Empedocles, I follow M. R. Wright's translation in *Empedocles: The Extant Fragments*, op. cit.

87. Aristotle, *Metaphysics* (1014b35) in McKeon, ed., *Basic Works of Aristotle*, op. cit.

88. The early Greeks often used *ousia* as a synonym for *physis* (nature) or to mean property (in the legal sense).

89. On Derrida's textual strategies of reading and writing, see *Dissemination*, op. cit. and *Margins of Philosophy*, trans. Alan Bass (Chicago, IL: U of Chicago P, 1982).

90. On the nature (*physis*) and convention (*nomos*) debate, see Richard D. McKirahan, *Philosophy Before Socrates* (Indianapolis, IN: Hackett Publishing, 1994), pp. 390–413.

91. G.E.R. Lloyd, "The Invention of Nature" in Lloyd, *Methods and Problems in Greek Science* op. cit., pp. 431–32.

92. Sidney Feshbach, "Empedocles: The Phenomenology of the Four Elements in Literature," in Anna-Teresa Tymieniecka, ed., *Poetics of the Elements in the Human Condition: The Airy Elements* (Dordrecht, Netherlands: Kluwer Academic, 1988), p. 23.

93. Ibid., p. 25.

94. See, for example, Rachel Carson, *Silent Spring* (New York: Ballantine Books, 1962) and Barry Commoner, *The Closing Circle* (New York: Bantam Books, 1971). For a discussion of these individuals and issues related to pollution and pollution politics, see Yaakov Garb, "The Politics of Nature in Rachel Carson's *Silent Spring*" in David Macauley, *Minding Nature*, op. cit. and Andrew Feenberg, "The Commoner-Ehrlich Debate," in Macauley, *Minding Nature*, op. cit.

95. See Marvin S. Soroos, *The Endangered Atmosphere: Preserving a Global Commons* (Columbia: U of South Carolina P, 1977); Robin Clarke, *Water: The International Crisis* (Cambridge, MA: MIT Press, 1993); John M. Donahue and Barbara Rose Johnston, *Water, Culture, and Power: Local Struggles in a Global Context* (Covelo, CA: Island Press, 1998); William Meyer, *Human Impact on the Earth* (Cambridge, UK: Cambridge UP, 1996); and Alan Wellburn, *Air Pollution and Acid Rain* (New York: Wiley, 1988).

96. In the case of air pollution, for example, wind transports polluted air from one bioregion, state, and country to another. Thus, the problem can no longer be viewed entirely as a local one that does not affect other areas. See, Hilary French, "You Are What You Breathe," in Lester R. Brown, *The Worldwatch Reader* (New York: W.W. Norton, 1991).

97. See, for example, Jacques Leslie, "Running Dry: What happens when the world no longer has enough freshwater?" *Harpers* (July 2000), pp. 37–52.

98. Mary Douglas, *Purity and Danger: An Analysis of Concepts of Pollution and Taboo* (New York: Praeger, 1966).

99. Pollution has sometimes been considered to include seminal emission apart from coition.

100. See Robert Parker, *Miasma: Pollution and Purification in Early Greek Religion* (Oxford, UK: Clarendon, 1983).

101. J. Donald Hughes, *Pan's Travail* (Baltimore, MD: Johns Hopkins UP, 1994), p. 52.

102. Herodotus, *Histories* (1.174). Cited in Hughes, *Pan's Travail*, op. cit., p. 51.

103. See generally, Robert Sallares, *The Ecology of the Ancient Greek World*, op. cit. and Hughes, *Pan's Travail*, op. cit.

104. Plato, *Critias*, in *The Collected Dialogues*, op. cit., p. 1216 (111b).

105. See Iamblichus, *Vita Pythagoras* (110), where the notion of purification has strong religious aspects and occurs through *mousike* (music, including dance, performance, and poetry).

106. See, for example, Plato's *Sophist* (226a) in which *katharsis* (purification) involves the removal of evil in the soul and is compared with the practice of medicine, which seeks to do the same. Socrates also speaks of cleansing the soul through *elenchos* (interrogative questioning).

107. See, especially, Aristotle's *Poetics* and the well-known view of tragedy as causing a homeopathic *katharsis* (purification) of the *pathe* (emotions) of fear and pity.

108. See fr. 98 and 105. In Empedocles' view, blood contains the most perfect and equal blend of the elements, and through it inspiration and respiration take place.

109. See J. W. Jones, *Law and Legal Theory of the Greeks* (Oxford, UK: Clarendon, 1956), p. 255.

110. Sophocles, *The Theban Plays*, trans. E. F. Watling (New York: Penguin, 1974), 1424–28.

111. Euripides, *Medea and Other Plays*, trans. Philip Vallacott. (New York: Penguin, 1963), 1327–28.

112. These currents, of course, are by no means unique to environmentalists and they are found to one degree or another in most, if not all, political and philosophical movements.

113. For a discussion of some of these tendencies, see David Macauley, "Greening Philosophy and Democritizing Ecology," in Macauley, *Minding Nature*, op. cit., pp. 1–23.

114. Douglas, *Purity and Danger*, op. cit., p. 5.

115. Ibid. (italics added), p. 35. In fairness, Douglas may not intend "elements" to mean the four elements, although it is possible to read it this way.

116. On the possibility of reform in this area, see Robert N. Stavins and Bradley W. Whitehead, "Market-based Incentives for Environmental Protection," in Louis Pojman, *Environmental Ethics*, op. ed., pp. 401–07.

117. See Langdon Winner, *The Whale and the Reactor* (Chicago, IL: U of Chicago P, 1986) and Neil Evernden, *The Social Creation of Nature*, op. cit.

118. See, for example, Karl Grossman, "Environmental Racism" in Donald Van DeVeer and Christine Pierce, *The Environmental Ethics and Policy Book*, 2nd ed. (Belmont, CA: Wadsworth, 1998), pp. 553–59. Grossman illustrates how hazardous wastes often are dumped in Black and Native American communities in the United States.

119. For work of interest on this dimension of pollution, see Robert R. Higgins, "Race, Pollution, and the Mastery of Nature," *Environmental Ethics* 16.3 (1994), pp. 251–64; Robert D. Bullard, ed. *Unequal Protection: Environmental Justice and Communities of Color* (San Francisco, CA: Sierra Club Books, 1994); and Robert D. Bullard, *Dumping in Dixie: Race, Class and Environmental Quality* (Boulder, CO: Westview Press, 1990).

120. Timothy Morton, "Shelley's Green Desert," *Studies in Romanticism* 35.3 (1996).

121. Some Deep Ecologists are given toward this kind of characterization, seeking to preserve a pristine, untouched "nature" free of all human activity.

122. See Hippocrates, *Air, Water, Places*, trans. W.H.S. Jones, Loeb Classical Library (Cambridge, MA: Harvard UP, 1948) and *Ancient Medicine*, trans. W.H.S. Jones, Loeb Classical Library (Cambridge, MA: Harvard UP, 1948).

123. Jacques Derrida, *Of Grammatology*, trans. Gayatri Spivak (Baltimore, MD: Johns Hopkins UP, 1967), p. 102.

124. See the emerging literature of post-structuralist ecology such as Verena Andermatt Conley, *Ecopolitics: The Environment in Poststructuralist Thought* (New York: Routledge, 1997); Michael E. Soulé and Gary Lease, eds., *Reinventing Nature?: Responses to Postmodern Deconstruction* (Washington, DC: Island Press, 1995); Michael Zimmerman, *Contesting Earth's Future: Radical Ecology and Postmodernity* (Berkeley: U of California P, 1994); Jane Bennett and William Chaloupka, eds., *In the Nature of Things: Language, Politics, and the Environment* (Minneapolis: U of Minnesota P, 1993); Max Oelschlaeger, *The Idea of Wilderness* (New Haven, CT: Yale UP, 1991), esp. Chapter Ten. See also the literature of critical theory and ecology such as Steven Vogel, *Against Nature*, op. cit. and my review of this work in *Capitalism, Nature, Socialism* 9.1 (1998).

125. For a discussion of the relation of philosophy to root and tree metaphors, see Mary Tiles, "Images of Reason in Western Culture" in Eliot Deutsch, *Introduction to World Philosophies* (Upper Saddle River, NJ: Prentice Hall, 1997), pp. 211–18.

126. Think, for example, of the metaphor of branching in the well-known taxonomic work of anatomist and paleontologist, Georges Cuvier.

127. Gilles Deleuze and Félix Guattari, *A Thousand Plateaus*, op. cit., p. 15. Compare on this point, Albert the Great, who advanced a theory, to which was commonly subscribed in the Middle Ages, that in clearing away a wooded area for agricultural use it is incumbent to remove all rhizomes from cut trees (e.g., through fire) for fear that they will use up the nourishment of the surrounding soil. See Albert the Great, *De Vegetabilibus*, Bk. VII, ed. Peter Jammy (Lyons: France, 1651), pp. 488–89.

128. Ibid., p. 20. For a helpful analysis of Deleuze and Guattari, see Steven Best and Douglas Kellner, *Postmodern Theory: Critical Interrogations* (New York: Guilford, 1991).

129. Thought, Deleuze and Guattari claim, is decidedly non-arborescent, as is short-term memory (unlike long-term memory). Thus, one needs to replace psychoanalysis with what they term elsewhere *schizoanalysis*, which treats the unconscious as a-centered, productive and free-flowing (not symbolic, representational, or structural) and "subjects" or individuals as "desiring machines." What they call rhizomatics, schizoanalysis, and nomadology are closely related as breaks from representation, repression, and roots.

130. Foucault looks at issues related to the roots of language, letters, and alphabetic writing—through which "the history of men is entirely changed"—in *The Order of Things*, op. cit., p. 104ff.

131. For example, following the work of Walter Ong in *Orality and Literacy: The Technologizing of the Word* (New York: Methuen, 1982) and Marshall McLuhan in *The Gutenberg Galaxy* (Toronto, Canada: U of Toronto P, 1962)—or alternatively, Derrida who is critical of such perspectives—one might explore the effect of the element qua letter (along with the accompanying alphabet and writing culture) on environmental "literacy" and by extension, our understandings of the natural world.

132. The literature of cybernetic organisms and the human–machine interface is growing. For an early contribution, see Donna Harroway, "The Cyborg Manifesto" in *Simians, Cyborgs, and Women: The Reinvention of Nature* (New York: Routledge, 1991).

133. Deleuze and Guattari, *A Thousand Plateaus*, op. cit., pp. 10–11.

134. See Stephen Jay Gould's works, such as *Wonderful Life*, for a view of evolution that resonates at times with the rhizome model. Gould argues evolution is less like a ladder, a cone of increasing diversity, or tree and more like a bush (without a trunk) budding contingent branches.

135. Ibid., p. 238.

136. A becoming, however, between heterogeneous terms—which for them is completely real and lacking in a subject distinct from itself—is closer to what they term *involution* (not to be understood as regression) rather than traditional evolution in that it is creative and rhizomatic.

137. Gilles Deleuze and Félix Guattari, *What is Philosophy?*, trans. Hugh Tomlinson and Graham Burchell (New York: Columbia UP, 1994), p. 88.

138. Ibid., p. 85. See also Deleuze and Guattari, *A Thousand Plateaus*, op. cit., p. 339, where they see Empedocles "sinking too deeply into the earth."

139. On Deleuze's naturalistic ontology, see Patrick Hayden, "Gilles Deleuze and Naturalism: A Convergence with Ecological Theory and Politics," *Environmental Ethics* 19.2 (1997), pp. 185–204. See also Robert Mugerauer "Deleuze and Guattari's Return to

Science as a Basis for Environmental Philosophy," in Bruce V. Foltz and Robert Frodeman, eds., *Rethinking Nature*, op. cit., pp. 180–204.

140. Félix Guattari, *The Three Ecologies* (London, UK: Athlone Press, 2001).

Interstice: Ice and Snow

1. Henry David Thoreau, quoted in Mariana Gosnell, *Ice: The Nature, the History, and the Uses of an Astonishing Substance* (New York: Knopf, 2005), p. 12.
2. Ibid., p. 4.
3. Samuel Coleridge, *The Rime of the Ancient Mariner and Other Poems* (New York: Dover, 1992), p. 5ff.
4. Richard E. Byrd, *The National Geographic Magazine*, October 1947.
5. Stephen Pyne, *The Ice: A Journey to Antarctica* (Iowa City: U of Iowa P, 1986), p. 3.
6. Ibid., p. 3.
7. Barry Lopez, *Arctic Dreams: Imagination and Desire in a Northern Landscape* (New York: Bantam 1996), p. 206.
8. John Broder and Andrew Revkin, "Warming May Wipe Out Most Polar Bears, Study Says," *New York Times*, September 8, 2007, p. A11.
9. Gretel Ehrlich *The Future of Ice: A Journey into Cold* (New York: Pantheon, 2004), p. 56.
10. For literature on the subject, see Laura Martin, "Eskimo Words for Snow: A case study in the genesis and decay of an anthropological example," *American Anthropologist* 88.2 (1986), pp. 418–423; and Geoffrey Pullman, *The Great Eskimo Vocabulary Hoax* (Chicago, IL: U of Chicago P, 1991).
11. Jay Griffiths, *Wild: An Elemental Journey* (New York: Penguin, 2006), p. 107.
12. Stephen Pyne, *The Ice*, op. cit., p. 19.
13. Maurice Merleau-Ponty, *The Visible and Invisible*, op. cit., p. 218.
14. Wallace Stevens, "The Snow Man" in *The Palm at the End of the Mind*, ed. Holly Stevens (New York: Vintage, 1972), p. 54.

Chapter 4: Plato's *Chora*-graphy of Earth, Air, Fire, and Water

1. For the Greek, I rely on *Plato*, Vol. IX, trans. R. G. Bury (Cambridge, MA: Loeb Classical Library, 1929). For the English translation, I turn to the rendering in Plato, *Timaeus*, trans. Francis Cornford, op. cit. I also have consulted Francis Cornford, *Plato's Cosmology: The Timaeus of Plato* (London, UK: Routledge & Kegan Paul, 1948); A. E. Taylor, *A Commentary on Plato's Timaeus* (Oxford, UK: Oxford UP, 1928); and W. K. Guthrie, *A History of Greek Philosophy*, Vol. 5 (Cambridge, UK: Cambridge UP, 1986).
2. My translation diverges here from that of Cornford.
3. See Gabriela R. Carone, "Plato and the Environment," *Environmental Ethics* 20 (1998), pp. 115–133; Thomas M. Robinson and Laura Westra, eds., *The Greeks and the Environment*, op. cit.; Geoffrey Lloyd, "Plato as a Natural Scientist," *Journal of Hellenic Studies* 88 (1968), pp. 78–92; Daniel Dombrowski, "Was Plato a Vegetarian?" *Apeiron* 18.1 (1984).

4. The implicit steps to this argument can be reconstructed as follows:

1. The universe consists of a body because what comes to be must have bodily form (31b).

2. Bodies are tangible and visible (Ibid).

3. Tangibility and visibility require light and solidity, and hence depend on the elements, fire and earth, which provide for these bodily properties (Ibid).

4. The primary bodies cannot be singular because the world is tangible and visible, thereby requiring at least two elements (implicit, Ibid).

5. Two elements, however, are insufficient to form the body of the universe because a third is necessary to unite them (31 b–c).

6. These three need to be in proportion, and the best type of bond is a proportion that forms a unity of means and extremes (31c–32a).

7. Thus, a continued geometrical proportion is required because it is the most perfect kind of proportion in that any one of the numbers can be a first, middle, or last term (Ibid).

8. Three terms and one mean, however, are insufficient because the body of the universe is not a plane surface but solid in form, as are all primary bodies (32a–b) (following Steps 2 and 3).

9. Solid bodies are conjoined by two means, not one (32b).

10. Thus, there must be two other primary bodies between fire and earth if these two elements (deduced in Step 3) are to be connected (required by Step 5) (Ibid).

11. We can identify these two additional bodies as air and water (Ibid). (Plato posits the names of these two bodies without deriving them via attributes.)

12. Because these elements must be set into proportion (Step 6) insofar as it is possible, we arrive at the relational sequence: fire is to air as air is to water *and* air is to water as water is to earth (32b).

5. Plato's proportions do not seem to properly fit with the construction of the four solids later in the dialogue (53c–55c) and their attendant distribution to earth, air, fire, and water (55d–56c).

6. In later commentary, controversy exists concerning the actual number of elements in Plato's system. Although the *Timaeus* clearly focuses on four primary bodies, Aristotle once attributes three to Plato in a work he calls Plato's *Classifications*. Xenocrates accords him with a system of five.

7. *Timaeus* (32b–c). The figure of the frame returns when the Demiurge "frames" the four elements with "greatest possible perfection" (53b). In Chapter Eight, we consider Heidegger's notion of "enframing" as it relates to the natural world.

8. Plotinus also later represents nature (*physis*) as being without hands or feet, and as making without these appendages. The universe is spoken of, too, as an organism, a single, living being who dances and whose ballet is not wholly unlike the cosmological movements that occur in the *Timaeus*. See especially *Ennead* III.8, "Nature, Contemplation and the One" in Plotinus, *Enneads*, trans. A. H. Armstrong (Cambridge MA: Harvard UP, 1966).

9. See chapter 1 on the Gaia hypothesis and James Lovelock, *Gaia*, op. cit.

10. Space or place, however, is antecedent ontologically to time and thus more primordial.

11. In a later treatment of the generation of animals, Plato claims these creatures change from one into another, shifting their respective places with gains or losses in understanding (92c).

12. This interpretation is consistent with the Atomistic understanding of the cosmos as having its origin in chance permutations of atoms that collide with one another.

13. It is what Aristotle will call spontaneity (*to automaton*) in the *Physics*.

14. For an elaboration of the notion of constrained constructivism, see N. Katherine Hayles' article in Michael E. Soulé and Gary Lease, eds., *Reinventing Nature?* (Washington, DC: Island Press, 1995).

15. Mendeleyev, quoted in Paul Strathern, *Mendeleyev's Dream: The Quest for the Elements* (New York: Berkley, 2000), p. 286.

16. Plato later accounts for dreams and prophetic divination in the *Timaeus* by explaining them physiologically through the workings of the liver, which is the medium through which the rational part of the soul conveys thoughts as images (71a–72b).

17. See Aristotle's *Metaphysics* (1000a1ff), where elements are spoken of as "atomic sounds."

18. Letters (*stoicheia*) and syllables are also discussed in the *Cratylus* (421ff), a dialogue that takes up the theme of the relation between language and reality and the theory that a word should depict its referent. Socrates warns us that "we should remember that if a person goes on analyzing names into words, and inquiring also into the elements out of which the words are formed, and keeps on always repeating this process, he who has to answer him must at last give up the inquiry in despair" (421e). They are also considered in the *Statesman* (277 ff) and in the *Sophist* (266b). The idea of the ABC (the letters) recurs in, among other places, Book Two of Francis Bacon's *Of the Advancement of Learning*. It is the task of science to ascertain the "true forms," which are no more numerous than the letters of the alphabet. See *Selected Writings of Francis Bacon*, ed. Hugh G. Dick (New York: Modern Library, 1955).

19. "ΚΟΣΜΟΣ" is Greek for cosmos.

20. On this last point concerning writing and Plato, see Jacques Derrida, "Plato's Pharmacy" in *Dissemination*, op. cit.

21. Again, we see imagination enter into the account of the elements, which are also connected with dreams for Plato.

22. We will turn shortly to the notion of the *chora*.

23. John Sallis makes a case for interpreting earth more generally as providing a political frame, via the location of the city, in which to understand the dialogue. See Sallis, *Chorology*, op. cit., pp. 138–45.

24. See Aristotle, *On the Heavens* (306a2).

25. For an interpretation that complicates Plato's strong distinction between the sensible and intelligible, showing how *chora* both founds and displaces this division, see John Sallis, *Chorology*, op. cit.

26. Strictly speaking, of course, the ideal model does not lie within the *chora*.

27. Paul Virilio, *Open Sky*, op. cit., p. 150.

28. The image of wax is taken up by Plato in the *Theaetetus* (190e–195b) and later employed by Descartes in *The Meditations* (AT 30–32).

29. Recall here the issue of the construction and crafting of the elements and nature in Empedocles' works and Presocratic thought more generally, as discussed in Chapters One and Two.

30. The Receptacle, as Cornford has pointed out, is *not* an Aristotelian substrate "out of which" (*ex hou*) things come.

31. See Edward Casey, *The Fate of Place* (Berkeley: U of California P, 1997), pp. 32–49 for an articulation of this position.

32. A. E. Taylor defends this point in *A Commentary on Plato's Timaeus*, op. cit.

33. Martin Heidegger, *Introduction to Metaphysics*, op. cit., p. 66. For an interesting treatment of the *chora* and choric space/place that cannot be considered here, see Jacques Derrida's essay in *On the Name*, trans. David Wood et al., ed., Thomas Dutoit (Stanford, CA: Stanford UP, 1995).

34. For an account of the Greek *polis* as belonging to a golden era, see Hans Jonas, *The Gnostic Religion* (Boston, MA: Beacon Press, 1963). For a critical view of the *polis* in relation to environmental philosophy, see Jim Cheney, "In the Shadow of Ancient Ruins: Hellenism and Gnosticism in Contemporary Environmental Ethics," *Environmental History Review*, op. cit.

35. See Plato, *The Republic*, trans. Allen Bloom (New York: Basic, 1968), Bk. VII.

36. On the relationship between women and nature, see Carolyn Merchant, *The Death of Nature*, op. cit. Some of my thoughts on the subject appear in David Macauley, "On Women, Animals and Nature," *American Philosophical Association Newsletter on Philosophy and Feminism*, 1990 (3), pp. 116–27 and Macauley, "Echoes to Ecofeminism, *American Philosophical Association Newsletter on Philosophy and Feminism* 1 (1991), pp. 82–85.

37. For an examination of Plato's view of women, see Nancy Tuana, ed., *Feminist Interpretations of Plato* (University Park: Pennsylvania State UP, 1994) and Luce Irigaray, *An Ethics of Sexual Difference*, trans. C. Burke and G. C. Gill (Ithaca, NY: Cornell UP, 1993).

38. On the Pythagoreans, see G. S. Kirk et al., *Presocratic Philosophers*, op. cit., pp. 214–38.

39. We return to the theme of domestication in Chapter Seven. On the place of animals in human culture, see Paul Shepard, *The Others: How Animals Made us Human* (Washington, DC: Island Press, 1996).

40. As painter Henri Matisse said, "L'exactitude n'est pas la vérité" (Exactitude is not the truth).

41. Heraclitus also gives a place to play: "Eternity (*aion*) is a child playing" (DK 52).

42. See William S. Sax, ed., *The Gods at Play* (Oxford, UK: Oxford UP, 1995).

43. John Huizinga, *Homo Ludens: A Study of the Play Element in Culture* (Boston, MA: Beacon Press, 1950), p. 212.

44. On this point, see Mircea Eliade, *Myth and Reality* (New York: Harper Colophon, 1975), pp. 142–43 and Eliade, *The Sacred and the Profane*, op. cit.

45. Leo Frobenius, paraphrased by John Huizinga, *Homo Ludens*, op. cit., p.16.

46. Indeed, one finds that play has a definite, if marginal, place in the history of philosophy from the ironic play of Socrates and the performances of the Sophists to perennial language games and logical puzzles; from the aphorisms and jests of Nietzsche to the verbal puns of Derrida.

47. Huizinga, *Homo Ludens*, op. cit., p. 3.

48. See Plotinus, III.8, *Enneads*, op. cit.

49. For a discussion relevant to Plato's elements, see W. Heisenberg, "Platons Vorstellungen von den kleinstein Bausteinen der Materie und die Elementarteilchen der modernen Physik," *Im Umkreis der Kunst. Eine Festschrift für Emil Pretorius* (Germany: Insel-Verlag, 1953), pp. 137–40.

50. Paul Friedländer speculates that Plato may have vaguely anticipated Heisenberg's uncertainty principle because all is indeterminate at the level below the order of the primary bodies (elements). The Receptacle is responsible for what resists order in nature. See his *Plato: An Introduction*, trans. Hans Meyerhoff (Princeton, NJ: Princeton UP, 1969), p. 251.

51. See Paul Friedländer, *Plato*, op. cit. for further comparisons.

52. See Luc Brisson and F. Walter Meyerstein, *Inventing the Universe* (Albany: SUNY P, 1995).

53. There is the suggestion in the *Laws* that nature (*physis*) is misapplied to the elements and that when done so we are speaking only of a "so-called" nature—since "if we can show that soul came first—that it was not fire, nor air, but soul which was there to begin with—it will be perfectly true to say that it is the existence of soul which is eminently *natural*" (892c). This remark accords with an earlier statement made about the position under examination and the suggestion that nature (*physis*) is but a name given the elements. "Presumably one who reasons thus holds that fire and water, earth and air, are the most primitive origins of all things—*nature* being just the name he gives to them" (891c).

54. In the *Timaeus*, however, this something else is neither soul nor the Demiurge. The movement (*kinesis*) of the elements (or the "watery," "fiery," "airy" and "earthy" parts) derives instead from the "lack of uniformity" of the Receptacle's discontented contents.

55. For the link between modern science and the attempted control of nature, see William Leiss, *The Domination of Nature* (Boston, MA: Beacon Press, 1972).

56. Husserl mentions Euclidian geometry along with Greek mathematics and Greek science as "fragments, beginnings of our developed science." Edmund Husserl, *The Crisis of the European Sciences and Transcendental Phenomenology*, trans. David Carr (Evanston, IL: Northwestern UP, 1970), p. 21.

57. The notion of Plato's mathematization of nature should not be overdrawn because his mathematics is rooted in Pythagorean ideas, which are dissimilar in certain respects to modern, Cartesian and post-Cartesian thought. In fact, there are some important qualitative dimensions to the Pythagorean worldview.

58. Edmund Husserl, *Crisis*, op. cit., p. 21.

59. On the "unwritten doctrines," see J. N. Findlay, *Plato: The Written and Unwritten Doctrines* (New York: Humanities Press, 1974).

60. Think of the work in science and computer science—especially the study of fractals—to find and fit ideal geometric shapes onto nature.

61. Alfred North Whitehead, *The Concept of Nature*, op. cit., p. 19.
62. Alfred North Whitehead, *Process and Reality* (London, UK: Free Press, 1978), p. 383.
63. A possible exception here is the work of the Cambridge Platonists. One also should note the Aristotelian dimensions to Whitehead's work as well.
64. Alfred North Whitehead, *Process and Reality*, op. cit., p. 103.
65. Alfred North Whitehead, *Science and the Modern World* (New York: Free Press, 1967), p. 108.
66. Whitehead, *Process and Reality*, op. cit., p. 241.
67. Ibid., p. 89 (italics added).
68. This sketch of Whitehead's philosophy of nature and "process ecology" is admittedly very brief so as not to encumber the discussion of Plato with a prolonged excursus.

Interstice: Cloud

1. Oscar Wilde, "The Decay of Lying," in *De Profundis* (New York: Penguin Classics, 1976).
2. Richard Hamblyn, *The Invention of Clouds: How an Amateur Meteorologist Forged the Language of the Skies* (New York: Farrar, Straus & Giroux, 2001).
3. Johann Wolfgang von Goethe, quoted in Hamblyn, *The Invention of Clouds*, op. cit., p. 213.
4. William Shakespeare, *Hamlet* (New York: Penguin Classics 2001), scene ii, p. 83.
5. Edward Abbey, *Desert Solitaire*, op. cit., p. 135.
6. Ibid., p. 136.
7. Ronald Parkinson, *John Constable* (London, UK: V and A Publications, 2003), p. 9. See also Edward Morris, *Constable's Clouds* (Edinburgh, UK: National Galleries of Scotland, 2006) and Kurt Badt, *John Constable's Clouds* (London, UK: Routledge & Kegan Paul, 1950).
8. John Ruskin, *The Elements of Drawing* (New York: Dover, 1972), pp. 128–29.
9. Enoch, quoted in Jean-Pierre Verdet, *The Sky: Mystery, Magic, and Myth* (New York: Harry N. Abrams, 1992), p. 107.
10. On clouds as cultural emblems, see Jacqueline Taylor Basker, "The Cloud as Symbol: Destruction or Dialogue," *Cross Currents*, Spring 2006.
11. Aristophanes, *Four Plays by Aristophanes*, trans. William Arrowsmith et al. (New York: Penguin, 1994), p. 7ff.
12. Aristotle, *Meteorlogica*, trans. H. D. P. Lee (Cambridge, MA: Harvard UP, 1975).
13. René Descartes, quoted in Hamblyn, *The Invention of Clouds*, op. cit., pp. 29–30.
14. Gaston Bachelard, *Air and Dreams*, trans. Edith Farrell and C. F. Farrell (Dallas, TX: Dallas Institute, 1988), p. 185.
15. Basho, untitled haiku, in Nancy Wilson Ross, *The World of Zen* (New York: Vintage Books, 1960), p. 264.
16. Gaston Bachelard, *Air and Dreams*, op. cit., p. 190.

17. Percy Bysshe Shelley, "The Cloud," in *The Complete Poems of Percy Bysshe Shelley* (New York: Modern Library, 1994), p. 638.

Chapter 5: The Place of the Elements and the Elements of Place: Aristotle's Natural Household

1. George Santayana, *The Life of Reason*, Vol. 1 (New York: Charles Scribners, 1905), p. 21.
2. See especially Murray Bookchin, *The Ecology of Freedom*, op. cit. and *The Philosophy of Social Ecology*, op. cit.
3. Plato, *Timaeus*, op. cit., 54a–b.
4. John Randall suggests that if Plato's *Timaeus* is a creation story, Aristotle's *De Caelo* might be viewed as "uncreation or eternal myth." See John Randall, *Aristotle* (New York: Columbia UP, 1960), p. 147.
5. For Greek to English translations, I have consulted Richard McKeon, ed., *The Basic Works of Aristotle*, op. cit.; Aristotle, *The Physics*, trans. and commentary P. Wicksteed and F. M. Cornford (Cambridge, MA: Harvard UP, 1957); Aristotle, *Meteorlogica*, op. cit.; and Aristotle, *De Generatione et Corruptione*, trans. C. J. F. Williams (Oxford, UK: Oxford UP, 1982). For valuable commentary, I have benefited from Harold Joachim, *Aristotle on Coming-to-be and Passing-away* (*De Generatione Et Corruptione*), trans. and commentary (Oxford, UK: Clarendon, 1922); W. D. Ross, *Aristotle's The Physics, Text with Commentary* (Oxford, UK: Oxford UP, 1955); W. D. Ross, *Aristotle* (London, UK: Methuen, 1968); John Randall, *Aristotle*, op. cit.; Friedrich Solmsen, *Aristotle's System of the Physical World* (Ithaca, NY: Cornell UP, 1960); Sheldon Cohen, *Aristotle on Nature and Incomplete Substance* (Cambridge, UK: Cambridge UP, 1996); Mary Louise Gill, *Aristotle on Substance: The Paradox of Unity* (Princeton, NJ: Princeton UP, 1989); Aristotle, *De Generatione et Corruptione*, trans. C.J.F. Williams, op. cit.; M. R. Wright, *Cosmology in Antiquity* (London, UK: Routledge, 1995). Textual references and citations are to Richard McKeon, ed., *The Basic Works of Aristotle*, unless otherwise stated.
6. Due to limitations of space and the focus on more philosophical dimensions of Aristotle's work, we do not consider in detail the *Meteorology*.
7. It is only possible to adumbrate Aristotle's philosophy of nature because we are concerned mainly with those dimensions that relate to the elements.
8. Karl Jaspers, quoted in Edward Casey, *Getting Back into Place*, op. cit., p. 314.
9. See Sir Thomas Heath, ed., *The Thirteen Books of Euclid's Elements* (New York: Dover, 1956). In the thirteenth section of this work, Euclid discusses in some detail the five Platonic bodies, four of which are correlated with the elements of earth, fire, air, and water.
10. Euclid, for example, defines the line as "breathless length" (definition 2, Bk. 1) and this same definition is cited and criticized by Aristotle in his *Topics* (143b11ff).
11. There has been a great amount of debate as to whom Aristotle has in mind with this infinite body, which is denser than air but finer than water. Although most ancient commentators associated it with Anaximander, most modern writers (e.g., David Ross) reject this correlation.

12. See especially Harold Cherniss, *Aristotle's Criticism of Presocratic Philosophy* (New York: Octagon, 1964) and Cherniss, *Aristotle's Criticism of Plato and the Academy* (Baltimore, MD: Johns Hopkins UP, 1944).

13. Aristotle finds his way to these conclusions by reasoning through the horns of a series of possible dilemmas first concerning the duration of the process of dissolution and then concerning the "stuff" from which they might be generated.

14. In the *Physics*, Aristotle also rejects the arguments for the notion of the void as existing separately from bodies, and as occupied by a body or as in bodies, and he continues to hold to this position in *De Caelo*.

15. Having decided against Empedocles on the question of the eternality and genesis of the elements, it is important to point out that in *On Generation and Corruption*, Aristotle further distinguishes between *generation*—a new substance is created from a substratum with a different name; e.g., air from water or plant from seed—and *alteration*—a physical substance changes its properties. In Aristotle's interpretation, Empedocles' theory reduces both kinds of change to aggregation and separation of unchanging parts, ignoring the vital distinction between generation and alteration.

16. According to Aristotle, Plato's efforts to provide specific shapes for the four elements is ill founded, first of all, because the theory is unable to fill the whole of space since it recognizes more elements than it is able to generate. In addition, the shape of an element cannot be maintained because if it did persist the simple bodies, which are formed in part by the place they inhabit, would not be in continuous contact with the containing Receptacle. Moreover, Plato's elements cannot produce a continuous body such as flesh or bone because their collocation is incapable of producing a continuum. Finally, the shapes of the elements are not in accordance with the natural properties of the bodies to which they are assigned. In Aristotle's view, fire, in particular, presents a problem for Plato because he does not take into consideration fire's upward motion, believing that it should be allotted the pyramidal shape as the most mobile element since the pyramid offers both the least number of contact points and the least stability.

17. Throughout his corpus, Aristotle raises additional objections to Empedocles' cosmology.

1. He argues Empedocles' elements are not really four but two, contrasting air, water and earth (i.e., matter) with fire (330b20ff).

2. Aristotle considers the two forces, love and strife, to be on same level and of the same quantity as corporeal elements (314a16ff).

3. He objects to Empedocles' view on the basis that growth is not possible unless it occurs by addition (e.g., fire increases by fire) but that this is not the way growth actually happens (333a35ff).

4. Aristotle criticizes Empedocles for his use of poetic language (e.g., fr. 55, "Earth's sweat, the sea" which Aristotle misunderstands).

5. He asserts that Empedocles' account of motion is vague (333b22ff).

6. Aristotle refutes the notion that the soul consists of elements (409b19ff).

7. He expresses horror at those who believe the heavens were created: "Anaxagoras made the world come into being once, Empedocles many times" (984a, 279b 17).

8. Finally, Aristotle credits Empedocles with identifying loosely two of the four causes that Aristotle explicates, but he asserts that Empedocles does not use them consistently, scientifically or sufficiently (985a1ff), a claim that is related to his broader charge against the Presocratics that they tend to collapse the four causes into one, namely, the material, in their search for an *arche* (governing principle).

18. Milan Kundera, *The Unbearable Lightness of Being*, trans. Michael Henry Heim (New York: Harper & Row, 1984), p. 6.

19. This position distinguishes Aristotle's view from those of his predecessors, who did not generally recognize the use of absolute terms, treating bodies only relatively. Thus, according to Aristotle, both Plato and the Atomists ignore absolute lightness while the monists cannot explain either absolute weight or lightness.

20. Plato denies this possibility because he characterizes the universe as being similar in every way, and so does not acknowledge a true up or down. Interestingly, there is a current controversy in cosmology over the question of directionality in the universe.

21. See W. D. Ross, *Aristotle*, op cit. on this point.

22. M. R. Wright, *Cosmology in Antiquity*, op. cit., p. 104.

23. St. Augustine, *Confessions*, trans. Rex Warner (New York: New American Library, 1963), Bk. 13, Chapter Eight, p. 322.

24. Aristotle introduces the distinction between things that occupy a place naturally (without constraint) and unnaturally (although constrained), a distinction that becomes important in his explanation of the movements of the elements and relates more generally to the complexities surrounding nature (*physis*) and prime matter (*prote hyle*).

25. This characterization above is inexact because Aristotle believes that if one were to move the earth to the place of the moon, the disparate parts of earth would move (i.e., return) to the earth's present location rather than to the similar "earthy" parts of the moon. Husserl provides a different perspective on the issue of the place of the earth in some of his later writings, raising the question of what do two earths mean?" See especially, "Foundational Investigations of the Phenomenological Origin of the Spaciality of Nature," trans. Fred Kersten, in *Husserl: Shorter Works*, ed., Peter McCormick and Frederick Elliston (Notre Dame, IN: U of Notre Dame P, 1981).

26. As Jean Piaget learned, children until about the age of seven are quasi-Aristotelians who believe via common sense observations of phenomena that objects fall to the ground because that is where they "naturally belong." See Morris Berman, *The Reenchantment of the World* (New York: Bantam Books, 1981), p. 25.

27. Aristotle's proviso that "none of these things moves itself" is a reference to the *Physics*. See Bk. 7 (1.241b24) and Bk. 8 (4.254b7ff).

28. See Aristotle, *Physics* (212b14). In *De Caelo*, Aristotle also expresses a lococentric view in his critique of Empedocles when he asks, for instance, "When the elements were separated off by Hate, what caused the earth to keep its place?" (295a30ff) or responds to the claim that the vortex maintains the earth's repose with the question, "where would it have moved to but for the vortex? It could not move infinitely" (300b2).

29. We argue later that contact is a central notion in Aristotle's theory of the elements.

30. Bloom applies his theories mainly to poetry and literature, but they are also applicable theoretically to philosophers. See Harold Bloom, *The Anxiety of Influence: A Theory of Poetry* (New York: Oxford UP, 1973) and *Poetry and Repression: Revisionism from Blake to Stevens* (New Haven, CT: Yale UP, 1976).

31. Carrying capacity is the number (or biomass) of organisms that a habitat can support. Maximum (or subsistence) density is the largest number of individuals who can survive in the habitat, while the optimum (or safe) density number involves greater security in terms of food, protection from predators, and fluctuations in resources.

32. Lucy Lippard, *The Lure of the Land: Senses of Place in a Multicentered Society* (New York: The New Press, 1997), p. 23.

33. Herman Melville, *Moby Dick* (London, UK: J. M. Dent, 1907), p. 52.

34. See David Macauley, "Hannah Arendt and the Politics of Place: From Earth Alienation to *Oikos*" in Macauley, *Minding Nature*, op. cit.

35. For a discussion of some of the current questions and issues regarding ecosystem balance and disruption, holism and stability, see Daniel Botkin, *Discordant Harmonies*, op. cit.

36. For vivid short stories of this experience, see Loren Eiseley, "The Brown Wasps" in Eiseley, *Night Country* (New York: Macmillan, 1971) and E. B. White, "Once More to the Lake" in *Essays of E. B. White* (New York: HarperCollins, 1941).

37. Edward Casey, *Getting Back into Place*, op. cit., p. 307.

38. I have borrowed the term "topoclasm" from E. V. Walter, *Placeways: A Theory of the Human Environment* (Chapel Hill: U of North Carolina P, 1988), p. 215.

39. Lucy Lippard, *The Lure of the Land*, op. cit., p. 4.

40. Peter Berg and Raymond Dasmann, "Reinhabiting California" in *Reinhabiting a Separate Country: A Bioregional Anthology of Northern California*, ed. Peter Berg (San Francisco, CA: Planet Drum Foundation, 1978), pp. 217–18.

41. Gary Snyder, *The Practice of the Wild*, op. cit., p. 38.

42. Kirkpatrick Sale, *Dwellers in the Land* (San Francisco: Sierra Club Books, 1985). On this work, see David Macauley, "Review of *Dwellers in the Land*," *The Animals' Agenda* (July/August, 1988).

43. See Andrew Light, "On the Irreplaceability of Place," *Worldviews: Environment, Culture, Religion* 2.3 (1998), pp. 179–84; Donald Alexander, "Bioregionalism: Science or Sensibility?," *Environmental Ethics* 12.2 (1990), pp. 161–73; Andrew Brennan, "Bioregionalism: A Misplaced Project?," *Worldviews: Environment, Culture, Religion* 2.3 (1998), pp. 215–37; and Mick Smith, *An Ethics of Place* (Albany: SUNY P, 2001).

44. See Edward Casey, *The Fate of Place*, op. cit., pp. 69–70.

45. Luce Irigaray, "Place, Interval: A Reading of Aristotle, *Physics* IV" in *The Ethics of Sexual Difference*, op. cit., p. 35.

46. Ibid., p. 52.

47. Roszack speculates that it was "as if the first thing modern science had to do was to destroy the symbol of vision-flight. Bacon very nearly says as much in the *Novum Organum* as part of his open warfare on imagination. 'The understanding,' he insists, 'must not be supplied with wings, but rather hung with weights to keep it from leaping and flying.'" Theodore Roszak, *Where the Wasteland Ends* (New York: Anchor, 1973), pp. 330–31.

Interstice: Heat and Cold

1. Alphonso Lingis, *The Imperative* (Bloomington: Indiana UP, 1998), p. 14.
2. On relevant theories about the universe, see Neil deGrasse Tyson and Donald Goldsmith, *Origins: Fourteen Billion Years of Cosmic Evolution* (New York: W.W. Norton, 2004).
3. Thomas Mann, *The Magic Mountain*, quoted in G. Johnson, *Fire in the Mind*, op. cit., p. 208.
4. *Bhagavad Gita*, op. cit., 2.14, p. 31.
5. Joseph Campbell, *Myths to Live By* (New York: Bantam Books, 1978), p. 254.
6. Ralph Waldo Emerson, "May-Day," in *Poems of Ralph Waldo Emerson* (Oxford, UK: Elibron Classics, 2005), p. 177.
7. Aristotle, quoted in Liba Taub, *Ancient Meterology* (London, UK: Routledge, 2003), p. 100.
8. Edward Abbey, *Desert Solitaire*, op. cit., p. 147.
9. Richard Nelson, quoted by Jay Griffiths, *Wild: An Elemental Journey*, op. cit., p. 107.
10. Wallace Stevens, "The Snow Man," *The Palm at the End of the Mind*, op. cit., p. 54.
11. Gretel Ehrlich, *The Future of Ice: A Journey Into Cold*, op. cit., p. 4.
12. Gaston Bachelard, *The Psychoanalysis of Fire*, op. cit., pp. 74–75.
13. T. S. Eliot, "Little Gidding," in *Collected Poems, 1909–1962* (New York: Harcourt Brace Jovanovich, 1991), 173 ff.

Chapter 6: The Economy and Ecology of the Aristotelian Elements

1. See Aristotle, *Physics*, Bk. 1, ch. 5.
2. See, for example, Aristotle, *Meteorology*, Bk. IV (389a29ff).
3. Aristotle, *De Generatione et Corruptione*, trans. C.J.F. Williams, op. cit., p. 158.
4. The contraries are pairs of contrasting qualities not contrasting *qualia* (properties of sensory experiences). In the *Meteorology*, Aristotle refers to them as *dynameis* (powers).
5. Aristotle fails to notice that brittle things might still contain small amounts of moisture.
6. See C.J.F. Williams in Aristotle, *De Generatione et Corruptione*, op. cit., p. 159.
7. An exception again is the questionable Book IV of the *Meteorology*, where Aristotle describes them as *hyle* (matter) and as *dynameis* (powers).
8. See G.E.R. Lloyd, *Early Greek Science: Thales to Aristotle* (New York: W. W. Norton, 1970), p. 107.
9. See Aristotle, *De Generatione et Corruptione*, trans. C.J.F. Williams, op. cit., p. 160.
10. For Aristotle, the physical opposites are central as well to his biological works, where he discusses, for example, the "inborn heat" that maintains animal life. The opposites, hot and cold, also come to the philosophical fore again in Renaissance naturalism in the

works of Bernardino Telesio and Giodano Bruno, who operate within a modified Aristotelian framework, where the contraries become active principles that work upon a passive matter. Girolamo Cardano develops a hylozoist philosophy, arguing that the metals produced in the interior of the earth arise through the mutual reactions of the three elements of earth, water, and air and that all things tend toward the form of gold. As in the *Timaeus*, the world is conceived as an animate organism. In the process of world formation, the heaven (a seat of warmth) is separated from the sublunary world (a place of cold and wet elements). Telesio also subscribed to a hylozoist theory in which the fundamental causes of natural events are the warm and cold elements. For Heinrich Cornelius Agrippa, man unites in himself three worlds: the terrestrial world of elements, the world of heavenly bodies and the spiritual world. Humans serve as an ontological bond between these realms.

11. See Aristotle, *De Generatione et Corruptione*, trans. C.J.F. Williams, op. cit., p. 160. Opposition of the kind we find in Aristotle's theory of contraries is not entirely lacking in Empedocles' philosophy where qualitative attribution operates, though it usually takes the form of dark–bright and dry–wet pairings. Earth is hard and heavy; water is dark and cold; and qua sun, fire is hot and white (fr. 21). Aristotle's theory of contrariety (and the elements), however, is manifestly distinguishable from earlier views. On this count, he clearly challenges the monistic, dyadic, triadic and tetradic schemes of his predecessors.

12. On the transformation of the elements, I follow the analysis of Mary Louise Gill, *Aristotle on Substance: The Paradox of Unity*, op. cit. See also Sheldon M. Cohen, *Aristotle on Nature and Incomplete Substance*, op. cit.

13. The term *overpowered* suggests a kind of warring, strife and struggle of the elements. For further thoughts on this imagery, see Chapters One and Two, this volume.

14. Homoeomerous bodies have parts that are like one another and also like the whole, of which they are parts.

15. As Aristotle points out, Empedocles considers compounds in terms of *composition*—being akin to a wall formed of bricks or stones—so that his "mixture" is composed of unchanging "elements" whose parts are juxtaposed to one another. He thereby avoids the matter of generation just as he skirts it with the four sempiternal elements. At the same time, those who propose a single matter for all their elements have the difficult problem of explaining how a compound can be formed from two of them together (334b3ff).

16. See Aristotle, *De Generatione et Corruptione*, trans. C.J.F. Williams, op. cit., pp. 175–76.

17. On the different sense of potentiality, see Aristotle, *De Anima*, Bk. II.5.

18. See C. J. Williams' exegesis in Aristotle, *De Generatione et Corruptione*, op. cit., p. 177.

19. See Aristotle, *Meteorology* (382aff) for a differing perspective.

20. In *Categories*, Aristotle writes: "Another mark of substance is that it has no contrary" (3b24).

21. It should be noted this point flies in the face of some of his ideas elsewhere on the elements.

22. For differing views on the prime matter controversy, see Hugh R. King, "Aristotle Without *Prima Materia*," *Journal of the History of Ideas* XVII (1956), pp. 370–89; W. Charlton, "Prime Matter—A Rejoinder," *Phronesis* XXVIII (1983), pp. 197–211 and Charlton, *Aristotle's Physics, Books I and II* (Oxford, UK: Clarendon Aristotle Series, 1970), especially the appendix; Friedrich Solmsen, "Aristotle and Prime Matter: A Reply to Hugh

R. King," *Journal of the History of Ideas* XIX (1958), pp. 243–52; H. M. Robinson, "Prime Matter in Aristotle," *Phronesis* IX (1974), pp. 168–188. Also of interest to this debate is P. Suppes, "Aristotle's Concept of Matter and Its Relation to Modern Concepts of Matter," *Synthese* 28 (1974), pp. 27–50; B. Jones, "Aristotle's Introduction of Matter," *Philosophical Review* 83 (1974), pp. 474–500 and Mary Gill, *Aristotle on Substance*, op. cit.

23. Later, the Scholastics considered prime matter as "pure potentiality" at the opposite end of the metaphysical continuum issuing from God, who is "pure actuality."

24. For a consideration of causality in Aristotle, especially in relation to the Presocratics, see Harold Cherniss, *Aristotle's Criticism of Presocratic Philosophy*, op. cit., Chapter Three. For a discussion of the four causes, see D. J. Allan, "Causality Ancient and Modern," *Proceedings of the Aristotelian Society* 39 (1965), pp. 1–18 and M. Hocutt, "Aristotle's Four Becauses," *Philosophy* 49 (1974), pp. 385–99.

25. See Aristotle, *Metaphysics*, Bk. Alpha.

26. See Aristotle, *Metaphysics*, Bk. Lambda and *Physics*, Bk. 8.

27. See Aristotle, *On Generation and Corruption* Bk. I.3, op. cit.

28. Other passages in *On Generation and Corruption* that seem to support prime matter include: 322b11ff, 328a19ff, and 334a15ff.

29. On *ekeininos* (that-en), see C.J.F. Williams' commentary in Aristotle, *De Generatione et Corruptione*, op. cit., p. 152.

30. See Aristotle, *Physics*, 209b11ff and *On Generation and Corruption*, 329a13ff.

31. See Aristotle, *Topics*, Bk. 6.

32. For this provocative question and the suggestion about the role of earth in relation to the status of prime matter, I am indebted to John Rist, *The Mind of Aristotle* (Toronto, Canada: U of Toronto P, 1989).

33. See Aristotle, *On Generation and Corruption*, II.4, op. cit.

34. See Plato's *Phaedo*, trans. R. S. Bluck (London, UK: Routledge & Kegan Paul, 1955).

35. There are additional passages that strongly belie the notion of prime matter, but there is not time to explore all of them. See, for example, *On Generation and Corruption* (I.317b23ff).

36. Later, *aether* is the *quinta essentia* of medieval thought.

37. See Charles Kahn, *Anaximander and the Origins of Greek Cosmology*, op. cit.

38. Aristotle denies the validity of Anaxagoras' equation of *aether* with fire.

39. Homer, for example, speaks of the "ever-secure home of the gods" in the heavens.

40. For a brief sketch of several difficulties raised by the fifth element, see G.E.R. Lloyd, *Early Greek Science*, op. cit., pp. 111–12.

41. For a helpful discussion of the fifth element, see Solmsen, *Aristotle's System of the Physical World* op. cit.

42. For Aristotle's distinction between "position" and "place" in the *Physics*, see Bk. IV.

43. The explanation of action-passion is advanced in *On Generation and Corruption*, Bk. I.9, and it depends on the distinction between the actual or potential possession by a body of a given quality and on the variations in the intensity or degree that may exist in different parts of the body with instances of potential possession.

44. Aristotle leaves out the sense of smell in this consideration.

45. Compare here Empedocles' treatment of the emergence and composition of flesh as a blend of the elements in their most equal proportions. See fr. 83 of *Peri Phuseos* (*On Nature*).

46. See Aristotle, *De Anima*, Bk. II.10, op cit.

47. Aristotle's claims regarding touch and flesh appear problematic from a modern perspective, particularly the assertion that flesh is not an organ of perception but instead a medium.

48. See Aristotle, *On Generation and Corruption*, Bk. II.2–3.

49. There does seem to be some similarity here as to the way the mean functions in the *Nicomachean Ethics*, a book that is connected with *De Anima* in more ways than might be first apparent. The mean in Aristotle's ethics is of course not an arithmetic mean nor is it a middle point as to what is best. On the mean in Aristotle's ethics, see *Nicomachean Ethics*, Bk. II.6–9.

50. For helpful thoughts related to the subject of contact, see Cynthia Freeland, "Aristotle on the Sense of Touch," in Martha Nussbaum and Amelie Oksenberg Rorty, *Essays on Aristotle's De Anima* (Oxford, UK: Clarendon, 1992).

51. Although fire is usually not touched directly, its heat and presence is immediately felt.

52. Maurice Merleau-Ponty, *The Visible and Invisible*, op. cit., p. 76, italic added.

53. Walter Ong, *The Presence of the Word* (New Haven, CT: Yale UP, 1967), pp. 169–70.

54. J. J. Gibson, *The Ecological Approach to Visual Perception*, op. cit.

55. Kent Bloomer and Charles Moore, *Body, Memory and Architecture* (New Haven, CT: Yale UP, 1977), quoted in E. V. Walter, *Placeways*, op. cit., p. 134, italics added.

56. On the idea of an "epistemology of contact," see Laura Dassow Wall, *Seeing New Worlds: Henry David Thoreau and Nineteenth-Century Natural Science* (Madison: U of Wisconsin P, 1995), p. 147.

57. Place, like touch, is also deeply connected with human feelings and emotions, a fact that is evident in the experience of a loss of place. We return to the notion of touch in Chapter Eight.

58. See Wallace Stevens, "Anecdote of Men by the Thousand" in *The Palm at the End of the Mind*, op. cit.

59. Due to space constraints, we will forgo consideration of Aristotle's critique of earlier thinkers on the soul.

60. One might speculate as to whether the earth is a body in some sense, especially given the insights of the Gaia hypothesis. See J. E. Lovelock, *Gaia*, op. cit.

61. Aristotle uses "body" in numerous senses, and it is often difficult to determine whether it is equivalent to a composite of matter and form, of which the soul is part and parcel, or whether it is simply the matter of the composite. He seems to intend that if it is perceptible at all, "body" is a composite.

62. This distinction becomes a route for Aristotle to posit an intellect over and above the passive one and to separate it from the body.

63. To cite but one example of the complex relationship between—or idea of—"living" and "nonliving" in terms of the parts of an organism, trees are arguably not alive in their entirety because only a small percentage of their matter is actually growing.

64. One brief but important criticism: Prior to the introduction of the active intellect, Aristotle held thinking to be integrally related to, and an outgrowth of, the "lesser" functions of the soul—that is, the capacities for nutrition, appetite, sensation, and so on. In this regard, the passive intellect is completely consonant with these bodily aspects. Aristotle, however, then tells us that there is a sense in which thought creates the things it understands and that this intelligence is said to be (a) separable from matter, (b) immortal, and (c) indestructible. Hence, it is also separable from the body and thus essentially inconsistent with the general account he offers throughout the *De Anima*, including his definition of soul, which is "the first actuality of a natural body with organs." This split is similar to one that occurs in the account of *eudaimonia* (happiness or flourishing) in the *Nicomachean Ethics*, Bks. I and X.

65. This is the basis and background for his criticism of those thinkers who do not properly differentiate the kinds of soul. Every "higher" (more developed) soul presupposes the existence of the "lesser" souls. In this regard, those souls with the capacity for perception also possess the capacity for nutrition.

66. Unfortunately, space does not permit a full consideration of the Atomists in this work.

67. There is some controversy over the authenticity of Bk. IV of *Meteorology*. For a discussion of this debate, see Friedrich Solmsen, *Aristotle's System of the Physical World*, op. cit., p. 393 ff.

68. Frederick Woodbridge, *Aristotle's Vision of Nature* (New York: Columbia UP), p. 59.

69. Physical contact is, moreover, precluded with *aether*.

70. See Martin Heidegger, "On the Being and Conception of *Physis* in Aristotle's *Physics* B, 1," trans. Thomas J. Sheehan, in *Man and World* 4.9 (1976), pp. 219–70.

71. It is this latter sense of the term that Plato employs in, for example, the *Republic* (525c) or *Parmenides* (132d).

72. Heidegger has called attention to the fact that something of vital and animating importance has been lost in the translation of Greek words into Latin and other Roman languages and particularly in the translation of *physis* to the Latin, *natura*, meaning "birth" or "to be born." In his words, "it marks the first stage in the process by which we cut ourselves off and alienated ourselves from the original Greek philosophy." See Martin Heidegger, *Introduction to Metaphysics*, op. cit., p. 13. *Physis*, he claims, denotes "self-blossoming emergence . . . opening up, unfolding, that which manifests itself in such unfolding and perseveres and endures in it" (Ibid., p. 14). It "originally encompassed heaven as well as earth, the stone as well as the plant, the animal as well as man, and it encompassed human history as a work of men and the gods; and ultimately and first of all, it meant the gods themselves as subordinated to destiny" (Ibid). Thus, the early senses of the word and their transformations must be borne in mind as we think about the natural world.

73. In many ways, Aristotle's notion of nature (*physis*) is an attempt to revive and reconstruct the older Ionian view of nature and to offer a defense of genesis and motion with which nature is closely bound. To this extent, his arguments are directed against the Eleatics—who denied the reality of motion and change—and Empedocles and the atomists—who rejected coming-to-be.

74. See Susanne Foster, "Aristotle and the Environment," *Environmental Ethics* 24.4 (2002), pp. 409–28 and Laura Westra and Thomas Robinson, eds., *Greeks and the Environment*, op. cit.

75. See especially Murray Bookchin, *The Ecology of Freedom*, op. cit. and Bookchin, *The Philosophy of Social Ecology*, op. cit. For further consideration of social ecology, see David Macauley, "Evolution and Revolution: The Ecological Anarchism of Kropotkin and Bookchin," in Andrew Light, ed., *Social Ecology After Bookchin*, op. cit.

76. See John Randall, *Aristotle*, op. cit.; Susan Okin, *Women in Western Political Thought* (Princeton, NJ: Princeton UP, 1979); and Andrew Light, ed., *Social Ecology After Bookchin*, op. cit.

Interstice: Light and Shadow

1. Hans Blumenberg, "Light as a Metaphor for Truth," in David Michael Levin, ed., *Modernity and the Hegemony of Vision* (Berkeley: U of California P, 1993), p. 31.

2. *Bhagavad Gita*, op. cit., 11.11–12, p. 99.

3. Peter Pesic argues that the notion of *Fiat lux* should not be interpreted as God generating a source of light since the sun is not created until the fourth day in the Biblical account, but of "calling forth light as the primal act of *seeing*." See Pesic, *Sky in a Bottle*, op. cit., p. 10.

4. Arthur Zajonc, *Catching the Light* (Oxford, UK: Oxford UP, 1993), pp. 97–98.

5. J. J. Gibson, *The Ecological Approach to Visual Perception*, op. cit., p. 51.

6. John Milton, *Paradise Lost* (Indianapolis, IN: Hackett, 2003), line 171, p. 118.

7. Empedocles, *On Nature*, trans. William Leonard, *The Fragments of Empedocles*, op. cit. fr. 88.

8. Plato, *Symposium*, trans. Michael Joyce in Plato, *Collected Dialogues of Plato*, op. cit., 219a.

9. Johann Wolfgang von Goethe, *Scientific Studies* in *Goethe's Collected Works*, ed. and trans. Douglas Miller, Vol. 12 (Princeton, NJ: Princeton UP, 1988), p. 158.

10. Johann Wolfgang von Goethe, *Goethe's Color Theory*, ed. Rupprecht Matthaei and Herman Aach (New York: Van Nostrand, 1971), p. 76.

11. Barry Lopez, *Arctic Dreams*, op. cit., p. 233.

12. Marius von Senden, *Space and Sight: The Perception of Space and Shape in the Congenitally Blind before and after Operation*, trans. Peter Heath (Glencoe, IL: Free Press, 1960).

13. See David Michael Levin, ed., *Modernity and the Hegemony of Vision*, op. cit.

14. Maurice Merleau-Ponty, *Phenomenology of Perception*, op. cit., p. 68.

15. See Thomas Flynn, "Foucault and the Eclipse of Vision" in David Michael Levin, ed., *Modernity and the Hegemony of Vision*, op. cit., p. 273ff.

16. Friedrich Nietzsche, *Thus Spoke Zarathustra*, op. cit., p. 289.

17. "Negative Ontology" is a phrase used by David Michael Levin, *The Opening of Vision: Nihilism and the Postmodern Situation* (New York: Routledge, 1988), p. 424.

18. Martin Heidegger, "The Age of the World Picture" in *The Question Concerning Technology*, op. cit., p. 154.

19. Emmanuel Levinas, "Reality and its Shadow" in Sean Hand, ed., *The Levinas Reader* (Oxford, UK: Blackwell, 1989), p. 137 and p. 141.

20. David Michael Levin, *The Opening of Vision*, op. cit., pp. 429-430.
21. Victor I. Stoichita, *A Short History of the Shadow* (London, UK: Reaktion Books, 1997).
22. J. C. Lavatar, quote in Victor I. Stoichita, *A Short History of the Shadow*, op. cit., p. 157.
23. John Ruskin, quoted in Rosemary Verey, *The Garden in Winter* (London, UK: Frances Lincoln, 2002), p. 25.
24. Diane Ackerman, *A Natural History of the Senses*, op. cit., p. 245.
25. Carl Jung, *Psychology and Religion: East and West*, trans. Gerhard Adler and R.F.C. Hull (Princeton, NJ: Princeton UP, 1970) in *Collected Works*, Vol. 11, p. 131.
26. Carl Jung, *Psychological Reflections*, trans. R.F.C. Hull and Jolanda Jacobi (Princeton, NJ: Princeton UP, 1973), p. 217.
27. John Locke, *Essay Concerning Human Understanding* (London, UK: Elibron Classics, 2006) Bk. II, Ch. VIII, par. 5., p. 134.

Chapter 7: Domestication of the Elements

1. Stephen J. Pyne, "Consumed by Either Fire or Fire," in Conway et al., eds., *Earth, Air, Fire and Water*, op. cit., p. 86.
2. Gaston Bachelard, *Water and Dreams*, op. cit., p. 95.
3. Wislawa Szymborska, "Water" in *View with a Grain of Sand*, op. cit., p. 29.
4. Georg W. F. Hegel, *The Philosophy of Nature*, quoted in William Leiss, *The Domination of Nature*, op. cit., p. 125.
5. Stephen Budiansky, The *Covenant of the Wild: Why Animals Chose Domestication* (New Haven, CT: Yale UP, 1999).
6. I have borrowed this expression from Yi Fu Tuan, *Dominance and Affection* (New Haven, CT: Yale UP, 1984).
7. Peter J. Wilson, *The Domestication of the Human Species* (New Haven, CT and London, UK: Yale UP, 1988), p. 153.
8. Theophrastus, *Enquiry into Plants*, trans. A. F. Hort (Cambridge, MA: Loeb, 1916).
9. Ibid., p. 173.
10. On issues of gender and technology, see Patrick D. Hopkins, ed., *Sex/Machine* (Bloomington: Indiana UP, 1999).
11. See *Tao Te Ching*, trans. Stephen Mitchell, op. cit., chap. 78.
12. The literature on ecological feminism is relevant in this regard. See, for example, Carolyn Merchant, *The Death of Nature*, op. cit.
13. See Colin Ward, *Reflected in Water: A Crisis of Social Responsibility* (London, UK: Cassell, 1997), pp. 83–90.
14. Ivan Illich, H_2O *and the Waters of Forgetfulness*, op. cit., p. 1.
15. This definition follows one by John B. Jackson, whose work is developed in David Nye, ed., *Technologies of Landscape* (Amherst: U of Massachusetts P, 2000).
16. Simon Schama, quoted in David Nye, ed., *Technologies of Landscape*, op. cit., p. 4. It is more accurate, I think, to see the relation between land (earth) and culture

(world) as interactive and dialectical rather than to posit a "before" and "after" in an ongoing process.

17. Anne Spirn, "Constructing Nature: The Legacy of Frederick Law Olmstead" in William Cronon, ed., *Uncommon Ground* (New York: W. W. Norton, 1996), p. 98.

18. David Rothenberg, *Hand's End: Technology and the Limits of Nature* (Berkeley: U of California P, 1993), p. 194.

19. One also wonders whether it might in fact matter at times that we have this cognitive awareness, for it likely does at least complicate our aesthetic judgments knowing that the fluid is monitored and adjusted like an "organic machine" or a municipal water system. In the same way, it can make an important aesthetic or ethical difference knowing that a tree is plastic (rather than biological), that a forest has been replanted (rather than flourishing as old growth), or that a flower is an exotic newcomer to an ecosystem (rather than native to the place). For relevant articles on ecological restoration, see Martin Krieger, "What's Wrong with Plastic Trees?" and Robert Elliot, "Faking Nature" in Louis Pojman, *Environmental Ethics: Readings in Theory and Application* (Belmont, CA: Wadsworth, 2001), pp. 218–34.

20. Rothenberg claims there is no great damage to environment, but it may be that we just cannot see the harm either because it is below ground or it occurred in the historical past.

21. For photographs of the house, see Lynda S. Wagonner, *Falling Water: Frank Lloyd Wright's Romance with Nature* (New York: Universe, 1996).

22. Martin Heidegger, *The Question Concerning Technology*, op. cit., p. 16.

23. Ibid., pp. 16–17.

24. Martin Heidegger, *Poetry, Language, Thought*, op. cit.

25. Ibid., pp. 37–38.

26. On the de-meandering of streams, see Kenneth R. Olwig, "Reinventing Common Nature" in Cronon, ed., *Uncommon Ground*, op. cit., pp. 404–07.

27. Biophilia is the notion that humans have an innate affiliation with the natural world and biological life in particular that has arisen through evolution, a love and affinity that can affect our aesthetic preferences. See Stephen Kellert and Edward Wilson, eds., *The Biophilia Hypothesis* (Washington, DC: Island Press, 1993).

28. There are, it appears, very few straight lines in the natural world, at least at our perceptual level. Even trees do not necessarily grow at distinct right angles to the earth.

29. David Nye, *Technologies of the Landscape*, op cit.

30. Langdon Winner, *The Whale and the Reactor* (Chicago, IL: U of Chicago P, 1986).

31. Al Wright, quoted in Blaine Harden, *A River Lost* (New York: W.W. Norton, 1997).

32. Richard White, *The Organic Machine* (New York: Hill & Wang, 1996).

33. Ibid., p. x.

34. See Hannah Arendt, *The Human Condition* (Chicago, IL: U of Chicago P, 1958) on the distinction between work and labor.

35. Interestingly, as White points out, just as not all human energy is fruitfully realized in successful efforts (e.g., fishing), so only two percent of the river's potential energy eventuates in work via erosion, transportation or deposition of matter; the rest is kinetic energy expressed and dissipated as friction against the bed, banks, and river itself.

36. Richard White, *The Organic Machine*, op. cit., p. 112.
37. Ibid., p. 41.
38. See Lewis Mumford, *Technics and Civilization* (New York: Harcourt, Brace & World, 1963) and *Myth of the Machine* (New York: Harcourt, Brace and World, 1967). See also David Macauley, "Greening Philosophy and Democratizing Ecology" and Ramachandra Guha, "Lewis Mumford, the Forgotten American Environmentalist" in Macauley, ed., *Minding Nature*, op. cit.
39. White, *The Organic Machine*, op. cit., p. 108, italics added.
40. See Langdon Winner, *Autonomous Technology* (Cambridge, MA: MIT Press, 1977).
41. Richard White, *The Organic Machine*, op cit., p. 110.
42. Ibid., p. 110.
43. See Steven Vogel, *Against* Nature, op. cit. and Michael Pollan, *Second Nature*, op. cit.
44. Julie Stauffer, *The Water You Drink* (Gabriola Island, BC, Canada: New Society Publishers, 2004), pp. 93–99.
45. See Marc Reisner, *Cadillac Desert: The American West and Its Disappearing Water* (New York: Penguin, 1986). On efforts to privatize water resources in places like Stockton, California, India and Bolivia, along with community resistance movements, see the documentary, "Thirst," which appeared on WHYY, channel 12 in Philadelphia, July 18, 2004.
46. " 'Just say No to H_2O,' " *The New York Times*, September 2, 2001.
47. The medical community, however, has not found any health benefits to this therapy. See Carol Sorgen, "The Rise of Oxygen Bars," <http://www.my.webmd.com/content/article/48/39188?src+Inktomi&condition=Alternative%20Medicine>.
48. For this section, I have benefited greatly from Corby Kummer's informative article, "Carried Away," *New York Times Magazine*, August 30, 1998, pp. 38–61.
49. Interestingly, bottled water is legally considered a food product. Brian Howard, "What's in your Bottled Water?," August 28, 2003, reprinted from *E: The Environmental Magazine* at <http://www.hartfordadvocate.com>.
50. Corby Kummer, "Carried Away," op. cit.
51. These challenges call to mind analogous problems: the fact that greenhouse gases have literally changed the chemical content of the air and atmosphere—as measured by samples taken on mountaintops and from frozen ice cores—and that, according to Jacques Ellul, technological processes have actually altered the chemical structure of bread, the staff of life in many parts of the world. See Bill McKibben, *The End of Nature* (New York: Anchor Books, 1989) and Jacques Ellul, *The Technological Society* (New York: Vintage, 1967).
52. Editorial, "In Praise of Tap Water," *New York Times* (August 1, 2007), A 19. Due to the ecological and financial waste generated by bottled water and the fact that tap water is healthy to drink, the mayor of San Francisco prohibited municipal agencies and departments from buying bottled water in 2007.
53. Pacific Institute, "Bottled Water and Energy: A Fact Sheet," <http://www.hartfordadvocate.com>.
54. On the notion of revenge effects, see Edward Tenner, *Why Things Bite Back* (New York: Vintage, 1997).
55. Ivan Illich, H_2O *and the Waters of Forgetfulness*, op. cit., pp. 75–76.
56. Ibid., p. 76.

57. Michael Oakeshott, quoted in Neil Evernden, *The Social Creation of Nature*, op. cit., p. 159.

58. On "reverse adaptation," see Langdon Winner, *Autonomous Technology*, op. cit. See also Edward Tenner, *Why Things Bite Back: Technology and the Revenge of Unintended Consequences*, op. cit.

59. Illich, H_2O *and the Waters of Forgetfulness*, op. cit., p. 7.

60. Paul Virilio, *Open Sky*, op. cit., p. 22.

61. Ibid., p. 5.

62. Roald Hoffman, "The Bering Bridge" in *Writing on Air*, op. cit., p. 45.

63. Arendt's notion of alienation, though sharing affinities with existentialist and Marxist conceptions, entails the idea of being at home on the earth and in the world. It involves a loss of roots or a common, shared sense of place that includes a sphere of meaningful pursuits secured by tradition against the tides of change.

64. Hannah Arendt, *The Human Condition*, op. cit., p. 1. For a more complete discussion of the phenomena of earth alienation, see David Macauley, "Hannah Arendt and the Politics of Place: From Earth Alienation to *Oikos*" in Macauley, ed., *Minding Nature*, op. cit., ch. 5.

65. Arendt, *The Human Condition*, op. cit., p. 10.

66. Ibid., p. 262.

67. Yaakov Garb, "Perspective or Escape? Ecofeminist Musings on Contemporary Earth Imagery" in Irene Diamond and Gloria Orenstein, eds. *Reweaving the World: The Emergence of Ecofeminism* (San Francisco, CA: Sierra Club, 1990), p. 270. Garb argues that a "distancing, disengaged, abstract, and literalizing epistemology is quintessentially embodied in the whole Earth image where the visual mode of understanding is applied to the entire planet" (p. 267).

68. Martin Heidegger, "Only a God can save us: *Der Speigel's* interview with Martin Heidegger" in *Philosophy Today* XX (1976), p. 277.

69. Michael Zimmerman, *Contesting Earth's Future*, op. cit., p. 75.

70. Lewis Thomas, *Lives of a Cell* (New York: Bantam, 1975).

71. William Cronin, *Changes in the Land: Indians, Colonists, and the Ecology of New England* (New York: Hill & Wang, 1983).

72. See Katey Palmer, "Return of the Natives," *Earth First!* (December 21, 1988), p. 26.

73. Neil Evernden, *The Social Creation of Nature*, op. cit., p. 120.

74. Peter Kareiva et al., "Domesticated Nature," *Science Magazine* (June 2007), pp. 1866–69.

75. G.W.F. Hegel, quoted in David Michael Levin, *The Opening of Vision*, op. cit. p. 153.

76. Paul Virilio, *Open Sky*, op. cit., p. 41.

77. Hannah Arendt, *The Human Condition*, op. cit., p. 134.

78. Bill McKibben, *The End of Nature*, op. cit., p. 48.

79. McKibben's argument in *The End of Nature* also contains questionable religious appeals and claims, linking the notion of nature with a conception of and belief in God. He speaks, for example, of earth as "a museum of divine intent" and writes about how we "apprehend God in nature" (p. 72).

80. Langdon Winner, *The Whale and the Reactor*, op. cit., p. 3.

81. Max Horkheimer and Theodor Adorno, *Dialectic of Enlightenment* (New York: Continuum, 1987), pp. 5–6.
82. Lucretius, *On the Nature of the Universe*, op. cit.
83. See Philip Ball, *Life's Matrix*, op. cit.
84. John Donne, "An Anatomie of the World," in *"The Complete Poetry and Selected Prose of John Donne,"* ed. Charles M. Coffin (New York: Modern Library Classics, 2001), p. 186.
85. Robert Boyle, quoted in Philip Ball, *Life's Matrix*, op. cit., p. 115.
86. René Descartes, *Discourse on Method*, trans. Donald A. Cress (Indianapolis, IN: Hackett, 1980), p. 33.
87. T. B. Bottomore, ed., *Marx's Early Writing* (New York: McGraw-Hill, 1964), pp. 359–60.
88. On the contested veracity of the claim that Chief Seattle actually wrote these words, see Carolyn Merchant, *Radical Ecology* (New York: Routledge, 1992), pp. 121–22 and Shepard Krech III, *The Ecological Indian*, op. cit., p. 214.
89. On the ecological dimensions of Stoic philosophy, see Jim Cheney, "The Neo-Stoicism of Radical Environmentalism," *Environmental Ethics* 11 (1989) and William O. Stephens, "Stoic Naturalism, Rationalism, and Ecology," *Environmental Ethics* 16 (1994). On the physical views of the Stoics more generally, see S. Sambursky, *The Physics of the Stoics* (London, UK: Routledge & Kegan Paul, 1959). On the surviving excerpts of the Stoics, see *Stoicorum Veterum Fragmenta*, 4 vol., ed. H. von Arnim (Leipzig, Germany: Teubner, 1905–24). A useful anthology is Moses Hadas, ed., *The Essential Works of Stoicism* (New York: Bantam, 1961).
90. Paracelsus, *Philosophia ad Athenienses*, quoted in Merchant, *The Death of Nature*, op. cit., p. 119.
91. This brief characterization of Paracelsus' view relies on Carolyn Merchant's discussion in *The Death of Nature*, op. cit.
92. Georg W. F. Hegel, *Philosophy of Nature*, ed., M. J. Petry, Vol. 2 of *Encyclopedia of the Philosophical Sciences*, op. cit.
93. Georg W. F. Hegel, *Phenomenology of Spirit*, trans. A. V. Miller (Oxford, UK: Oxford UP, 1977), sect. 492. Hegel considers the elements in passing in the sections, "Observing Reason" (sect. 255) and "Culture and its Realm of Actuality" (sect. 492).
94. Georg W. F. Hegel, *Lectures on the History of Philosophy*, Vol. 1, op. cit.

Interstice: Night

1. Gaston Bachelard, *Water and Dreams*, op. cit., p. 101.
2. Wallace Stevens, "Six Significant Landscapes," in *Palm at the End of the Mind*, op. cit., p. 16.
3. Jonathan Franzen, *The Corrections* (New York: Farrar, Straus & Giroux, 2001), p. 11.
4. Gaston Bachelard, *Water and Dreams*, op. cit., p. 101.
5. Ranier Maria Rilke, "Evening" in *Selected Poetry of Rainer Maria Rilke*, op. cit., p. 13.

6. Alphonso Lingis, *The Imperative*, op. cit., pp. 9–10.
7. Gaston Bachelard, *Water and Dreams*, op. cit., p. 101.
8. Gaston Bachelard, *The Poetics of Reverie*, op. cit., p. 145.
9. Erich Neumann, *The Great* Mother, quoted in Levin, *The Opening of Vision*, op. cit., p. 348.
10. Emmanuel Levinas, "There is: existence without existents," in Sean Hand, ed., *The Levinas Reader* (Oxford, UK: Blackwell, 1989), p. 30.
11. Ibid., p. 31.
12. Vincent van Gogh, Letter to Wilhelmina van Gogh, Sept., 1888, in *Letters of Vincent van Gogh: 1886–1890*, trans. and ed., Robert Harrison (Aldershot, UK: Scolar Press, 1977), no. W07.
13. Julian Green, quoted in Brassai and Paul Morand, *Paris By Night* (Bullfinch Press, 2001).
14. To my mind at least, the philosopher, too, has often exhibited a bit of the vampire in his or her persona: witness the historical focus on or obsession with death; the fascination with eternity; the proclivity toward unusual diets; the work routinely performed in withdrawal or seclusion; the typical pallor of the skin; the tendency to suddenly attack opponents; and so forth.
15. Hesiod, *Theogony*, trans. Dorothea Wender, op. cit., lines 744–45 and 756–57.
16. See L. Taran, *Parmenides: A Text with Translation, Commentary and Critical Essays* (Princeton, NJ: Princeton UP, 1965).
17. *Tao Te Ching*, trans. Stephen Mitchell, op. cit., Chapters One and Twenty Eight.
18. *Rig Veda*, trans. Wendy Doniger O'Flaherty (London, UK: Penguin Books, 1981), 10.129 and 10.127.
19. Erazim Kohák, *The Embers and the Stars* (Chicago, IL: U of Chicago P, 1984), p. 34.
20. Howard C. Hughes, *Sensory Exotica: A World Beyond Human Experience* (Cambridge, MA: MIT Press, 2001), pp. 18–30
21. Henry Beston, op. cit., p. 168.
22. See Joe Bower, "The Dark Side of Light," *Utne Reader*, August 2000.
23. Immanuel Kant, *Observations on the Feeling of the Beautiful and Sublime*, trans. John T. Goldthwait (Berkeley: U of California P, 2004).
24. Michelangelo, "Sonnet to Darkness" in David Park, *The Fire Within the Eye* (Princeton: Princeton UP, 1997), p. 339.
25. William Shakespeare, *A Midsummer Night's Dream* (New York: Washington Square Press, 2004), Act 3, Scene 2, lines 177–180, p. 95.
26. David Michael Levin, *The Opening of Vision*, op. cit., p. 353.
27. Alphonso Lingis, *The Imperative*, op. cit., p. 10.
28. Henry Beston, *The Outermost House*, op. cit., p. 171.
29. Ludwig Wittgenstein, quoted in "The Painter's Keys," <http://quote.robertgenn.com/auth_search.php?name=LU>.
30. Novalis, *Hymns to the Night*, trans. D. Higgins (New York: Treacle Press, 1978), pp. 14, 33.
31. Diane Ackerman, *A Natural History of the Senses*, op. cit., p. 245.

Chapter 8: In Touch With the Sensuous World: The Reclamation of the Elemental in Continental Philosophy

1. For relevant discussions, see Michael Zimmerman, "What Can Continental Philosophy Contribute to Environmentalism?" in Bruce Folz and Robert Frodeman, eds., *Rethinking Nature*, op. cit.; Zimmerman, *Contesting Earth's Future*, op. cit.; Diane Michelfelder, "Contemporary Continental Philosophy and Environmental Ethics: A Difficult Relationship?" in Folz and Frodeman, eds., *Rethinking Nature*, op. cit. and Steven Vogel, "Nature as Origin and Difference: On Environmental Philosophy and Continental Thought," *Philosophy Today* 24 suppl. (1998), pp. 169–81.
2. Gaston Bachelard, *The Poetics of Space*, op. cit.
3. Gaston Bachelard, *The Psychoanalysis of Fire*, op. cit.
4. Gaston Bachelard, *On Poetic Imagination and Reverie: Selections from Gaston Bachelard*, ed., Colette Gaudin (Dallas, TX: Spring Publications, 1987), p. xxvii.
5. Gaston Bachelard, *Water and Dreams*, op. cit.
6. Ibid., p. 5.
7. See, for example, Poe's presentation of the sublime sea in "Into the Maelström," *Great Short Works of Edgar Allan Poe*, ed., G. R. Thompson (New York: Harper & Row, 1970).
8. Gaston Bachelard, *Water and Dreams*, op. cit., p. 79.
9. Gaston Bachelard, *Air and Dreams*, op. cit., p. 5
10. Gaston Bachelard, *The Psychoanalysis of Fire*, op. cit., p. 178.
11. See Chapter One on the connection among water, language, and thought.
12. Gaston Bachelard, *Psychoanalysis of Fire*, op. cit., p. 7.
13. Ibid., p. 16.
14. Gaston Bachelard, *Lautreamont*, trans. Robert S. Dupree (Dallas, TX: Dallas Institute Publications, 1986).
15. Gaston Bachelard, *La Flamme d'une chandelle* (Paris, France: Presses Universitaires de France, 1961).
16. Gaston Bachelard, *Air and Dreams*, op. cit., p. 185.
17. Ibid., p. 242.
18. Edmond Vandercammen, quoted in Bachelard, *The Poetics of Reverie*, op. cit., p. 118.
19. For a reading of Nietzsche as ecological thinker, see Max O. Hallman, "Nietzsche's Environmental Ethics," *Environmental Ethics*, op. cit., 99–125. One of the weaknesses with Hallman's interpretation is that it ignores the force of the Bachelard's assessment, namely that Nietzsche is often in flight from the earth, even if he advises us to remain faithful to it.
20. Gaston Bachelard, *Earth and Reveries of Will*, op. cit. Bachelard's *Earth and Reveries of Repose* is not yet translated. See *La Terre et les rêveries du repos* (Paris, France: Jose Corti, 1948).
21. Gaston Bachelard, *Earth and Reveries of Will*, op. cit., p. 59.
22. Ibid., p. 101.
23. Charles H. Kahn, ed., *The Art and Thought of Heraclitus*, op. cit., frag. 10, p. 33.
24. Gaston Bachelard, *La Terre et les rêveries du repos*, op. cit., p. 300.
25. Ibid., p. 291.

26. Bachelard, *On Poetic Imagination and Reverie*, op. cit., p. 87. According to Colette Gaudin, Bachelard used to remark, "I would like to develop a philosophy that has no point of departure, a philosophy that *is* not a point of departure." Compare the remarks by Deleuze and Guattari, such as "Freud tried to approach crowd phenomena from the point of view of the unconscious, but he did not see clearly, he did not see that the unconscious itself was fundamentally a crowd" or "A rhizome has no beginning or end; it is always in the middle, between things, interbeing, *intermezzo*. The tree is filiation, but the rhizome is alliance, uniquely alliance. The tree imposes the verb 'to be,' but the fabric of the conjunction carries enough force to shake and uproot the verb 'to be.' Where are you going? Where are you coming from? What are you heading for? These are totally useless questions." Deleuze and Guattari, *A Thousand Plateaus*, op. cit., pp. 29 and 25.

27. Interestingly, we find something akin to this "worlding" and "fouring" in Taoism, to which Heidegger looked later in his life.

28. Martin Heidegger, *Poetry, Language, Thought*, op. cit., p. 151.

29. See Martin Heidegger, *Introduction to Metaphysics*, op. cit. for a more complete characterization.

30. Martin Heidegger, "The Origin of the Work of Art" in *Poetry, Language, Thought*, op. cit.

31. Ibid., p. 150. One might also turn this idea on its head by noticing that it is the earth (and a new understanding of it) that will likely "save" us rather than the other way around, especially given that "rescuing" it so consciously and deliberately will likely invite further disaster, something from which we and the earth could be spared.

32. Implicit, of course, in Heidegger's remarks is a critique of modern technology, which is developed more fully elsewhere. See Heidegger, *The Question Concerning Technology*, op. cit.

33. With respect to the divinities and dwelling, it might be pointed out that in Jewish theology, one finds—despite the transcendental element—a common substitution of "place" (*makom*) for the name of God (as in holy place, *makom kadosh*) which suggests that for some individuals and cultures the divinities are always already dwelling on earth, beneath the sky and with mortals. On Heidegger's relation to religion, see F. Schalow, *Heidegger and the Quest for the Sacred* (Dordrecht, Netherlands: Kluwer, 2001); Ben Vedder, *Heidegger's Philosophy of Religion: From God to Gods* (Pittsburgh, PA: Duquesne UP, 2006); and Benjamin Crowe, *Heidegger's Religious Origins* (Bloomington: Indiana UP, 2006).

34. See Michael Soulé and Bruce Wilcox, eds., *Conservation Biology* (Sunderland, MA: Sinauer Press, 1980), p. 8.

35. See Yvonne Baskin, *The Work of Nature*, op. cit.

36. Heidegger's notion of authenticity is problematic, though the idea cannot be examined here.

37. This thought finds echoes in his essays, "The Thing" and "Letter on Humanism." See Martin Heidegger, *Basic Writings*, ed., David Farrell Krell (New York: Harper & Row, 1977).

38. Martin Heidegger, "Letter on Humanism" in *Basic Writings*, op cit.

39. See Luce Irigaray, *The Forgetting of Air in Martin Heidegger*, op. cit.

40. Wallace Stevens, "Anecdote of the Jar," *The Palm at the End of the Mind*, op. cit., p. 46. In the poem, a jar is placed atop a Tennessee hill, where its mere presence organizes a world and makes the "slovenly wilderness" rise up to it and "surround

that hill." On Heidegger's bridge and jug, see "The Thing" in *Poetry, Language, Thought*, op. cit.

41. See Langdon Winner, *The Whale and the Reactor* (Chicago, IL: U of Chicago P) and Don Ihde, "De-romanticizing Heidegger" in his *Post-phenomenology* (Evanston, IL: Northwestern UP, 1993).

42. Heidegger's view of death is closely related to his thinking about technology and the possibility of finding an ecological ethos in his later work. One might reasonably claim, in fact, that technology and in particular medical technology, can be seen in many ways as an attempt to overcome, forestall or control death. As Heidegger puts it in the *Holzwege*, technology is "the firm negation of death." See Heidegger, *Holzwege* (Frankfurt, Germany: Klosterman, 1972). But it is not simply technology that is responsible; rather it is our relationship to the earth and world more generally which permits this negation to occur: "It is not the much discussed atom bomb, as one particular kind of killing-machine, that is so deadly. What has long menaced man with death, even with the death of his essence, is the absolute pure willing, in the sense of the conscious imposition of man's will upon everything." Technology, according to Heidegger, is the culmination and closure of western metaphysics and thus overcoming metaphysics means at the same time radical questioning and perhaps "destruction" of invasive, restrictive technologies and a movement toward ecological and more liberating ones. Technology, he says, "devours the earth in the exhaustion and consumption and change of what is artificial. Technology drives the earth beyond the developed sphere of its possibility into such things which are not longer a possibility and are thus the impossible." See Heidegger, *The End of Philosophy*, trans. Joan Staumbaugh (New York: Harper & Row), p. 100.

43. This is a topic that returns us to our earlier engagement in the first chapter with framing earth, fire, air and water in the work of the ancient Greeks.

44. Martin Heidegger, *Discourse on Thinking*, op. cit., p. 50.

45. Martin Heidegger, *Being and Time*, op. cit., p. 100.

46. See Heidegger, "The Age of the World Picture" in *Question Concerning Technology*, op. cit.

47. Martin Heidegger, *Question Concerning Technology*, op. cit., p. 7.

48. Martin Heidegger, *Poetry, Language, Thought*, op. cit., p. 23.

49. Martin Heidegger, *Being and Time*, op. cit., p. 220.

50. Martin Heidegger, *Poetry, Language, Thought*, op. cit., p. 145.

51. Martin Heidegger, "Memorial Address," in *Discourse on Thinking*, op. cit., p. 47.

52. Ibid., pp. 48–49.

53. Ibid., p. 53.

54. Ibid., p. 57. Elsewhere, Heidegger writes, "if we lose the earth, of course, we also lose the roots."

55. Martin Heidegger, *Introduction to Metaphysics*, op. cit., p. 3.

56. A related and, no doubt, more serious, issue regarding Heidegger's use of root and earth metaphors concerns the political question and his relationship to National Socialism with its "Blut und Boden" ideology, a subject that cannot be taken up here. On the controversial relation between ecological thought and fascism generally, see Anna Bramwell, *Blood and Soil: R. Walther Darre and Hitler's Green Party* (Abbotsbrook, UK: Bourne End,

1985) and Anna Bramwell, *Ecology in the 20th Century: A History* (New Haven, CT: Yale UP, 1989).

57. See Jacques Derrida, *Margins*, op. cit., pp. 111–136; Theodor Adorno, *Negative Dialectics*, trans. E. B. Ashton (New York: Seabury Press, 1973), p. 62; Walter Kaufmann, *From Shakespeare to Existentialism* (Garden City, NY: Anchor Books, 1960), pp. 339–69 and Jürgen Habermas, *The Philosophical Discourse of Modernity*, trans. Frederick G. Lawrence (Cambridge, MA: MIT Press, 1987), pp. 131–60 as well as Allen Megill, *Prophets of Extremity* (Berkeley: U of California P, 1985), pp. 120–25. Walter Kaufman, for example, argues that Heidegger seeks solace in archaism, claiming that the greatest fault of his treatment of the Presocratics is that they become authorities for him but that in philosophy there is no room for such authority.

58. Martin Heidegger, "What is Metaphysics" in *Basic Writings*, op. cit.

59. Martin Heidegger, "Letter on Humanism" in Ibid.

60. Martin Heidegger, *Being and Time*, op. cit., pp. 21–22 (italics added).

61. For example, in "The Thinker as Poet," Heidegger speaks about singing and thinking as "stems" which "grow" out of Being toward "truth" (a word related etymologically in English to tree, as in that which is firm and straight) and connects them to Hölderlin's "trees of the woods." Alternatively, in the essay, "Language," the tree is spoken of as uniting the fourfold in a world understood in a nonmetaphysical sense. See *Poetry, Language, Thought*, op. cit., pp. 13 and 201. Plato's *Timaeus* calls humans "heavenly trees" as well, growing with their roots (or heads) upward into the sky (90a). Democritus, on the other hand, spoke of plants and trees as having their heads rooted in the earth (68b).

62. See Martin Heidegger, *The Question of Being*, trans. William Klubuck and Jean T. Wilde (New Haven, CT: College and UP, 1958). This is a point made by David Farell Krell. Cited in Hwa Yol Jung, "Heidegger's Way with Sinitic Thinking" in Graham Parkes, ed., *Heidegger and Asian Thought* (Honolulu: U of Hawaii P, 1987).

63. All of the eco-philosophical implications of Heidegger's thought cannot be explored here. I focus in the main on his reworking of the elements into a fourfold. Elsewhere, I relate his thought to Hannah Arendt's reflection on the phenomena of earth alienation. See David Macauley, "Out of place and Outer Space: Hannah Arendt on Earth Alienation," *Capitalism, Nature, Socialism* 3.4 (1992), pp. 19–45.

64. For a more general discussion of Heidegger's relationship to deep ecology and ecological currents, see the work of Michael Zimmerman, particularly "Toward a Heideggerian Ethos for Radical Environmentalism," *Environmental Ethics* 5 (1983), pp. 99–131. See also Zimmerman, *Contesting Earth's Future*, op. cit.; Zimmerman, "Rethinking the Heidegger-Deep Ecology Relation," *Environmental Ethics* 15.3 (1993), pp. 195–224; and "Martin Heidegger: Antinaturalistic Critic of Technological Modernity," in David Macauley, *Minding Nature*, op. cit. For another insightful treatment, see Bruce Foltz, *Inhabiting the Earth: Heidegger, Environmental Ethics, and the Metaphysics of Nature* (Atlantic Highlands, NJ: Humanities Press, 1995).

65. It should be pointed out that Heidegger's thought is not without its share of problems for thinking about the natural world. To summarize very briefly a few of the difficulties: (a) a residual or latent anthropocentrism often exists in his work; (b) *Dasein* is not strictly understood as humans though in fact it comes to mean no one or nothing other than the human; (c) there is a glaring lack of the "mit-Sein" (being-with) and intersubjectivity;

(d) Heidegger denies animals the capacity for language; and (e) his earth/world opposition is usually put in terms of a competitive battle or striving rather than characterized as cooperative or symbiotic.

66. Maurice Merleau-Ponty, *The Visible and the Invisible*, op. cit., p. 139.

67. Ibid., p. 147.

68. Aristotle, *De Anima*, op. cit., II, 7. 418a31ff.

69. Maurice Merleau-Ponty, *Themes from Lectures at the College de France, 1952–1960*, op. cit.

70. Maurice Merleau-Ponty, "Husserl et la notion de Nature," *Revue de Métaphysique et de Morale*, op. cit. and *Themes from Lectures at the College de France, 1952–60*, op. cit.

71. Maurice Merleau-Ponty, *Visible and Invisible*, op. cit., pp. 218, 267, 140, 218, 223.

72. Maurice Merleau-Ponty, *Phenomenology of Perception*, op. cit., p. 52ff.

73. Merleau-Ponty also values *ambiguity* (in contrast to Cartesian certainty), *experience* (the world as lived through, not simply what one thinks) and *expression* (an alternative to representational thought).

74. For a monumental and encyclopedic treatment of touch—especially in relation to the body and by way of a critique of intuitionism within phenomenology—that, unfortunately, cannot be considered here, see Jacques Derrida, *On Touching*, trans. Christine Irizarry (Palo Alto, CA: Stanford UP, 2005).

75. Emmanuel Levinas, *Totality and Infinity: An Essay on Exteriority*, trans. Alphonso Lingis (Pittsburgh, PA: Duquesne UP, 1969), p. 131.

76. Levinas himself seems to withhold from this possibility, contrasting the element to the face [*visage*] because with a face an existent appears in a personal rather than impersonal form.

77. Ibid., p. 131.

78. Ibid., p. 135.

79. Ibid., p. 131.

80. John Sallis, "Levinas and the Elemental," *Research in Phenomenology* 28 (1998), p. 152ff.

81. Ibid., p. 137.

82. Ibid., p. 132–33.

83. Alphonso Lingis, *The Imperative*, op. cit. See also Lingis, "Imperatives," in M. C. Dillon, ed., *Mereleau-Ponty Vivant*, op. cit.

84. Alphonso Lingis, *The Imperative*, op. cit., p. 16.

85. Ibid., p. 73.

86. Ibid., p. 155.

87. Ibid., p. 31.

88. Ibid., pp. 15–16.

89. Ibid., p. 17.

90. Ibid., p. 19.

91. Ibid., p. 21.

92. Ibid., p. 22.

93. Alphonso Lingis, *Foreign Bodies* (New York: Routledge, 1994), p. 42.

94. Ibid., p. 189.

95. One might compare here Umberto Eco's *The Island of the Day Before*, trans. William Weaver (New York: Penguin Books, 1996), which also involves a mythical island and the play of elements and elemental forces.

96. Alphonso Lingis, *The Imperative*, op. cit. p. 22.

97. Graham Harman, *Guerrilla Metaphysics: Phenomenology and the Carpentry of Things* (Chicago and La Salle, IL: Open Court, 2005), p. 60.

98. Ibid., p. 68. See also Alexander E. Hooke and Wolfgang W. Fuchs, ed., *Encounters with Alphonso Lingis* (Lanham, MD: Lexington Books, 2003).

99. Luce Irigaray, quoted in Tasmin Lorraine, *Irigaray and Deleuze: Experiments in Visceral Philosophy* (Ithaca, NY: Cornell UP, 1999), p. 227; quote from Irigaray, *Sexes and Genealogies*, trans. Gilliam C. Gill (New York: Columbia UP, 1985), p. 57.

100. Luce Irigaray, *Marine Lover of Friedrich Nietzsche*, trans. Gillian C. Gill (New York: New York UP, 1991), p. 58 and Luce Irigaray, *Why Different?*, eds., Luce Irigaray and Sylvere Lotringer, trans. Camille Collins (New York: Semiotext(e), 2000), p. 118.

101. Margaret Whitfield, *Luce Irigaray: Philosophy in the Feminine* (New York: Routledge, 1991), p. 62.

102. Tasmin Lorraine, *Irigaray and Deleuze*, op. cit.

103. Luce Irigaray, *Why Different?*, op. cit., p. 130. It also seems to be the case that antagonisms and hatred may be generated through the air. Nietzsche proclaimed provocatively, "Nothing is worse than the smell of an ill-constituted soul," and observed that what often separates people is that they can't stand each other's smell.

104. Luce Irigaray, *The Forgetting of Air in Martin Heidegger*, op. cit., p. 2.

105. Luce Irigaray, *The Sex Which is Not One* (Ithaca, NY: Cornell UP, 1985), p. 107.

106. Irigaray, *The Forgetting of Air*, op. cit., p. 8.

107. Ibid., p. 11.

108. Irigaray points out that in Empedocles' cosmology, air is the first element separated off by what is sometimes translated as "hatred."

109. Ibid., p. 15.

110. Luce Irigaray, *Why Different?*, op. cit., p. 133. See Irigaray, *Between East and West: From Singularity to Community*, trans. Stephen Pluhacek (New York: Columbia UP).

111. In fairness to Nietzsche, he may use "earth" to mean the place of all natural places (and elements) rather than as a singular element.

112. Mary Daly, *Pure Lust: Elemental Feminist Philosophy* (Boston, MA: Beacon Press, 1984), p. 257.

113. Mary Daly, *Quintessence . . . Realizing the Archaic Future* (Boston, MA: Beacon Press, 1998).

114. Edward Casey, *Getting Back into Place*, op. cit., p. xiii.

115. Ibid., p. xv.

116. Ibid., p. 237.

117. Ibid., p. 265.

118. Edward Casey, *Representing Place: Landscape Painting and Maps* (Minneapolis: U of Minnesota P, 2002), p. 33.

119. Ibid., p. 35.

120. Ibid., p. 37.

121. Ibid.
122. Ibid., p. 39.
123. John Sallis, *Force of Imagination: The Sense of the Elemental* (Bloomington: Indiana UP, 2000). Less directly, Sallis engages the elemental world in *Stone*, op. cit. and *Chorology*, op. cit.
124. Sallis, *Force of Imagination*, op. cit., p 149.
125. Ibid., p. 154.
126. Ibid., p 155.
127. Ibid., p. 192. Heidegger is quoted by Sallis, *Force of Imagination*, op. cit., p. 195.
128. Joyce Carol Oates, "Marya," quoted in Stefan Klein, "Time Out of Mind," *New York Times*, March 17, 2008.
129. For an exploration of this subject, see Sara Ebenreck, "Opening Pandora's Box: The Role of Imagination in Environmental Ethics," *Environmental Ethics* 18.1 (1996), pp. 3–18.
130. The emphasis on "nature's return" is especially evident in Sallis' essay, "Levinas and the Elemental," *Research in Phenomenology*, op. cit., p. 152ff.
131. In a footnote, Sallis writes: "Though the difference between the depth of a thing and that of an element is marked by Levinas, it is immediately assimilated to the global opposition between existence and existent... This assimilation allows Levinas, in turn, to link the recession of the elemental to the *il y a*... the result is not only, as Levinas intends, to deprive elemental nature of the capacity for heterogeneous provocation but also to efface the specificity of the elemental. Levinas' further step, identifying the depth of the elemental with 'the materiality of the elemental non-I' and with "the fathomless obscurity of matter... risks reinscribing the entire analysis of the elemental within the most classical philosophical conceptuality." Sallis, *Force of the Imagination*, op. cit., p. 159, fn. 17.
132. Although not treated separately here, David Michael Levin's rich tapestry of work merits special mention as well for its attentive and creative insights regarding elemental subjects such as light, breath, shadow, earth, and night. See Levin, *The Opening of Vision*, op. cit.; *The Body's Recollection of Being* (London, UK: Routledge & Kegan Paul, 1985); and *Before the Voice of Reason: Echoes of Responsibility in Merleau-Ponty's Ecology and Levinas's Ethics* (Albany: SUNY P, 2008).
133. Friedrich Nietzsche, *On the Genealogy of Morals*, trans. Walter Kaufmann (New York: Vintage, 1969), p. 80.
134. Yi-Fu Tuan, *Passing Strange and Wonderful* (Washington, DC: Island Press, 1993), pp. 112–13.
135. Gaston Bachelard, *The Poetics of Reverie*, op. cit., p. 176.
136. Ibid., p. 177.

Interstice: Space

1. Thomas G. Bergin, "Space Prober," launched into space on a satellite called "Traac," November 14, 1961.
2. "Genesis," 11: 4 in *The Oxford Study Bible*, op. cit., p. 20.

3. Immanuel Kant, *Prolegomena to Any Future Metaphysic*, quoted in Joseph Campbell, *The Inner Reaches of Outer Space* (New York: Harper & Row, 1986), p. 27.

4. Immanuel Kant, *The Critique of Practical Reason*, trans. Thomas Abbot (Sioux Falls, SD: NuVision, 2005), p. 125.

5. Galileo Galilei, *Siderius Nuncius*, trans. Albert van Helden (Chicago, IL: U of Chicago P, 1989), p. 89.

6. Gaston Bachelard, *Air and Dreams*, op. cit., pp. 175–76.

7. Rainer Maria Rilke, "The First Elegy," *Duino Elegies* in *The Selected Poetry of Rainer Maria Rilke*, op. cit., p. 151.

8. Albert Einstein, quoted in Michael I. Sobel, *Light* (Chicago, IL: U of Chicago P, 1987), p. 137.

9. Issa, Untitled haiku, quoted in Nancy Wilson Ross, *The World of Zen*, op. cit. p. 117.

10. Johannes Kepler, Letter to Galileo Galilei, April, 1610, quoted in David F. Noble, *The Religion of Technology: The Divinity of Man and the Spirit of Invention* (New York: Penguin Books, 1999), p. 117.

11. Giuseppe Ungaretti, quoted in Joseph Campbell, *Myths to Live By*, op. cit., p. 242.

12. T. S. Eliot, "Four Quartets," in *Collected Poems, 1909–1962* (New York: Harcourt Brace Jovanovich, 1991), p. 173ff.

13. William W. Reade, *The Martyrdom of Man* (New York: Elibron Classics, 1872), p. 514.

14. Chandogya Upanishad, in *The Upanishads*, ed., Eknath Easwaran (Tomales, CA: Nilgiri Press, 2007), p. 139.

15. Archibald MacLeish, "The End of the World" in Paul Negri, ed., *Great Short Poems* (New York: Dover, 2000), p. 51.

Chapter 9: Revaluing Earth, Air, Fire, and Water: Elemental Beauty, Ecological Duty, and Environmental Policy

1. Koun Yamada, *The Gateless Gate: The Classic Book of Zen Koans* (Sommerville, MA: Wisdom Publications, 2004).

2. Sigmar Groeneveld, Lee Hoinacki, Ivan Illich and friends, "Declaration on Soil," *Whole Earth Review*, 1991.

3. Gary Snyder, *The Practice of the Wild*, op. cit., p. 31.

4. See, for example, Michel Serres, *The Natural Contract*, trans. Elizabeth MacArthur and William Paulson (Ann Arbor: U of Michigan P, 1995).

5. See Andrew Light and Eric Katz, eds., *Environmental Pragmatism* (New York: Routledge, 1996).

6. Holmes Rolston III, "Environmental Ethics in Antarctica," *Environmental Ethics* 24.2 (2002), p. 133.

7. Ibid., pp. 133–34.

8. Edward Abbey, *The Monkey Wrench Gang* (New York: HarperCollins, 2000), Chapter Five.

9. Thoreau, *Walden and Other Writings*, ed., op. cit., p. 117.

10. For work on the philosophical, environmental, political, and aesthetic aspects of walking, see David Macauley, "Walking the Elemental Earth: Phenomenological and Literary Foot Notes," *Annalecta Husserliana* 71 (2001), pp. 15–31; "Walking the City: Peripatetic Practices and Politics," *Capitalism, Nature, Socialism* 11.4 (2000), pp. 3–43; and "A Few Foot Notes on Walking," *The Trumpeter: Journal of Ecosophy* 10.1 (1993), pp. 14–16.

11. On the two major frameworks in environmental aesthetics, see Allen Carlson, *Aesthetics and the Environment: The Appreciation of Nature, Art and Architecture* (New York: Routledge, 2002) and Arnold Berleant, *The Aesthetics of the Environment* (Philadelphia, PA: Temple UP, 1995).

12. For one such attempt to develop a middle way between the cognitivist and engagement aesthetic views, see Ronald Moore, "Appreciating Natural Beauty as Natural" in Allen Carlson and Arnold Berleant, eds., *The Aesthetics of Natural Environments*, op. cit.

13. Holmes Rolston, "Aesthetic Experience of Forests" in Allen Carlson and Arnold Berleant, eds., *The Aesthetics of Natural Environments*, op. cit., p. 186.

14. Yi-Fu Tuan, *Passing Strange and Wonderful*, op. cit., p. 155.

15. Edward Abbey, *Desert Solitaire*, op. cit., p. 33.

16. Jean Baudrillard, *On Seduction*, trans. Brian Singer (New York: St. Martin's, 1990), p. 104.

17. William Desmond, *Being and the Between* (Albany: SUNY P, 1995), p. 278. See also William Desmond, *Philosophy and Its Others* (Albany: SUNY P, 1990), especially pp. 269–90. There, Desmond speaks in passing of the elemental in connection with song, sleep, death, and time. The elemental holds forth the promise of "a refreshed relatedness to being in its otherness" (p. 270). "Lose the elemental, life greys," he suggests (p. 272).

18. Hans-Erik Larsen, *The Aesthetics of the Elements: Imaginary Morphologies in Texts and Paintings*, trans. Kenneth Tindall (Oxford, UK: Aarhus UP, 1996), p. 5.

19. Ibid., p. 13.

20. See, for example, Andy Goldsworthy, *Time* (New York: Harry N. Abrams, 2000); *Stone* (New York: Harry N. Abrams, 1998); *Wood* (New York: Harry N. Abrams, 1996) and *Andy Goldsworthy: A Collaboration with Nature* (New York: Harry N. Abrams, 1991). For a documentary film on Goldsworthy, see "Rivers and Tides: Working with Time," directed by Thomas Riedelsheimer (Edinburgh, UK: Skyline Productions, 2003).

21. James Hatley, "*Techne* and *Phusis*: Wilderness and the Aesthetics of the Trace in Andrew Goldsworthy," *Environmental Philosophy* 2.2 (2005), p. 6.

22. Jacques Derrida, *Of Grammatology*, op. cit., p. 167.

23. Jacques Derrida, *Speech and Phenomena*, trans. David Allison (Evanston, IL: Northwestern UP, 1973), p. 86.

24. Jacques Derrida, *Margins*, trans. Alan Bass (Chicago, IL: U of Chicago P, 1982), p. 15.

25. Andy Goldsworthy and Terry Friedman, eds., *Hand to Earth* (New York: Harry N. Abrams, 2004), epigraph.

26. Jay Griffiths, *Wild: An Elemental Journey*, op. cit., p. 2.

27. Ibid.

28. Ibid.

29. Nigel Hoffman, *Goethe's Science of Living Form: The Artistic Stages* (Hillsdale, NY: Adonis Press, 2007).

30. See Camille Paglia, *Sexual Personae* (New Haven, CT: Yale UP, 1990), pp. 222–226 and G. Wilson Knight, *The Imperial Theme* (New York: Routledge, 1984), pp. 227–44.
31. Shakespeare, *Julius Caesar* (New York: Washington Square Press, 2004), line 5.55.68.
32. Shakespeare, *Sonnets* (New York: Washington Square Press, 2004), sonnets 44 and 45.
33. T. S. Eliot, "The Wasteland" and "Four Quartets" in *Collected Poems, 1909–1962* (New York: Harcourt Brace Jovanovich, 1991), pp. 51ff and 173 ff.
34. Henry David Thoreau, "Walking" in *Walden and Other Writings*, op. cit., p. 619.
35. Gary Snyder, "As for Poets," *Turtle Island* (New York: New Directions, 1974), pp. 87–88.
36. Antonin Artaud, "The New Revelation of Being" in *Artaud Anthology*, ed. Jack Hirschman (San Francisco, CA: City Lights Publishers, 1963).
37. Richard Nirenberg concludes, "Those in power ought to read the poets," a line that implicitly recalls Shelley's famous remark, "Poets are the unacknowledged legislators of the world." See Nirenberg, "H," op. cit.
38. See, for example, Heide Fasnacht, *Drawn to Sublime* (New York: Kent Press, 2004).
39. See Samantha Rippner, *The Prints of Vija Celmins* (New York: Metropolitan Museum of Art, 2002).
40. Philippe Soupault, quoted in Gaston Bachelard, *Earth and Reveries of Will*, op. cit., p. 36.
41. Space does not permit an exploration of the elements in astrology or alchemy. On alchemy, see, for example, Michael Sendivogius, *New Light of Alchemie*, trans. J.F.M.D. (London, UK: Thomas Williams, 1650). In the thirteenth century, Albertus Magnus tried to demonstrate the influence of the four elements on geological phenomena, as well.
42. See Camille Paglia, *Sexual Personae*, op. cit., p. 223.
43. Like Oliver Sacks, who has written of his love for the periodic table, Primo Levi has drawn on the modern view of the chemical—rather than the classical—elements, sketching interesting and sometimes haunting connections between such elements as argon, hydrogen, zinc, potassium, nitrogen, and carbon and basic human traits such as courage, humor, greed, and forgiveness. Primo Levi, *The Periodic Table of Elements*, op. cit.
44. See Hugo Grotius, *The Rights of War and Peace*, trans. A. C. Campbell (New York: M. W. Dunne, 1901).
45. Alice Outwater, *Water: A Natural History* (New York: Basic, 1997).
46. See P. H. Gleick, *The World's Water* (Washington, DC: Island Press, 2004).
47. See Marq De Villiers, *Water*, op. cit., pp. 276–313.
48. Tracy Staedter, "Water From Air, Low-Tech Style," *Discovery News*, June 15, 2007.
49. On living machines, see Steve Lerner, *Eco-Pioneers* (Cambridge, MA: MIT Press, 1997).
50. On these ideas and other practical proposals, see Paul Hawken, Amory Lovins and L. Hunter Lovins, *Natural Capitalism* (Boston, MA: Little, Brown, 1999).
51. See David Appell, "The Darkening Earth," *Scientific American*, August 2, 2004.

52. See Ross Gelbspan, *Boiling Point* (New York: Basic, 2004) for an analysis of the politics of global warming, as well as an articulation of policy proposals to fund the transfer of renewable energy to developing nations, change subsidies from fossil fuel to alternative energy sources, and greatly improve emission standards.

53. On wind power, see Marc de Villiers, *Windswept: The Story of Wind and Weather* (New York: Walker, 2007) and Jan DeBlieu, *Wind*, op. cit.

54. George W. Bush actually helped to encourage the use of wind power while governor of Texas. On Bush's environmental record, see Robert F. Kennedy Jr., *Crimes Against Nature* (New York: HarperCollins, 2004).

55. Stan Cox, "America's Air-Conditioned Nightmare," <http://www.altnet.org/story/38154>.

56. See Janine Benyus, *Biomimcry*, op. cit.

57. On alternative policies and practices for the land and agriculture, see William Vitek and Wes Jackson, eds., *Rooted in the Land* (New Haven, CT: Yale UP, 1996) and Wes Jackson, Wendell Berry and Bruce Colman, eds., *Meeting the Expectations of the Land* (San Francisco, CA: North Point Press, 1984).

58. Elizabeth Barrett Browning, *Aurora Leigh*, quoted in R. H. Blyth, *Zen in English Literature and Oriental Classics* (New York: E. P. Dutton, 1960), p. 1.

59. Johann Wolfgang von Goethe, "Toward a Theory of Weather" in *Scientific Studies* in *Goethe's Collected Works*, op. cit., p. 147.

60. Percy Bysshe Shelley, "A Defence of Poetry," (1821) in Edmund D. Jones, *English Critical Essays* (London, UK: Oxford UP, 1947), p. 131.

61. See Paul T. Anastas and John C. Warner, *Green Chemistry: Theory and Practice* (Oxford, UK: Oxford UP, 2000).

62. On hydrogen options, see Seth Dunn, ed., *Hydrogen Futures: Toward a Sustainable Energy System* (Washington, DC: Worldwatch Institute, 2001).

63. Edward Abbey, *Desert Solitaire*, op. cit., pp. 42–43.

64. Tom Robbins, *Even Cowgirls Get the Blues*, op. cit., p. 103.

65. Jan DeBlieu, *Wind*, op. cit., p. 3.

66. "The Four" in D. H. Lawrence, *The Complete Poems of D.H. Lawrence*, Vol. 2, ed. Vivian de Sola Pinto and Warren Roberts (New York: Viking, 1964), p. 706.

67. The expressions, "natural aliens," "rogue primates" and "robo-*sapiens* derive respectively from Neil Evernden, *The Natural Alien*, op. cit.; John A. Livingston, *Rogue Primate* (Boulder, CO: Roberts Rinehart Publisher, 1995); and Peter Menzel and Faith D'Aluisio, *Robo sapiens: Evolution of New Species* (Cambridge, MA: MIT Press, 2001).

Index

Abbey, Edward, 54–55, 173–174, 204, 337, 340, 354
Ackerman, Diane, 249, 291
Adams, Ansel, 53–54
Adler, Mortimer, 2
Adorno, Theodor W., 277
aesthetics, 338–345; cognitivist model of, 339; engagement model of, 339
aether: etymology of, 227
aether (ether), 5, 81, 187–188, 225–228. *See also* fifth element
air, 25–35; Anaximenes on, 26–27, 32, 33, 362n. 82; Aristotle on, 190, 191, 213–214, 217–218; Bachelard on, 297–298; biological characteristics of, 29, 31–32; breathing of, 26, 30–31, 32; cultural interpretations of, 33; Derrida on, 32; differentiated characteristics of, 27, 29; Empedocles on, 107, 109–110, 114, 115; environmental action on, 348–350; gases of, 29, 31–32; Hegel on, 280–281; ideogram for, 61; Irigaray on, 30, 316–318; layers of, 27; metaphysical properties of, 33; movements of, 27–28, 29–30; Plato on, 145–146, 148–150, 152–153, 154, 161–163; pollution of, 34–35; preclassical view of, 362n. 86. *See also* sky
Air and Dreams (Bachelard), 295
air conditioning, 349–350
airsheds, 27
Alcmaeon, 114–115
alienation: earth, 25, 273, 405n. 63; place, 196–197; world, 273
Allegory of Cave, 166

altruism, 121
ambient light, 244–245
Anapanasati Sutra (Buddha), 31
Anaxagoras, 69, 327
Anaximander, 64, 87–88, 109, 158; on opposition, 69, 163
Anaximenes: on air, 26, 32, 33, 362n. 82; on clouds, 175–176; on cosmos, 147; on elemental transformation, 154
animals: Aristotle on, 259; cold-blooded, 202; domestication of, 258, 274; Empedocles on, 120–122; experimentation on, 121; night and, 287; Plato on, 148, 160, 161, 259; warm-blooded, 201–202
animism, 116, 373n. 105
Antarctica, 138–139, 140–141, 336–337
anthropocentrism, 335
Antony and Cleopatra (Shakespeare), 343–344
Apache, 79
apparent horizon, 64
archetypes, 66–67
Archidoxis (Paracelsus), 279–280
Archimedes, 90
Arctic, 139, 140
Arctic Dreams (Lopez), 139
Arendt, Hannah, 273, 275
Aristophanes, 176
Aristotle, 8, 179–199, 209–242; on aether, 187–188, 225–228; on air, 190, 191, 213–214, 217–218; on animals, 259; on body, 70, 183, 236; on boundary/limit, 192–193, 195–196; on breath, 32; on change, 185, 195, 213–216, 223–225,

Aristotle *(continued)*
  239–240; on composite bodies, 190–191; on compound bodies, 216–218; on contact, 210, 228–233; on contraries, 69, 185, 209–216, 225, 396n. 10; on earth, 190, 191, 213, 217, 222–223; ecology and, 238–242; on elemental definitions, 182–183; on elemental generation, 183–186; on elemental self-domestication, 195; on elemental transformation, 213–216, 224–225; vs. Empedocles, 181, 183, 184–185, 393n. 17; on evolution, 119–120; on fifth element, 187–188, 225–228; on fire, 40–41, 190, 191, 212, 213, 217–218; on flesh, 231, 232, 308; on form, 189–190, 192; geocentrism and, 240; on heat, 204; on heaviness, 186–188, 191, 211; on home-place, 197; on hot-cold, 209–213, 216–217, 222; on impossible elemental transformations, 215–216; on interval, 192; on knowledge, 237–238; on letters, 60; on light, 245; on lightness, 186–187, 211; on locomotion, 189, 190; on matter, 191–192, 194; on monism, 183–184; on movement, 180, 187–191, 195, 226, 241; naturalism and, 240–242; on nature, 181, 240–242, 400n. 73; on perception, 231–232; on place, 63, 65, 180, 188–199, 234, 394n. 24; vs. Plato, 181, 183–184, 212, 393n. 16; on prime matter, 218–225; on rapid irreversible elemental transformation, 215; on rapid reversible elemental transformation, 214, 224; on rock, 57; on senses, 230–232, 237–238; on sight, 233–234; on slow reversible elemental transformation, 214, 224; on soul, 234–238; on *stoicheia*, 182–183; on substratum, 221; on thinking, 237, 400n. 64; on touch, 210, 228–233; on up and down, 65, 187, 189, 193; on water, 190, 213–214, 217; on weight, 185, 186–188, 191, 211; on wet-dry, 209–213

Armstrong, Neil, 331

art: calligraphic, 62; clouds in, 174; earth in, 18, 22, 321; elemental themes in, 345; environmental, 341–342; ice in, 142; landscape in, 320–321; light in, 320; lightning in, 177; night in, 285–286; nude in, 260; shadow and, 249, 250; snowball, 141; stone, 54; water in, 48, 320–321

Atlas Complex, 298–299

atmosphere: etymology of, 29

atom, 70, 166–167

Atomism, 70, 162–163, 167, 239

Augustine of Hippo, 188

autochthones, 25

Bachelard, Gaston, 5, 8, 294, 325; on air, 297–298; on ancient texts, 85; botanical metaphors of, 299–300; on clouds, 176, 178; on constellations, 329; on earth, 22, 298–299; on fire, 37, 42, 206, 297; on imagination, 66–67; on night, 283, 284; poetics of, 295–300; on reverie, 66–67; on rock, 57, 58; on sky, 28; on touch, 234; on union, 256; on water, 46–47, 296–297

banishment: for pollution, 129

bats, 287–288

Baudrillard, Jean, 340

beauty, 338–345

Being and Time (Heidegger), 300–301, 306, 307

Bentham, Jeremy, 96

Beston, Henry, 1, 288

Bhagavad Gita, 30, 203, 244

Bible: clouds in, 175; light in, 244; water in, 45

Big Bang model, 167

biocentrism, 335–336

biophilia, 403n. 27

bioregionalism, 198

biotechnology, 274

bipedalism, 25, 26

Bjornerud, Marcia, 52

Blake, William, 42, 56–57, 64, 204, 364n. 119

blindness, 247

Bloch, Ernst, 116, 242
Bloom, Harold, 296
Blumenberg, Hans: on light, 244
Blur Building, 175
Bodin, Jean, 71
body, 70–71; Aristotle on, 70, 183, 236; humors of, 71; Irigaray on, 316; Plato on, 70, 145; of universe, 147
body temperature, 201–202, 203–204
Bohr, Neils, 166
Bookchin, Murray, 115, 241–242
books, 133
bottled water, 267–270
bowel movement, 24
Boyle, Robert, 72–73, 278
breath: Aristotle on, 32; Self as, 29, 77
breathing, 26, 30–31, 32
bridge, 262, 303–304
Browne, Thomas, 80
Browning, Robert, 30
Buddha: on breath, 31; Dafu, 56
Buddhism: architecture in, 75–76; elements in, 78; sky burial in, 33–34
buildings, 258–259
Bush, George W., 349
Byrd, Richard, 138
Byron, Lord, 289

Callicott, J. Baird, 117
Campbell, Joseph, 203
Camus, Albert, 57
Caravaggio, 249
cardinal directions, 65
carrying capacity, 195, 395n. 31
Carson, Rachel, 126
Casey, Edward, 8, 294, 313; on horizon, 64; on mapping, 22–23; on place, 197, 319–321
caves, 24–25, 287–288; allegory of, 166
Celmins, Vija, 48, 345
change: Anaximenes on, 154; Aristotle on, 185, 195, 213–216, 223–225, 239–240; Empedocles on, 110–113, 154; Heraclitus on, 154; Plato on, 152–155, 160–163, 239; rhizomatic, 134
chanting, 31

character: cold and, 206–207
chemistry, 72–74
chiaroscuro, 249
Chief Seattle, 278–279
China: elemental conceptions in, 74–75
chiromancy, 345
chora, 156–160
Christianity, 53, 80; light in, 244
Church, Frederic Edwin, 142, 320
Cicero, 85
Clarke, Arthur C., 39, 44–45
class, 131
Claudel, Paul, 344
climate change, 205
climbing, 56–57
cloud forests, 177–178
clouds, 173–178; color of, 174; cultural interpretations of, 174–175; forecasting by, 177; intellectual considerations of, 175–176; types of, 176–177
Cocteau, Jean, 42
cognition, 343
cold, 201–202, 205–207; character and, 206–207
Coleridge, Samuel Taylor, 138, 175
color, 246; black and, 291; cloud, 174; sky, 28, 177
Columbia River, 265–266
Commoner, Barry, 126
complexes, 150–152
compost, 17
Confessions (Augustine), 188
conflict. *See* strife
Constable, John, 174
constrained constructivism, 148–150
contact: Aristotle on, 210, 228–233; body-element, 71
contextualism, 370n. 50
contraries: Aristotle on, 69, 185, 209–216, 225, 396n. 10
Cornford, Francis M., 88–89, 152–153
cosmo-centrism, 332
cosmogony, 79–81
Cox, Stan, 349
Cratylus (Plato), 151
creation myths, 79–81

Crisis of the European Sciences, The (Husserl), 168–169
Critias (Plato), 128
Critique of Practical Reason (Kant), 328
cyborgs, 134

Dafu, 56
Dalton, John, 72
Daly, Mary, 318–319
darkness, 285, 292; prolonged, 290; sudden, 290
Darwin, Charles, 17
Davies, Peter Maxwell, 138
Da Vinci, Leonardo, 327–328
De Anima (Aristotle), 210, 229, 230, 235
DeBlieu, Jan, 355
De Chazal, Malcolm, 27
deforestation, 98, 274
Deleuze, Gilles, 7, 131–136, 294; on earth, 21; on naturalism, 136; on Presocratics, 118; on stone, 57; on thought, 64
Delicate Arch, 354
de Maria, Walter, 177
Democritus, 147
Denmark: landscape aesthetics in, 263
Derrida, Jacques: on air, 32; on earth, 21; on fire, 42, 364n. 117; on fourfold frame, 83, 373n. 98; on horizon, 65; on roots, 132; on stone, 57; on trace, 342
Descartes, René, 26, 150; on clouds, 176; on domestication, 278; on light, 243–244, 245; on soul, 236
desertification, 274
Desmond, William, 340–341
Diels, Hermann, 119
diet: fire and, 39
Dillard, Annie, 58
Diogenes, 109, 235
dirt, 17, 130
disease, 70, 71, 165
Döbereiner, Johann, 370n. 51
Dogon, 174–175
domestication, 2, 4, 8, 86, 255–281; of animals, 274; commodification and, 278; vs. domination, 258; of Earth, 274; of fire, 39, 40, 41, 255–256; of gene, 274; of humans, 258–259; of outer space, 329; of sky, 271–272; of water, 90–91, 256–271
domination: of nature, 257, 258
Donne, John, 278
Double Negative, 22
Douglas, Mary, 130
dreams, 66, 150–151
Durkheim, Émile, 88

Earth, 15; alienation from, 25, 273; Deleuze and Guattari on, 21; Hesiod on, 20–21; overdomestication of, 274; personification of, 16
earth, 14–25; alienation from, 405n. 63; Aristotle on, 190, 191, 213, 217, 222–223; in art, 18, 22, 321; Bachelard on, 298–299; creative images of, 22; Derrida on, 21; differentiated characteristics of, 15, 16; as egg, 20, 86; Empedocles on, 107, 109–110, 114, 115; environmental action on, 350–351; fire effects on, 37–38; generative characteristics of, 20–22, 25; geo-philosophic characteristics of, 21–22; Hegel on, 281; Heidegger on, 21, 24, 301; holes in, 19–20; horizons of, 16; human-related topography of, 18–19; Husserl on, 21; ideogram for, 61; layers of, 16; mapping of, 22–23; personification of, 16; physical/emotional awareness of, 23–24; placeholding aspect of, 18; Plato on, 21, 145–146, 148–150, 152–153, 154–155, 159, 161–163; profile of, 16; psychological levels of, 15; Ross on, 21–22; Sallis on, 22; vs. sky, 19; vs. world, 24
earth: etymology of, 16
Earth and Reveries of Will (Bachelard), 295
Earth Art, 22
Earth-Mapping (Casey), 319
earthquake, 19
eclipse, 290
eco-centrism, 335, 336

ecological sensibility, 103–104, 376n. 2
ecology, 2; Aristotle and, 238–242; Empedoclean relevance to, 113–115; existential, 35; feminist, 318–319; gray, 275; Haeckel on, 121–122; Heideggerian, 306–307
egg: earth as, 20, 86
Ehrlich, Gretel, 140, 206
electrical lights, 288
element(s), 1–9, 59–91, 324–325; aesthetics and, 338–345; archetypical characterization of, 66–67; bodily, 70–71; chemical, 72–74; Chinese conceptions of, 74–76; cognition and, 343; in creation myths, 79–81; cultural interpretations of, 74–81, 352–354; vs. the elemental, 324–325; ethics and, 334–338; four-frame of, 81–84; geography of, 63–66 (*see also* place); history of, 277–279; humors and, 71; Indian conceptions of, 76–78; Japanese conceptions of, 74–76; linguistic representation of, 60–63; Maori conceptions of, 79; materiality of, 69–70; metaphorical use of, 60–61, 68; Native American conceptions of, 65, 78–79; vs. nature, 3–4; opposite, 67–69 (*see also* opposition); Persian conceptions of, 78; root, 72; social construction of, 84–91; substantive, 69–72. See also air; earth; fire; *stoicheia;* water
elemental, the, 324–325
Elemental Passions (Irigaray), 316, 318
elemental sensibility, 310–312
Elements (Euclid), 183
Eliade, Mircea, 33, 46, 113, 172
Eliasson, Olafur, 48, 250
Eliot, T. S., 207, 331, 344
Emerson, Ralph Waldo, 34, 50; on heat, 204; on horizon, 65; on language, 61
empathy, 120–122
Empedocles, 7, 103–136; on air, 107, 109–110, 114, 115; on animal empathy, 120–122; vs. Aristotle, 181, 183, 184–185, 393n. 17; on change, 110–113, 154; on compounds, 397n. 15; contemporary relevance of, 113–115; cosmology of, 110–113; death of, 380n. 54; on earth, 107, 109–110, 114, 115; elemental cosmology of, 110–113; environmental actions of, 117–119; on environmental ethics, 122–124; on equality, 113–115; on evolution, 119–120; on fire, 107, 109–110, 114, 115; four elements of, 106–110, 113–114; on light, 245; on love, 110–113, 116, 119, 124; metaphoric language of, 116, 124; on metempsychosis, 124; *On Nature,* 104, 105–106, 107, 110, 134–135; on nature, 124–126; on opposites, 397n. 11; on organic unity, 115–117; on pollution, 129, 131; *The Purifications,* 104, 105–106, 120–121, 129, 134–135; Pythagorean influence on, 114; rhizomata of, 72, 106–110, 115, 124, 125–126; on senses, 108, 115; as shaman-magician, 7, 118–119; on soul, 235; on strife, 110–113, 116, 129–130; on water, 107, 109–110, 114, 115; water clock of, 90
Empedocles complex, 37, 297
encircling horizon, 64
End of Nature, The (McKibben), 275–276
energy: heat as, 204–205; hydroelectric, 262, 266; solar, 251
enjoyment, 310–312
environmental action, 345–352; on air, 348–350; on earth, 350–351; by Empedocles, 117–119; on fire, 351–352; on water, 346–348
environmental ethics, 334–338; in Aristotelian thought, 241–242; Orphic influence in, 123–124; panpsychism and, 117; in Presocratic thought, 122–124; in Pythagorean thought, 123; in Stoic thought, 279
environmental movements, 129–131
epistemological luddism, 266
equality: Empedocles on, 113–115
Eschmann, E. W., 55
Euclid, 183
Euthyphro (Plato), 128

Evernden, Neil, 122
evolution: Aristotle on, 119–120; Deleuze and Guattari on, 135–136; Empedocles on, 119–120; Whitehead on, 171
excrement, 24
exercise: breathing with, 30
exosphere, 27
exotherm, 202
eye: Empedocles on, 245; light processing by, 245; Plato on, 148

factory farming, 121
Fahrenheit, Daniel, 202
Fallingwater, 262
Fasnacht, Heide, 345
Fate of Place, The (Casey), 319
feet, 378n. 28
feminism, 318–319
feng shui, 61–62
Feshbach, Sidney, 125–126
fifth element, 187–188, 225–228. See also aether (ether)
fire, 36–42; Aristotle on, 40–41, 190, 191, 212, 213, 217–218; Bachelard on, 37, 42, 206, 297; Derrida on, 42, 364n. 117; domestication of, 36, 37, 39, 40, 41, 255–256; ecological functions of, 37–38, 41; Empedocles on, 107, 109–110, 114, 115; environmental action on, 351–352; geography of, 40–41; Hegel on, 280–281; Heidegger on, 41–42; Heraclitus on, 36–37, 41–42; historical analysis of, 38–40; ideogram for, 61; industrial, 41; myths about, 37; Native American use of, 38; place of, 40–41; Plato on, 36, 145–146, 147, 148–150, 152–153, 154, 155–156, 161–163; poetic figure of, 41–42; stages of, 40; Stoics on, 279
fire: etymology of, 37
five elements, 74–78, 180
flesh: Aristotle on, 231, 232, 308; Merleau-Ponty on, 234, 308
flood motif, 45
fog, 176–177

Foreign Bodies (Lingis), 314
forests, 95; fire effects on, 37–38, 41; loss of, 98–99, 274; sacred, 127
Forgetting of Air in Martin Heidegger (Irigaray), 316
form: Aristotle on, 189–190, 192
formism, 370n. 50
Forms: in Plato, 155, 156, 167, 170
Foucault, Michael, 248
fountains, 262–263
four-thought, 1–3, 81–84
Francis of Assisi, 80
Frazier, James, 95
free will, 34–35
Freud, Sigmund, 110
Friday (Tournier), 314–315
Fromm, Harold, 34–35
Frost, Robert, 23, 42, 53
Fulton, Hamish, 22
funerary practice, 33–34, 55, 96
Fuseli, Henry, 286

Gaia hypothesis, 34, 147
Galileo, 169, 329
Gaudin, Colette, 295, 299–300
Gellis, Sandy, 286
gender, 131; of Earth, 16, 160; place and, 198–199; in *Timaeus*, 160; water associations with, 259–260
gene: domestication of, 274
geocentrism, 240
geography. See place
geometry: in *Timaeus*, 160–163, 169
Getting Back Into Place (Casey), 319
Gibson, James J., 65
Gleick, Peter, 347
Glenn, John, 276
Goethe, Johann Wolfgang von, 343; on clouds, 175; on color, 246; on elements, 353; on light, 245; on Luke Howard, 173; on sky color, 28
Gogh, Vincent van, 285–286
Golden Bough, The (Frazier), 95
Goldsworthy, Andy, 53, 141, 250, 341–342

Gorgias (Plato), 146
Gosnell, Mariana, 137
graveyard, 55
gray ecology, 275
Green, Julian, 286
Greene, Mott, 89–90
greenhouse gases, 349, 404n. 51
Griffiths, Jay, 140–141, 343
Grotius, Hugo, 346
Guattari, Félix, 7, 131–136, 294; on earth, 21; on stone, 57
Guthrie, W. K. C., 374n. 122

Haeckel, Ernst, 121–122
hail, 177
Halys River, 89–90, 374n. 125
Hamlet (Shakespeare), 173
haptein, 233
Hardin, Garrett, 346
hardwood, 97
Harman, Graham, 315–316
Harrison, Robert Pogue, 95
hate, 86
Hatley, James, 342
Hawthorne, Nathaniel, 53
Hayden Planetarium, 329
health, 114–115
heartwood, 96
heat, 201–205
heaviness: Aristotle on, 185, 186–188, 190, 191, 211
Hebel, Johann Peter, 306
Hebrews, 175
Hegel, Georg Wilhelm Friedrich, 275; on elements, 3–4, 280–281; on philosopher's stone, 52
Heidegger, Martin, 8; on breath, 32; on *chora*, 159; on divinities, 301–302; on dwelling, 300–303, 305; on earth, 21, 24, 301; on earth from space, 274; ecologism of, 306–307; on elemental terms, 60; etymological investigations of, 305; on fire, 41–42; on fourfold frame, 83, 294, 300–308; on ground/grounding, 306, 307; on horizon, 65; on language, 305, 400n. 72; on mortality, 302, 410n. 42; on Rhine River, 262; root metaphors of, 306–307; on shadow, 248; on sky, 301; on stone, 57; on stone bridge, 303–304; on technology, 304–305; on truth, 244
Heisenberg, Werner, 167
Heizer, Michael, 22
Heraclitus, 19, 110; on change, 154; death of, 380n. 54; on fire, 36–37, 41–42; on heat, 203; on opposition, 67, 68–69, 163; on social world, 159; on soul, 36–37, 235; on war, 68, 87, 110, 163; on water, 46, 49
Herder, Johann Gottfried von, 71
Hero, 90
Hesiod, 20–21, 63, 85–86, 109, 287
Hildegard von Bingen, 29
Hillman, James, 295
Hinduism: elemental conceptions in, 76–78; fourfold frame in, 82–83; heat in, 204; light in, 244; play in, 164; Self in, 29, 77, 371n. 68
Hippocrates, 31
Hiroshima, 250
H_2O, 270–271
H_2O and the Waters of Forgetfulness (Illich), 270
Hoffman, Nigel, 343
Hoffman, Roald, 272
Hoffman complex, 37
Hölderin, Friedrich, 42, 297, 323
holes: earthen, 19–20
Holocaust, 42
homeotherm, 201
home-place, 197
Homer: cosmology of, 109; on earth, 21; on night, 287
Hopkins, Gerald Manley, 34
horizon, 64–65; night and, 285
Horkheimer, Max, 63, 277
hot-cold: Aristotle on, 209–213, 216–217, 222
Howard, Luke, 173, 176
Hubble Telescope, 329

Hughes, Donald, 123
Hugo, Victor, 291
Huizinga, John, 164–165
humans, 25; breathing of, 26; domestication of, 258–259; speech of, 26, 27; water of, 45
humors, 71
Husserl, Edmund, 7, 294; on earth, 21; on mathematization of nature, 168–170; on place, 394n. 25
Hutton, James, 362n. 90
hydroelectric energy, 262, 266
Hygeia, 131
hygron, 212
hylozoism, 32–33, 116, 167

Ibsen, Henrik, 66
ice, 137–142; functions of, 141–142; sounds of, 138; types of, 138–139
idealism, 149
ideograms, 61–62
igneous rock, 54
Iliad (Homer), 109
Illich, Ivan, 5, 260, 263, 270
illumination, 244–245
imagination: Bachelard on, 66–67; Larsen on, 341; Sallis on, 321–323
implicit horizon, 64–65
impurity, 128, 129. See also pollution
incest, 85
India: elemental conceptions in, 76–78; fourfold frame in, 82–83. See also Hinduism
In Praise of Shadows (Tanizaki), 248–249
insomnia, 289–290
International Shadow Project, 250
Introduction to Metaphysics (Heidegger), 306
Inuit, 140
Inupiat, 140
ionosphere, 27
Irigaray, Luce, 8, 294, 316–319; on air, 30, 316–318; on elements, 316–317; on feminine, 198–199

Japan: elemental conceptions in, 75–76
Jaspers, Karl, 181

Jonas, Hans, 242
Julius Caesar (Shakespeare), 344
Jung, Carl, 15, 66
justice, 87–88; Presocratics on, 87, 123; Pythagoreans on, 114

Kaaba, 52–53
Kabbalah, 32
Kant, Immanuel, 288, 328
Kepler, Johannes, 330
Khayyám, Omar, 78
King Lear (Shakespeare), 322–323
knowledge: Aristotle on, 237–238; Empedocles on, 115–117; Plato on, 150–153, 155–156
Koyukon, 205
Kropotkin, Peter, 121
Kundera, Milan, 186

Land Art, 22
landscape, 260–264; Casey on, 319–321; Schama on, 260
Lane, Fritz Hugh, 320–321
language, 27, 60–63; of elements, 60–63, 68; Emerson on, 61; Heidegger on, 305, 400n. 72; Irigaray on, 316; Nabokov on, 368n. 13; natural phenomena and, 151; Plato on, 150–151
Larsen, Hans-Erik, 341
Last Child in the Woods (Louv), 99
Lavoisier, Antoine, 72, 73
Lawrence, D. H., 355
Laws, The (Plato), 21, 149, 164, 167–168, 390n. 53
Lectures on the History of Philosophy (Hegel), 3
Leopold, Aldo, 98, 332
letters, 60–63, 150–151, 166, 388n. 18
Levi, Primo, 417n. 43
Levin, David Michael, 248, 289
Levinas, Emmanuel, 8; on elemental sensibility, 310–312; on shadow, 248
Lévy-Bruhl, Lucien, 88
l'heure bleue, 246
light, 243–251; in art, 320; ecological, 245; Empedocles on, 245; human-generated, 288; ocular processing of,

245; Plato on, 243, 245; properties of, 244–245; religious interpretations of, 244; stilling of, 251
lightness: Aristotle on, 185, 186–187, 186–188, 190, 191, 211
lightning, 177
limestone caverns, 24–25
Lingis, Alphonso, 8, 312–316; on elements, 313–314; on hot and cold, 202; on Incan stone cutters, 56; on night, 284; on perception, 312
Lippard, Lucy, 196, 197
Little Prince, The (Saint-Exupéry), 23
Locke, John, 250
locomotion: Aristotle on, 189, 190, 195
Logan, William Bryant, 17, 20
London, Jack, 206
Long, Richard, 22
Lopez, Barry, 139, 247
Louv, Richard, 99
love, 86; Empedocles on, 110–113, 116, 119, 124; Plato on, 146
Lovelock, James, 34, 319
Lucretius, 379n. 52; on conflict, 68
luminocentrism, 248, 272
lunar rocks, 53
Lyotard, Jean-François, 295

Macbeth (Shakespeare), 98
Machu Picchu, 55–56
MacLeish, Archibald, 332
Malouf, Joan, 35
mandala, 66
Mandarin, 61–62
Mann, Thomas, 203
Maori, 79
mapping, 22–23, 64
Marine Lover of Friedrich Nietzsche (Irigaray), 316, 318
marriage, 85–86
Mars, 35, 337
Marx, Karl, 278–279
mass, 188
mathematical sciences: Husserl on, 168–170; Plato on, 168
matter, 69–70; Aristotle on, 191–192, 194, 218–225

Maxwell, James Clerk, 5, 85
McKibben, Bill, 275–276
McLuhan, Marshall, 206
mean: Aristotelian, 233, 399n. 49; touch as, 233
meaning: technology and, 275–277
mechanism, 370n. 50
Medea (Euripides), 129
media: McLuhan on, 206
meditation, 31
Melissus, 109
Melville, Herman, 45, 196, 284
member: etymology of, 309
Mendeleyev, Dmitri, 150
Merleau-Ponty, Maurice, 8, 294, 308–310; on earth, 19, 21; on elements, 308–309; on flesh, 234, 308; on high-altitude thinking, 274; on horizon, 65; on ice, 142; on inhabitation, 310; on phenomenal field, 309–310; on self, 309; on sight, 234; on vision, 247–248
metamorphic rock, 54
Metaphysics (Aristotle), 182, 183, 221–222, 240
Meteorology (Aristotle), 176, 180, 240
miasma, 127, 128
Michaels, Walter Benn, 58
Michelangelo, 54, 288–289
microcosm, 147
Midsummer Night's Dream, A (Shakespeare), 289
mind: panpsychic, 115–117; Plato on, 167
mining, 19, 128
Moby Dick (Melville), 45, 196, 284
monism, 183–184
moon, 328, 331, 337
Moore, Thomas, 19
morality, 87–88
mortality: Heidegger on, 302, 410n. 42
mountains, 56–57
movement: of air, 27–28, 29–30; Aristotle on, 187–191, 195, 226, 241; Empedocles on, 112–113; of water, 47. *See also* change
mud, 24, 299
Muir, John, 94
Mumford, Lewis, 266

myths: about fire, 37; about rocks, 57; about water, 45–46; creation, 79–81

Nagasaki, 250
Nagy, Gregory, 34
Native Americans: elemental conceptions of, 65, 78–79; fire use by, 38
naturalism: dialectal, 241–242; philosophical, 240–242
nature: Aristotle on, 181, 240–242, 400n. 73; domination of, 257, 258; vs. elements, 3–4; Empedocles on, 124–126; end of, 275–276; intuited, 169; mathematization of, 168–170; Plato on, 144–145; scientific, 169; social construction of, 84–91
nature deficit disorder, 99
Nazca lines, 18–19
nazism, 42
necessity: Plato on, 148–150
Neumann, Erich, 284
Niagara Falls, 261
Nicomachean Ethics (Aristotle), 233
Nietzsche, Friedrich, 57; on air, 298; on earth, 25; on recurrence, 113; on vision, 248; on water, 43; on weight, 186
night, 283–292; animals at, 287; artifical lighting and, 288; philosophic thought and, 286–287; space and, 284–285
Nirenberg, Richard, 62–63, 344–345
nirvana, 78, 94
nomos: vs. *physis,* 125
Northern Lights, 246–247
Novalis, 44, 291
nude: in art, 260
Nye, David, 264

Oakeshott, Michael, 270
Oates, Joyce Carol, 323
objectivity: touch and, 234; Whitehead on, 171–172
oceans, 44–45, 47–48
ocular-centrism, 247
Oedipus Rex (Sophocles), 129
om mantra, 83
On Breath (Aristotle), 32

On Generation and Corruption (Aristotle), 180, 209–210, 211, 216, 219–220, 223, 228–229, 393n. 15
On Nature (Empedocles), 104, 105–106, 107, 110, 134–135
On the Heavens (De Caelo) (Aristotle), 180, 187–188, 193–194, 223–224
On the Soul (Aristotle), 180
Oppenheim, Dennis, 250
opposition, 67–69, 163; Anaxagoras on, 69; Anaximander on, 69, 163; Aristotle on, 69, 209–216, 225, 396n. 10; Empedocles on, 397n. 11; Heraclitus on, 67, 68–69, 163; Parmenides on, 69; Pythagoreans on, 69
organicism, 370n. 50
organic rain, 29
Orpheus, 123–124
outer space, 327–332
Outwater, Alice, 347
oxygen, 31–32

Paglia, Camille, 345
palmistry, 345
panentheism, 116
panexperientalism, 116
panpsychism, 115–117
pansensism, 116
pantheism, 116
Paracelsus, 279–280
Parmenides, 110, 113; on night, 287; on opposition, 69, 186
Parmenides (Plato), 156
perception: Aristotle on, 231–232; Lingis on, 312
Periodic Table of Elements, 5, 150
Persia: elemental conceptions of, 78
personifying, 373n. 105
Peru: Machu Picchu of, 55–56; Nazca lines of, 18–19
Pesic, Peter, 28
petrifaction, 54
pet rocks, 58
Phaedo (Plato), 155
Phenomenology of Spirit (Hegel), 280–281
Philebus (Plato), 146

Philosopher's Stone, 52
Philosophy Addressed to the Athenians, The (Paracelsus), 279–280
Philosophy of Nature, The (Hegel), 3, 280
photosynthesis, 245
Physics (Aristotle), 192–194, 229
Pierce, Franklin, 278–279
Piercy, Marge, 21
place(s), 63–66; alienation from, 196–197; Aristotle on, 63, 65, 188–199, 234, 394n. 24; Casey on, 319–321; gender and, 198–199; Husserl on, 394n. 25; Plato on, 63, 156–160, 194–195
plankton, 48
plants: Empedocles on, 120–122
plastic bottles, 269–270
Plath, Sylvia, 26
Plato, 5, 7, 143–172; on air, 145–146, 148–150, 152–153, 154, 161–163; on animals, 148, 160, 259; vs. Aristotle, 181, 183–184, 212, 393n. 16; on cave, 57, 166; on change, 152–155, 160–163, 239; on *chora*, 156–160; on conflict, 163; constrained constructivism of, 148–150; on cyclical transformations, 153–155; on Demiurge, 149, 156–157, 167, 169–170; on disease, 71, 165; on dream, 66, 150; on earth, 21, 145–146, 148–150, 152–153, 154–155, 159, 161–163; on elemental construction, 160–163; on fire, 36, 145–146, 147, 148–150, 152–153, 154, 155–156, 161–163; on Forms, 155, 156, 167, 170; on fourfold frame, 82; geometry in, 160–163; on knowledge, 150–153, 155–156; on letters, 60, 150–151, 166; on light, 243, 245; on love, 146; on mathematical sciences, 168; on nature, 144–145; on necessity, 148–150; on place, 63, 156–160, 194–195; on play, 163–165; on pollution, 128; on powers, 147; on qualities, 153, 155, 165–166; on sensation, 163; on shadows, 248; on sky color, 28; on social world, 159; on soul, 145, 148, 149–150, 168, 236; on things in themselves, 155–156; on time,

148; on water, 145–146, 148–150, 152–153, 154, 161–163; on world's body, 145, 146, 147–148
play, 163–165
Pliny the Elder: on earth, 19; on shadow, 249; on water, 366n. 154
Plotinus, 165, 388n. 8
pneuma, 279
Poe, Edgar Allan, 15, 296, 345
polis, 159, 196, 198
Politics (Aristotle), 196, 240
Pollan, Michael, 97
pollution, 1, 126–131; air, 34–35; dromospheric, 271–272; elemental alienation and, 196–197; Empedocles on, 129; ethnic/racial dimensions of, 131; idea of, 127, 128–129, 131; mining-related, 128; physical, 126–127; prohibitions against, 127–128; water, 49, 126–127, 128, 269
pollution: etymology of, 127
polyethylene terephthalate, 267
Pound, Ezra, 94
powers: Plato on, 147
Presocratics, 7, 103–104; Deleuze on, 118; environmental ethics and, 122–124; on justice, 87, 123. *See also* Empedocles
Priestley, Joseph, 5, 73
prime matter, 218–225
primordial depth, 65–66
primordial sea/waters, 45, 46
process: Whitehead on, 170–172
Process and Reality (Whitehead), 170
profile: earth, 16
Prometheus, 36
Protagoras (Plato), 36
Psychoanalysis of Fire, The (Bachelard), 295
psychology: archetypes in, 66–67; earth symbolism in, 15; shadow, 249–250
Ptolemy, 90
Purifications, The (Empedocles), 104, 105–106, 120–121, 129, 134–135
Puritanism, 130
purity, 127, 129–130. *See also* pollution
Pyne, Stephen, 38–40, 41, 138–139, 141, 255, 335

Pythagoreans, 167; environmental ethics and, 123; on four, 82; on justice, 114; opposites and, 69

qualities: Plato on, 153, 155, 165–166
Quintessence (Daly), 319

race, 131
radiant light, 244–245
rain, 177
Receptacle: in Plato, 63, 86, 156–160
recycling: Empedocles on, 123
regolith, 16
re-inhabitation, 198
Rembrandt, 286
Representing Place (Casey), 319
Republic, The (Plato), 155, 159; Allegory of Cave of, 166
re-story-ation, 5
reverie, 66–67
Rhine River, 262
rhizomata, 7, 72, 106–110, 115, 124, 125–126
rhizomes, 7, 108, 131–136
Rig Veda, 23, 45, 287
Rilke, Ranier Maria, 15, 35, 58, 123–124, 284, 329, 358n. 3
Ringing Rocks Park, 54
Rist, John, 6
rivers: Heidegger on, 262; human work and, 265–266; re-meandering of, 263
Robbins, Tom, 48–49, 354–355
rock, 51–58
Rolston, Holmes, 95, 336–337, 339–340
Rome, 263
Romeo and Juliet (Shakespeare), 26
roots, 108, 122; Derrida on, 132; Empedocles on, 72, 106–110; Heidegger on, 306–307
Ross, Stephen David, 21–22
Roszak, Theodore, 119, 199, 395n. 47
Rothenberg, David, 261–262
Rubáiyát, 78
Rumi, 31
Ruskin, John, 20, 48, 174, 249

Rutherford, Ernest, 166

Saint-Exupéry, Antoine de, 23
Sallis, John, 8, 22, 294; on elements, 322–323; on imagination, 321–323; on Levinas, 311; on stone, 57–58
Samkhya, 77–78
Santayana, George, 179
sapwood, 96
Sartre, Jean Paul, 57
Schama, Simon, 260
schizoanalysis, 385n. 129
scientific elements, 4–5
sculpture, 54
seas, 44–45, 47–48
seasons, 203
seawater, 45
sedimentary rock, 54
seduction, 340
Self: Hindu, 29, 77, 371n. 68
self: Merleau-Ponty on, 309
Seneca, 19; on clouds, 176; on wind, 29
senses: Aristotle on, 230–232, 237–238; Empedocles on, 108, 115; Levinas on, 310–312; Lingis on, 313–314; Plato on, 163
sensible horizon, 64
Serres, Michel, 335
sex, 85–86
shadows, 248–250
Shakespeare: *Antony and Cleopatra*, 343–344; *Hamlet*, 173; *Julius Caesar*, 344; *King Lear*, 322–323; *Macbeth*, 98; *A Midsummer Night's Dream*, 289; *Romeo and Juliet*, 26; *Timon of Athens*, 24
shaman-magician: Empedocles as, 7, 118–119
shan shui, 62
Sharp, Thomas, 324
Shelley, Percy Bysshe, 175, 178, 353
shivering, 206
Shubin, Neil, 45
sight, 233–234
Simic, Charles, 58
Sisyphus, 57
Skeptical Chymist, The (Boyle), 278

Skjern River, 263
Skrbina, David, 116
sky: color of, 28, 177; cultural interpretations of, 28, 33; domestication of, 271–272; vs. earth, 19; Heidegger on, 301; "indoor," 28. *See also* air
sky: etymology of, 28
sky burial, 33–34
Sky in a Bottle (Pesic), 28
Sloterdijk, Peter, 24
Smithson, Robert, 22
snow, 139–142; functions of, 141–142; types of, 140–141
Snyder, Gary, 44, 96, 199, 335, 344
softwood, 97
soil: biological activity of, 17; profile of, 16; psychological, 15
soil: etymology of, 16–17
solar eclipse, 290
solar energy, 251
Sophist (Plato), 156
soul: Anaximenes on, 33; Aristotle on, 234–238; Descartes on, 236; Diogenes on, 235; Empedocles on, 235; Heraclitus on, 36–37, 235; Plato on, 145, 148, 149–150, 168, 236
space, 327–332
space travel, 273–274, 327–328, 330
speech, 26, 27
Sphere: Empedocles on, 112, 123
sphere: Plato on, 147
Spiral Jetty, 22
stars, 328; Aristotle on, 228
Steiner, George, 307
Stevens, Wallace, 25, 205, 234, 283, 303
stoicheia, 3, 60, 108, 143, 151, 152, 165, 319, 388n. 18; Aristotle on, 182–183. *See also* element(s)
Stoics, 279
stone, 51–58; cultural uses of, 52–53, 55–56; funerary use of, 55; poetic figure of, 58
stratosphere, 27
strife, 68, 87; Empedocles on, 110–113, 116, 129–130; Plato on, 163

substratum, 221
sulfur dioxide, 349
sun, 245–246; artificial, 250
Swineburne, Algernon Charles, 296
syllables, 150–152, 166, 388n. 18
Szymborska, Wislawa, 24, 28, 49, 51, 256

tactility: Empedocles on, 108
Tanizaki, Junichiro, 248–249
Taoism: night in, 287; water in, 43–44; wood in, 94
Tao Te Ching, 43–44, 85, 287
technology, 36, 39–40, 41; Heidegger on, 304–305; meaning and, 275–277; water-related, 260–267
telescope, 329
temperature: body, 201–202, 203–204; environmental, 203–204; planet, 205
tenebroso, 249
Thales: death of, 380n. 54; on stone, 52, 364n. 126; on water, 43, 89–90, 374n. 125
Theaetetus (Plato), 150
Theogony (Hesiod), 287
Theophrastus, 33, 258
thinking: Aristotle on, 237, 400n. 64; Deleuze on, 64
Thomas, Dylan, 58, 292
Thompson Indians, 79
Thoreau, Henry David, 37, 338, 344
Thousand Plateaus, A (Deleuze and Guattari), 132–136
Three Characters, The, 74–75
thunder, 177
Timaeus (Plato), 143–145. *See also* at Plato
time: geologic, 20; Plato on, 148; Sallis on, 323
Timon of Athens (Shakespeare), 24
Totality and Infinity (Levinas), 310
touch: Aristotle on, 210, 228–233; Bachelard on, 234; objectivity and, 234
Tournier, Michel, 314–315
trace, 342
trees, 93–96; Bachelard on, 299–300; cultural uses of, 97; loss of, 98–99

tribes, 88–89
troposphere, 27
Tuan, Yi-Fu, 340
Tudge, Colin, 96
Turner, J. M. W., 345
Twain, Mark, 49, 272
2001: A Space Odyssey, 330

Unbearable Lightness of Being, The (Kundera), 186
universe: end of, 202–203; Plato on, 147–148
Upanishads, 30, 77, 83, 332
Updike, John, 18

Valentine, Basil, 18
Vaughan Williams, Ralph, 138
Venerable Bede, 20
Vico, Giambattista, 27, 80–81
Virilio, Paul, 157, 271, 275
Visible and the Invisible, The (Merleau-Ponty), 308
vision, 245, 247–248
Vlastos, Gregory, 123
vocabulary: elemental, 60–63, 68
volcanoes, 118, 380n. 56

walking, 338
war, 68, 87; Empedocles on, 110; Heraclitus on, 68, 87, 110, 163
Watair, 347
water, 43–50; Aristotle on, 190, 213–214, 217; in art, 48, 320–321; artesian, 268; Bachelard on, 46–47, 296–297; biological characteristics of, 47–48; bottled, 267–270; in Buddism, 44; cultural interpretations of, 45–46, 257–258; differentiated characteristics of, 46; domestication of, 90–91, 256–271; Eastern philosophy on, 43–44; Empedocles on, 107, 109–110, 114, 115; environmental action on, 346–348; filtration of, 269; gender associations with, 259–260; geographic distribution of, 47, 49; ground, 268; Hegel on, 280–281; Heraclitus on, 46, 49; vs. H_2O, 270–271; ideogram for, 61; landscape aesthetics and, 260–264; metaphorical use of, 60–61; mineral, 268, 269; movements of, 47; mythological uses of, 45–46; Nietzsche on, 43; plastic bottles for, 269–270; Plato on, 145–146, 148–150, 152–153, 154, 161–163; poetic figure of, 46–47, 49, 60–61; pollution of, 49, 126–127, 128, 269; re-meandering of, 263; Roman use of, 263; spring, 268; in Taoism, 43–44; tap, 268, 269; technologizing of, 89–90, 260–264; Thales on, 43, 89–90, 374n. 125; work and, 265–267
Water and Dreams (Bachelard), 295
watercraft, 260–264
weather, 29–30
weight: Aristotle on, 185, 186–188
Weil, Simone, 104
Weinstein, Norman, 50
Weintraub, Linda, 49
wet-dry: Aristotle on, 209–213, 222
White, Richard, 265, 266
Whitehead, Alfred North, 2–3, 7, 170–172, 294
Whitfield, Margaret, 316
Wilde, Oscar, 173
Wilson, Peter, 258
wind, 27–28, 29–30. *See also* air
wind energy, 349
Winner, Langdon, 264, 266, 276
Wittfogel, Karl, 90–91
Wittgenstein, Ludwig, 151, 291
woman/women: place and, 198–199; Plato on, 160; water associations with, 259–260
wood, 93–99; petrifcation of, 54–55; types of, 96–97; utilitarian uses of, 97–98
wood-air breathing, 35
Woodbridge, Frederick, 5, 240
Woolf, Virginia, 18
work, 265–267
world: alienation from, 273; vs. earth, 24

worms, 17
Wright, Frank Lloyd, 262

Xenophanes of Colophon, 20
xeron, 212

yoga, 23–24, 30, 204

Your Inner Fish (Shubin), 45

Zen Buddhism: stone figures in, 53; on trees, 94; on water, 44
Zimmerman, Michael, 274
zodiac, 259
Zoroastrians, 244